Professional CDO Programming

Daniel J. Mitchell
Siegfried Weber
Donald Xie

Wrox Press Ltd. ®

Professional CDO Programming

Published by Wrox Press Ltd, Arden House, 1102 Warwick Road, Acocks Green,
Birmingham, B27 6BH, UK
Printed in the United States
ISBN 1-861002-0-68

Trademark Acknowledgements

Credits

Authors
Daniel J. Mitchell
Siegfried Weber
Donald Xie

Additional Material
Sue Mosher
Diane Poremsky
John Schenken
Ken Slovak
John Wootton

Technical Editors
Craig Berry
Dev Lunsford
Daniel Maharry

Technical Reviewers
Robert Chang
Mikael Friedlitz
Davide Marcato
Daniel J. Mitchell
Sue Mosher
Christian Nagel
Christophe Nasarre
Nik Okuntseff
Kenn Scribner
Julian Templeman
Helmut Watson

Managing Editor
Joanna Mason

Development Editors
Dominic Lowe
Greg Pearson

Project Manager
Sophie Edwards

Design/Layout
Tom Bartlett
Mark Burdett
Jonathan Jones
John McNulty

Figures
William Fallon
Jonathan Jones

Index
Diane Brenner
Martin Brooks
Andrew Criddle

Cover
Chris Morris

About the Authors

Daniel J. Mitchell

Dan Mitchell has been programming since a 3.5k memory upgrade was a big deal – he studied Mathematics and Computation at Oxford, discovering that there's a whole lot more math involved than he'd expected, then went on to spend the next few years making a living writing video games (where there's still a whole lot more math involved than he'd expected...). He currently lives in Canada, where he spends time wrestling with the intricacies of Exchange programming, and was recently made a Microsoft Most Valuable Professional as recognition for the time he's spent helping others in the same boat.

Siegfried Weber

Siegfried Weber is a ten-year veteran of the IT business. He started as a Novell NetWare network administrator, and later focused on messaging. At the end of 1996 he joined the Microsoft Exchange Community and started working with Microsoft Exchange Server 5.0 and Active Messaging.

He is now a freelance consultant doing Exchange & Outlook training and also planning, implementing and installing Exchange and Outlook in enterprise environments. Apart from these activities, he's also researching and developing Groupware and Workflow solutions using Microsoft Collaboration Data Objects, Exchange Server Scripting and Routing, Outlook and Active Server Pages.

Because of his his continuous contribution to the online community, with his Web site CDOLive (www.cdolive.com), and to several online discussion forums and mailing lists, Microsoft invited him in August 1999 to become a Microsoft Most Valuable Professional.

Donald Xie

Donald Xie has 12 years experience in software development. Currently, he is a project leader in Rio Tinto Research and Technology Development in Perth, Australia. He is specialized in creating enterprise-strength applications. You can reach Donald at donald@iinet.net.au.

Dedications:

To my wife, Iris, and our daughters, Belinda and Clare. I love them.

Acknowledgements

I really must thank everyone who made this book possible. They are Joanna Mason, Greg Pearson, Daniel Maharry, Dev Lunsford, and Sophie Edwards from Wrox Press, the technical reviewers, and of course the other authors and contributors.

I would also like to thank the following people for their tremendous support throughout my career: Steve Filmer for teaching me how to serve customers in the best possible way, Vic Currell for guiding me with his vision of providing a competitive edge to business, Mark Bennett and Philip Hingston for helping me to understand the importance and potential of collaborating between people and in businesses, and especially Jesse Liberty for encouraging me to write.

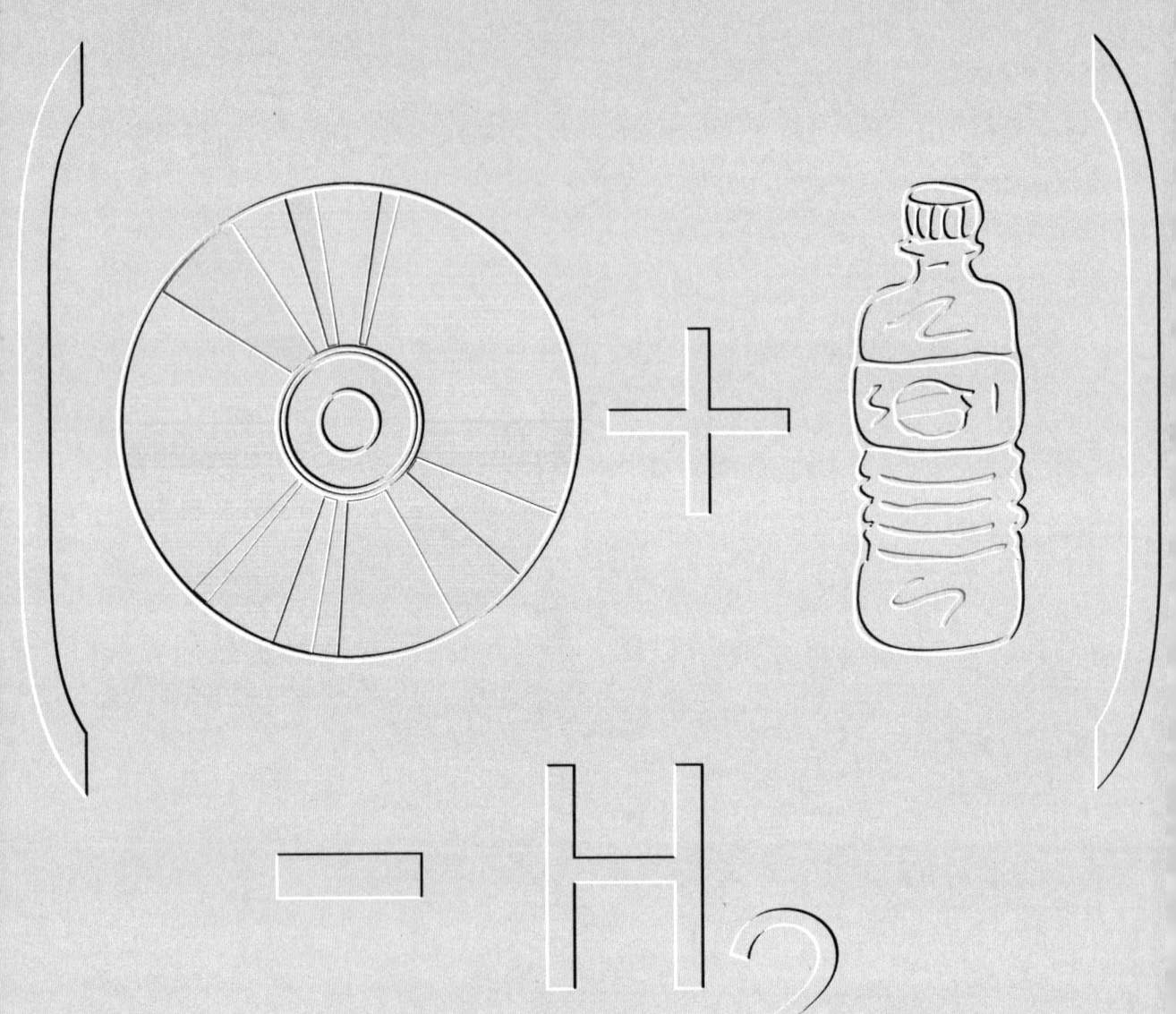

Table of Contents

Table of Contents

Chapter 3: Managing Information Stores   57

Chapter 4: Managing Address Books   101

Chapter 5: Managing Messages   139

Chapter 6: Managing Schedules 217

Chapter 7: Managing Rules and Folder Permissions   283

Chapter 8: CDO For NT Server – CDONTS   309

Chapter 9: Working with the CDO Rendering Library 351

Chapter 10: Formats and Patterns 377

Chapter 11: Views 393

Chapter 14: Using CDO from C++   477

Chapter 16: The Future of CDO   601

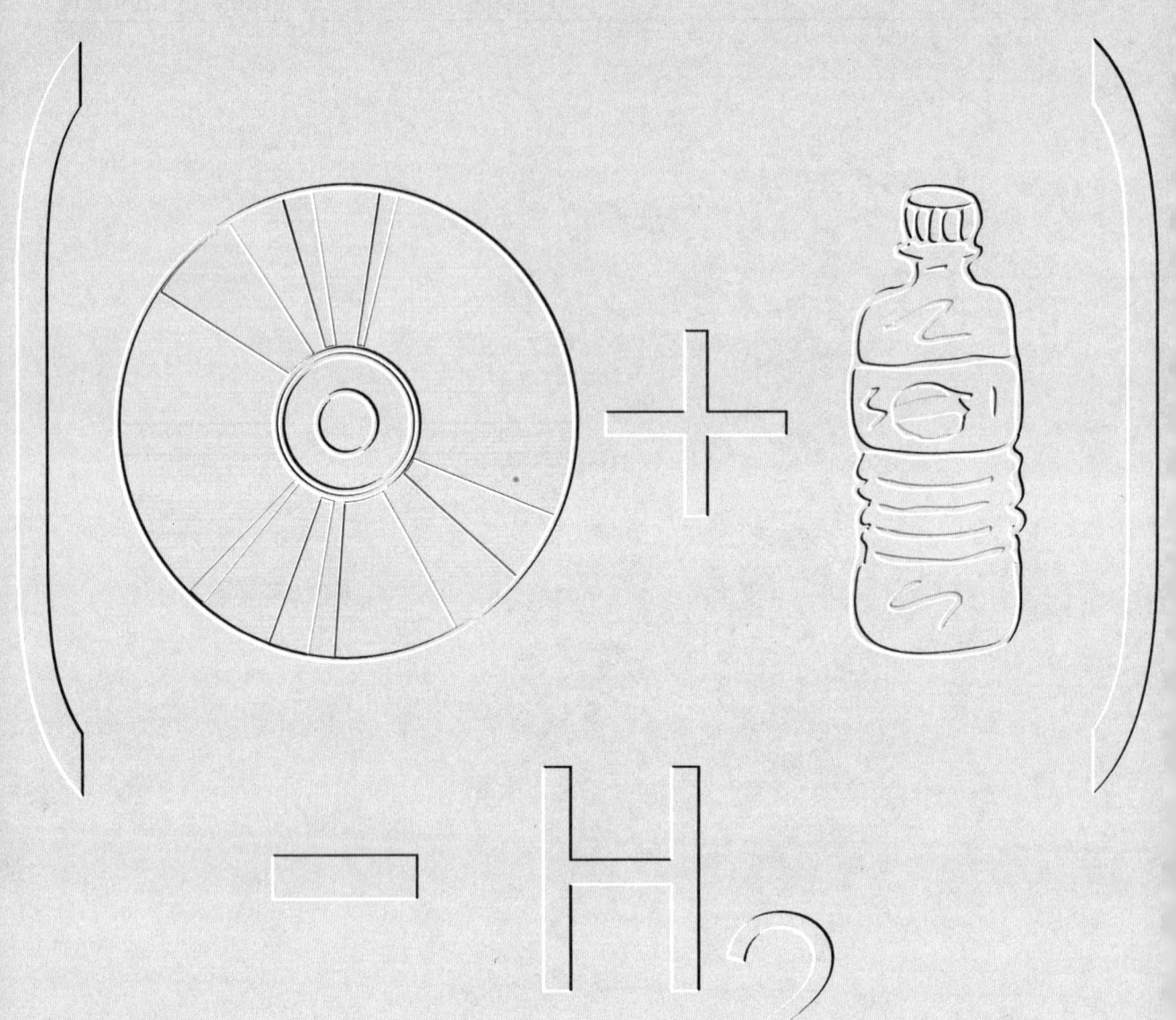

Introduction

Nowadays, e-mail is in use in almost every business in the world – it's hard to imagine how people could have got things done back when they had to transfer files by sending a floppy disk through the post, and when messages took days (if not weeks) to get from one person to another. And where there's new technology, there are new opportunities to take advantage of that technology.

At the simplest level, you could simply install a Microsoft Exchange Server somewhere on your network, distribute Outlook to all your users, and then sit back and leave them to it. Of course, Exchange and Outlook aren't the only way to implement mail; there's Lotus Notes as the most obvious competitor or Netscape's SuiteSpot set of tools for a start. We won't discuss those in any detail here, however – they're all fine products, but CDO is designed for use in a Microsoft environment, which means Exchange Server and Outlook.

Once you've installed the basic Microsoft mail services, if you only want the basic functionality that Outlook provides, that's fine and you can stop there. But what do you do if you want to, say:

- ❑ Add functionality to an existing application to let it send mail?
- ❑ Build a web-based interface to your contacts database?
- ❑ Leverage the scheduling features of Outlook to automatically have meeting rooms display information for the meetings due to happen there?
- ❑ Automatically send mail to an administrator warning when disk space gets low on a server?
- ❑ Monitor users' mailboxes for space used and warn them when they get near to quota?

The CDO libraries will let you do all of this, and pretty much anything else mail-related that you might want.

What is this book about?

This book will cover all the current CDO libraries:

❑ The main CDO library, used to send/read mail, calendar, address book and contact information.

❑ The CDO Rendering library, used to format mail items as HTML for web pages.

❑ The CDONTS library used to send mail to Internet mail servers without needing Exchange.

❑ The external components provided to change access levels on, and add rules to folders.

We'll cover the object models used in these libraries, and provide sample code to demonstrate how to use them in real life applications. CDO has a reasonably simple object model if you look at it purely in terms of the number of different types of object – but there are an unfortunate number of subtle aspects to what you can and cannot do. We explain these restrictions as we come across them, and, where applicable, give suitable workarounds.

Who is this book for?

This book is aimed, fundamentally, at anyone who wants to write code to leverage the power of Microsoft Exchange Server and use the mail systems it provides.

The only prior knowledge assumed is a basic understanding of the concepts behind e-mail and how it works, and some experience with using Microsoft Outlook. We assume a reasonable level of competence in Visual Basic programming; this is not a VB programming book, nor do you need to be an expert but you should know what a form is, what a module is, and how to write simple VB applications. The chapters concerning the CDO Rendering and CDONTS libraries also assume knowledge of ASP, as they are primarily web-based, but again you need not be an expert to follow through the examples in this book.

If you already have some experience with CDO, you may find some of the basic material familiar, but there's enough in-depth coverage that you're almost certain to see something you didn't already know; and, as already mentioned, we explain a number of subtleties that you may not be aware of.

The other sort of developer that will find this useful is the developer in the position I was in about nine months ago – the developer who's been wrestling with the complexities of Extended MAPI and is wondering why there isn't an easier way to do all this stuff. CDO is that way – in a lot of ways, if you're in this situation, you're ideally placed to read this, because you know the underlying details, but don't want to have to deal with them all...

What does this book cover?

A rough outline of the book is as follows:

- ❑ We start with a quick look at the history and origins of CDO, and a general overview of the assorted CDO libraries.

- ❑ Chapters 2 to 6 look at the main object model for CDO, messages, logging in and out, calendaring, and people. As a companion piece, Chapter 7 looks at how to manage inbox rules and folder permissions programmatically.

- ❑ In Chapter 8, we'll look at CDONTS, a cut down version of CDO designed to work with non-MAPI-based SMTP mail servers.

- ❑ Chapters 9 to 13 look at the CDO Rendering library and how we use it in ASP scripts to create web-based interfaces to Exchange. In demonstration, we'll look at Microsoft's Outlook Web Access and then an original case study, both of which use this technology.

- ❑ Chapters 14 and 15 look at using CDO in Visual C++ applications and accessing the MAPI APIs that underlie the CDO technology. To demonstrate, we've included a large case study incorporating messaging into an NT Service.

What do I need to use this book?

To summarize, you need an Exchange Server running at least version 5.0 or later as a server, and a machine with Outlook 97 or later installed on it to develop on. Chapter 1 specifies exactly what you need to do to have the correct DLLs installed, but this is a rough minimum requirement.

Hardware specifications are pretty loose – on the client side, if you can run Outlook happily, you can run programs using CDO just as happily. Requirements for an Exchange Server vary enormously with the number of users it's intended to support, but, again, your code using CDO will respond as quickly (or as slowly) as any other program talking to the Exchange Server does, so if Outlook takes a minute to view your Inbox, you should expect your CDO-based code to take about the same.

For development, we assume you're using Visual Basic 6.0 (and Visual C++ 6.0 as appropriate) – if you want to develop ASP pages, you'll need Internet Information Server 4.0 and your favorite ASP editor, be it Notepad, Visual InterDev, or something else entirely.

Conventions

We use font style and layout to distinguish the different types of information in the book; here are samples of these and an explanation of what each of them signifies:

- ❑ **Important words** are in a bold font.

- ❑ Words that appear onscreen, such as menu selections or options, appear in a similar font to that used onscreen (assuming a default Windows installation, that is), for instance the File | New menu. If you should select a submenu from a main menu, we use the vertical-bar (pipe) character to separate them (|).

- ❑ Code keywords appearing in the main body of text appear in this font, for instance we might say "to create a Session object, you should type Set objSession = New Session".

- ❑ Blocks of code to enter appear as follows:

```
' Create a session object we can log in to
Dim s As MAPI.Session
Set s = New MAPI.Session
```

- ❑ If we're altering existing bits of code, the new code appears as follows:

```
Dim n As Integer
For n = 1 to 10
    Debug.Print n
    ' Now we actually do something
    DoSomething(n)
Next
```

> **This sort of box is used to highlight important details that may crop up during discussion of something; anything in one of these boxes is vital information that you should be sure to take note of.**

Background information, asides and references appear in text like this.

Feedback

Please tell us what you think about this book – either return the reply card in the back of the book, or e-mail any comments to feedback@wrox.com.

All the source code files and project files for the examples are available for download at http://www.wrox.com. See Appendix H for exact instructions on how to access them.

We've made every possible effort to ensure that no typos or factual mistakes are in the book, but if one should have slipped through, you can find errata on our web site at http://www.wrox.com – if you find an error that isn't reported there, please let us know about it so we can update things appropriately.

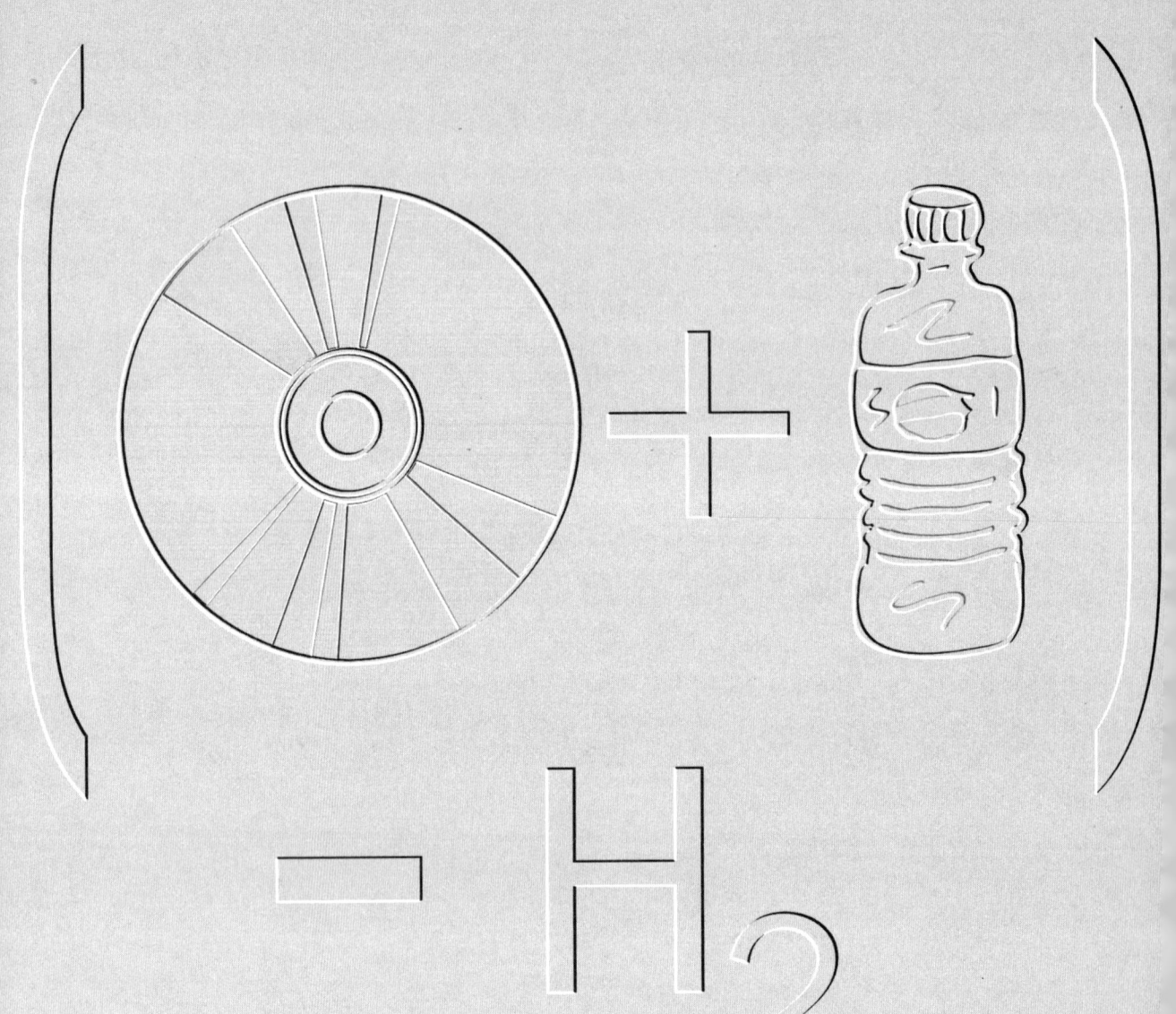

$$\left(+ \right) - H_2$$

Introducing the CDO Libraries

So what is CDO? Well, it stands for **Collaboration Data Objects**, and is essentially a set of object libraries you should use if you want to do any of the following:

- Write a web-based message board for intranet users.
- Automatically send mail to track sales and orders for your products.
- Centralize contact information to let all your users share a contact database.
- Add a guest book to your web site.
- Implement an automated response system to handle frequently-asked helpdesk questions.
- Set meeting rooms to automatically display relevant information for the upcoming meeting.
- Monitor server status and send warning mail to the administrator when problems arise.

And that's far from all you can do – from something as simple as automatically mailing customers when a product upgrade is available, to something as complex as implementing an entire web-based collaboration and messaging system, CDO will provide you with the tools you need.

In order to work with CDO libraries, you'll need a message store. **Microsoft Exchange Server** provides a message store architecture ideally suited to storing multiple messages and accessing them rapidly in exactly the way that mail-enabled applications require – while standard database servers may have more versatility, they are not fundamentally designed to handle mail transportation and storage from the ground up, as Exchange Server is.

Key to our choice of running CDO samples against Exchange is the fact that while CDO should work with any Messaging Application Programming Interface (MAPI) compliant system, it uses many Exchange-specific features to manage and access the data. This creates problems when you use CDO libraries with messaging systems other than Exchange.

Because CDO is designed to support the Microsoft COM specification, you can use CDO from a wide variety of languages: Visual Basic, C/C++, Delphi, Visual J++, JavaScript (ECMAScript), VBScript, ASP, and many more. This means that your application development is not constrained by language issues; you can take the information we provide in this book and apply it to any application you may be writing or want to write.

In this chapter, we'll be looking at:

❑   A historical recap of the development and origins of CDO

❑   An overview of the different flavors of CDO

❑   Where to get the different CDO Libraries

❑   A list of which products include which CDO version

❑   A brief glance at the features of each library and what they're all for

First, it would be a good idea to look at what collaboration actually is.

What is a Collaboration Application?

In today's business world, companies need to communicate effectively to gain and maintain competitive advantages. Internally, they need to coordinate activities involving different business units. Externally, they need to establish and improve good relationships with customers and suppliers. Modern interpersonal messaging technologies such as telephone, fax, and e-mail provide reliable and efficient services to satisfy our needs.

The IT industry continues to provide the infrastructure necessary to allow businesses to communicate and collaborate. Microsoft Exchange Server, Lotus Notes, and other messaging systems offer reliable and powerful services for people and organizations to communicate with each other, while messaging clients such as Microsoft Outlook allow people to maintain contact information, send and receive messages, organize schedules and meetings, and share information. Collectively, messaging servers and clients form collaboration applications that spread over local area networks, wide area networks, and the Internet.

While shrink-wrapped applications provide the capability for users to perform common tasks, there is always demand for customized applications that best satisfy the specific requirements of an organization. Building such collaboration applications requires the ability to programmatically access message stores and manage messaging data. The Microsoft CDO 1.21 and CDO Rendering libraries provide well-defined object models that allow application developers to communicate with Microsoft Exchange Servers and provide users access to data stored on those servers.

The Origins of CDO

Given its full name – Collaboration Data Objects 1.21 Library – it wouldn't be particularly surprising if you believed that CDO was a fairly new technology. In this guise it may be, but in the long view, CDO is actually Microsoft's fourth generation Messaging API.

Simple MAPI

While Microsoft provided a variety of mail systems in the past, the first one that included any sort of API for programmers was Microsoft Mail 3.0 for Windows, released for Windows 3.0, 3.1 and 3.11 (Windows for Workgroups). This e-mail system introduced the **Simple Messaging Application Programming Interface**, or Simple MAPI for short.

> *At the time, it was actually just called MAPI, but with the introduction of Extended MAPI a while later, the original interface was renamed to avoid confusion.*

Simple MAPI provided very basic functionality – you could log in and out of the system, read messages from your inbox, view the address book, and send plain text messages with file attachments. This may not seem like a lot, but at the time it was a great step forward – it meant that applications supporting Simple MAPI such as Word 2.0 could now have, for instance, File | Send... menu options.

Simple MAPI is still useful if you want to write very simple mail applications, and is still supported – for instance the Microsoft MAPI controls for Visual Basic are just a wrapper for Simple MAPI, and you can even use the functions directly from Visual Basic if need be.

What's more, remnants of the original API still remain – the original mail systems used a separate password to protect your mailbox, and you will still find a password argument used in the logon methods of CDO, even though now it serves no purpose. We won't look at Simple MAPI in this book, but it's an important part of the history of CDO.

Purely for historical completeness, it would be rude not to mention the **CMC** (Common Messaging Calls) API. This was another simple messaging API, specified by the XAPIA consortium – the group behind the X.400 specification. CMC was intended to be usable with any mail system; programmers would write to the CMC API, and versions of CMC would then talk to the different underlying mail systems as appropriate, be it Microsoft Mail, Banyan Vines, Hewlett-Packard OpenMail, or whatever. In practice, CMC is very rarely used due to lack of support; should you come across it anywhere, you will at least now know what it is.

Extended MAPI

In the first quarter of 1996, Microsoft released Exchange Server 4.0 – the first version of Exchange Server, despite the numbering. This replaced Microsoft Mail **Post Office** with a more flexible, more powerful server. With the release of Exchange Server 4.0 came a new mail API, **Extended MAPI 1.0**. The 'official' name for this is simply MAPI 1.0, but to keep things clear, it is still referred to as Extended MAPI from time to time, in order to retain the distinction between this and Simple MAPI.

> **Extended MAPI is the underlying system on top of which every Exchange-based mail system produced since 1996 runs.**

This key fact means that using Extended MAPI in your applications does have its advantages – write it once and it will work on any recent Microsoft mail system. But, naturally, it also has its downsides. Extended MAPI is a complex API with a steep learning curve. To make matters worse, it doesn't support a **dispatch interface**, just a plain COM interface – this translates to meaning that it can only be used from C or C++, not Visual Basic/VBScript, and so on (although, with some wrestling, it can be used with Delphi).

If you need the features of Extended MAPI, nothing else will suffice. However, CDO is much simpler to work with for the vast majority of tasks you will need to perform. It is also possible to write "hybrid" code in your apps that uses CDO for most of the work and also Extended MAPI when absolutely necessary; this is covered in more detail in Chapter 14.

However, by the time Extended MAPI was released, the Visual Basic community had become large enough that it was obvious that some way was needed to allow those programmers to access the new, more powerful features beyond the basic ones available in Simple MAPI. The library written to allow that is what we now know as CDO – though, as we'll see, it has had various names over the years.

Extended MAPI is a very low-level interface; you can talk to the objects stored on the Exchange Server directly, with no wrappers to interfere with your code. This makes it the most powerful way to write Exchange Server-enabled applications, because there are no restrictions on what you can do.

Early Versions of CDO

With the release of Microsoft Windows Messaging with Microsoft Windows 95 and Microsoft Windows NT 4.0, and later Exchange Client 4.0, Microsoft released a new library called **OLE Messaging 1.0**.

The OLE in OLE Messaging stands for "Object Linking and Embedding", and was the general term used at the time for the architecture that would later become COM. In this context, "OLE Messaging" simply means a messaging system that uses the standard OLE interfaces to access it. At the time, OLE was one of the technologies that Visual Basic used to communicate with external components, and so this was the first non-trivial (not Simple MAPI) messaging library for Visual Basic users.

After the success of Microsoft Exchange Server 4.0, Microsoft recognized the need to provide greater functionality and programmability to their customers, releasing Microsoft Exchange Server 5.0 in the first quarter of 1997. This version of Exchange Server introduced a great deal of new Internet features (like the first version of Outlook Web Access, called "Exchange Active Server Components"). It also brought with it a new version (1.1) of the OLE Messaging Library, which was renamed to **Active Messaging**.

Where CDO Is Now

With the release of Microsoft Exchange Server 5.5 in the last quarter of 1997, Microsoft again responded to developers crying for a technology with more power and functionality that was afforded them in the Active Messaging 1.1 Library. They had seen that capabilities far beyond simple messaging were needed, stretching into the areas of calendaring, collaboration, and workflow. Outlook had provided these in one way or another for a long time (longer still if you count Schedule+), but there had not previously been a way for programmers to take advantage of these features. In response, Microsoft replaced the Active Messaging 1.1 Object Library with the **Collaboration Data Objects 1.2 Object Library**.

The current version of CDO is actually version 1.21, which shipped as the first release of CDO with a client, namely Outlook 98 – this fixes some bugs in CDO 1.2. As such, if we refer to CDO 1.2, this can also be taken to mean CDO 1.21.

> *To add to the confusion, there is more than one version of CDO 1.21; Exchange Server Service Packs tend to contain even newer versions. The definitive latest version is the one you can download from Microsoft, though, at*
> `http://www.microsoft.com/exchange/55/downloads/CDO.htm`

As a final summary to the history of CDO, we'll look in slightly more detail at how CDO and MAPI interact – for now, we're still only talking about 'pure' CDO. As we'll see, there are a few libraries that have a claim to the name.

> *Note that SMTP is cited here as the protocol layer just as an example; any mail protocol could sit under here (a Lotus Notes connector, for instance) – this is just the way that the Exchange Server sends/receives messages to/from the outside world.*

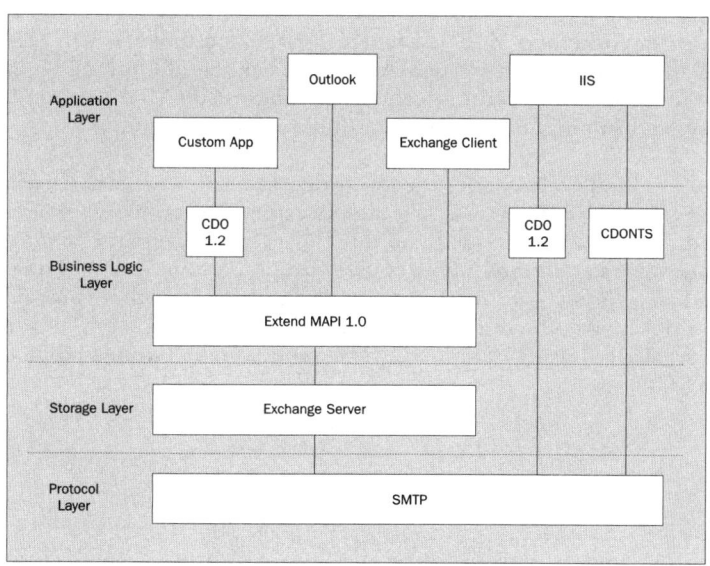

You can see that Outlook, the Exchange Client, and CDO all use MAPI to talk to the Exchange server.

Versions of MAPI and Where to Get Them

Since CDO in all its versions uses MAPI as the underlying messaging system to talk to Exchange Server, you must have the MAPI messaging system installed to use CDO's features. This is important for application developers who want to use CDO to build stand-alone applications that need access to an Exchange Server-based mailbox.

While you can download the CDO for Exchange DLL from the Microsoft web site, this does not contain the underlying MAPI system that CDO needs to talk to Exchange. It's not possible to simply distribute MAPI32.DLL, either – Microsoft's license forbids it, for one thing, and for another even if you did try this it wouldn't work because there are registry settings required which only come with a proper installation of MAPI.

There is a version of the Windows Messaging System available for download from Microsoft's web site – however, that version is very old and Microsoft do not recommend using this with CDO. Similarly, Exchange Client 5.0 (the precursor to Outlook 97) comes with a MAPI system, but that is also sufficiently old that there's no guarantee it won't fail.

Essentially, you will have to install Outlook 97, 98, or 2000. You can try using earlier versions or the freely distributable MAPI subsystem, but those are unsupported, and you may well hit mysterious problems. We don't recommend you do this, and this book is written assuming you have installed a version of Outlook to get your MAPI subsystem.

> Note that if you have Outlook 98 or Outlook 2000 installed, you have to make sure you have them installed in **Corporate or Workgroup Mode**, as opposed to **Internet Mail Only Mode**.

Beginning with Outlook 98, Microsoft developed two different versions of the Outlook client. The CW or "Corporate or Workgroup Mode", version is dedicated to work with Microsoft Exchange Server (5.0 and upwards) because it is the MAPI-based version of Outlook 98/2000. This is also the version you need to install if you want to connect to a Microsoft Mail postbox-based server, or to Novell Groupwise, and so on; it is basically the "full" version of Outlook.

The IMO, or Internet Mail Only Mode, version is dedicated to work with Mail servers which support the Internet standards for messaging and directory access, like POP3, IMAP4, and LDAP. It does not provide any MAPI subsystem and therefore can't access an Exchange Server-based mailbox. Note that you can still mail Internet users using Outlook in CW mode, as long as your Exchange Server is set up to talk to the Internet – the restriction is that you can't talk to non-Internet users in IMO mode. Of course, if your Exchange Server is set up to support Internet mail standards, you can talk to it using Outlook in IMO mode, though at this point you would probably be better off using CW mode.

CDO Versions and the Products They Ship With

Microsoft has released many different versions of its messaging client and server products. Indeed, pretty much each new messaging product from Microsoft has contained a new version of CDO as you can see from the following table.

CDO Library	Where found
CDO 1.0a	Exchange 4.0, early Outlook 97
CDO 1.1	Exchange 5.0, later Outlook 97
CDO 1.2	Exchange 5.5, Outlook 98 or 2000
CDO 1.21	Exchange 5.5 Service Packs 1-3
CDONTS	Internet Information Server 4.0
CDO Win2K	Windows 2000
CDO Exchange 2K	Exchange 2000

Knowing this history is quite important – each new variant of CDO has also brought with it new functionality, so the choice for developing CDO applications for a company is quite simple. Given that the machines in the company are not necessarily all up to date, you can

❑ Write your CDO application to the earliest version of CDO on the network, or

❑ Redistribute the latest version of CDO (1.21) across the network, having downloaded it from Microsoft's website.

Either way should guarantee that your application will work on all the systems you are writing for. Providing you have the MAPI subsystem installed, as described above, redistribution is the easiest way to go. As mentioned earlier, you can find the latest version of cdo.dll at http://www.microsoft.com/exchange/55/downloads/CDO.htm. To install it, just download the appropriate version for your machine, copy it to your Windows system directory (\Windows\System or \WinNT\System32 in the appropriate drive), and register it. To do this, open a MS-DOS command prompt window, change into the directory you copied the DLL into, and type

```
.\regsvr32 cdo.dll
```

The .\ in front of regsvr32 avoids possible problems if your Windows system directory isn't in the path.

The Different CDO Libraries

There are a large number of different libraries with "CDO" in their name. Until this point, we've only talked about "CDO 1.2", the main library intended for talking to an Exchange Server. There is actually an assortment of other libraries in this family. Here is a summary of the differences between them, and giving the abbreviations we'll be using to refer to them later on. We also list the names of the DLLs containing the various versions:

- ❏ **CDO1.0**. OLE Messaging, `OLEMSG.DLL`. Obsolete (see above).

- ❏ **CDO1.1**. Active Messaging. `ACTMSG32.DLL`. Obsolete (see above).

- ❏ **CDO1.2 (1.21)**. The main CDO library for talking to Exchange Server. `CDO.DLL`.

- ❏ **CDONTS**. The CDO for NT Server library – this is used to talk to an SMTP/POP3 server to handle Internet mail. `CDONTS.DLL`.

- ❏ **CDOR**. The CDO Rendering library, used to render CDO messaging objects into HTML for use in web pages. `CDOHTML.DLL`.

- ❏ **CDOW2K**. CDO for Windows 2000 – this follows up on CDONTS, and provides added functionality for MIME messages and NNTP (Usenet)) newsgroups. Originally known as CDO 2.0. `CDOSYS.DLL`.

- ❏ **CDOE2K**. CDO for Exchange 2000 (formerly called Exchange Platinum) – this extends CDOW2K to provide OLEDB database connectivity to the Exchange Server and objects thereon. Originally known as CDO 3.0. `CDOEX.DLL`.

CDOW2K and CDOE2K are not backwards compatible with CDO 1.21 – however, Exchange 2000 still ships with a version of CDO 1.21 you can use if you need backwards compatibility.

> Note that at the time this book goes to press neither Microsoft Windows 2000 nor Microsoft Internet Information Server 5.0 (IIS) have been released, so all information provided about CDO for Windows 2000 are subject to change by Microsoft without any notice.

In more detail, we have:

Feature	CDO1.21	CDOR	CDONTS	CDOW2K	CDOE2K
Based on OLEDB					YES
Based on MAPI	YES	YES			
Supports profiles	YES	YES			
Supports authenticated users	YES	YES			YES

Feature	CDO1.21	CDOR	CDONTS	CDOW2K	CDOE2K
Supports address book access	YES	YES			YES
Supports remote server access	YES	YES			YES
Supports SMTP access	Not directly[1]		YES	YES	YES
Supports NNTP access				YES	YES
Supports Outlook calendar access	Partially[2]	Partially[2]			YES
Supports Outlook contact access	Partially[3]	Partially[3]			YES
Supports Outlook task access					
Supports Outlook journal access					
Supports HTML rendering		YES			
Supports MHTML messages			YES	YES	YES
Supports NewMail object			YES	YES	
Can be called from ASP	YES	YES	YES	YES	YES
Compatible with IIS 4.0	YES	YES	YES		
Compatible with IIS 5.0	YES	YES	YES	YES	YES
Compatible with MCIS (Microsoft Commercial Internet System	YES		YES	YES	YES
Compatible with CDO 1.1 applications	YES	YES			

[1]. You can mail Internet users if your Exchange server is configured to allow this.

[2]. Only supports calendar access to the calendar for the primary mailbox.

[3]. Not native in the object model, and only in the primary mailbox's contacts folder.

Summary

Hopefully this short overview of the CDO libraries has given you an idea of what they are and what they're for. Don't let the fact that there are lots of so-called CDO libraries get confusing. For a start, we won't be using the Windows 2000 and Exchange 2000 versions, since they're not properly out yet, so we're down to three: CDO 1.21, CDONTS, and the CDO Rendering library.

We'll be looking at each of them separately, starting with 'pure' CDO. There should be no excuse for getting them confused by the time we reach the end of the book, since you'll have used each library in its own context.

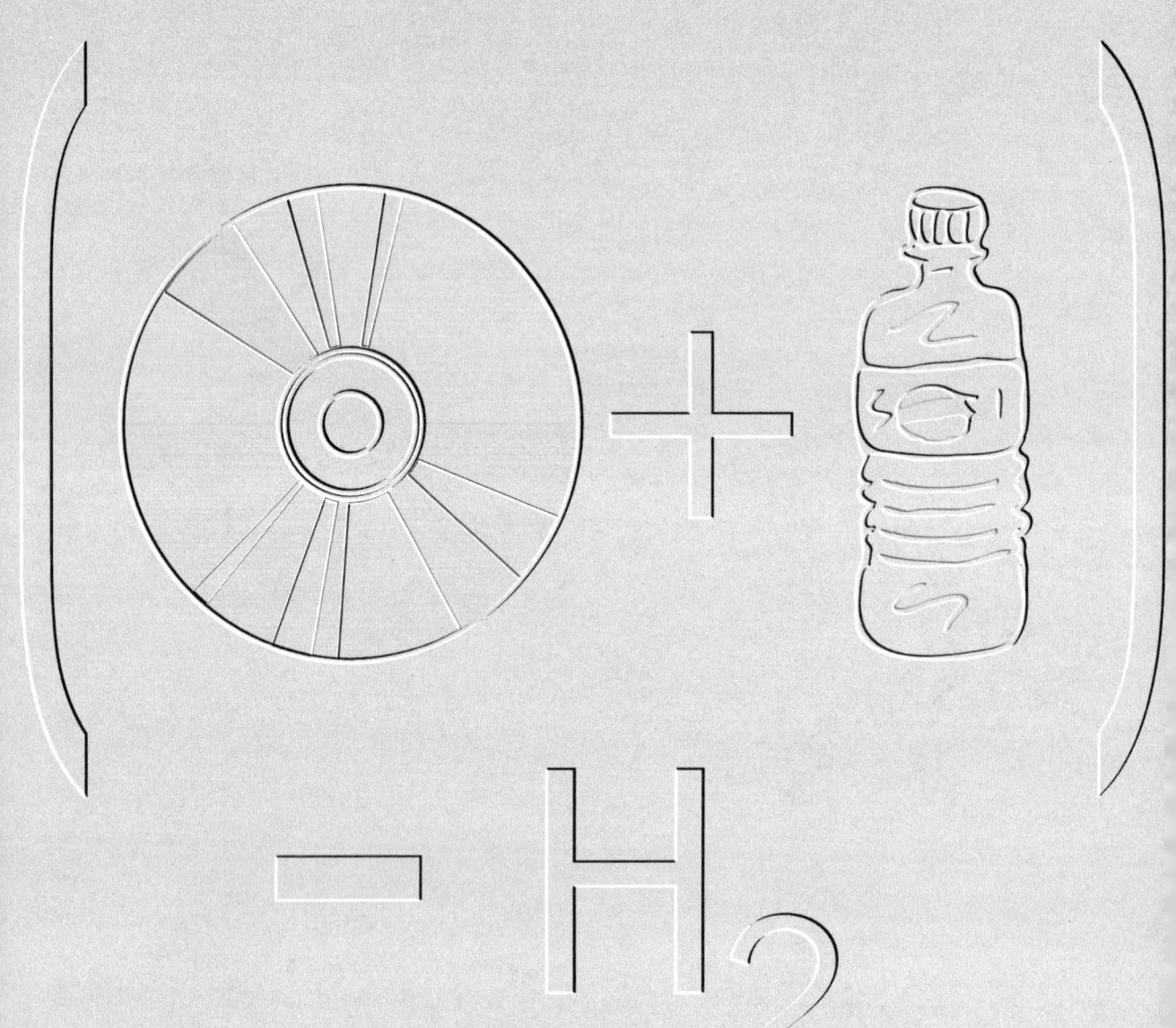

2

The CDO 1.21 Library

Introduction

In chapter 1, we were introduced to the CDO library family. The CDO libraries form the building blocks of collaboration applications. We learned what CDO libraries are and how we identify the dynamic linked libraries (DLLs) we need for developing our applications. More importantly, we know a little bit about how the current CDO libraries fit into the big picture of building collaboration applications with Microsoft Exchange Server, MAPI and Extended MAPI, CDO, standard Microsoft Windows applications, and Internet and Intranet applications. In this and the following chapters, we'll be looking specifically at the CDO 1.21 for Exchange library.

The CDO 1.21 Library

In this section, we start our journey by exploring the first of the CDO libraries: the CDO 1.21 library. We'll look at the CDO 1.21 object model and then move on to see each of the objects in action. This will present a clear picture of the object hierarchy and demonstrate how the objects relate to each other. We'll build a sample application designed to demonstrate the objects in CDO 1.21, and in the following chapters we'll expand the project as we look into each object in more detail. By the end of it, we'll have built an application that contains a subset of the features available in Microsoft Outlook, but more importantly we'll have gained an understanding of the uses of the CDO 1.21 object model.

This chapter will introduce the object model as a whole, and then move to discuss the `Session` object, which is the root object of the CDO 1.21 library. From now until the end of chapter 6, when we say 'CDO', we're referring specifically to the CDO 1.21 library unless specified otherwise.

CDO Architecture

The CDO 1.21 library lets us programmatically perform tasks that you can perform using Microsoft Outlook and Exchange Server, such as sending mail, checking free/busy information, and scheduling appointments. We might be writing an application that needs to offer our users the ability to post documents to public folders on the Exchange Server. Or, we might have an application that allows our sales representatives to arrange their appointments with management and customers.

CDO is an object-oriented interface to the Microsoft Exchange Server. If you are familiar with ADO, CDO plays the same role for Exchange application programmers as ADO does for database application programmers. Conceptually, CDO is a layer between an application and the Exchange Server, as illustrated in the following figure.

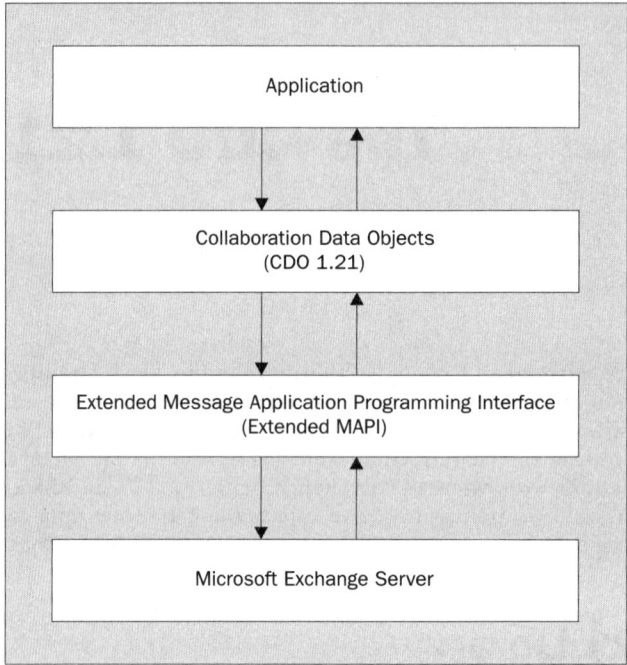

Your application communicates with CDO to perform tasks such as creating messages and accessing folders. As far as application developers are concerned, CDO represents an Exchange Server. Conceptually, CDO communicates with the Exchange Server to perform tasks requested by applications. However, CDO does not talk to the Exchange Server directly. As described in the last chapter, it uses the Extended Messaging Application Programming Interface, or Extended MAPI, to communicate to the Exchange Server.

CDO provides an object-oriented interface to the MAPI framework. It makes it easy for programmers to build messaging applications by providing a COM interface that can be accessed in a standard way by using high-level programming languages. Although we can also use CDO from other languages such as C or even Assembly that do not have direct support for COM, we'd have to put in a lot more effort to get them to work properly.

CDO Limitations

The CDO library makes it easier to work with Microsoft Exchange Server than plain MAPI does. For instance, it wraps up some of the undocumented MAPI Appointment properties so we can manage appointments easily. An indication of this is obvious when you read the CDO documentation. However, it does not really offer any extension to MAPI. It relies on MAPI to perform all messaging tasks. For instance, when we ask CDO to retrieve a message from a user's mailbox, it calls the relevant MAPI functions to actually retrieve the message from an Exchange Server and packs the returned message in a `Message` object. The client program can then access the message easily in code. While other programming languages such as C++ and Delphi can access MAPI as COM classes directly, CDO provides a uniform mechanism for all languages.

While CDO provides a convenient way to work with MAPI-compliant message stores, it does not expose the full MAPI functionality. For example, CDO does not provide a notification service to inform the client application when mail arrives. While this and some of the other limitations are expected to be fixed in CDO for Exchange 2000 (formerly CDO 3.0), we have to work with them when working with CDO 1.21.

CDO also has irregularities and bugs that could cause unexpected problems in applications. I will show you many of the common problems you'll encounter when programming with the CDO library as we meet them. But now, let's look at the CDO object model.

The CDO Object Model

Applications communicate with CDO using a set of well-defined and inter-related objects. The CDO 1.21 Library is represented as a hierarchy of objects as shown here.

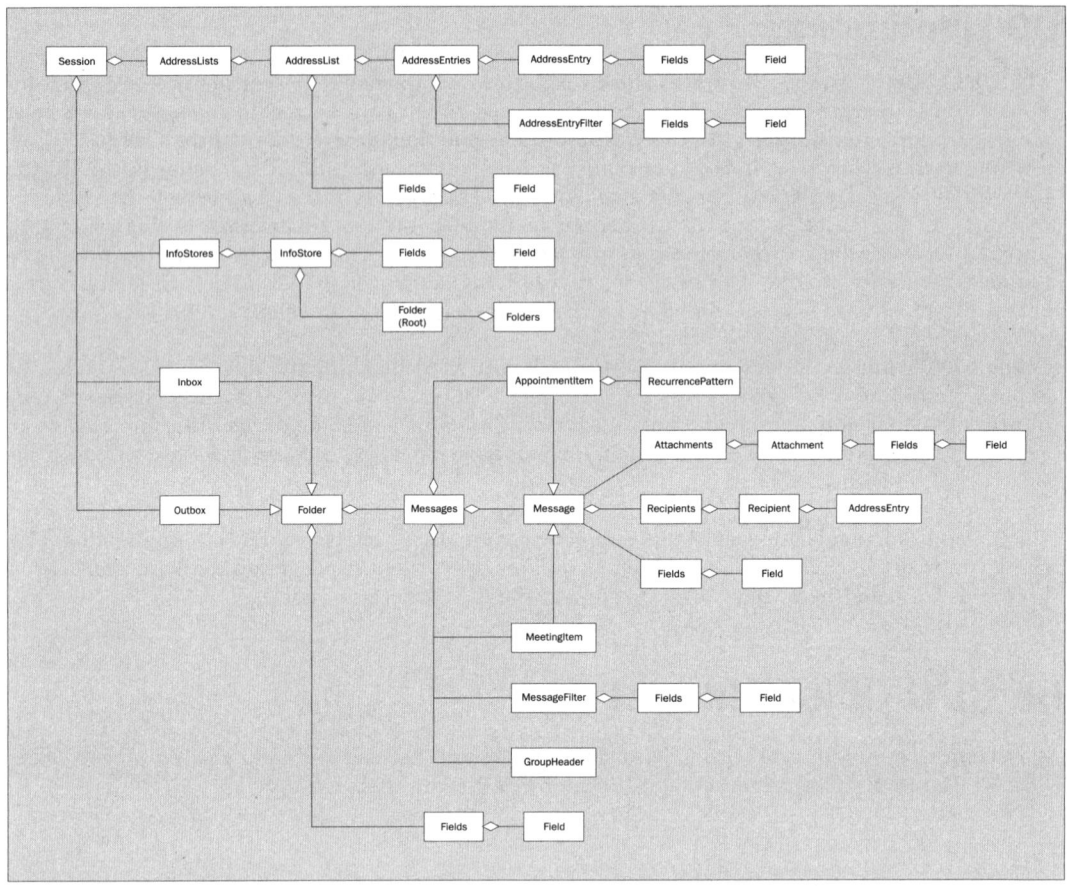

This somewhat frightening diagram represents the CDO 1.21 object model. If you're familiar with the Unified Modeling Language (UML), you should find the above diagram relatively easy to read. Please feel free to skip the following backgrounder in UML and move right along into the next section. If you're not familiar with the UML, here is a brief description of what you need to know in order to read the above diagram.

Unified Modeling Language (UML)

The UML specifies a set of notations, symbols, and diagrams to describe systems and their internal organization. One kind of UML diagram is called a class diagram, and it describes the class properties, methods, and class relationships. The object model diagram above is actually a class diagram representing the CDO object model.

Classes

In the above diagram, a rectangle represents a class, with its name displayed inside the rectangle. Each class relates to one or more other classes. The line connecting the two classes represents the relationship between them. The diagram above shows two different types of relationship between classes – **aggregation** and **generalization**.

Aggregation

A line with a diamond represents an aggregation. The class attached to the diamond 'aggregates' the class at the other end. For example, the Session class aggregates an AddressList class, a Folder class, and an InfoStores class. That is, the Session class defines properties that represent an instance of the AddressList class, an instance of the InfoStores class, and two instances of the Folder class.

Generalization

A line with a triangle represents a Generalization/Specialization relationship. The class attached to the triangle is the general, or the **base**, class; the class at the other end is the specialized form of the general class. In the above diagram, the Message class is the base class and the AppointmentItem and MeetingItem classes are **specialized**, or **derived**, classes. They inherit all properties and methods of the Message class. They also have their own properties and methods that are not relevant to the Message class.

That's all we need to know about the UML in order to understand the CDO object model as shown above. I will explain a few more UML features when we need them later on. For a more detailed discussion on UML, see Instant UML, ISBN 1861000871, also by Wrox Press.

Back to the Object Model

This chapter is going to focus on the Session object. As CDO's root object, it's the natural place to start. Before going into too much detail about that, though, we'll just introduce a few of the objects you can see in the diagram above.

In the top left corner is the Session object. All other objects are accessible by navigating through the object model starting with the Session object. It has two direct child objects, an AddressLists collection and an InfoStores collection.

If you are familiar with object-oriented technology, you will find that the term Class might be better suited to describe the objects in the CDO Library. While I would generally prefer to distinguish between the term Class and Object, I find it is easier to use the term Object to represent both the type of the object and an instance of the object when describing the CDO Library. This is also the convention used in the CDO Library documentation. Therefore I will use the term Object in general, unless I need to distinguish between the type and the instance in certain cases. In those cases, the term Class is used to represent the type of the object, and the term Object is used to represent an instance of the class.

The AddressLists collection contains all AddressList objects in the Library. An AddressList object may represent a Global Address List (GAL) or a Personal Address Book (PAB). In each AddressList object, we will have a collection of AddressEntry objects that represent the information about a person, a company, or a distribution list. An AddressEntries collection also contains an AddressEntryFilter object, which specifies the search criteria of the AddressEntries.

The `InfoStores` collection contains all `InfoStore` objects. An `InfoStore` object is the root of a collection of `Folder` objects in a message store. However, instead of containing a `Folders` collection directly, it contains a folder – `RootFolder` – which in turn contains a collection containing all folders in the store. Typically, each user has a private `InfoStore`, representing his mailbox on the Exchange Server, and a public `InfoStore`. The private `InfoStore` usually contains folders that are private to the user such as Inbox, Outbox, and the Calendar folder. A public `InfoStore` stores the public folders managed by the underlying message store.

In CDO, the `Folder` structure is recursive; that is, each folder can contain sub-folders. Each sub-folder can also have sub-sub-folders, and so on. A `Folder` object contains a collection of messages accessible through its `Messages` property. Watch out, though – in CDO, the word 'message' is really a broad term because it could refer to an e-mail message, a Word document, a contact record, an appointment, or anything that you can keep in a folder. We'll work with the most common types of messages in later chapters.

The above diagram also shows that the `Session` object contains an `Inbox` object and an `Outbox` object. They are actually both normal folders stored in an `InfoStore` representing a user's mailbox, but since they are used so frequently, the CDO `Session` object provides two properties for direct access to them.

That's it for our quick tour – we'll be looking in more detail at the objects in the following chapters. Common to all the objects, though, are four properties, which we'll look at right now.

Common Properties

Each CDO object defines a set of properties. Four of these properties are common to all the CDO objects, so we'll examine them right up front. They are the `Application`, `Class`, `Parent`, and `Session` properties.

The Application Property

The `Application` property always returns the string "Collaboration Data Objects", regardless of the CDO object you're checking. If you use a mixture of CDO and other objects in your application, the `Application` property provides a way of identifying the parent application or library of an object.

The `Application` property is read-only and can be queried as follows:

```
strCDOApplication = obj.Application
```

The Class Property

The `Class` property returns a `Long` integer representing the type (class) of the current object. The CDO Library defines a set of constants, defined in an enumeration type `CdoObjectClass`, that represents the object types. For example, a CDO `Message` object returns `CdoMsg` (3) as its class. For a complete listing of `CdoObjectClass` constants, see the `CdoObjectClass` section in Appendix B

> *In the* `CdoObjectClass` *section in Appendix B, you will see a constant* `CdoUnknown`. *It turns out that no object in the CDO 1.21 Library actually returns this constant when its* `Class` *property is queried. More detailed discussion about this constant is beyond the scope of this book, though, and it really doesn't affect us, so we can just leave this constant alone.*

The Parent Property

The `Parent` property returns an object's immediate parent object. For instance, a `Message` object's `Parent` property returns the `Messages` collection of the `Folder` object where the message is stored. This code snippet displays the class of the current CDO object's parent.

```
Debug.Print obj.Parent.Class
```

where `obj` represents whatever object you're working with. Note that the `Parent` property returns the logical parent object. For instance, an `Inbox` object's `Parent` property returns the current `Session` object instead of the `Folders` collection in the user's mailbox information store.

The Session Property

The `Session` property always returns the `Session` object current to the object you're querying. Since all CDO objects except the `Session` object itself must be created within the context of the current `Session` object, this property should never return `Nothing`. We will see how to establish a CDO session later in this chapter. A `Session` object's `Session` property returns a reference to itself.

On the subject of sessions, it's about time we moved on to look at the `Session` object.

The CDO Session Object

In CDO, we must create a `Session` object before we can access any of the other CDO objects. The `Session` object represents the connection between your application and the Exchange Server. When you say it like that, it's obvious why a `Session` object is necessary – without it, we wouldn't have a connection to the Exchange Server and so wouldn't be able to access anything on it! The `Session` object itself has a set of properties and methods as shown in the following figure:

SESSION	
Properties	**Type**
AddressLists	AddressLists
Application	String
Class	Long
CurrentUser	AddressEntry
Inbox	Folder
InfoStores	InfoStores
Name	String
Outbox	Folder
OperatingSystem	String
OutOfOffice	Boolean
OutOfOfficeText	String
Parent	Object
Session	Session
Version	String
Methods	
AddressBook	GetFolder
CompareIds	GetInfoStore
CreateConversationIndex	GetMessage
DeliverNow	GetOption
GetAddressEntry	Logoff
GetAddressList	Logon
GetArticle	SetLocaleIDs
GetDefaultFolder	SetOptions
Events	

Child Objects

The Session object has four child objects that you can access directly through its properties. They are AddressLists, InfoStores, Inbox, and Outbox. From those direct child objects, you can get to all CDO objects programmatically. Their relationships are shown below.

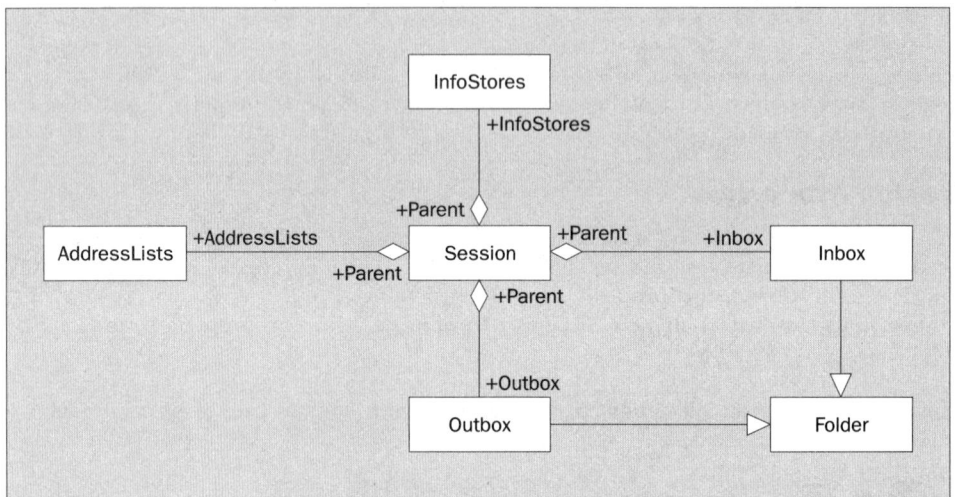

As the diagram above shows, you can access each child object using the relevant property of the Session object. Conversely, to get to the Session object from the child objects, you can simply use the Session or Parent properties as we saw earlier. The above figure only shows the Parent property, but remember that the current Session object can always be accessed from any CDO objects through their Session property.

Both Inbox and Outbox are just special instances of the CDO Folder object. The other two child objects are actually collections – AddressLists is a collection that stores all available address lists such as the Global Address List (GAL) and the Personal Address Book (PAB) in a given user profile. InfoStores is another collection, this time of information stores. It contains all public and private folders in the given profile.

Inbox and Outbox are folders that represent the message inbox and outbox (respectively) of the user. Although the above figure shows that Inbox and Outbox as special forms of the Folder object, they really behave just like simple Folder objects. You can access the Inbox and Outbox folders from the Session object through its Inbox and Outbox properties, respectively.

There are several other methods of accessing the Inbox or Outbox folder, which we'll deal with in a later chapter.

Other Properties

In addition to the four child objects, the `Session` object also has a set of other properties. Let's take a look at them now.

- ❑ `CurrentUser` – The `CurrentUser` property returns the currently logged on user as a CDO `AddressEntry` object, which we will cover in a later chapter. If you have just created a CDO `Session` object but have not logged on, or if you have logged off, this will return `Nothing` and a CDO error `CdoE_Not_Initialized` (&H80040605) will be raised.

- ❑ `MAPIObject` – The `MAPIObject` property returns an `IUNKNOWN` pointer to the current `Session` object. This is accessible to C++ applications, but not Visual Basic applications since Visual Basic does not support the `IUNKNOWN` pointer.

- ❑ `Name` – Returns the Profile Name. If you try to retrieve this property without first logging on, you will also get the `CdoE_Not_Initialized` error.

- ❑ `OperatingSystem` – The `OperatingSystem` property returns the name, version, and build information of the operating system on which your CDO application is running. For instance, running a CDO application on a Windows NT 4 Workstation, the `OperatingSystem` property returns something similar to:

  Microsoft Windows NT(TM) 4.0.1381

  This property *is* accessible without having to log on first.

- ❑ `OutOfOffice` and `OutOfOfficeText` – `OutOfOffice` returns `True` if the current user has indicated that they are not currently in the office. In Microsoft Outlook 97, 98, and 2000, we can specify whether we are out of office and create a text message to provide some details of our availability or other information. Depending on the rules created, when Exchange Server receives a message, it may automatically generate a reply with this out-of-office message. The `OutOfOfficeText` property of the `Session` object returns this text.

```
If objSession.OutOfOffice Then
    Debug.Print objSession.OutOfOfficeText
End If
```

Methods

The `Session` object also has a set of methods that perform various CDO session-related tasks.

- ❑ `AddressBook` – The `AddressBook` method displays a dialog box with all entries in the address book.

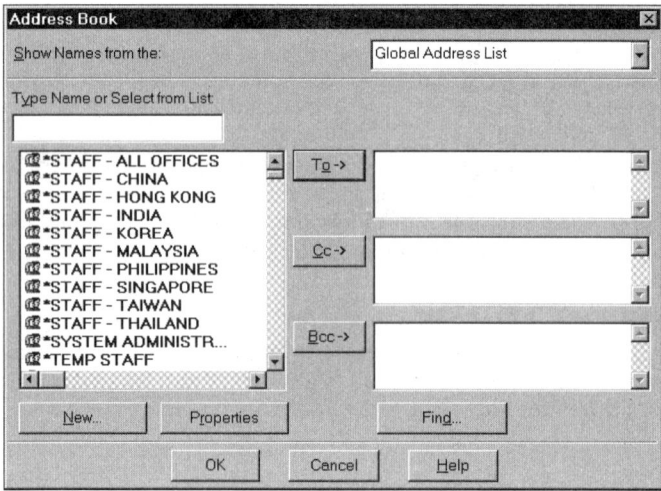

This is the same dialog box Microsoft Outlook displays when you click on the `AddressBook` button on the toolbar. We will see how we use this method in the chapter on messages, where it's more appropriate.

❑ `CompareIDs` – When a CDO object represents a message, a folder, or any other object that is stored on Microsoft Exchange Server, it is said to be a **persistent object**. That is, its state is saved between sessions. Such objects have an `ID` property of type `String`. It is a unique string of hexadecimal characters that identifies the object on the Exchange Server.

The `CompareIDs` method of the CDO `Session` object compares the unique identifiers of two CDO objects.

```
If objSession.CompareIDs(obj1.ID, obj2.ID) Then
    Debug.Print "obj1 and obj2 refer to the same object"
Else
    Debug.Print "obj1 and obj2 does not refer to the same object"
End If
```

If both CDO objects refer to the same physical object in Exchange Server, this method returns `True`. Note that the IDs themselves are not necessarily identical, since they are created by CDO when the objects are created. That's OK, though – as long as `obj1` and `obj2` represent the same object on the Exchange Server, this method will return `True`.

❑ `CreateConversationIndex` – When posting messages to public folders, you can specify a conversation topic. When users reply to this message, the responses also use the same conversation topic. This allows applications such as Microsoft Outlook to display related messages in a hierarchy, or a message thread. Each message in the thread, including the original message, has an unique index indicating the order of messages. The `CreateConversationIndex` method creates a `String` that is a valid CDO conversation index. We will see how we use this method in Chapter 5.

❏ DeliverNow – The DeliverNow method forces all undelivered messages created in the current session to be delivered immediately. You can call this method before logging out of the session to save the user from being asked whether they want to send the messages. However, this method might take a while to return as it is a synchronous operation. That is, it will not return until all messages have been transmitted to the underlying messaging system.

❏ GetAddressEntry – The GetAddressEntry method returns an AddressEntry object by its ID.

```
Set objAddressEntry = objSession.GetAddressEntry(strAddressEntryID)
```

❏ GetAddressList – The GetAddressList method retrieves the GAL or a PAB. We will learn more about this method when we go on to look at managing address books in a later chapter.

❏ GetArticle and GetMessage – The GetMessage method returns a message with the specified MessageID. It is one of the most frequently used methods and will be covered in detail in Chapter 4.

The GetArticle method retrieves a message specified by the Article ID, which is a Long integer assigned to a new message. The GetMessage method is often preferred to this method.

❏ GetDefaultFolder – The GetDefaultFolder method returns the default folder for a given folder type. It accepts a CDO constant representing a folder type listed in the following table. Although CDO is independent of the client application, some of the folder types only apply to Microsoft Outlook. These folders are shown in bold in the table below.

Folder Type	CDO Constant	Value
Calendar	CdoDefaultFolderCalendar	0
Inbox	CdoDefaultFolderInbox	1
Outbox	CdoDefaultFolderOutbox	2
Sent Items	CdoDefaultFolderSentItems	3
Deleted Items	CdoDefaultFolderDeletedItems	4
Contacts	CdoDefaultFolderContacts	5
Journal	CdoDefaultFolderInbox	6
Notes	CdoDefaultFolderInbox	7
Tasks	CdoDefaultFolderInbox	8

We will see more on this method in Chapter 3. There is also a CDO bug related to this method, which will be covered in the Logon Methods section later in this chapter.

❑ GetFolder – The GetFolder method returns the folder specified by a pair of Folder ID and InfoStore IDs. We will use this method in Chapter 3.

❑ GetInfoStore – The GetInfoStore method returns the InfoStore object specified by an InfoStore ID.

❑ GetOption and SetOption – These two methods are used in conjunction with the CDO Rendering Library. The SetOption method specifies how the CDO Container and Object Renderers render the Calendar in HTML format. The GetOption method retrieves the settings. We will see more about these two methods later in this chapter. The CDO Rendering library is covered in a later section of this book.

❑ Logon and Logoff – The Logon method logs onto the Exchange Server. We'll be looking at the Logon method in more detail in the next section; because it takes so many parameters, there are a number of ways to log on. Logoff is simpler – it simply logs the current session off.

❑ SetLocaleIDs – The SetLocaleIDs method sets the current Session object's locale. When this method is called, the Session object sets the proper locale of the log-on profile. Therefore, it must be called before logging onto the Exchange Server.

That is the Session object in a nutshell. The first thing we need to use the Session object for is usually at log-on. Before we start our sample application, let's examine the issues that arise when we consider logging onto the Exchange Server. We'll look at the Logon method and profiles before seeing how to create the entry point for our project – the log-on form.

The Logon Method

There are many log-on options. The Session object's Logon method has the following syntax:

```
gobjSession.Logon(Optional ProfileName As String = "", _
        Optional ProfilePassword As String = "", _
        Optional ShowDialog As Boolean = True, _
        Optional NewSession As Boolean = True, _
        Optional ParentWindow As Long = 0, _
        Optional NoMail As Boolean = False, _
        Optional ProfileInfo As String = "")
```

It would actually be too complicated to explain what all the parameters do here, simply because they're all inter-related. What we will do is look at various combinations, and hopefully that way you'll come to understand what all the parameters are for. You can see that all the parameters are optional, though, so you can call the Logon method without passing any arguments:

```
objSession.Logon
```

If you try this, you will get a dialog box asking which mail profile you want to use. A mail profile is a set of user-specific settings that define such things as the available services and address books. It can be created using the Mail control in the Windows Control Panel. If you have an Outlook or Windows Inbox icon on your desktop, you can also access the profile list by right-clicking it and selecting Properties on the context menu.

Note that a profile does not necessarily link to an Exchange Server because you can create a profile in Internet-only mode with SMTP e-mail functions. If a profile needs to connect to an Exchange Server, it must connect to an existing mailbox. In this case, the Exchange Server verifies that the user has access permission to the mailbox when the profile is created. Once you select a profile, the Logon method will try to connect to the Exchange Server specified in that profile and open the mailbox.

As described above, looking at all the parameters of the Logon method would be less efficient than gleaning that knowledge from a discussion of the most commonly used ways of logging on, so let's examine a few.

Using a Specific Existing Profile

Firstly, we can log on using an existing profile. This is accomplished by specifying a profile name and optionally a password:

```
ObjSession.Logon ProfileName:="MS Exchange Settings", _
        ProfilePassword:="MyPassword"
```

> *The above statement uses named arguments. In case you haven't seen these before (and apologies if you have), instead of supplying arguments in order, you can supply them by name as seen above. That means no unsightly (and confusing) string of commas when you only want to supply the last argument.*

Note that profiles are not password-protected. A password used to be required using the 16-bit Windows for Workgroups mail, but it's not used any more. CDO simply ignores the password. For this Logon method to work, we must not specify a ProfileInfo value (which is used to create a temporary profile for the current CDO session). If we do, CDO will use that value instead of the profile name we specified. This is because there can only be one log-on session, that is, you *either* use an existing profile *or* you create a temporary profile – not both. CDO always assumes that you want to create a temporary profile if you pass both parameters.

The ShowDialog argument is ignored once we pass in the ProfileName value. ShowDialog usually pops up a dialog box asking for a profile to be selected, but in this case we've already told it which one to use, so there's no need. See how it gets complicated?

The NewSession argument specifies whether CDO should create a new session for this login. If it is True (which is the default), CDO will create a new session. Otherwise, it will use an existing session if there is one or create a new one when it cannot find one.

CDO and MAPI Sessions

OK, now you might be wondering what's going on. I mean, the `Logon` method is a method of the `Session` object, right? So what's with creating a *new* session? Well, some developers distinguish a CDO session from a MAPI session. When they say a MAPI session, they mean a connection to an Exchange Server. On the other hand, creating a *CDO* session just means creating a new CDO `Session` object and logging onto an Exchange Server. This log-on may not actually establish a new connection to an Exchange Server – it could use an existing one.

In that sense, the `NewSession` argument specifies whether we need to establish a new connection to the Exchange Server. If you already have Outlook or other CDO applications running on your machine and therefore already have a connection to the Exchange Server, you might want to share the same connection in your application to reduce the load on the Exchange Server and network traffic. From now on, we'll simply use the term 'session' to mean 'CDO session'.

Back to the log-on we're in the middle of – the `ParentWindow` argument is also ignored, as it is only useful when the `ShowDialog` argument is used. As we've said, the `ShowDialog` argument is being ignored, so let's move on.

The `NoMail` argument specifies whether or not the session to be created should connect to a MAPI spooler to send and receive messages.

> *A MAPI spooler is a process responsible for sending and receiving messages from an underlying messaging system such as the Internet or a Fax system. An Exchange Server usually uses a MAPI spooler to communicate to the messaging system transport provider in order to deliver and receive messages. If the underlying messaging system is unavailable, the MAPI spooler stores outgoing messages and delivers them when the messaging system becomes available again. While it is possible to bypass the MAPI spooler if the message store connects to a transport provider directly, the details are beyond the scope of this book.*

Please note that even if `NoMail` is set to `True` (meaning that we cannot send and receive mail through a MAPI spooler), we can still access messages in the Inbox. This is useful when you use one mailbox for a group of users in your application and you only want grant certain people in the group the right to send emails through this mailbox. You can set `NoMail` to `False` for those users who are allowed to send mail, and to `True` for those who are not.

Bug in Shared Profiles

If the profile used here is also used by Outlook 98 and Outlook 2000, you may encounter an error `CdoE_No_Support` when calling the session object's `GetDefaultFolder` to find the Calendar folder. A profile is said to be 'used by Outlook' if a user has used this profile in Outlook at least once. To solve this problem, you will need to either create a temporary profile to use in your application as described later in this chapter, or use a profile that is not used by Outlook 98 or 2000.

We will see how to create a temporary profile in a minute. The `GetDefaultFolder` method and the Calendar folder will be covered in later chapters.

Asking for an Existing Profile

It is sometimes useful to have more than one profile. For instance, Microsoft Outlook allows you to select a profile to use when it starts. By default, Outlook uses one profile – normally the first profile created on a machine – automatically. You can change this by selecting Outlook's **Tools** menu and clicking **Options**. When the **Options** dialog shows up, click the **Mail Services** tab. You can then change the **Startup Settings** as shown in the following dialog.

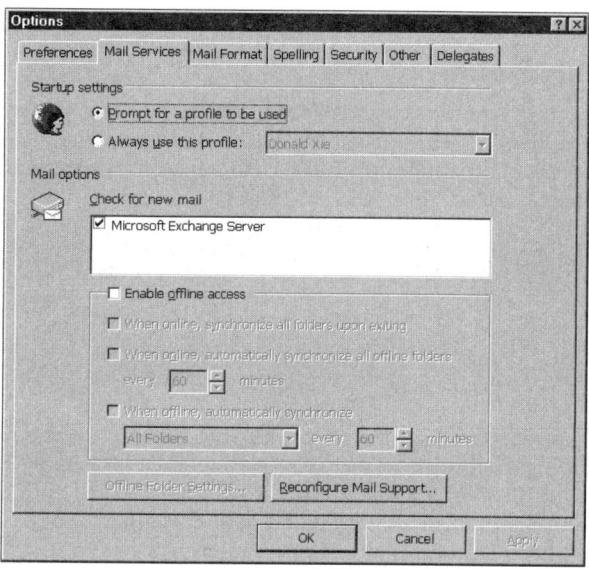

CDO provides the functionality for us to offer our users the same service. To use this, you should set the `ShowDialog` argument to `True`:

```
objSession.Logon ShowDialog:=True
```

or simply

```
objSession.Logon
```

since `ShowDialog` is `True` by default. In this case, we must not pass a `ProfileName` or a `ProfileInfo`, since either of them will cause CDO to ignore the `ShowDialog` argument. We do not need to specify a password here. CDO will use the setting stored in the profile to connect to various servers. CDO will also use the `NewSession` argument value to determine whether or not it will establish a new connection to the Exchange Server.

The `ParentWindow` argument comes into play in this case. You can pass it a window handle to set its parent to that window. A window handle is a `Long` integer assigned by Windows when a form is loaded into memory. You can determine a form's window handle through its `hWnd` property at run time. A value of -1 makes the current active window as the parent of the dialog. This is useful when you want to force the user to select a profile before proceeding. The default value is 0, which means that the dialog is application modal. That is, all forms in the application are suspended until this dialog is closed. This ensures that your user must select a profile before proceeding with any other tasks.

Creating a Temporary Profile

Sometimes you don't actually want to create profiles for a CDO application. For instance, you might want to provide your users with the ability to connect to their mailboxes from any machine on your network. In this case, creating a profile for each user on every machine could be an administrative nightmare. A better approach is to ask your users to enter their mailbox alias to connect to their mailboxes. CDO can then create a temporary profile for the current session and destroy it when the user logs off.

To generate a temporary profile, we specify the `ProfileInfo` parameter.

```
objSession.Logon ProfileInfo:="MyExchServer" & vbLF & "MailboxAlias"
```

The `ProfileInfo` is a string that consists of three parts. The first is the name of the Exchange Server. The second is always a linefeed character. And the last is an existing mailbox alias that is used to create a temporary profile. Do not use the mailbox's Display Name (such as Donald Xie), use its alias (for example, XieD) instead. Otherwise you will get a `CdoE_Logon_Failed` error. A user's mailbox alias is specified by Exchange Server administrators when the mailbox is created. You can find out a user's mailbox alias in Outlook by looking up the entry in the Global Address List.

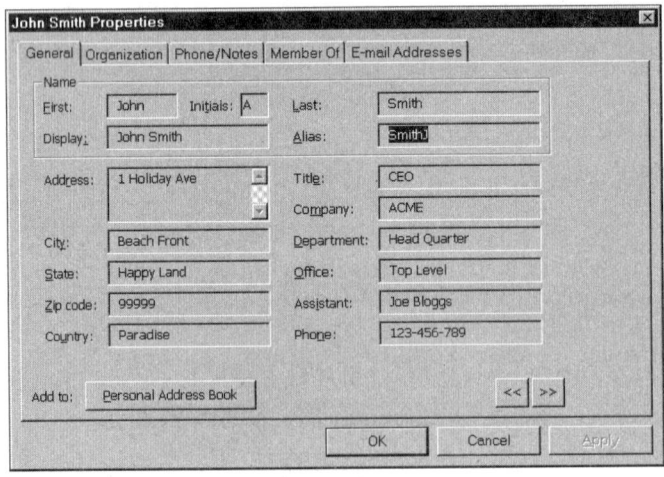

As we saw before, passing a `ProfileInfo` parameter causes CDO to ignore both the `ProfileName` and `ShowDialog` parameters. The `ProfilePassword` and `ParentWindow` parameters are also ignored implicitly. Since temporary profiles are created when the user logs in and destroyed when they log off, CDO will always establish a new connection to the Exchange Server so the `NewSession` parameter does not have any effect.

Here, we can better see the advantage of using named arguments. If we don't, we will end up doing this:

```
objSession.Logon , , , , , , "MyExchServer" & vbLF & "MailboxAlias"
```

As you can see, it's not that easy to read.

Anonymous Log-on

One of the most common CDO techniques is to let the users log on anonymously. This is useful when we develop web-based CDO applications. For instance, if we use Microsoft Internet Information Server (IIS) and Microsoft Exchange Server to implement an unrestricted online discussion group, we do not want to create a profile, permanent or temporary, for each user since they can be anybody on the Internet. There is really no need to keep track of who the users are either; they can remain anonymous if they want. We'll see an example of anonymous log-on in Chapter 13.

Just like logging on using temporary profiles, we also specify the `ProfileInfo` string to create an anonymous log-in. This time, we will need to provide a bit more information to CDO.

```
strProfileInfo = "/o=" & EnterpriseName & _
        "/ou=" & SiteName & _
        "/cn=Configuration/cn=Server" & _
        "/cn=" & ServerName & vbLf & vbLf & "anon"

objSession.Logon ProfileInfo:=strProfileInfo
```

Note that this will only work with web-based applications where your users log on to Microsoft Internet Information Server anonymously. It does not work if your web server requires users to log on using either basic authentication or Windows NT Challenge/Response authentication. Similarly it will not work in native Windows applications. In the last two cases, the Exchange Server verifies the current user against the Windows NT domain and rejects any attempt to connect anonymously.

The two `vbLf` characters and the literal string "anon" after the `ServerName` are mandatory. You must follow this exact syntax for anonymous log-on to work. When you install a Microsoft Exchange Server, the server is located in a Site, which in turn belongs to an Organization. For instance, let's say your company, ACME Group Limited, has offices in three countries: US, UK, and Australia. When setting up a server, say ACMEPerth, in Perth, Australia, it might belong to the ACMEAustralia site. The organization name might be ACMEGroup. To connect to this server, your `ProfileInfo` string will be

```
/o=ACMEGroup/ou=ACMEAustralia/cn=Configuration/cn=Server/cn=ACMEPerth[vbLf]
[vbLf]
anon
```

As usual, the best and most effective way of learning to use CDO to create messaging and collaboration applications is to actually build one. In our sample application, we will allow the user to log on using either a stored profile or a dynamically created (temporary) profile. We'll see an example of logging on anonymously in Chapter 13. We will create a Log On form to allow our users to log onto the Exchange Server.

Learning by Example – the Sample Application

The CDO 1.21 library provides a hierarchy of objects that can be accessed using Microsoft Visual Basic and other programming languages that recognize the COM architecture. To understand the techniques we can use to build CDO applications, we will work through a sample project that demonstrates the structure, capability, and problems of the CDO 1.21 Library.

What We'll Achieve

We'll be using Microsoft Visual Basic to build this sample CDO application. While we can learn by building an application using other programming languages such as C++ or Java, Visual Basic provides an excellent rapid application development (RAD) environment that helps us to get to the CDO Library easily and quickly. Therefore we will not have to spend too much time on tasks (like creating a user interface) that don't directly relate to exploring the CDO Library. Chapter 15 discusses CDO with C++.

This application will provide a subset of the messaging and collaboration functionality we find in messaging client applications such as Microsoft Outlook. It aims to demonstrate common methods of using CDO objects in Visual Basic applications.

We will start by working with the `Session` object in this chapter. In the next chapter, we will add the ability of navigating through the CDO information stores and folders. We'll examine issues like adding, copying, and deleting folders. We will also learn to access hidden CDO properties using the `Fields` collection and the `Field` object.

Chapter 4 will show how we can access and manipulate address books and address entries with CDO. We will learn to access the GAL and the PAB. We will create new address entries and edit existing address entries in the PAB. We will also discuss the issues of accessing the Outlook Contacts folder.

In chapter 5, we add the ability to create messages, send e-mail messages to other people, and post messages to public folders. We will see how we can sort and filter messages, add and extract attachments, and resolve recipients.

We will conclude our CDO sample project in chapter 6 where we add the ability to create appointments and organize meetings to it. We will also spend some time discussing the creation of recurring appointments.

Getting Started

Let's start building our project. Fire up Visual Basic and create a Standard EXE project. We will give it a very descriptive name, `CDOSample`. Since this is a CDO application, we will need to add a reference to the CDO library. To add a reference to a library, select the Project menu item and click References.

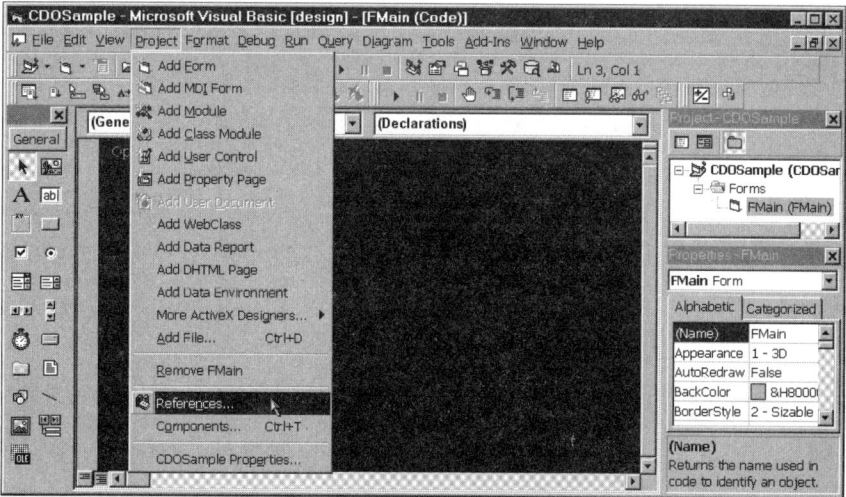

When the References dialog pops up, scroll down the Available References list and check Microsoft CDO 1.21 Library.

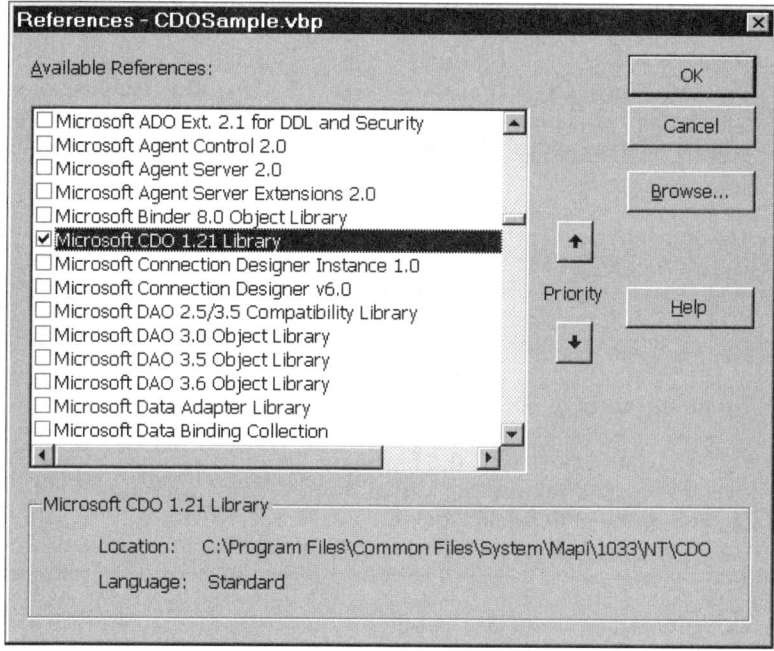

Just a note on using the Object Browser: you can either press *F2* in the Visual Basic IDE or select the View menu item and click Object Browser to bring up the Object Browser. If you also use it, be sure to select the MAPI library when checking CDO objects because that is how the CDO library is referenced. You will not find a library called CDO in the Object Browser.

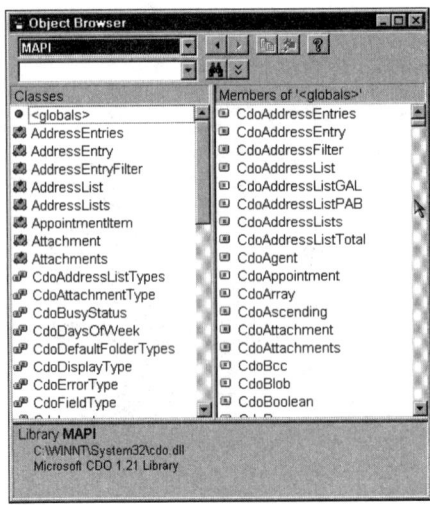

The Common Module

Add a standard module to the project and name it MCommon. We will use this module to store application-wide settings and utility functions.

The very first step of running a CDO application is almost always to create a Session object and log on to the Exchange Server. This Session object will be used throughout the application, so it seems sensible to make it an application-wide global object. We can then use it whenever we need to.

```
Option Explicit

Public Const gcstrServer As String = "Server" & vbLf

Public gobjSession As MAPI.Session
```

You should substitute the name of your server for the word 'Server' above.

It is also often a good technique to cache the Exchange Server name in the system registry and load it up when we log on. You can use the Visual Basic GetSetting function to read Windows registry entries. If we ever need to replace one Exchange Server with another, we can easily change its registry entry to point to the new server and our application will continue to work. In this sample application, however, we'll just hard-code it into the application by assigning it to a constant.

The Log-On Form

Before we start to build the log-on form, let's look at the steps we need to go through to log on to the Exchange Server. When the application starts, the application will display a log-on form. The user then supplies either their profile name or mailbox alias. The form will have a `Logon` method that will deal with the actual log-on process. When the log-on operation is completed, it sets the CDO `Session` object, `gobjSession`, that we defined previously in `MCommon`. This object will be available throughout the life of our CDO Sample application.

Of course, we might encounter an error during the log-on process due to, say, an invalid profile name. The user may also cancel the log-on. When either of those events occur, we can either force the user to log on again or stop the application.

Rename `Form1` to `FLogon` and add several controls to it so that it looks like the following figure. In this and subsequent chapters, we'll use diagrams like this to show what controls you need to add, and what properties you need to change. Note that such things as `Text` and `Caption` properties are not given, as they should be obvious from the screenshot itself. We've also only showed changes to the defaults, except in certain cases where the default value is essential to make the control work the way we want it to. In those cases we'll show these values as well.

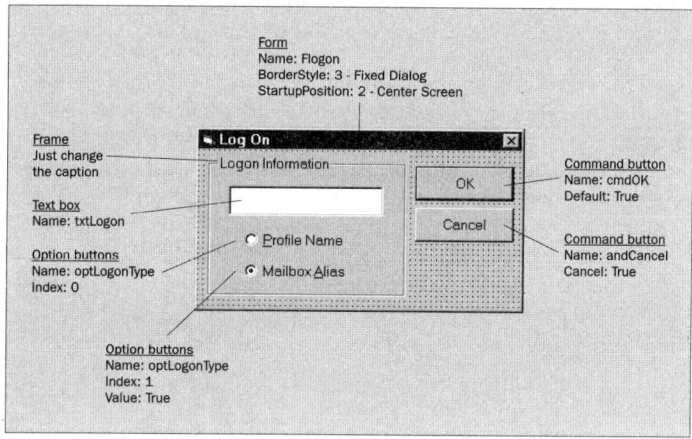

Recall that this form will have a `Logon` method that will use CDO to perform the tasks of actually logging on to an Exchange Server, we will put the code that performs the log-on operations in this method.

```
Private Function Logon() As Boolean
    On Error GoTo ErrHandler

    Set gobjSession = New MAPI.Session
    With gobjSession
        Select Case True
            Case optLogonType(0).Value
                ' Logon using existing profile
                .Logon ProfileName:=txtLogon.Text

            Case optLogonType(1).Value
                .Logon ProfileInfo:=gcstrServer & txtLogon.Text, _
                    ShowDialog:=False
```

```
        End Select
    End With

    ' We have logged on
    Logon = True

ExitFunc:
    Exit Function

ErrHandler:
    ' Display an error and ask the user to log on again
    MsgBox "Invalid Profile Name or Mailbox Alias , try again!", , "Logon"
    txtLogon.SetFocus
    SendKeys "{Home}+{End}"

    Resume ExitFunc
End Function
```

First, we create a new `Session` object. You'll recall that we declared the object in the `MCommon` module. We didn't instantiate it, though, as we want to do that here. Next, the code checks the log-on type. If the user indicates that they wish to log on using a stored profile, we call the `Session` object's `Logon` method and pass in the profile name (as entered in the text box) to the `ProfileName` parameter. Otherwise, we will build the profile string by concatenating the server name and mailbox alias and pass it to the `Logon` method of the `Session` object.

If we logged on successfully, we return `True` to the calling routine. If there is an error, we display an error message and return `False`. Here we apply a little user-friendliness feature by highlighting the text box content and put the focus back on it. This is done by sending a combination of the *Home* and *End* keys. The user can then reenter the profile name or alias straight away without having to reach for their mouse.

We can then code the `cmdOK_Click` event handler to call this method.

```
Private Sub cmdOK_Click()
    If Logon() Then
        Unload Me
    End If
End Sub
```

If we have logged on successfully, we dismiss the log-on form and proceed with other tasks. Otherwise, we will wait for the user to try again.

If the user decides that they don't want to log on, they can click on the Cancel button and we will terminate the application. We will see how this is done in a minute. For now, the `cmdCancel_Click` event handler is fairly simple. Add this code to the log-on form (we'll alter it later):

```
Private Sub cmdCancel_Click()
    On Error Resume Next

    Unload Me
End Sub
```

So the log-on process is simple, and it seems almost too good to be true. Well, like everything else in life, if something seems too good to be true, it is. There is a problem with this approach, and it is not our fault.

Ensuring Successful Log-on

CDO has a very interesting behavior where it may defer the error reporting on log-on. If we cannot log on for whatever reason, the `Session` object's `Logon` method does not always raise an error. In many cases, it will just silently execute without much complaint. Only when you try to perform some other operations using the `Session` object will it surprise you with an error.

There is no documentation on when this will definitely happen, but it does happen. We will have to perform a little more testing to ensure that the log-on process has indeed been successful. One reliable workaround is to actually try to access the user's Inbox. If we can do this, we can be sure that the log-on process is indeed fine.

Please note that since the Inbox is stored in a user's mailbox on an Exchange Server, this only works when we log on as a user who has a mailbox on the Exchange Server. An anonymous user does not have a mailbox, so we cannot use this to verify a successful anonymous log-on. We can, however, try to access the root public folder. If we can access the root public folder, we are fine. Otherwise, we have not logged in properly. For details about performing anonymous access to public folders, please see Chapter 13.

Testing whether or not we can access the logged-on user's Inbox is actually quite simple. The CDO `Session` object exposes an `Inbox` property that returns a reference to the logged-on user's Inbox folder. All we need to do in our program is to assign it to a CDO `Folder` object. If the `Session` object's `Logon` method fails, attempting to assign its `Inbox` property to a `Folder` object will definitely raise an error. If it does not raise an error, we're home free.

Let's modify the `Logon` method of the log-on form to perform this additional checking.

```
Private Function Logon() As Boolean
    On Error GoTo ErrHandler

    ' For testing log-on only
    Dim objFolder   As MAPI.Folder

    Set gobjSession = New MAPI.Session
...
        End Select

        ' Ensure that we have actually logged on since the
        ' Logon method might not report an error even if
        ' the log-on fails
        Set objFolder = .Inbox
    End With
...
ExitFunc:
    ' Clean up
    Set objFolder = Nothing
    Exit Function
...
```

So the solution is to define a `Folder` object and assign it the `Session` object's `Inbox`. Before we exit the function, we should set this object to `Nothing` to release the reference to the Inbox folder. While it is generally good programming practice to explicitly release any object reference that is no longer in use, it is particularly important in CDO programming because we might not be able to log off properly if references to any objects in the current session are not released before the `Logoff` method is invoked. It doesn't really matter in this function as Visual Basic will destroy this reference when it goes out of scope, but we should leave nothing to chance.

Logging Off

It is logical at this point that we also create a `Logoff` method. We'll actually put this method in the `MCommon` module as a public method, so that it can be called from anywhere in the application.

```
Public Sub Logoff()
   On Error Resume Next

   If Not gobjSession Is Nothing Then
      gobjSession.Logoff
      Set gobjSession = Nothing
   End If
End Sub
```

It checks whether the `Session` object is valid. If so, it calls the `Session` object's `Logoff` method. Because a valid `Session` object doesn't tell us whether or not we are logged in successfully, it might raise an error if we try to log off when we're not logged on, if you see what I mean. But since we're trying to log off anyway, we're not concerned about this error. The line:

```
   On Error Resume Next
```

takes care of this. We then set the `Session` object to `Nothing` to avoid a memory leak here. Setting the `Session` object to `Nothing` releases the memory it occupies. However, there is a bug in Extended MAPI that does not release a MAPI session properly and therefore causes a memory leak. Unfortunately, this is out of our control. We just have to do the best we can in our own applications.

Back to our application, setting the `Session` object to `Nothing` actually has one additional purpose in our application. The CDO `Session` object does not provide a shrink-wrapped method for us to check whether it is connected to an Exchange Server. While there are many ways of testing its connection state, such as trying to access the logged-on user's Inbox, the best way to make sure that we always have a connection to the Exchange Server is to instantiate the `Session` object just before we log on, and release it right after we disconnect. That means that if we have a valid `Session` object, we are connected.

This is a rather simplistic statement, because it is possible that the Exchange Server might crash, or the network could break down during a session. Although such exceptions are preventable, I will not get into detail here to keep our application focused. In addition, if something went wrong and we do not release the Session object, we might run into trouble when attempting to log on again.

No doubt you're wondering what would happen if something goes wrong in the `Logon` method of the log-on form. We should look after this situation by calling the `Logoff` method in the error handler of the `Logon` method.

```
Private Function Logon() As Boolean
   On Error GoTo ErrHandler

   ' For testing log-on only
```

```
        Dim objFolder As MAPI.Folder

            ' If we have logged on previously, log off now
            Logoff

            Set gobjSession = New MAPI.Session
    ...
    ErrHandler:
            ' Logoff to release the object reference
            Logoff

            ' Display an error and ask the user to log on again
    ...
    End Function
```

We also call the `Logoff` method just before instantiating the `Session` object, just to cover our backs. We should also do the same when the user clicks the `Cancel` button.

```
    Private Sub cmdCancel_Click()
        On Error Resume Next

            ' Explicitly logoff just in case
            Logoff

            Unload Me
    End Sub
```

The Startup Module

Now the log-on form is completed, we will write the code to load this form when the application starts. We'll keep this code in a new module, so add a second standard module and call it `MStartup`. This will be the entry point of the application. We'll create a `Main` method and change the Startup Object of the project to `Sub Main`. You can do this by going into the **Project Properties** dialog as shown in the following figure.

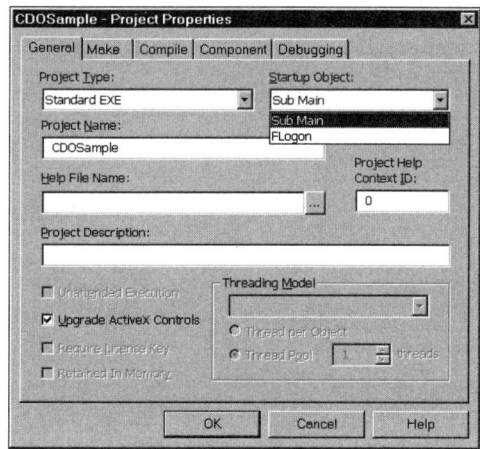

The `Main` method simply loads up the `Logon` form and waits for it to finish.

```
Private Sub Main()
    Dim frmLogon As FLogon

    Set frmLogon = New FLogon
    frmLogon.Show vbModal
    Set frmLogon = Nothing

    If Not gobjSession Is Nothing Then
        ShowMainForm
    End If
End Sub
```

It creates an instance of the log-on form and shows it as a modal form. This is necessary since we must log on first before performing any other operations.

After the user unloads this form by either logging on successfully or canceling the form, the `Main` method releases the reference to this form to free up the memory. It then tests whether or not the global `Session` object is valid since we know that it will be set to `Nothing` if not connected. If it is connected, we call the `ShowMainForm` method that loads the main form of the application. For now, the `ShowMainForm` method will simply display a message box and log off. Add it to the `MStartup` module and we'll alter it later.

```
Private Sub ShowMainForm()
    Msgox "Connected!"
    Logoff
End Sub
```

Now we've seen how to instantiate a `Session` object and use it to log onto the Microsoft Exchange Server, it's time to take a closer look at the properties and methods of the CDO `Session` object.

The Sample Project's Main Form

The main form will be the central location for working with our application. Add a new form to the project, and call it `FMain`. We are going to use a TreeView control to display all `InfoStore` objects and folders in the `Session` object's `InfoStores` collection. To use the TreeView control, we will need to add the Microsoft Windows Common Controls 6.0 to our toolbar by right-clicking and selecting **Components...** from the pop-up menu.

Now add a TreeView control to the main form and name it `tvwFolders`. We will need to change several properties of the control as shown here.

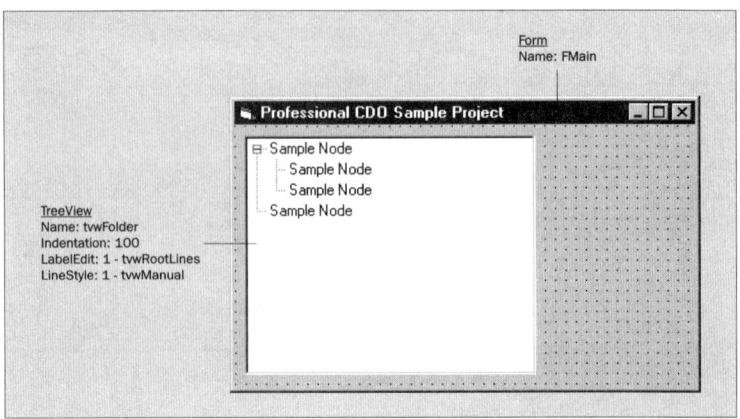

After you change the TreeView control's `Indentation` property to 100, Visual Basic may immediately change it to 99.77 due to its internal design. This is fine. You can leave all other properties as default or set them as you like.

Information Stores

Now open the code window of `FMain` and add a procedure `ShowInfoStores` to it.

```
Private Sub ShowInfoStores()
    On Error GoTo ErrHandler

    Dim objStore As MAPI.InfoStore

    tvwFolders.Nodes.Clear
    For Each objStore In gobjSession.InfoStores
        Call tvwFolders.Nodes.Add(Key:=objStore.ID, Text:=objStore.Name)
    Next

ExitFunc:
    Set objStore = Nothing
    Exit Sub

ErrHandler:
    MsgBox "Error [" & FormatHex(Err.Number) & "]: " & Err.Description

    Resume ExitFunc
End Sub
```

In this procedure, we display the name of each `InfoStore` object in the tree view as we traverse through the collection. Note that the TreeView control requires that each node have a unique key. Since the `ID` property of each info store object is always unique, we can use it as the key of the node. This `ID` can be used to retrieve an info store object using the `Session` object's `GetInfoStore` method.

Tracking and Handling Errors

If there is an error, we'd ideally like to display the error number in hexadecimal format. This is not a requirement but a convenience, since both the CDO and MAPI documentations list error codes in hexadecimal format. Showing errors in this format helps us to find the error description in the documentation easily.

The `FormatHex` function converts an error code to a string representing an 8-digit hexadecimal number. Since this is a heavily-used function throughout the application, we should place it in the `MCommon` module so we can use it at any time.

```
' Format a long integer to an 8 digit hex string such as &H12345678
'
Public Function FormatHex(lngNumber As Long) As String
    Dim strPadding As String
    Dim strHex As String
```

```
      strHex = CStr(Hex(lngNumber))
      strPadding = "00000000"
      FormatHex = "&H" & Left(strPadding, 8 - Len(strHex)) & strHex
   End Function
```

We can then display error codes in hexadecimal format, using a subprocedure we'll write in a minute. Since this is a sample project aiming to demonstrate the CDO objects, we won't handle errors as comprehensively as we would in a production system. In most cases, we will simply display a message box showing the rather cryptic CDO error description as shown here:

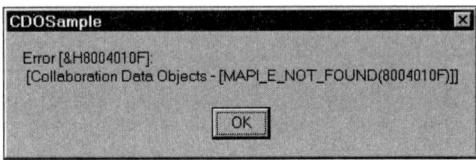

This shows the MAPI error constant and value in hexadecimal format. You can translate a MAPI error constant to a CDO error constant by replacing MAPI_E with CdoE. For instance, the corresponding CDO error constant is CdoE_Not_Found.

For convenience, we'll add a ReportError procedure in MCommon and simply call this when required.

```
' Display a message box to report an error
'
Public Sub ReportError(Err As VBA.ErrObject)
   MsgBox "Error [" & FormatHex(Err.Number) & "]: " & _
         vbCrLf & Err.Description
End Sub
```

The ShowInfoStores method in FMain will simply call this function when an error occurs.

```
Private Sub ShowInfoStores()
...
ErrHandler:
   Call ReportError(Err)
   Resume ExitFunc
End Sub
```

Displaying Information Stores

Depending on the requirements of your application, you might want to display the info store list when the form loads. This is what we will do in this sample application. Add this code snippet, which is the Form_Load event handler of FMain, to the main form:

```
Private Sub Form_Load()
   Call ShowInfoStores
End Sub
```

Since this is the main form of our application, it makes sense to log off when this form unloads. We can do this in the form's `QueryUnload` event handler.

```
Private Sub Form_QueryUnload(Cancel As Integer, UnloadMode As Integer)
    On Error Resume Next
    Logoff
End Sub
```

We do not care if an error occurs here; we just unload the form anyway.

Now the basic functionality of the main form is done, we just need to load it up when the application starts. Go back to the `MStartup` module and modify the `ShowMainForm` procedure to instantiate and load the `FMain` form.

```
Private Sub ShowMainForm()
    On Error GoTo ErrHandler

    Dim frmMain As FMain
    Set frmMain = New FMain
    frmMain.Show

ExitFunc:
    Set frmMain = Nothing
    Exit Sub

ErrHandler:
    Call ReportError(Err)
    Resume ExitFunc
End Sub
```

We can now save the project and run it to have a quick look at what shows up when we log on. First, log-on using an existing profile and the output will be similar to the following screen shot.

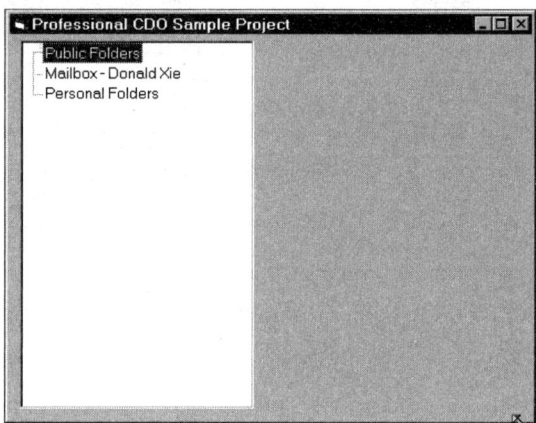

This screen shot shows that the profile contains three info stores. The first of these is a Public Folders info store, containing all public folders maintained in the Exchange Server. We will see more about public folders in a later chapter. We also see a Mailbox store that represents all folders in the logged-on user's mailbox stored on the Exchange Server.

The third store is the personal folder store that contains folders that are included in the profile and stored locally on the user's PC. If you do not see a personal folder store, you might not have it in your profile. You can verify this by going into the Windows Control Panel and opening the Mail applet. By default, it displays the information services included in the default profile.

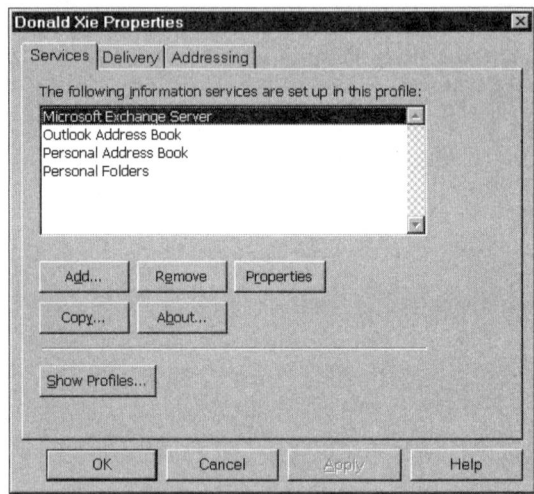

If the Personal Folders entry is not listed, you can click the **Add** button to add it to the profile.

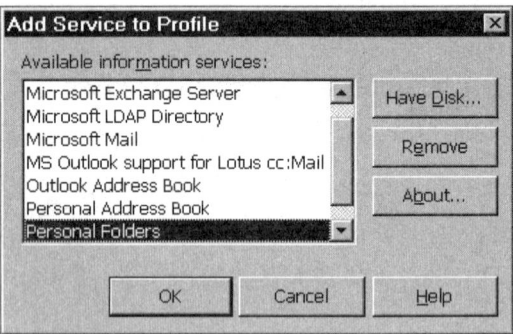

If you have more than one profile, you can click on the **Show Profiles** button to see a list of all profiles.

Once you add the Personal Folders to your profile, the sample application will display it in the info store list.

The Personal Folders store, however, does not show up if you log on using a temporary profile. This is because the Personal Folders store specifically belongs to a profile. Temporary profiles do not contain personal folders since such profiles are created and destroyed dynamically. That means that they cannot contain any local settings.

CurrentUser, Application, and Version Properties

We can personalize our main form by displaying the currently logged-on user's name and CDO version information. This can be done in the `Form_Load` event handler. Make the following changes to the code in the main form:

```
Private Sub Form_Load()
    With gobjSession
        Me.Caption = .CurrentUser.Name & " - " & _
                .Application & " v" & .Version
    End With

    Call ShowInfoStores
End Sub
```

The `CurrentUser` property of the `Session` object is an `AddressEntry` object representing the current user. It has a `Name` property that stores the display name of the user. We will see more about `AddressEntry` objects in the next chapter.

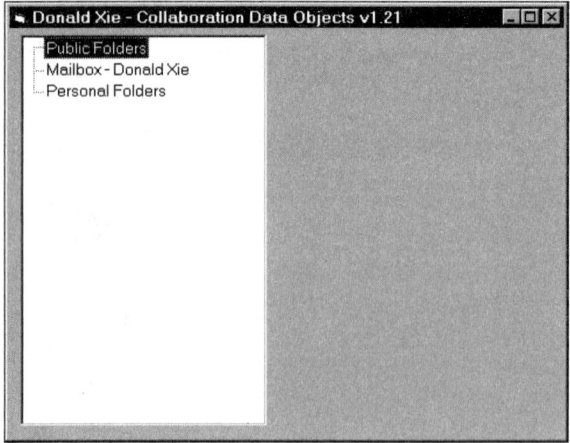

Session Options and GetOption/SetOption Methods

One of the most common uses of the CDO library (and its companion, the CDO Rendering library) is to enable the collaboration of people over the Internet or an intranet. The CDO library allows an application to connect to an Exchange Server, while the CDO Rendering library renders the messages and other items to proper HTML format so that the users can use their web browsers to view the messages. The `Session` object contains a set of display options that are most commonly used by the CDO Rendering library to format the display. These options can be obtained or modified using the `Session` object's `GetOption` and `SetOption` methods.

We will see more about the CDO Rendering library later on in the book. If you are using Microsoft Outlook, you can view most of the settings by going into Tools | Options | Calendar Options.

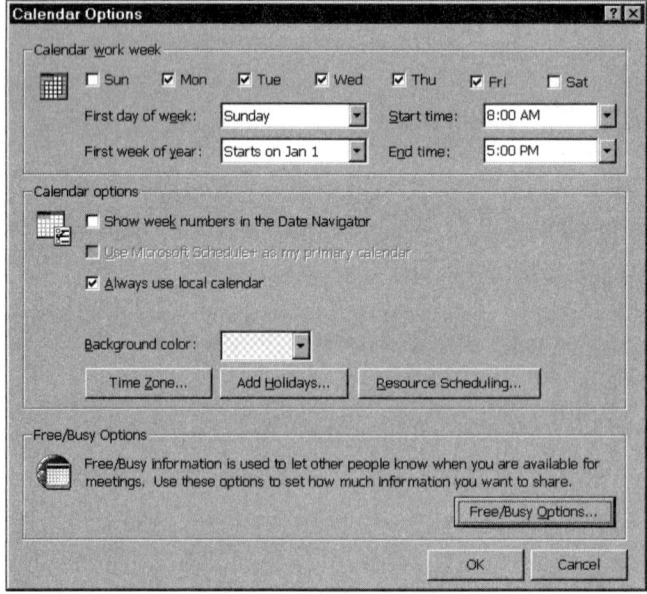

For now, let's have a quick look at what those options in the CDO Session object are, and how we can retrieve them.

Option	Value Type	Value
CalendarStore	String	Specifies where the user's Calendar folder is stored. It can be either "Outlook" or "SchedulePlus".
WorkingDays	Long	CdoMonday, CdoTuesday, etc. You can use the bitwise OR operator to specify a combination of days. The default is *CdoMonday Or CdoTusday Or ... Or CdoFriday*, which is 62.
FirstDay OfWeek	Long	1. Monday 2. Tuesday ... 7. Sunday (Default)
BusinessDay EndTime	Variant (vbDate)	HH:MM AM/PM (HH:MM) Default is 5:00 P.M. (17:00)
BusinessDay StartTime	Variant	HH:MM AM/PM (HH:MM) Default is 9:00 A.M. (09:00)
FreeBusyMonths	Long	Default is 3
Is24HourClock	Boolean	True – 24 Hour Clock False – 12 Hour Clock (Default)
TimeZone	Long	See ContainerRender object in the CDO Rendering Library

The Options Form

Let's get back to our project and add another new form to the project to display those options. Name the new form FOption and add a ListView control and a command button to it. The following figure and table show the form and its controls.

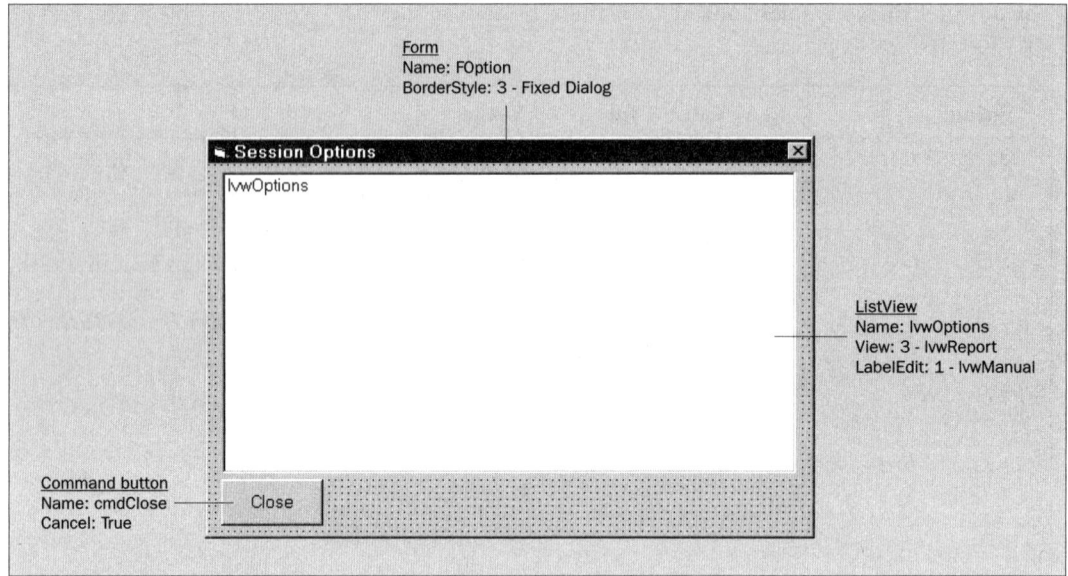

Now add the following code to the `FOption` form.

```
Option Explicit

Private Sub cmdClose_Click()
   Unload Me
End Sub

Private Sub Form_Load()
   ShowOptions
End Sub

Private Sub ShowOptions()
   On Error GoTo ErrHandler

   Dim arrOptions As Variant
   Dim nodOption As MSComctlLib.ListItem
   Dim lngIndex As Long

   With lvwOptions.ColumnHeaders
      .Clear
      .Add Text:="Option"
      .Add Text:="Value"
   End With

   arrOptions = Array("CalendarStore", _
               "WorkingDays", _
               "FirstDayOfWeek", _
               "BusinessDayStartTime", _
               "BusinessDayEndTime", _
               "FreeBusyMonths", _
```

```
                        "Is24HourClock", _
                        "TimeZone")

        With lvwOptions.ListItems
            .Clear
            For lngIndex = 0 To UBound(arrOptions)
                Set nodOption = .Add(Text:=arrOptions(lngIndex))
                nodOption.SubItems(1) = _
                    gobjSession.GetOption(arrOptions(lngIndex))
            Next
        End With

ExitFunc:
    Exit Sub

ErrHandler:
    Call ReportError(Err)
    Resume ExitFunc
End Sub
```

The main procedure is `ShowOptions`, which displays the options and their values on the ListView control, `lvwOptions`. First, it sets up the headers represented by the `ColumnHeaders` property. We will have two columns: Option for the name string of the option, and Value for the option's value.

It then creates a string array storing the name of the available options. Note that there is no CDO constant that represents any of the option names, so we will use the literal values here. The `ShowOptions` method then retrieves the option values using the `Session` object's `GetOption` method and displays them in the ListView control.

The `FreeBusyMonths` option is new with Microsoft Exchange Server 5.5 Service Pack 2. If you receive an error `CdoE_Invalid_Parameter` (which equates to `&H80070057` and corresponds to the MAPI error constant `MAPI_E_InvalidArg`) when trying to access this option, you should check whether Exchange Server Service Pack 2 is installed on your server machine and whether the version number of `CDO.DLL` on the client machine is 5.5.2448.0 or later. You can check for this version number by right-clicking the `CDO.DLL` file in your WinNT\System32 or Windows\System folder and selecting Properties.

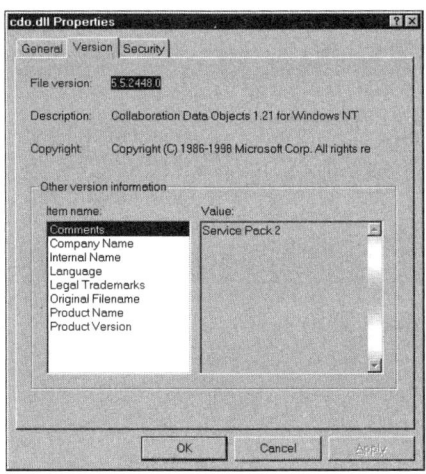

Before we can run it, we need to find a way to load this form from the main form. We'll add a menu to FMain in the Visual Basic IDE through the Menu Editor button on the toolbar or from the Tools menu. The menu we are creating has the following items.

Menu Item Caption	Name
&File	mnuFile
E&xit	mnuFileExit
&Tools	mnuTools
&Options	mnuToolsOptions

We will add more items to the menu as we progress. For now, add these two procedures to the FMain form.

```
Private Sub mnuFileExit_Click()
    Unload Me
End Sub

Private Sub mnuToolsOptions_Click()
    Dim frmOption As FOption
    Set frmOption = New FOption
    frmOption.Show vbModal
    Set frmOption = Nothing
End Sub
```

That's all we need for the moment. When you run the project and select Options from the Tools menu, you should see a display similar to the following:

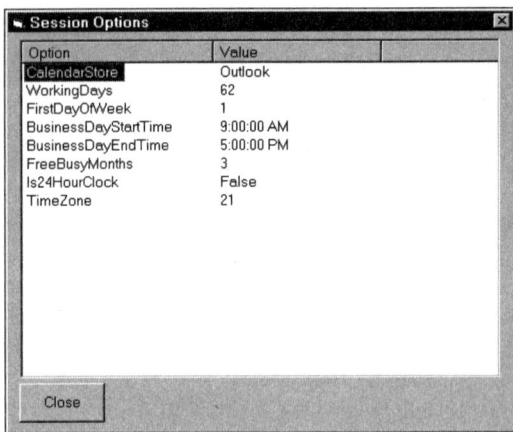

The SetOptions method allows you to set the options.

```
gobjSession.SetOption OptionName, OptionValue
```

CDO does not restrict the value of options set by the SetOptions method. You, as a programmer, are responsible for ensuring that the values are meaningful. Assigning invalid values to options may cause unexpected errors. For instance, the FreeBusyMonths option specifies the number of months during which a user's calendar information will be made available to other users. In CDO applications, we can retrieve such information by using the GetFreeBusy methods of the AddressEntry and Recipient objects. Because the Exchange Server must save all appointments and meetings within that period, setting the FreeBusyMonths option to a large number can consume a large amount of memory on the server.

Summary

In this chapter, we've introduced the CDO 1.21 library and its object model. The CDO 1.21 library provides the ability for applications to access Microsoft Exchange Server and other MAPI-compliant message stores. We can use CDO to create custom messaging and collaboration applications that serve the need of corporations and people to communicate and share information.

We have created a sample project that we'll use to demonstrate the CDO Session object and its properties and methods. In particular, we learned to create a CDO session to connect to Exchange Servers. This is just the beginning; we'll use this sample project to learn more CDO programming techniques in the following chapters.

In the next chapter, we will extend the sample application to access information stores and folders.

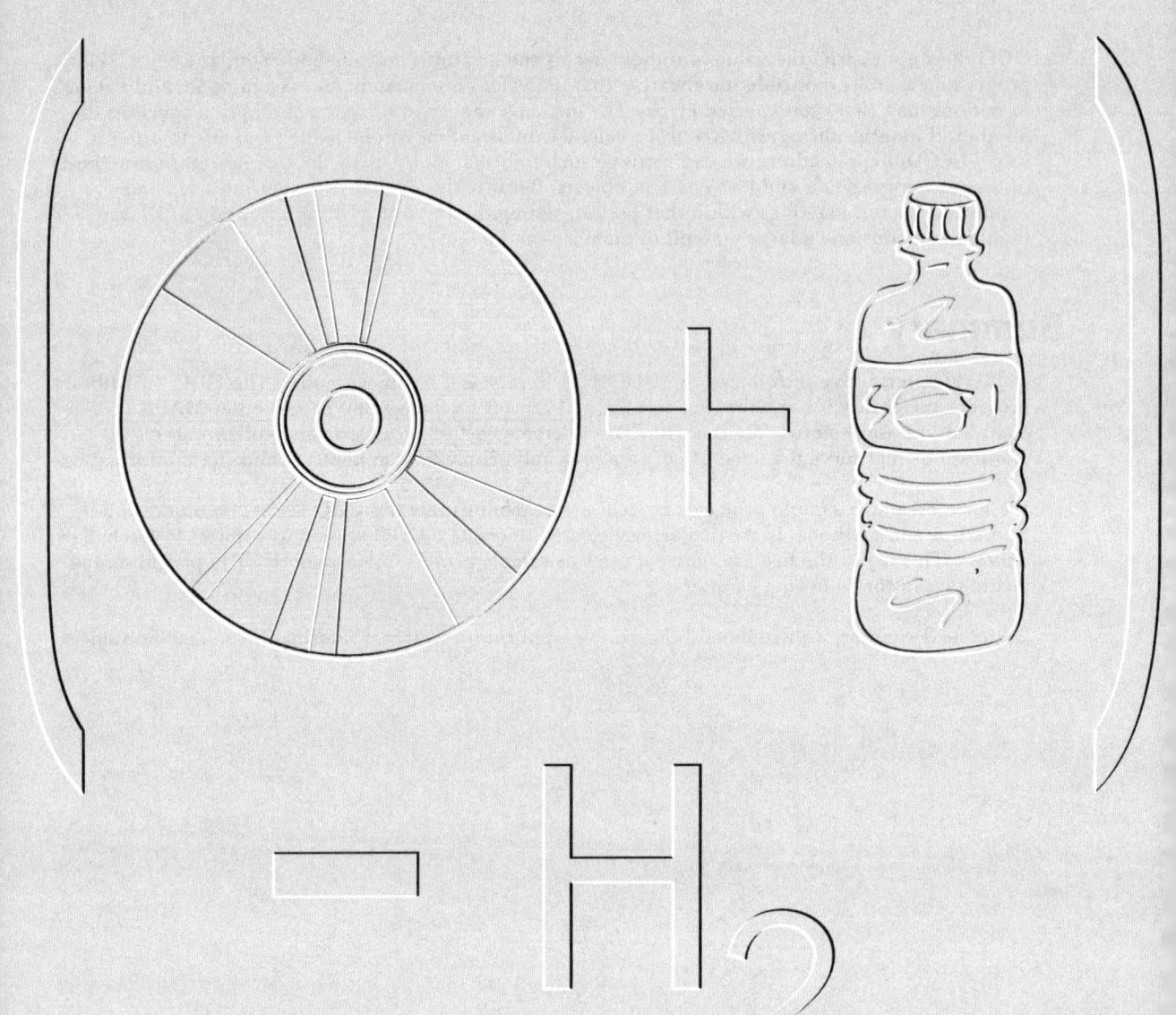

3

Managing Information Stores

Introduction

In the first chapter, we introduced the process of logging onto the Microsoft Exchange Server using the CDO `Session` object. The CDO Sample application we created in the first chapter currently only demonstrates the very basics of CDO applications – namely, how a CDO application connects to an Exchange Server with the `Session` object. Once we have established a connection, we can then proceed to access messages, appointment items, and the other information stored on the Exchange Server.

In this chapter, we'll learn about CDO information stores and `Folder` objects. First, we'll look at the CDO `InfoStores` collection and the `InfoStore` object. We'll improve upon our sample project, enabling it to access the root folders of information stores. Next, we'll look into the `Folders` collection and the `Folder` object, followed by more improvements to the sample project showing how we can use them in practice. Lastly, we'll learn to access hidden properties of CDO objects using the `Fields` collection and the `Field` object.

Before we get down to altering our application, we should look at the concept and structure of CDO Information Stores.

Information Stores

Microsoft Exchange Server provides information stores that store e-mail messages, public folder postings, appointments, and meeting schedules. A public information store provides a hierarchy of public folders to store information that may be used by some or all users in an organization. A private information store contains a user's mailbox, organized into folders such as the user's Inbox and Calendar folders.

As usual, the CDO library provides object-oriented methods to get access to these information stores. In addition, it also enables us to access a user's personal information store, called Personal Folders, stored locally on a user's PC. CDO treats this personal information store just like other stores (such as Public Folders and the Mailbox). As described in Chapter 2, a user's personal information store is associated with a profile and is only available when the user is logged in using the corresponding profile.

Regardless of where the information stores are physically located, we can use the CDO Library to access them. All information stores accessible to a CDO session are contained in an InfoStores collection. This collection is exposed as the CDO Session object's InfoStores property.

Each information store contains a collection of folders. The CDO library defines a Folders collection and a Folder object that represent the folder collections and individual folders, respectively. The following diagram shows the relationship between information stores and folders in the CDO object model:

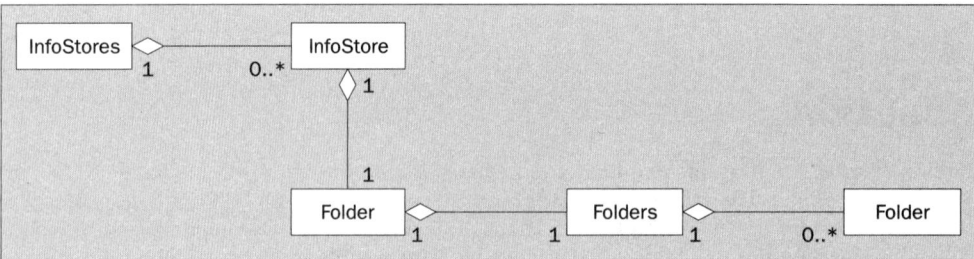

You're probably wondering what the ones and zeros are on this diagram. Well, it's all to do with how many instances of a class are allowed in an aggregation. For instance, an InfoStores collection can contain zero or more InfoStore objects. The allowed or required number of instances is called the **multiplicity** of the association. In UML, a multiplicity of exactly one is shown as 1, and a multiplicity of zero or more is shown as 0..*. More generically, a multiplicity in a range from m to n is represented as m..n.

So the first aggregation in the above figure shows that an InfoStores collection may contain any number of InfoStore objects. In theory, an InfoStores collection can be empty. That is, it may not contain any InfoStore objects at all. In reality, however, an empty collection is useless because CDO does not allow us to add new information stores to a collection.

The second and third aggregations are a little strange. They specify that an InfoStore object contains exactly one Folder object, which in turn contains exactly one Folders collection. It might be more straightforward if an InfoStore object simply contained a Folders collection, bypassing the middle man. However, this is just how the CDO object model is defined. The folder in the middle is called the Root Folder of an information store. It is the root of all folders in the store.

The last aggregation is simple: a `Folders` collection may contain zero or more `Folder` objects. Folders are recursive, that is, a folder can contain a collection of subfolders. In CDO, a `Folder` object has a `Folders` property that returns a reference to a CDO folder collection that contains all its subfolders.

The InfoStores Collection

The `InfoStores` collection is perhaps the simplest collection in the CDO Library. In addition to the four properties that are common to all CDO objects, it has only two additional properties:

INFOSTORES	
Properties	**Type**
Application	String
Class	Long
Count	Long
Item	InfoStore
Parent	Session
Session	Session
Methods	

The `Count` property returns the number of `InfoStore` objects in the current `InfoStores` collection. The `Item` property has two variations, both of which return an `InfoStore` object in the collection:

```
Set objInfoStore = colInfoStores.Item(Index)
Set objInfoStore = colInfoStores.Item(StoreName)
```

The first syntax accepts a Long integer representing the index of an `InfoStore` object. Like standard Visual Basic collections, all CDO collections are one-based. That is, the index of the first object in a collection is always 1. The second syntax accepts a string that is the name of an `InfoStore` object.

Another similarity of all CDO collections and Visual Basic collections is that the `Item` property is always the default property of collections. That means the two statements above are equivalent to:

```
Set objInfoStore = colInfoStores(Index)
Set objInfoStore = colInfoStores(StoreName)
```

The CDO `InfoStores` collection does not have any methods. You cannot add `InfoStore` objects to, or remove them from, the collection.

The InfoStore Object

An `InfoStore` object represents an information store where folders and messages are stored.

INFOSTORE	
Properties	**Type**
Application	String
Class	Long
Fields	Fields
ID	String
Index	Long
MAPIOBJECT	IUnknown
Name	String
Parent	InfoStores
ProviderName	String
RootFolder	Folder
Session	Session
Methods	
IsSameAs	

❑ The `Fields` Collection – The `Fields` property returns a collection of `Fields` that stores the various attributes of the `InfoStore` object. We will see the `Fields` collection and the `Field` object in more detail later in this chapter.

❑ The `ID` Property – The `ID` property returns the unique identifier of the current `InfoStore` object. It is assigned by an Exchange Server and does not change from one session to another.

❑ The `Index` Property – The `Index` property returns the index of this `InfoStore` object in the `InfoStores` collection. It can be used to retrieve this object from the collection through the `InfoStores` collection's `Item` property as described in the previous section.

❑ The `MAPIOBJECT` Property – The `MAPIOBJECT` property returns an `IUNKNOWN` pointer to the current `Session` object. This is accessible to C++ applications, but not Visual Basic applications since Visual Basic does not support the `IUNKNOWN` pointer.

❑ The `Name` Property – The `Name` property returns the name of the current `InfoStore` object. We can also use it to find this object from the parent `InfoStores` collection through the `Item` property.

❑ The `ProviderName` Property – The `ProviderName` property returns the name of the underlying message store where the current `InfoStore` object resides. For the Public Folders and user's Mailbox stores on an Exchange Server, this property returns 'Microsoft Exchange Server'. The 'Personal Folders' store's `ProviderName` is always 'Personal Folders'.

❑ The `RootFolder` Property – As we saw mentioned previously, the `InfoStore` object does not directly expose a `Folders` collection. It does expose a `RootFolder` property, though, and this returns a `Folder` object containing a collection of all folders in the current `InfoStore` object.

However, if your application runs as a Windows NT Service such as an Active Server Pages (ASP) application running on Microsoft Internet Information Server (IIS), you cannot use this property to access Microsoft Exchange Server Public Folders. In this scenario, the `RootFolder` property of the Public Folders `InfoStore` always returns `Nothing`. We will discuss a workaround later in the book.

❑ The IsSameAs Method – The IsSameAs method checks whether two InfoStore objects refer to the same physical information store in an Exchange Server.

```
If objInfoStore.IsSameAs(InfoStore2) Then
```

It returns True if the current InfoStore object and InfoStore2 refer to the same information store.

Working with the CDO Sample Project

Now we know what the InfoStores collection and InfoStore object are, let's modify the CDO sample project to display the root folders of each information store in a profile.

Accessing Root Folders

We have seen that the CDO Session object's InfoStores property returns a collection of information store objects. To access the root folders, we can modify the ShowInfoStores method in the FMain form:

```
Private Sub ShowInfoStores()
    On Error GoTo ErrHandler

    Dim objStore As MAPI.InfoStore
    Dim objFolder As MAPI.Folder
    Dim nodStore As MSComctlLib.Node

    tvwFolders.Nodes.Clear
    For Each objStore In gobjSession.InfoStores
        Set nodStore = tvwFolders.Nodes.Add(Key:= objStore.ID, Text:=objStore.Name)
        Set objFolder = objStore.RootFolder
        Call tvwFolders.Nodes.Add(Relative:=nodStore, _
                    Relationship:=tvwChild, _
                    Key:=objStore.ID & "," & objFolder.ID, _
                    Text:=objFolder.Name)
        nodStore.Expanded = True
    Next

ExitFunc:
    Set nodStore = Nothing
    Set objFolder = Nothing
    Set objStore = Nothing
    Exit Sub

ErrHandler:
    Call ReportError(Err)
    Resume ExitFunc
End Sub
```

We want to display the root folder of an information store as a sub-node of the store node in the TreeView since `RootFolder` is a child object of the information store. Therefore we need to get hold of a reference to the store node in the tree. We firstly declare an object, `nodStore`, that is an instance of the TreeView `Node` class. It is then used to reference the new node added to the TreeView control's `Nodes` collection:

```
Set nodStore = tvwFolders.Nodes.Add(Key:=objStore.ID, Text:=objStore.Name)
```

We then get a reference to the root folder and assign it to `objFolder`. We can now add a sub-node to `nodStore` using the `TreeView.Nodes.Add` method. We just need to pass in `nodStore` as the parent node and specify that the new node is a child of it.

As explained in the last chapter, each `Node` object in a TreeView must have a unique string value in its `Key` property. In CDO, a folder's ID is only unique within an information store. That is, two folders in different stores may have the same ID. Thus we use a combination of store ID and folder ID to ensure the uniqueness of node keys. If you're wondering what a CDO ID value looks like, here is a sample ID string:

```
000000001A447390AA6611CD9BC800AA002FC45A0300C0B86B30DBD611CEB31700AA00574CC6000000
0000020000
```

You'll never know if I just made that up, or if it's a real one. That's the beauty of unique identifiers!

As you'll see later, we will also use the Node's `Key` value when we need to retrieve the associated `Folder` object. In this sample project, we will always use a comma as a delimiter to the IDs, so it would be a good idea to define it as a constant rather than using the literal string. This is more descriptive and makes our code more readable. We'll add a public constant declaration in `MCommon`:

```
Option Explicit
Public Const gcstrIDDelimiter As String = ","
```

We can then replace the literal string "," in our `ShowInfoStores` procedure with `gcstrIDDelimiter`:

```
Private Sub ShowInfoStores()
...
    For Each objStore In gobjSession.InfoStores
        Set nodStore = tvwFolders.Nodes.Add(Key:=objStore.ID, Text:=objStore.Name)
        Set objFolder = objStore.RootFolder
        Call tvwFolders.Nodes.Add(Relative:=nodStore, _
                    Relationship:=tvwChild, _
                    Key:=objStore.ID & gcstrIDDelimiter & objFolder.ID, _
                    Text:=objFolder.Name)
        nodStore.Expanded = True
    Next

ExitFunc:
...
```

If you now run the program, you should see an output similar to this:

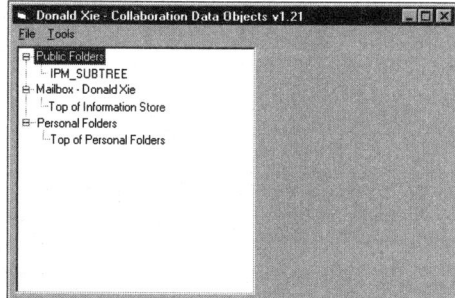

As you can see from the sample output, the root folder in each information store has a different name. While the RootFolder property plays an important role in navigating the information store and folder structure, we do not usually care about it as much as we do with the real folders.

It's back to the theory for a short while. Now we know how to get the root folders, we should really look into the CDO Folders collection and CDO Folder object in more detail. Once we understand them, we can move on to discuss the important task of how to get hold of all the folders in an information store.

Folders

Messages and other items are stored in folders. A CDO folder is analogous to a file system folder where files reside. A CDO folder stores e-mail messages, contact information, appointment items, and so on. A CDO Folder object exposes a Folders property that returns a reference to a CDO Folders collection consisting of all its top-level subfolders and their subfolders recursively.

The Folders Collection

The CDO Folders collection provides properties and methods to allow applications to navigate the collection and access each folder in the collection.

FOLDERS	
Properties	**Type**
Application	String
Class	Long
Count	Long
Item	Folder
Parent	Folder
RawTable	IUnknown
Session	Session
Methods	
Add	
Delete	
GetFirst	
GetLast	
GetNext	
GetPrevious	
Sort	

The Count and Item Properties

The Count property returns the number of folders in the current Folders collection. The Item property returns a Folder object. It has two variations:

```
Set objFolder = colFolders.Item(Index)
Set objFolder = colFolders.Item(SearchValue)
```

The first syntax is straightforward – you pass in a number representing an index, and it returns the folder at that location in the collection. The second syntax is not that clear-cut. It accepts a string and finds the next folder in the collection with the sorting property greater than or equal to the search value. By default, the sorting property is the folder name. This can be overridden by the property specified in the Sort method.

The problem with the second syntax is that it does not always behave as you would have expected. That is, the underlying folder table on the Exchange Server might not be sorted in alphabetic order. For instance, Exchange Server sorts public folders in non-alphabetic order. Therefore, you should use the second syntax with caution.

A more reliable method is to loop through the folder collection yourself and compare the sorting property with the search value. For instance:

```
For Each objFolder In objFolders
    ' Perform a case insensitive search
    If StrComp(objFolder.Name, SearchValue, vbTextCompare) >= 0 Then
        Exit For
    End If
Next
```

Although this method is more reliable, it could be slow if the folder collection contains a large number of folders.

The Sort Method

The Sort method sorts the Folders collection using the SortOrder specified.

```
colFolders.Sort([SortOrder] [, PropTag]
colFolders.Sort([SortOrder] [, PropertyName]
```

SortOrder Constant	Value	Order
CdoNone	0	Do not sort
CdoAscending	1	Sort in ascending order
CdoDescending	2	Sort in descending order

The first syntax sorts the collection on a standard MAPI property specified by the property tag. The second syntax sorts or a user-defined property specified by the property name. We will see more on MAPI property tags and user-defined fields later in this chapter when we discuss the `Field` object. If neither the property tag nor the property name is specified, it sorts the collection using the property specified in the previous `Sort` operation. If the collection has not been sorted previously, it is sorted on folder names.

The `Sort` method does not always succeed. If the Exchange Server does not support a specific sort, this method raises an `CdoE_TOO_COMPLEX` (`&H80040117`) error.

Navigating the Folders Collection

As we saw in Chapter 2, all CDO collection objects support the Visual Basic `For Each ... Next` construct. However, this is not the only method of traversing the collection. Visual Basic collections allow us to access each of their elements through an index. For instance:

```
Dim colBooks As Collection
Dim lngIndex As Long

' Populate the collection - code omitted for simplicity

' Access elements in the collection
For lngIndex = 1 To colBooks.Count
    Debug.Print colBooks(lngIndex)
Next
```

The same technique is applicable to all CDO collections. For example, we could rewrite the `ShowInfoStores` method using this technique. If you like, you can make these changes to the project to see it in action, but don't save it this way.

```
Private Sub ShowInfoStores()
   On Error GoTo ErrHandler

   Dim colStores As MAPI.InfoStores
   Dim objStore As MAPI.InfoStore
   Dim objFolder As MAPI.Folder
   Dim nodStore As MSComctlLib.Node
   Dim lngIndex As Long

   tvwFolders.Nodes.Clear
   Set colStores = gobjSession.InfoStores

   For lngIndex = 1 To colStores.Count
       Set objStore = colStores(lngIndex)
       Set nodStore = _
          tvwFolders.Nodes.Add(Key:=objStore.ID, Text:=objStore.Name)
       Set objFolder = objStore.RootFolder
       Call tvwFolders.Nodes.Add(Relative:=nodStore, _
                    Relationship:=tvwChild, _
                    Key:=objStore.ID & gcstrIDDelimiter & objFolder.ID, _
                    Text:=objFolder.Name)
       nodStore.Expanded = True
```

```
        Next

    ExitFunc:
        Set nodStore = Nothing
        Set objFolder = Nothing
        Set objStore = Nothing
        Set colStores = Nothing
        Exit Sub

    ErrHandler:
        Call ReportError(Err)

        Resume ExitFunc
    End Sub
```

The reason you shouldn't save the method looking like this is because this technique has limitations when used in CDO collections. We'll discuss these limitations now:

CDO Collection Limitations

Some CDO collections are said to be **Large Collections**. A large collection is one where an accurate count of the number of members is not kept. For example, an Exchange Server might host a huge number of public folders. This is especially true when it is set up as a news server that hosts Internet newsgroups. If you have used Internet Newsgroups, you would have noticed the number of newsgroups is quite extraordinary – a rough estimation shows more than 25,000. You could imagine, then, that the Folders collection could be said to be a large collection. You'd be right. In CDO, the AddressEntries and Messages collections are also large collections.

As described above, CDO does not always maintain an accurate count of the number of elements in a large collection. This has two implications. First, you need to check the value returned by the Count property before using it in your application. If its value is &H7FFFFFFF (or 2^{31} -1), it does not contain the valid count.

```
    lngNumOfFolders = objFolders.Count
    If lngNumOfFolders = &H7FFFFFFF Then
        MsgBox "Cannot determine the exact number of folders in the collection"
    End If
```

In a 32-bit environment, you can check this value against the predefined CDO Type Library constant CdoMaxCount which equates to &H7FFFFFFF. However, this constant is not available for other environments.

The second implication is that you should avoid using the For...Next loop like this because the Count might be incorrect:

```
    For lngIndex = 1 To colFolders.Count
        Debug.Print colFolders(lngIndex).Name
    Next
```

If the `Count` is not accurate, the above loop may go past the last folder in the collection and cause a `Script Out Of Scope` error. It is preferred that we use the `For Each...Next` loop. Some CDO collections including `Folders` also provide a set of four Get methods: `GetFirst`, `GetPrevious`, `GetNext`, and `GetLast`, that can be used to navigate the collection.

The GetFirst, GetLast, GetNext, GetPrevious Methods

These four methods provide the ability to navigate `Folders` collections. For instance, you can navigate forwards:

```
Set objFolder = objFolders.GetFirst
Do
    Debug.Print objFolder.Name
    Set objFolder = objFolders.GetNext
Loop Until objFolder Is Nothing
```

Note that the Get methods alone don't actually *move* the current object (for example, `objFolder`) – you have to `Set` the object as well. The following code, then (which never actually sets `objFolder` to the next item) will cause an endless loop (because `objFolder` will always point to the first folder in the collection):

```
Set objFolder = objFolders.GetFirst
Do
    Debug.Print objFolder.Name
Loop Until objFolder.GetNext Is Nothing
```

The RawTable Property

The `RawTable` property returns an `IUnknown` pointer to the table that stores the `Folders` collection on the Exchange Server. It is not accessible to Visual Basic applications.

The Add Method

The `Add` method creates a new folder in the current folders collection and returns a reference to the newly created folder. We will see how it works later when we get back to working on our sample application.

The Delete Method

The `Delete` method deletes all folders in the collection. It does not delete the collection itself.

The Folder Object

The `Folder` object represents a folder in an information store.

FOLDER	
Properties	**Type**
Application	String
Class	Long
Fields	Fields
FolderID	String
Folders	Folders
HiddenMessages	Messages
ID	String
MAPIOBJECT	IUnknown
Messages	Messages
Name	String
Parent	Object
Session	Session
StoreID	String
Methods	
CopyTo	
Delete	
IsSameAs	
MoveTo	
Update	

Properties

- ❑ `Fields` – The `Fields` property returns a `Fields` collection that stores the various attributes of the current `Folder` object. We will see more on the CDO `Fields` collection later in this chapter.

- ❑ `FolderID` – The `FolderID` property returns the unique identifier of the parent folder of the current `Folder` object.

- ❑ `Folders` – The `Folders` property returns a collection of subfolders in the current folder. If a folder does not contain subfolders, the `Count` property of its `Folders` collection returns 0.

- ❑ `HiddenMessages` – The `HiddenMessages` property returns a collection of messages that are not visible to messaging clients. These messages are typically used to store folder associated information created by MAPI. Some messaging clients such as Microsoft Outlook also use hidden messages to implement rules. Folder rules are covered in Chapter 7.

- ❑ `ID` and `Name` – The `ID` property returns the unique identifier of the current folder object. The `Name` property returns the name of the current folder.

- ❑ `MAPIOBJECT` – The `MAPIOBJECT` property returns an `IUNKNOWN` pointer to the current Session object. This is accessible to C++ applications, but not VB applications since Visual Basic does not support the `IUNKNOWN` pointer.

- ❑ `Messages` – The Messages property returns a collection of messages in the current folder. We will examine messages in Chapter 5.

- ❑ `StoreID` – The `StoreID` property returns the unique identifier of the `InfoStore` object to which the current folder belongs.

Methods

❑ CopyTo and MoveTo – The CopyTo and MoveTo methods copy the current folder and all messages in it to a new folder. The difference is that the MoveTo method also removes the original folder from its parent Folders collection. We will see how those methods work later when we extend our sample project.

❑ Delete – The Delete method removes the current folder and all subfolders from its parent Folders collection. We will also use this method later in the sample object.

❑ IsSameAs – The IsSameAs method checks whether two Folder objects refer to the same physical folder on an Exchange Server.

```
If objFolder.IsSameAs(objFolder2) Then
```

It returns True if the current Folder object and objFolder2 refer to the same folder.

❑ Update – If you have changed any properties of a folder, you must call its Update method to save the changes to the Exchange Server.

Folders in the CDO Sample Project

After our second bite of theory, it's time to get back to our sample project. First, we'll see a method for displaying folders recursively. It should become obvious why we'd want to do that.

Displaying Folders Recursively

The ShowFolder method we're going to create will be used to display all the folders present in the underlying info stores. Since folders are recursive, potentially containing many levels of nested subfolders, it's nearly impossible to tell how many levels there will be. For this reason, it's natural to code a recursive method that will call itself, showing all the subfolders of the current folder. That way, if any subfolders have subfolders, the method will simply call itself again, until it's done everything. Anyway, here's the code. Add this to the FMain form module:

```
Private Sub ShowFolder(nodParent As MSComctlLib.Node, _
                objFolder As MAPI.Folder)
    On Error GoTo ErrHandler
    Dim objSubFolder As MAPI.Folder
    Dim nodFolder As MSComctlLib.Node

    Set nodFolder = tvwFolders.Nodes.Add( _
        Relative:=nodParent, Relationship:=tvwChild, _
        Key:=objFolder.StoreID & gcstrIDDelimiter & objFolder.ID, _
        Text:=objFolder.Name)

    For Each objSubFolder In objFolder.Folders
        ShowFolder nodFolder, objSubFolder
    Next

ExitFunc:
    Set nodFolder = Nothing
    Set objSubFolder = Nothing
    Exit Sub

ErrHandler:
    Call ReportError(Err)
    Resume ExitFunc
End Sub
```

Its first parameter is the parent TreeView node under which this folder will be displayed. The second parameter is the current folder object to be displayed.

Apart from (or maybe because of) its recursive nature, the method itself is simple enough. Firstly, it adds a new node under that parent node in the TreeView control, `tvwFolders`. Next, it traverses through each of its subfolders and calls itself recursively to display each subfolder.

We also need to modify the `ShowInfoStores` method slightly to call the `ShowFolder` method, passing in the node and root folder to get the whole thing started:

```
Private Sub ShowInfoStores()
...
    For Each objStore In gobjSession.InfoStores
        ' Display the information store
        Set nodStore = tvwFolders.Nodes.Add(Key:=objStore.ID, Text:=objStore.Name)

        ' Display folders in the store
        Call ShowFolder(nodStore, objStore.RootFolder)
        nodStore.Expanded = True
    Next

ExitFunc:
...
```

A warning before you run the project: it may take a long time if any of the information stores have a large number of folders. In particular, the Public Folders store is likely to contain many folders. You can use Outlook to find out whether this is the case. If so, you might want to filter out the information store by modifying the `ShowInfoStores` method as shown here.

```
    For Each objStore In gobjSession.InfoStores
        ' Display the information store
        Set nodStore = tvwFolders.Nodes.Add(Key:=objStore.ID, Text:=objStore.Name)
        If objStore.Name <> "Public Folders" Then
            ' Display folders in the store
            Call ShowFolder(nodStore, objStore.RootFolder)
            nodStore.Expanded = True
        End If
    Next
```

If you run the project with public folders included and expand all the folders in the tree view, you will see an output similar to the following:

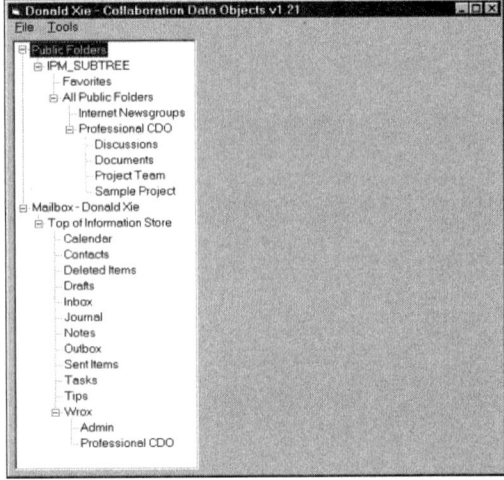

> You might find that you get an 'unexpected' error – MAPI_E_NOT_FOUND – while the public folders are being enumerated. This probably just means that certain folders aren't accessible to your profile. You'll probably find that you still get a display that looks like the screenshot, but you should consider adding error handling to get around this minor problem.

It looks quite promising except for just one thing: displaying the root folders themselves really has no meaning for us. Since this can be easily fixed, let's do it right now.

First, modify the ShowFolder method to add a third parameter, IsRootFolder:

```
Private Sub ShowFolder(nodParent As MSComctlLib.Node, _
                objFolder As MAPI.Folder, _
                Optional IsRootFolder As Boolean = False)
    On Error GoTo ErrHandler

    Dim objSubFolder    As MAPI.Folder
    Dim nodFolder       As MSComctlLib.Node

    If IsRootFolder Then
        Set nodFolder = nodParent
    Else
        Set nodFolder = tvwFolders.Nodes.Add( _
            Relative:=nodParent, Relationship:=tvwChild, _
            Key:=objFolder.StoreID & gcstrIDDelimiter & objFolder.ID, _
            Text:=objFolder.Name)
    End If

    For Each objSubFolder In objFolder.Folders
        Call ShowFolder(nodFolder, objSubFolder, IsRootFolder:=False)
    Next
    ...
```

As you can see, the change is really quite simple. We check whether the folder is a root folder. If it is, we simply assign the parent node to nodFolder, which will be used as the parent node in subsequent ShowFolder calls. If it is not a root folder, we add a node to the tree and pass the newly added node as the parent node in subsequent ShowFolder calls.

We then just need to modify the `ShowInfoStores` method again to indicate that it will pass in root folders to the `ShowFolder` call.

```
Private Sub ShowInfoStores()
...
    For Each objStore In gobjSession.InfoStores
        ' Display the information store
        Set nodStore = _
            tvwFolders.Nodes.Add(Key:=objStore.ID, Text:=objStore.Name)

        ' Display folders in the store
        Call ShowFolder(nodStore, objStore.RootFolder, IsRootFolder:=True)
        nodStore.Expanded = True
    Next

ExitFunc:
...
```

If you run the program again, you'll see a more sensible folder tree:

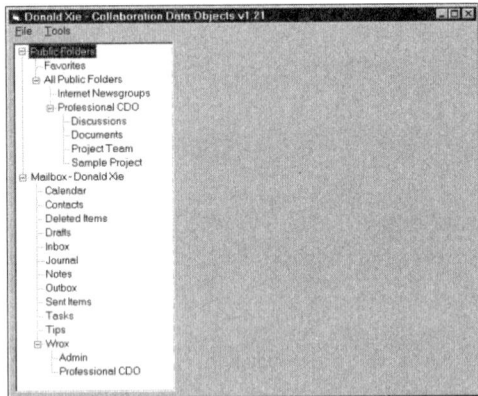

Navigating Using the Get Methods

We can also navigate around folder collections using the `Folders` collection's Get methods. The following code snippet shows a modified `ShowFolder` method. The only change to it is to use the Get methods instead of the `For Each ... Next` loop. It's up to you whether you make this change or not – the program will behave the same in either case.

```
Private Sub ShowFolder(nodParent As MSComctlLib.Node, _
                    objFolder As MAPI.Folder, _
                    Optional IsRootFolder As Boolean = False)
    On Error GoTo ErrHandler

    Dim colFolders    As MAPI.Folders
    Dim objSubFolder  As MAPI.Folder
    Dim nodFolder     As MSComctlLib.Node
    If IsRootFolder Then
        Set nodFolder = nodParent
    Else
        Set nodFolder = tvwFolders.Nodes.Add( _
            Relative:=nodParent, Relationship:=tvwChild, _
            Key:=objFolder.StoreID & gcstrIDDelimiter & objFolder.ID, _
```

```
            Text:=objFolder.Name)
        End If

'     For Each objSubFolder In objFolder.Folders
'         Call ShowFolder(nodFolder, objSubFolder, IsRootFolder:=False)
'     Next

        Set colFolders = objFolder.Folders
        Set objSubFolder = colFolders.GetFirst
        Do While Not objSubFolder Is Nothing
            Call ShowFolder(nodFolder, objSubFolder, IsRootFolder:=False)
            Set objSubFolder = colFolders.GetNext
        Loop

ExitFunc:
        Set nodFolder = Nothing
        Set objSubFolder = Nothing
        Set colFolders = Nothing

        Exit Sub

ErrHandler:
        Call ReportError(Err)
        Resume ExitFunc
End Sub
```

As you can see if you run it, the result is identical. Which one to use is a matter of your own personal preference.

The `ShowFolder` code itself is straightforward, but it actually shows a very important point in CDO programming. Let's see just what that is.

Create Temporary Objects Yourself

The code fragment that navigates the folders uses a temporary object, `colFolders`, to store a reference to the subfolder collection:

```
        Set colFolders = objFolder.Folders
        Set objSubFolder = colFolders.GetFirst
        Do While Not objSubFolder Is Nothing
            Call ShowFolder(nodFolder, objSubFolder, IsRootFolder:=False)
            Set objSubFolder = colFolders.GetNext
        Loop
```

We could have written the code as follows:

```
        Set objSubFolder = objFolder.Folders.GetFirst
        Do While Not objSubFolder Is Nothing
            Call ShowFolder(nodFolder, objSubFolder, IsRootFolder:=False)
            Set objSubFolder = objFolder.Folders.GetNext
        Loop
```

This saves us from creating a temporary object, right? Well, yes, it does save us from creating one temporary object explicitly. However, it could cause many more temporary objects to be created. The way Visual Basic handles object navigation is that it implicitly creates a temporary object each time it encounters a dot (.). Therefore on the first line, it creates a temporary Folders collection when it reaches the second dot in objFolder.Folders.GetFirst. It calls the temporary Folders collection's GetFirst method and assigns the first folder in the collection to objSubFolder. The temporary Folders collection is then destroyed.

What's important is that this process is repeated for *each* call to objFolder.Folders.GetNext. If objFolder has 50 subfolders, Visual Basic will create and destroy 50 instances of temporary folder collections. Since object creation and deletion are expensive operations, this code fragment is very inefficient. If we look at the whole picture, we know that the ShowFolder method is called recursively. You can imagine how this inefficiency would propagate. Explicitly creating a temporary collection (colFolders) thus saves you quite a few CPU cycles and memory allocations.

An alternative to creating a temporary object explicitly is to create it implicitly, but to ensure that it is created only once using the With statement:

```
With objFolder.Folders
    Set objSubFolder =.GetFirst
    Do While Not objSubFolder Is Nothing
        Call ShowFolder(nodFolder, objSubFolder, IsRootFolder:=False)
        Set objSubFolder =.GetNext
    Loop
End With
```

When Visual Basic parses the With statement, it creates a temporary folder collection that references objFolder.Folders. It then calls this temporary folder collection's GetFirst and GetNext methods. It doesn't destroy it until the End With statement. Whether to create a temporary object explicitly or implicitly is a matter of coding style. What we should always avoid is letting Visual Basic create and destroy excessive numbers of temporary objects.

Now we've seen how we can traverse through the CDO information store and folder hierarchy. CDO also provides us with the ability to add, copy, and delete folders. Let's take a look at that now.

Managing Folders

Using CDO, we can add, copy, and delete folders in the Folders collection object. To add a subfolder to a folder, we call the Add method of the folder's Folders property:

```
Set objSubFolder = objParentFolder.Folders.Add(strSubFolderName)
```

Unlike normal Visual Basic collections, the CDO Folders collection does not have a Remove method. We delete a folder from a Folders collection using the Folder object's Delete method:

```
objSubFolder.Delete
```

This deletes objSubFolder and any messages it contains, and any subfolders it may have (along with any messages in them).

We can also copy an existing folder to another folder's subfolder collection using the originating folder's CopyTo method:

```
Set objCopiedFolder = objFolder.CopyTo(strNewParentFolderID _
                                [, strNewStoreID] _
                                [, strNewFolderName] _
                                [, blnShouldCopySubFolders])
```

Where:

- ❑ objFolder is the original folder to be copied.

- ❑ objCopiedFolder is a reference to the copy of objFolder.

- ❑ strNewParentFolderID is the ID of the folder where objFolder will be copied into.

- ❑ strNewStoreID is the ID of the destination information store. If the new parent folder is in a different store than that of objFolder, we need to specify the new store ID in this parameter.

- ❑ strNewFolderName is the name of the copy. By default, objCopiedFolder will have the same name as objFolder, unless you specify a different name by specifying this parameter.

- ❑ blnShouldCopySubFolders specifies whether or not all subfolders of objFolder should also be copied. By default, this is True and all subfolders are copied.

The MoveTo method is simpler:

```
Set objMovedFolder = objFolder.MoveTo(strNewParentFolderID [, strNewStoreID])
```

It moves objFolder to live under the folder specified by strNewParentFolderID, which can even be in a different information store. After the move is completed, the original folder is deleted. That means that you cannot use objFolder any more – it doesn't point to anything valid.

Folders in the Sample Project

Let's look at each of the methods by example. We'll create a toolbar on the main form (FMain) and add some buttons to it that perform the copy and move operations. In addition, we'll add more buttons that will perform other tasks later on in the progress of the project. Toolbar buttons can be graphical, that is, they can display images. To use images for toolbar buttons, we will need to add them to an ImageList control first. We can then bind the Toolbar to the ImageList.

One little inconvenience of using the Toolbar and ImageList controls is that once you bind a Toolbar to an ImageList, you can only add new images to the ImageList. You cannot rearrange the image order or remove images from it unless you unbind the list first. You can unbind the list, rearrange or delete images, and then rebind it. However, once you have unbound the list, you lose all relationships between toolbar buttons and images. That means that when you bind the image list to the toolbar again, you'll have to reconfigure all the toolbar buttons to use the correct images.

To get around this, we'll create an ImageList control that contains *all* the images we'll be using in FMain, not just those on the toolbar. Then we'll create a Toolbar control bound to it. If we use the Key property of the images (that is, we give them code names) instead of the Index, we can ignore the ordering of images in the ImageList and simply refer to each by name.

The Interface

Open the main form `FMain` in the CDO Sample project and add an ImageList control and a Toolbar control to the form. It doesn't matter where the ImageList goes as it's invisible at run time.

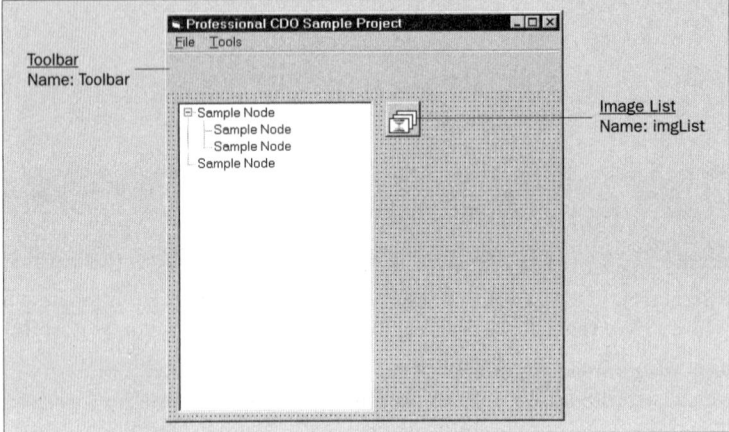

Name the ImageList and Toolbar controls `imgList` and `Toolbar`, respectively, and click on the `Custom` property of the ImageList control:

You could also right-click on the ImageList and go to **Properties** – both bring up the same property page. In `imgList`'s property page, leave the settings on the **General** tab at their default values. On the Images tab, you just click the Insert Picture button to add a picture.

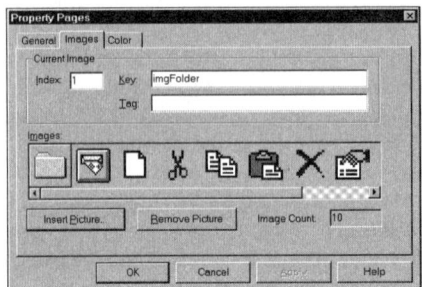

The table shows the images we'll use in `FMain`. The `Index` of the images is not important, as we've said before; we'll be using their `Key` properties. We won't use all of the images here, though – some of them will be used in later chapters. Add these pictures to the image list. If you do not want the images, and ultimately the toolbar, to take up too much space, you can set all image size to 16 by 16 on the ImageList control's Property Pages *before* adding any images to the list.

Index	File Path: Program Files\Microsoft Visual Studio\Common\Graphics\...	Key
1	`Icons\Win95\Clsdfold.ico`	imgFolder
2	`Bitmaps\Assorted\Mail.bmp`	imgMessage
3	`Bitmaps\TlBr_W95\New.bmp`	imgNew
4	`Bitmaps\TlBr_W95\Cut.bmp`	imgCut
5	`Bitmaps\TlBr_W95\Copy.bmp`	imgCopy
6	`Bitmaps\TlBr_W95\Paste.bmp`	imgPaste
7	`Bitmaps\TlBr_W95\Delete.bmp`	imgDelete
8	`Bitmaps\TlBr_W95\Prop.bmp`	imgProp
9	`Icons\Arrows\Arw07up.ico`	imgArrowUp
10	`Icons\Arrows\Arw07dn.ico`	imgArrowDown

Now click open the Toolbar control's Property Page and set its `ImageList` property to `imgList`, and its `Style` property to 1 – tbrFlat, as shown:

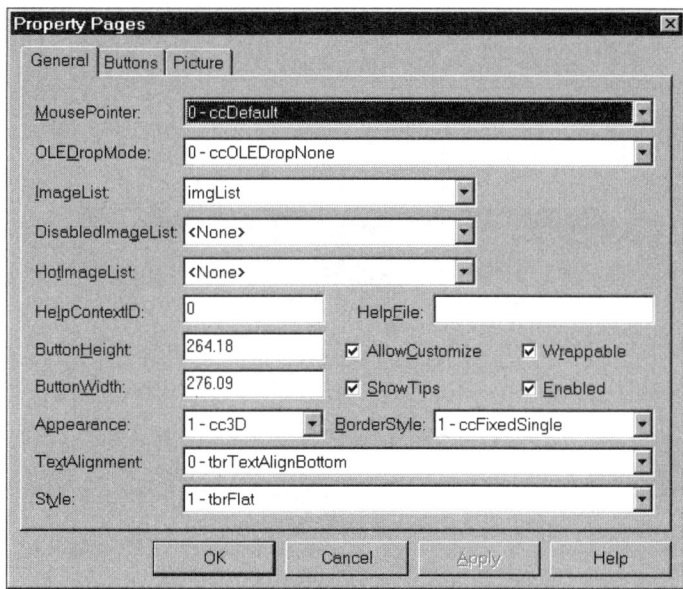

Now click on the Buttons tab and click Insert Button:

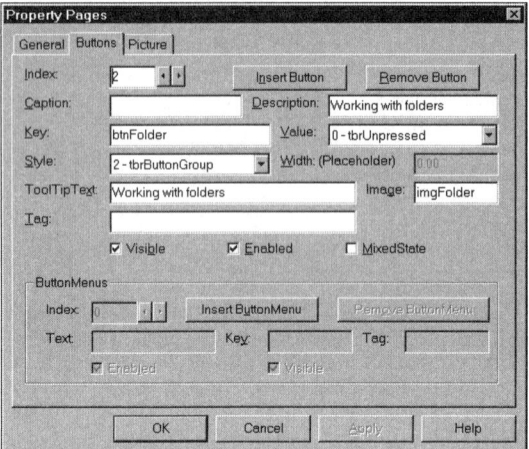

Insert a series of 13 'buttons' (some of them are actually separator bars, as you'll see). Change the properties of the new buttons as shown here:

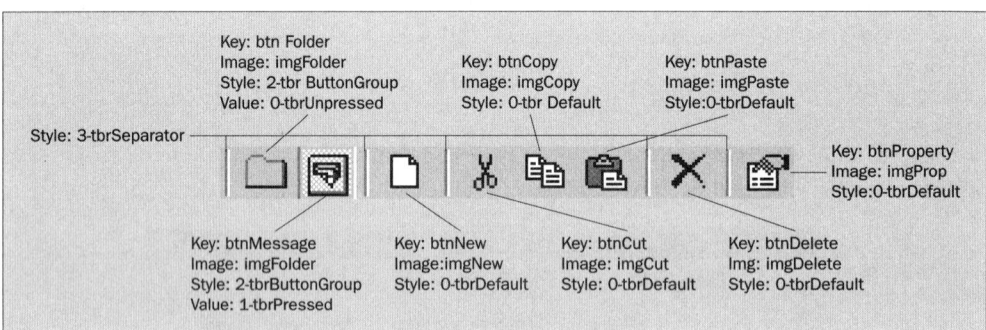

When you have created the buttons, your form should look like this:

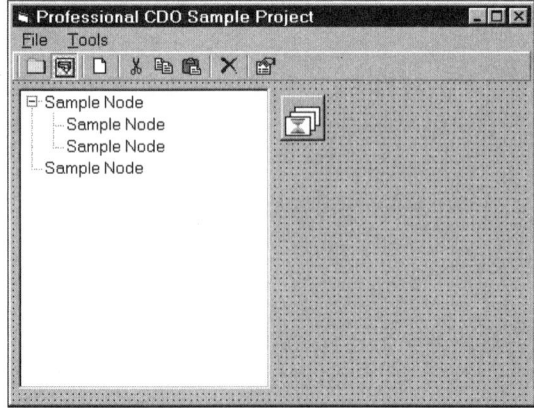

The **Folder** and **Message** buttons indicate whether we are working on folders or messages. In this chapter, we'll be using the other buttons for manipulating folders only. When we start working with messages later on, we'll also use them to handle the messages.

The user can press the **New** button to add a new folder. The **Cut** button is not used in this chapter. The **Copy** and **Paste** buttons can be used in combination to copy folders. The **Delete** button allows the user to delete a folder. And the **Property** button will show a property window listing all the properties of the selected folder.

Before we move on, let's add a `Form_Resize` event handler procedure to resize the folder tree view control when the form is resized. First, though, we'll add a constant, `gclngEdge`, to the `MCommon` module. It's a long integer that specifies the distance between the edge of the form and the tree view control and other controls. We will use this constant in other forms as well.

```
Option Explicit

Public Const gcstrServer As String = "Server" & vbLf
Public Const gclngEdge As Long = 60

Public gobjSession As MAPI.Session
```

Next, add the `Form_Resize` procedure to `FMain`:

```
Private Sub Form_Resize()
    On Error Resume Next

    With tvwFolders
        .Move gclngEdge, Toolbar.Height + gclngEdge
        .Height = ScaleHeight - tvwFolders.Top - gclngEdge
    End With
End Sub
```

When the user increases or decreases the height of `FMain`, the folder tree will be resized accordingly. We're not going to worry about making the list view wider and narrower with the form in this project, but you can if you want.

Now add the following constant declarations to the `General` section of `FMain`:

```
Private Const mcstrButtonKeyFolder As String = "btnFolder"
Private Const mcstrButtonKeyMessage As String = "btnMessage"
Private Const mcstrButtonKeyNew As String = "btnNew"
Private Const mcstrButtonKeyCut As String = "btnCut"
Private Const mcstrButtonKeyCopy As String = "btnCopy"
Private Const mcstrButtonKeyPaste As String = "btnPaste"
Private Const mcstrButtonKeyDelete As String = "btnDelete"
Private Const mcstrButtonKeyProperty As String = "btnProperty"

Private Enum WorkingObjectTypeEnum
    wotFolder = 1
    wotMessage = 2
End Enum
```

The constants are initialized with string values representing the `Key` property of the toolbar buttons we will be using in the program. The `WorkingObjectTypeEnum` specifies the two working modes our form will have, whether we're working with folders or with messages. We'll also write a little function that returns the current working object type:

```
Private Function WorkingObject() As WorkingObjectTypeEnum
    If Toolbar.Buttons(mcstrButtonKeyFolder).Value = tbrPressed Then
        WorkingObject = wotFolder
    Else
        WorkingObject = wotMessage
    End If
End Function
```

With the user interface elements in place, let's turn our attention to actually writing code to manage our folders.

Adding Folders

The Add Folder button in our CDO Sample application will allow the user to select a folder on the folder tree and add a subfolder to it. If the user selects an information store from the tree, the program will create a new top-level folder in the store's `RootFolder`.

First, add a `NewFolder` method to the `FMain` form:

```
Private Sub NewFolder()
    On Error GoTo ErrHandler

    Dim objStore As MAPI.InfoStore
    Dim objParentFolder As MAPI.Folder
    Dim nodParent As MSComctlLib.Node
    Dim arrIDs() As String
    Dim strFolderName As String

    ' There should always be a currently selected node
    Set nodParent = tvwFolders.SelectedItem
    arrIDs = Split(nodParent.Key, gcstrIDDelimiter)
    If UBound(arrIDs) > 0 Then
        ' It's a Folder
        Set objParentFolder = gobjSession.GetFolder(arrIDs(1), arrIDs(0))
    Else
        ' It's an InfoStore
        Set objStore = gobjSession.GetInfoStore(arrIDs(0))
        Set objParentFolder = objStore.RootFolder
    End If

    strFolderName = InputBox("Enter the new folder name")
    If Len(strFolderName) > 0 Then
        Call objParentFolder.Folders.Add(strFolderName)
        Call ShowInfoStores
    End If

ExitFunc:
    Set nodParent = Nothing
```

```
        Set objParentFolder = Nothing
        Set objStore = Nothing
        Exit Sub

    ErrHandler:
        Call ReportError(Err)
        Resume ExitFunc
    End Sub
```

The NewFolder function firstly finds the currently selected node, tvwFolders.SelectedItem, on the TreeView control. Next, it examines the Key property of the selected node to see whether it represents an information store or a folder. Recall that, the way we've set it up, an information store node's Key property contains its ID, while a folder node's Key property contains its parent stores ID and its own ID separated by a comma. That means that we can distinguish them by checking the Key property. Just to remind you, the following code snippet is taken from the ShowFolder method and shows how a folder node's Key property is constructed.

```
Set nodFolder = tvwFolders.Nodes.Add( _
        Relative:=nodParent, Relationship:=tvwChild, _
        Key:=objFolder.StoreID & gcstrIDDelimiter & objFolder.ID, _
        Text:=objFolder.Name)
```

There are many ways of extracting the store and folder IDs. One of the easiest methods is to use the new Split function in Visual Basic 6. The (simplified) syntax as we use it in the code above has the following form:

```
StringArray = Split(SourceString, Delimiter)
```

It splits SourceString by the specified Delimiter string and assigns each resulting sub-string to an element in a zero-based, variable-length string array.

```
Dim arrIDs() As String
...
arrIDs = Split(nodParent.Key, gcstrIDDelimiter)
```

If the node represents an information store, its Key property does not contain a comma so the resulting arrIDs will have only one element. But for a folder store, the resulting string will contain two elements – the first is its parent information store ID and the second is its own ID. So we can check the upper bound of the array to determine the node type:

```
If UBound(arrIDs) > 0 Then
    ' It's a Folder
    Set objParentFolder = gobjSession.GetFolder(arrIDs(1), arrIDs(0))
Else
    ' It's an InfoStore
    Set objStore = gobjSession.GetInfoStore(arrIDs(0))
    Set objParentFolder = objStore.RootFolder
End If
```

If the node represents an information store, we call the `Session` object's `GetInfoStore` method with the following syntax:

```
Set objStore = objSession.GetInfoStore(strStoreID)
```

To create a top-level folder in an information store, we need to get its `RootFolder` so that we can add a new folder to its `Folders` collection.

If the node represents a folder, we call the `Session` object's `GetFolder` method with the following syntax:

```
Set objFolder = objSession.GetFolder(strFolderID, strStoreID)
```

Checking TreeView Node Type

Many functions in `FMain` will use this method to distinguish and retrieve information store or folder objects. It would be a good idea to make this method an independent function so we can use it easily later on. We will define an Enum, `FolderNodeTypeEnum`, in the General section to help the readability of the code as well. Put all this code in `FMain`:

```
Private Enum FolderNodeTypeEnum
    fntStore = 1
    fntFolder = 2
End Enum


Private Function GetFolderNodeType(ByRef StoreID As String, _
                        ByRef FolderID As String) As FolderNodeTypeEnum
    Dim nodFolder As MSComctlLib.Node
    Dim arrIDs() As String

    Set nodFolder = tvwFolders.SelectedItem
    If Not nodFolder Is Nothing Then
        arrIDs = Split(nodFolder.Key, gcstrIDDelimiter)
        If UBound(arrIDs) = 0 Then
            GetFolderNodeType = fntStore
        Else
            FolderID = arrIDs(1)
            GetFolderNodeType = fntFolder
        End If
        StoreID = arrIDs(0)
    End If

    Set nodFolder = Nothing
End Function
```

The `GetFolderNodeType` function returns the type of node to the calling function. It also returns the store ID and, if the node represents a folder, the folder ID through the two `ByRef` parameters. The calling function can then use those IDs to retrieve the information store or folder object.

We can then modify the `NewFolder` function to call `GetFolderNodeType`:

```
Private Sub NewFolder()
    On Error GoTo ErrHandler

    Dim objParentFolder As MAPI.Folder
    Dim strFolderName As String
    Dim strStoreID As String
    Dim strFolderID As String

    If GetFolderNodeType(strStoreID, strFolderID) = fntStore Then
        ' It's an InfoStore
        Set objParentFolder = gobjSession.GetInfoStore(strStoreID).RootFolder
    Else
        ' It's a Folder
        Set objParentFolder = gobjSession.GetFolder(strFolderID, strStoreID)
    End If

    strFolderName = InputBox("Enter the new folder name")
    If Len(strFolderName) > 0 Then
        Call objParentFolder.Folders.Add(strFolderName)
        Call ShowInfoStores
    End If
...
```

The `NewFolder` method asks the user for the new folder's name using Visual Basic's `InputBox`. Once we get the folder's name, we call the `Add` method of the parent folder's `Folders` collection. Finally, we call the `ShowInfoStores` method to redisplay the folder tree.

The CDO `Folders` collection's `Add` method returns a reference to the newly-created folder. This allows us to modify it if necessary. For instance, we could add a message to it like this:

```
Set objFolder = objParentFolder.Folders.Add(strFolderName)
Set objNewMessage = objFolder.Messages.Add(Subject:="Important Notice")
```

This method of adding folders will work as long as the current user has the permission to create subfolders in the selected folder. If the user does not have such permission, CDO will raise an error, `CdoE_No_Access` (&H80070005). You can use Microsoft Outlook to find out the user's permission on any folders. Just right-click on a folder in the folder list tree diagram and click on **Properties**. Then click on the **Permissions** tab, as shown here:

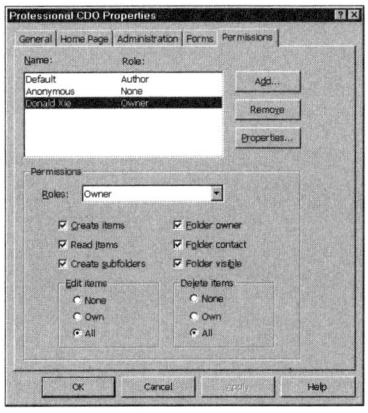

See Chapter 7 for more details about programmatically managing folder permissions.

Now we have the `NewFolder` method that creates new folders, we just need to hook it up to the `NewFolder` toolbar button. Add this code to `FMain`'s code module:

```
Private Sub Toolbar_ButtonClick(ByVal Button As MSComctlLib.Button)
    On Error GoTo ErrHandler

    Select Case Button.Key
        Case mcstrButtonKeyFolder, mcstrButtonKeyMessage
            ' Will check button state in WorkingObject

        Case mcstrButtonKeyNew
            If WorkingObject = wotFolder Then
                Call NewFolder
            Else
                ' Creating a new message
            End If

        Case Else
            ' Do nothing
    End Select

ExitFunc:
    Exit Sub

ErrHandler:
    Call ReportError(Err)
    Resume ExitFunc
End Sub
```

Deleting Folders

Our CDO Sample application will also provide the user with the ability to select a folder on the Tree View list and click the Delete button on the toolbar to delete it. Let's start coding this with the `DeleteFolder` function:

```
Private Sub DeleteFolder()
    On Error GoTo ErrHandler

    Dim objFolder As MAPI.Folder
    Dim strStoreID As String
    Dim strFolderID As String
    Dim strPrompt As String

    If GetFolderNodeType(strStoreID, strFolderID) = fntFolder Then
        Set objFolder = gobjSession.GetFolder(strFolderID, strStoreID)

        strPrompt = "Delete the " & tvwFolders.SelectedItem.Text & " folder"
        If objFolder.Folders.Count > 0 Then
            strPrompt = strPrompt & " and all subfolders"
        End If
        strPrompt = strPrompt & "?"
```

```
        If MsgBox(strPrompt, vbYesNo) = vbYes Then
            Call objFolder.Delete
            Call ShowInfoStores
        End If

        Set objFolder = Nothing
    End If

ExitFunc:
    Exit Sub

ErrHandler:
    Call ReportError(Err)
    Resume ExitFunc
End Sub
```

We use the same technique as in the NewFolder function to determine whether or not the user has selected a folder node on the folder tree. If a folder node is selected, we ask the user to confirm the deletion. This function then retrieves the folder using the CDO Session object's GetFolder function and calls the Folder object's Delete method to remove it. Finally, it calls the ShowInfoStores method to refresh the folder tree.

This code aims to demonstrate how to check whether a folder has any subfolders by checking its Folders property that contains its subfolders. This means it must call the GetFolder method to actually retrieve the folder from the Exchange Server and then display the name of the folder when it asks for confirmation. A slightly better approach might be to check the folder tree node to see if it has any child nodes. The latter approach has an advantage: we can ask for user confirmation *before* calling the GetFolder method – therefore we wouldn't need to call it if the user decided not to delete the folder. This would save a potential network round trip for CDO to go to the server and retrieve the Folder object.

As with the NewFolder function, we also need to link up the DeleteFolder function to the Delete button on the toolbar.

```
Private Sub Toolbar_ButtonClick(ByVal Button As MSComctlLib.Button)
...
        Case mcstrButtonKeyNew
            If WorkingObject = wotFolder Then
                Call NewFolder
            Else
                ' Creating a new message
            End If


        Case mcstrButtonKeyDelete
            If WorkingObject = wotFolder Then
                Call DeleteFolder
            Else
                ' Delete a message
            End If


        Case Else
            ' Do nothing
    End Select
...
```

Copying Folders

Adding and deleting folders is pretty straightforward stuff. Copying folders is slightly more complicated, since we need to know both the source folder *and* its new parent folder. There are many elegant user interface design methods to make this process easy and intuitive. One of them is to provide the user with the ability to drag the folder to be copied and drop it under its new parent. This is the method Microsoft Outlook uses.

Since this book is about CDO programming, we won't discuss the user interface issues in much detail. We'll use an implementation that is easier to code (even though it is less intuitive to actually use), simply to keep the focus on CDO. In this implementation, the user must first select the folder to be copied and click the Copy button. The program will cache the folder when the Copy button is clicked. The user will then need to select the new parent folder and click the Paste button. The cached folder will be copied after the user has clicked the Paste button.

To do this, we'll create two functions. The CopyFolder function is called when the user selects the source folder and clicks the Copy button. The PasteFolder function is then called when the user selects the new parent folder and clicks Paste.

Firstly, we will need to define a form-level object in FMain to hold a reference to the folder to be copied. Add the shaded code to FMain:

```
Option Explicit

Private Const mcstrButtonKeyNewFolder   As String = "btnNewFolder"
Private Const mcstrButtonKeyNewEmail    As String = "btnNewEmail"
Private Const mcstrButtonKeyNewPosting  As String = "btnNewPosting"
Private Const mcstrButtonKeyCopy        As String = "btnCopy"
Private Const mcstrButtonKeyPaste       As String = "btnPaste"
Private Const mcstrButtonKeyDelete      As String = "btnDelete"

' The current working folder
Private mobjFolder As MAPI.Folder
```

Next, add the CopyFolder function to FMain:

```
Private Sub CopyFolder()
    On Error GoTo ErrHandler

    Dim strStoreID As String
    Dim strFolderID As String

    If GetFolderNodeType(strStoreID, strFolderID) = fntFolder Then
        Set mobjFolder = gobjSession.GetFolder(strFolderID, strStoreID)
    End If

ExitFunc:
    Exit Sub

ErrHandler:
    Call ReportError(Err)
    Resume ExitFunc
End Sub
```

This function should be starting to look familiar by now. It checks to see if the user has selected a node representing a folder. If they have, this function calls the Session object's GetFolder method to retrieve the selected folder and saves it in the form-level object, mobjFolder.

Now that we have the source folder, the user can then select a destination parent folder (or an information store if the source folder is to be copied to a top-level folder). They can then click the **Paste** button to invoke the PasteFolder function to actually perform the copy. Let's add that function to FMain now:

```
Private Sub PasteFolder()
   On Error GoTo ErrHandler

   Dim objParentFolder As MAPI.Folder
   Dim strStoreID    As String
   Dim strFolderID    As String

   Screen.MousePointer = vbHourglass

   ' Only paste if we have already selected the source folder
   If Not mobjFolder Is Nothing Then
      If GetFolderNodeType(strStoreID, strFolderID) = fntStore Then
         Set objParentFolder = gobjSession.GetInfoStore(strStoreID).RootFolder
      Else
         Set objParentFolder = gobjSession.GetFolder(strFolderID, strStoreID)
      End If

      If gobjSession.CompareIDs(objParentFolder.ID, mobjFolder.FolderID) Then
         MsgBox "Cannot copy to the same parent folder"
      Else
         If gobjSession.CompareIDs(mobjFolder.StoreID, _
                        objParentFolder.StoreID) Then
            Call mobjFolder.CopyTo(objParentFolder.ID)
         Else
            Call mobjFolder.CopyTo(objParentFolder.ID, objParentFolder.StoreID)
         End If
         Set mobjFolder = Nothing

         Call ShowInfoStores
      End If
   End If

ExitFunc:
   Screen.MousePointer = vbDefault
   Set objParentFolder = Nothing
   Exit Sub

ErrHandler:
   Call ReportError(Err)
   Resume ExitFunc
End Sub
```

Since a copy operation could take some time to complete, we would do well to provide a visual clue to indicate that the copy operation is being executed. A simple way of doing this is to change the mouse pointer to an hourglass while we are copying and reset it when the operation is completed.

We also need to make sure that the user has already selected a folder to be copied:

```
If Not mobjFolder Is Nothing Then
```

We then check whether the user has selected a tree node representing the new parent folder, or a node representing an information store. In the latter case, the source folder will be copied to the destination store's RootFolder. That is, it becomes a top-level folder in the destination store's RootFolder.

If the user selects a folder node, the corresponding folder will be the parent folder. We can retrieve it using the Session object's GetFolder method. If the user selects an information store node, its RootFolder will be the parent folder. We can get the corresponding InfoStore object and return a reference to its root folder using its RootFolder property.

```
Set objParentFolder = gobjSession.GetInfoStore(arrIDs(0)).RootFolder
```

The Folder object's CopyTo method has an optional parameter specifying the parent information store ID. This parameter is required if the source folder is in a different store than the destination. One way of figuring out whether the source and destination store are the same is to use the CDO Session object's CompareIDs function:

```
objSession.CompareIDs(ID1 As String, ID2 As String)
```

This function can be used to compare any objects such as information stores, folders, and messages. It returns True if ID1 and ID2 refer to the same object on the Exchange Server, even if the two IDs are not themselves identical.

If the new parent folder is the same as the current parent folder of the selected folder, CDO will return an error, CdoE_COLLISION (&H80040604), indicating that the folder already exists. Therefore we need to prevent this from happening. The CDO Folder object has a FolderID property that returns the ID of the current folder's parent folder. So we again call the CompareIDs method to verify whether the two are actually the same. If so, we simply display a message. Otherwise, we call the source folder's CopyTo method to copy itself to the new location.

```
If gobjSession.CompareIDs(mobjFolder.StoreID, objParentFolder.StoreID) Then
    Call mobjFolder.CopyTo(objParentFolder.ID)
Else
    Call mobjFolder.CopyTo(objParentFolder.ID, objParentFolder.StoreID)
End If
```

In fact, this step is not strictly necessary. Even if the source and destination stores are the same, we can still pass the store ID to the CopyTo method with no side effect or performance penalty. We could replace the above code snippet with just one statement:

```
Call mobjFolder.CopyTo(objParentFolder.ID, objParentFolder.StoreID)
```

Feel free to do so if you like. Once we are done, we set the source folder to Nothing to release the reference. This is more of a design decision than a technical requirement. It would be perfectly valid to keep mobjFolder so that the user could copy it again.

Finally, we call the `ShowInfoStores` function again to reload the folder tree.

Looking at this function closely, you will find that it is not necessary to actually get the parent folder object at all. The CDO `Folder` object's `CopyTo` method only needs the parent folder and store ID, not the actual folder and store objects. So we can rewrite this function without getting the folder and store object explicitly:

```
Private Sub PasteFolder()
...
    ' Only paste if we have already selected the source folder
   If Not mobjFolder Is Nothing Then
      If GetFolderNodeType(strStoreID, strFolderID) = fntStore Then
         strFolderID = gobjSession.GetInfoStore(strStoreID).RootFolder.ID
      End If

      If gobjSession.CompareIDs(strFolderID, mobjFolder.FolderID) Then
         MsgBox "Cannot copy to the same parent folder"
      Else
         Call mobjFolder.CopyTo(strFolderID, strStoreID)
         Set mobjFolder = Nothing
         Call ShowInfoStores
      End If
   End If
...
```

This saves us from getting the parent folder object if the user selects a folder as the new parent. We'll still have to query the server for the root folder if the user selects an information store. In any case, this approach may be slightly faster.

A restriction of the `CopyTo` method is that you may not be able to copy a folder back to itself, or any subfolder of itself. Doing so may cause a MAPI error – `MAPI_W_Partial_Completion` (`&H00000A68`). While it would be desirable to prevent this error from happening, the error handling routine in `PasteFolder` does the job here.

To finish off the copying folder task, let's modify the toolbar control's `ButtonClick` event to call the `CopyFolder` and `PasteFolder` functions:

```
Private Sub Toolbar_ButtonClick(ByVal Button As MSComctlLib.Button)
...
    Case mcstrButtonKeyNew
        If WorkingObject = wotFolder Then
            Call NewFolder
        Else
            ' Create new messages
        End If

    Case mcstrButtonKeyCopy
        If WorkingObject = wotFolder Then
            Call CopyFolder
        Else
            ' Copy a message
        End If
```

```
        Case mcstrButtonKeyPaste
           If WorkingObject = wotFolder Then
               Call PasteFolder
           Else
               ' Paste a message
           End If

        Case mcstrButtonKeyDelete
           If WorkingObject = wotFolder Then
               Call DeleteFolder
           Else
               ' Delete a message
           End If

    ...
```

Accessing Hidden Properties

We've seen that we can retrieve and assign ordinary properties in various CDO objects. For example, we can retrieve the ID property of information store and folder objects. We can also assign the Name property of folder objects.

While the CDO object model exposes a rich set of properties for all CDO objects that's sufficient for everyday use, each CDO object also has more (relatively less used) properties that are not directly exposed. For instance, a Folder object has a property that specifies the type of items contained in it. This property cannot be directly accessed because the folder object does not have a ContentType (or similar) property.

While these hidden properties are not frequently used, they can be very useful in certain circumstances. For instance, if we want to display a list of items contained in a folder, we would like to know what properties of those items should be displayed. If a folder contains messages, we might want to display the sender and subject of those messages. On the other hand, for contact and address items, we might want to display the contact's name and e-mail addresses. The aforementioned 'content type' property is thus very useful in this situation.

In this section, we'll see how to access such hidden properties of CDO objects.

Fields Collection and Field Object

Many CDO objects contain a Fields collection, which contains a list of Field objects representing the attributes, or properties, of the parent object.

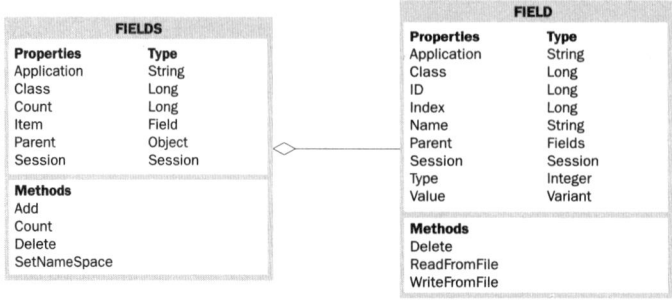

Standard CDO Fields

CDO defines a set of standard fields for each type of objects. These standard fields are identified by their IDs, which correspond to a MAPI property tag. But what is a MAPI property tag?

CDO defines a collection of 32-bit integer constants for predefined MAPI properties. We can use those constants when we want to refer to a MAPI property in Visual Basic applications. For instance, if we want to retrieve the Display Name of an `AddressEntry`, we can use:

```
objAddressEntry.Fields.Item(CdoPR_DISPLAY_NAME).Value
```

`CdoPR_DISPLAY_NAME` maps to the MAPI Property Tag PR_DISPLAY_NAME. To use this in ASP, however, you must use the value directly. For example, you will need to use `&H3001001E` instead of `CdoPR_DISPLAY_NAME` in an ASP page:

```
objAddressEntry.Fields.Item(&H3001001E).Value
```

You can find out the value of a CDO constant from the CDO documentation or using the Object Browser.

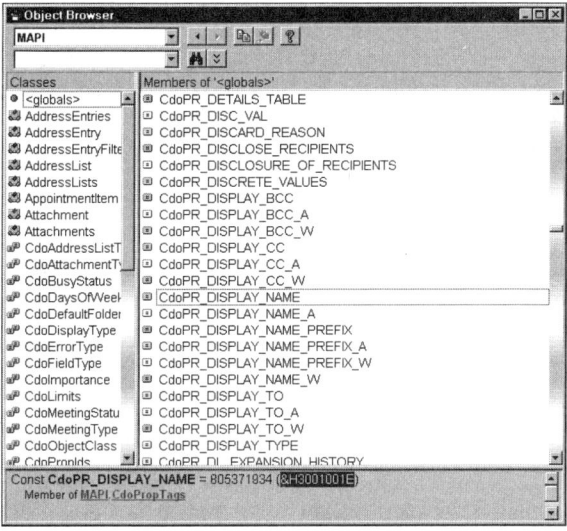

In addition to MAPI property tags, Microsoft Exchange Server also defines a set of property tags. If your application connects to an Exchange Server, you can use those properties in your application too. However, Exchange Server property tags do not have equivalent CDO constants, so you'll need to use the numeric values of the property tags in your program. A good practice is to define your own constants for the property tags used in your application.

Custom Fields

While most objects (such as `Message` and `Folder`) contain a set of standard fields when the object is created, others (such as `MessageFilter` and `AddressEntryFilter`) contain no fields by default. You can add fields to the `Fields` collection in an object by using the `Add` method. For instance, the CDO `AddressEntry` object has a set of standard properties, like a person's name and company she works for.

An example: if you worked for an automobile mechanic company, your company might want to record the most recent vehicle service date so that you can send out service reminders. You could add a field, `LastServiceDay`, to the customer address entries to handle this.

If the `Add` method is successful, it returns a reference to the newly created `Field` object. This is similar to the `Add` method of any standard Visual Basic collection.

Adding Fields to the Fields Collection

The `Add` method has two flavors. The first accepts a MAPI property tag and a value for the field. This creates a `Field` object that corresponds to a predefined MAPI property.

```
Set objField = colFields.Add(PropTag, Value)
```

`PropTag` is a `Long` integer that specifies a MAPI property tag. `Value` specifies the value of the field. The type of `Value` is determined by the MAPI property.

The second version of the `Add` method creates a user-defined field:

```
Set objField = colFields.Add(Name, Type [, Value] [, PropsetID])
```

The first parameter specifies the name of the field. This can be used to retrieve the field from the `Fields` collection later on.

```
strAuthorName = objMessage.Fields ("Author").Value
```

Note that the length of the field name must not exceed 120 characters, or CDO will raise an error – `CdoE_CALL_FAILED (&H80040005)`.

The second parameter specifies the type of the field. This is not required in the first syntax since CDO knows the types of all predefined MAPI properties. But when creating a user-defined field, you need to inform CDO of the field type. The following table lists all field types supported by CDO.

Field Type	Visual Basic Type	Value
Empty (Not initialized)	vbEmpty	0
Short Integer (2 bytes)	vbInteger	2
Long Integer (4 bytes)	vbLong	3

Field Type	Visual Basic Type	Value
8 Byte Integer scaled by 10,000	vbCurrency	6
Single precision floating point number	vbSingle	4
Double precision floating point number	vbDouble	5
8 Byte floating point number representing date/time value. The integer portion represents the date, and the fraction represents the time.	vbDate	7
String	vbString	8
Boolean	vbBoolean	11
Variant data containing objects or other primitive types	vbVariant	12
Unknown binary object	vbBlob	65
Array	vbArray	8192

You need to be careful when creating a field with an array type. You must always provide a concrete data type to specify the type of element in the array. For example, if you want to create a field that can contain a string array, you need to specify the type as `vbArray + vbString`, not just `vbArray`.

While you can specify an `Empty` field while creating it, you will never get back a field that contains uninitialized data. CDO will decide and assign a field type for you when you assign a value to the field. If you don't assign a value to a new `Empty` field, CDO will not save that field.

On that note, the third parameter assigns the value to the new field. It is optional, that is, you can add a field to a collection and assign its value later. For example,

```
Set objField = colFields.Add("Author", vbString)
objField.Value = "Donald Xie"
```

This is the equivalent of

```
Set objField = colFields.Add("Author"; vbString, "Donald Xie")
```

Finally, the fourth parameter specifies a Property Set, or Namespace, in which this field should be placed.

> *A Property Set is a namespace where a set of properties is defined. This helps to resolve the name conflicts that might arise. For instance, you might use the name "Required" to specify a Field storing the names of documents that must be read before attending the meeting defined in a MeetingItem. You might also potentially use the same name to specify another Field that contains the knowledge (say, Visual Basic or COM) that meeting attendees must have. You can define two property sets, one which contains the field for required documents and the other contains the field for required knowledge.*

It might sound silly because we can simply name those fields RequiredDocuments and RequiredKnowledge respectively, to avoid the trouble of defining property sets. That is, as long as you have control over the property names. However, this might not be the case if you use third-party CDO components in your application, or if you want to define a field with the same name as the predefined property names. For example, if you post a Microsoft Word document to a public folder, the Exchange Server creates a message and stores the document author's name in a field named "Author". If you need to define another field, also called Author, to store the person who actually posted the message, you will have a name conflict.

Each property set is identified with a globally unique identifier (GUID) that is assigned when the property set is created. MAPI defines several property sets. By default, CDO uses the one represented by the GUID constant PS_Public_String. This property set contains document summary information, such as the Author of a Word document.

Microsoft Outlook also defines several property sets used in the private folders. They are listed in the following table.

Constant	ID (String)	Properties in
CdoPropSetID1	0220060000000000C000000000000046	Appointment items
CdoPropSetID2	0320060000000000C000000000000046	Task items
CdoPropSetID3	0420060000000000C000000000000046	Contact items
CdoPropSetID4	0820060000000000C000000000000046	Common properties in Appointment, Contact and Task items
CdoPropSetID5	2903020000000000C000000000000046	Generic
CdoPropSetID6	0E20060000000000C000000000000046	Note items
CdoPropSetID7	0A20060000000000C000000000000046	Journal items

Setting the Default PropertySet

The CDO Fields collection has a SetNamespace method:

```
Call colFields.SetNamespace(PropsetID)
```

It specifies a property set (represented by the PropsetID parameter) as the default property set in the current Fields collection. The PropsetID is a GUID that uniquely identifies a property set. The selected property set remains in force until the next SetNamespace call.

The Item property and Add method access Field objects in the current Fields collection from the default property set of the collection, unless you override it with the optional PropsetID parameter when accessing them.

By default, the MAPI `PS_Public_Strings` property set is used. If you call this method with an empty string as the `PropsetID`, it resets the default property of the current collection to the MAPI `PS_Public_Strings` property set.

Retrieving a Field from a Fields Collection

Similar to standard Visual Basic collections, the CDO `Fields` collection has an `Item` property that retrieves a `Field` from a `Fields` collection. This property has three variations:

```
Set objField = colFields.Item(Index)
Set objField = colFields.Item(PropTag)
Set objField = colFields.Item(Name, [PropsetID])
```

The first syntax accepts an integer and returns the *Index*[th] `Field` object in the collection. It raises an error – `Script Out Of Range (9)` – if the Index value is not valid. Here is how you work with a field in the collection using its index. We're assigning the `Field`'s `Value` property to a variable in this case:

```
varVariable = objMessage.Fields.Item(1).Value
```

The second syntax accepts a `Long` integer specifying a MAPI Property Tag.

The third syntax retrieves a custom `Field` object. The first parameter is the name of the field. It can only be used for user-defined fields. That is, you cannot use it to retrieve the standard MAPI properties supported by CDO, for instance the `DisplayName` of an `AddressEntry`. The second parameter is optional. It specifies the property set associated with the field to be retrieved.

If you need to retrieve a custom `Field` object defined in a property set other than `PS_Public_String` (the default), you need to pass the property set's GUID as the second parameter. Here is an example of using the third syntax with the default property set:

```
strAuthor = objMessage.Fields.Item("Author").Value
```

Finally, `Item` is the default property of all CDO collections, so the following two statements are syntactically equivalent:

```
strAuthor = objMessage.Fields.Item("Author").Value
strAuthor = objMessage.Fields("Author").Value
```

Deleting a Field from a Fields Collection

The CDO `Field` object has a `Delete` method that deletes the current `Field` object from its parent `Fields` collection. Only an optional or user-defined field can be deleted; standard properties cannot be deleted.

The ReadFromFile Method

The `ReadFromFile` method reads a file and replaces the content of the field with the content of the file.

```
Call objFolder.ReadFromFile(FileName As String)
```

This method is only valid if the field type is `vbString` or `vbBlob`. The `FileName` parameter must be the full path and name of a file, for example:

```
C:\CDOApps\Data\Authors.txt
```

The WriteToFile Method

```
Sub WriteToFile(FileName As String)
```

The `WriteToFile` method writes the field value to a file specified by the `FileName` parameter. Like `ReadFromFile`, this method is only valid in fields with type `vbString` or `vbBlob`. It overwrites the content of the file with the field value. Again, the `FileName` parameter should contain the full path and name of the destination file.

Using Fields in the Sample Project

The `Fields` collection of a CDO object contains very useful information about that object. We will add a utility form to our CDO Sample project to list all the fields of a given CDO object. As usual in our sample application, the aim is to demonstrate the use of the various objects. You'll probably come up with many custom uses for `Field` objects.

Open the CDO Sample project and add a new form, calling it `FFields`. We will use a `ListView` control on this form to display the field objects:

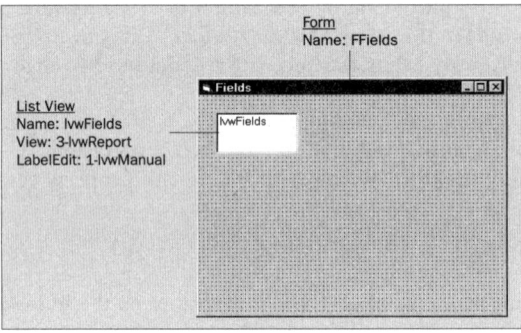

Add the following method, `ShowFields`, to the form's code module:

```
Private Sub ShowFields(obj As Object)
    On Error Resume Next

    Dim colFields As MAPI.Fields
    Dim objField As MAPI.Field
    Dim itmField As MSComctlLib.ListItem

    Set colFields = obj.Fields

    With lvwFields.ColumnHeaders
        .Clear
        .Add Text:="ID"
        .Add Text:="Name"
        .Add Text:="Value"
    End With
```

```
      With lvwFields.ListItems
         .Clear
         For Each objField In colFields
            Set itmField = .Add(Text:=FormatHex(objField.ID))
            itmField.SubItems(1) = objField.Name
            itmField.SubItems(2) = objField.Value
         Next
      End With

      With lvwFields
         .SortKey = 0
         .SortOrder = lvwAscending
         .Sorted = True
      End With

      Set itmField = Nothing
      Set objField = Nothing
      Set colFields = Nothing
   End Sub
```

Because this is for displaying the fields in the given object only, we will just ignore any errors that might arise. If we cannot get to a field for whatever reason, we can't display it anyway, so we may as well ignore it. The ListView will have three columns – ID, Name, and Value – to display our Field objects' ID, Name, and Value properties. We then loop through the Fields collection of the given object and display the corresponding properties of each field. To help us to read the fields easily, we will sort the fields by their IDs.

Since we need to pass an object to this form, we'll code a ShowForm method that accepts this ID, calls ShowFields, and loads the form. Add this code to the FFields code module:

```
   Public Sub ShowForm(obj As Object)
      Call ShowFields(obj)
      Call Me.Show(vbModal)
   End Sub
```

To make the list easier to read, let's code the form's Resize event, allowing us to resize the ListView to occupy the whole form:

```
   Private Sub Form_Resize()
      On Error Resume Next

      lvwFields.Move 0, 0, ScaleWidth, ScaleHeight
   End Sub
```

Now the form is ready, we need to make some changes to the main form to show this form. Add this code, the ShowFolderProperties method, to the FMain form:

```
   Private Sub ShowFolderProperties()
      Dim objFolder As MAPI.Folder
      Dim frmFields As FFields
      Dim strStoreID As String
      Dim strFolderID As String
```

```
      If GetFolderNodeType(strStoreID, strFolderID) = fntFolder Then
         ' It's a Folder
         Set objFolder = gobjSession.GetFolder(strFolderID, strStoreID)

         Set frmFields = New FFields
         Call frmFields.ShowForm(objFolder)

         Set frmFields = Nothing
         Set objFolder = Nothing
      End If
   End Sub
```

This method checks whether the user has selected a folder. If they have, it creates a new instance of
FFields and calls its ShowForm method with the selected folder object. Finally, we need to modify the
toolbar's ButtonClick event handler to call this method when the user clicks the **Property** button:

```
Private Sub Toolbar_ButtonClick(ByVal Button As MSComctlLib.Button)
...

      Case mcstrButtonKeyDelete
         If WorkingObject = wotFolder Then
            Call DeleteFolder
         Else
            ' Delete a message
         End If

      Case mcstrButtonKeyProperty
         If WorkingObject = wotFolder Then
            Call ShowFolderProperties
         Else
            ' Show Message Properties
         End If

      Case Else
         ' Do nothing
...
```

That's it. You can run the project, select a folder from the folder tree and click the **Property** button to
display a list of field objects in the folder's Fields collection, as you can see below. The example is
from the Calendar folder.

The highlighted field corresponds to the MAPI property `CdoPR_CONTAINER_CLASS`, and it has a value of `IPF.Appointment`. By examining this property, you will be able to tell that it contains appointments. Some fields correspond to CDO object properties. For example, field `&H3001001E` corresponds to the `Name` property of the CDO `Folder` object.

Summary

In this chapter, we have worked with information stores and folders using CDO. CDO organizes messages and other storable items into folders, which are stored in information stores. Getting data from Exchange Servers programmatically with CDO requires us to find stores and folders before we can actually access the messages.

We have added the capability of navigating information stores and folders to our sample project. We have also seen how we can retrieve information stores and folders directly using the CDO `Session` object's `GetInfoStore` and `GetFolder` methods. The CDO `Session` object also provides direct access to the Inbox and Outbox folders in a user's mailbox through its `Inbox` and `Outbox` properties.

Accessing the information stores and folders is just a start. We have also learned how to create new folders, copy folders, and delete existing folders. In the next chapter, we will go through another top-level CDO collection, `AddressLists`, to find out how to access and manage address information.

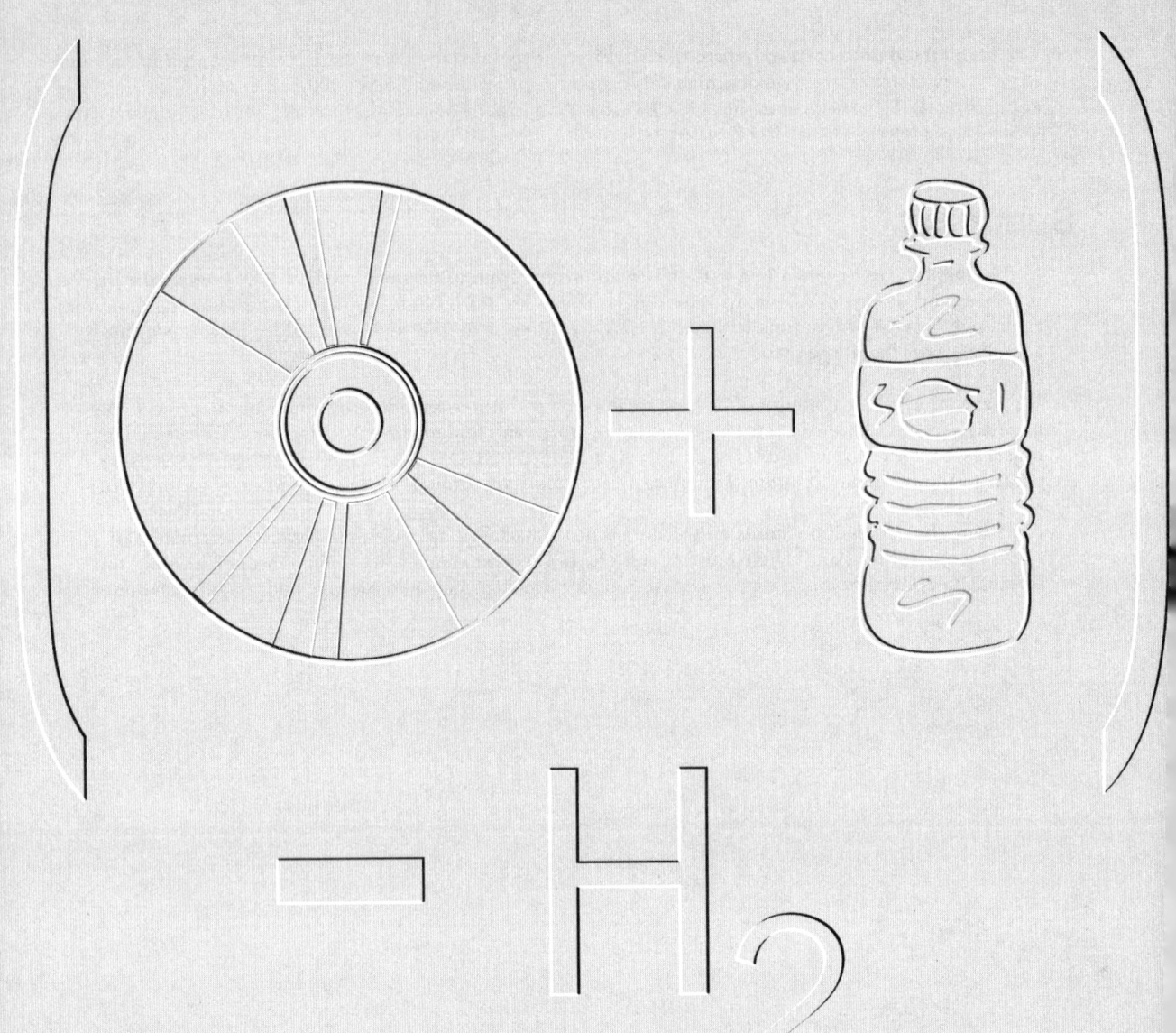

4

Managing Address Books

Introduction

In chapter 2, we saw that the CDO `Session` object has four directly accessible child objects. In the last chapter, we learned to access the `InfoStores` property to access the information stores and folders. Inbox and Outbox are just two of the most commonly used folders. We will work with creating and managing messages in chapter 6. In this chapter, though, we'll look deep into the `Session` object's `AddressLists` property, which is a collection of all address lists.

Address data is represented in CDO `AddressEntry` objects. Each `AddressEntry` object may represent a individual person or a distribution list. Address entries are organized into different address lists. A MAPI Messaging user profile can contain several address lists. Typically, it contains at least the Global Address List (GAL) and optionally a Personal Address Book (PAB).

The Global Address List (GAL)

The GAL is created and maintained by your Microsoft Exchange Server administrator. It typically consists of all users who have a mailbox on the Exchange Server. Because of the integrated security model employed by Windows NT and Exchange Server, you can only create a mailbox for a user if they belong to the Windows NT Domain where the Exchange Server is located or if the user is in a trusted domain. You may also set up a mailbox with public access, that is, a mailbox that is associated with 'Everyone'. However, you *can* add a user to a Windows NT Domain without assigning them a mailbox.

The GAL is accessible to all users with a mailbox on the Exchange Server. When you create a CDO session and log on using either an existing profile or a dynamically generated profile, the GAL is accessible through the `Session` object's `AddressLists` collection property.

Users normally do not have permission to modify this list. This access restriction is reflected in the CDO library which does not support the modification of the GAL. That is, you cannot use CDO to add, edit, or remove addresses contained in the GAL.

In addition to the GAL, an Exchange Server administrator can create additional address lists and assign permissions to relevant users. Those additional address lists then become accessible to users who have the proper permission. The `Session` object's `AddressLists` collection contains the GAL and any additional address lists. Like the GAL, such address lists are generally not modifiable by users who are not Exchange Server administrators. It will also possibly contain the Personal Address Book, depending on the log-on method. We'll look into that address list soon.

Accessing the GAL using CDO

First, though, a bit about how you can gain access to the GAL using the CDO `Session` object's `GetAddressList` method.

```
Set objGAL = objSession.GetAddressList(CdoAddressListGAL)
```

The `GetAddressList` method is different from other `Session` object Get methods. As we have seen, we can use the `Session` object's `GetInfoStore` and `GetFolder` methods to retrieve an information store object and a folder object, respectively, by passing in their unique IDs.

The `GetAddressList` method, however, has a different parameter specification. Its only parameter is a Long integer that specifies the type of address list. In fact, it only accepts two values, 0 and 1. To get the GAL, you pass in 0 (represented by the CDO constant `CdoAddressListGAL`). If you are writing an ASP application, which doesn't have these constants available, you can either use the literal number 0 or define your own constant for it.

The Personal Address Book (PAB)

Unlike the GAL, a user's Personal Address Book is created and maintained by the individual user. When you create a MAPI profile, you have the option to include a PAB in the profile. Alternatively, you can add the PAB to an existing profile by bringing up the profile property page and click the Add button on the Services tab.

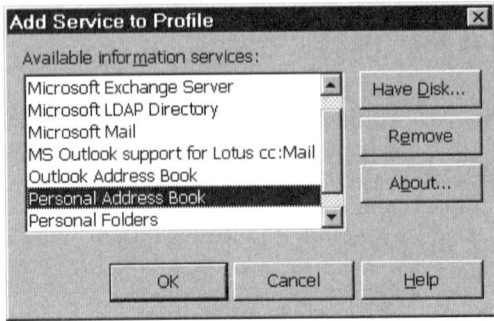

The PAB of one user is normally not accessible by other users, because it's stored locally on the user's machine (just like Personal Folders). A PAB is only accessible to a CDO application when it logs on using an existing profile that contains a PAB. A dynamically created profile does not contain a PAB and therefore cannot access one.

In general, an ASP application uses either anonymous access or a temporary profile to log in. That means your users cannot access their PABs. If your application really needs to have the ability to access PABs, you can get around this limitation by creating a profile either for each user or one for all users. However, such workarounds are rarely required.

Accessing the PAB using CDO

In a similar way as is used to access the GAL, you can use the `Session` object's `GetAddressList` method to retrieve a reference to the PAB:

```
Set objPAB = objSession.GetAddressList(CdoAddressListPAB)
```

`CdoAddressListPAB` is another CDO constant, this time with the value of 1. Recall that the `GetAddressList` method will only accept values of 0 or 1.

PAB? Which One?

You can choose not to add the PAB to a user profile. If you do decide to add the PAB to a user profile, it is the one and only PAB in that profile. However, you should be aware of a strange behavior of the `GetAddressList` method.

A MAPI profile may be used by either your CDO application or Microsoft Outlook, or it can be shared by both. If your users do not use Microsoft Outlook, you will not have any problem calling the `GetAddressList` method to access the PAB. If the PAB is included in the profile, you will get a reference to it using the `GetAddressList` method. Otherwise, you will receive an error `CdoE_CALL_FAILED` (`&H80004005`).

If a user also uses Microsoft Outlook in addition to your application, the situation is quite different. It is common and convenient to use the same profile in your CDO application and Outlook. In this case, calling the `GetAddressList(CdoAddressListPAB)` method always returns an address list that represents the Outlook Contacts folder, not the local PAB. This means that you cannot use this method to access the PAB at all. You can see this behavior by logging in using a profile that has been used by Outlook.

```
Debug.Print gobjSession.GetAddressList(CdoAddressListPAB).Name
```

So how do we work around this problem? We know that we can use neither a dynamically created profile (because it does not have access to the PAB) nor an existing profile that is shared by Outlook (because of the Contacts problem). A possible solution is to create a profile that is used solely by our application. We can do this by manually creating a profile and making sure that the user does not use it for Outlook.

This solution, however, is not very convenient since there is no way in which we can create a permanent MAPI profile programmatically using CDO. We must create it manually. Even then we can never be sure that the user will not inadvertently use it when starting Outlook.

103

The better solution is not to use the GetAddressList() method to access the PAB. Instead, we will see how to access the PAB from the Session object's AddressLists property later in this chapter. For now, let's have a quick look at the CDO Address Book structure and object model.

Address Book Structure

In CDO, you can access address book entries through the Session object's AddressLists property, which returns an AddressLists collection. The AddressLists collection contains several AddressList objects such as the GAL, the PAB, and any other address lists. This is the only way to access address lists other than the GAL and the PAB. Each AddressList object has an AddressEntries property that returns a collection of AddressEntry objects. The diagram below illustrates these relationships.

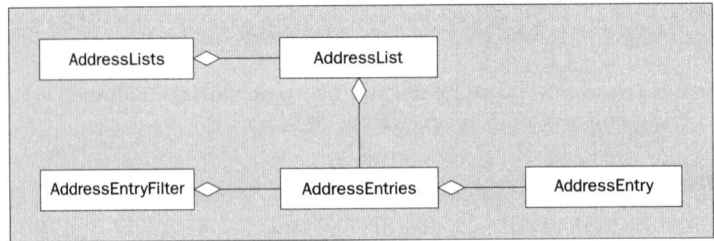

The AddressEntryFilter object is always associated with an AddressEntries collection. It allows us to specify search criteria to the AddressEntries collection so that only relevant entries show up when we navigate through the collection.

The AddressLists Collection

Like the InfoStores collection, the AddressLists collection is a very simple object in the CDO library. It has only six properties and defines no methods at all.

ADDRESSLISTS	
Properties	**Type**
Application	String
Class	Long
Count	Long
Item	AddressList
Parent	Session
Session	Session
Methods	
Events	

In addition to the four CDO common properties, it only implements two more – the Count and the Item properties. The Count property returns the number of AddressList objects in the AddressLists collection. The Item property returns an AddressList object in the collection. It accepts either a Long integer and retrieves the Index[th] AddressList in the collection, or else it accepts a String and retrieves an AddressList with the given name.

Since it does not have any methods, you cannot use CDO to add or remove address lists in the collection. That is, the `AddressLists` collection is read-only – so you can't programmatically create address lists.

The AddressList Object

An `AddressList` object contains a collection of addresses representing people, organizations, or distribution lists.

ADDRESSLIST	
Properties	**Type**
AddressEntries	AddressEntries
Application	String
Class	Long
Fields	Fields
ID	String
Index	Long
IsReadOnly	Boolean
Name	String
Parent	AddressLists
Session	Session
Methods	
IsSameAs	

❑ The `AddressEntries` Property – These addresses are contained in an `AddressEntries` collection returned by the `AddressList` object's `AddressEntries` property. This property is read-only so you cannot assign an `AddressEntries` collection to it. You can, however, add, modify, or remove address entries in the collection if the current user has the permission to do so.

❑ The `ID` and `Name` Properties – An `AddressList` object has an `ID` property that returns the unique ID string of the address list. It also has a `Name` property which returns the name of the address list. The GAL always has a name of Global Address List and the PAB is always named Personal Address Book. As I mentioned earlier, if a profile is shared by Microsoft Outlook, we can access its Contacts folder. Although it is confusing when the CDO `Session` object's `GetAddressList(CdoAddressListPAB)` method returns the Contacts folder, the ability to access the Contacts folder is quite useful. This folder is represented as an address list named Contacts. Since the names of the GAL, the PAB, and the Contacts folder are never changed, we can use them to access their corresponding address lists in the collection.

❑ The `Index` Property – The `Index` property returns the index of the current `AddressList` object in its parent `AddressLists` collection. The first `AddressList` in the collection has an `Index` value of 1.

❑ The `IsReadOnly` Property – The `AddressList` object has an `IsReadOnly` property. It returns `True` for the GAL and `False` for the PAB and the Outlook Contacts folder. Please note that although the Outlook Contacts folder is accessible to a CDO application and modifiable, we cannot use the CDO Library to modify it directly. We will see what happens when we try to modify the Outlook Contacts folder later.

❑ The `IsSameAs` Method – The `IsSameAs` method returns `True` if the current `AddressList` object and `AddressList2` refer to the same physical address list. For instance, if the Global Address List is the first `AddressList` object in the `objAddrLists` collection, the following code will print `True`.

```
Set objAddrList1 = objAddrLists(1)
Set objAddrList2 = objAddrLists("Global Address List")
Debug.Print objAddrList1.IsSameAs(objAddrList2)
```

The AddressEntries Collection

The CDO `AddressEntries` collection is accessible through an `AddressList` object's `AddressEntries` property. It contains a list of address entries in the parent address list.

ADDRESSENTRIES	
Properties	
Application	String
Class	Long
Count	Long
Filter	AddressEntryFilter
Item	Address Entry
Parent	AddressList
RawTable	IUnknown
Session	Session
Methods	
Add	
Delete	
GetFirst	
GetLast	
GetNext	
GetPrevious	
Sort	
Events	

Properties

❑   `Count` and `Item` – The `Count` property returns the number of `AddressEntry` objects in the `AddressEntries` collection. Please note that an `AddressEntries` collection is a large collection. This means that its `Count` property is not always reliable.

The `Item` property returns an `AddressEntry` object.

```
Set objAddrEntry = colAddrEntries.Item(lngIndex)
Set objAddrEntry = colAddrEntries.Item(strSearchValue)
```

If you pass it a Long integer, it returns the `AddressEntry` object in that position specified by the value of `lngIndex`. If you pass it a String, it returns the next `AddressEntry` object after the current cursor location in the collection, that has a current sorting property value greater than or equal to `strSearchValue`.

By default, the address list is sorted by the address entries' display name in ascending order. Therefore using the second syntax on an address list that has not been sorted returns the next entry with the matching `Name` property value, which is stored in the `CdoPR_DISPLAY_NAME` field.

If there is no matching `AddressEntry` object in the collection, an error `CdoE_NOT_FOUND` (&H8004010F) is raised. This could happen if the matching `AddressEntry` object is filtered out in the `Filter` object.

❑ `Filter` – The `AddressEntries` collection has a `Filter` property that returns a reference to the `AddressEntryFilter` object associated with the current collection. You can use the `AddressEntryFilter` object to set the search criteria of the collection. For instance, you can filter out any entries that do not belong to a certain company. This property is read-only so you cannot assign it with a `Filter` object created elsewhere. You will see an example of using the `AddressEntryFilter` later in our sample application.

❑ `RawTable` – The `RawTable` property returns an `IUnknown` pointer to the underlying MAPI table on the Exchange Server. This is accessible to C++ applications, but not Visual Basic applications since Visual Basic does not support the `IUNKNOWN` pointer.

Methods

❑ `Add` – The `AddressEntries` collection has an `Add` method that allows us to add entries to the collection. We will see how this method works when we extend our CDO Sample project later on.

❑ `Delete` – The `Delete` method physically deletes *all* `AddressEntry` objects in the collection and sets the current `AddressEntries` collection's `Count` property to zero. The collection itself is not deleted, though, so you can add more address entries to it as normal.

❑ `Sort` – You can sort an `AddressEntries` collection using its `Sort` methods.

```
colAddrEntries.Sort [SortOrder], [PropTag]
colAddrEntries.Sort [SortOrder], [Name]
```

It sorts the address entries in the collection using the `SortOrder` specified.

SortOrder Constant	Value	Order
CdoNone	0	Do not sort
CdoAscending	1	Sort in ascending order (default)
CdoDescending	2	Sort in descending order

It sorts the collection on either the standard MAPI property specified by the property tag (for example, `CdoPR_COMPANY_NAME`) or the user-defined property specified by the property name (for example, "Business Unit"). If neither the property tag nor the property name are specified, it sorts the collection using the property specified in the previous `Sort` operation. If the collection has not been sorted previously, it is sorted on the property `CdoPR_COMPANY_NAME`, which is exposed as the `Name` property of `AddressEntry` objects.

The `Sort` method does not always succeed. If the underlying message store does not support a specific sort, this method raises a CdoE_TOO_COMPLEX (&H80040117) error. If the parent `AddressList` object is read-only, the `Sort` method also fails with the same error.

❑ `GetFirst`, `GetLast`, `GetNext`, `GetPrevious` – These four methods are similar to their counterparts in the `Folders` collection. If you need to traverse the collection forwards and backwards, the `For Each … Next` loop does not work, so you will need to use these methods.

The AddressEntry Object

An `AddressEntry` object normally stores information about, well, an address entry. It may be a distribution list that itself contains a list of address entries. You can examine the `AddressEntry` object's `DisplayType` property to find out whether the `AddressEntry` object is an address or a distribution list.

ADDRESSENTRY	
Properties	
Address	String
Application	String
Class	Long
DisplayType	Long
Fields	Fields
ID	String
Manager	AddressEntry
MAPIObject	IUnknown
Members	AddressEntries
Name	String
Parent	Object
Session	Session
Type	String
Methods	
Delete	
Details	
GetFreeBusy	
IsSameAs	
Update	
Events	

Properties

❑ `DisplayType` – The name of this property is somewhat misleading. It returns the type of address entry object, not how the address entry should be displayed. It can have the following values:

DisplayType Constant	Value	Description
CdoUser	0	A user belonging to the local messaging system
CdoRemoteUser	6	A user belonging to the remote messaging system
CdoDistList	1	A public distribution list
CdoPrivateDistList	5	A private distribution list
CdoForum	2	A public folder
CdoAgent	3	An automated agent
CdoOrganization	4	An organizational unit

While CDO defines all seven types listed above, you can only use the `AddressEntries` collection's `Add` method to add two types of address entries, `CdoUser` and `CdoPrivateDistList`. Other types of address entries must be added using message store-specific utilities such as the Microsoft Exchange Server Administrator.

❑   `Members` – If an address entry object is a distribution list, its `Members` property returns a collection of all its child address entries. This can also contain distribution lists.

❑   `Address` and `Type` – The `AddressEntry` object splits a full address such as `SMTP:name@domain.com` into two parts. Its `Type` property returns the address type, for example `SMTP`, while its `Address` property stores the address value, for example `name@domain.com`. CDO determines the destination and messaging system using the full address.

❑   `Name` – The `Name` property returns the display name of the current `AddressEntry` object.

❑   `Manager` – Microsoft Exchange Server provides the ability to specify a manager for an `AddressEntry` – this is nothing more sinister than the person's manager. Although, of course, for some people, there *is* nothing more sinister than their managers…! The `Manager` property returns a reference to the manager's `AddressEntry` object. If you have not assigned the `Manager` field, this property returns `Nothing`.

❑   `MAPIOBJECT` – The `MAPIOBJECT` property returns an `IUNKNOWN` pointer to the current `Session` object. This is accessible to C++ applications, but not Visual Basic applications since Visual Basic does not support the `IUNKNOWN` pointer.

Methods

❑   `Delete` – You can delete an `AddressEntry` object from the parent `AddressEntries` collection using its `Delete` method. This permanently removes the entry represented by `AddressEntry` object from the message store.

❑   `Details` – The `Details` method displays a dialog box showing detailed information about the current `AddressEntry` object. We will see how we can use this method later in the sample project.

❑   `GetFreeBusy` – As a collaboration library, CDO provides the ability to get the availability of the person described by an address entry in a specified period.

```
strFreeBusy = objAddrEntry.GetFreeBusy(StartTime, EndTime, Interval)
```

Both the `StartTime` and `EndTime` parameters are `Variants`. They specify the date and time values in `vbDate` format. They specify the starting and ending time of the period. The `Interval` parameter is a `Long` integer that specifies the length of time slots in minutes.

The `GetFreeBusy` method returns the availability of the user in the period from `StartTime` to `EndTime`. The `Interval` parameter specifies the length of time slot in minutes. For instance, if you need to know the user's availability from 8am to 10am on September the 15th in half-hour slots, you can call this method as follows:

```
strAvail = objAddrEntry.GetFreeBusy("8:00:00 09/15/1999", _
                    "10:00:00 09/15/1999", 30)
```

The returned string contains four characters, because 4 half-hour slots were specified. The first represents the user's availability from 8:00 to 8:30, the second from 8:30 to 9:00, the third from 9:00 to 9:30, and the fourth from 9:30 to 10:00. Each character may have one of the following four values:

Character	CDO Constant	Meaning
0	CdoFree	The user is free in the whole time slot
1	CdoTentative	The user has one or more tentative commitments in the whole or a part of the time slot
2	CdoBusy	The user has one or more confirmed commitments in the whole or a part of the time slot
3	CdoOutOfOffice	The user is out of the office in the whole or a part of the time slot

If there is an overlapping of commitments in a time slot, the GetFreeBusy method returns the highest value. For instance, if the user is busy from 8:30 to 8:45 and has a tentative appointment from 8:45 to 9:30, the second character in the returned string will be 2.

The Interval parameter must be greater than or equal to 1, otherwise you will receive an error: CdoE_INVALID_PARAMETER (&H80070057).

Most message stores restrict the length of the period for which the schedule information is published, for performance reasons. For instance, Microsoft Outlook only publishes a maximum of three months. You can change this setting in Outlook if it connects to an Exchange Server 5.5 with Service Pack 2.

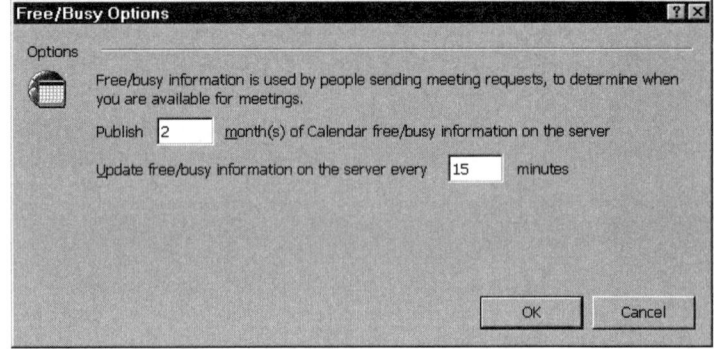

If you specify the period from StartTime to EndTime to be longer than three months, the GetFreeBusy method might return a string containing all zeros for time slots after the maximum period. This maximum period may be changed in the Session object's SetOption method with type FreeBusyMonths. However unless you are confident that the underlying message store supports this option, you should limit the length of the search period to avoid getting inaccurate results. You should also limit the number of time slots to prevent the application from consuming a huge amount of memory. For instance, calling the method for three months in 1-minute intervals will take up hundreds of megabytes of your user's memory.

❑ Update – The Update method saves the changes made to the AddressEntry object to the message store.

```
Call objAddrEntry.Update([MakePermanent] [,RefreshObject])
```

CDO uses its own memory cache to store the changes to AddressEntry objects to improve performance. If the MakePermanent parameter is True, CDO commits the changes to the message store and flushes the cache. Otherwise, the Update method simply flushes the cache without committing the change.

The RefreshObject parameter determines whether the cache should be reloaded from the message store. If it is True, CDO reloads address data from the message store. If the change is not committed, reloading data causes all changes to be lost and effectively cancels the change.

The effects of possible combinations of the MakePermanent and RefreshObject parameters are listed in the following table:

	RefreshObject = True	RefreshObject = False
MakePermanent = True	Commit all changes to the message store and reload the object from the message store so that changes made by other processes will be visible immediately.	Save the change to the message store but do not refresh the cache with possible changes made by other processes.
MakePermanent = False	Reload AddressEntry data from the message store, thus canceling the change.	Flush the cache.

The AddressEntryFilter Object

Each AddressEntries collection has an associated AddressEntryFilter object. You can use this object to specify the search criteria or restrictions on the address entry collection. For instance, you can specify that you only need the entries that belong to a certain company.

ADDRESSENTRYFILTER	
Properties	**Type**
Address	String
Application	String
Class	Long
Fields	Fields
Name	String
Not	Boolean
Or	Boolean
Parent	AddressEntries
Sessions	Session
Methods	
IsSameAs	

You cannot create an AddressEntryFilter object. You can only assign an AddressEntryFilter object with the Filter property of an existing AddressEntries collection.

```
Dim objAddrEntryFilter As MAPI.AddressEntryFilter
Set objAddrEntryFilter = _
    objSession.AddressLists("Global Address List").AddressEntries.Filter
```

By default, an `AddressEntries` collection has an `AddressEntryFilter` object that has no filtering criteria. You specify the filtering criteria by setting the `AddressEntryFilter`'s `Address`, `Name`, `Not`, and `Or` properties. You can also add `Field` objects to its `Fields` collection to specify further restrictions.

Filtering Address Entries

In CDO, an address list may contain hundreds or even thousands of address entries. Scrolling through such a large number of entries to find an entry doesn't make it very easy for your users. But there are two ways of helping them out.

The first is to sort the address list in a predefined order. For example, we can sort the list alphabetically by its address entry's display name.

```
Call colAddrEntries.Sort(CdoAscending, CdoPR_DISPLAY_NAME)
```

The second way to ease the search is to use the CDO `AddressEntryFilter` object. Let's take a look at the ways that we can do this.

Filtering by Address Entry Properties

The CDO `AddressEntryFilter` object has an `Address` property that specifies the full address of the address entries to be filtered. If you assign it a string representing a full mail address, only `AddressEntry` objects that have the matching full address will be accessible.

Another property of the `AddressEntryFilter` object is the `Name` property. By assigning a value to the `Name` property, only `AddressEntry` objects with display names containing a sub-string that matches the specified value will be included. For instance, assigning the `Name` property with the value "Jo" will find address entries with display names "John", "Joe", and so forth.

If you want to filter the collection by other properties, you can add the corresponding MAPI property tag or user-defined property name to the `Fields` collection of the `AddressEntryFilter` object.

The filter is applied when you set its properties and modify its `Field` objects. The `Fields` of each address entry in the collection are compared with the corresponding `Field` objects in the filter to determine whether the entry should be accessible to the application.

Filtering by Combined Properties

By default, address entries satisfying all specified matching criteria are included. In the following code snippet, only entries for people who reside in the UK and work for Wrox are accessible.

```
With objAddrEntryFilter
    .Fields("Company") = "Wrox"
    .Fields("Country") = "UK"
End With
```

The `Not` property specifies whether the filter restrictions should be negated. Note that you cannot specify a negative matching criteria like this:

```
objAddEntryFilder.Fields("Company") <> "Wrox"
```

...because this is an invalid expression. You must use the `Not` property. The following code snippet causes the `AddressEntries` collection to filter *out* people who reside in UK and work for Wrox.

```
With objAddrEntryFilter
    .Fields("Company") = "Wrox"
    .Fields("Country") = "UK"
    .Not = True
End With
```

Because the `Not` property negates all individual restrictions, you cannot mix positive and negative criteria, such as finding people who live in the UK but do not work for `Wrox`.

The `Or` property specifies whether entries that satisfy at least one restriction will be accessible. Entries for people who work for Wrox or reside in UK will be accessible in the following code fragment.

```
With objAddrEntryFilter
    .Fields("Company") = "Wrox"
    .Fields("Country") = "UK"
    .Or = True
End With
```

The `Not` property has higher precedence than the `Or` property. Therefore if both `Not` and `Or` are `True`, restrictions are negated and then ORed.

```
With objAddrEntryFilter
    .Fields("Company") = "Wrox"
    .Fields("Country") = "UK"
    .Or = True
    .Not = True
End With
```

So here, address entries representing people who do not work for Wrox or do not reside in the UK are included.

The `Filter` property of an `AddressEntries` collection may be set to `Nothing`, thus removing all restrictions applying to the collection. However, the filter object itself is persistent and remains attached to the collection. When it is referenced later, an empty filter object is returned.

```
Set objAddrEntries.Filter = Nothing    ' Remove all restrictions
Set objFilter = objAddrEntries.Filter  ' Gets an empty filter
```

Now we have acquired a good overview of the address book objects, it's time to see how we actually use them in our CDO Sample application.

The CDO Sample Application

Here, we'll be adding the ability to display, edit, and filter address entries to the CDO Sample project. More specifically, the users of this application will be able to see all address lists and entries in a profile. They will also be able to add, edit, and remove address entries in the PAB.

The figure below shows a design-time screenshot of the form we'll create to work with address lists. The top combo box contains all address lists in the profile. The text box below it can be used to enter a display name to filter the address list. The next tree view control displays a hierarchy of the address entries in the selected address list.

The text boxes on the right (as well as the label shown selected here) display the properties of the selected address entry. It is also used for creating new and editing existing address entries. An address entry's e-mail address consists of two parts, the type and the address.

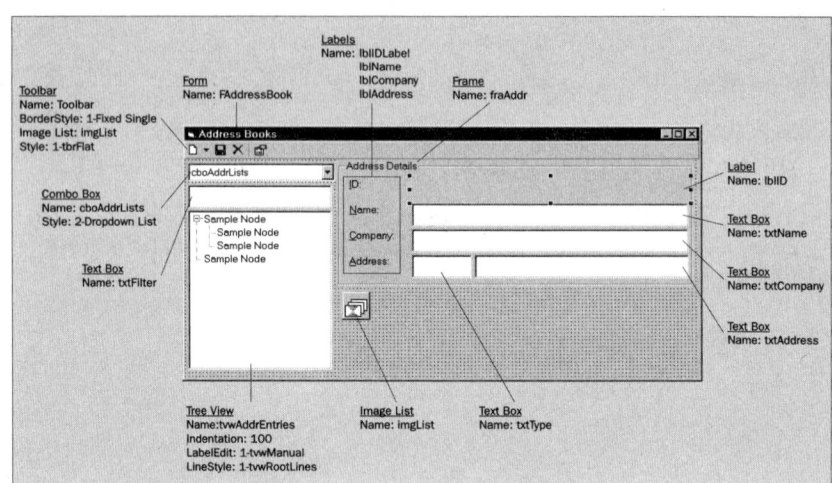

User Interface

We start by adding a new form, `FAddressBook`, to the CDO Sample project. Add the controls as shown in the screenshot above.

As we did in `FMain`, we will use a toolbar to host several buttons that, when clicked, perform various tasks. So we again need to add an ImageList control to store the images for the buttons.

Index	File Path	Key
1	Bitmaps\TlBr_W95\New.bmp	imgNew
2	Bitmaps\TlBr_W95\Save.bmp	imgSave
3	Bitmaps\TlBr_W95\Delete.bmp	imgDelete
4	Bitmaps\TlBr_W95\Prop.bmp	imgProp

Now add the following buttons to the toolbar:

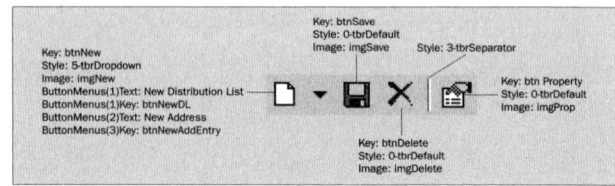

The Form Code

Next, we need to add the following form-level constants and object to the `FAddressBook` form:

```
Option Explicit

Private Const mcstrNewAddrEntry As String = "New address entry ..."
Private Const mcstrButtonKeyNewDL As String = "btnNewDL"
Private Const mcstrButtonKeyNewAddrEntry As String = "btnNewAddrEntry"
Private Const mcstrButtonKeySave As String = "btnSave"
Private Const mcstrButtonKeyDelete As String = "btnDelete"
Private Const mcstrButtonKeyProperty As String = "btnProperty"

Private mobjCurrentList As MAPI.AddressList
```

The `mcstrNewAddrEntry` constant stores the string we will be showing on `lblID` when we add new address entries. The button key constants store the keys of buttons on the toolbar. The `mobjCurrentList` object stores a reference to the currently selected address list collection.

Now add the event handlers to the form:

```
Private Sub Form_Load()
   On Error Resume Next

   Call ShowAddrLists
End Sub

Private Sub Form_Resize()
   On Error Resume Next

   cboAddrLists.Move gclngEdge, Toolbar.Height + gclngEdge, _
     ScaleWidth - fraAddr.Width - gclngEdge * 3
   txtFilter.Move gclngEdge, _
     cboAddrLists.Top + cboAddrLists.Height + gclngEdge, _
     cboAddrLists.Width

   With tvwAddrEntries
    .Move gclngEdge, _
       txtFilter.Top + txtFilter.Height + gclngEdge, _
       cboAddrLists.Width
    .Height = ScaleHeight - .Top - gclngEdge
   End With

   fraAddr.Move ScaleWidth - fraAddr.Width - gclngEdge, _
     Toolbar.Height
End Sub

Private Sub Form_QueryUnload(Cancel As Integer, UnloadMode As Integer)
   On Error Resume Next
   Set mobjCurrentList = Nothing
End Sub
```

When the form loads, it calls the `ShowAddrLists` method to display the address lists. We will see this method in a moment. When it unloads, it releases the reference stored in `mobjCurrentList`. The `Resize` event handler resizes the controls on the form.

Navigating, Filtering and Displaying Address Lists

When the form loads, it fills the combo box, `cboAddrLists`, with the names of all the address lists in the profile. It also fills the tree view control, `tvwAddrEntries`, with address entries from the GAL. Let's add a new method, `ShowAddrLists`, that will display the address lists in the combo box `cboAddrLists`.

```
Private Sub ShowAddrLists(Optional strDisplayListName As String = "")
    On Error Resume Next

    Dim colAddrLists As MAPI.AddressLists
    Dim objAddrList As MAPI.AddressList

    Set colAddrLists = gobjSession.AddressLists
    Call cboAddrLists.Clear
    Call tvwAddrEntries.Nodes.Clear

    For Each objAddrList In colAddrLists
      If objAddrList.Name <> "Recipients" Then
         Call cboAddrLists.AddItem(objAddrList.Name)
      End If
    Next
    If Len(strDisplayListName) > 0 Then
       cboAddrLists.Text = strDisplayListName
    Else
      cboAddrLists.ListIndex = 0
    End If

    Set objAddrList = Nothing
    Set colAddrLists = Nothing
End Sub
```

It accepts an optional parameter that specifies the name of an address list. This will be the address list selected in `cboAddrLists`. Address entries in this address list will then be displayed in `tvwAddrEntries`. If this parameter is not passed in, we select the first list in the collection. Note that we don't want to display any address list named Recipients because, in most cases, it is identical to the GAL.

We first get the `Session` object's `AddressList` collection. The name of each address list in this collection is added to `cboAddrLists`. Setting the combo box's `Text` or `ListIndex` property triggers its `Click` event, so let's add that now:

```
Private Sub cboAddrLists_Click()
    On Error GoTo ErrHandler

    Dim Button As MSComctlLib.Button
    Dim EnableButton As Boolean
```

```
      Set mobjCurrentList = gobjSession.AddressLists.Item(cboAddrLists.Text)
      Call ShowAddrList(mobjCurrentList)

      EnableButton = Not mobjCurrentList.IsReadOnly
      For Each Button In Toolbar.Buttons
        If Button.Key <> mcstrButtonKeyProperty Then
           Button.Enabled = EnableButton
        End If
      Next
      Set Button = Nothing

   ExitFunc:
      Exit Sub

   ErrHandler:
      Call ReportError(Err)
      Resume ExitFunc
   End Sub
```

In this event handler, we set `mobjCurrentList` to the address list with the selected name in the combo box. This address list is displayed in `tvwAddrEntries` by our code in the `ShowAddrList` method, which we will see right after this. Note that it's not the same as the `ShowAddrLists` method we've just coded! We then get the address list's `IsReadOnly` property. If it is `False` (that is, the list is modifiable), we enable all the buttons in the toolbar. Otherwise, we disable the **New**, **Save**, and **Delete** buttons so that the users know that they cannot make any changes to the entries in the list.

Add this code to the form:

```
   Private Sub ShowAddrList(objAddrList As MAPI.AddressList, _
          Optional strNameFilter As String = "")
      On Error Resume Next

      Dim nodAddrList As MSComctlLib.Node

      Call tvwAddrEntries.Nodes.Clear
      With objAddrList
       Set nodAddrList = tvwAddrEntries.Nodes.Add(Key:=.ID, Text:=.Name)
       Call ShowAddrEntries(nodAddrList, .AddressEntries, strNameFilter)
       nodAddrList.Expanded = True
      End With

      Set nodAddrList = Nothing
   End Sub
```

The `ShowAddrList` method accepts two parameters. The first is the address list to be displayed. The second is optional. It accepts an address entry display name used to filter the address list.

Filtering Address Entries with the AddressEntryFilter Object

The `ShowAddrList` method first adds the name of the address list to the address entry tree. It then calls the `ShowAddrEntries` method to display all entries in its `AddressEntries` property. The name filter is passed to the `ShowAddrEntries` method, which we'll add now:

```
Private Sub ShowAddrEntries(nodParent As MSComctlLib.Node, _
             colAddrEntries As MAPI.AddressEntries, _
             Optional strNameFilter As String = "")
  On Error Resume Next

  Dim objAddrEntry As MAPI.AddressEntry
  Dim nodAddrEntry As MSComctlLib.Node
  Dim objAddrFilter As MAPI.AddressEntryFilter

  Call colAddrEntries.Sort(CdoAscending, CdoPR_DISPLAY_NAME)

  If Len(strNameFilter) > 0 Then
    Set objAddrFilter = colAddrEntries.Filter
    objAddrFilter.Name = strNameFilter
  Else
    Set colAddrEntries.Filter = Nothing
  End If

  For Each objAddrEntry In colAddrEntries
    Set nodAddrEntry = tvwAddrEntries.Nodes.Add(nodParent, tvwChild, _
        nodParent.Key & gcstrIDDelimiter & objAddrEntry.ID, objAddrEntry.Name)

    If objAddrEntry.DisplayType = CdoDistList Or _
       objAddrEntry.DisplayType = CdoPrivateDistList Then
      Call ShowAddrEntries(nodAddrEntry, objAddrEntry.Members)
      nodAddrEntry.Expanded = True
    End If
  Next

  Set objAddrFilter = Nothing
  Set nodAddrEntry = Nothing
  Set objAddrEntry = Nothing
End Sub
```

Firstly, it sorts the address entries in the `AddressEntries` collection by their display names. An address entry's display name is exposed by its `Name` property. Since the `Sort` method requires a MAPI property tag, we use the corresponding MAPI property `CdoPR_Display_Name`.

The `Sort` method does not always succeed. For instance, the Outlook Contacts folder cannot be sorted. Incidentally, that folder always appears sorted, so the inability to sort the entries is not a problem. We just ignore it, by the use of the `On Error Resume Next` statement.

Next, we check whether the name filter is empty. If it is not, we assign its value to the `Name` property of the associated address entry filter object. Assigning the `Name` property affects the collection immediately. If the name filter is empty, we set the `AddressEntries` collection's filter to `Nothing` to remove any previous filters.

This method then adds the name of each entry in the collection to the address entry tree. Since the ID of each address entry is unique, we could just use it as the key of the tree node. However, we need to know its parent ID if we need to delete it later, so we need to store its parent's ID. Therefore we will concatenate the parent node's key and the current entry's ID and assign the combined string to the node's key. As we saw in Chapter 3, the IDs are also separated by a comma so that we can easily parse a node's key to a string array using the Split function.

If an address entry is a distribution list, the ShowAddrEntries method calls itself recursively and passes in the address entry collection returned in the distribution list's Members property.

In our CDO Sample application, a user can type a string into the txtFilter box and filter the displayed address list. We catch any changes to the txtFilter.Text value and call the ShowAddressList method to actually filter the list. Add this block of code to the form:

```
Private Sub txtFilter_Change()
    On Error GoTo ErrHandler
    Call ShowAddrList(mobjCurrentList, txtFilter.Text)

ExitFunc:
    Exit Sub

ErrHandler:
    Call ReportError(Err)
    Resume ExitFunc
End Sub
```

Please note that we cannot apply the filter in this procedure as follows.

```
' This does not work since the Filter is lost when passed along
Private Sub txtFilter_Change()
    Dim objAddrFilter As MAPI.AddressEntryFilter
    Set objAddrFilter = mobjCurrentList.AddressEntries.Filter
    objAddrFilter.Name = txtFilter.Text
    Call ShowAddrList(mobjCurrentList)
    Set objAddrFilter = Nothing
End Sub
```

The problem with this approach is that the filter is lost when we call the ShowAddrList method. That is, we can't pass address entry collections with filters across functions. So we must pass the filter string to the ShowAddrList method and eventually to the ShowAddrEntries method. Only then can we apply the filter.

Now we've sorted out displaying the address lists. We also need to display address entry properties when the user clicks on a node in the address entry tree.

Accessing Address Entry Properties

When the user clicks an address entry node, the tree view control's `NodeClick` event fires:

```
Private Sub tvwAddrEntries_NodeClick(ByVal Node As MSComctlLib.Node)
   On Error GoTo ErrHandler

   Dim arrIDs() As String
   Dim strEntryID As String

   arrIDs = Split(Node.Key, gcstrIDDelimiter)
   strEntryID = arrIDs(UBound(arrIDs))
   Call ShowAddrEntry(strEntryID)

ExitFunc:
   Exit Sub

ErrHandler:
   Call ReportError(Err)
   Resume ExitFunc
End Sub
```

It parses the node key into an array of IDs. Since the last ID in the array is the ID of the selected address entry, we call the `ShowAddrEntry` method and pass this ID to it. Add the `ShowAddrEntry` method now:

```
Private Sub ShowAddrEntry(Optional strID As String = "")
   On Error Resume Next

   Dim objAddrEntry    As MAPI.AddressEntry

   ' Clear all fields
   lblID.Caption = mcstrNewAddrEntry
   txtName.Text = ""
   txtCompany.Text = ""
   txtType.Text = ""
   txtAddress.Text = ""

   If Len(strID) > 0 Then
     Set objAddrEntry = gobjSession.GetAddressEntry(strID)
     With objAddrEntry
        lblID.Caption = .ID
        txtName.Text = .Name

        txtCompany.Text = objAddrEntry.Fields(CdoPR_COMPANY_NAME).Value
        If Err <> 0 Then
           Err.Clear
           txtCompany.Text = ""
        End If

        txtType.Text = .Type
        txtAddress.Text = .Address
     End With
     Set objAddrEntry = Nothing
   End If
End Sub
```

The `strID` parameter specifies the ID of the address entry object to be displayed. If it is not passed, we are creating a new address entry.

First, we clear all the address entry detail fields. If an ID is passed, we call the `Session` object's `GetAddressEntry` method to retrieve the `AddressEntry` object from the Exchange Server. We then fill the fields on the form with the corresponding properties of the address entry object.

As we saw when we looked at the `AddressEntry` object, CDO splits a full address into two parts. The `Type` property returns the address type, like `SMTP`. The `Address` property stores the address value, like `name@domain.com`.

In addition to the display name and messaging address, an address entry usually contains other information about a person such as company name, postal address and telephone number. These properties are not directly accessible in CDO since the CDO `AddressEntry` object does not expose a set of corresponding properties. We need to access them through the `AddressEntry`'s `Fields` collection.

MAPI defines a set of standard address entry property tags for such common address properties. For instance, the company name is represented by a MAPI property tag `CdoPR_Company_Name`. So we can retrieve this property from the `AddressEntry` object's `Fields` collection:

```
txtCompany.Text = objAddrEntry.Fields(CdoPR_COMPANY_NAME).Value
```

However, there is a problem. If the company property has not been entered for this address entry, the above statement will raise an error `CdoE_NOT_FOUND (&H8004010F)`. We aren't reporting such errors to our users; simply presenting them with an empty company field is more than enough.

While we could create our own address entry property form to display all properties of an address entry, just as we do for the few properties we've chosen to display on `FAddressBook`, there is a better way of handling this. The CDO `AddressEntry` object has a `Details` method that displays a dialog box containing all the standard properties of an address entry. This dialog box differs for address entries in the GAL and the PAB:

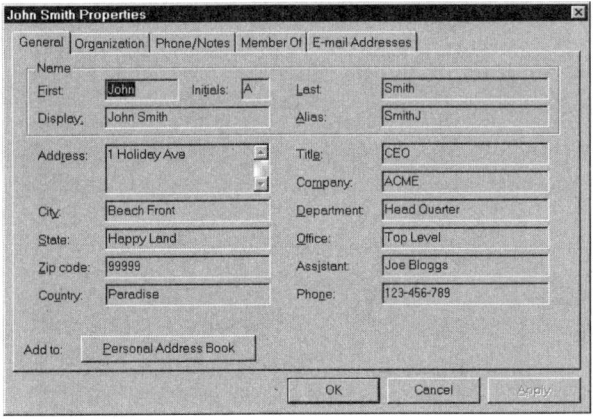 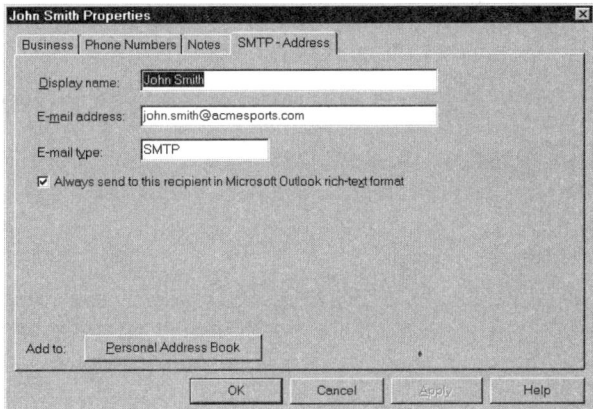

The second dialog box does more than just display the properties. You can also use it to modify properties of address entries in the PAB. Modification to the address entries is managed automatically by CDO, so you don't need to write any code.

In the FAddressBook form, we will allow the user to click the Show Properties button on the toolbar to display this dialog. Clicking this button fires the toolbar's ButtonClick event, so we need to add the following code to its event handler:

```
Private Sub Toolbar_ButtonClick(ByVal Button As MSComctlLib.Button)
    On Error GoTo ErrHandler

    Dim nodSelected As MSComctlLib.Node
    Dim arrIDs()    As String

    Set nodSelected = tvwAddrEntries.SelectedItem
    arrIDs = Split(nodSelected.Key, gcstrIDDelimiter)

    Select Case Button.Key
     Case mcstrButtonKeyProperty
        Call ShowAddrEntryDetails(arrIDs)

     Case Else

    End Select

ExitFunc:
    Set nodSelected = Nothing
    Exit Sub

ErrHandler:
    Call ReportError(Err)
    Resume ExitFunc
End Sub
```

Here we simply parse the selected node's Key into a string array and pass it to the ShowAddrEntryDetails method, which we also need to add:

```
Private Sub ShowAddrEntryDetails(arrIDs() As String)
    On Error Resume Next

    Dim objAddrEntry As MAPI.AddressEntry
    Dim strEntryID As String

    If UBound(arrIDs) > 0 Then
        ' Only show Address Entry details
        strEntryID = arrIDs(UBound(arrIDs))
        Set objAddrEntry = gobjSession.GetAddressEntry(strEntryID)
        Call objAddrEntry.Details
        If Err.Number <> CdoE_USER_CANCEL Then
            Call ShowAddrEntry(objAddrEntry.ID)
        End If
    End If

    Set objAddrEntry = Nothing
End Sub
```

We extract the currently selected address entry's `ID` from the ID array and call the `Session` object's `GetAddressEntry` method to retrieve the address entry object. We then call its `Details` method to display the dialog box.

If the user clicks OK to acknowledge the Details dialog, the changes made will be committed to the Exchange Server. We should also update the detail fields. But if the user clicks Cancel to dismiss the dialog, CDO will raise an error – `CdoE_USER_CANCEL` (`&H80040113`) – so we handle this and don't update the displayed detail fields. One nice feature of this dialog is that if users click the Apply button, the changes will be saved just as we expect. If they then click the Cancel button, no error will be raised, so the `ShowAddrEntry` method will still be called.

Linking the FMain and FAddressBook

To test what we have done so far to the address book form, `FAddressBook`, we need to link this form to the main form. We can add a menu item, **Address Books**, to the **Tools** menu on `FMain`.

We can then add this event handler to `FMain`:

```
Private Sub mnuToolsAddrBooks_Click()
    FAddressBook.Show vbNormal
End Sub
```

If you run the project now, you should see all available address lists and their address entries. The next thing we need to do is to add the code that will enable our users to add address entries and distribution lists to their address lists.

Adding Address Entries and Distribution Lists

To add an address entry or a distribution list to an address list, users must select either the current address list or a distribution list in the address list. They then click on either the **New Distribution List** or the **New Address** button. The new distribution list or address will be added as either a top-level entry in the address list or an entry in the selected distribution list.

When the **New Distribution List** or the **New Address** button is clicked, the toolbar's `ButtonMenuClick` event is triggered. We need to add the following code snippet to the address book form:

```
Private Sub Toolbar_ButtonMenuClick(ByVal ButtonMenu As MSComctlLib.ButtonMenu)
    On Error GoTo ErrHandler

    Dim nodParent As MSComctlLib.Node
    Dim arrIDs() As String

    Select Case ButtonMenu.Key
        Case mcstrButtonKeyNewDL
            Set nodParent = tvwAddrEntries.SelectedItem
            arrIDs = Split(nodParent.Key, gcstrIDDelimiter)
            Call AddDistList(arrIDs)

        Case Else
            ' Do nothing
    End Select

ExitFunc:
    Exit Sub

ErrHandler:
    Call ReportError(Err)
    Resume ExitFunc
End Sub
```

If the user clicked the **New Distribution List** button, we retrieve the currently selected item. This will be the parent of the new distribution list. We then call the `AddDistList` method and pass it the array containing the IDs of the current node and its parents.

If the user clicked the **New Address** button, we simply call the `ShowAddrEntry` method. This method is covered in the next section.

Now add the following code snippet to the address book form:

```
Private Sub AddDistList(arrIDs() As String)
    On Error GoTo ErrHandler

    Const cstrDLType As String = "MAPIPDL"
    Dim colAddrEntries As MAPI.AddressEntries
    Dim objParentEntry As MAPI.AddressEntry
    Dim objAddrEntry As MAPI.AddressEntry
    Dim strDLName As String

    strDLName = InputBox("Enter new Distribution List name:")
    If Len(strDLName) > 0 Then
        If UBound(arrIDs) = 0 Then
            ' The user has selected the current Address List
            Set colAddrEntries = mobjCurrentList.AddressEntries
        Else
```

```
            ' The user has selected an AddressEntry node
         Set objParentEntry = _
            gobjSession.GetAddressEntry(arrIDs(UBound(arrIDs)))

            ' Only add DL if the parent address entry is a DL
         If objParentEntry.DisplayType = CdoPrivateDistList Then
            Set colAddrEntries = objParentEntry.Members
         End If
      End If

      If Not colAddrEntries Is Nothing Then
         Set objAddrEntry = colAddrEntries.Add(cstrDLType, strDLName)
         Call objAddrEntry.Update
         If Not objAddrEntry Is Nothing Then
            Call ShowAddrLists(tvwAddrEntries.Nodes(arrIDs(0)).Text)
         End If
      End If
   End If

ExitFunc:
   Exit Sub

ErrHandler:
   ' CDO does not support adding DLs to DLs in
   ' the Outlook Contacts folder
   MsgBox "Can't add distribution list [" & _
      FormatHex(Err.Number) & "]:" & Err.Description
   Resume ExitFunc
End Sub
```

After the user enters the new distribution list name, the AddDistList function examines the array of IDs passed in to see whether or not the user has decided to add the new distribution list to the current address list. If the array contains only one ID, we're adding this new distribution list as a top-level distribution list in the current address list. Thus the new distribution list should be added to the AddressEntries collection of the address list.

If the array contains more than one ID, the user has selected an existing distribution list as the parent of the new distribution list. In this case, the new distribution list should be added to the Members collection of the selected distribution list. We must ensure that the parent address entry is a private distribution list by checking its DisplayType property. We can only use CDO to modify private distribution lists.

If an AddressEntry object is a distribution list, its Members property returns a collection of all its child address entries, which may also be distribution lists. That is, we can have nested distribution lists. You can send mails to both the parent and the child distribution lists. If you send a mail to the parent distribution list, the mail also goes to all people in the child distribution list.

Once we have the parent AddressEntries collection for the new distribution list, we add the new distribution list to it by calling the collection's Add method.

Adding a Distribution List

The `AddressEntries` collection's `Add` method adds an `AddressEntry` object to the collection. This is the only way in CDO to create a new address entry.

```
Set objAddrEntry = colAddrEntries.Add(Type [, Name] [, Address])
```

The `Type` parameter does not specify the `DisplayType` of the new address entry. Instead, it is a string that specifies the type of the actual address of the `AddressEntry` object. CDO does not restrict the value of this parameter so you can assign anything you like. However, the Exchange Server needs to use this information to resolve the destination of any messages sent to this address entry. Therefore you will need to ensure that you enter a value that is recognized and supported by the Exchange Server or any other underlying message store. In general, most message systems support standard message types such as SMTP, X400 and FAX. For Exchange Server, the type of a private distribution list is always MAPIPDL.

Both the `Name` and the `Address` parameters are optional. The `Name` parameter, if given, specifies the display name of the new `AddressEntry` object. The `Address` parameter specifies the actual address. Microsoft Exchange Server assigns distribution lists with internal addresses so we should not specify an address here. Messages sent to a distribution list are passed to all its members.

In the `AddDistList` method, we pass the type, `MAPIPDL`, and the name to the `Add` method. We then call the returned object's `Update` method to commit the change to the Exchange Server. Once the new distribution list is added to the Exchange Server, we call the `ShowAddressLists` to refresh the address entry tree. We pass it the name of the current address list to `ShowAddressLists` so this list will be displayed.

Now you can save your changes and run your project to test this function. It should work with the PAB without any problems. Before we move on, if you are tempted to try this out in the Outlook Contacts folder, you need to be aware of a limitation of CDO.

The Outlook Contacts Folder

Although distribution lists in both the PAB and the Outlook Contacts folder are private distribution lists, we can use CDO only to directly modify the private distribution lists in the PAB. If you attempt to add a new distribution list to the Outlook Contacts folder, CDO will use automation to invoke the Outlook application to perform the task.

That is, if your users have Outlook installed on their machine, your application will load Outlook to add the distribution list. Otherwise, there will be no Contacts in the address list collection anyway, because the Contacts folder is only available when Outlook is installed.

You can test this process on your development machine. First, check your Outlook's option to ensure that it will prompt for a profile when it starts. You can select Options from the Tools menu and click the Mail Services tab:

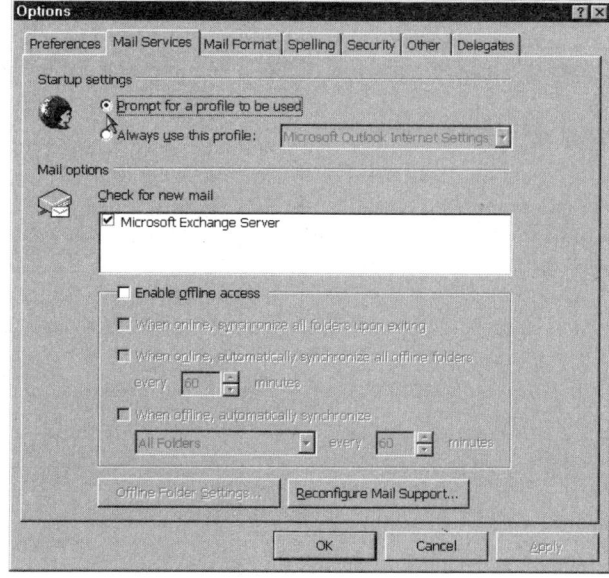

Make sure that you select the Prompt for a profile to be used option and close Outlook. When you run the CDO sample project and try to add a distribution list to the Outlook Contacts folder, you will see a dialog box asking you which profile you want to use:

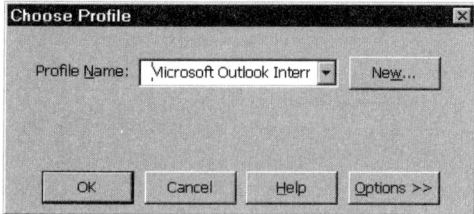

This proves that Outlook is called by CDO when you try to add a distribution list to the Outlook Contacts folder.

There are two limitations when dealing with the Outlook Contacts folder:

1. While you can add a top-level address entry (or contact) to the Outlook Contacts folder using Outlook automation, such entries are not visible to CDO. The new contact shows up in the Contacts folder in Outlook but not in your CDO application. However, you can see the new contact as a message in your Contacts folder. You can try this after we complete the next chapter, Managing Messages.

2. You cannot use CDO to implicitly call Outlook through automation to add address entries and distribution lists to distribution lists in the Outlook Contacts folder. Doing so will result in an error CdoE_NO_SUPPORT (&H80040102). If you need to do this, you should consider using Outlook automation directly from your application.

In general, you should not use CDO to modify the Outlook Contacts folder. While we could modify our sample application to disable the change buttons when the Outlook Contacts folder is selected, I will leave it as is for simplicity. Let's turn our attention to adding new address entries.

Adding Address Entries

When users click the New Address button on the toolbar, we should clear the detail fields so that they can enter the relevant information. When they are done, they can click the Save button to commit the changes. To do all this, we just need to add a couple of lines to the toolbar's ButtonMenuClick event handler:

```
Private Sub Toolbar_ButtonMenuClick(ByVal ButtonMenu As MSComctlLib.ButtonMenu)
    On Error GoTo ErrHandler

    Dim nodParent As MSComctlLib.Node
    Dim arrIDs() As String

    Select Case ButtonMenu.Key
        Case mcstrButtonKeyNewDL
            Set nodParent = tvwAddrEntries.SelectedItem
            arrIDs = Split(nodParent.Key, gcstrIDDelimiter)
            Call AddDistList(arrIDs)

        Case mcstrButtonKeyNewAddrEntry
            Call ShowAddrEntry

        Case Else
            ' Do nothing
    End Select

ExitFunc:
    Exit Sub

ErrHandler:
    Call ReportError(Err)
    Resume ExitFunc
End Sub
```

When users click the New Address button, we will just call the ShowAddrEntry method without passing in an ID to clean up the detail fields.

After they have entered the address details, they will click the Save button to save the new address entry. This triggers the toolbar's ButtonClick event. Add the highlighted code below to handle the Save button.

```
Private Sub Toolbar_ButtonClick(ByVal Button As MSComctlLib.Button)
    On Error GoTo ErrHandler

    Dim nodSelected As MSComctlLib.Node
    Dim arrIDs() As String

    Set nodSelected = tvwAddrEntries.SelectedItem
    arrIDs = Split(nodSelected.Key, gcstrIDDelimiter)
```

```
        Select Case Button.Key
            Case mcstrButtonKeySave
                Call SaveAddrEntry(arrIDs)

            Case mcstrButtonKeyProperty
                Call ShowAddrEntryDetails(arrIDs)

            Case Else

        End Select

ExitFunc:
    Set nodSelected = Nothing
    Exit Sub

ErrHandler:
    Call ReportError(Err)
    Resume ExitFunc
End Sub
```

The **Save** button actually serves two purposes: to save a new address entry and to save changes to an existing address entry. The `SaveAddrEntry` method handles this process. What we need to do in the `ButtonClick` event handler is to parse the IDs of the currently selected node and pass it to the `SaveAddrEntry` method:

```
Private Sub SaveAddrEntry(arrIDs() As String)
    Dim objParentEntry As MAPI.AddressEntry
    Dim strNodeID As String

    strNodeID = arrIDs(UBound(arrIDs))
    If IsNewEntry Then
        ' This is a new entry, the currently selected node is the parent.
        If UBound(arrIDs) = 0 Then
            ' The user selected an Address List,
            Call AddEntry(mobjCurrentList.AddressEntries)
        Else
            ' The user selected an Address Entry. We need to ensure
            ' that it is a Distribution List
            Set objParentEntry = gobjSession.GetAddressEntry(strNodeID)
            If objParentEntry.DisplayType = CdoPrivateDistList Then
                Call AddEntry(objParentEntry.Members)
            End If
        End If
    Else
        ' Modify the currently selected node.
    End If

    Call ShowAddrLists(tvwAddrEntries.Nodes(arrIDs(0)).Text)

    Set objParentEntry = Nothing
End Sub
```

We first extract the ID of the currently selected node and check whether or not we are adding a new address entry using the `IsNewEntry` function:

```
Private Function IsNewEntry() As Boolean
    IsNewEntry = (lblID.Caption = mcstrNewAddrEntry)
End Function
```

This function simply checks the ID in the `Details` frame. If it is equal to the string "New address entry...", we are adding a new address entry. Otherwise, we are saving the changes made to an existing entry.

We will see how to save an existing entry in a minute. If we are adding a new address entry, we will check whether the new entry should be added to the address list as a top-level entry or an entry in a distribution list. This is achieved by examining the array of IDs, similar to the way we do it in the `AddDistList` method. If this is going to be a top-level entry, we call the `AddEntry` method and pass in the current address list's `AddressEntries` collection. Otherwise, we must make sure that the currently selected node is a private distribution list and pass its `Members` collection to the `AddEntry` method:

```
Private Sub AddEntry(colAddrEntries As MAPI.AddressEntries)
    On Error GoTo ErrHandler

    Dim objAddrEntry As MAPI.AddressEntry

    Set objAddrEntry = colAddrEntries.Add(txtType.Text, txtName.Text, _
                    txtAddress.Text)
    With objAddrEntry
        Call .Fields.Add(CdoPR_COMPANY_NAME, txtCompany.Text)
        Call .Update
        lblID.Caption = .ID
    End With

ExitFunc:
    Set objAddrEntry = Nothing
    Exit Sub

ErrHandler:
    MsgBox "Can't add address entry [" & _
        FormatHex(Err.Number) & "]:" & Err.Description
    Resume ExitFunc
End Sub
```

Like the `AddDistList` method, we call the `AddressEntries` collection's `Add` method to create a new address entry in the collection. This time we also pass the e-mail address into the `Add` method. We then need to add the company name to the newly created address entry's `Fields` collection. Again, we call the `Update` method to commit the change.

Editing Address Entries

When your users click an address entry node in the tree, the selected properties of that address entry are displayed in the Details frame. They can then modify some of them and click the Save button to save the changes. As we have seen in the last section, the `SaveAddrEntry` method is invoked. We need to make the following changes to this method:

```
Private Sub SaveAddrEntry(arrIDs() As String)
...
        End If
      End If
    Else
      ' Modify the currently selected node.
      If UBound(arrIDs) > 0 Then
        Call SaveEntry(strNodeID)
      End If
    End If

    Call ShowAddrLists(tvwAddrEntries.Nodes(arrIDs(0)).Text)

    Set objParentEntry = Nothing
End Sub
```

If the currently selected node represents an address entry in the list, we call the `SaveEntry` method to save the changes made to an existing address entry:

```
Private Sub SaveEntry(strEntryID As String)
  Dim objAddrEntry As MAPI.AddressEntry

  Set objAddrEntry = gobjSession.GetAddressEntry(strEntryID)
  With objAddrEntry
    ' Only allow changes to address entries
    If .DisplayType = CdoUser Then
      .Type = txtType.Text
      .Name = txtName.Text
      .Address = txtAddress.Text
      Call .Fields.Add(CdoPR_COMPANY_NAME, txtCompany.Text)
      Call .Update
    End If
  End With

  Set objAddrEntry = Nothing
End Sub
```

If the selected node represents an address entry, we assign the changes to its `Type`, `Name`, and `Address` to the corresponding properties of the address entry object. Assigning changes to properties in the `Fields` collection is a bit tricky. If the company name field is not in the collection, we would get an error if we tried this statement:

```
objAddrEntry.Fields(CdoPR_Company_Name).Value = txtCompany.Text
```

In that case, we must use the `Fields` collection's `Add` method to add a new field to the collection:

```
Call objAddrEntry.Fields.Add(CdoPR_COMPANY_NAME, txtCompany.Text)
```

Luckily, it turns out that the `Add` method will also work even if the field already exists in the collection. If the field already exists, the `Add` method will just modify its value with the new value. Therefore we can use the `Add` method regardless of whether or not the field already exists. That is quite a nice feature, and it saves us from having to do a lot of cross-checking.

It would be nice if we could also add fields to distribution lists as well. Unfortunately, CDO does not let you do so. Attempting to do so results in a `CdoE_NO_ACCESS` error.

As we saw before, we can also use the `AddressEntry` object's `Details` method to modify address entry properties. It even allows us to change distribution lists. So unless you need to add some custom properties, using the `Details` method might be the best choice. At the very least, it will save you a bit of extra coding.

Deleting Address Entries

While we can add and edit address entries in the PAB, we haven't yet dealt with how to delete address entries from it. There are some problems with the `Delete` method of the CDO `AddressEntry` object. First we'll start to add the functionality to delete an address entry and then we can discuss those problems as they arise.

In our project, the user can select an address entry or a distribution list from the address entry tree and click the `Delete` button to remove it. let us add the following statements to the toolbar's `ButtonClick` event handler on `FAddressBook`:

```
Private Sub Toolbar_ButtonClick(ByVal Button As MSComctlLib.Button)
    On Error GoTo ErrHandler

    Dim nodSelected As MSComctlLib.Node
    Dim arrIDs() As String

    Set nodSelected = tvwAddrEntries.SelectedItem
    arrIDs = Split(nodSelected.Key, gcstrIDDelimiter)

    Select Case Button.Key
        Case mcstrButtonKeySave
            Call SaveAddrEntry(arrIDs)

        Case mcstrButtonKeyDelete
            If MsgBox("Remove " & nodSelected.Text & " from PAB?", _
                vbQuestion Or vbYesNo) = vbYes Then
                Call DeleteAddrEntry(arrIDs)
            End If

        Case mcstrButtonKeyProperty
            Call ShowAddrEntryDetails(arrIDs)
```

```
        Case Else
            ' Shouldn't get here

    End Select

ExitFunc:
    Set nodSelected = Nothing
    Exit Sub

ErrHandler:
    Call ReportError(Err)
    Resume ExitFunc
End Sub
```

After the user clicks the **Delete** button, we ask them to confirm this action. If they answer **Yes**, we will call the `DeleteAddrEntry` method and pass the ID array to it. We need to add this method to `FAddressBook`:

```
Private Sub DeleteAddrEntry(arrIDs() As String)
    On Error GoTo ErrHandler

    Dim colAddrEntries As MAPI.AddressEntries
    Dim objParentEntry As MAPI.AddressEntry
    Dim objAddrEntry As MAPI.AddressEntry
    Dim strParentID As String
    Dim strEntryID As String

    Select Case UBound(arrIDs)
        Case 0
            ' Can't delete Address List

        Case 1
            ' Top-level Address Entry
            Set colAddrEntries = mobjCurrentList.AddressEntries

        Case Is > 1
            ' Parent is a DL
            strParentID = arrIDs(UBound(arrIDs) - 1)
            Set objParentEntry = gobjSession.GetAddressEntry(strParentID)
            If objParentEntry.DisplayType = CdoPrivateDistList Then
                Set colAddrEntries = objParentEntry.Members
            End If
    End Select

    If Not colAddrEntries Is Nothing Then
        strEntryID = arrIDs(UBound(arrIDs))
        For Each objAddrEntry In colAddrEntries
            If gobjSession.CompareIDs(objAddrEntry.ID, strEntryID) Then
                Call objAddrEntry.Delete
                Call ShowAddrLists(tvwAddrEntries.Nodes(arrIDs(0)).Text)
                Exit For
            End If
        Next
```

```
      End If

ExitFunc:
    Set objAddrEntry = Nothing
    Set objParentEntry = Nothing
    Set colAddrEntries = Nothing
    Exit Sub

ErrHandler:
    Call ReportError(Err)
    Resume ExitFunc
End Sub
```

First, we need to find the parent address entry collection of the selected address entry. We check the type of the selected address entry by examining the ID array that's passed in. If there is only one ID in the array, the user has selected the address list itself. Since we cannot delete an address list, we will have to pass on this.

If there are two IDs in the array, the selected entry is a top-level entry. So its parent is the current address list's AddressEntries collection. Otherwise, it is an entry in a distribution list and its parent is the distribution list's Members collection. We can retrieve the distribution list using the Session object's GetAddressEntry method.

Once we have found the parent address entry collection, we loop through the collection to find the entry. We then call its Delete method to remove itself from the collection. The Delete operation happens immediately so there is no need to call the entry's Update method.

Sounds simple enough, but you might be wondering why we go through all this trouble to find the address entry object's parent collection. Why can't we just use the Session object's GetAddressEntry method to retrieve the entry and call its Delete method to delete it?

There are a couple of issues worth mentioning in deleting an address entry. First, unlike the EditEntry method, we do not use the Session object's GetAddressEntry function to retrieve the AddressEntry object from the Exchange Server:

```
'
' This does not work!
'
Private Sub DeleteAddrEntry1(arrIDs() As String)
    Dim objAddrEntry   As MAPI.AddressEntry
    Set objAddrEntry = gobjSession.GetAddressEntry(arrIDs(UBound(arrIDs)))
    If Not objAddrEntry Is Nothing Then
        Call objAddrEntry.Delete
        Call ShowAddrLists
    End If

    Set objAddrEntry = Nothing
End Sub
```

Running this will result in an error. This is because the `Delete` method of the CDO `AddressEntry` object is only valid when the current address entry is accessed from an `AddressEntries` collection. If you call this method on an address entry that is retrieved using the CDO `Session` object's `GetAddressEntry` method as we do here, it will fail with an error `MAPI_W_PARTIAL_WARNING` (2664). This is actually a MAPI warning that seems to indicate that the whole process is not completed. Unfortunately it actually means that the deletion operation has failed completely. It does not have a corresponding CDO error code.

You may wonder why the `MAPI_W_PARTIAL_WARNING` code is represented as a decimal number, 2664, instead of the normal 8-digit hexadecimal code. The reason is that CDO passes error and warning codes to Visual Basic differently. MAPI returns both error and warning codes as 32-bit integers to CDO. CDO passes the error codes to Visual Basic applications as normal 32-bit integers that are equivalent to the corresponding CDO constants. For instance, a `MAPI_E_INVALID_PARAMETER` (&H80070057) error is passed to Visual Basic applications unchanged, that is a Visual Basic application receives &H80070057 as the error code. This value is equivalent to the corresponding CDO constant `CdoE_INVALID_PARAMETER`. So you can test for this error with this:

```
If Err.Number = CdoE_INVALID_PARAMETER Then
    Debug.Print "Invalid parameter"
End If
```

However, when CDO receives a MAPI warning and passes it to a Visual Basic application, it takes only the low-order 16-bit value of the warning code and adds decimal value 1000 to it. It then passes the sum to Visual Basic applications. For example, CDO receives the `MAPI_W_PARTIAL_COMPLETION` warning code (&H00040680) and extracts the low-order 16-bit value (&H0680, or 1664). It then adds 1000 to it and passes the result (2664) to Visual Basic applications. To test for this warning in your Visual Basic applications, you should take the corresponding CDO constant, `CdoW_PARTIAL_COMPLETION`, which is also(&H00040680) and extract its low-order 16-bit value using the bitwise AND operator:

```
CdoW_PARTIAL_COMPLETION & &HFFFF
```

You can then add 1000 to this value and compare it with the error code you receive:

```
If Err.Number = CdoW_PARTIAL_COMPLETION & &HFFFF + 1000 Then
    Debug.Print "The operation has not completed successfully"
End If
```

The Item Method

The second issue is not directly related to the `Delete` method, it is a problem with the CDO `AddressEntries` collection's `Item` method. The CDO documentation states that you can access an address entry object in a collection by passing it a search string:

```
Set objAddrEntry = colAddrEntries.Item(SearchString)
```

This asks CDO to find the first entry that matches the SearchString according to its current Sort property. For example, if the current sorting property is the entry ID and the sort order is ascending, it should return the next entry with an ID greater than or equal to the SearchString. Therefore since the address entry ID corresponds to MAPI property tag CdoPR_ENTRYID, we should be able to do this:

```
Call colAddrEntries.Sort(CdoAscending, CdoPR_ENTRYID)
Set objAddrEntry = colAddrEntries.GetFirst
Set objAddrEntry = colAddrEntries.Item(strID)
If Not objAddrEntry Is Nothing Then
    Call objAddrEntry.Delete
    Call ShowAddrLists
End If
```

However, running this code results in a CdoE_INVALID_PARAMETER (&H80070057) error on this line:

```
Set objAddrEntry = colAddrEntries.Item(strID)
```

In fact, there is a bug in this code even if the above worked. If the address entry we were looking for has the smallest ID in the collection, the above code would have missed it because the search starts at the next entry after the first. Of course, we can check the ID of the first address entry to fix this problem. Nevertheless, this method does not work so we should use the methods demonstrated in the DeleteAddrEntry method since that always works.

Summary

In this chapter, we have learned to access address entries contained in address lists. CDO provides the ability to add, modify, and delete address entries and distribution lists in the PAB. We have also seen how CDO and Outlook work together to provide limited access to the Outlook Contacts folder.

Address entries, especially those in the GAL, have many attributes that are not directly exposed by the CDO AddressEntry object. While we could access them using the AddressEntry object's Fields collection programmatically, its Details method provides a more consistent look and feel for displaying and editing address entries.

The CDO AddressEntry object is an essential component of the CDO object model. Other CDO objects including messages, appointment items, and meeting items contain AddressEntry objects to store user-related information such as message sender and meeting organizers. In the next chapter, we will work with CDO Message objects.

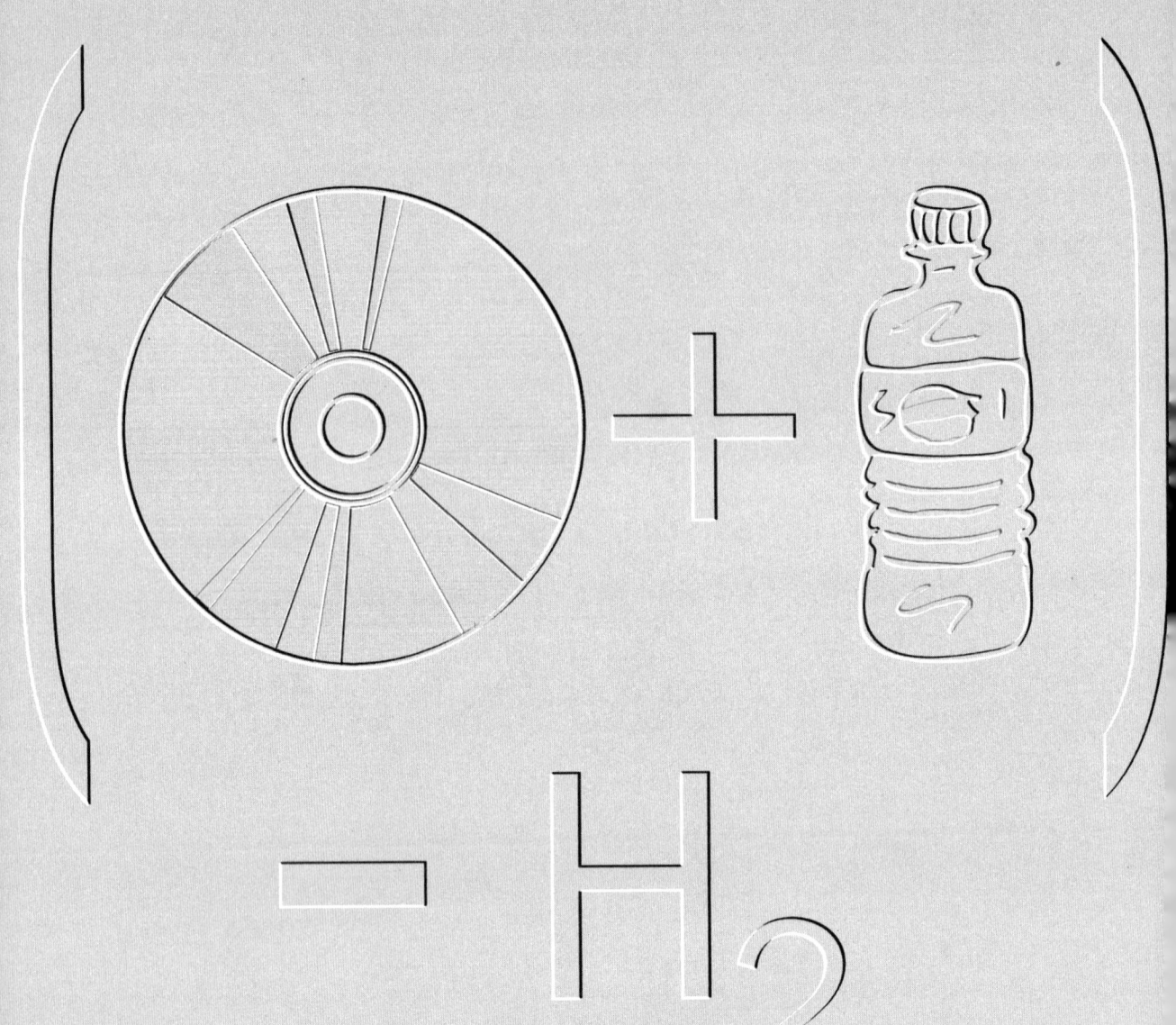

5

Managing Messages

Introduction

In Chapter 3, we learned to navigate and manage information stores and folders using CDO. In the last chapter, we looked at address books and address entries. These objects provide us with the foundation on which we can build useful CDO applications.

This chapter introduces one of the most commonly used CDO objects – the `Message` object. We'll be looking at the message hierarchy, including the `Messages` collection, the `Message` object, the `MessageFilter` object, the `Recipients` collection, the `Recipient` object, the `Attachments` collection, and the `Attachment` object. We will start by examining each of the objects in detail. Once we understand them, we will extend our CDO sample project further to include the ability to display and send messages.

CDO Message Structure

In CDO, each folder contains a collection of messages. A CDO `Folder` object's `Messages` property returns a `Messages` collection containing all `Message` objects in the folder. Like the `AddressEntries` collection we saw last chapter, the `Messages` collection has a corresponding `MessageFilter` object that can be used to filter the messages in the collection.

Each CDO `Message` object contains a collection of recipients associated with the message and a collection of message attachments. The recipient and attachment collections are exposed as the `Message` object's `Recipients` and `Attachments` properties, respectively. The following figure illustrates the relationship among all these objects.

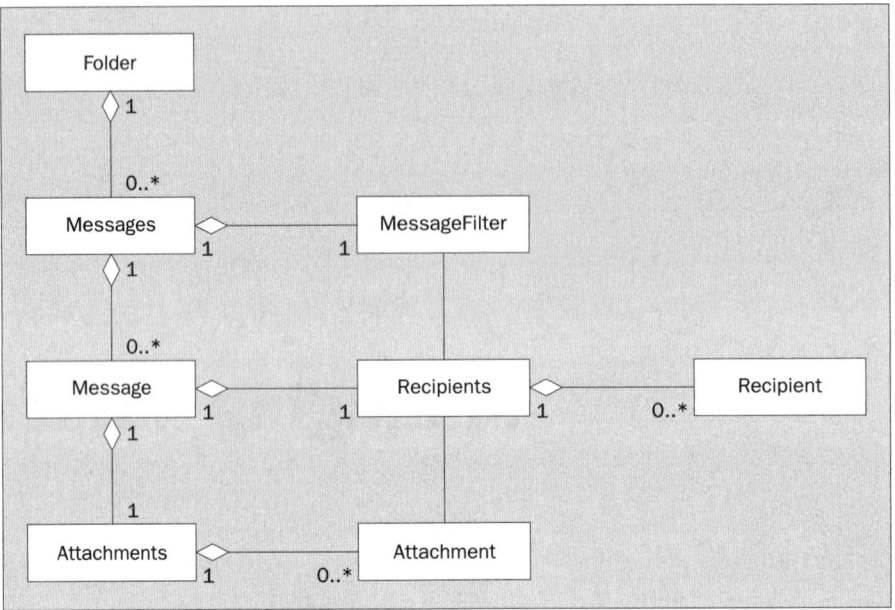

The Messages Collection

A `Folder` object's `Messages` collection contains all messages in that folder. This raises a question: how are we going to access appointments and other non-message items in certain folders?

Since we can store different types of items in a folder, a CDO `Messages` collection can actually contain more than just what we'd think of as messages. For instance, the `Messages` collection of the Calendar folder contains appointments. We will see how to handle appointment and meeting items in the next chapter.

The `Messages` collection has the properties and methods shown here:

MESSAGES	
Properties	**Type**
Application	String
Class	Long
Count	Long
Filter	MessageFilter
Item	Object
Parent	Field
RawTable	IUnknown
Session	Session
Methods	
Add	
Delete	
GetFirst	
GetLast	
GetNext	
GetPrevious	
Sort	
Events	

The Count Property

The `Count` property returns the number of `Message` objects in the `Messages` collection. Like the `Folders` collection, the CDO `Messages` collection is a large collection. That means that CDO might not always maintain an accurate count on the message numbers. You should thus be aware that this property does not always return the correct number of `Message` objects in the collection.

The Item Property

The `Item` property has two variations:

```
Set obj = colMessages.Item(Index)
Set obj = colMessages.Item(SearchValue)
```

The first syntax is straightforward – you pass in a number representing an index, and the corresponding message in the collection is returned. The second syntax passes in a string containing a search value. It only works with collections containing `Message` objects. Depending on the sorting order applied to the `Messages` collection using the `Sort` method, this syntax returns the next `Message` object that has the sorting property greater than or equal to the `SearchValue`.

You might have noticed that in the code snippets above the object is named `obj`, rather than the conventional `objMessage`, to store the return value. I've done this for a reason. We've seen briefly that in CDO, a message can be virtually any object that can be stored in a folder in the underlying message store. The `Item` property of the `Messages` collection therefore can return any one of the following four types of objects.

- ❑   `Message`
- ❑   `AppointmentItem`
- ❑   `MeetingItem`
- ❑   `GroupHeader`

If the `Messages` collection is created by the CDO Rendering library objects, it could contain `GroupHeader` objects from the Calendar folder. We will see more on the CDO Rendering library later in the book, so we'll leave the `GroupHeader` object for now.

The other three objects could be returned from a `Messages` collection instantiated by CDO library objects. An `AppointmentItem` represents a user appointment in the Calendar folder, while a `MeetingItem` represents a meeting request or a meeting response. We will see more about handling them in the next chapter. From now on, I will use the term "message" to represent all items that can be stored in a folder. Just remember that the message could well be a CDO `Message`, an `AppointmentItem`, or a `MeetingItem`.

The Filter Property

The `Filter` property returns the `MessageFilter` object associated with the current collection. Each `Messages` collection has an empty `Filter` by default. You can modify this filter to add restrictions to the collection, or you can set the `Messages` collection's `Filter` property to another `MessageFilter` object.

The RawTable Property

The `RawTable` property returns an `IUnknown` pointer to the table that stores the `Folders` collection on the Exchange Server. It is not accessible to Visual Basic applications.

The Sort Method

The `Sort` method sorts the `Messages` collection using the `SortOrder` specified.

```
Call colMessages.Sort([SortOrder] [, PropTag]
Call colMessages.Sort([SortOrder] [, FolderName]
```

SortOrder Constant	Value	Order
CdoNone	0	Do not sort
CdoAscending	1	Sort in ascending order
CdoDescending	2	Sort in descending order

The first syntax sorts the collection on a standard MAPI property specified by the property tag. The second syntax sorts on a user-defined property specified by the property name. If neither the property tag nor the property name is specified, it sorts the collection using the property specified in the previous `Sort` operation. If the collection has not been sorted previously, it is sorted on folder names.

The `Sort` method does not always succeed. If the Exchange Server does not support a specific sort, this method raises an `CdoE_TOO_COMPLEX` (&H80040117) error.

The Add Method

The `Add` method creates a new message in the current `Messages` collection and returns a reference to the newly created message. After you use this method to create a new message, you must call either the `Update` or the `Send` method of the new message, otherwise it will not be saved. We will see how it works later when we further modify our sample application.

The Delete Method

The `Delete` method physically deletes *all* messages in the collection. It does not delete the collection itself.

The GetFirst, GetLast, GetNext, GetPrevious Methods

These four methods are similar to their counterparts in the `Folders` and `AddressEntries` collection. They provide the ability to navigate around the `Messages` collection.

The Message Object

The `Message` object is arguably the most programmed CDO object. Almost all CDO applications come down to accessing and manipulating messages. So not surprisingly, the `Message` object has the largest number of properties and methods (well, except for the `AppointmentItem` object, but as we saw early on, the `AppointmentItem` object is really a specialized version of the `Message` object anyway).

MESSAGE	
Properties	**Type**
Application	String
Attachments	Attachments
Categories	StringArray
Class	Long
ConversationIndex	String
ConversationTopic	String
DeliveryReceipt	Boolean
Encrypted	Boolean
Fields	Fields
FolderID	String
ID	String
Importance	Long
MAPIObject	IUnknown
Parent	Messages
ReadReceipt	Boolean
Recipients	Recipients
Sender	AddressEntry
Sensitivity	Long
Sent	Boolean
Session	Session
Signed	Boolean
Size	Long
StoreID	String
Subject	String
Submitted	Boolean
Test	String
TimeCreated	Variant
TimeExpired	Variant
TimeLastModified	Variant
TimeReceived	Variant
TimeSent	Variant
Type	String
Unread	Boolean
Methods	
CopyTo	Update
Delete	
Forward	
IsSameAs	
MoveTo	
Options	
Reply	
ReplyAll	
Send	
Events	

The `Message` object is the fundamental building block of a message store. A message store is worth nothing without the ability to store and retrieve messages. In CDO, a message can contain virtually any object that can be stored in a folder on an Exchange Server. For instance, a message could represent an e-mail message in the Inbox or a person's contact information in the Contacts folder. It could also contain a Microsoft Word document or an Access database.

To retrieve a message, we can either use the CDO `Session` object's `GetMessage` method or traverse through a message collection. If you know the message ID, you can call the `GetMessage` method to access the message.

Message Object and GetMessage Method

The `GetMessage` method returns a message with a given ID and optionally an information store ID.

```
Set obj = gobjSession.GetMessage(MessageID [, StoreID])
```

It is not necessary to pass the store ID to the `GetMessage` method when the folder is in the user's mailbox. If the message is in another store, such as somewhere in a public or private folder, we must specify the store ID. This method is one of the most frequently used methods, and it seems simple enough. However, it is not as easy as it appears.

The `GetMessage` method can return a `Message` object, an `AppointmentItem` object, or a `MeetingItem` object. Unless you are certain that the `MessageID` represents a particular type of item, you cannot simply assign the returned object to a specific object. For example:

```
Dim objMessage As MAPI.Message
Set objMessage = objSession.GetMessage(strMessageID)
```

This might cause a Type Mismatch error (13) if the object returned by the `GetMessage` method is an `AppointmentItem` or a `MeetingItem`. If you remember that every CDO object has a `Class` property that tells its type, you can easily implement a workaround.

```
Dim obj As Object
Dim objMessage As MAPI.Message
Dim objAppointmentItem As MAPI.AppointmentItem
Dim objMeetingItem As MAPI.MeetingItem

Set obj = objSession.GetMessage(strMessageID)
Select Case obj.Class
   Case CdoAppointment
      Set objAppointmentItem = obj
   Case CdoMeeting
      Set objMeetingItem = obj
   Case CdoMsg
      Set objMessageItem = obj
End Select
```

The following table lists the three CDO type constants and their values. You can find a comprehensive listing of CDO object type constants in the `CdoObjectClass` section of Appendix B.

Constant	Value
CdoAppointment	26
CdoMeetingItem	27
CdoMsg	3

You might expect that with the polymorphism feature implemented in programming languages such as Visual Basic and C++, the following code snippet would work.

```
Dim objMessage As MAPI.Message
Dim objAppointmentItem As MAPI.AppointmentItem

Set objAppointmentItem = objSession.GetMessage(MessageID)
Set objMessage = objAppointmentItem
```

But if the actual item is a `Message` object, this line will fail:

```
Set objAppointmentItem = objSession.GetMessage(MessageID)
```

This is perhaps understandable as you cannot set the subclass object to the base class object in Visual Basic, and downcasting in C++ is usually not a good technique.

On the other hand, if the actual item is an `AppointmentItem`, the above line will work but the next line causes a Type Mismatch error:

```
Set objMessage = objAppointmentItem
```

This is somewhat surprising given that the CDO documentation says that the `AppointmentItem` class is a subclass of the `Message` class. So it seems that this inheritance is implemented as containment, that is, the `AppointmentItem` class actually contains the `Message` class and exposes all properties and most methods of the `Message` class. It also defines a set of additional properties and methods required for managing appointments. A `MeetingItem` has the similar problem. We will see each object in more detail in the next chapter.

There is another problem with the `GetMessage` method. If you log on using a stored profile that is also used by Outlook 98, the `GetMessage` method always returns a `Message` object, even if the item itself is an `AppointmentItem` or a `MeetingItem` object. That is, `obj.Class` always returns 3. The workaround is to either create a CDO-only profile, that is a profile that is never used by Outlook or use a dynamically created temporary profile when logging on.

But wait, there's more. The `GetMessage` method only returns `AppointmentItem` objects from the Calendar folder. While CDO allows you to create `AppointmentItem` objects in other folders (such as a public folder), it cannot retrieve it as an `AppointmentItem`. That is, you can still access the properties and methods of the `Message` object, but not the `AppointmentItem`-specific properties and methods. The `GetMessage` method always returns a `Message` object from folders other than the default Calendar folder in the private information store.

Message Object Types

Even a true `Message` object might actually be one of many types. You can check the message type through its `Type` property. By default, CDO sets this property to `IPM.Note` for e-mail messages and `IPM.Post` for public folder postings. Here IPM stands for InterPersonal Message, a term used in MAPI to indicate that the message is intended for human use.

The `Type` property typically contains several parts, each separated by a dot (`.`). CDO accepts any string for this property, but it is preferable to use the standard convention. For instance, a message posted to a Contacts public folder can have the `Type` property set to `IPM.Contact` and a document posted as `IPM.Document`. If you assign a message's `Type` property with a non-standard string such as `My.Personal.Mail`, it will be saved to the message as is. That is, CDO does not attempt to verify or change this property. Your application can take advantage of this to perform some specific operations, such as checking whether a mail has been composed and sent using your application. However, other applications might not recognize the message properly. For example, Outlook might display a warning message while trying to open the message:

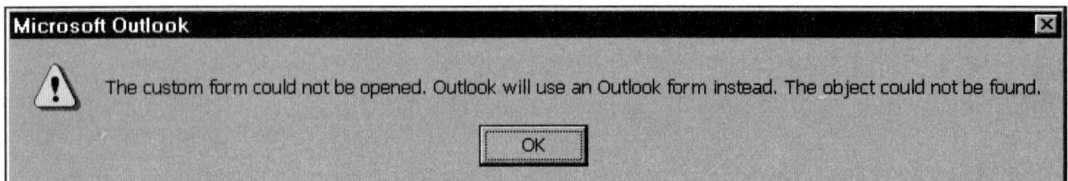

The following table lists the Message Types of items in the special Outlook folders. We will see examples of messages with `IPM.Document` in a moment – there are no special folders for this type.

Folder	Message Type
Calendar	`IPM.Appointment`
Tasks	`IPM.Task`
Contacts	`IPM.Contact`
Notes	`IPM.StickyNote`
Journal	`IPM.Activity`

Accessing Appointments

Note that the type of message found in the Calendar folder is `IPM.Appointment`. It may sound quite strange that CDO defines a type of CDO `Message` object to represent the appointment items while appointment items are represented by, and can be retrieved as, CDO `AppointmentItem` objects that have a few more specific properties and methods. So why does CDO define such a message type? There are two reasons.

First, as we saw above, CDO only supports retrieving `AppointmentItem` objects from the default calendar folder, that is, the Calendar folder in the user's mailbox. While we can use Outlook to create private and public folders using `AppointmentItems` as illustrated below, CDO will only return `Message` objects from those folders.

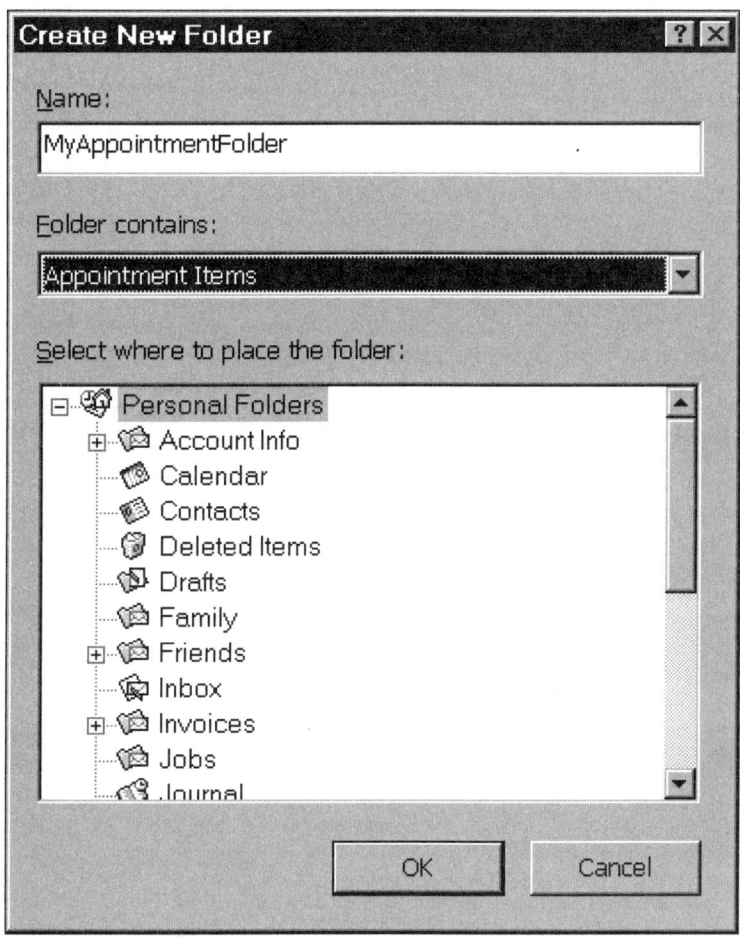

Second, you must use the CDO `Session` object's `GetDefaultFolder` method to retrieve the default `Calendar` folder in order to retrieve `AppointmentItem` objects from it. For example,

```
Set objCalendarFolder = gobjSession.GetDefaultFolder(CdoDefaultFolderCalendar)
```

If you simply loop through the folders in the user's mailbox, you will only get `Message` objects from the Calendar folder. That can be awkward, and it really seems like another bug to me.

In Chapter 2, we briefly encountered a CDO bug that causes the `GetDefaultFolder` call to fail if we log on using a profile that is shared with Microsoft Outlook. Several methods to retrieve an appointment as an CDO `AppointmentItem` object from the default Calendar folder are illustrated in the following flow diagram.

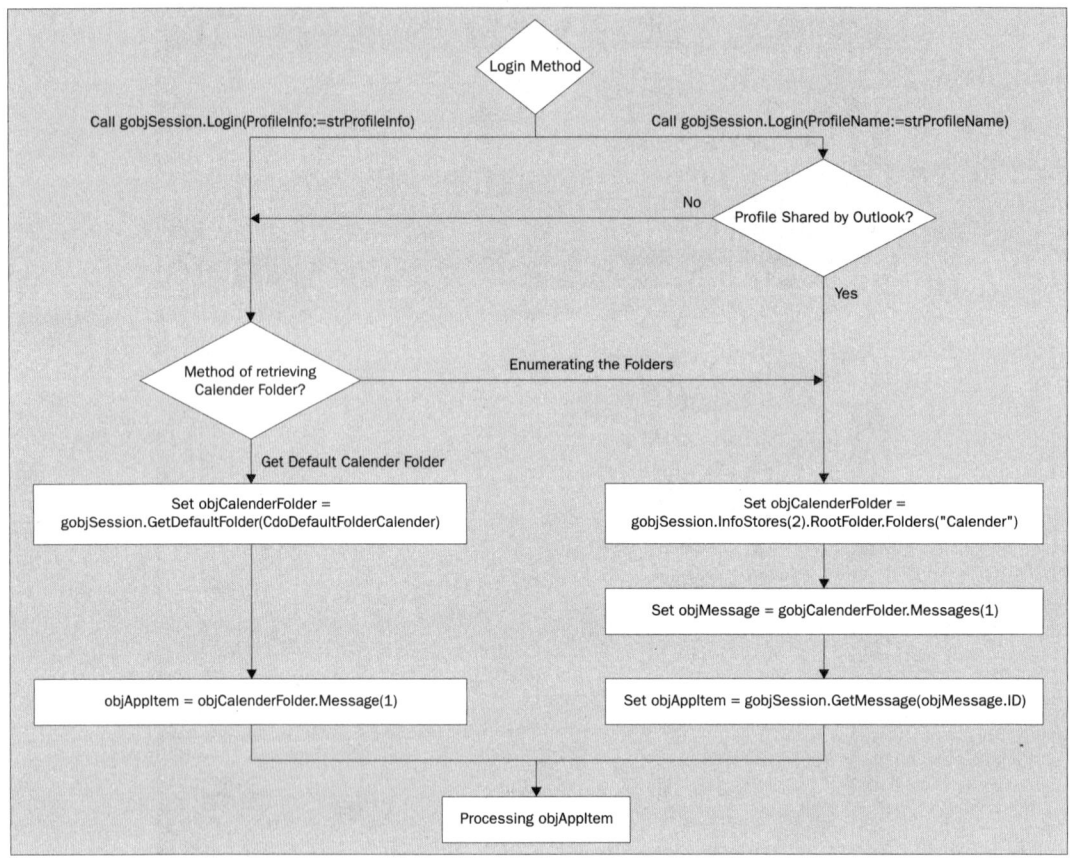

The above diagram assumes that the user's mailbox is the second `InfoStore` in the `Session` object's `InfoStores` collection. If we log in using a temporary profile or an existing profile that is not shared by Outlook, we have two choices. First, we can call the CDO `Session` object's `GetDefaultFolder` method to retrieve the default Calendar folder and get an appointment from its `Messages` collection. Second, we can retrieve the calendar `folder` by enumerating the Folder collection of the mailbox's root folder.

If we log in using a profile shared with Outlook, the `GetDefaultFolder` method does not work. Therefore we must enumerate the folder collection as with the second method above. We can then obtain a `Message` object representing an appointment item. Finally, we call the CDO `Session` object's `GetMessage` method and pass it the ID of the `Message` object to retrieve the appointment as a CDO `AppointmentItem` object.

Once we get hold of the `AppointmentItem` object, we can access its properties and invoke its methods. The next chapter, Managing Schedules, goes into detail on managing appointments. For now, let's look briefly at how to access OLE documents.

Accessing OLE Documents

Using Exchange Server and Outlook, you can post an OLE document to a public or a private folder by dragging it from Windows Explorer and dropping it into a folder. Examples of OLE documents include Microsoft Word documents, Microsoft Excel worksheets, and Visio diagrams.

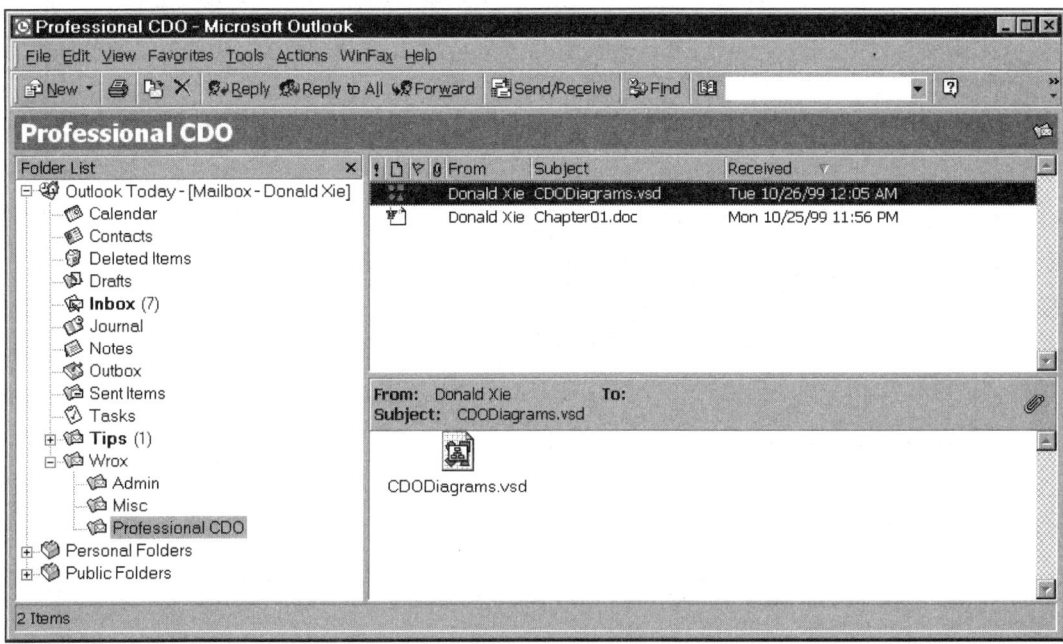

A document posted to a folder is always retrieved as a CDO `Message` object with type `IPM.Document.*`. For instance, the type of a message containing a Microsoft Word 97 document is `IPM.Document.Word.Document.8`. Note that Outlook displays the icon associated with the host application of the document in the top-right message list pane, instead of a message icon with an attachment. Although the document is stored on the Exchange Server as a normal message with an attachment, Outlook recognizes that it really represents a document. When you use CDO to access that message, you will get a message with the document as a binary attachment. You can access document properties using the `Message` object's `Fields` collection.

```
With objMessage
    If .Type Like "IPM.Document*" Then
        strDocAuthor = objMessage.Fields("Author").Value
    End If
End With
```

The `Like` operator accepts the wildcard character * when comparing two strings. For instance, the above `If` condition is `True` if the message type is `IPM.Document.Word.Document.8` or `IPM.Document.Visio.Drawing.5`. The following figure shows a sample list of OLE document properties.

ID	Name	Value
&H801A001E		9.0
&H801B000B		False
&H801F000B		False
&H80200003		0
&H80220003		0
&H80F4001E	Title	Professional CDO Programming
&H80F5001E	Author	Donald Xie
&H80F6001E	Template	ProfTrig97.dot
&H80F7001E	LastAuthor	Donald Xie
&H80F8001E	RevNumber	3
&H80F9001E	AppName	Microsoft Word 8.0
&H80FA001E	EditTime	12 Minutes
&H80FB0040	CreateDtmRo	9/21/99 11:37:00 PM
&H80FC0040	LastSaveDtm	10/25/99 11:55:00 PM
&H80FD0003	PageCount	1
&H80FE0003	WordCount	1113
&H80FF0003	CharCount	6345
&H81000003	Security	0
&H8101001E	Company	ACME Ltd
&H81020003	LineCount	52
&H81030003	ParCount	12
&H8104000B	Scale	False
&H8105000B	LinksDirty	False
&H8106101E	DocParts	
&H8109001E	Subject	CDO

The IDs of the OLE document custom fields do not correspond to any MAPI property tags; they are OLE document-specific.

The Categories Property

The `Categories` property specifies or returns a set of application-defined message attributes. These attributes can be used to access a subset of messages in a folder.

To assign the attributes, you must first create an array of a particular data type and fill it with attribute values. You then assign the array to the `Categories` property.

```
Dim arrCategories(2) As String
arrCategories(0) = "Marketing Plan"
arrCategories(1) = "Europe"
arrCategories(2) = "Promotion"

objMessage.Categories = arrCategories
```

This is simple enough. Retrieving the `Categories` property is a bit trickier. You must define a `Variant` array (not an array of `Variants` or an array of `Strings`), and access the elements through this `Variant` array.

```
Dim arrCategories As Variant
' NOT Dim arrCategories(2) As Variant
' NOT Dim arrCategories(2) As String

arrCategories = objMessage.Categories
```

Accessing elements in the `Categories` array is even trickier – you need to remember to use an extra pair of parentheses before specifying the index.

```
For lngIndex = 0 To UBound(objMessage.Categories)
    Debug.Print objMessage.Categories()(lngIndex)
Next
```

This is because the `Categories` property is implemented as a property function, instead of a plain public property value. So you must use the proper property accessing syntax.

The ConversationTopic and ConversationIndex Properties

A conversation is a group of messages that relate to a common topic. In CDO, the common topic is stored in the `ConversationTopic` of all messages participating in the conversation. This provides an easy way of grouping, or **threading**, the messages.

It is conventional that the messages appear in the order they are created. CDO provides the `ConversationIndex` property to record this order. Naturally, it relates to the time the message is created. The `ConversationIndex` is a string containing a hexadecimal number. We can use the CDO `Session` object's `CreateConversationIndex` method to generate a conversation index. You will see more about this later when we work with public folder postings in the sample application.

The DeliveryReceipts and ReadReceipts Properties

These two properties specify the message delivery notification options. If the `DeliveryReceipts` property is set to `True`, a delivery notification is sent to the message originator when the message is delivered to each recipient. If the `ReadReceipts` property is set to `True`, a read notification is sent to the message originator when each recipient reads the message.

The Encrypted and Signed Properties

While the `Encrypted` and the `Signed` properties are defined in CDO, they are implemented by Exchange Server. If you set one of these properties to `True`, CDO simply passes it as a request to the underlying Exchange Server for processing. CDO itself does not attempt to encrypt or digitally sign the message.

However, even if a received message's `Encrypted` or `Signed` property is `True`, it does not necessarily mean that the message is indeed encrypted or digitally signed. It is a mere indication that the message was intended to be encrypted or digitally signed when it was initially created.

The FolderID and StoreID Properties

The `FolderID` and `StoreID` properties return the unique IDs of the folder and information store where this message is stored.

The ID Property

The `ID` property returns the unique ID of the message.

The Importance Property

The `Importance` property specifies the importance of the message. It can have one of the following values:

Constant	Value
CdoLow	0
CdoNormal	1
CdoHigh	2

By default, CDO assigns new messages the importance of `CdoNormal`.

The MAPIOBJECT Property

The `MAPIOBJECT` property returns an `IUNKNOWN` pointer to the current `Message` object. This is accessible to C++ applications, but not Visual Basic applications since Visual Basic does not support the `IUNKNOWN` pointer.

The Sender Property

The `Sender` property is an `AddressEntry` object that specifies the sender of the message. It may seem simple enough, but CDO actually defines two senders for each message: one is the actual message sender, and the other is the person on whose behalf the message was sent. For instance, an assistant can send a message on behalf of his boss.

When a message is created, the `Sender` property is set to the current user of the session. She is sending this message on behalf of herself. If she wish to send it on behalf of her boss, we need to set the `Sender` in CDO twice. The first time sets her boss, and the second sets herself. The `ImpersonateMessage` function example illustrates the steps in setting the `Sender` property to send the message on behalf the manager of the current user:

```
Function ImpersonateMessage(TheMessage As MAPI.Message)
    Dim objCurrentUser As MAPI.AddressEntry
    Set objCurrentUser = mobjSession.CurrentUser
    Set TheMessage.Sender = objCurrentUser.Manager   ' Sending on behalf of Boss
    Set TheMessage.Sender = objCurrentUser            ' Myself
    Set objCurrentUser = Nothing
End Function
```

The Sensitivity Property

The `Sensitivity` property specifies the Sensitivity of messages. It has one of the following values:

Constant	Value
CdoNoSensitivity	0
CdoPersonal	1
CdoPrivate	2
CdoConfidential	3

By default, CDO assigns this property a value of `CdoNoSensitivity`.

The Sent and Submitted Properties

In CDO, a message can be in one of four states: **new**, **saved**, **submitted**, and **sent**. When a message is created and saved to the Exchange Server, it is **saved**. This is normally achieved by calling the `Update` method of the `Message` object. The `Sent` property indicates whether the message has been sent. You can set this property before calling the `Send` method to categorize the message. The `Send` method sends the message, sets the `Sent` property to `True` and turns this property into a read-only property.

The message is said to be **submitted** when it is submitted to the underlying MAPI system. The `Submitted` property is usually used when a user posts messages directly into public folders. We will see examples of posting to public folders later in this chapter.

The Size Property

The `Size` property returns the total bytes of the current message. It contains the size of all attachments, fields, and other properties of the current message. Since Exchange Server does not know the size of the message until it is saved, this property is only valid after either the `Update` or the `Send` method is called.

The Subject and Text Properties

The `Subject` and `Text` properties contain the subject and the body of the current message.

The TimeCreated, TimeExpired, TimeLastModified, TimeReceived, and TimeSent Properties

The `TimeCreated` property returns the date and time the message is first saved. It is set when the `Update` or `Send` method is called for the first time. The `TimeLastModified` property returns the date and time the message was last saved.

The `TimeSent` property specifies the date and time the message was sent. It is represented with the sender's local system time. The `TimeReceived` property specifies the date and time the message was received in the receiver's local mail system. For an e-mail message, this property is set automatically by MAPI. However, MAPI will not set it if the message is posted to a Public folder. In this case, the message originator can set it to the time the message is sent.

The `TimeExpired` property specifies the date and time the message becomes invalid. The receiver can decide what to do when the message has expired. For example, it could delete the message once its expiry time is passed.

The Unread Property

The Unread property specifies whether or not the current message has been read by the current user. When you set this property to False to signify that it has been read, the message is flagged as read in the Exchange Server. The client, however, might not be updated straight away. So your user might not see the change immediately.

The Update and Send Methods

The Update method saves changes to the message store. It has two optional parameters.

```
Call objMessage.Update([MakePermanent] [, RefreshObject])
```

CDO uses its own memory cache to store the changes to Message objects to improve performance. If the MakePermanent parameter is True, CDO commits the changes to the message store and flushes the cache. Otherwise, the Update method simply flushes the cache without committing the change.

The RefreshObject parameter determines whether the cache should be reloaded from the message store. If it is True, CDO reloads address data from the message store. If the change is not committed, reloading data causes all changes to be lost and effectively cancels the change.

The effects of the possible combinations of the MakePermanent and RefreshObject properties are listed in the following table.

	RefreshObject = True	RefreshObject = False
MakePermanent = True	Commit all changes to the message store and reload the object from the message store so that changes made by other processes will be visible immediately	Save the change to the message store but do not refresh the cache with possible changes made by other processes.
MakePermanent = False	Reload AddressEntry data from the message store, thus cancel the change	Flush the cache.

The Send method submits the message to MAPI and initiates a transmission. It has three optional parameters.

```
Call objMessage.Send([SaveCopy] [, ShowDialog] [,ParentWindow])
```

The SaveCopy parameter indicates whether a copy of the message should be saved in the Exchange Server, for example, in the Sent Items folder. If the ShowDialog parameter is set to True, CDO will display a modal dialog box allowing the user to modify either the message recipients or contents. The ParentWindow parameter is only meaningful when the ShowDialog parameter is set to True. It specifies the parent window that will be disabled until the dialog box is closed. By default, it is set to zero so that all windows in the current application are disabled while the dialog box is displayed. We will use the ShowDialog option later in the sample application.

The `Send` method moves the current message to the Outbox folder and sets the message's `Submitted` property to `True`. When the underlying messaging system picks up the message from the Outbox and passes it to the transport system, it sets the message's `Sent` and `Unread` properties to `True`. The receiving messaging system will set the received message's `Submitted` method back to `False`.

When `ShowDialog` is `True`, the user may decide to close the dialog box without sending the message. This will cause an error message `CdoE_USER_CANCEL` (`&H80040113`), so it is a good idea to catch this error and perform appropriate actions in case the user does not send the message. For example, you can call the `Update` method to save the message so that the user can send it later.

The Reply, ReplyAll, and Forward Methods

The `Reply` method creates a new message as a reply to the current message and adds the current message's `Sender` to the new message's `Recipients` collection. It returns a reference to the new message so that you can modify it before sending it. The `ReplyAll` method is similar with one difference: it adds the current message's `Sender` and all recipients to the new message's `Recipients` collection. Finally, the `Forward` method creates a new message that can be used to forward the current message. We will use them later in our sample application.

The CopyTo and MoveTo Methods

Both the `CopyTo` and `MoveTo` methods copy the current message to another folder. The `MoveTo` method also deletes the original message. As with all these methods, we will see how they work later.

The Delete Method

The `Delete` method removes the current message from the message collection.

```
Call objMessage.Delete([ShouldMoveToDeletedItemsFolder])
```

You can specify the `ShouldMoveToDeletedItemsFolder` parameter to indicate whether CDO should move the message to the Deleted Items folder. It is `False` by default, but it is generally good manners to move it to the Deleted Items folder so that the user can recover it if required.

The Options Method

The `Options` method displays a dialog box so that the user can change message submission options.

```
Call objMessage.Option([ParentWindow])
```

The optional `ParentWindow` specifies the parent window of the dialog box. The following figure shows the option dialog box.

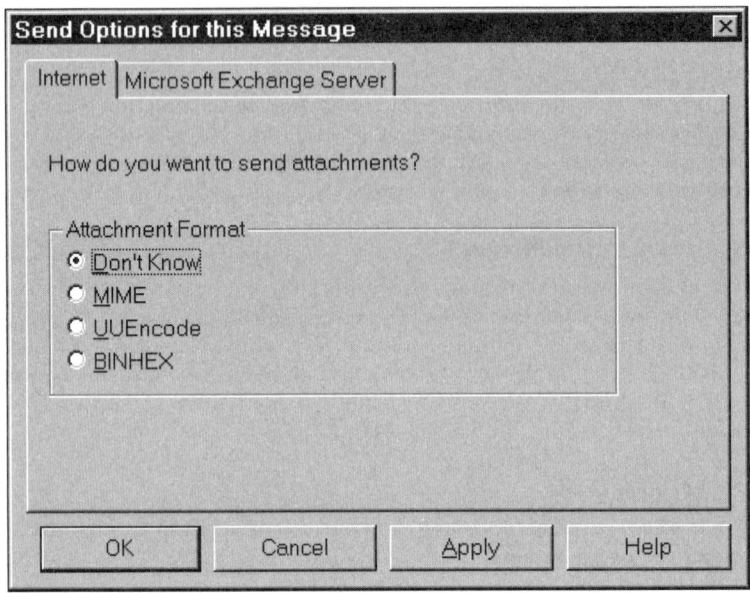

Here you can specify the attachment type. You can also specify other Exchange Server specific options using the Microsoft Exchange Server tab, as shown in the following figure.

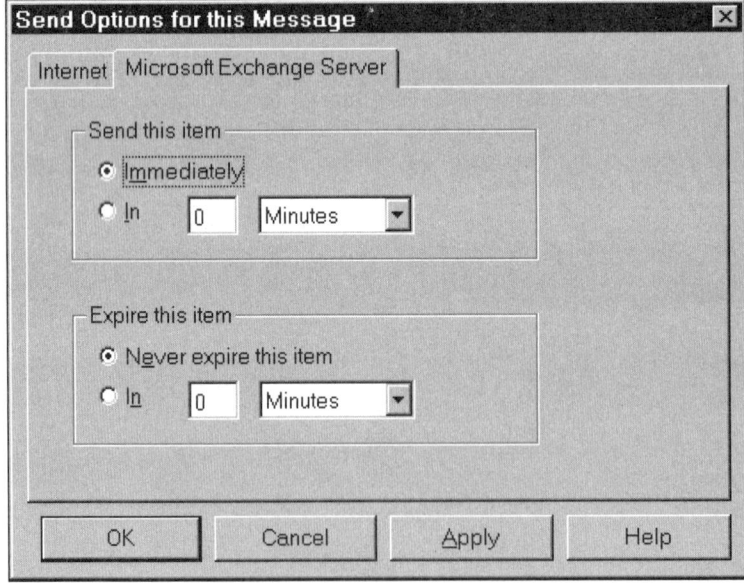

The MessageFilter Object

A `MessageFilter` object is associated with a `Messages` collection to specify the search criteria of the messages in the collection. `Messages` that match the search criteria will be accessible through the `For Each` syntax or the `Messages` collection's `Get` methods. The `GetMessage` method of the `Session` object is not affected by the message filters.

MESSAGEFILTER	
Properties	**Type**
Application	String
Class	Long
Conversation	String
Fields	Fields
Importance	Long
Not	Boolean
Or	Boolean
Parent	Messages
Recipients	String
Sender	String
Sent	Boolean
Session	Session
Size	Long
Subject	String
Text	String
TimeFirst	Variant
TimeLast	Variant
Type	String
Unread	Boolean
Methods	
IsSameAs	
Events	

Apart from the four common CDO properties, `Application`, `Class`, `Parent`, and `Session`, most of the `MessageFilter` object properties correspond to the `Message` properties with the same name. The `Conversation`, `Importance`, `Sent`, `Type`, and `Unread` properties specify that only messages that have the specified property values are included. For example, if you assign the `MessageFilter`'s `Importance` property to `CdoHigh`, only messages with high importance will be included in the filtered collection.

The `Not` and `Or` properties are similar to their counterparts in the `AddressEntryFilter` object. The `Not` property negates all individual restrictions, while the `Or` property specifies whether the filter restrictions should be ORed, that is, whether messages that satisfy at least one restriction will be accessible.

The Sender and Recipients Properties

The `Sender` property is a string. Only messages sent by people whose name (the `AddressEntry` object's `Name` property) contains the specified string are included. The `Recipients` property is also a string. If you assign it a value, only messages that have at least one recipient whose name (the `Recipient` object's `Name` property) contains the specified string are included. We will see the `Recipient` object in a moment.

The Subject and Text Properties

If you assign the `Subject` property with a string value, only messages containing the specified string in their `Subject` property are included. The `Text` property also specifies that only messages containing the specified string in their body text are included.

The TimeFirst and TimeLast Properties

If you specify the `TimeFirst` property, only messages that are received (the `Message` object's `TimeReceived` property) at or since the specified time are included. The `TimeLast` property, on the other hand, indicates that only messages that are received at or before the specified time are included.

The Size Property

Only messages larger than the specified `Size` are included. You can set the `Not` property to `True` to include only the smaller messages.

The IsSameAs Method

```
objMsgFilter.IsSameAs(objMsgFilter2)
```

The `IsSameAs` method returns `True` if `objMsgFilter` and `objMsgFilter2` refer to the same physical `MessageFilter` object.

The Recipients Collection

Each message can be sent to one or more recipients. The `Recipients` collection of a message contains all intended recipients of the message.

RECIPIENTS	
Properties	**Type**
Application	String
Class	Long
Count	Long
Item	Recipient
Parent	Message
RawTable	IUnknown
Resolved	Boolean
Session	Session
Methods	
Add	
AddMultiple	
Delete	
GetFirstUnresolved	
GetFreeBusy	
GetNextUnresolved	
Resolve	
Events	

The Count and Item Properties

The `Count` property returns the number of `Recipient` objects in the collection. The `Item` property returns a `Recipient` object in the collection. Note that it only accepts a `Long` integer as the index in the collection.

The RawTable Property

The `RawTable` property returns an `IUnknown` pointer to the underlying MAPI table representing the `Recipients` collection on the Exchange Server. This is accessible to C++ applications, but not Visual Basic applications since Visual Basic does not support the `IUNKNOWN` pointer.

The Resolve Method and the Resolved Property

The `Resolve` method attempts to resolve all `Recipient` objects in the collection.

```
Call colRecips.Resolve([ShowDialog])
```

The optional `ShowDialog` parameter indicates whether CDO should show a dialog box asking the user to manually resolve ambiguous recipients. It is `True` by default.

The `Resolve` method invalidates any references to the recipients in the collection. If you have a variable holding a reference to a `Recipient` object in the collection, the reference becomes invalid after this method is called. In general, try to release such references before calling this method.

The `Resolved` property returns `True` if all recipients in the collection represent valid `AddressEntry` objects.

The Add Method

The `Add` method creates a new `Recipient` object in the collection and returns a reference to the newly created object. It has the following syntax.

```
Set objRecip = colRecips.Add([Name] [,Address] [, Type] [, EntryID)
```

Parameter	Value	Description
Name		The Display Name of the recipient. The value of this parameter is assigned to the new Recipient's `Name` property.
		This parameter is ignored if `EntryID` is present.
Address		The full address of the recipient. If this parameter is specified, it must contain the full address such as `SMTP:john@city.net`. The value of this parameter is assigned to the new `Recipient's Address` property.
		This parameter is ignored if `EntryID` is present.
Type	CdoTo = 1	The type of the recipient. The value of this parameter is assigned to the new `Recipient's Type` property.
	CdoCc = 2	
	CdoBcc = 3	
EntryID		The unique ID of an `AddressEntry` object. If this parameter is specified, `Name` and `Value` parameters are ignored. `Recipient` objects added using `EntryID` need not be resolved.

Note that the `Add` method does not accept an `AddressEntry` object, therefore you cannot add an `AddressEntry` object to the `Recipients` collection directly. For example, this does not add the `AddressEntry` object representing the current user to the collection:

```
Call objMessage.Recipients.Add(mobjSession.CurrentUser)
```

159

Since the default property of an `AddressEntry` object is its `Name`, the above code is equivalent to the following code.

```
Call objMessage.Recipients.Add(Name:=mobjSession.CurrentUser.Name)
```

You must call the `Resolve` method before sending the message.

```
Set objRecipient = objMessage.Recipients.Add(mobjSession.CurrentUser)
objRecipient.Resolve
```

We will see how to `Resolve` a `Recipient` object shortly. Alternatively, you can pass in the `CurrentUser`'s ID to the `EntryID` parameter.

```
objMessage.Recipients.Add EntryID:=mobjSession.CurrentUser.ID
```

The AddMultiple Method

The `AddMultiple` method adds multiple recipients to the `Recipients` collection in one call.

```
Call colRecips.AddMultiple(Name [, Type])
```

The `Name` parameter is a string containing a list of recipient display names or addresses, each separated by a semicolon. Since the recipients are added using either their display names or addresses, you must call either each recipient's or the collection's `Resolve` method to resolve their addresses.

The Delete Method

The `Delete` method deletes all `Recipient` objects in the collection.

The GetFirstUnresolved and GetNextUnresolved Methods

The `GetFirstUnresolved` method finds the first unresolved `Recipient` object in the collection. If all recipients have been resolved, this method returns `Nothing`.

The `GetNextUnresolved` method finds the next unresolved `Recipient` object in the collection. The `GetFirstUnresolved` method must be called before this method is called. If all recipients in the collection have been resolved, this method returns `Nothing`.

You generally use these methods to perform two operations:

- ❏ Resolve each `Recipient` object after they have been added to the collection
- ❏ Modify `Recipient` objects that cannot be resolved

The GetFreeBusy Method

```
strFreeBusy = colRecips.GetFreeBusy(StartTime, EndTime, Interval)
```

The `GetFreeBusy` method returns the *combined availability* of the recipients in the collection in the period from `StartTime` to `EndTime`. More precisely, it returns the combined availability of all `AddressEntry` objects contained in the `Recipient` objects in the current collection. We will see more detail on retrieving the `AddressEntry` object's free/busy status in the next chapter.

The Recipient Object

A Recipient object contains information about a recipient of a message. It contains an AddressEntry object that can be accessed through its AddressEntry property.

RECIPIENT	
Properties	**Type**
Address	String
AddressEntry	AddressEntry
AmbiguousNames	AddressEntries
Application	String
Class	Long
DisplayType	Long
ID	String
Index	Long
MeetingResponseStatus	Long
Name	String
Parent	Recipients
Session	Session
Type	Long
Methods	
Delete	
GetFreeBusy	
IsSameAs	
Resolve	
Events	

The AddressEntry, Address, ID, and Name Properties

The AddressEntry property returns the AddressEntry object representing the recipient. When this property is accessed, the recipient is resolved. If the recipient cannot be resolved, accessing this property will cause an error: CdoE_AMBIGUOUS_RECIP (&H80040700).

One very useful technique in using this property is to assign a valid AddressEntry object to the recipient. For instance,

```
Set objRecipient = objMessage.Recipients.Add
Set objRecipient.AddressEntry = mobjSession.CurrentUser
```

The Recipient object exposes the commonly used properties of its child AddressEntry. If you wish to change a property, for instance the postal code property, of a recipient's AddressEntry object, you might try to do this:

```
objRecipient.Name = "Joe Bloggs"
objRecipient.Resolve

objRecipient.AddressEntry.Fields(CdoPR_Postal_Code) = "99999"
objRecipient.AddressEntry.Update
```

Unfortunately this does not work – the change is never saved. The correct way of doing this is to create an `AddressEntry` object explicitly and use it to update the property.

```
Dim objAddrEntry As MAPI.AddressEntry

objRecipient.Name = "Joe Bloggs"
objRecipient.Resolve

Set objAddressEntry = objRecipient.AddressEntry
objAddressEntry.Fields(CdoPR_Postal_Code) = "99999"
objAddressEntry.Update

Set objRecipient.AddressEntry = objAddressEntry
```

This works just fine.

The AmbiguousNames Property

If the current recipient cannot be resolved with the `Resolve` method, the `AmbiguousNames` property returns an `AddressEntries` collection containing possible suggestions to resolve the recipient. You can display a list and ask the user to select one from the list. You can also programmatically examine this collection and add or remove entries in it before presenting the list to the user.

This property returns `Nothing` if the recipient is resolved, or there is no suggestions by CDO. In general, you should first call the `Resolve` method and only use this property if there is an error.

The Index Property

The `Index` property returns the index of this recipient in the `Recipients` collection.

The MeetingResponseStatus Property

The `MeetingResponseStatus` property is used when the parent message of the collection is an `AppointmentItem` object. We will see more on this in the next chapter.

The Type Property

The `Type` property specifies the type of recipient. It can have one of the following three values:

Constant	Value
CdoTo	1
CdoCc	2
CdoBcc	3

The Delete Method

The `Delete` method removes the recipient from the parent `Recipients` collection.

The GetFreeBusy Method

The `GetFreeBusy` method returns the availability of the recipient in the period from `StartTime` to `EndTime`. The `Interval` parameter specifies the length of time slot in minutes. More precisely, it returns the availability of the enclosed `AddressEntry` objects. We will see more details on retrieving the `AddressEntry` object's free/busy status in the next chapter.

The IsSameAs Method

```
objRecip.IsSameAs(objRecip2)
```

The `IsSameAs` method returns `True` if `objRecip` and `objRecip2` refer to the same physical `AddressEntry` object.

The Resolve Method

The `Resolve` method attempts to resolve the current `Recipient` object.

```
Call objRecip.Resolve([ShowDialog])
```

The optional `ShowDialog` parameter indicates whether CDO should show a dialog box asking the user to manually resolve if the recipient has an ambiguous name.

Unlike the `Recipients` collection's `Resolve` method (which invalidates references to the recipients in the collection), the `Resolve` method of the `Recipient` object does not invalidate references to itself or other recipients in the collection. The current recipient is resolved against the current user's address books.

If the recipient is a custom address that does not belong to any of the address books, the `Resolve` method creates a temporary `AddressEntry` object and assigns it an ID. However, it does not, and cannot, validate the address.

The Attachments Collection

The `Attachments` collection stores a list of attachments in a `Message` object. It allows users to attach objects such as files or messages to messages.

ATTACHMENTS	
Properties	**Type**
Application	String
Class	Long
Count	Long
Item	Attachment
Parent	Message
Session	Session
Methods	
Add	
Delete	

The Count and Item Properties

The `Count` property returns the number of `Attachment` objects in the collection. The `Item` property returns an `Item` with a given index in the collection.

The Add Method

The `Add` method creates an `Attachment` object in the collection and returns a reference to the newly added `Attachment` object. It has the following syntax:

```
Set objAttachment = colAttachments.Add([Name] [, Position] [, Type] [, Source]
```

The `Name` parameter specifies the display name of the attachment.

The `Position` parameter specifies the offset from the beginning of the message text where the attachment should be placed. The first character in the message text is 1. If `Position` is 0, as is the default, the attachment will not be displayed within the message. A value of –1 indicates that the attachment should be placed by CDO without using the `Position` parameter.

The `Type` and `Source` parameters specify the type of the attachment and the corresponding path to the attachment object in the file system. The valid values of the `Type` parameter and possible `Source` parameter format are listed in the following table. These values are defined in the `CdoAttachmentType` enumerated type.

Type	Source
CdoFileData (1)	The full path and file name of the attachment object. The location of attachment source can be the local file system such as `C:\My Documents\Proposal.doc`, or the network file system such as `\\Server\Documents\Proposal.doc`. The content of the file is included in the attachment and sent to the recipients. In the `AddAttachment` method, we specify the full path and file name returned in the common dialog's `FileName` property.
CdoFileLink (2)	The `Source` parameter format is identical to `CdoFileData`. However, the content of the file is not included in the attachment. If a recipient does not have access to the file system where the actual document resides, she cannot access the file contents. This means that messages with this type of attachments should only be send to recipients who have access to the file system, for example, recipients on the LAN.
CdoOLE (3)	The `Source` parameter format is identical to `CdoFileData` except that the file must be a valid OLE DocFile. Its content is included in the attachment and sent to the recipient.
CdoEmbeddedMessage (4)	The attachment is itself a message. The `Source` parameter specifies the ID of the message. The whole message is included in the attachment and sent to the recipients.

Note, when you specify the type of the new attachment is `CdoOLE`, the source must be a valid OLE docfile, not just an OLE file. An OLE docfile is a file created using the OLE `IStorage` and `IStream` interface. Microsoft Word documents and Excel spreadsheets are two examples of OLE docfiles, while bitmaps are an OLE file but not an OLE docfile. Generally, the `CdoFileData` type works with all types of attachment files.

The Delete Method

The `Delete` method removes all `Attachment` objects from the collection. The deletion is not committed until the `Update` or the `Send` method of the message is called. You can cancel the deletion by not calling any of those two methods.

The Attachment Object

An `Attachment` object represents one attachment in the message. It can either be a file, a message, or a link to a file. The content of the attached files may be included in the `Attachment` objects, or only links to those files may be included.

ATTACHMENT	
Properties	**Type**
Application	String
Class	Long
Fields	Fields
Index	Long
MAPIObject	IUnknown
Name	String
Parent	Attachments
Position	Long
Session	Session
Source	Variant
Type	Long
Methods	
Delete	
IsSameAs	
ReadFromFile	
WriteToFile	

The Index Property

The `Index` property returns the index of the current `Attachment` object in the parent `Attachments` collection.

The MAPIOBJECT Property

The `MAPIOBJECT` property returns an `IUNKNOWN` pointer to the current `Attachment` object. This is accessible to C++ applications, but not Visual Basic applications since Visual Basic does not support the IUNKNOWN pointer.

The Name, Position, Type, and Source Properties

These four properties have the same meaning as the four parameters in the `Attachments` collection's `Add` method.

The Delete Method

The `Delete` method removes the current attachment from the parent message's `Attachments` collection.

```
Call objAttachment.Delete
```

You should normally release all references to the current `Attachment` object before calling its `Delete` method.

This method immediately updates the parent `Attachments` collection. All remaining `Attachment` objects are re-indexed and the collection's `Count` property is updated.

The IsSameAs Method

```
objAttachment.IsSameAs(objAttachment2)
```

The `IsSameAs` method returns `True` if `objAttachment` object and `objAttachment2` refer to the same physical `Attachment` object in the Exchange Server.

The ReadFromFile Method

The `ReadFromFile` method reads a file and replaces the content of the attachment with the content of the file.

```
Call objAttachment.ReadFromFile(FileName)
```

This method is only valid if the attachment type is either `CdoDataFile` or `CdoOLE`. The `FileName` parameter must be the full path and name of a file. For example,

```
C:\CDOApps\Data\Authors.txt
```

The WriteToFile Method

The `WriteToFile` method saves the attachment to a file specified by the `FileName` parameter.

```
Call objAttachment.WriteToFile(FileName)
```

Like `ReadFromFile`, this method is only valid if the attachment type is either `CdoDataFile` or `CdoOLE`. It overwrites the content of the file with the attachment content. Again, the `FileName` parameter should contain the full path and name of the destination file. Please note that CDO does not warn if the file already exists, so you might need to display a warning yourself to ask the user to confirm it.

The CDO Sample Application

In this chapter, we will add the ability to display and sort messages to the CDO Sample project. The main form, `FMain`, will display messages in a selected folder in a ListView control. We will extend the capability of the Cut, Copy, and Paste buttons on the toolbar to copy and move messages.

Because different types of messages have different properties, we will display the most important properties of each types of messages. For instance, we might want to display the sender, message subject, and received time for messages in the inbox and display start time, end time, and appointment subject for appointment items in the Calendar folder. I will introduce a technique that allows us to display different types of messages polymorphically using the Visual Basic `Interface` feature. As you will see later, this technique makes it easy to display and sort messages. The figure opposite shows a sample screenshot of `FMain`.

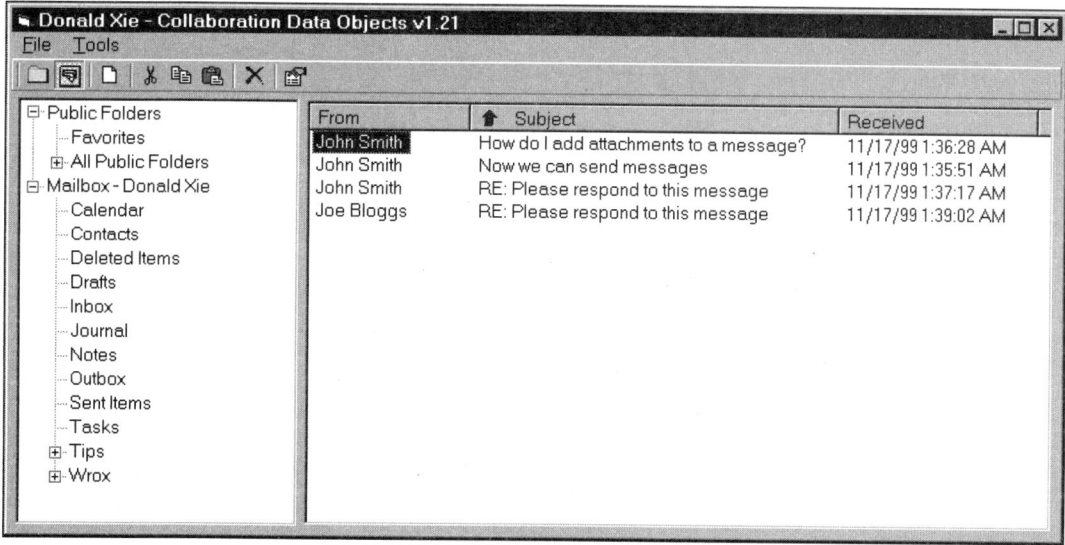

We will also create a new message form that provides our users with the ability to create new messages. It will also be used to view, reply and forward existing messages. The following figure shows the message form displaying a message.

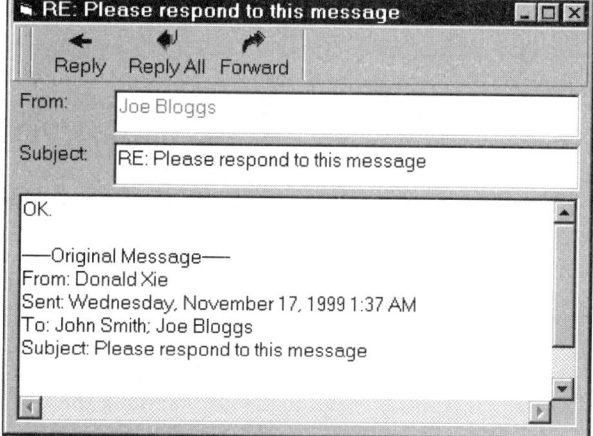

First, let's add a ListView control to the main form, FMain. When a user selects a folder in the folder tree, we will display a selected set of properties of messages in the selected folder in this control.

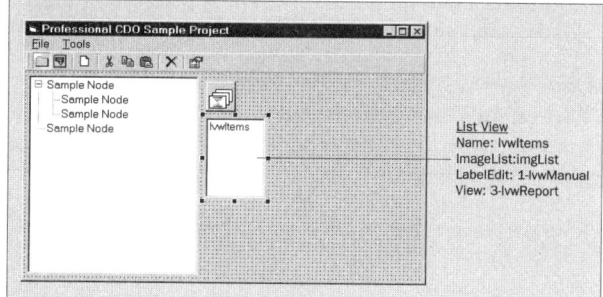

Note that the control is not full-size here. We will size it properly in code so when users resize the form, this control is resized properly.

Next, add the following code to the `Form_Resize` procedure so that the list view control is resized properly.

```
Private Sub Form_Resize()
    On Error Resume Next

    With tvwFolders
        .Move gclngEdge, Toolbar.Height + gclngEdge
        .Height = ScaleHeight - tvwFolders.Top - gclngEdge
    End With

    With lvwItems
        .Move tvwFolders.Left + tvwFolders.Width + gclngEdge, tvwFolders.Top
        .Width = ScaleWidth - .Left - gclngEdge
        .Height = tvwFolders.Height
    End With
End Sub
```

There is a user interface design issue. Since different folders can contain different types of items, we will want to display different properties depending on the type of items in the folder. For instance, we might want to display the sender, message subject, and received time for messages in the inbox and display start time, end time, and appointment subject for appointment items in the Calendar folder.

Displaying Messages Polymorphically

One solution is to check the folder type and display the desired items. This means that we will need to use a `Select Case` block whenever we need to display the items. To make matters worse, we are going to allow the user to click on `lvwItems`' column headers to sort the items. Every time we want to redisplay a folder, we would have to check which property the current message collection should be sorted on.

A better solution is to display the items polymorphically. We will define a set of Visual Basic classes. Each class will be responsible for handling the display of one type of item. For instance, we will define a `CMessageFolder` class and a `CCalendarFolder` to display e-mail messages and appointments, respectively. These classes implement an interface that defines a set of methods to show and sort messages. When the user selects a folder, we will create an instance of its corresponding class to display the items in the folder.

It might sound complex on paper, but you will find it actually quite easy to implement and use. More importantly, if you ever decide to change the display requirements of one type of folders, you only need to change one class.

To keep our application simple, we will only create three concrete classes to handle e-mail messages, appointment items, and messages in the Outlook Contacts folder. As described in the last chapter, we can access address entries in the Outlook Contacts folder as messages. Figure 4.2 illustrates the class relationship.

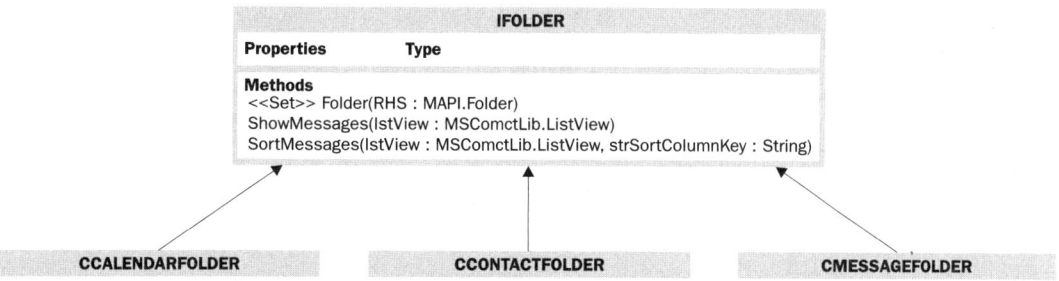

As mentioned in Chapter 1, a line with a triangle represents a generalization/specialization relationship. In programming languages such as C++ that support inheritance, this relationship is usually implemented as a pair of base and derived classes. For instance, the CCalendarFolder derives from the base class IFolder.

Since Visual Basic does not support inheritance, we need to use its Implements feature to implement this relationship. You will see how we achieve this in our sample project in a moment.

From now on, I will refer IFolder as the **Interface Class** as it defines the interface that must be implemented by the CCalendarFolder, CContactFolder, and CMessageFolder classes. The latter three classes are referred as **Concrete Classes** because they actually perform the operations to show and sort messages. Their instances are consequently said to be concrete objects.

Defining the Interface Class

Without further ado, let us add a class module to the project and name it IFolder. This is our interface class. It has two public methods and one write-only property.

```
Option Explicit

Public Property Set Folder(RHS As MAPI.Folder)
End Property

Public Sub ShowMessages(lstView As MSComctlLib.ListView)
End Sub

Public Sub SortMessages(lstView As MSComctlLib.ListView, _
            strSortColumnKey As String)
End Sub
```

The Property Set Folder procedure assigns a CDO Folder object to a concrete object so that the concrete object will have a reference to the folder it will need to manage. Its parameter RHS stands for Right Hand Side and simply represents the right operand of the Set statement:

```
Set obj.Folder = objFolder ' RHS = objFolder
```

The client object can call the `ShowMessages` method of a concrete object to actually display the items in the folder to the ListView control passed in as an argument. The `SortMessages` method also passes the ListView control and the column to be sorted.

Note that this implementation dictates that our utility classes can only be used to display items in a ListView. While there are techniques to relax such restrictions so that they can display items in any controls, they have nothing to do with CDO so I will not go into detail.

The `SortMessages` accepts a string that specifies on which column the items in the folder should be sorted. This is because the client objects such as `FMain` only have access to the ListView, not to the actual display methods. When a user clicks on a column header to sort this column, the main form only knows which column is clicked. It does not know which property the column represents. As long as it passes the clicked column, the utility class can figure out which property the items should be sorted on.

This will become clearer when we look at the implementation of the concrete utility classes. First on the list is the `CMessageFolder` class.

Displaying Message Objects

The `CMessageFolder` class is responsible for displaying the CDO `Message` objects. Add a new class module, `CMessageFolder`, to the project and add the following declarations to its `General` section.

```
Implements IFolder

Private Const mcstrPartyKey As String = "Party"
Private Const mcstrPartyTextFrom As String = "From"
Private Const mcstrSubjectKey As String = "Subject"
Private Const mcstrSubjectText As String = "Subject"
Private Const mcstrTimeKey As String = "Time"
Private Const mcstrTimeTextReceived As String = "Received"

Private mobjFolder As MAPI.Folder
Private mcolProps As Collection
```

It implements the `IFolder` interface, that is, it will implement all methods and properties declared in the `IFolder` interface class.

> *If you're not familiar with implementing interfaces and suchlike, try VB COM, ISBN 1861002130, also by Wrox Press.*

We can use it to display the sender, message subject, and time received properties of messages. While this is fine for a folder (such as the Inbox) that stores received messages, it is not quite right for the Sent Items folder. Displaying the sender of messages in the Sent Items folder is pretty much useless since the sender is always the user of the current mailbox. The sent items do not have a received time either since the received time is only set by the recipient's message store.

We could solve this by checking whether the working folder is the Sent Items folder and then display different properties such as `TimeSent`, `Recipient`, and so on. This is the reason why I use the term Party in this class because we could display the message recipients for the Sent Items folder and the message sender for other folders. We could also design a new concrete class `CSentItemFolder` to handle the Sent Items folder. In any case, we will not worry about this little drawback here in order to keep our project simple.

The `mobjFolder` object holds a reference to the current folder to be displayed. It can be set in the `Property Set` procedure of our new class. Note that the declaration of this property is changed from:

```
Public Property Set Folder(RHS As MAPI.Folder)
```

in the `IFolder` class to:

```
Private Property Set IFolder_Folder(RHS As MAPI.Folder)
```

in our concrete class. This is a Visual Basic requirement for implementing interfaces. The concrete class must implement methods declared in the interface class as such. You will see that we will also follow this requirement for the `ShowMessages` and `SortMessages` methods. Add this `Property Set` procedure to the class:

```
Private Property Set IFolder_Folder(RHS As MAPI.Folder)
    Set mobjFolder = RHS
End Property
```

`mcolProps` is a collection that stores the list view `lvwItems` column header keys and the MAPI property tags representing the properties to be displayed on each column. When we sort a CDO `Messages` collection, we must pass a MAPI property tag to its `Sort` method. When the user clicks on one of the column headers, we will sort the messages on the property in that column.

When we create a `CMessageFolder` object, we initialize the `mcolProps` collection. When the object is destroyed, we also delete this collection.

```
Private Sub Class_Initialize()
    On Error GoTo ErrHandler

    Set mcolProps = New Collection
    mcolProps.Add CdoPR_SENT_REPRESENTING_NAME, mcstrPartyKey
    mcolProps.Add CdoPR_NORMALIZED_SUBJECT, mcstrSubjectKey
    mcolProps.Add CdoPR_MESSAGE_DELIVERY_TIME, mcstrTimeKey

ExitFunc:
    Exit Sub

ErrHandler:
    Err.Raise FormatHex(Err.Number), Err.Source, Err.Description
    Resume ExitFunc
End Sub

Private Sub Class_Terminate()
    On Error Resume Next

    Set mcolProps = Nothing
    Set mobjFolder = Nothing
End Sub
```

The `CdoPR_SENT_REPRESENTING_NAME` property stores the display name of the message sender. The `CdoPR_MESSAGE_DELIVERY_TIME` property stores the time the message is delivered to the recipient's mailbox. This corresponds to the `Message` object's `TimeReceived` property.

A message's subject corresponds to the `CdoPR_SUBJECT` property. CDO does not support sorting on this property. To sort a message collection by subject, we must use the `CdoPR_NORMALIZED_SUBJECT` property. This property stores the message subject without any prefix such as RE: or FW:. This makes sense because sorting messages by their normalized subject means that we will group the replies and forwards with the original message, rather than just in a big group of RE:... messages.

When messages in a folder are displayed in the list view for the first time, it is not sorted. Since we will display different properties of items in different folders depending on their type, we should recreate the column headers to display the property names that are relevant to the items to be displayed. We use the `ShowHeaders` method to display the column headers. Add the following code to the `CMessageFolder` class:

```
Private Sub ShowHeaders(lstView As MSComctlLib.ListView)
    On Error GoTo ErrHandler

    Dim hdrColumn As MSComctlLib.ColumnHeader

    With lstView.ColumnHeaders
        ' Recreate all the column headers
        .Clear
        Set hdrColumn = .Add(Key:=mcstrPartyKey, Text:=mcstrPartyTextFrom)
        hdrColumn.Tag = CdoNone
        Set hdrColumn = .Add(Key:=mcstrSubjectKey, Text:=mcstrSubjectText)
        hdrColumn.Tag = CdoNone
        Set hdrColumn = .Add(Key:=mcstrTimeKey, Text:=mcstrTimeTextReceived)
        hdrColumn.Tag = CdoNone
    End With

ExitFunc:
    Set hdrColumn = Nothing
    Exit Sub

ErrHandler:
    Err.Raise FormatHex(Err.Number), Err.Source, Err.Description
    Resume ExitFunc
End Sub
```

We firstly clear all existing headers and add headers for the three properties to be displayed: sender, subject, and the time received. We assign each new column header a key that will be used later to indicate which column the message will be sorted on. We use the column header's `Tag` property to store the current sort order. Since this is the first time the messages are being displayed, they aren't sorted. We should store `CdoNone` in their `Tag`s. The other constants we will be using are `CdoAscending` and `CdoDescending`. Passing these constants to the `Sort` method of the message collection will sort the messages in ascending and descending order, respectively.

The next step is to display the messages. We will add a new method, `ShowMessages`, to the `CMessageFolder` class to do this.

```
Private Sub ShowMessages(lstView As MSComctlLib.ListView)
    On Error GoTo ErrHandler

    Dim colMessages As MAPI.Messages
    Dim objMessage As MAPI.Message
    Dim itmMessage As MSComctlLib.ListItem

    Set colMessages = mobjFolder.Messages
    With lstView.ListItems
        .Clear

        For Each objMessage In colMessages
            Set itmMessage = .Add(Text:=objMessage.Sender.Name)
            With itmMessage
                .Tag = objMessage.StoreID & gcstrIDDelimiter & objMessage.ID
                .SubItems(1) = objMessage.Subject
                .SubItems(2) = objMessage.TimeReceived
            End With
        Next
    End With

ExitFunc:
    Set colMessages = Nothing
    Set objMessage = Nothing
    Set itmMessage = Nothing
    Exit Sub

ErrHandler:
    Err.Raise FormatHex(Err.Number), Err.Source, Err.Description
    Resume ExitFunc
End Sub
```

It's pretty straightforward. We clear all the rows and then add each message to the list. We store the message ID, and the ID of the information store where the message is stored, in the list item's `Tag` property so we can retrieve the message. Later in this chapter, we will add the ability to display a message when the user selects one from the list.

Since the `CMessageFolder` class implements the `IFolder` interface, we should implement the two methods defined in the `IFolder` interface. The first is the `ShowMessages` method, which is named `IFolder_ShowMessages` in the `CMessageFolder` class.

```
Private Sub IFolder_ShowMessages(lstView As MSComctlLib.IListView)
    On Error GoTo ErrHandler

    ShowHeaders lstView
    ShowMessages lstView

ExitFunc:
    Exit Sub

ErrHandler:
    Err.Raise FormatHex(Err.Number), Err.Source, Err.Description
    Resume ExitFunc
End Sub
```

It just delegates the display task to the ShowHeaders and ShowMessages methods. Even though we don't actually sort the messages at this stage, we must at least implement a bare-bones SortMessages method – Visual Basic will complain if we don't. Now, add this code too:

```
Private Sub IFolder_SortMessages(lstView As MSComctlLib.IListView, _
                    strSortColumnKey As String)
End Sub
```

Since we will be instantiating different concrete message display utility classes including CMessageFolder, CCalendarFolder, and CContactFolder, it's desirable that the client objects (such as FMain) do not have to know how to handle the instantiation. Therefore, we should create a simple class factory that will manage this for us.

The Class Factory

The class factory accepts a CDO Folder object from the client and creates a proper utility object that is suitable for displaying items in the folder. Add a new class CUtilityFactory to the project and add the following code to its General section.

```
Private Const mcstrClassAppointment As String = "IPF.Appointment"
Private Const mcstrClassContact As String = "IPF.Contact"
Private Const mcstrClassNote As String = "IPF.Note"
```

The three constants correspond to the CdoPR_CONTAINER_CLASS property of the CDO Folder object. This property specifies the type of folders. While message type strings start with IPM, folder type strings start with IPF. Depending on this property, we will instantiate different types of utility classes.

This class has only one method, GetUtility, that accepts either a folder or a pair of folder and store IDs, creates and returns a proper utility object to the calling object.

```
Public Function GetUtility(Optional Folder As MAPI.Folder, _
                Optional FolderID As String, _
                Optional StoreID As String) As IFolder
    On Error Resume Next

    Dim objFolderUtility   As IFolder
    Dim strFolderClass     As String
    Dim objCalendarFolder  As MAPI.Folder

    If Folder Is Nothing Then
        Set Folder = gobjSession.GetFolder(FolderID, StoreID)
        If Err <> 0 Then
            ' Cannot get folder, bail out
            Exit Function
        End If
    End If

    strFolderClass = Folder.Fields(CdoPR_CONTAINER_CLASS).Value
```

```
      If Err <> 0 Then
         Err.Clear
         strFolderClass = mcstrClassNote
      End If

      Select Case strFolderClass
         Case mcstrClassAppointment
            Set objCalendarFolder = _
               gobjSession.GetDefaultFolder(CdoDefaultFolderCalendar)
            If Err.Number = 0 Then
               If gobjSession.CompareIDs(objCalendarFolder.ID, Folder.ID) Then
                  Set Folder = objCalendarFolder
                  Set objFolderUtility = New CCalendarFolder
               Else
                  Set objFolderUtility = New CMessageFolder
               End If
            Else
               Err.Clear
               Set objFolderUtility = New CMessageFolder
            End If

            Set objCalendarFolder = Nothing

         Case mcstrClassContact
            Set objFolderUtility = New CContactFolder

         Case mcstrClassNote
            Set objFolderUtility = New CMessageFolder

         Case Else
            Set objFolderUtility = New CMessageFolder
      End Select

      Set objFolderUtility.Folder = Folder
      Set GetUtility = objFolderUtility
      Set objFolderUtility = Nothing
   End Function
```

There are several places where errors may occur. We will handle them inline. If the user does not pass in a folder, we will use the folder and store IDs pair to obtain a folder. If there is an error in getting the folder, we simply exit the function. Note that this could cause problems in the client object since this returns `Nothing`. So it would be very useful to raise an error when this happens. Here, though, we're just going to assume that we will always receive correct parameter values, just to keep it simple.

Once we get the folder, we'll try to read its `CdoPR_CONTAINER_CLASS` property by reading its value from the folder's `Fields` collection (because the `Folder` object does not directly expose this property). The Inbox, as well as some other folders, might not have this property since it can store virtually any type messages such as meeting request and normal e-mail messages. Therefore trying to access this property may fail. While it is possible to manage such exceptions when we actually display the individual messages in the folder, we will just assume that it contains message items for now. So if this fails, we set the message class to normal messages and plan to instantiate a `CMessageFolder` object later.

Once we have found out the folder type, we will instantiate the appropriate utility class to handle the folder. If the folder contains appointment items, we see whether it is the default calendar folder. To do this, we need to get the default calendar folder using the `Session` object's `GetDefaultFolder` method. Since this may fail if we log on using a profile that is shared with Outlook, we will catch the error here. If it is successful, we see whether the folder that's passed in is the same as the default calendar folder. One way of testing this is to use the `Session` object's `CompareIDs` method. Another method is to use the `Folder` object's `IsSameAs` method. For instance,

```
If Folder.IsSameAs(objCalendarFolder) Then
```

If both objects are referring to the same folder, we set `Folder` to the default calendar folder so that we can retrieve `AppointmentItem` objects from it. We also create a `CCalendarFolder` object to display it. Otherwise, we will have to settle for only retrieving `Message` objects from it. In this case, we will create a `CMessageFolder` object.

If the `GetDefaultFolder` call fails, we will also have to use a `CMessageFolder` object to read the `Message` objects from this folder.

The rest of the code is simple, we simply create a `CMessageFolder` object for all other folders unless it is a folder that stores contact information.

Changing the Main Form

Now we have a message-displaying utility class, `CMessageFolder`, capable of displaying messages in a folder. We also have a class factory that knows how to instantiate the appropriate utility class according to the type of folder it receives. We need to modify the main form, `FMain`, to use this class. First, add a form-level object, `mobjFolder`, that will hold a reference to an instance of the class.

```
' The display utility object for the current folder
Private mobjFolderUtility As IFolder
```

We declare it as an instance of our interface class, `IFolder`. This allows us to polymorphically display and sort different types of messages. When the user clicks a node in the folder tree, we will display the messages in the selected folder. Add a new method, `ShowContents`, to `FMain` to do this.

```
Private Sub ShowContents(Optional Folder As MAPI.Folder, _
                Optional Node As MSComctlLib.Node)
    Dim objFactory As CUtilityFactory
    Dim strStoreID As String
    Dim strFolderID As String

    Set objFactory = New CUtilityFactory

    If Folder Is Nothing Then
        If GetFolderNodeType(strStoreID, strFolderID) = fntFolder Then
            Set mobjFolderUtility = _
                objFactory.GetUtility(StoreID:=strStoreID, FolderID:=strFolderID)
        End If
    Else
        Set mobjFolderUtility = objFactory.GetUtility(Folder:=Folder)
```

```
        End If

        If Not mobjFolderUtility Is Nothing Then
            mobjFolderUtility.ShowMessages lvwItems
        End If

        Set objFactory = Nothing
End Sub
```

This method accepts either an optional CDO `Folder` object or a `Node` object in the folders tree. We first create a class factory object. If a `Folder` object is passed in, we can create a utility object by simply calling the factory object's `GetUtility` method and passing it the `Folder` object. Otherwise, we check to ensure that the currently selected node represents a folder. If `Node` represents a folder, we call the factory object's `GetUtility` method and pass it the `folder` and `storeID` pair.

Once we get a utility object, we call its `ShowMessages` method to display the folder contents. Note that the `ShowContents` method does not have any knowledge on the type of the folder and how the contents should be displayed. This level of isolation is perfect in such situations because it will be very easy to create new utility classes. We only need code the new utility class and change the class factory; the client object, `FMain` in this case, need not be touched at all.

The last step is to link up the folder tree's `NodeClick` event handler to the `ShowContents` method on the main form, `FMain`.

```
Private Sub tvwFolders_NodeClick(ByVal Node As MSComctlLib.Node)
    On Error GoTo ErrHandler

    Call ShowContents

ExitFunc:
    Exit Sub

ErrHandler:
    Call ReportError(Err)
    Resume ExitFunc
End Sub
```

There is not much to say about this code snippet. If you are itching to try out the program now, you can either comment out the instantiation of other utility classes in the class factory or create two skeleton utility classes, `CCalendarFolder` and `CContactFolder`. If you choose the latter approach, your skeleton utility classes will look like the following:

```
Option Explicit

Implements IFolder

Private Property Set IFolder_Folder(RHS As MAPI.Folder)
End Property

Private Sub IFolder_ShowMessages(lstView As MSComctlLib.IListView)
End Sub

Private Sub IFolder_SortMessages(lstView As MSComctlLib.IListView, _
                strSortColumnKey As String)
End Sub
```

They won't actually do anything, but they have implemented the `IFolder` interface required by the class factory. We will implement the `CContactFolder` class later in this chapter and the `CCalendarFolder` class in the next chapter. If you run the program now, you can see the results as expected.

Take a break. When we come back, we will implement the functions that will sort the messages.

Intermission

Anyone for ice cream?

Sorting Messages

Welcome back. Our `CMessageFolder` class is now capable of displaying the messages in a folder. The next thing we'll need to do is add the ability for the class to display the messages in a certain order. It will need to sort the messages and then display them in the sorted order.

While it is easy to ask the user on what property the messages should be sorted, and in what order, it is more user-friendly if we could add a bit of intelligence to our display class. We will allow the user to click on the header of a column in the message list. Our class will be smart enough to find out what the current sort order is on the property that is displayed in the selected column. If the message list is already sorted on this property, it will then reverse the sort order and redisplay the list. This is similar to the way Outlook displays messages.

When the messages are sorted, we should let our user know the sort order using some kind of visual clue. One way of doing this is to use the column header's `Icon` property to show an arrow. An up arrow means the messages are sorted in ascending order and a down arrow indicates descending order. To be able to display the icon, we need to bind the message list view to an image list control that contains to arrow images. Since we already added the two arrow icons to the image list, `imgList`, in `FMain`, in Chapter 2, we can just bind the list view control to `imgList`.

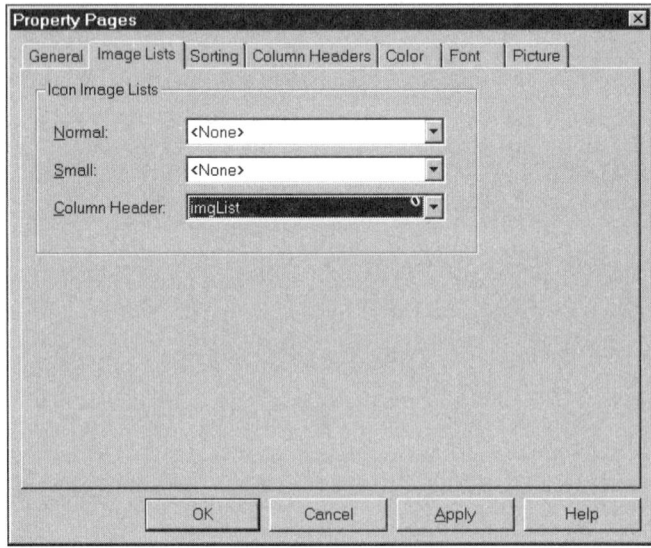

After this is done, we can assign an arrow to a column header at run time. Since the three CDO sort order constants, CdoNone (0), CdoAscending (1), and CdoDescending (2), have continuous values, we can store the arrow image keys in an array to simplify the process of assigning the images. Because all our utility classes will be using those images, put the array in the common module, MCommon.

```
Public garrSortOrder(CdoNone To CdoDescending) As String

' Initialize the sort order array with the key of images to be displayed
Public Function InitSortOrderArray()
    garrSortOrder(CdoNone) = ""
    garrSortOrder(CdoAscending) = "imgArrowUp"
    garrSortOrder(CdoDescending) = "imgArrowDown"
End Function
```

The Sub Main procedure in MStartUp calls the InitSortOrderArray to initialize garrSortOrder so that it is ready for use.

```
Private Sub Main()
    Dim frmLogon As FLogon

    Set frmLogon = New FLogon
    frmLogon.Show vbModal
    Set frmLogon = Nothing

    If Not gobjSession Is Nothing Then
        Call InitSortOrderArray
        ShowMainForm
    End If
End Sub
```

To start the sorting process, we will need to know which column is selected. The IFolder interface provides the client object with a SortMessages method that, in addition to accepting the display list view object, accepts the key of the column header that is clicked. We can pass this to the ShowHeaders method and let it figure out the property and current sort order. It will return the property and the new sort order. We can then pass them to the ShowMessages method to sort and redisplay the messages.

First up, modify the ShowHeaders method in the CMessageFolder class as shown here.

```
Private Sub ShowHeaders(lstView As MSComctlLib.ListView, _
            Optional SortColumnKey As String = "", _
            Optional ByRef SortOrder As Long = MAPI.CdoNone, _
            Optional ByRef SortPropTag As Long = 0)
    On Error GoTo ErrHandler

    Dim blnShouldSort As Boolean
    Dim hdrColumn As MSComctlLib.ColumnHeader
    Dim lngCurrentSortOrder As Long

    blnShouldSort = (Len(SortColumnKey) > 0)
```

```
    With lstView.ColumnHeaders
      If blnShouldSort Then
        ' Get the property to be sorted
        SortPropTag = mcolProps(SortColumnKey)

        ' Retrieve the current sort order
        lngCurrentSortOrder = .Item(SortColumnKey).Tag

        ' Sort in ascending order by default
        If lngCurrentSortOrder = CdoAscending Then
           SortOrder = CdoDescending
        Else
        ' CdoNone or CdoDescending
           SortOrder = CdoAscending
        End If
      End If

      ' Recreate all the column headers
      .Clear
   ...
```

It now accepts the column header key as a parameter and two more parameters, SortOrder and SortPropTag, by reference. The latter two are output parameters that will be used to return the property tag and order for sorting. I made all three optional so that the existing code will continue to work.

If the column header key is not passed, we will not sort the messages. In this case, we will return 0 as the property to be sorted and CdoNone as the sort order to indicate that we should not sort the messages.

If a column key is passed, we first retrieve the property associated with that column. We do this by looking up the mcolProps collection using the column key as the key to the collection item. Since we use the ColumnHeader's Tag property to store the current sort order, we can get the current sort order by checking this property of the selected column header. If the current sort order is already ascending, we will set the new sort order to descending. Otherwise we set it to ascending.

The rest of this method is unchanged. You might be wondering why we do not save the correct sort order to the header's Tag property and display the appropriate icon. The reason is that sorting messages is not always successful. CDO does not support sorting messages by some of the MAPI properties. Since we do not know whether or not the messages can be sorted on the selected property in this method, we will have to leave it to the ShowMessages method after the sorting is done.

We are also going to change the ShowMessages method in the CMessageFolder class quite significantly.

```
    Private Sub ShowMessages(lstView As MSComctlLib.ListView, _
              Optional ByVal SortOrder As Long = MAPI.CdoNone, _
              Optional ByVal SortPropTag As Long)
      On Error GoTo ErrHandler

      Dim colMessages As MAPI.Messages
      Dim objMessage As MAPI.Message
      Dim itmMessage As MSComctlLib.ListItem
      Dim hdrColumn  As MSComctlLib.ColumnHeader
```

```
Set colMessages = mobjFolder.Messages

If SortOrder <> CdoNone Then
    ' Sort the message and handle the possible error inline
    On Error Resume Next
    colMessages.Sort SortOrder, SortPropTag

    ' The error is likely to be CdoE_TOO_COMPLEX, but
    ' we will catch all errors here
    If Err.Number = 0 Then
    ' Sort OK - display the sort order on the column header
        For Each hdrColumn In lstView.ColumnHeaders
            With hdrColumn
                If mcolProps(.Key) = SortPropTag Then
                    .Tag = SortOrder
                    .Icon = garrSortOrder(SortOrder)
                    Exit For
                End If
            End With
        Next
    Else
        ' Sort failed, we should still display the messages unsorted
        Err.Clear

        ' The message collection may no longer be valid, so we need
        ' to reset the reference
        Set colMessages = mobjFolder.Messages
    End If

    ' Reset the error handler
    On Error GoTo ErrHandler
End If

' Display the messages
With lstView.ListItems
    .Clear

'    For Each objMessage In colMessages
'        Set itmMessage = .Add(Text:=objMessage.Sender.Name)
'        With itmMessage
'            .Tag = objMessage.StoreID & gcstrIDDelimiter & objMessage.ID
'            .SubItems(1) = objMessage.Subject
'            .SubItems(2) = objMessage.TimeReceived
'        End With
'    Next

    Set objMessage = colMessages.GetFirst
    Do While Not objMessage Is Nothing
        Set itmMessage = .Add(Text:=objMessage.Sender.Name)
        With itmMessage
            .Tag = objMessage.StoreID & gcstrIDDelimiter & objMessage.ID
            .SubItems(1) = objMessage.Subject
            .SubItems(2) = objMessage.TimeReceived
        End With

        Set objMessage = colMessages.GetNext
    Loop
End With
```

```
ExitFunc:
    Set colMessages = Nothing
    Set objMessage = Nothing
    Set itmMessage = Nothing
    Set hdrColumn = Nothing
    Exit Sub

ErrHandler:
    Err.Raise FormatHex(Err.Number), Err.Source, Err.Description
    Resume ExitFunc
End Sub
```

If we should sort the messages, we call the `Messages` collection's `Sort` method. If CDO does not support sorting on the given property, this method will raise a `CdoE_TOO_COMPLEX` (&H80040117) error. If we do not get an error, we can save the new sort order to the column header's `Tag` property and display the appropriate icon on the header. If the `Sort` method fails, the message collection object may no longer be valid. We must reset it to the folder's `Messages` collection so that we can still display them later.

Previously, we used the Visual Basic `For Each` statement to enumerate the messages in the collection. Unfortunately this will not display the message in the sorted order, so we've commented out that section. We will need to use the message collection's `GetFirst` and `GetNext` methods. Do not use the `For … Next` statement:

```
For lngIndex = 1 To colMessages.Count
Next
```

Remember that the CDO `Messages` collection is a large collection and its `Count` property does not always return the correct number of messages in the collection.

The last change to the `CMessageFolder` class is to add code to the `IFolder_SortMessages` method.

```
Private Sub IFolder_SortMessages(lstView As MSComctlLib.IListview, _
                    strSortColumnKey As String)
    On Error GoTo ErrHandler

    Dim lngSortOrder   As Long
    Dim lngSortPropTag As Long

    ShowHeaders lstView, strSortColumnKey, lngSortOrder, lngSortPropTag
    ShowMessages lstView, lngSortOrder, lngSortPropTag

ExitFunc:
    Exit Sub

ErrHandler:
    Err.Raise FormatHex(Err.Number), Err.Source, Err.Description
    Resume ExitFunc
End Sub
```

We call the `ShowHeaders` method to work out the sort property and order. The `ShowMessages` method takes care of the sorting and displaying of messages for us.

We only need to make one change to the main form. We need to program the message list view object's `ColumnClick` event handler to invoke the utility object. Add this to `FMain`:

```
Private Sub lvwItems_ColumnClick(ByVal ColumnHeader As MSComctlLib.ColumnHeader)
    Call mobjFolderUtility.SortMessages(lvwItems, ColumnHeader.Key)
End Sub
```

We can now try out the sample application to display and sort messages. If you implemented the skeleton `CContactFolder` and `CCalendarFolder` classes earlier, no messages are displayed in the Contacts and Calendar folders. However, if you simply commented out the corresponding case statements in the `CUtilityFactory` class, all contact and appointment items will be shown as messages. The following screen shot shows messages in the Inbox sorted in ascending order by their subject:

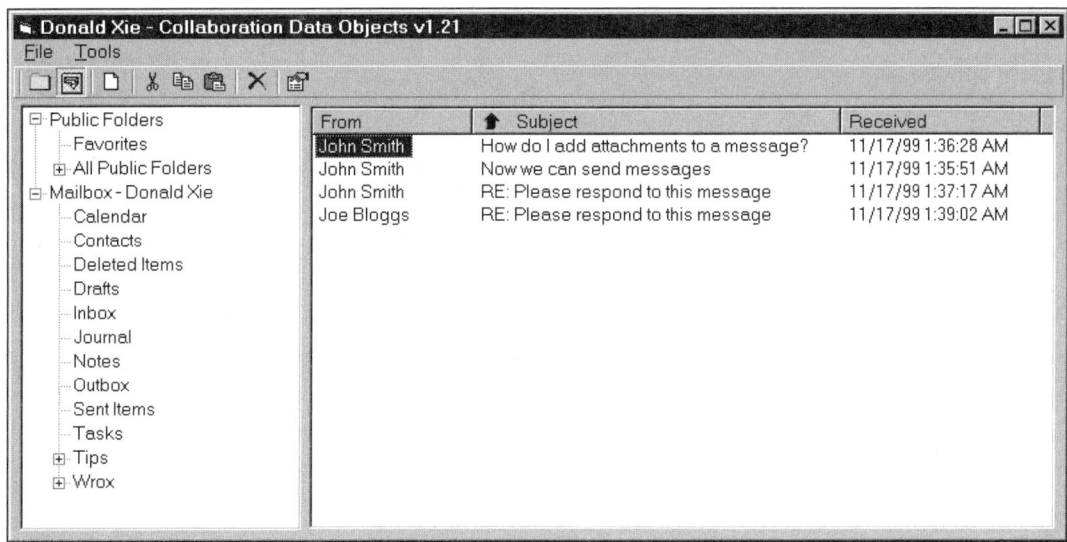

Displaying and Sorting Contacts

We have done one of the three utility classes. In this section, we will implement the `CContactFolder` class.

The `CContactFolder` class is almost a carbon copy of the `CMessageFolder` class. The only difference is that the `CContactFolder` class will display different properties for contacts. While the default contact folder is only available when we use a profile shared by Microsoft Outlook, we can create public and private folders of type `IPF.Contact` using CDO alone. We can use this class to display messages in all available `IPF.Contact` folders.

> *CDO has problems dealing with distribution lists in Outlook Contacts folders. If you have Contacts folders rather than a PAB, you may have to handle the errors it throws up. For simplicity, we haven't done so here.*

Even though the messages in the contact folders are really address entries, CDO returns `Message` objects containing all the properties in their `Fields` collection from those folders. As we saw in Chapter 4, we can access the default contact folder and retrieve `AddressEntry` objects through the `Session` object's `AddressLists` collection. Unfortunately, we cannot access other contact folders in the same fashion.

The CDO `Message` object directly exposes properties common to mail messages. Almost all common contact information such as name and company must be accessed through the `Fields` collection.

Since the `CContactFolder` class is virtually the same as the `CMessageFolder` class, I will not repeat the description here. If you have not done so already with the dummy classes, add a new class module named `CContactFolder` to the CDO Sample project and copy and paste the code from `CMessageFolder` into it. Then, you'll have to make a few changes to it, first in the General Declarations:

```
Option Explicit

Implements IFolder

Private Const mcstrCompanyKey As String = "Company"
Private Const mcstrCompanyText As String = "Company"
Private Const mcstrNameKey As String = "Name"
Private Const mcstrNameText As String = "Name"

Private mobjFolder As MAPI.Folder
Private mcolProps   As Collection

Private Sub Class_Initialize()
    On Error GoTo ErrHandler

    Set mcolProps = New Collection
    mcolProps.Add CdoPR_COMPANY_NAME, mcstrCompanyKey
    mcolProps.Add CdoPR_DISPLAY_NAME, mcstrNameKey

ExitFunc:
    Exit Sub

ErrHandler:
    Err.Raise FormatHex(Err.Number), Err.Source, Err.Description
    Resume ExitFunc
End Sub
```

...and then in the `ShowHeaders` method:

```
Private Sub ShowHeaders(lstView As MSComctlLib.ListView, _
            Optional strSortColumnKey As String = "", _
            Optional SortOrder As Long = MAPI.CdoNone, _
            Optional SortPropTag As Long = 0)
    On Error GoTo ErrHandler

    Dim blnShouldSort As Boolean
    Dim hdrColumn As MSComctlLib.ColumnHeader
    Dim lngCurrentSortOrder As Long
```

```
            blnShouldSort = (Len(strSortColumnKey) > 0)

        With lstView.ColumnHeaders
          If blnShouldSort Then
             ' Get the property to be sorted
             SortPropTag = mcolProps(strSortColumnKey)

             ' Retrieve the current sort order
             lngCurrentSortOrder = .Item(strSortColumnKey).Tag

             ' Sort in ascending order by default
             If lngCurrentSortOrder = CdoAscending Then
               SortOrder = CdoDescending
             Else
                ' CdoNone or CdoDescending
               SortOrder = CdoAscending
             End If
          End If

          ' Recreate all the column headers
          .Clear
          Set hdrColumn = .Add(Key:=mcstrNameKey, Text:=mcstrNameText)
          hdrColumn.Tag = CdoNone
          Set hdrColumn = .Add(Key:=mcstrCompanyKey, Text:=mcstrCompanyText)
          hdrColumn.Tag = CdoNone
        End With

    ExitFunc:
        Set hdrColumn = Nothing
        Exit Sub

    ErrHandler:
        Err.Raise FormatHex(Err.Number), Err.Source, Err.Description
        Resume ExitFunc
    End Sub
```

As you can see here, instead of displaying the message sender, subject, and received time, we display the contact's display name and company name. You might be wondering why we're not displaying one of the most important contact properties, the e-mail address. The reason is that CDO does not provide an easy way to figure out where the e-mail address is stored. For instance, the e-mail address of a contact in the Outlook Contacts folder is stored with ID &H8049001E in its Fields collection. That differs from where the e-mail address of a contact in a public folder is kept; here, the ID is &H8025001E.

You can test this by using the **Property** button on the toolbar to display properties for a selected message. First, add two new methods, GetMessage and ShowMessageProperties, to the main form, FMain:

```
    Private Sub ShowMessageProperties()
        Dim objMessage As MAPI.Message
        Dim frmFields As FFields

        Set objMessage = GetMessage()
```

```
    Set frmFields = New FFields
    Call frmFields.ShowForm(objMessage)

    Set frmFields = Nothing
    Set objMessage = Nothing
End Sub

Private Function GetMessage() As MAPI.Message
    Dim itmMessage As MSComctlLib.ListItem
    Dim arrIDs() As String

    Set itmMessage = lvwItems.SelectedItem
    If Not itmMessage Is Nothing Then
      arrIDs = Split(itmMessage.Tag, gcstrIDDelimiter)
      Set GetMessage = gobjSession.GetMessage(arrIDs(1), arrIDs(0))
    End If

    Set itmMessage = Nothing
End Function
```

The `GetMessage` function parses the selected item's `Tag` property to retrieve the message ID and information store ID. It then calls the `Session` object's `GetMessage` method to retrieve the corresponding message and returns it to the calling object.

The `ShowMessageProperties` function uses the `GetMessage` function to retrieve the message and instantiates the `FField` form to display message properties.

We will also need to call this method when the property button is pressed:

```
Private Sub Toolbar_ButtonClick(ByVal Button As MSComctlLib.Button)
   On Error GoTo ErrHandler
...

      Case mcstrButtonKeyProperty
         If WorkingObject = wotFolder Then
            Call ShowFolderProperties
         Else
            Call ShowMessageProperties
         End If

      Case Else
...
```

That is it about the utility classes for the day. We will leave the `CCalendarFolder` class to the next chapter when we explore the CDO `AppointmentItem` object. Let's turn our attention to managing individual messages.

Creating, Reading and Responding to Messages

Messages are a core component of a collaboration application. The CDO library provides a rich set of message manipulation operations. In the previous sections, we have gone through the process of getting the messages. The next step is to add enough functionality to our sample application to actually create and process the messages.

In this section, we will look at how we can perform the following tasks using CDO:

❑ Create and send new e-mail messages

❑ Create new public folder postings

❑ Reply to and forward e-mail messages

❑ Reply to public folder postings

❑ Add and retrieve attachments to and from messages

❑ Copy messages

❑ Move messages

❑ Delete messages

The Message Form

Let us start by adding yet another form to the project. This form will be used to display existing messages and create new messages.

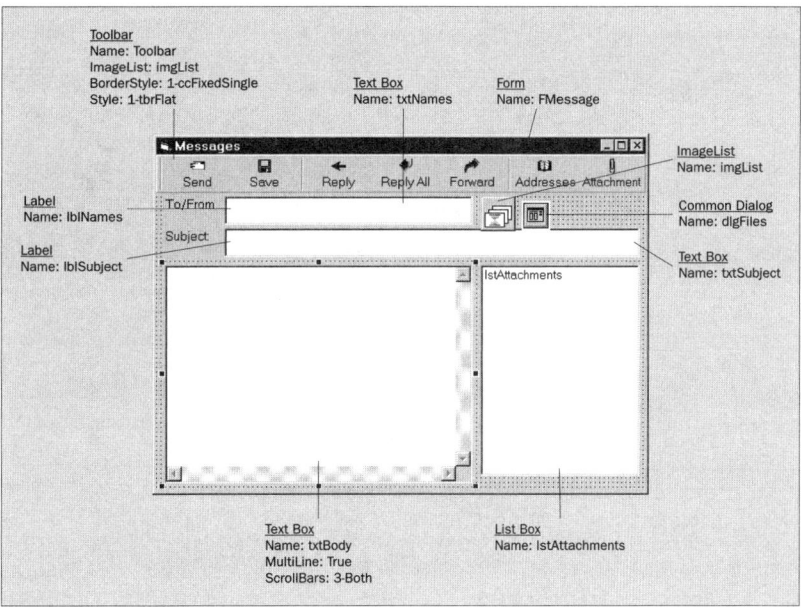

As usual, the `ImageList` control contains images to be used for toolbar buttons. To keep it simple, we will just use the bitmaps and icons shipped with Visual Basic. The file paths listed in the following table are subfolders of the `Common\Graphics` folder in Visual Studio.

Index	File Path	Key
1	Icons\Mail\mail03.ico	imgSend
2	Bitmaps\TlBr_W95\Save.bmp	imgSave
3	Icons\Arrows\arw08lt.ico	imgReply
4	Icons\Arrows\arw09lt.ico	imgReplyAll
5	Icons\Arrows\arw09rt.ico	imgForward
6	Icons\Writing\book02.ico	imgAddrBook
7	Icons\Office\clip01.ico	imgAttach

The price we pay for using images shipped with Visual Basic is that some of them aren't particularly intuitive in representing the function of the toolbar buttons. Therefore we will specify the `Caption` property of each toolbar button, as shown in the following screenshot:

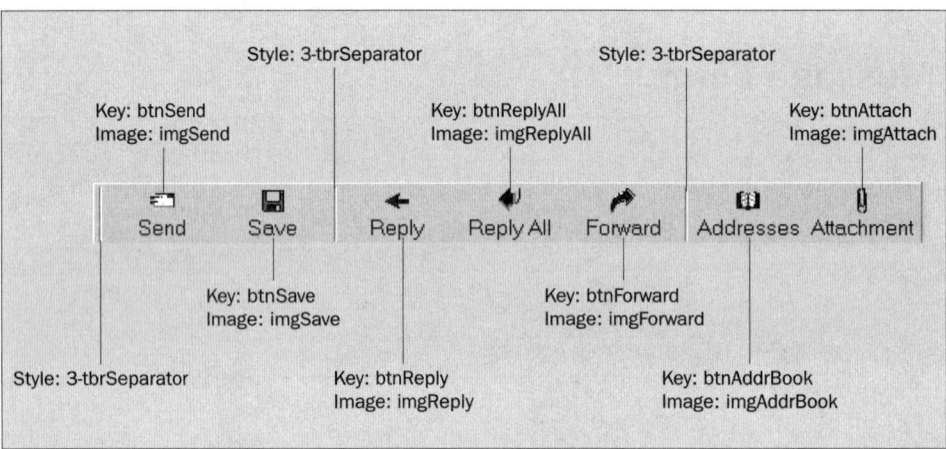

We will also need to define the constants to be used in this form:

```
Option Explicit

Private Const mcstrButtonKeySend As String = "btnSend"
Private Const mcstrButtonKeySave As String = "btnSave"
Private Const mcstrButtonKeyReply As String = "btnReply"
Private Const mcstrButtonKeyReplyAll As String = "btnReplyAll"
Private Const mcstrButtonKeyForward As String = "btnForward"
Private Const mcstrButtonKeyAddrBook As String = "btnAddrBook"
Private Const mcstrButtonKeyAttach As String = "btnAttach"
Private Const mcstrButtonTextAddAtt As String = "Add Attachment"
Private Const mcstrButtonTextSaveAtt As String = "Save Attachment"
```

```
Private Const mcstrTo As String = "To:"
Private Const mcstrFrom As String = "From:"

Private mobjFolder As MAPI.Folder
Private mobjMessage As MAPI.Message
Private mblnIsEmail As Boolean
```

Depending on whether or not we are creating a new message or displaying an existing message, the **Names** text box will display the recipient names or sender name. Consequently, we display either "To" or "From" as the caption accordingly. We will also use this form for posting messages to public folders.

The `mobjFolder` constant stores the folder where the message is stored or will be posted. The `mobjMessage` constant stores a reference to the current message. The `mblnIsEmail` indicates whether the message is an e-mail message or a posting since sending e-mail and posting to public folders require different processing procedures. We only display and accept a subset of message attributes here but it should be very easy to extend this form to provide a more polished user interface.

We will look at how to handle e-mail messages in the next section and how to handle messages in public folders in a later section.

Handling E-Mail Messages

We start working with e-mail messages. E-mail messages are created in either the user's Inbox or Outbox folders.

Adding New Messages

When we create a new message, we will show **To:** on the **To/From** label. The user can click the **Addresses** button to select recipients from address lists; we will see how in a moment. They can also type the recipients' names into `txtNames` directly. We will use CDO to resolve the recipients before we send out the message.

Since we will be allowing the user to add attachments to the message, we will display **Add Attachment** on the **Attachment** button. When the user clicks this button, we will show an **Open File** dialog so that they can pick a file and attach it to the message. The user can choose to save the message at any time. When they're ready, they can send the message. We will add a method, `InitControls`, to our new form to handle this:

```
Private Sub InitControls()
    Toolbar.Buttons(mcstrButtonKeySave).Visible = True
    Toolbar.Buttons(mcstrButtonKeyReply).Visible = False
    Toolbar.Buttons(mcstrButtonKeyReplyAll).Visible = False
    Toolbar.Buttons(mcstrButtonKeyForward).Visible = False
    With Toolbar.Buttons(mcstrButtonKeyAttach)
        .Visible = True
        .Caption = mcstrButtonTextAddAtt
    End With
```

189

```
        lblNames.Caption = mcstrTo

    If mblnIsEmail Then
        Me.Caption = "New E-mail Message"
        Toolbar.Buttons(mcstrButtonKeyAddrBook).Visible = True
        Toolbar.Buttons(mcstrButtonKeySend).Visible = True
    Else
        ' New public folder postings
    End If
End Sub
```

When creating new messages, the user may need to use the **Addresses** and **Add Attachment** buttons, so we enable those two buttons.

Displaying Messages

When we display an existing message on this form, things are slightly different. We will display From: on the To/From label and the recipients in `txtNames`. Since there is no need to look up any recipients here, we will hide the lookup button, `cmdLookup`.

The message subject and body will be displayed in `txtSubject` and `txtBody`, respectively. If the message has attachments, we will display their names in the attachment list box, `lstAttachments`. We will allow the user to select an attachment in the list and save it to the hard disk. Therefore we will display **Save Attachment** on `cmdAttachment`. We will also hide the **Save** and **Send** buttons.

The `ShowMessage` method displays a message passed in as an argument:

```
Private Sub ShowMessage()
    Dim objAtt As MAPI.Attachment

    Toolbar.Buttons(mcstrButtonKeySend).Visible = False
    Toolbar.Buttons(mcstrButtonKeySave).Visible = False
    Toolbar.Buttons(mcstrButtonKeyReply).Visible = True
    Toolbar.Buttons(mcstrButtonKeyReplyAll).Visible = True
    Toolbar.Buttons(mcstrButtonKeyForward).Visible = True
    Toolbar.Buttons(mcstrButtonKeyAddrBook).Visible = False

    lblNames.Caption = mcstrFrom
    txtNames.Enabled = False

    With mobjMessage
        ' Display the message
        Me.Caption = .Subject
        txtNames.Text = .Sender.Name
        txtSubject.Text = .Subject
        txtBody.Text = .Text

        lstAttachments.Clear

        If .Attachments.Count > 0 Then
            For Each objAtt In .Attachments
                lstAttachments.AddItem objAtt.Name
                lstAttachments.ItemData(lstAttachments.NewIndex) = objAtt.Index
            Next
```

```
        With Toolbar.Buttons(mcstrButtonKeyAttach)
                .Visible = True
                .Caption = mcstrButtonTextSaveAtt
            End With
        Else
            ' If there is no attachment, don't show the
            ' Save Attachment button.
            Toolbar.Buttons(mcstrButtonKeyAttach).Visible = False
        End If
    End With
End Sub
```

This procedure is slightly more complex. We first set up the controls on the form and then display the relevant properties. Since we are just displaying an existing message, there is no need for the **Send** or **Save** button. We check whether there is any attachment in the message. If there is, we add the name of each attachment to the attachment list and save its index in the `Attachments` collection to the `ItemData` array of the list. This will be later used to retrieve the attachment object. If there is no attachment, we hide the **Save Attachment** button.

Showing the Message Form

With the display functions done, we add a public method `ShowForm` to the message form. This is the only public method the client object can call:

```
Public Sub ShowForm(Folder As MAPI.Folder, Optional Message As MAPI.Message)
    On Error GoTo ErrHandler

    Call CheckFolder(Folder)
    If Not Message Is Nothing Then
        Set mobjMessage = Message
        Call ShowMessage
    Else
        Call InitControls
    End If

    Me.Show vbModal

ExitFunc:
    Exit Sub

ErrHandler:
    Call ReportError(Err)
    Resume ExitFunc
End Sub
```

The `CheckFolder` method checks the folder, as we'll see in a minute. If it is either the Inbox or the Outbox, we assume that the users are creating or displaying an e-mail message. There are two ways of creating outbound messages using CDO. The first is to add it to the Outbox and the second is to add it to the Inbox. If you add it to the Inbox, CDO will actually move it to the Outbox when you call its `Send` method, so adding them to the Outbox would seem to make more sense. Please note that you must create new messages in the Outbox when using CDONTS, so it would be a good idea to get into the habit of creating new messages in the Outbox.

We will see how CDONTS works in Chapter 8.

Either way, CDO will pick it up and send it when we call the message's Send method. In fact, CDO will move new messages from any folder in the Mailbox store to the Outbox when you call their Send methods and then send the messages. If, however, the message is created in a folder in a different store, calling its Send method will result in a CdoE_COMPUTED (&H8004011A) error. In the FMessage form, if the folder is neither the Inbox nor the Outbox, we will assume that the users are dealing with a message in a public or private folder. Add this code for the CheckFolder method to your form:

```
Private Sub CheckFolder(Folder As MAPI.Folder)
    Dim objFolder As MAPI.Folder

    Set mobjFolder = Nothing
    mblnIsEmail = False

    Set objFolder = gobjSession.Inbox
    If gobjSession.CompareIDs(Folder.ID, objFolder.ID) Then
        mblnIsEmail = True
    Else
        Set objFolder = gobjSession.Outbox
        If gobjSession.CompareIDs(Folder.ID, objFolder.ID) Then
            mblnIsEmail = True
        End If
    End If
    Set objFolder = Nothing

    If mblnIsEmail Then
        Set mobjFolder = gobjSession.Outbox
    Else
        Set mobjFolder = Folder
    End If
End Sub
```

It sets mblnisEmail to True for e-mail messages or False for public folder postings.

We're then dumped back into the ShowForm method, which now checks whether a CDO Message object is passed in. If so, it calls the ShowMessage method to display the selected properties. Otherwise it calls InitControls to set up the controls on the form. It then loads and shows the form.

Looking Up Recipients

When you send a message, you need to specify who the recipients are. You can simply enter an e-mail address or you can select recipients from address lists. In this section, we will see how to provide the recipient lookup function on our message form.

The CDO `Session` object has a method, `AddressBook`, that displays a dialog box complete with all the entries in the relevant address book:

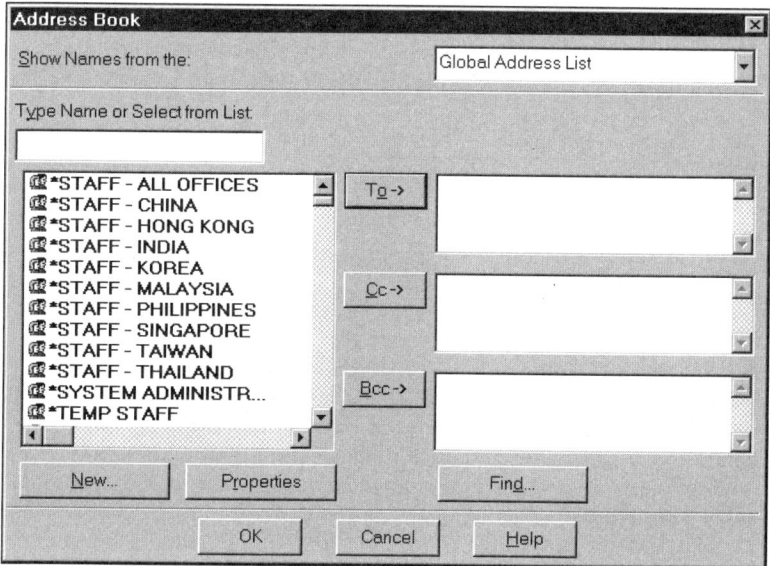

We can select one or more entries including individuals and distribution lists from the list. Once a user has clicked on OK, a `Recipients` collection is returned. It's used like this (don't worry, I'll tell you when you need to add code to your project):

```
Dim colRecipients As MAPI.Recipients
Set colRecipients = objSession.AddressBook
```

If the user clicks the **Cancel** button to dismiss the dialog, a CDO error `CdoE_User_Cancel` (`&H80040113`) is returned, so you will need to have a proper error handling routine in place. One solution is to use `On Error Resume Next` and examine the returned `Recipients` collection:

```
On Error Resume Next
Set colRecipients = objSession.AddressBook
If Not colRecipients Is Nothing Then
   ' The user clicked the OK button
Else
   ' The user clicked the Cancel button
End If
```

Note that even if the user has not selected any entries, as long as they click the **OK** button, `colRecipients` will not be `Nothing`. If you want to ensure that the user has selected at least one entry, check the `Count` property of the `colRecipients` instead:

```
On Error Resume Next
Set colRecipients = objSession.AddressBook
If Not colRecipients Is Nothing Then
   ' The user clicked the OK button
   If objRecipients.Count > 0 Then
```

```
      ' The user has selected at least one entry
    Else
      ' No entry is selected
    End If
  Else
      ' The user clicked the Cancel button
  End If
```

The AddressBook method has the following full syntax:

```
Set colRecipients = objSession.AddressBook([Recipients] [, Title] [, OneAddress] _
              [, ForceResolution] [, RecipLists]
              [, ToLabel] [, CcLabel] [, BccLabel] _
              [, ParentWindow])
```

If we pass in a Recipients collection, the dialog box will be displayed with all entries in the collection pre-selected. For instance, we can pass in a message's Recipients collection so the user need not reselect the recipients that have already been added to the message. The user can then add entries to or remove entries from the collection. By default, the dialog box does not have a title. We can specify a title by passing in a Title string. We can also restrict the user to only be able to select one address entry from the list by setting the OneAddress argument to True. The ForceResolution parameter indicates whether CDO should resolve selected names before closing the dialog.

The RecipLists parameter specifies how the dialog displays the selected entries. There are three command buttons and selection lists: To, Cc, and Bcc, which correspond to the RecipLists value 3. An AddressBook dialog with RecipLists value 1 displays the To button and selection list only, and one with value 2 displays the To and Cc buttons and selection lists. You can also change the captions of those buttons by specifying the ToLabel, CcLabel, and BccLabel parameters.

ParentWindow is the window handle of the parent window. You can assign any window as the ParentWindow of the dialog box. The user must dismiss the dialog box before she can enter anything in the ParentWindow. If you pass it the value 0, the user can proceed to interact with other windows before returning to this dialog box.

> **Please note that the CDO documentation states that the value zero causes the dialog box to be application modal. It does not. Instead, the dialog becomes non-modal. This is an error in documentation and perhaps a bug in CDO because your user can close all windows in your application before closing this dialog. Leaving this dialog displayed prevents your application from being unloaded from the memory. When the user finally gets around to closing this dialog, your application will crash horribly.**

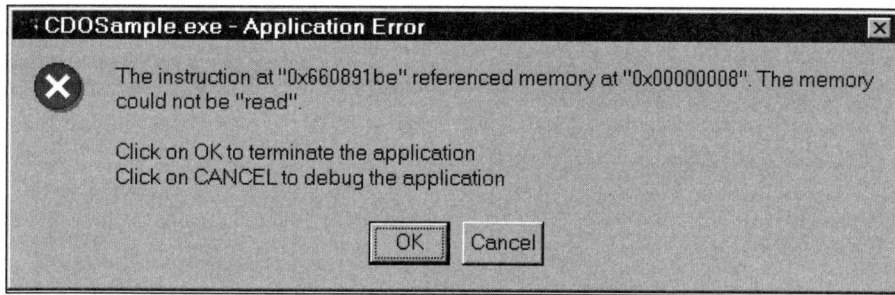

The solution to this problem is to pass the window handle of the current form to this method. Let us get back to our sample application and see how to use this dialog. Add this procedure to your `FMessage` form:

```
Private Sub Toolbar_ButtonClick(ByVal Button As MSComctlLib.Button)
    On Error GoTo ErrHandler

    Select Case Button.Key
        Case mcstrButtonKeySend
            Call SendMessage

        Case mcstrButtonKeySave
            SaveMessage

        Case mcstrButtonKeyReply
            Call Reply

        Case mcstrButtonKeyReplyAll
            Call ReplyAll

        Case mcstrButtonKeyForward
            Call Forward

        Case mcstrButtonKeyAddrBook
            Call LookupAddressBook

        Case mcstrButtonKeyAttach
            If Button.Caption = mcstrButtonTextAddAtt Then
                Call AddAttachment
            Else
                Call SaveAttachment
            End If
    End Select

ExitFunc:
    Exit Sub

ErrHandler:
  Call ReportError(Err)
  Resume ExitFunc
End Sub
```

```
Private Sub LookupAddressBook()
    On Error GoTo ErrHandler

    Dim strRecipients As String
    Dim lngLastSemicolon As Long
    Dim objRecipient As MAPI.Recipient
    Dim colRecipients As MAPI.Recipients

    ' Don't show error box if the user click Cancel on the AddressBook dialog box
    On Error Resume Next
    Set colRecipients = gobjSession.AddressBook(ParentWindow:=Me.hWnd)
    If Err <> 0 Then
     Err.Clear
    End If

    ' Reset the error handler
    On Error GoTo ErrHandler

    If Not (colRecipients Is Nothing) Then
        strRecipients = Trim(txtNames.Text)
        If Len(strRecipients) > 0 Then
            strRecipients = strRecipients & gcstrRecipDelimiter
        End If

        For Each objRecipient In colRecipients
            strRecipients = strRecipients & objRecipient.Name & gcstrRecipDelimiter
        Next

        ' Remove the last semicolon if any
        lngLastSemicolon = InStrRev(strRecipients, gcstrRecipDelimiter)
        If lngLastSemicolon > 0 Then
            strRecipients = Left(strRecipients, lngLastSemicolon - 1)
        End If
        txtNames.Text = strRecipients
    End If

ExitFunc:
    Exit Sub

ErrHandler:
    Call ReportError(Err)
    Resume ExitFunc
End Sub
```

`gcstrRecipDelimiter` is a constant specifying the delimiter separating the recipient names. Since it will be used in the appointment form introduced in the next chapter, we should define it as a global constant in the `MCommon` module:

```
Public Const gcstrRecipDelimiter As String = ";"
```

We will see each of the above methods in a moment. When the user clicks the lookup button, we display the address book dialog and make it modal to the message form. It only shows the To: button for simplicity. We turn off our error handler to make sure that it will not display an error if the user clicks Cancel. After the dialog closes, we append the names of selected recipients to the recipient list shown in the `txtNames` box. The recipients' names are separated by semicolons. We will see in a moment that using semicolons as name delimiters comes in handy when we add recipients to the message's recipient collection.

Next, we add the ability to allow the user to add attachments to the message by adding a method, AddAttachment, to the form:

```
Private Sub AddAttachment()
    ' Open the Open File dialog to let the user to
    ' select a file and insert it as an attachment
    With dlgFiles
        .Flags = cdlOFNExplorer Or _
            cdlOFNFileMustExist Or _
            cdlOFNHideReadOnly Or _
            cdlOFNLongNames Or _
            cdlOFNPathMustExist
        .Filter = "All Files (*.*)|*.*"
        .CancelError = False
        .InitDir = App.Path
        .ShowOpen

        ' If the message hasn't been saved, we must save it
        ' before we can add attachment to it.
        If Len(.FileName) > 0 Then
            Call SaveMessage

            ' Add attachment
            Call mobjMessage.Attachments.Add(Name:=.FileTitle, _
                        Type:=CdoFileData, _
                        Source:=.FileName)

            ' Display the file name in the attachment list
            lstAttachments.AddItem .FileTitle
        End If
    End With
End Sub
```

We use the Windows Common Dialog control to display an Open File dialog to allow the user to add one file to the message. We assign the Flags property with predefined values in the Windows Common Dialog control. You can find a complete list of flags in the MSDN Library under Common Dialog Control. Setting the dialog's CancelError to False prevents Visual Basic from displaying an error when the user clicks the Cancel button to dismiss the dialog. If the user has selected a file, we need to add it to the message.

We can only add attachments to existing messages. Therefore we need to ensure that we have a valid Message object. The SaveMessage method will create a new Message object if there isn't already one. We will see how this method is implemented shortly. We then add the attachment to the message by adding it to the message's Attachments collection.

The Add method creates an Attachment object in the collection and returns a reference to the newly added Attachment object. The Name parameter specifies the display name of the attachment. We will use the attached file's file name as returned in the common dialog's FileTitle property.

After the attachment has been added to the message, we add its name to the attachment list box on the form.

Saving Messages

The `SaveMessage` method does two things. It creates a new message if necessary and assigns the message with properties entered in the form.

```
Private Sub SaveMessage()
    If mobjMessage Is Nothing Then
      Set mobjMessage = mobjFolder.Messages.Add
    End If

    With mobjMessage
      .Subject = txtSubject.Text
      .Text = txtBody.Text

      If mblnIsEmail Then
          ' The Recipients collection might already contain
          ' recipients from a previous save, so let us clear
          ' it first and then add recipients again.
          Call .Recipients.Delete
          Call .Recipients.AddMultiple(txtNames.Text, CdoTo)
          Call .Recipients.Resolve

          Call .Update
      Else
          ' Save posting
      End If
    End With
End Sub
```

We first check whether we already have a valid message. If not, we will get one by calling the `Add` method of the message collection in the folder. CDO will pick it up and send it when we call the message's `Send` method.

Assigning the subject and body to a message is straightforward. To add recipients to it, we first clear any existing recipients and then add the selected recipients in the `txtNames` box to it. We can add one recipient at a time using the `Recipients` collection's `Add` method:

```
Set objRecip = objMessage.Recipients.Add(RecipName, RecipType)
```

`RecipName` is the display name of a recipient and `RecipType` is the recipient type. The acceptable recipient types are `CdoTo` (1), `CdoCc` (2), and `CdoBcc` (3).

While adding one recipient at a time is acceptable, the CDO `Recipients` collection defines another more convenient method, `AddMultiple`.

```
objMessage.Recipients.AddMultiple(RecipNames, RecipType)
```

`RecipNames` is a string containing a list of recipient display names or addresses, each separated by a semicolon. If you specify a recipient by his display name, it must be resolvable, meaning that it must contain a string that unambiguously identifies the recipient.

If you specify a recipient with his address, the address should be the full address in the form `AddressType:AddressString`. For instance, `SMTP:john_smith@server.com`. The only case where you can omit the address type is if it is SMTP. CDO will treat any addresses without an address type specifier as SMTP addresses.

`RecipType` is the same as its namesake in the `Add` method. Since we separate each recipient by a semicolon anyway, `AddMultiple` is perfect.

We then should resolve the recipients to ensure that each recipient is reachable by calling the `Recipients` collection's `Resolve` method. If a recipient cannot be resolved, CDO will display a dialog box asking the user to take action. For instance, if one of the recipient's name is 'someone', you will see a dialog box similar to this:

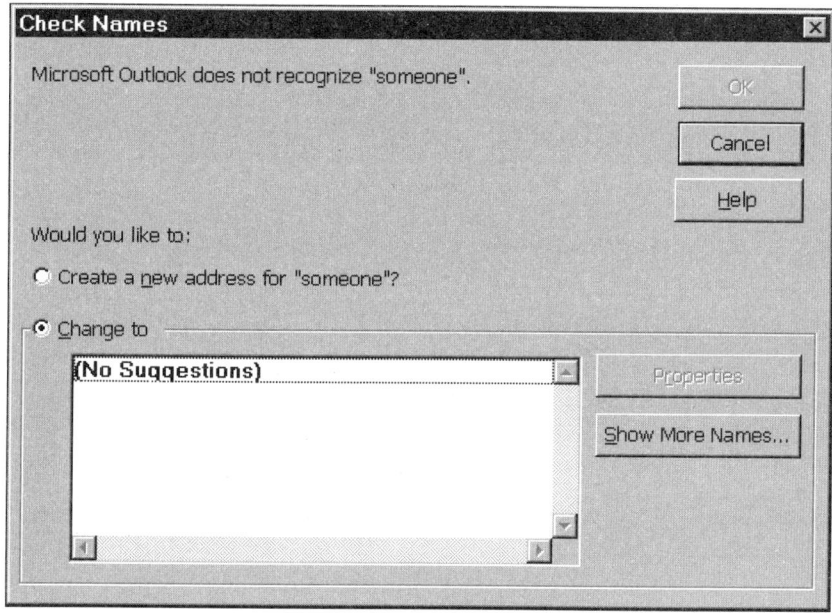

The `Resolve` method does not resolve SMTP addresses since it would have to look up the destination server. If the server were valid, it would have to connect to the server to verify the recipient. This is not practically viable, as there is no guarantee that all SMTP servers support verifications. In fact, the only reliable way of verifying a SMTP address is to actually send it an e-mail and check whether or not it gets bounced. CDO always regards SMTP addresses as valid and the `Resolve` method always succeeds.

The `Recipients` collection's `Resolve` method checks all recipients in the collection. If you want to resolve a recipient separately, you can call the recipient's `Resolve` method which is similar to the `Resolve` method of the recipient collection.

Calling the `Messages` collection's `Add` method and assigning properties and recipients does not automatically save the message. We must call the message's `Update` method to commit the changes.

Sending Messages

After the user has prepared the new message, they'll probably want to send it. The SendMessage method takes care of this task. Add this code to the message form:

```
Private Sub SendMessage()
    Call SaveMessage
    Call mobjMessage.Send
    Unload Me
End Sub
```

It could not be easier. We make sure that we save everything and then call the Send method to send the message. Note that the Send method saves the message before actually sending it, so it is not necessary to call the Update method explicitly as in the SaveMessage method. After the message has been sent, we close the message form and return to the main form.

In FMessage form, users can save a message either by clicking the Save button or by adding attachments to it. If they decide to cancel the message by closing the message form without sending it, they will have a message sitting in their Outbox. A good practice is to ask them whether or not they want to discard the message. We do this in the form's QueryUnload event handler:

```
Private Sub Form_QueryUnload(Cancel As Integer, UnloadMode As Integer)
    On Error Resume Next

    If Not mobjMessage Is Nothing Then
        If Not mobjMessage.Sent Then
            Select Case MsgBox("Discard the message?", _
                    vbQuestion Or vbYesNoCancel)
            Case vbYes
                mobjMessage.Delete

            Case vbNo
                ' Just leave it

            Case vbCancel
                Cancel = True
            End Select
        End If

        If Not Cancel Then
            Set mobjMessage = Nothing
        End If
    End If
End Sub
```

Because we would not want to bother the user if the message has been sent, we will test the message's Sent property before presenting the message box. As you would expect, it returns False if the message has not been sent. In that case, we display the message box and ask for instructions. If the user selects to discard the message, we call the message's Delete method to remove it. Otherwise, we will just leave it there. To be a bit more fancy, we also allow the user to select Cancel so the message form remains open. In the latter case, we will leave the message as well so that the user can continue working on it.

If the message has been sent, its `Sent` property should be `True` and the Visual Basic message box should not be displayed. Unfortunately, this is not how it works. If you try it out, you will see the message box regardless of whether or not the message has been sent. Why's this?

It turns out that the message's `Send` method invalidates the object. While the message object is still in memory, any attempt to access its properties will cause a `CdoE_INVALID_OBJECT` (`&H80040108`) error. In the `QueryUnload` event handler, we've said that we want to ignore all errors:

```
On Error Resume Next
```

When we test a sent message's `Sent` property...

```
If Not mobjMessage.Sent Then
```

...CDO raises an error. Since the error is ignored, the message box is displayed. To fix this, we need to test the `Err` object. Change the procedure as follows:

```
Private Sub Form_QueryUnload(Cancel As Integer, UnloadMode As Integer)
    On Error Resume Next

    If Not mobjMessage Is Nothing Then
        If Not mobjMessage.Sent Then
            If Err.Number = 0 Then
                Select Case MsgBox("Discard the message?", _
                        vbQuestion Or vbYesNoCancel)
                    Case vbYes
                        mobjMessage.Delete

                    Case vbNo
                        ' Just leave it

                    Case vbCancel
                        Cancel = True
                End Select
            End If
        End If

        If Not Cancel Then
            Set mobjMessage = Nothing
        End If
    End If
End Sub
```

This will also work when we use this form to display existing messages because we can safely query the message's `Sent` property and it is always set to `True`.

Now, we will see how we extract and save attachments in messages.

Saving Attachments

We have already seen how to display messages and their attachments. Saving attachments is not a very demanding job either. Add a new method, `SaveAttachment`, to the form:

```
Private Sub SaveAttachment()
    Dim objAtt As MAPI.Attachment
    Dim lngIndex As Long

    ' Save an attachment to disk
    If lstAttachments.ListIndex > 0 Then
        lngIndex = lstAttachments.ItemData(lstAttachments.ListIndex)
        Set objAtt = mobjMessage.Attachments(lngIndex)
        If Not objAtt Is Nothing Then
            With dlgFiles
                .FileName = objAtt.Name
                .Flags = cdlOFNExplorer Or cdlOFNHideReadOnly Or cdlOFNLongNames
                .Filter = "All Files (*.*)|*.*"
                .CancelError = False
                .InitDir = App.Path
                .ShowSave

                objAtt.WriteToFile .FileName
            End With
        End If
    End If

    Set objAtt = Nothing
End Sub
```

The user can select an attachment in the attachment list box and click the **Save Attachment** button. Since we saved the index of each attachment in the list box's `ItemData` array, we can use it to retrieve the selected attachment from the message's `Attachments` collection. We then display a **Save File** dialog to ask the user for the location to save the file. Finally, we call the attachment's `WriteToFile` method and pass it the full path and file name. This method writes the attachment to the specified file.

Linking Up the Message Form

So our message form is ready for creating and displaying e-mail messages. Let's modify the main form to link up the message form to it. We start by modifying the toolbar's `ButtonClick` event handler and adding a new method, `NewMessage`. Add this code to `FMain`:

```
Private Sub Toolbar_ButtonClick(ByVal Button As MSComctlLib.Button)
    On Error GoTo ErrHandler

    Select Case Button.Key
        Case mcstrButtonKeyFolder, mcstrButtonKeyMessage
            ' Will check button state in WorkingObject

        Case mcstrButtonKeyNew
            If WorkingObject = wotFolder Then
                Call NewFolder
            Else
```

```
            Call NewMessage
        End If

    Case mcstrButtonKeyDelete
...


Private Sub NewMessage()
    Call ShowMessageForm
End Sub

Private Sub ShowMessageForm(Optional Message As MAPI.Message)
    Dim frmMessage As FMessage
    Dim objFolder As MAPI.Folder
    Dim strStoreID As String
    Dim strFolderID As String

    If GetFolderNodeType(strStoreID, strFolderID) = fntFolder Then
        Set objFolder = gobjSession.GetFolder(strFolderID, strStoreID)

        Set frmMessage = New FMessage
        Call frmMessage.ShowForm(objFolder, Message)
        Set frmMessage = Nothing

        Call ShowContents(Folder:=objFolder)
        Set objFolder = Nothing
    End If
End Sub
```

Note that the user must click the "Working with messages" button to enable the message functions.
After that, they can select the **New** button to bring up the message form for creating a new message.
When they double-click a message in the message list, we will also display the selected message in the
message form. Add this code to `FMain`:

```
Private Sub lvwItems_DblClick()
    On Error GoTo ErrHandler
    Call ShowMessage

ExitFunc:
    Exit Sub

ErrHandler:
    Call ReportError(Err)
    Resume ExitFunc
End Sub

Private Sub ShowMessage()
    ShowMessageForm GetMessage
End Sub

Private Sub ShowMessageForm(Optional Message As MAPI.Message)
    Dim frmMessage As FMessage
    Dim objFolder As MAPI.Folder
    Dim strStoreID As String
    Dim strFolderID As String
```

```
If GetFolderNodeType(strStoreID, strFolderID) = fntFolder Then
    Set objFolder = gobjSession.GetFolder(strFolderID, strStoreID)

    Set frmMessage = New FMessage
    Call frmMessage.ShowForm(objFolder, Message)
    Set frmMessage = Nothing

    Call ShowContents(Folder:=objFolder)
    Set objFolder = Nothing
End If
End Sub
```

It might seem a bit silly to simply pass calls from `ShowMessage` to `ShowMessageForm`. We're doing this because we will be working with appointment and meeting items later on. We'll have `ShowAppForm` and `ShowMeetingForm` procedures, both called by `ShowMessage`. Otherwise, the code here is very simple. Next, we will look at how to reply to and forward messages.

Replying to Messages

We reply to an e-mail message by calling its `Reply` method. This creates a new message as a reply to the current message. It adds the current message's `Sender` to the new message's `Recipients` collection. However, it does not copy the message body, that is, the `Text` property to the new message. So if you want this functionality, you're going to have to perform it in code. Consistent with the convention, the `Reply` method doesn't copy any of the message attachments either.

Since we have already learned to construct and send a new message, we will use a different approach to reply to a message in `FMessage`. Add this code to the message form:

```
Private Sub Reply()
    ' Ignore CdoE_User_Cancel (&H80040113)
    On Error Resume Next

    Dim objReply As MAPI.Message

    If mblnIsEmail Then
        Set objReply = mobjMessage.Reply
        With objReply
            .Subject = "RE: " & mobjMessage.Subject
            .Text = vbCrLf & mobjMessage.Sender.Name & " wrote: " & vbCrLf & _
                mobjMessage.Text
            .Send ShowDialog:=True    ' Send it
        End With
        Set objReply = Nothing
    Else
        ' Reply to a posting in a public folder
    End If
End Sub
```

The CDO `Message`'s `Reply` method returns a reference to the reply message. While it automatically adds the original message's `Sender` to its `Recipients`, it does not fill the `Subject` and `Text` properties automatically. We simply add a "RE: " prefix to the original message's subject and copy its body to the new message. We then call the `Send` method and specify its `ShowDialog` property to `True`.

The `Send` method has three optional parameters:

```
objMessage.Send([SaveCopy] [, ShowDialog] [, ParentWindow])
```

The `SaveCopy` parameter indicates whether a copy of the message should be saved in the local message store, for example in the Sent Items folder. It is `True` by default. If the `ShowDialog` parameter is set to `True`, CDO will display a modal dialog box allowing the user to modify the message before it is sent. The `ParentWindow` parameter is only meaningful when the `ShowDialog` parameter is set to `True`. It specifies the parent window that will be disabled until the dialog box is closed. By default, it is set to zero so that all windows in the current application are disabled while the dialog box is displayed.

Since we have set the `ShowDialog` property to `True`, we will see a dialog box as shown here:

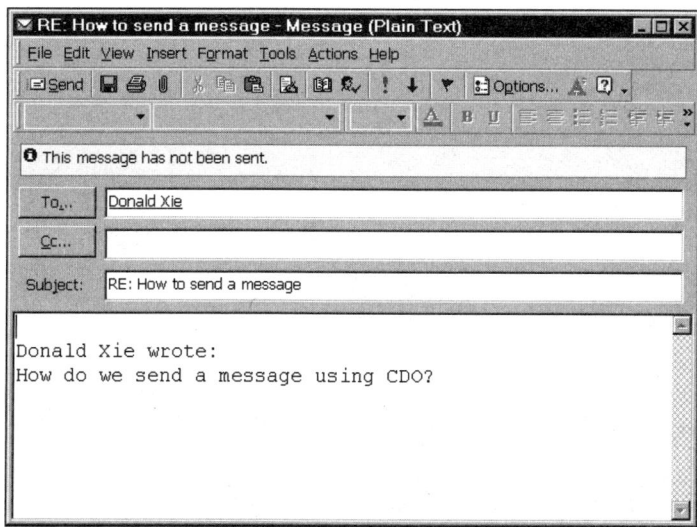

The user can then modify the message and click the **Send** button to actually send it. If they choose not to send the message, they can just close the dialog. However, this raises a CDO error `CdoE_User_Cancel` (&H80040113). We can just ignore this error here.

The CDO `Message` object also has a `ReplyAll` method that is similar to the `Reply` method with one difference: it adds the current message's Sender and all recipients to the new message's `Recipients` collection. Let's add our own `ReplyAll` procedure:

```
Private Sub ReplyAll()
   On Error Resume Next

   Dim objReply As MAPI.Message
   Set objReply = mobjMessage.ReplyAll
   With objReply
      .Subject = "RE: " & mobjMessage.Subject
      .Text = vbCrLf & mobjMessage.Sender.Name & " wrote: " & vbCrLf & _
         mobjMessage.Text
      .Send ShowDialog:=True      ' Send it
   End With
   Set objReply = Nothing
End Sub
```

Our `ReplyAll` method is very similar to our `Reply` method, so I will not explain it further.

Forwarding Messages

We can forward a message by calling its `Forward` method. It creates a new message that can be used to forward the current message. It returns a reference to the new message so that you can modify it before sending it. It copies most properties, including attachments, of the current message to the new message. The two notable omissions are the message text and recipients. It is easy to understand why the `Recipients` collection is not copied since, by convention, you do not want to forward the message to people who have already received it. However, it is puzzling why the message text is not copied as well because almost all mail clients copy the original message's text. After all, why would you want to forward a message without its text? Of course, it is easy to overcome this problem. Add a new subprocedure to the `FMessage` form:

```
Private Sub Forward()
    On Error Resume Next

    Dim objForward As MAPI.Message
    Set objForward = mobjMessage.Forward()

    With objForward
        .Subject = "FW: " & mobjMessage.Subject
        .Text = vbCrLf & "Original Message: " & vbCrLf & mobjMessage.Text
        .Send ShowDialog:=True
    End With
    Set objForward = Nothing
End Sub
```

Now we have seen how to send and read e-mail messages. Using CDO, we can also posting new messages to public folders. The next section demonstrates how.

Handling Public Folder Postings

The title of this section might be slightly misleading since we can post not only to public folders, but also to private folders. CDO offers the same procedure for posting to both public and private folders. There is no difference whatsoever. However, posting to public folders is by far the more common use so I will continue to use the term "Public Folder" here.

Creating New Postings

When we post a message to a public folder, we do not call the message's `Send` method. There is no need to look up the recipients either because the message is not mailed. Therefore we can hide the **Send** and **Addresses** buttons.

Of course, we need to know which folder the message will be posted to. As we did in the last section, the folder is passed in to the `ShowForm` method and assigned to the `mobjFolder` object. We will display its name in the `txtName` text box. Since it does not make sense to allow the user to change the folder name here, we need to disable this text box. Change the `InitControls` method:

```
Private Sub InitControls()
    Toolbar.Buttons(mcstrButtonKeySave).Visible = True
    Toolbar.Buttons(mcstrButtonKeyReply).Visible = False
    Toolbar.Buttons(mcstrButtonKeyReplyAll).Visible = False
    Toolbar.Buttons(mcstrButtonKeyForward).Visible = False
    With Toolbar.Buttons(mcstrButtonKeyAttach)
```

```
            .Visible = True
            .Caption = mcstrButtonTextAddAtt
      End With

      lblNames.Caption = mcstrTo

      If mblnIsEmail Then
          Me.Caption = "New E-mail Message"
          Toolbar.Buttons(mcstrButtonKeyAddrBook).Visible = True
          Toolbar.Buttons(mcstrButtonKeySend).Visible = True
      Else
          Me.Caption = "New Posting"
          txtNames.Text = mobjFolder.Name
          txtNames.Enabled = False
          Toolbar.Buttons(mcstrButtonKeyAddrBook).Visible = False
          Toolbar.Buttons(mcstrButtonKeySend).Visible = False
      End If
  End Sub:
```

Displaying Posted Messages

E-mail messages and messages posted in public folders are essentially the same, as far as CDO is concerned. So the ShowMessage method is virtually unchanged with one exception: we will hide the ReplyAll and Forward buttons. While we could use the ReplyAll button to reply to both the message originator and the public folder, it should be very easy to create two messages, one to be sent as an e-mail to the originator and another to be posted to the folder. Since we have already covered sending e-mails in the last section and will learn how to post a message to a folder, I will leave this functionality out to avoid duplications – with a similar decision for the Forward button. Make the following change to the ShowMessage procedure:

```
  Private Sub ShowMessage()
      Dim objAtt As MAPI.Attachment

      Toolbar.Buttons(mcstrButtonKeySend).Visible = False
      Toolbar.Buttons(mcstrButtonKeySave).Visible = False
      Toolbar.Buttons(mcstrButtonKeyReply).Visible = True
      Toolbar.Buttons(mcstrButtonKeyReplyAll).Visible = mblnIsEmail
      Toolbar.Buttons(mcstrButtonKeyForward).Visible = mblnIsEmail
      Toolbar.Buttons(mcstrButtonKeyAddrBook).Visible = False

      lblNames.Caption = mcstrFrom
      txtNames.Enabled = False

      With mobjMessage
          ' Display the message
          Me.Caption = .Subject
          txtNames.Text = .Sender.Name
          txtSubject.Text = .Subject
          txtBody.Text = .Text

          lstAttachments.Clear

          If .Attachments.Count > 0 Then
              For Each objAtt In .Attachments
                  lstAttachments.AddItem objAtt.Name
                  lstAttachments.ItemData(lstAttachments.NewIndex) = objAtt.Index
              Next
```

```
With Toolbar.Buttons(mcstrButtonKeyAttach)
            .Visible = True
            .Caption = mcstrButtonTextSaveAtt
        End With
    Else
        ' If there is no attachment, don't show the
        ' Save Attachment button.
        Toolbar.Buttons(mcstrButtonKeyAttach).Visible = False
    End If
    End With
End Sub
```

Posting New Messages

Posting to public folders is a very different process from sending e-mail. The most obvious difference is that we only need to call the `Update` method (instead of the `Send` method). But before we post it, we will need to set a few properties. Let's modify the `SaveMessage` method to show an example of this process to make our discussion easier:

```
Private Sub SaveMessage(Optional ShouldCloseForm As Boolean = False)
    If mobjMessage Is Nothing Then
        Set mobjMessage = mobjFolder.Messages.Add
    End If

    With mobjMessage
        .Subject = txtSubject.Text
        .Text = txtBody.Text

        If mblnIsEmail Then
            ' The Recipients collection might already contain
            ' recipients from a previous save, so let us clear
            ' it first and then add recipients again.
            Call .Recipients.Delete
            Call .Recipients.AddMultiple(txtNames.Text, CdoTo)
            Call .Recipients.Resolve

            Call .Update
        Else
            .ConversationTopic = .Subject
            .ConversationIndex = gobjSession.CreateConversationIndex()
            .Sender = gobjSession.CurrentUser
            .Sent = True
            .Submitted = False
            .Unread = True
            .TimeSent = Now
            .TimeReceived = .TimeSent

            Call .Update
            If ShouldCloseForm Then
                Unload Me
            End If
        End If
    End With
End Sub
```

First, we need to assign the `ConversationTopic` property. When other users reply to this message, their messages will have the same conversation topic so the related message can be grouped.

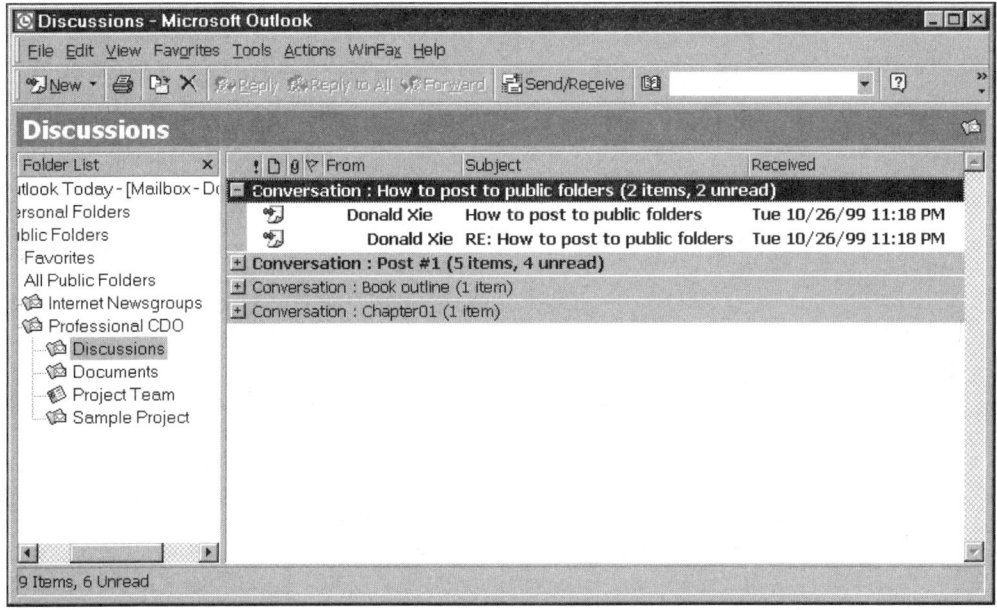

The order of messages in a conversation thread is set according to their `ConversationIndex` which is a string. CDO can generate a unique and valid conversation index automatically for us through the `Session` object's `CreateConversationIndex` method:

```
strConvIndex = objSession.CreateConversationIndex([ParentIndex])
```

If a `ParentIndex` is not passed in, this method creates a new top-level conversation. If a `ParentIndex` is present, the returned string is used to create a new conversation under the parent object.

Unlike e-mail messages, the `Sender` property of public folder postings is not set automatically, so we must set it manually here. We also need to set the `Sent` and `Unread` properties to `True`, and the `Submitted` property to `False`. The `TimeSent` and `TimeReceived` properties should both be set to the same time. You can set them to any time you like, but it makes sense to set them to the time when the message is posted.

Apart from CDO issues, we also have a little user interface problem. We can invoke this method two ways – when the user first adds an attachment, or when the user clicks the **Save** button. In the first case, we want to keep the form open. In the second, however, we want to close the form. So we add an optional parameter, `ShouldCloseForm`, to it and only unload the form if the parameter is `True`. We will also need to modify the `ButtonClick` event handler, adding this `Case` statement in with the rest:

```
' In Private Sub Toolbar_ButtonClick(ByVal Button As MSComctlLib.Button)
    Case mcstrButtonKeySave
        Call SaveMessage(ShouldCloseForm:=True)
```

Replying to Posted Messages

We can also reply to posted messages in public folders. It follows the same procedure as we did when posting new messages:

```
Private Sub Reply()
    ' Ignore CdoE_User_Cancel (&H80040113)
    On Error Resume Next

    Dim objReply    As MAPI.Message

    If mblnIsEMail Then
        Set objReply = mobjMessage.Reply
        With objReply
            .Subject = "RE: " & mobjMessage.Subject
            .Text = vbCrLf & mobjMessage.Sender.Name & " wrote: " & vbCrLf & _
                mobjMessage.Text
            .Send ShowDialog:=True     ' Send it
        End With
        Set objReply = Nothing
    Else
        Set objReply = mobjFolder.Messages.Add
        With objReply
            .ConversationTopic = mobjMessage.ConversationTopic
            .ConversationIndex = _
                gobjSession.CreateConversationIndex(mobjMessage.ConversationIndex)
            .Subject = "RE: " & .ConversationTopic
            .Text = "This is a reply to " & _
                mobjMessage.Sender.Name & "'s message:" & vbCrLf & _
                mobjMessage.Text
            .Sender = gobjSession.CurrentUser
            .Sent = True
            .Submitted = False
            .Unread = True
            .TimeSent = Now
            .TimeReceived = .TimeSent
            Call .Update
        End With
        Set objReply = Nothing

        Unload Me
    End If
End Sub
```

The only real difference is the way it calls the `Session` object's `CreateConversationIndex` method. Here we pass the original message's `ConversationIndex` property as its parent topic. CDO then automatically generates a new conversation index that is recognized as a reply to the original message.

That is all for the message form. Before we leave, we can add a form resizing event handler to it so the controls on the form will resize with the form:

```
Private Sub Form_Resize()
    On Error Resume Next

    lblNames.Move gclngEdge, Toolbar.Height + gclngEdge
    With txtNames
        .Move lblNames.Left + lblNames.Width + gclngEdge, lblNames.Top
        .Width = ScaleWidth - .Left - gclngEdge
    End With

    lblSubject.Move gclngEdge, lblNames.Top + lblNames.Height + gclngEdge
    With txtSubject
        .Move lblSubject.Left + lblSubject.Width + gclngEdge, lblSubject.Top
        .Width = ScaleWidth - .Left - gclngEdge
    End With

    With txtBody
        .Move gclngEdge, lblSubject.Top + lblSubject.Height + gclngEdge
        .Height = ScaleHeight - .Top - gclngEdge
    End With

    If Toolbar.Buttons(mcstrButtonKeyAttach).Visible Then
        With lstAttachments
            .Move ScaleWidth - .Width - gclngEdge, txtBody.Top
            .Height = txtBody.Height
            .Visible = True
            txtBody.Width = ScaleWidth - .Width - gclngEdge * 3
        End With
    Else
        lstAttachments.Visible = False
        txtBody.Width = ScaleWidth - gclngEdge * 2
    End If
End Sub
```

We have learned to create, reply, and forward messages. We can also copy, move, or delete messages.

Copying and Moving Messages

In Chapter 3, we learned to copy a folder by copy-and-pasting. We will use this method to copy a message to a different folder. To move a message from one folder to another, we can first select a message using the Cut button. We then select the destination folder and click the Paste button to move it. Since we need to distinguish between copying and moving, let us define an Enum, CutCopyTypeEnum, in FMain to specify the type of operation:

```
Private Enum CutCopyTypeEnum
    cctNone = 0
    cctCut = 1
    cctCopy = 2
End Enum
```

We also need a reference to the message to be copied or moved and a form-level variable that specifies the operation in `FMain`:

```
Private mobjMessage As MAPI.Message
Private mcctCutCopy As CutCopyTypeEnum
```

Now add a `CutMessage` and a `CopyMessage` methods to `FMain`:

```
Private Sub CutMessage()
    Set mobjMessage = GetMessage
    mcctCutCopy = cctCut
End Sub

Private Sub CopyMessage()
    Set mobjMessage = GetMessage
    mcctCutCopy = cctCopy
End Sub
```

Both the `CutMessage` and the `CopyMessage` methods assign the selected message to the form-level object `mobjMessage`. The `CutMessage` method then specifies that we should be moving the message, while the `CopyMessage` method specifies that we should be copying the message.

The user can then select the destination folder and click the **Paste** button. This invokes the `PasteMessage` method to actually copy or move the message.

```
Private Sub PasteMessage()
    Dim objCopy As MAPI.Message
    Dim strStoreID As String
    Dim strFolderID As String

    If Not mobjMessage Is Nothing Then
        If GetFolderNodeType(strStoreID, strFolderID) = fntFolder Then
            Select Case mcctCutCopy
                Case cctNone
                    ' Ignore

                Case cctCut
                    Call mobjMessage.MoveTo(strFolderID, strStoreID)

                Case cctCopy
                    Set objCopy = mobjMessage.CopyTo(strFolderID, strStoreID)
                    Call objCopy.Update
                    Set objCopy = Nothing
            End Select

            Call ShowContents
        End If
    End If

    Set mobjMessage = Nothing
    mcctCutCopy = cctNone
End Sub
```

We check whether a message has been selected and, if so, check whether the destination node represents a folder, since we cannot move a message to an information store. If the message is to be moved, we call its MoveTo method, passing it the folder and store IDs. This method takes effect immediately and invalidates the original message, mobjMessage. You must make sure that you don't use it again. If you need a reference to the new message in the destination folder, you can assign the returned object of the MoveTo method:

```
Set objMoved = mobjMessage.MoveTo(strFolderID, strStoreID)
```

If the message is to be copied, we call the CopyTo method (which is slightly different from the MoveTo method). The copied message in the destination folder is not saved until you call its Update method. Either way, after we are done, we set mobjMessage to Nothing just like we did when copying a folder.

Now modify the ButtonClick event handler in FMain to hook up those methods:

```
Private Sub Toolbar_ButtonClick(ByVal Button As MSComctlLib.Button)
    On Error GoTo ErrHandler

    Select Case Button.Key
        Case mcstrButtonKeyFolder, mcstrButtonKeyMessage
            ' Will check button state in WorkingObject

        Case mcstrButtonKeyNew
            If WorkingObject = wotFolder Then
                Call NewFolder
            Else
                Call NewMessage
            End If

        Case mcstrButtonKeyCut
            If WorkingObject = wotFolder Then
                ' Not implemented
            Else
                Call CutMessage
            End If

        Case mcstrButtonKeyCopy
            If WorkingObject = wotFolder Then
                Call CopyFolder
            Else
                Call CopyMessage
            End If

        Case mcstrButtonKeyPaste
            If WorkingObject = wotFolder Then
                Call PasteFolder
            Else
                Call PasteMessage
            End If
```

```
Case mcstrButtonKeyDelete
   If WorkingObject = wotFolder Then
      Call DeleteFolder
   Else
      Call DeleteMessage
   End If

Case mcstrButtonKeyProperty
   ...
```

Now let's move on and look at deleting messages.

Deleting Messages

Deleting a message is as simple as calling its `Delete` method. Let us add the `DeleteMessage` method to `FMain` and see how it works:

```
Private Sub DeleteMessage()
   Dim objMessage As MAPI.Message

   Set objMessage = GetMessage
   If MsgBox("Delete message " & objMessage.Subject & "?", _
         vbQuestion Or vbYesNo) = vbYes Then
      Call objMessage.Delete
      Call ShowContents
   End If
   Set objMessage = Nothing
End Sub
```

It retrieves the selected message and asks the user for confirmation. If confirmed, it simply calls the message's `Delete` method to delete the message. Finally, it refreshes the message list using the `ShowContents` method.

Summary

CDO messages can be more than just e-mail messages. They can store other types of information such as documents and contact data. In this chapter, we have learned to display messages polymorphically in different formats depending on their types. While we haven't covered every single type of message, the techniques we saw will help you to define your own message display utilities.

We have also learned to create new e-mail messages and public folder postings. We can programmatically construct and send messages by providing custom message entry forms. In addition, CDO offers a send message dialog that helps to simplify this process. Replying to and forwarding messages are easy to do, although they need a bit of extra programming. We can also copy, move, and delete messages programmatically using CDO.

A CDO `Message` object is the most common item in messaging and collaboration applications, it is just one of the three CDO objects that can be stored in folders. The other two objects are `AppointmentItem` and `MeetingItem`, which are more specific types of objects. In the next chapter, we will see how to create appointments and schedule meetings.

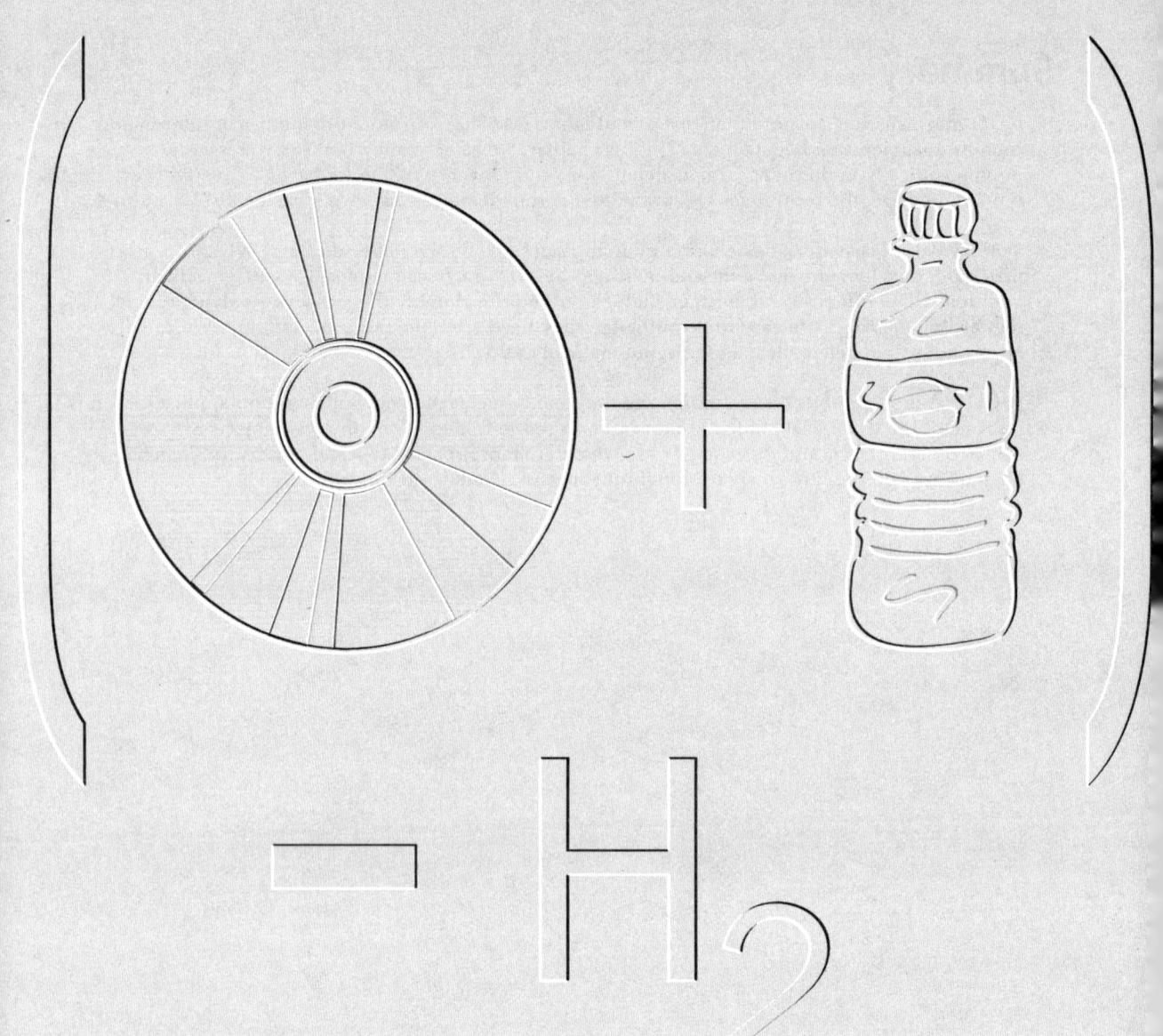

6

Managing Schedules

Introduction

In the last chapter, we experimented with the CDO `Message` and related objects to send, receive and manipulate e-mail messages and public folder postings. This chapter introduces two specialized message objects, the `AppointmentItem` and `MeetingItem` objects.

A CDO `Message` object represents items such as an e-mail message or a public folder posting. As we have seen, a message can be anything that can be stored in a folder, including items that are stored in a user's Calendar folder. Such items normally represent appointments in the user's schedule. As we would expect, appointment items and meeting items have some unique properties that are generally not relevant to other types of messages. Examples of those properties are the starting and ending times of the appointment. CDO defines a specialized object, `AppointmentItem`, that exposes such specific properties in addition to the properties that are common to all messages.

Imagine what you do to organize a meeting without using a computer. You find a time and work out a list of people you would like to be in the meeting. You can go around and ask them whether they can attend the meeting. They will check their diary and tell you if the time is OK with them. If they all accept, the meeting will be on. Otherwise, you reschedule the meeting and repeat the process until you find a suitable time. This process is modeled in Outlook and CDO.

In CDO, we can create an appointment and send it to all the participants. When the request arrives at each participant's mailbox, it appears as a `MeetingItem` object of the `IPM.Schedule.Meeting.Request` type. The receivers can check the meeting time and other attributes and decide whether they will accept or decline the meeting request. If they decide to accept a meeting request, they can either respond to the request by sending a reply or just accept a meeting without sending a reply. Either way, CDO creates an appointment in their Calendar folder. If they decline, you may want to reschedule the meeting to a time that is acceptable for all intended attendees.

In this chapter, we will cover the last three CDO objects:

        AppointmentItem

        RecurrencePattern

        MeetingItem

We will also complete our CDO sample project by adding the ability to perform the following tasks:

        Creating appointments

        Editing recurrence patterns

        Creating meeting requests

        Responding to meeting requests

First, let's take a look at the structure of CDO scheduling objects.

CDO Scheduling Object Structure

Three CDO objects, `AppointmentItem`, `RecurrencePattern`, and `MeetingItem`, help us to perform our scheduling tasks. Both the `AppointmentItem` and the `MeetingItem` object have their own special properties and methods in addition to those defined in the `Message` object. The `RecurrencePattern` object is always associated with an `AppointmentItem` and specifies how the `AppointmentItem` will recur:

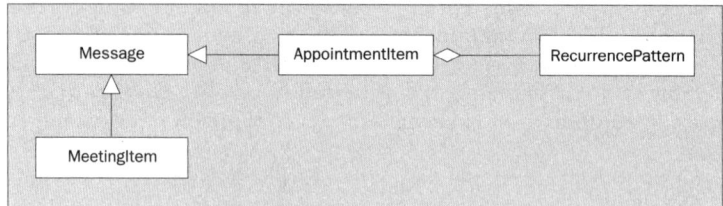

How the AppointmentItem and MeetingItem Objects Work

The `AppointmentItem` and `MeetingItem` objects work together to provide CDO applications with the ability to organize meetings. To create a meeting, we create an `AppointmentItem` object and add all intended recipients to it. When we call its `Send` method, CDO creates a `MeetingItem` object from it. This `MeetingItem` object contains an `AppointmentItem` object with all properties having the same values as in the original `AppointmentItem` object. Please note that although the associated `AppointmentItem` object and the original `AppointmentItem` object have the same property values, they are two different objects.

All recipients receive this MeetingItem object in their Inbox. Although they may modify the associated AppointmentItem's properties, such changes are not automatically propagated to the meeting organizer and other recipients. In other words, if you are not the meeting organizer, you cannot change meeting schedule using CDO.

When they accept the meeting, CDO creates an AppointmentItem object with changes in their Calendar folder. If they decide to accept the meeting without responding to it, that is the end of the process. If they respond, a new MeetingItem object is created and sent to the meeting organizer. This MeetingItem object also contains an AppointmentItem object with possible changes. Again, its associated AppointmentItem object is a different object to the AppointmentItem object saved in their Calendar folder even though they have the same property values.

The response arrives in the meeting organizer's Inbox as a MeetingItem object. While the meeting organizer can examine the associated AppointmentItem object's properties for any differences, he must manually update the original AppointmentItem object if necessary.

The AppointmentItem Object

In Outlook, you can create appointments in any folder that is created to contain appointments. While a typical way of creating appointments is to create it in the Calendar folder in our mailboxes, we can also create public or private folders that can store appointment information in Microsoft Outlook as shown here. While a typical way of creating appointments is to create it in the Calendar folder in our mailboxes, we can also create public or private folders that can store appointment information in Microsoft Outlook as shown here:

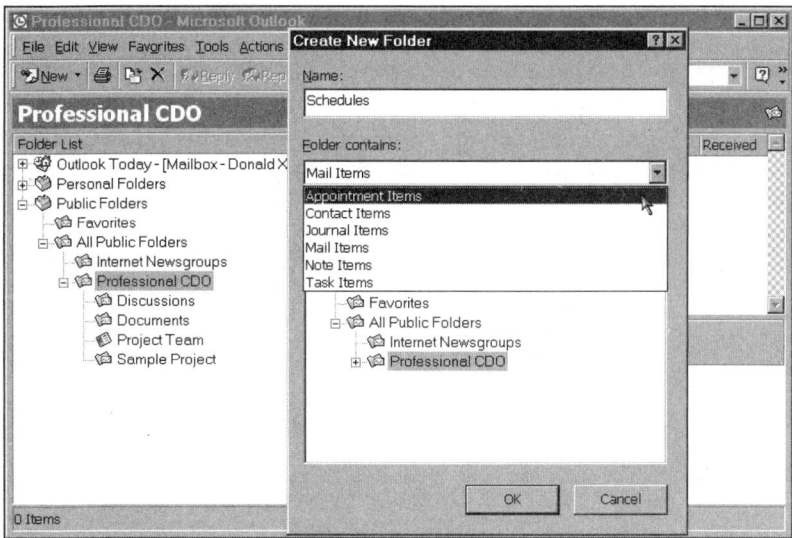

However, you can only access appointments in the user's default Calendar folder as AppointmentItem objects using CDO. To access appointments in other folders, CDO always returns Message objects with Type properties set to IPM.Appointment. The object will still contain all message and AppointmentItem properties in its Fields collection, so we can access them programmatically. In this chapter, we will only deal with appointments stored in the default Calendar folder because we have already seen how to access properties in a Fields collection.

The `AppointmentItem` object has all properties of the `Message` object. It also supports most of `Message` object methods except those listed below:

CopyTo

Forward

MoveTo

Options

Reply

ReplyAll

When an `AppointmentItem` object represents a meeting request, the recipients receive a `MeetingItem` object created from it by CDO. The following figure shows the additional properties and methods unique to the `AppointmentItem` object:

APPOINTMENTITEM	
Properties	**Type**
AllDayEvent	Boolean
BusyStatus	Long
Duration	Long
EndTime	Variant
IsRecurring	Boolean
Location	String
MeetingResponseStatus	Long
MeetingStatus	Long
Organizer	AddressEntry
ReminderMinuteBeforeStart	Long
ReminderSet	Boolean
ReplyTime	Variant
ResponseRequested	Boolean
StartTime	Variant
Methods	
ClearRecurrencePattern	
GetRecurrencePattern	
Respond	

The AllDayEvent, StartTime, EndTime, and Duration Properties

The `StartTime` and `EndTime` properties specify the starting and ending data/time of an appointment. They are all Visual Basic `Variants` with `vbDate` subtypes. The `Duration` property returns the duration of the appointment in minutes. It is a read-only property and is automatically calculated from the `StartTime` and `EndTime` property values by CDO.

The `AllDayEvent` property indicates whether or not the appointment will take a full day. An appointment may last several days. For example, if you are heading out for a round-the-world trip, you can mark it as an all-day event for 3 months.

The BusyStatus Property

This property indicates how the appointment will appear in your calendar. It can have one of the following four values:

CDO Constant	Value	Meaning
CdoFree	0	The user is free in the whole time slot
CdoTentative	1	The user has one or more tentative commitments in the whole or a part of the time slot

CDO Constant	Value	Meaning
CdoBusy	2	The user has one or more confirmed commitments in the whole or a part of the time slot
CdoOutOfOffice	3	The user is out of the office in the whole or a part of the time slot

The IsRecurring Property and the GetRecurrencePattern and ClearRecurrencePattern Methods

The `IsRecurring` property returns `True` if the appointment is a recurring appointment. The `GetRecurrencePattern` method returns the associated `RecurrencePattern` object that specifies how the appointment will recur. The `ClearRecurrencePattern` method makes the appointment non-recurring and sets the `IsRecurring` property to `False`. We will see more on this later when we update our sample project.

The Organizer and Location Properties

The `Organizer` property returns an `AddressEntry` object representing the user who creates the appointment. It is set to the current user by CDO when the appointment is created. The `Location` property is a string that specifies where the appointment will take place.

The ReminderSet and ReminderMinutesBeforeStart Properties

The `ReminderSet` property indicates whether or not a reminder is set for the appointment. If it is `True`, the `ReminderMinutesBeforeStart` property specifies how many minutes before the appointment starting time the reminder should fire.

The MeetingStatus Property

The `MeetingStatus` property specifies whether this appointment represents a meeting. It can take one of the following four values, as specified in the `CdoMeetingStatusTypes` enum.

CDO Constant	Value	Meaning
CdoNonMeeting	0	This is not a meeting. It is scheduled for the current user only.
CdoMeeting	1	This is a meeting request. You must set the `MeetingStatus` property to `CdoMeeting` before sending out a meeting request.
CdoMeetingReceived	3	This appointment represents a meeting and the meeting request has been received by the recipients.
CdoMeetingCanceled	5	This appointment represents a meeting. You can send a request to cancel the meeting by setting the `MeetingStatus` property to `CdoMeetingCanceled`.

The ResponseRequested Property

The `ResponseRequested` property specifies whether the meeting organizer wishes to receive a response. It is merely an indication of the meeting organizer's intention, rather than an enforceable request.

The MeetingResponseStatus Property

This property indicates if this appointment represents a meeting request, and if so, what response it has received. You can access this property in the original appointment and the appointment associated with a response to the meeting response. This property can take of the following values defined in the `CdoResponseStatus` enum.

CDO Constant	Value	Meaning
CdoResponseNone	0	Returned from the original appointment in Outlook only. This appointment does not represent a meeting.
CdoResponseNotResponded	5	Same as above, but in Microsoft Schedule+ only.
CdoResponseOrganized	1	Returned from the original appointment in Outlook only. This appointment represents a meeting.
CdoResponseAccepted	3	Returned from an `AppointmentItem` object associated with a meeting response. The recipient has accepted the request.
CdoResponseTentative	2	Returned from an `AppointmentItem` object associated with a meeting response. The recipient has tentatively accepted the request.
CdoResponseDeclined	4	Returned from an `AppointmentItem` object associated with a meeting response. The recipient has declined the request.

The ReplyTime Property

When a recipient of a meeting request accepts a meeting, CDO creates an appointment in their Calendar folder. The `ReplyTime` property of the appointment returns the date/time when the reply is sent. Its value is not specified if the recipient accepts the meeting but has not sent a reply. It is not meaningful in the original appointment in the meeting organizer's Calendar folder.

The Respond Method

You can only call the `Respond` method of an `AppointmentItem` object that is associated with a `MeetingItem`:

```
Set objMeetingItem = objAppItem.Respond(RespondType)
```

The `Respond` type has one of the following three values defined in the `CdoResponseStatus` enum:

CDO Constant	Value	Meaning
CdoResponseAccepted	3	Accept the meeting request
CdoResponseTentative	2	Tentatively accept the meeting request
CdoResponseDeclined	4	Decline the meeting request

This method creates a new `MeetingItem` object and sends it to the meeting organizer.

The RecurrencePattern Object

In CDO, an `AppointmentItem` object is a message with additional properties. It may contain an optional `RecurrencePattern` object that encapsulates whether and how the appointment recurs in the future. For instance, if you are a team leader, you can set up a meeting with your team members at 4 o'clock every Friday afternoon to review the progress of your project. You create an appointment and set it to recur once a week, on Friday afternoons.

The `RecurrencePattern` object has a set of properties (but no methods); many of them have the same meaning as the same properties of the `AppointmentItem` object:

RECURRENCEPATTERN	
Properties	**Type**
Application	String
Class	Long
DayOfMonth	Long
DayOfWeekMask	Long
Duration	Long
EndTime	Variant
Instance	Long
Interval	Long
MonthOfYear	Long
NoEndDate	Boolean
Occurances	Long
Parent	AppointmentItem
PatternEndDate	Variant
PatternStarDate	Variant
RecurrenceType	Long
Session	Session
StartTime	Variant
Methods	

While most properties are self-explanatory, some of them such as `DayOfWeekMask` and `Instance` are quite complex and inter-related to each other. We will examine each property in detail when we create a recurrent pattern entry form in our sample application, and they really will make more sense in that context, so we won't look at them here.

The MeetingItem Object

The `MeetingItem` object itself is very simple. In addition to the normal message properties and methods, it has one extra property and two extra methods:

MEETINGITEM	
Properties	**Type**
MeetingType	Long
Methods	
GetAssociatedAppointment	
Respond	

The MeetingType Property

The new property on the CDO `MeetingItem` object is `MeetingType`. It has two possible values, `CdoMeetingRequest` (1) and `CdoMeetingResponse`. When a `MeetingItem` object is created from a call to an `AppointmentItem`'s Send method, its `MeetingType` is set to `CdoMeetingRequest`. When you respond to a meeting request, the `MeetingType` is set to `CdoMeetingResponse`.

The GetAssociatedAppointment Method

This method returns the appointment object associated with the meeting object. It is not the same `AppointmentItem` object from which this meeting object is created, because that appointment stays in the appointment creator's mailbox. If a meeting request is sent to multiple recipients, each recipient receives a different `AppointmentItem` object although most of the properties will have the same value.

The Respond Method

After you have decided to accept or decline a meeting request, you call the `Respond` method:

```
Set objRespMeetingItem = objMeetingItem.Respond(RespondType)
```

The `Respond` type takes one of the following three values, as defined in the `CdoResponseStatus` enum:

CDO Constant	Value	Meaning
CdoResponseAccepted	3	Accept the meeting request
CdoResponseTentative	2	Tentatively accept the meeting request
CdoResponseDeclined	4	Decline the meeting request

When you send an `AppointmentItem` object to a recipient, CDO creates a `MeetingItem` object containing a copy of that `AppointmentItem` object, sets its `MeetingType` property to `CdoMeetingRequest` (1), and delivers the `MeetingItem` to the recipient. In a CDO application, we can respond to a meeting request by calling the `Respond` method of either the `MeetingItem` object or its associated `AppointmentItem` object. Both methods create a new `MeetingItem` object as a response to the meeting request.

When we call the `MeetingItem`'s `Respond` method, CDO creates another `MeetingItem` object and sets its `MeetingType` property to `CdoMeetingResponse` (2). The `Type` property of the new response `MeetingItem` stores the type of the recipient's response as shown in the following table:

RespondType	Type
CdoResponseAccepted	IPM.Schedule.Meeting.Resp.Pos
CdoResponseTentative	IPM.Schedule.Meeting.Resp.Tent
CdoResponseDeclined	IPM.Schedule.Meeting.Resp.Neg

Querying User Availability

While it is possible to send out meeting requests and check the attendees' response to decide whether a meeting will go ahead, it's useful that the meeting organizer can check each intended participant's availability for a given time period *before* sending the meeting request. If you are organizing a meeting, you will appreciate the convenience of knowing other people's schedules so that you can arrange the meeting at a time when everyone is free. This ability is modeled in CDO where you can retrieve the free/busy status of yourself and other users.

The CDO `AddressEntry` object and `Recipient` object provide a `GetFreeBusy` method that returns the availability of a user in a time period. The `Recipients` collection also has the same method, but in this case it returns the collective free/busy status of all recipients in the collection:

```
strAvail = Object.GetFreeBusy(StartTime, EndTime, Interval)
```

The `Interval` parameter specifies the length of time slot in minutes. For instance, if you need to know a user's availability from 8am to 10am on September the 15th in half-hour slots, you can call this method as follows:

```
strAvail = objAddrEntry.GetFreeBusy("8:00:00 09/15/1999", _
              "10:00:00 09/15/1999", 30)
```

The returned string contains four characters, the first representing the user availability between 8:00 to 8:30, the second from 8:30 to 9:00, the third from 9:00 to 9:30, and the fourth from 9:30 to 10:00. Each character may have one of the following four values:

Character	CDO Constant	Meaning
0	CdoFree	The user is free in the whole time slot
1	CdoTentative	The user has one or more tentative commitment in the whole or a part of the time slot
2	CdoBusy	The user has one or more confirmed commitment in the whole or a part of the time slot
3	CdoOutOfOffice	The user is out of office in the whole or a part of the time slot

If there is an overlapping of commitments in a time slot, the `GetFreeBusy` method returns the highest value. For instance, if the user is busy from 8:30 to 8:45 and has a tentative appointment from 8:45 to 9:30, the second character in the returned string will be 2. You can refine your query by specifying a smaller time interval to obtain a more accurate result.

The `Interval` parameter must be greater than or equal to 1, otherwise, you will receive an error: `CdoE_Invalid_Parameter` (&H80070057).

The `GetFreeBusy` method of the `Recipients` collection returns the *combined availability* of the recipients in the collection in the period from `StartTime` to `EndTime`. For instance, if one recipient in the collection is busy from 8:00 to 8:15, while another is free from 8:00 to 9:00, the collection is flagged as busy between 8:00 to 8:30.

Most message stores restrict the length of period in which the schedule information is published for performance reasons. For instance, Microsoft Exchange Server and Outlook only publish a maximum of three months:

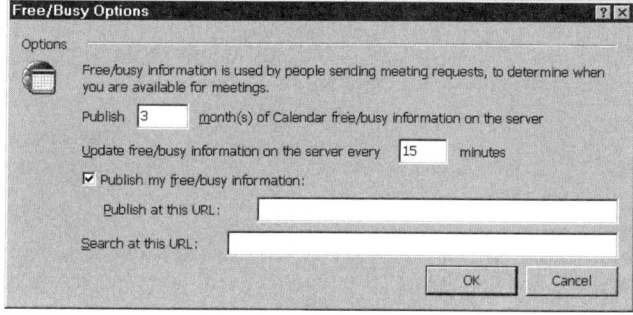

If you specify the period from StartTime to EndTime to be longer than three months, the GetFreeBusy method may return a string containing all zeros for the time slots after the maximum period. This maximum period may be changed in the Session object's SetOption method with type 'FreeBusyMonths'. However unless you are confident that underlying messaging store supports this option, you should limit the length of the search period to avoid getting inaccurate results.

One problem with the GetFreeBusy method is that you cannot get the free/busy status of a user if he has never logged in using Outlook or other messaging clients such as an Exchange Client. Calling this method on such a mailbox will cause a CdoE_NOT_FOUND (&H8004010F) error. There are three workarounds.

The first is to ask the user to log on using a messaging client so that his free/busy information becomes available.

The second is to programmatically create a test appointment in the user's Calendar folder in your application, query his free/busy status, and delete the test appointment. However, it is not always possible to create appointments in other users' mailboxes unless the current user has access permission to those mailboxes.

The last and perhaps most practical solution is to catch the CdoE_NOT_FOUND error and assume that a user is free if querying his free/busy status causes this error. This is practical because this error only occurs if the user has no appointment at all.

Managing Appointments and Meetings in the Sample Project

In this chapter, we will implement the CCalendarFolder utility class we were talking about in the previous chapter to facilitate the display of the default Calendar folder. We will also create several new forms to allow the users to create and modify appointments, check other users' availability, send meeting requests, and respond to meeting requests. We'll start with the CCalendarFolder class.

The CCalendarFolder Utility Class

As you would have expected, the CCalendarFolder class is very similar to the two other utility classes we wrote, CMessageFolder and CContactFolder. In fact, it is the simplest of the three, because the Messages collection in the default Calendar folder cannot be sorted using CDO. The appointments in the default Calendar folder are always sorted in ascending order on their StartTime property, which corresponds to MAPI property tag CdoPR_START_TIME. CDO does not support the sorting of AppointmentItems in the Calendar folder on any other properties, not even sorting them in descending order on CdoPR_START_TIME.

So we could just implement the CCalendarFolder class like the other classes without sorting the messages. If a user were to click on a column, nothing would happen as far as the user was concerned. However, we can do better than that.

Instead of giving in to the CDO restriction, we can use the ListView control's own sorting ability to sort the list. If you have not created the CCalendarFolder class in your project in the previous chapter, then you'll need to add a new class module to the project and name it CCalendarClass. Let us look at how this class works, starting with the General section. Type in this code:

```
Option Explicit

Implements IFolder

Private Const mcstrStartDate As String = "StartDate"
Private Const mcstrEndDate As String = "EndDate"
Private Const mcstrSubject As String = "Subject"
Private Const mcstrStatus As String = "Status"


Private mobjFolder As MAPI.Folder
```

As usual, we must implement the `IFolder` interface so the main form can use this class polymorphically. Instead of having different constants for column header key and text, we will use the same constant for the `Key` and `Text` properties of each column header. We will display four appointment properties: the starting and ending date/time, the subject, and the status of the appointment. We still need the folder object for storing the parent folder.

Because we will not use the `Sort` method of the CDO `Messages` collection to sort the appointments, we no longer need to know the corresponding property tag for each property to be displayed. This means that there is nothing for the `Class_Initialize()` event handler to do. As a matter of style, we'll still leave an empty procedure there just to make our intention obvious. We'll leave the error handler there as well in case we need to enhance it later on:

```
Private Sub Class_Initialize()
    On Error GoTo ErrHandler

    ' Do nothing

ExitFunc:
    Exit Sub

ErrHandler:
    Err.Raise FormatHex(Err.Number), Err.Source, Err.Description
    Resume ExitFunc
End Sub

Private Sub Class_Terminate()
    On Error Resume Next

    Set mobjFolder = Nothing
End Sub
```

The `Set Folder` property procedure is identical to other utility classes. Because our intention is to use this class to handle appointment items in the default Calendar folder only, we could just as easily get that folder when the class is created. However, letting the client objects assign the folder property is more consistent with the implementation of the other utility classes. So add this property procedure:

```
Private Property Set IFolder_Folder(RHS As MAPI.Folder)
    On Error GoTo ErrHandler

    Set mobjFolder = RHS

ExitFunc:
```

```
      Exit Property

ErrHandler:
      Err.Raise FormatHex(Err.Number), Err.Source, Err.Description
      Resume ExitFunc
End Property
```

We'll leave the other two methods defined in the `IFolder` interface for a moment and think about how to use the ListView control's sorting functions. We'll look at the working steps in the next few paragraphs and present the full code listing right after that.

When we display the appointments for the first time, we need to recreate the column headers:

```
   With lstView.ColumnHeaders
      .Clear
      Set hdrColumn = .Add(Key:=mcstrStartDate, Text:=mcstrStartDate)
      hdrColumn.Icon = garrSortOrder(CdoAscending)

      Call .Add(Key:=mcstrEndDate, Text:=mcstrEndDate)
      Call .Add(Key:=mcstrSubject, Text:=mcstrSubject)
      Call .Add(Key:=mcstrStatus, Text:=mcstrStatus)
   End With
```

Since the appointments are always sorted by their starting time by CDO, we display the ascending order icon on the starting time column. Next, we add the appointment items to the list:

```
   With lstView.ListItems
      .Clear

      For Each objAppItem In mobjFolder.Messages
         Set itmAppItem = .Add(Text:=objAppItem.StartTime)
         With itmAppItem
            .Tag = objAppItem.StoreID & "," & objAppItem.ID
            .SubItems(1) = objAppItem.EndTime
            .SubItems(2) = objAppItem.Subject
            .SubItems(3) = arrFreeBusy(objAppItem.BusyStatus)
         End With
      Next
   End With
```

The CDO `AppointmentItem` object exposes the status of an appointment through its `BusyStatus` property. The `BusyStatus` property returns a `Long` integer that takes the following values:

Constant	Value
CdoFree	0
CdoTentative	1
CdoBusy	2
CdoOutOfOffice	3

Unless our users know CDO, displaying the numeric values will mean nothing to them. Fortunately, it is very easy to create an array of descriptive text to make the program more user-friendly:

```
arrFreeBusy = Array("Free", "Tentative", "Busy", "Out Of Office")
```

We can then get the corresponding description for each `BusyStatus` value using this array:

```
arrFreeBusy(objAppItem.BusyStatus)
```

Since we will also use this array in another form later on, let us create a function in the `MCommon` module to return this array. Add this to the `MCommon` module:

```
' In MCommon
Public Function FreeBusyArray() As Variant
    FreeBusyArray = Array("Free", "Tentative", "Busy", "Out Of Office")
End Function
```

If a user clicks on a column header after the appointments are displayed, we need not recreate the headers. We will just need to set the ListView's `SortKey` and `SortOrder` properties:

```
With lstView
    For Each hdrColumn In .ColumnHeaders
        If hdrColumn.Key = strSortColumnKey Then
            .Sorted = True
            .SortKey = hdrColumn.Index - 1
            .SortOrder = 1 - .SortOrder
            hdrColumn.Icon = garrSortOrder(.SortOrder + 1)
        Else
            hdrColumn.Icon = 0
        End If
    Next
End With
```

`strSortColumnKey` is the second parameter specified in the `IFolder`'s `SortMessages` method. It is the key of the column the user has clicked on. We just go through each column header and compare its `Key` property against this string. If they match, this is the column to be sorted on.

The ListView's `SortKey` property specifies the column index, where zero means the first column, one means the second column, and so forth. Strangely, the `Index` property of the `ColumnHeader` object returns 1 for the first column, 2 for the second column, and so on. So we subtract 1 from it and assign it to the `SortKey` property.

The `SortOrder` property of the ListView control has two values, `lvwAscending` (0) and `lvwDescending` (1). We can toggle this property like this:

```
lstView.SortOrder = 1 - lstView.SortOrder
```

Note that these two values are one less than the corresponding CDO values, `CdoAscending` (1) and `CdoDescending` (2). Therefore we assign the header column's `Icon` property with the image key stored in the `garrSortOrder` array by adding one to the `SortOrder` property value.

If the column, `hdrColumn`, is not the sort column, we remove any icon present by setting its `Icon` property value to 0. Now we've looked at the theory behind it, it's time to actually code the `ShowMessages` method as shown below:

```
Private Sub ShowMessages(lstView As MSComctlLib.ListView, _
        Optional strSortColumnKey As String = "")
   On Error GoTo ErrHandler

   Dim objAppItem As MAPI.AppointmentItem
   Dim hdrColumn As MSComctlLib.ColumnHeader
   Dim itmAppItem As MSComctlLib.ListItem
   Dim arrFreeBusy As Variant

   If Len(strSortColumnKey) = 0 Then
       ' Display the messages for the first time
       With lstView.ColumnHeaders
           .Clear
           Set hdrColumn = .Add(Key:=mcstrStartDate, Text:=mcstrStartDate)
           hdrColumn.Icon = garrSortOrder(CdoAscending)

           Call .Add(Key:=mcstrEndDate, Text:=mcstrEndDate)
           Call .Add(Key:=mcstrSubject, Text:=mcstrSubject)
           Call .Add(Key:=mcstrStatus, Text:=mcstrStatus)
       End With

       ' Display appointment items
       arrFreeBusy = FreeBusyArray
       With lstView.ListItems
           .Clear

           For Each objAppItem In mobjFolder.Messages
               Set itmAppItem = .Add(Text:=objAppItem.StartTime)
               With itmAppItem
                   .Tag = objAppItem.StoreID & "," & objAppItem.ID
                   .SubItems(1) = objAppItem.EndTime
                   .SubItems(2) = objAppItem.Subject
                   .SubItems(3) = arrFreeBusy(objAppItem.BusyStatus)
               End With
           Next
       End With
   Else
       ' No need to reload messages, simply sort the list
       With lstView
           For Each hdrColumn In .ColumnHeaders
               If hdrColumn.Key = strSortColumnKey Then
                   .Sorted = True
                   .SortKey = hdrColumn.Index - 1
                   .SortOrder = 1 - .SortOrder
                   hdrColumn.Icon = garrSortOrder(.SortOrder + 1)
               Else
                   hdrColumn.Icon = 0
               End If
           Next
       End With
```

```
      End If


ExitFunc:
    Exit Sub

ErrHandler:
    Err.Raise FormatHex(Err.Number), Err.Source, Err.Description
    Resume ExitFunc
End Sub
```

If the sort column key string is not passed, we are displaying the appointments for the first time. Otherwise, they are already displayed and should be sorted on the clicked column.

We could have done the same for the CMessageFolder and CContactFolder classes. However, as the aim of this sample project is to show what we can do with CDO, we used them to illustrate how we can sort messages using CDO. Here, though, we can see how to work around the limitations of CDO.

The two methods defined in the IFolder interface simply call this function to display and sort the appointments. So enter the following code snippet in the CCalendarFolder class:

```
Private Sub IFolder_ShowMessages(lstView As MSComctlLib.IListView)
    On Error GoTo ErrHandler

    ShowMessages lstView

ExitFunc:
    Exit Sub

ErrHandler:
    Err.Raise FormatHex(Err.Number), Err.Source, Err.Description
    Resume ExitFunc
End Sub

Private Sub IFolder_SortMessages(lstView As MSComctlLib.IListView, _
                strSortColumnKey As String)
    On Error GoTo ErrHandler

    ShowMessages lstView, strSortColumnKey

ExitFunc:
    Exit Sub

ErrHandler:
    Err.Raise FormatHex(Err.Number), Err.Source, Err.Description
    Resume ExitFunc
End Sub
```

You can now save and run the project to see how appointments in the default Calendar folder are displayed.

Remember the CDO bug that causes an error when we use the CDO `Session` object's `GetDefaultFolder` method to retrieve the default Calendar folder? To get around this, you should log on using either the `ProfileInfo` parameter or using a profile that is not shared by Microsoft Outlook. In fact, you should do this throughout this chapter.

The GetMessage Method

In the last chapter, we saw that the CDO `Session` object's `GetMessage` method may return one of the three types of message objects. However, our own `GetMessage` method in the main form, `FMain`, always returns a `Message` object:

```
Private Function GetMessage() As MAPI.Message
    Dim itmMessage As MSComctlLib.ListItem
    Dim arrIDs() As String

    Set itmMessage = lvwItems.SelectedItem
    If Not itmMessage Is Nothing Then
     arrIDs = Split(itmMessage.Tag, gcstrIDDelimiter)
     Set GetMessage = gobjSession.GetMessage(arrIDs(1), arrIDs(0))
    End If

    Set itmMessage = Nothing
End Function
```

Likewise the `ShowMessageProperties` method in `FMain`:

```
Private Sub ShowMessageProperties()
    Dim objMessage As MAPI.Message
    Dim frmFields As FFields

    Set objMessage = GetMessage()

    Set frmFields = New FFields
    Call frmFields.ShowForm(objMessage)

    Set frmFields = Nothing
    Set objMessage = Nothing
End Sub
```

They work just fine when we are working with normal messages represented by the CDO `Message` object. If, however, we try to use them to get an `AppointmentItem` object in the default Calendar folder, we will get a type mismatch error. We saw a workaround for this problem, but have not used it yet. Now that we're working with the `AppointmentItem` object, it's time to fix the problem:

```
Private Function GetMessage() As Object
    Dim itmMessage As MSComctlLib.ListItem
    Dim arrIDs() As String

    Set itmMessage = lvwItems.SelectedItem
    If Not itmMessage Is Nothing Then
        arrIDs = Split(itmMessage.Tag, gcstrIDDelimiter)
```

```
        Set GetMessage = gobjSession.GetMessage(arrIDs(1), arrIDs(0))
    End If

    Set itmMessage = Nothing
End Function

Private Sub ShowMessageProperties()
    Dim objMessage As Object
    Dim frmFields As FFields

    Set objMessage = GetMessage()

    Set frmFields = New FFields
    Call frmFields.ShowForm(objMessage)

    Set frmFields = Nothing
    Set objMessage = Nothing
End Sub
```

Handling Message, AppointmentItem and MeetingItems as Objects

There's actually more to fix than just that. We will also need to modify the `CutMessage`, `CopyMessage`, `PasteMessage`, and `DeleteMessage` methods in `FMain`. First, change the type of `mobjMessage` in `FMain` from `MAPI.Message` to `Object`:

```
Private mobjMessage As Object ' MAPI.Message
```

This takes care of the `CutMessage` and `CopyMessage` methods. We still need to modify the `PasteMessage` and the `DeleteMessage` methods:

```
Private Sub PasteMessage()
    Dim objCopy As Object ' MAPI.Message
    Dim strStoreID As String
    Dim strFolderID As String

...

Private Sub DeleteMessage()
    Dim objMessage As Object ' MAPI.Message

    Set objMessage = GetMessage
    If MsgBox("Delete message " & objMessage.Subject & "?", _
        vbQuestion Or vbYesNo) = vbYes Then
     Call objMessage.Delete
     Call ShowContents
    End If
    Set objMessage = Nothing
End Sub
```

The changes to the code are pretty minor, but if you try it now, you will find that they still don't seem to work because you will still be getting errors in the `PasteMessage` method. If you trace the error down, you will see that the `CopyTo` and `MoveTo` methods actually fail. Unfortunately, this is because CDO 1.21 does not support those methods for the `AppointmentItem` objects. So if you really need to copy or move appointments, you will have to do it all manually, in code. For instance, you can retrieve an appointment as a message and call its `CopyTo` or `MoveTo` method. Please remember that CDO can only access appointments in the default Calendar folder, so copying and moving appointment items to other folders might not be such a good idea in any case.

That's not to say that the changes we've just made aren't still useful – the `CopyTo` and `MoveTo` methods work fine with `MeetingItem` objects. Now let's move on and create a form to create and edit appointments.

The Appointment Form

As I mentioned before, a CDO `AppointmentItem` object is a specialized `Message` object. It inherits all properties and most methods of the `Message` object. We can create an appointment by adding a new `AppointmentItem` object to the default Calendar folder's `Messages` collection, just like we did with messages.

On the other hand, an `AppointmentItem` object has some unique properties and methods that are not available for normal `Message` objects. In this section, we will look at those properties and methods in detail, seeing how we can use them to our advantage. First, let's create an appointment entry form:

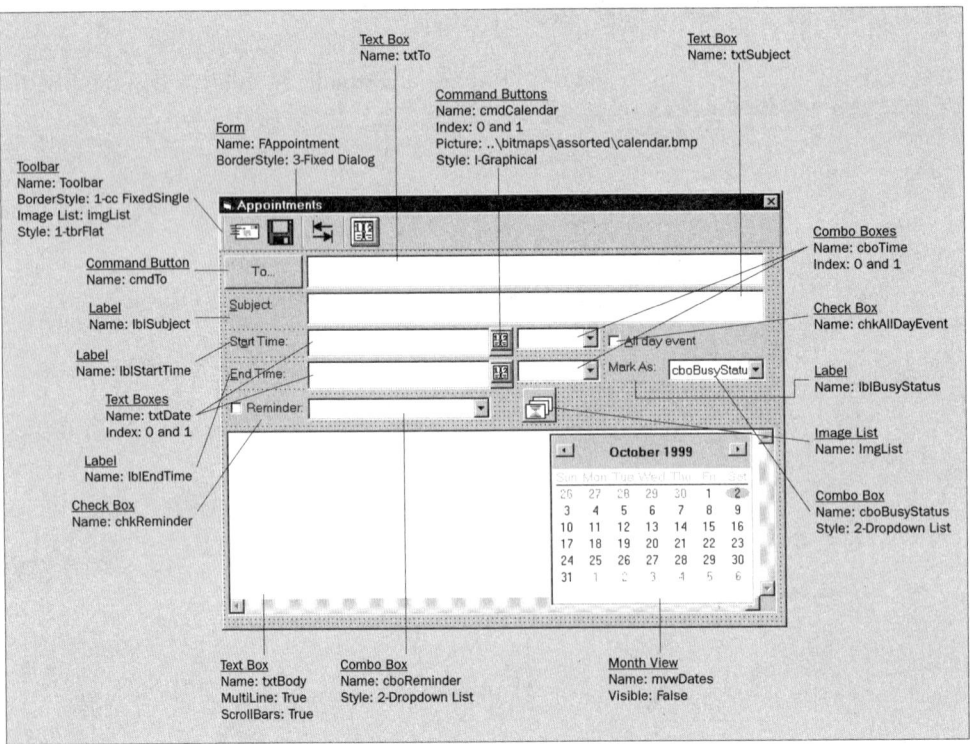

As usual, the ImageList control should contain the image files used by the toolbar buttons. The MonthView control is included in Microsoft Windows Common Controls-2, so you will need to add it to the project.

Index	File Path	Key
1	Icons\Mail\Mail03.ico	`imgSend`
2	Bitmaps\TlBr_W95\Save.bmp	`imgSave`
3	Icons\Computer\Key06.ico	`imgRecur`
4	Bitmaps\Assorted\Calendar.bmp	`imgCalendar`

And here's the toolbar:

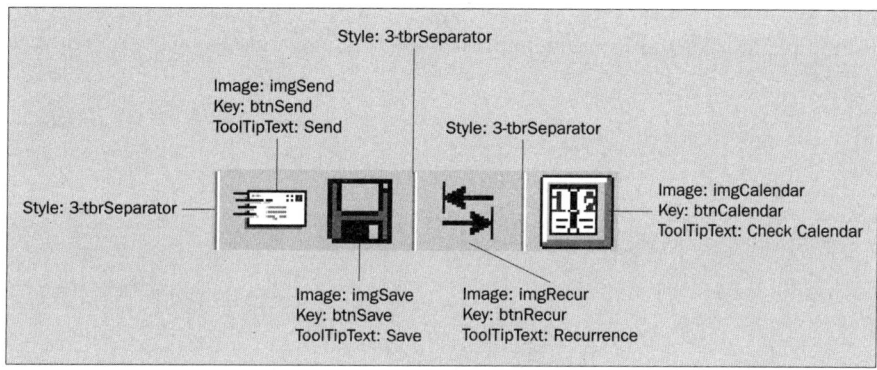

Making the Appointment Form Work

Add the following statements to the General section of the new form:

```
Option Explicit

Private Const mcstrButtonKeySend As String = "btnSend"
Private Const mcstrButtonKeySave As String = "btnSave"
Private Const mcstrButtonKeyRecur As String = "btnRecur"
Private Const mcstrButtonKeyCalendar As String = "btnCalendar"

Private mobjCalendar As MAPI.Folder
Private mobjAppItem As MAPI.AppointmentItem
```

The four constants correspond to the `Key` properties of buttons on the toolbar. This form will always work with the default Calendar folder, so we declare `mobjCalendar` to hold a reference to this folder. When the form loads, we call the `Session` object's `GetDefaultFolder` method to retrieve the default Calendar folder and assign it to `mobjCalendar`.

Add the following event handlers to the form:

```
Private Sub Form_Load()
    Set mobjCalendar = gobjSession.GetDefaultFolder(CdoDefaultFolderCalendar)
End Sub

Private Sub Form_QueryUnload(Cancel As Integer, UnloadMode As Integer)
    On Error Resume Next

    Set mobjCalendar = Nothing
    Set mobjAppItem = Nothing
End Sub
```

The second module-level object, `mobjAppItem`, holds a reference to the current working appointment object. On closing the form, we release both objects.

A user can enter recipients by either typing their names directly into the To text box, or clicking the To command button and selecting from the address books dialog. Add the relevant code now:

```
Private Sub cmdTo_Click()
    Call LookupAddressBook
End Sub

Private Sub LookupAddressBook()
    On Error GoTo ErrHandler

    Dim colRecipients As MAPI.Recipients

    ' Don't show error box if the user clicks Cancel on the AddressBook dialog box
    On Error Resume Next
    If Not mobjAppItem Is Nothing Then
        Set colRecipients = _
            gobjSession.AddressBook(Recipients:=mobjAppItem.Recipients, _
                        ParentWindow:=Me.hWnd)
    Else
        Set colRecipients = gobjSession.AddressBook(ParentWindow:=Me.hWnd)
    End If

    If Err <> 0 Then
        Err.Clear
    End If

    ' Reset the error handler
    On Error GoTo ErrHandler
    Call ShowRecipients(colRecipients)

ExitFunc:
    Exit Sub

ErrHandler:
    Call ReportError(Err)
    Resume ExitFunc
End Sub
```

```
Private Sub ShowRecipients(Recipients As MAPI.Recipients)
    Dim strRecipients As String
    Dim lngLastSemicolon As Long
    Dim objRecipient As MAPI.Recipient

    If Not (Recipients Is Nothing) Then
        For Each objRecipient In Recipients
            strRecipients = strRecipients & objRecipient.Name & gcstrRecipDelimiter
        Next

        ' Remove the last semicolon if any
        lngLastSemicolon = InStrRev(strRecipients, gcstrRecipDelimiter)
        If lngLastSemicolon > 0 Then
            strRecipients = Left(strRecipients, lngLastSemicolon - 1)
        End If
        txtTo.Text = strRecipients
    End If

    Set objRecipient = Nothing
End Sub
```

Since those methods are almost identical to their counterparts in the message entry form, FMessage, you should be familiar with them by now. The LookupAddressBook method calls the Session object's AddressBook method to display the address book dialog. After the user has selected some recipients from the list, this method returns a Recipients collection containing all selected recipients. The ShowRecipients method then displays all recipient names separated by semicolons.

The **Send** button is only visible when the user enters one or more recipients in txtTo. When it is visible, the user can send the specified recipients this appointment, which will be transformed into a meeting request. If no recipient is entered, the user can only save the appointment using the **Save** button. We will capture the Change event of txtTo to display or hide the **Send** button:

```
Private Sub txtTo_Change()
    Dim ShouldSend As Boolean

    If mobjAppItem Is Nothing Then
        ShouldSend = True
    Else
        If gobjSession.CompareIDs(gobjSession.CurrentUser.ID, _
                    mobjAppItem.Sender.ID) Then
            ShouldSend = True
        Else
            ShouldSend = False
        End If
    End If
    ShouldSend = ShouldSend And Len(Trim(txtTo.Text)) > 0

    Toolbar.Buttons(mcstrButtonKeySend).Visible = ShouldSend
End Sub
```

The user can click the **Recurrence** button to create or edit the recurrence pattern of the current appointment. We'll see how to manage the recurrence pattern object later on.

If you enter some recipients, you can check their availability during the period specified by the starting and ending date/time by clicking the Calendar button on the toolbar. Otherwise the Calendar button can be used to show the current user's own availability. We'll be looking at checking user availability later on, too.

The starting and ending date/times of the appointment are entered into a set of control arrays. Each control array contains two controls. The control with index 0 is for entering the starting date/time, while the one with index 1 is for entering ending date/time. To improve the code readability, we will define an enumeration type in MCommon:

```
' In MCommon
Public Enum DateTimeTypeEnum
    dttStartDateTime = 0
    dttEndDateTime = 1
    dttAllDateTime = 2
End Enum
```

I decided to put this type in MCommon because not only the appointment entry form, but also the recurrence pattern entry form and the meeting response form, will need to use it.

The dates are entered into the txtDate text boxes. To help users to enter the date easily, we display a MonthView control when a user clicks one of the Calendar command buttons. They can then select a date instead of having to enter the date by hand. Here's the code to display the calendar:

```
Private Sub cmdCalendar_Click(Index As Integer)
    With mvwDates
        If Index = dttStartDateTime Then
            ' Enter start date
            .Move txtDate(dttStartDateTime).Left, _
                txtDate(dttStartDateTime).Top + _
                txtDate(dttStartDateTime).Height + 30
        Else
            ' Enter end date
            .Move txtDate(dttEndDateTime).Left, _
                txtDate(dttEndDateTime).Top + _
                txtDate(dttEndDateTime).Height + 30
        End If

        .Tag = Index
        .Visible = Not .Visible
    End With
End Sub
```

The MonthView is invisible when the form loads. By default, its current day is always set to the day it is first added to the form at design time. While we can change this value at design time, the better approach is to set it to the correct day when the form loads:

```
Private Sub Form_Load()
    mvwDates.Value = Now
    Set mobjCalendar = gobjSession.GetDefaultFolder(CdoDefaultFolderCalendar)
End Sub
```

When a user clicks one of the two **Calendar** command buttons, we display the MonthView control under the proper `txtDate` text box so that the user can select a date from it. The `Tag` property of the MonthView control stores which of the two Calendar controls is clicked. Selecting a date from the control triggers the `DateClick` event, which we'll add now:

```
Private Sub mvwDates_DateClick(ByVal DateClicked As Date)
    mvwDates.Visible = False
    If mvwDates.Tag = dttStartDateTime Then
        txtDate(dttStartDateTime).Text = Format(DateClicked, gcstrDateFormat)
    Else
        txtDate(dttEndDateTime).Text = Format(DateClicked, gcstrDateFormat)
    End If
End Sub
```

It uses the MonthView's `Tag` property to work out which `txtDate` should get the selected date and displays the selected date there. `gcstrDateFormat` is a string specifying the date format – we'll define it in `MCommon`:

```
Public Const gcstrDateFormat As String = "ddd, mm/dd/yyyy"
Public Const gcstrTimeFormat As String = "h:mm ampm"
```

The second constant, `gcstrTimeFormat`, specifies the display format of time in hours and minutes. We will use it with the two `cboTime` controls that are populated with the times of day in 30-minute intervals. Since we will also use the same controls in the recurrence pattern entry form, let's add a procedure to `MCommon`:

```
Public Sub PopulateTimeComboBox(cboTime As ComboBox)
    Dim t As Date

    cboTime.Clear
    For t = CDate("12:00 am") To CDate("11:30 pm") Step CDate("0:30")
        cboTime.AddItem Format(t, "h:mm ampm")
    Next
Exit Sub
```

The above code adds a list of time value strings to the combo box, starting at 12:00 am and ending at 11:30 pm, in 30-minute intervals. You can change the start time, end time, and interval easily to suit your application's requirements.

In the `Form_Load` event handler, we populate the two `cboTime` controls using this method:

```
Private Sub Form_Load()
    mvwDates.Value = Now
    Call PopulateTimeCombo(dttAllDateTime)
    Set mobjCalendar = gobjSession.GetDefaultFolder(CdoDefaultFolderCalendar)
End Sub
```

```
Private Sub PopulateTimeCombo(ByVal DateTimeType As DateTimeTypeEnum)
    Dim ComboIndex As Long
    For ComboIndex = 0 To 1
        If DateTimeType = ComboIndex Or DateTimeType = dttAllDateTime Then
            Call PopulateTimeComboBox(cboTime(ComboIndex))
        End If
    Next
End Sub,
```

The All Day Event check box indicates whether this appointment should be scheduled for the full day. If this is checked, we will hide the two `cboTime` combo boxes, because there is no need to enter the starting and ending times if the appointment is going to take the whole day. Add the checkbox's `Click` event handler:

```
Private Sub chkAllDayEvent_Click()
    Dim lngIndex    As Long
    For lngIndex = 0 To 1
        cboTime(lngIndex).Visible = (chkAllDayEvent.Value = vbUnchecked)
    Next
End Sub
```

In Outlook, we can mark an appointment as one of the four possible statuses: free, tentative, busy, and out of office. Each of those four status settings is represented with a different color, helping us to see the availability easily. We can also use CDO to programmatically set and read this status setting; in this case, we're using the `cboBusyStatus` check box to allow the user to set the status of appointments. The `PopulateBusyStatusCombo` method in `FAppointment` populates this combo box. Make another change to the `Form`'s `Load` event handler, and add the `PopulateBusyStatusCombo` method:

```
Private Sub Form_Load()
    mvwDates.Value = Now
    Call PopulateTimeCombo(AllDateTime)
    Call PopulateBusyStatusCombo
    Set mobjCalendar = gobjSession.GetDefaultFolder(CdoDefaultFolderCalendar)
End Sub

Private Sub PopulateBusyStatusCombo()
    With cboBusyStatus
        .Clear
        .AddItem "Free"
        .AddItem "Tentative"
        .AddItem "Busy"
        .AddItem "Out Of Office"

        .Text = "Busy"
    End With
End Sub
```

We can also set a reminder of an appointment. Microsoft Outlook displays a dialog box at a specific time before the appointment's start time. The CDO `AppointmentItem` object has a pair of properties, `ReminderSet` and `ReminderMinutesBeforeStart`, to specify this setting. The `cboReminder` combo box will be filled with a list of arbitrary times for setting up the reminder. Let's add the following procedure to `MCommon`:

```
Public Sub PopulateReminderComboBox(cboReminder As ComboBox)
    With cboReminder
    .Clear
    .AddItem "0 minute"
    .ItemData(.NewIndex) = 0
    .AddItem "5 minutes"
    .ItemData(.NewIndex) = 5
    .AddItem "10 minutes"
    .ItemData(.NewIndex) = 10
    .AddItem "15 minutes"
    .ItemData(.NewIndex) = 15
    .AddItem "30 minutes"
    .ItemData(.NewIndex) = 30
    .AddItem "1 hour"
    .ItemData(.NewIndex) = 60
    .AddItem "2 hours"
    .ItemData(.NewIndex) = 120
    .AddItem "3 hours"
    .ItemData(.NewIndex) = 180
    .AddItem "4 hours"
    .ItemData(.NewIndex) = 240
    .AddItem "5 hours"
    .ItemData(.NewIndex) = 300
    .AddItem "6 hours"
    .ItemData(.NewIndex) = 360
    .AddItem "7 hours"
    .ItemData(.NewIndex) = 420
    .AddItem "8 hours"
    .ItemData(.NewIndex) = 480
    .AddItem "9 hours"
    .ItemData(.NewIndex) = 540
    .AddItem "10 hours"
    .ItemData(.NewIndex) = 600
    .AddItem "11 hours"
    .ItemData(.NewIndex) = 660
    .AddItem "12 hours"
    .ItemData(.NewIndex) = 720
    .AddItem "1 day"
    .ItemData(.NewIndex) = 1440
    .AddItem "2 days"
    .ItemData(.NewIndex) = 2880
    End With
End Sub
```

Again, we will actually populate the reminder combo box in the Form's Load event handler:

```
Private Sub Form_Load()
    mvwDates.Value = Now
    Call PopulateTimeCombo(AllDateTime)
    Call PopulateReminderComboBox(cboReminder)
    Call PopulateBusyStatusCombo
    Set mobjCalendar = gobjSession.GetDefaultFolder(CdoDefaultFolderCalendar)
End Sub
```

Since the AppointmentItem's ReminderMinutesBeforeStart property stores the number of minutes for the reminder, we save the number of minutes for each item in the combo box's ItemData array. Again, this procedure is included in MCommon because both the Appointment and Meeting forms will use it. If the reminder checkbox is checked, the reminder combo box is displayed. Otherwise, it is hidden. Let's implement that simple logic:

```
Private Sub chkReminder_Click()
    cboReminder.Visible = (chkReminder.Value = vbChecked)
End Sub
```

Now we have set up the bits and pieces of the form controls, it's time to turn our attention to creating and editing appointments.

Creating Appointments

Like other forms in the project, we will create a public ShowForm method that serves as the entry point to this form. In this section, we look at the process of creating a new appointment item. First, let's add a new public method, ShowForm, to FAppointment:

```
Public Sub ShowForm(Optional AppItem As MAPI.AppointmentItem)
    If Not AppItem Is Nothing Then
        ' Display the appointment
    Else
        Call NewAppointment
    End If

    Me.Show vbModal
End Sub
```

When we create a new appointment, we call this method without passing in an AppointmentItem object. The NewAppointment method creates default values for some of the controls on the form:

```
Private Sub NewAppointment()
    Me.Caption = "Create new appointment"
    Toolbar.Buttons(mcstrButtonKeySend).Visible = False
    Call ProcReminder(False)

    txtDate(dttStartDateTime).Text = Format(Now, gcstrDateFormat)
    txtDate(dttEndDateTime).Text = txtDate(dttStartDateTime).Text
    cboTime(dttStartDateTime).Text = Format(Now, gcstrTimeFormat)
    cboTime(dttEndDateTime).Text = Format(Now + CDate("0:30:00"), gcstrTimeFormat)
End Sub
```

When creating a new appointment, we hide the **Send** button and set the starting and ending times with the current date and time. By default, the reminder is not set:

```
Private Sub ProcReminder(ShouldSetReminder As Boolean)
    If ShouldSetReminder Then

    Else
        chkReminder.Value = vbUnchecked
        cboReminder.Visible = False
    End If
End Sub
```

Note that this form only includes a subset of common appointment properties. A user can enter the subject, body, starting and ending date/time, select the busy status, and set the reminder. When they're done, they click the **Save** button to save the appointment.

Saving an Appointment

Add the toolbar's `ButtonClick` event handler as follows:

```
Private Sub Toolbar_ButtonClick(ByVal Button As MSComctlLib.Button)
    Select Case Button.Key
        Case mcstrButtonKeySave
            Call SaveAppointment
            Unload Me

        Case mcstrButtonKeySend
            ' Send meeting request

        Case mcstrButtonKeyRecur
            ' Edit recurrence pattern

        Case mcstrButtonKeyCalendar
            ' Check free/busy status
    End Select
End Sub
```

The `SaveAppointment` method reads the values entered in the form controls and assigns them to the corresponding properties of the new `AppointmentItem` object:

```
Private Sub SaveAppointment()
    If mobjAppItem Is Nothing Then
      Set mobjAppItem = mobjCalendar.Messages.Add    ' No parameter allowed
    End If

    With mobjAppItem
        .Subject = txtSubject.Text
        .Text = txtBody.Text

        ' The Recipients collection might already contain
        ' recipients from a previous save, so let us clear
        ' it first and then add recipients again.
```

```
            Call .Recipients.Delete
            Call .Recipients.AddMultiple(txtTo.Text, CdoTo)
            Call .Recipients.Resolve

            ' No date validation here
            .StartTime = ToDate(txtDate(dttStartDateTime).Text & " " & _
                    cboTime(dttStartDateTime).Text)
            .EndTime = ToDate(txtDate(dttEndDateTime).Text & " " & _
                    cboTime(dttEndDateTime).Text)
            If .EndTime < .StartTime Then
                .EndTime = .StartTime + 1
            End If

            .AllDayEvent = (chkAllDayEvent.Value = vbChecked)
            .BusyStatus = cboBusyStatus.ListIndex

            If chkReminder.Value = vbChecked Then
                .ReminderSet = True
                .ReminderMinutesBeforeStart = _
                    cboReminder.ItemData(cboReminder.ListIndex)
            Else
                .ReminderSet = False
            End If

            .Update
        End With
    End Sub
```

When we are creating a new appointment, mobjAppItem is not instantiated until we call this method for the first time. It creates a new appointment by calling the message collection's Add method. This is the same as the way we create new messages. However, there is one difference. When calling the Add method to add a new appointment to the default Calendar folder, no parameter is allowed. Therefore we must assign the Subject and Text properties to the returned object. Adding recipients to an appointment is also identical to adding them to a normal message.

The StartTime and EndTime properties accept Visual Basic variants of type vbDate. We can generate such a variant by combining the value in txtDate and cboTime. It is not strictly necessary to convert the string into a date variable with CDate because Visual Basic will automatically convert the string into a vbDate type variant before assigning it to the StartTime or EndTime property. However, there is a little problem here.

Converting Strings to vbDate Variants

In order to provide a more user-friendly interface, we display the day of week in the txtDate text box when the user selects a date from the month view. This is done by applying the date display format constant we added to the MCommon module previously:

```
Public Const gcstrDateFormat As String = "ddd, mm/dd/yyyy"
```

Unfortunately, Visual Basic cannot convert a string containing the day of week to a vbDate variant. It will raise a Type Mismatch error when doing so. Therefore we need to remove the day from the concatenated string before assigning it to the StartTime or EndTime property. While there are a few ways of doing this, most of them are not straightforward.

In addition, the user can also type in the date directly without the day of week. For instance, they could enter 10/30/99 manually. This makes it a bit of a tedious job to fix the string. One of the easier workarounds is to try to convert it to a `Date` variable using the Visual Basic `CDate` function. Assuming that the date value is actually valid, the `CDate` function will only fail when the day of week is present. Add this function to the `MCommon` module:

```
Public Function ToDate(DateString As String) As Date
    On Error Resume Next

    Dim StartPos As Long

    ToDate = CDate(DateString)
    If Err.Number <> 0 Then
     Err.Clear
     ToDate = CDate(Mid(Format(DateString, gcstrDateFormat), _
             InStr(gcstrDateFormat, "mm")))
    End If
End Function
```

If the `CDate` function fails, we will need to remove the weekday from the string. Here I take a simplistic approach by assuming, again, that the user always enters the weekday at the beginning of the day value and follows the date format defined in `gcstrDateFormat` such as Fri, 10/29/1999. We can then remove the weekday string using the `Mid` function to trim off the first five characters. Of course, in a production program, we'd have to do a lot better than this, but for the purposes of learning CDO, this workaround is fine. Don't forget to add this procedure to the `MCommon` module.

In CDO, if `EndTime` is earlier than `StartTime`, the next `Update` call will fail with a `CdoE_INVALID_OBJECT` (&H80040108) error. Here I use a not-so-perfect workaround by assigning the `EndTime` to the day after `StartTime`, just so that the program doesn't get any more complex. A better approach would be to catch this error in the call to the appointment object's `Update` method and ask the user to re-enter the date/time values.

Setting up the `AllDayEvent` and `BusyStatus` flags is simple enough. If the reminder is set, we set the `ReminderSet` flag to `True` and assign the `ReminderMinutesBeforeStart` property. At last, we call the `Update` method to save the appointment to the Calendar folder.

After the appointment is saved, we close the form.

Sending Meeting Requests

The user can send an appointment to a list of recipients after selecting them by clicking the **Send** button on the `Toolbar` on `FAppointment`. So we need to add a new method, `SendMeeting`, to `FAppointment` and modify the `Toolbar`'s `ButtonClick` event handler to call this method.

```
Private Sub Toolbar_ButtonClick(ByVal Button As MSComctlLib.Button)
    Select Case Button.Key
        Case mcstrButtonKeySave
            Call SaveAppointment
            Unload Me

        Case mcstrButtonKeySend
```

```
            Call SendMeeting
            Unload Me

        Case mcstrButtonKeyRecur
            ' Edit recurrence pattern

        Case mcstrButtonKeyCalendar
            ' Check free/busy status
    End Select
End Sub


Private Sub SendMeeting()
    Call SaveAppointment

    With mobjAppItem
        .MeetingStatus = CdoMeeting
        Call .Send
    End With
    Set mobjAppItem = Nothing

    Unload Me
End Sub
```

It uses the `SaveAppointment` method to save the appointment and then calls the
`AppointmentItem` object's `Send` method. Just like when sending messages, it is not necessary to
call the `Update` method before calling the `Send` method, since the `Send` method saves the
appointment as well. On the other hand, *unlike* sending messages, we must set the appointment
object's `MeetingStatus` flag to `CdoMeeting` (1) before calling its `Send` method. When the `Send`
method is called, CDO creates a `MeetingItem` object containing the current `Appointment` object.
The `AddressEntry` object representing the appointment creator, or the `CurrentUser` of the
`Session` object, is assigned to the `MeetingItem` object's `Organizer` property.

By default, an `AppointmentItem` object's `MeetingStatus` is set to `CdoNonMeeting` (0). Sending
an appointment without setting its `MeetingStatus` flag to `CdoMeeting` causes a
`CdoE_No_Support` (&H80040102) error. If you wish to cancel a meeting, you can open the
corresponding appointment item in your Calendar folder, set its `MeetingStatus` to
`CdoMeetingCanceled`, and send it. Only a meeting's organizer can cancel the meeting. Please note
that deleting an appointment does not automatically send a meeting cancellation.

Although CDO documentation states that you should not send a meeting request to a distribution list,
I have not found any problem in doing so.

Reading Existing Appointments

The `FAppointment` form can also be used to display an existing appointment. All we need to do is
pass in an `AppointmentItem` object:

```
Public Sub ShowForm(Optional AppItem As MAPI.AppointmentItem)
    If Not AppItem Is Nothing Then
        Set mobjAppItem = AppItem
        Call ShowAppointment
    Else
```

```
      Call NewAppointment
    End If

    Me.Show vbModal
End Sub
```

```
Private Sub ShowAppointment()
    With mobjAppItem
        Me.Caption = "Appointment - " & .Subject
        Toolbar.Buttons(mcstrButtonKeySend).Visible = False

        Call ShowRecipients(.Recipients)
        txtSubject.Text = .Subject
        txtBody.Text = .Text
        txtDate(dttStartDateTime).Text = Format(.StartTime, gcstrDateFormat)
        txtDate(dttEndDateTime).Text = Format(.EndTime, gcstrDateFormat)

        If .AllDayEvent Then
            chkAllDayEvent.Value = vbChecked
            cboTime(0).Visible = False
            cboTime(1).Visible = False
        Else
            chkAllDayEvent.Value = vbUnchecked
            cboTime(0).Visible = True
            cboTime(1).Visible = True

            cboTime(0).Text = Format(mobjAppItem.StartTime, gcstrTimeFormat)
            cboTime(1).Text = Format(mobjAppItem.EndTime, gcstrTimeFormat)
        End If

        ProcReminder .ReminderSet
        cboBusyStatus.ListIndex = .BusyStatus
    End With
End Sub
```

The ShowAppointment method simply fills the form controls with the appointment's properties. We need to split the date and time components in the StartTime and EndTime properties. If it is an all-day event, the time combo boxes are hidden. The rest is self-explanatory.

That is all we're going to say about creating appointments and sending meeting requests. However, CDO provides the ability for us to find out people's availability and create recurring appointments. In the next section, we will learn more about retrieving the busy status of one or more users. Creating and editing recurring appointments is also covered in a later section.

Retrieving Free/Busy Status

We'll be using the `GetFreeBusy` method of the CDO `AddressEntry` object, the `Recipient` object, or the `Recipients` collection. First, add a new form, `FFreeBusy`, to the CDO Sample project:

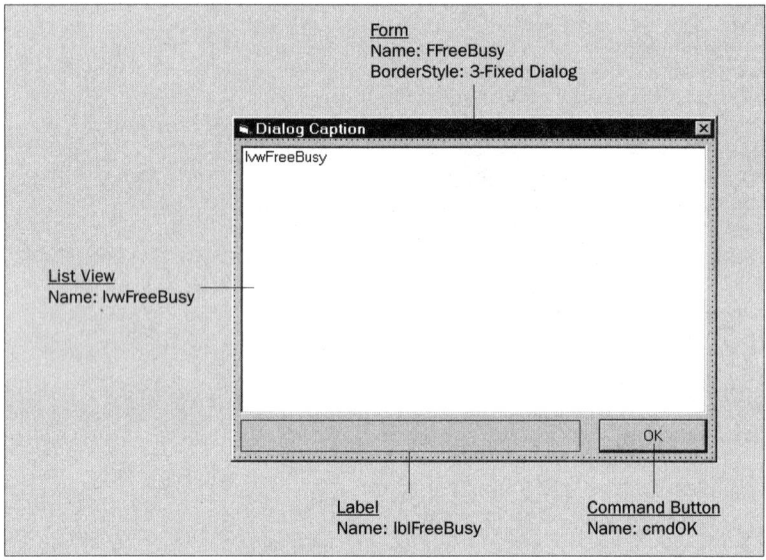

Compared to most of the other forms in the project, this one is very simple. It has just one ListView control, one label, and an OK button.

It will have a public `ShowForm` method that accepts an `Object`, a starting time, and an ending time. Add it to the form now:

```
Option Explicit

Public Sub ShowForm(AddrEntries As Object, _
        ByVal StartTime As Date, ByVal EndTime As Date)
    On Error Resume Next

    Dim arrFreeBusy   As Variant
    Dim strFreeBusy   As String
    Dim datStartTime  As Date
    Dim datEndTime    As Date
    Dim lngChar       As Long

    arrFreeBusy = FreeBusyArray

    Select Case AddrEntries.Class
        Case CdoRecipients
            If AddrEntries.Count > 1 Then
                Me.Caption = "Availability of all recipients"
            Else
```

```
            Me.Caption = "Availability of " & AddrEntries(1).Name
        End If

    Case CdoRecipient, CdoAddressEntry
        Me.Caption = "Availability of " & AddrEntries.Name

    Case Else
        Exit Sub
End Select

With lvwFreeBusy.ColumnHeaders
    .Add Text:="Start"
    .Add Text:="End"
    .Add Text:="Status"
End With

' This will fail if The mailbox has not been logged into
' with a mail client yet, as no Free/Busy information
' has yet been created for this mailbox.
strFreeBusy = AddrEntries.GetFreeBusy(StartTime, EndTime, 30)
If Err.Number = 0 Then
    With lvwFreeBusy.ListItems
        .Clear
        datStartTime = StartTime
        For lngChar = 1 To Len(strFreeBusy)
            datEndTime = datStartTime + CDate("0:30:00")
            With .Add(Text:=Format(datStartTime, gcstrTimeFormat))
                .SubItems(1) = Format(datEndTime, gcstrTimeFormat)
                .SubItems(2) = arrFreeBusy(CLng(Mid(strFreeBusy, lngChar, 1)))
            End With

            datStartTime = datEndTime
        Next
    End With

    strFreeBusy = AddrEntries.GetFreeBusy(StartTime, EndTime, _
                    DateDiff("n", StartTime, EndTime))
    lblFreeBusy = arrFreeBusy(CLng(strFreeBusy))
Else
    lblFreeBusy.Caption = "Free/Busy information is not available"
End If

Me.Show vbModal
End Sub
```

Since there is more than one CDO object that has the GetFreeBusy method, the ShowForm method uses late binding to allow for any of the three types of objects. If a Recipients collection is passed in, it displays the free/busy status of the collection unless there is only one recipient in the collection. Otherwise, it displays the recipient or address entry's name in the form caption.

To demonstrate the GetFreeBusy method in a bit more detail, it first displays the free/busy status in 30-minute slots on the ListView control, lvwFreeBusy. It then displays the overall status on the label lblFreeBusy.

The OK button simply closes the form:

```
Private Sub cmdOK_Click()
    Unload Me
End Sub
```

Since both FAppointment and the meeting form (to be created later) will use this form, let's add a public method to the common module, MCommon:

```
Public Sub ShowAvailability(AddrEntries As Object, _
                StartTime As Date, EndTime As Date)
    Dim frmFreeBusy As FFreeBusy
    Set frmFreeBusy = New FFreeBusy
    Call frmFreeBusy.ShowForm(AddrEntries, StartTime, EndTime)
    Set frmFreeBusy = Nothing
End Sub
```

It simply loads the FFreeBusy form and passes the AddressEntry, the Recipient object, or the Recipients collection it receives to the FFreeBusy's ShowForm method.

Now link up the FFreeBusy form to FAppointment by modifying the Toolbar's ButtonClick event handler in FAppointment:

```
Private Sub Toolbar_ButtonClick(ByVal Button As MSComctlLib.Button)
    Select Case Button.Key
        Case mcstrButtonKeySave
            Call SaveAppointment
            Unload Me

        Case mcstrButtonKeySend
            Call SendMeeting
            Unload Me

        Case mcstrButtonKeyRecur
            ' Edit recurrence pattern

        Case mcstrButtonKeyCalendar
            Call ShowFreeBusy
    End Select
End Sub


Private Sub ShowFreeBusy()
    Dim colRecipients    As MAPI.Recipients

    If Len(Trim$(txtTo.Text)) > 0 Then
        If mobjAppItem Is Nothing Then
            Set mobjAppItem = mobjCalendar.Messages.Add
        End If

        Set colRecipients = mobjAppItem.Recipients
        With colRecipients
            Call .Delete
```

```
            Call .AddMultiple(Trim$(txtTo.Text))
            Call .Resolve
        End With

        Call ShowAvailability(colRecipients, _
            ToDate(txtDate(dttStartDateTime).Text & " " & _
                cboTime(dttStartDateTime).Text), _
            ToDate(txtDate(dttEndDateTime).Text & " " & _
                cboTime(dttEndDateTime).Text))
        Call colRecipients.Delete
        Set colRecipients = Nothing
    Else
        Call ShowAvailability(gobjSession.CurrentUser, _
            ToDate(txtDate(dttStartDateTime).Text & " " & _
                cboTime(dttStartDateTime).Text), _
            ToDate(txtDate(dttEndDateTime).Text & " " & _
                cboTime(dttEndDateTime).Text))
    End If
End Sub
```

If no recipient is entered, the `ShowFreeBusy` method calls the `ShowAvailability` method to display the current user's availability. It obtains the starting and ending time from the starting and ending date/time entered on `FAppointment`.

If there are recipients, we need to create a `Recipients` collection. It creates a new appointment if there isn't one already, then adds the entered recipients to the `Appointment` object's `Recipients` collection. The `ShowAvailability` method then picks up this collection and displays its collective availability.

To test this form, create some appointments with different busy status for at least two mailboxes. The following screen shots show two users during a time period between 10am and 2pm:

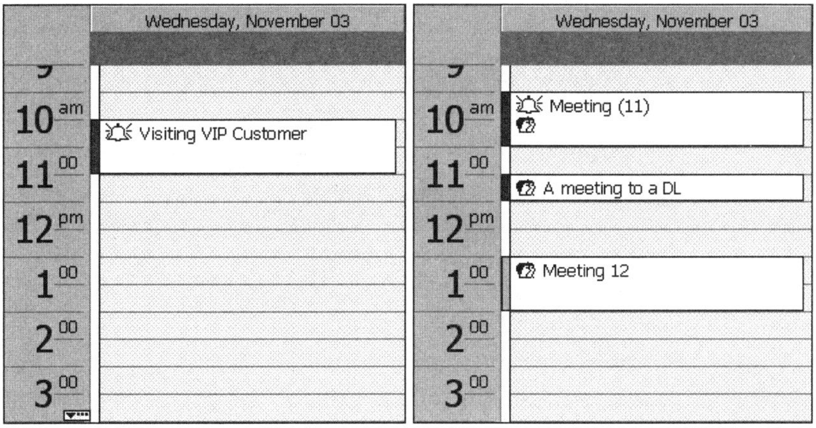

The above screen shots show that User 1 on the left will be out of the office between 10:30am to 11:30am. User 2 on the right has three appointments: the first two are marked as busy, while the third is tentative. Here is how the `FFreeBusy` form displays these results:

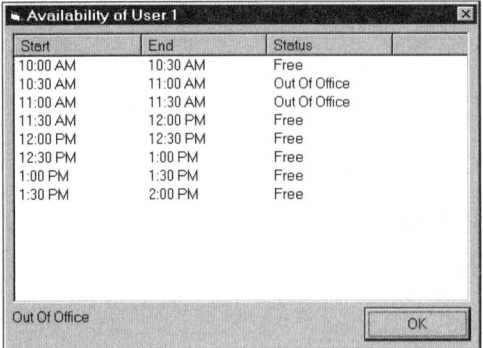
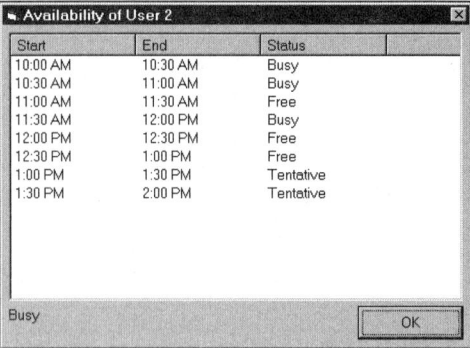

As you can see from the above figures, the overall free/busy status of each user is the highest value. For user 1, it is Out Of Office even though he is not out of office for the whole 4 hours. For user 2, it is Busy.

If you don't see the correct free/busy status in this form after adding in some test appointments for users 1 and 2, it is possible that their free/busy status has not been published. By default, updating the free/busy status to the Exchange Server is done every 15 minutes. You can check this setting in Outlook by selecting the Tools/Options menu and clicking the Calendar Options button:

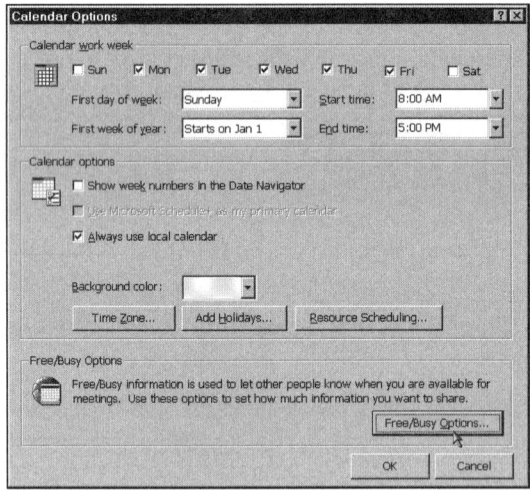

You can then click the Free/Busy Options button to open the Free/Busy Options form, which we saw earlier. While we cannot force the free/busy status to be updated to the Exchange Server, we can set the update interval to a shorter time period, such as one minute. This is useful when developing and testing applications, because it wouldn't be much fun if we had to wait 15 minutes each time we created or modified an appointment. In a production environment, however, we should set this option to a reasonable value to reduce load pressure on the server and network traffic. The default setting of 15 minutes is generally acceptable.

If we display the collective status of the two users, we will get the most committed state in each time slot:

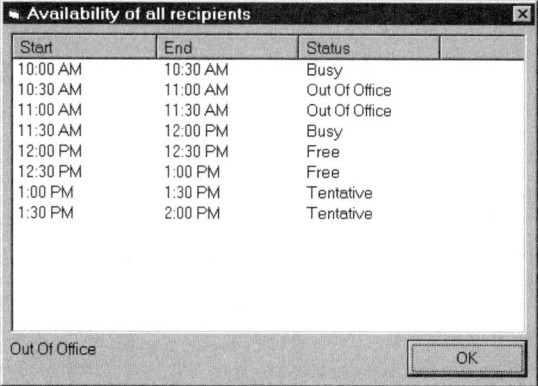

This example illustrates the power of the GetFreeBusy method. It allows us check out the free/busy status of any user in our messaging system. We can use this information to create well-behaved collaboration applications. For instance, we can check out the recipients' availability before scheduling meetings.

In the next section, we look into another extremely useful object, the RecurrencePattern object.

Managing Recurrence Patterns

A CDO AppointmentItem object has an associated RecurrencePattern object that specifies the AppointmentItem's recurrence characteristics. It contains a comprehensive set of properties indicating when, how often, and for how long the appointment will occur. There are several recurrence types.

Recurrence Types

The CDO RecurrencePattern object has a RecurrenceType property that specifies the frequency of the recurrence. It has one of the following values.

CdoRecurTypeDaily (0)

The appointment recurs once every few days. For instance, we can make an appointment recur once in every two days. The Interval property specifies the day interval.

CdoRecurTypeWeekly (1)

The appointment recurs on certain days of the week. The DayOfWeekMask property specifies the days. It can have a combination of any day or days from Sunday to Saturday. For instance, you can specify that an appointment shall occur every Monday and Thursday. The following table lists the CDO constants representing the days of the week:

CdoSunday	$1 = 2^0$
CdoMonday	$2 = 2^1$
CdoTuesday	$4 = 2^2$
CdoWednesday	$8 = 2^3$
CdoThursday	$16 = 2^4$
CdoFriday	$32 = 2^5$
CdoSaturday	$64 = 2^6$

As you would have expected, we can combine those constants to represent a combination of days using the bit-wise OR operator. For example, if an appointment should recur on both Sunday and Wednesday, we assign the DayOfWeekMask property with:

```
CdoSunday Or CdoWednesday = 9
```

If an appointment occurs on all working days, the DayOfWeekMask will be 62:

```
CdoMonday Or CdoTuesday Or CdoWednesday Or CdoThursday Or CdoFriday = 62
```

Furthermore, we can also specify the Interval property to indicate whether an appointment should recur weekly, fortnightly, and so forth.

CdoRecurTypeMonthly (2)

If an appointment is to recur on monthly basis, we set its recurrence pattern object's RecurrenceType to CdoRecurMonthly. The recurrence pattern object's DayOfMonth property specifies on which day of the month the appointment should occur. This property can have an integer value of 1 to 31, representing the first to the 31st day of the month. If you set the appointment to recur on the 31st day, it will actually happen on the last day of any month that has less than 31 days. For example, the appointment will recur on the 30th of June. Only one day can be specified. We can also set the Interval property to indicate whether an appointment recurs monthly, bi-monthly, and so on.

CdoRecurTypeMonthlyNth (3)

The suffix Nth of this constant denotes that this recurrence type allows us to set in which week of the month an appointment should recur. We can then use the DayOfWeekMask and Instance properties to specify the details. For example, if an appointment recurs on each Monday and Thursday of the second week, we can set the DaysOfWeekMask property to 17 (CdoMonday Or CdoThursday) and the Instance property to 2. Like the CdoRecurTypeMonthly type, we can also set the Interval property.

CdoRecurTypeYearly (4)

This type is similar to CdoRecurTypeMonthly. We can specify the MonthOfYear and DayOfMonth properties to indicate on which day of which month of the year an appointment should recur. It only accepts one day and month so you cannot specify multiple days or months of the year. The DayOfMonth property has the same value (1 to 31) as in CdoRecurTypeMonthly. The MonthOfYear property may have a value between 1 and 12. The Interval property further specifies the year interval.

CdoRecurTypeYearlyNth (5)

Like the `CdoRecurTypeMonthlyNth` type, this allows us to specify the `DayOfWeekMask` and `Instance` properties to indicate the days of which week of the month. We can also set the `MonthOfYear` and `Interval` properties as in `CdoRecurTypeYearly`.

The `RecurrenceType` property and the related properties are very flexible, but their capabilities aren't very clear since there are so many possible combinations. It would be easier to see if we actually tried using them, so that's exactly what we are going to do next.

The Sample Recurrence Entry Form

In this section, we will add a new form to the Sample CDO project that resembles most options found in the Microsoft Outlook **Appointment Recurrence** form. Be warned, though, this form is full of controls. We're going to have to build it bit by bit. Here's what we'll be trying to emulate:

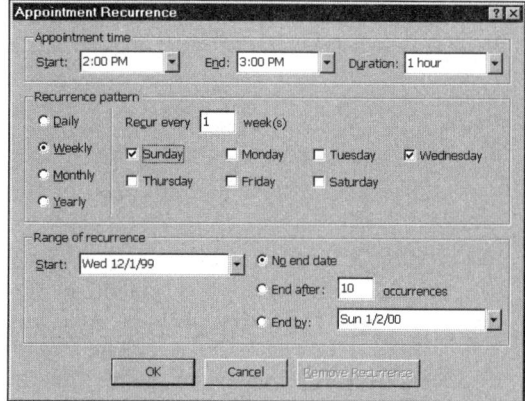

This incredibly powerful form allows a user to enter the starting and ending time of each occurrence, the recurrence frequency, and the time period in which the appointment should recur. We will recreate a very similar form to provide the most of the functionality. In the process of building this form, we will learn the use of the CDO `RecurrencePattern` object in more detail. Here is a screenshot that shows the basic framework of the `FRecurrence` form:

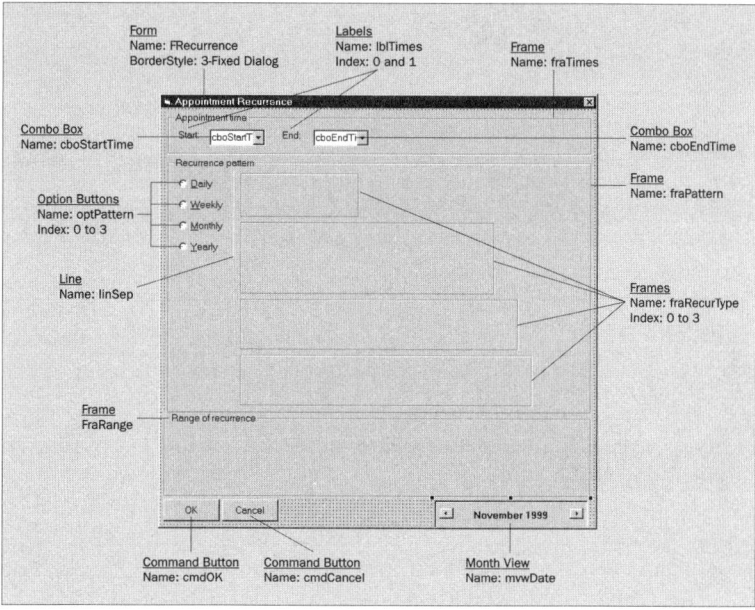

The `fraRecurType` array contains four frames in the Recurrence pattern frame. This is by far the most complex form in our project so I'm not listing all the controls in one batch. We'll build it up as we go along. When we discuss each of the frames, we'll add the controls contained in that frame so that we can reference them easily. Don't be intimidated by the form's apparent complexity though.

As usual, this form will define a public `ShowForm` method as its sole entry point. It also has two module-level objects, which we'll add first:

```
Option Explicit

' All weekdays =
' CdoMonday Or CdoTuesday Or CdoWednesday Or CdoThursday Or CdoFriday
Private Const mclngAllWeekdays As Long = 62

Private mobjAppItem As MAPI.AppointmentItem
Private mobjPattern As MAPI.RecurrencePattern
```

The `mobjAppItem` is the parent `AppointmentItem` object, and `mobjPattern` is the current working pattern. `mclngAllWeekdays` will be used to indicate that we want an appointment to recur on all weekdays.

Getting the Originating AppointmentItem Object

We access the recurrence pattern of an appointment through its `GetRecurrencePattern` method:

```
'
' Entry point to this form
'
Public Sub ShowForm(AppItem As MAPI.AppointmentItem)
    On Error GoTo ErrHandler

    If Not AppItem Is Nothing Then
      Set mobjAppItem = AppItem.GetRecurrencePattern.Parent
      Set mobjPattern = mobjAppItem.GetRecurrencePattern

      Call ShowPattern
      Me.Show vbModal
    End If

ExitFunc:
    Exit Sub

ErrHandler:
    Call ReportError(Err)
    Resume ExitFunc
End Sub
```

Since a `RecurrencePattern` is always attached to an `AppointmentItem`, this method requires the parent appointment object. This line:

```
Set mobjAppItem = AppItem.GetRecurrencePattern.Parent
```

may seem a little strange: it does not assign the passed in `AppItem` to `mobjAppItem`. This has to do with the way CDO handles the recurrences.

Modifying a Recurrence Pattern

When you create a new recurrence pattern, its parent appointment is called its **originating** appointment. To save this new pattern, you call its originating appointment's `Update` method. Once a recurrence pattern has been created, it can be accessed from any of the appointments in the recurring series using the `GetRecurrencePattern` method. However, if you modify a recurrence pattern, you must call its originating appointment object's `Update` method. If you call the `Update` method of any other appointment object in the series, only that appointment is changed. The series' recurrence pattern is not changed, that is, all other appointments in the recurring series remain unchanged.

A `RecurrencePattern` object's `Parent` property always returns its originating appointment object, not the appointment object from which this `RecurrencePattern` object is accessed. This provides a convenient way to retrieve the originating appointment object. Here the `ShowForm` method stores the originating appointment object in `mobjAppItem` so that when we call its `Update` method, we update the recurrence pattern of the series.

After caching the originating appointment object, the `RecurrencePattern` object itself is assigned to `mobjPattern`. The `ShowPattern` method displays the recurrence properties.

Accessing the Recurrence Pattern of an Appointment

But wait – what happens if the appointment is not recurring? In that case, the `GetRecurrencePattern` method creates a recurrence pattern for this appointment. This makes the appointment recurring and sets its `IsRecurring` flag to `True`. Please note that there is no `CreateRecurrencePattern` method that creates a new `RecurrencePattern` object for an `AppointmentItem`. There doesn't need to be, though, as you can just use `GetRecurrencePattern`.

The newly created recurrence pattern object is filled with default values that correspond to the relevant properties of the parent appointment object. For instance, the recurrence pattern's starting and ending time are set to the time portions of the starting and ending time of the parent appointment items. You can then change the `RecurrencePattern` object's properties as required.

This approach has an implication: you cannot use the `GetRecurrencePattern` method to test whether an appointment is recurring. If it wasn't, it becomes so anyway, so doing this won't work:

```
If objAppItem.GetRecurrencePattern Is Nothing Then ' Always False
```

...because this method will never return `Nothing`. The reliable way of testing this is to check the `AppointmentItem` object's `IsRecurring` property. Please note that once the `GetRecurrencePattern` method is called for the first time, a new recurrence pattern object is created and attached to the appointment. To make the appointment non-recurring, you must call its `ClearRecurrencePattern` method to delete the recurrence pattern. Calling this method automatically sets the `IsRecurring` property back to `False`.

The `GetRecurrencePattern` and `ClearRecurrencePattern` methods are the only methods for accessing and maintaining recurrence patterns.

Back to the code above, once we have set up the module-level objects, we call the `ShowPattern` method, which you should now add:

```
Private Sub ShowPattern()
    Call ShowTimes
    Call ShowRecurType
    Call ShowRange
End Sub
```

We will see each of the methods it calls in detail in a moment. The `Form_Load` event handler initializes the `mvwDate` control and populates various combo boxes with option values:

```
Private Sub Form_Load()
    mvwDate.Value = Now
    Call PopulateTimeComboBox(cboStartTime)
    Call PopulateTimeComboBox(cboEndTime)
    Call PopulateInstance(cboMonthInstance)
    Call PopulateInstance(cboYearInstance)
    Call PopulateDayofWeek(cboMonthlyDayOfWeek)
    Call PopulateDayofWeek(cboYearlyDayOfWeek)
    Call PopulateMonthOfYear
End Sub
```

Initializing Option Lists

The `PopulateTimeComboBox` method was explained earlier. The other methods are listed below.

```
Private Sub PopulateInstance(cboInstance As ComboBox)
    With cboInstance
        .AddItem "first"
        .AddItem "second"
        .AddItem "third"
        .AddItem "fourth"
        .AddItem "last"
    End With
End Sub
```

The `Instance` property specifies in which week of the month an appointment should occur. We can programmatically select an item from this combo box to show its current value. Because the `Instance` property requires a value between 1 and 5, we need to calculate this value from the selected item like this:

```
mobjPattern.Instance = cboInstance.ListIndex + 1
```

When we display the instance of an existing pattern, we calculate it like this:

```
cboInstance.ListIndex = mobjPattern.Instance - 1
```

The next method to look at is `PopulateDayOfWeek`. Type in this code:

```
Private Sub PopulateDayOfWeek(cboDayOfWeek)
    With cboDayOfWeek
        .AddItem "Sunday"
        .AddItem "Monday"
        .AddItem "Tuesday"
        .AddItem "Wednesday"
        .AddItem "Thursday"
        .AddItem "Friday"
        .AddItem "Saturday"
    End With
End Sub
```

If you review the possible values of the `DayOfWeekMask` property, you will notice that the constants are equal to the first six powers of 2. To retrieve a `DayOfWeekMask` value from this combo box, we use this code:

```
mobjPattern.DayOfWeekMask = 2 ^ cboDayOfWeek.ListIndex
```

To display an existing `DayOfWeekMask` property, we just do the reverse. We'll need a `Log2` function – add this function to `FRecurrence`:

```
Private Function Log2(ByVal n As Long) As Long
    Log2 = Log(n) / Log(2)
End Function
```

Then we can just use this:

```
cboDayOfWeek.ListIndex = Log2(mobjPattern.DayOfWeekMask)
```

The `PopulateMonthOfYear` method is straightforward, but it must populate two combo boxes in the control array `cboMonthOfYear`:

```
Private Sub PopulateMonthOfYear()
    Dim lngIndex As Long
    For lngIndex = 0 To 1
        With cboMonthOfYear(lngIndex)
            .AddItem "January"
            .AddItem "February"
            .AddItem "March"
            .AddItem "April"
            .AddItem "May"
            .AddItem "June"
            .AddItem "July"
            .AddItem "August"
            .AddItem "September"
            .AddItem "October"
            .AddItem "November"
            .AddItem "December"
        End With
    Next
End Sub
```

Getting the selected item in and out of these combo boxes, we can use code like the following:

```
cboMonthOfYear(0).ListIndex = mobjPattern.MonthOfYear - 1
mobjPattern.MonthOfYear = cboMonthOfYear(0).ListIndex + 1
```

We will use it later in the FRecurrence form. Now we have done the preliminary work, let's go back to our FRecurrence form user interface.

Displaying and Editing Starting and Ending Times

The first frame, fraTimes, contains two combo boxes, cboStartTime and cboEndTime. They correspond to the recurrence pattern object's StartTime and EndTime properties:

```
Private Sub ShowTimes()
    With mobjPattern
        cboStartTime.Text = Format(.StartTime, gcstrTimeFormat)
        cboEndTime.Text = Format(.EndTime, gcstrTimeFormat)
    End With
End Sub
```

The StartTime and EndTime properties contain both date and time portions. By default, their date portion is the same as the date in the originating appointment's StartTime and EndTime properties. In general, the date portion is not significant in recurrence pattern. However, the StartTime date portion must always be equal to the first day of the recurrence series. Here we only display the time portion, formatted to the time format we defined earlier.

When we save a recurrence pattern, we read the values in those combo boxes and assign the StartTime and EndTime properties as follows:

```
Private Sub SaveTimes()
    On Error GoTo ErrHandler

    With mobjPattern
        .StartTime = ToDate(Format(.StartTime, gcstrDateFormat) & " " & _
                cboStartTime.Text)
        .EndTime = ToDate(Format(.EndTime, gcstrDateFormat) & " " & _
                cboEndTime.Text)
    End With

ExitFunc:
    Exit Sub

ErrHandler:
    Call ReportError(Err)
    Resume ExitFunc
End Sub
```

The SaveTimes method preserves the existing date portion of each property and appends the times to the end of the time portion. As discussed in the Saving an Appointment section, the ToDate function takes care of converting the string to the vbDate format required by the StartTime and EndTime properties.

Working with Different Recurrence Types

The second frame, `fraPattern`, contains an option button array, `optPattern`, and four sub-frames. The `optPattern` array allows the user to select whether an appointment should recur daily, weekly, monthly, or yearly. On its own, it does not decide the recurrence type. We must also select an option in one of the four child frames to refine the recurrence type criteria. Let's look at each of them one by one in more detail.

Each of the four child frames corresponds to an `optPattern` button. For example, when the Daily option is chosen, the first child frame, `fraPattern(0)`, is displayed. All the others remain hidden. To improve the code readability, let's create an enumeration type in the General section of the form for identifying those frames:

```
' Determines which Recurrence Type frame should be visible
Private Enum RecurFrameTypeEnum
    rftDaily = 0
    rftWeekly = 1
    rftMonthly = 2
    rftYearly = 3
End Enum
```

For example, we can then refer to the daily child frame as `fraPattern(rftDaily)`. Showing and hiding the child frames are tasks that are better enclosed in a procedure in the `FRecurrence` form:

```
Private Sub ShowRecurTypeFrame(ByVal Index As Long)
    Const clngLeft As Long = 1260
    Const clngTop As Long = 180
    Dim lngIndex As Long

    optPattern(Index).Value = True
    For lngIndex = rftDaily To rftYearly
        With fraRecurType(lngIndex)
            If lngIndex = Index Then
                .BorderStyle = 0
                .Move clngLeft, clngTop
                .Visible = True
            Else
                .Visible = False
            End If
        End With
    Next
End Sub
```

The two constants, `clngLeft` and `clngTop`, contain arbitrary values for placing the sub-frames. You might want to modify them to fit your own controls. We pass the procedure the index of the child frame to be shown. It selects the proper `Pattern` option button on the left, moves this frame to the right place and makes it visible.

When a user selects one of the Recurrence Type option buttons, we also call this method to display the proper child frame:

```
Private Sub optPattern_Click(Index As Integer)
    Call ShowRecurTypeFrame(Index)
End Sub
```

Recurring Daily – CdoRecurTypeDaily

The first child frame, `fraRecurType(rftDaily)`, contains two options, represented in the following enumeration type, which you should add at this time:

```
Private Enum RecurrenceTypeOptionEnum
    ' Recurrence Types in Daily Recurrence Type frame
    rtoDaily = 0
    rtoWeekly = 1
End Enum
```

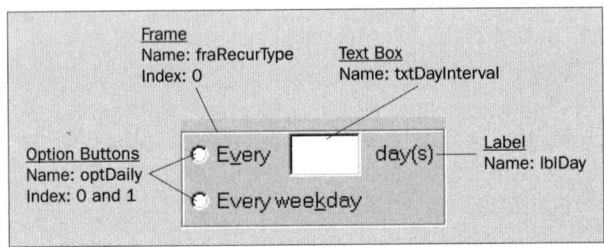

The first option, `optDaily(rtoDaily)`, matches nicely to the `CdoRecurTypeDaily` type. A user can enter the day interval in the textbox, `txtDayInterval`. This value can also be read from an existing pattern's `Interval` property. Add the following code:

```
Private Sub ShowRecurType()
    With mobjPattern
        Select Case .RecurrenceType
        Case CdoRecurTypeDaily
            Call ShowRecurTypeFrame(rftDaily)

            optDaily(rtoDaily).Value = True
            txtDayInterval.Text = .Interval
        End Select
    End With
End Sub
```

If the recurrence pattern object's `RecurrenceType` is `CdoRecurTypeDaily`, this function selects the first option and displays the day interval. Saving the recurrence type `CdoRecurTypeDaily` and day interval is simple:

```
Private Sub SaveRecurType()
    With mobjPattern
        Select Case True
            Case optPattern(rftDaily).Value
                If optDaily(rtoDaily).Value Then
                    ' Daily
                    .RecurrenceType = CdoRecurTypeDaily
                    .Interval = txtDayInterval.Text
                End If
        End Select
    End With
End Sub
```

It checks whether the `Daily` option is selected and, if so, whether the first option in the `Daily` child frame is selected. If both are true, it assigns `CdoRecurTypeDaily` to the `RecurrenceType` and the value in `txtDayInterval` to the `Interval` property.

The second option, every weekday, is actually a special case of `CdoRecurTypeWeekly`.

Recurring Weekly – CdoRecurTypeWeekly

The `DayOfWeekMask` property accepts values that represent multiple days. A common combination of days is to specify all working days. As explained in the Recurrence Types section, this combination is represented with a value 62. The `Daily` frame displays this special case of the weekly recurrence type:

```
Private Sub ShowRecurType()
    With mobjPattern
        Select Case .RecurrenceType
            Case CdoRecurTypeDaily
                Call ShowRecurTypeFrame(rftDaily)

                optDaily(rtoDaily).Value = True
                txtDayInterval.Text = .Interval


            Case CdoRecurTypeWeekly
                If .DayOfWeekMask = mclngAllWeekdays Then
                    Call ShowRecurTypeFrame(rftDaily)
                    optDaily(rtoWeekly).Value = True
                End If
        End Select
    End With
End Sub
```

So if the recurrence pattern's `RecurrenceType` is `CdoRecurTypeWeekly` and its `DayOfWeekMask` is 62, we should still display the Daily frame and select the second option. Saving it back to the pattern object is just as simple:

```
Private Sub SaveRecurType()
    With mobjPattern
        Select Case True
            Case optPattern(rftDaily).Value
```

```
              If optDaily(rtoDaily).Value Then
                  ' Daily
                  .RecurrenceType = CdoRecurTypeDaily
                  .Interval = txtDayInterval.Text
              Else
                  ' Weekly with all weekdays
                  .RecurrenceType = CdoRecurTypeWeekly
                  .DayOfWeekMask = mclngAllWeekdays
              End If
          End Select
      End With
  End Sub
```

The weekly recurrence type can be more flexible. It allows us to specify any combination of days and the week interval. The second child frame, `fraRecurType(rftWeekly)`, provides the user interface for managing this:

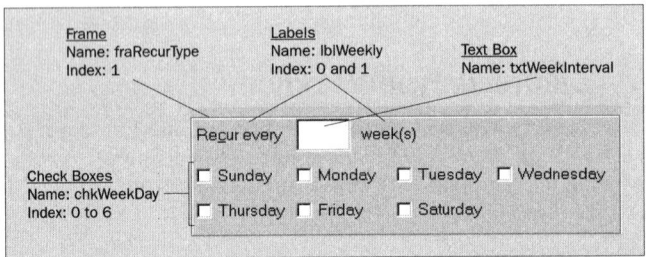

The `txtWeeklyInterval` box corresponds to the week interval value stored in the `Interval` property. Each check box shows whether a day of the week is selected in the recurrence pattern. As I explained before, the value of the weekday combination is calculated by using the bitwise OR operator:

```
CdoMonday Or CdoWednesday Or CdoFriday...
```

Extracting the day out of the combination requires some bit twiddling. For instance, to find out whether Monday is in the combination, we will do something like this:

```
If mobjPattern.DayOfWeekMask And CdoMonday = CdoMonday Then
    ' Monday is in the combination
```

Therefore we can display the `DayOfWeekMask` property by AND-ing it with each CDO weekday constant, as illustrated in the following code snippet.

```
Private Sub ShowRecurType()
    With mobjPattern
        Select Case .RecurrenceType
            Case CdoRecurTypeDaily
                Call ShowRecurTypeFrame(rftDaily)

                optDaily(rtoDaily).Value = True
                txtDayInterval.Text = .Interval
```

```
          Case CdoRecurTypeWeekly
              If .DayOfWeekMask = mclngAllWeekdays Then
                  Call ShowRecurTypeFrame(rftDaily)
                  optDaily(rtoWeekly).Value = True
              Else
                  optPattern(rftWeekly).Value = True
                  Call ShowRecurTypeFrame(rftWeekly)

                  txtWeekInterval.Text = .Interval

                  Dim lngIndex      As Long
                  Dim lngDayOfWeek    As Long
                  For lngIndex = 0 To 6
                     lngDayOfWeek = 2 ^ lngIndex

                     If (.DayOfWeekMask And lngDayOfWeek) = lngDayOfWeek Then
                        chkWeekDay(lngIndex).Value = vbChecked
                     Else
                        chkWeekDay(lngIndex).Value = vbUnchecked
                     End If
                  Next
              End If
          End Select
      End With
  End Sub
```

It makes the Weekly child frame, `optPattern(rftWeekly)`, visible and displays the `Interval` property. It then works out whether each check box should be checked, that is, if the corresponding weekday is in the combination. Because Sunday is the first checkbox in the array, its `Index` is 0. The corresponding CDO constant, `CdoSunday` is equal to 1, or 2^0. Similarly, the index of the Wednesday checkbox is 3 and `CdoWednesday` is 2^3. So if we go through each checkbox, we can get its corresponding CDO weekday constant by calculating the Index[th] power of 2. AND-ing the `DayOfWeekMask` property value with each CDO weekday constant tells us whether a day is included in the property.

Saving the weekday settings is a matter of OR-ing each CDO constant if its corresponding checkbox is checked:

```
  Private Sub SaveRecurType()
     With mobjPattern
        Select Case True
           Case optPattern(rftDaily).Value
              If optDaily(rtoDaily).Value Then
                 ' Daily
                 .RecurrenceType = CdoRecurTypeDaily
                 .Interval = txtDayInterval.Text
              Else
                 ' Weekly with all weekdays
                 .RecurrenceType = CdoRecurTypeWeekly
                 .DayOfWeekMask = mclngAllWeekdays
              End If

           Case optPattern(rftWeekly).Value
              Dim lngDayOfWeek As Long
```

```
                Dim lngIndex As Long

                .RecurrenceType = CdoRecurTypeWeekly
                .Interval = CLng(txtWeekInterval.Text)

                lngDayOfWeek = 0
                For lngIndex = 0 To 6
                    If chkWeekDay(lngIndex).Value = vbChecked Then
                        lngDayOfWeek = lngDayOfWeek Or 2 ^ lngIndex
                    End If
                Next
                .DayOfWeekMask = lngDayOfWeek
        End Select
    End With
End Sub
```

Recurring Monthly

The third child frame, `fraRecurType(rftMonthly)`, provides a user interface to the two monthly recurrence types, `CdoRecurTypeMonthly` and `CdoRecurTypeMonthlyNth`:

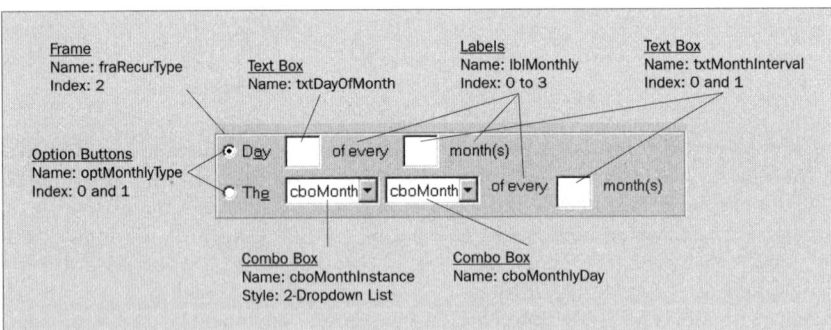

The first option allows a user to specify a day of the month and the month interval. This is exactly what the recurrence type `CdoRecurTypeMonthly` is about. The second option allows for selecting the day of week, the week of the month, and the month interval. Perhaps not surprisingly, this matches the set of properties available for the recurrence type `CdoRecurTypeMonthlyNth`. Let's add two more enumerated constants to the `RecurrenceTypeOptionEnum` type:

```
Private Enum RecurrenceTypeOptionEnum
    ' Recurrence Types in Daily Recurrence Type frame
    rtoDaily = 0
    rtoWeekly = 1

    ' Recurrence Types in Monthly Recurrence Type frame
    rtoMonthly = 0
    rtoMonthlyNth = 1
End Enum
```

Recurring Monthly – CdoRecurTypeMonthly

This recurrence type is quite simple. It allows us to specify on which day of the month an appointment should recur. Note that we can only specify one day, so you cannot use it to set the appointment to recur on the first and the 15th day of month, for example. As usual, it also accepts a month interval value.

The additional code in the `ShowRecurType` and the `SaveRecurType` methods demonstrates how to display and save the two properties relevant to this recurrence type:

```
Private Sub ShowRecurType()
    With mobjPattern
        Select Case .RecurrenceType
            Case CdoRecurTypeDaily
                Call ShowRecurTypeFrame(rftDaily)

                optDaily(rtoDaily).Value = True
                txtDayInterval.Text = .Interval

            Case CdoRecurTypeWeekly
...
                    End If
                Next
            End If

            Case CdoRecurTypeMonthly
                Call ShowRecurTypeFrame(rftMonthly)

                optMonthlyType(rtoMonthly).Value = True
                txtDayOfMonth.Text = .DayOfMonth
                txtMonthInterval(rtoMonthly).Text = .Interval
        End Select
    End With
End Sub


Private Sub SaveRecurType()
    With mobjPattern
        Select Case True
...
            Next
            .DayOfWeekMask = lngDayOfWeek

            Case optPattern(rftMonthly).Value
                If optMonthlyType(rtoMonthly).Value = True Then
                    .RecurrenceType = CdoRecurTypeMonthly
                    .DayOfMonth = CLng(txtDayOfMonth.Text)
                    .Interval = CLng(txtMonthInterval(rtoMonthly).Text)
                End If
        End Select
    End With
End Sub
```

Recurring Monthly – CdoRecurTypeMonthlyNth

The second option in the Monthly frame corresponds to the recurrence type `CdoRecurTypeMonthlyNth`. In this type, you can select the day of week and the week of month an appointment will occur. For instance, you can select the third Sunday of every two months. The day of the week is stored in the `DayOfWeekMask` property. However, it is not possible to select a combination of weekdays as we did with the `CdoRecurTypeWeekly` type:

```
Private Sub ShowRecurType()
    With mobjPattern
        Select Case .RecurrenceType
...

        Case CdoRecurTypeMonthly
            Call ShowRecurTypeFrame(rftMonthly)

            optMonthlyType(rtoMonthly).Value = True
            txtDayOfMonth.Text = .DayOfMonth
            txtMonthInterval(rtoMonthly).Text = .Interval

        Case CdoRecurTypeMonthlyNth
            Call ShowRecurTypeFrame(rftMonthly)

            optMonthlyType(rtoMonthlyNth).Value = True
            cboMonthInstance.ListIndex = .Instance - 1
            cboMonthlyDayOfWeek.ListIndex = Log2(.DayOfWeekMask)
            txtMonthInterval(rtoMonthlyNth).Text = .Interval
        End Select
    End With
End Sub
```

The `Instance` property stores the week of the month. The first week of the month is 1 and the last week is 5. This means that when we pick an item in the `cboMonthInstance` combo box that corresponds to the `Instance` property, we must subtract one from the `Instance` value by one to get the right item. To find the right item on the `cboMonthDayOfWeek` item list, we just call the `Log2` function as explained previously.

Once we understand this, saving the values back to those properties is fairly simple too.

> *The Instance value of 5 is a special value that signifies the last week of the month, even if there are only 4 full weeks in a month. For example, because there are only four Wednesdays in January 2000, the last Wednesday of January is actually the fourth Wednesday.*

```
Private Sub SaveRecurType()
    With mobjPattern
        Select Case True
...

        Case optPattern(rftMonthly).Value
            If optMonthlyType(rtoMonthly).Value = True Then
                .RecurrenceType = CdoRecurTypeMonthly
```

```
            .DayOfMonth = CLng(txtDayOfMonth.Text)
            .Interval = CLng(txtMonthInterval(rtoMonthly).Text)
        Else
            .RecurrenceType = CdoRecurTypeMonthlyNth
            .Instance = cboMonthInstance.ListIndex + 1
            .DayOfWeekMask = 2 ^ cboMonthlyDayOfWeek.ListIndex
            .Interval = CLng(txtMonthInterval(rtoMonthlyNth).Text)
        End If
    End Select
  End With
End Sub
```

Recurring Yearly – CdoRecurTypeYearly and CdoRecurTypeYearlyNth

The last child frame, `fraRecurType(rftYearly)`, is very similar. It also contains two options, one corresponding to the `CdoRecurTypeYearly` type and the other corresponds to the `CdoRecurTypeYearlyNth` type. The differences between those two types are analogous to those between `CdoRecurTypeMonthly` and `CdoRecurTypeMonthlyNth`, so I will not describe them separately:

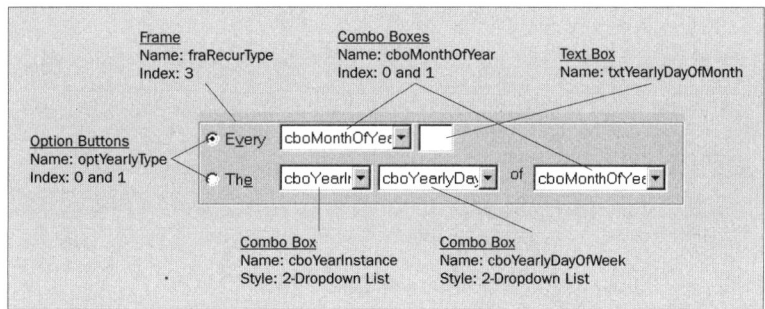

Before we continue, add two more enumerated constants to `RecurrenceTypeOptionEnum`:

```
Private Enum RecurrenceTypeOptionEnum
    ' Recurrence Types in Daily Recurrence Type frame
    rtoDaily = 0
    rtoWeekly = 1

    ' Recurrence Types in Monthly Recurrence Type frame
    rtoMonthly = 0
    rtoMonthlyNth = 1

    ' Recurrence Types in Yearly Recurrence Type frame
    rtoYear = 0
    rtoYearNth = 1
End Enum
```

The `CdoRecurTypeYearly` type allows us to select the day of the month and month of the year. The combo box, `cdoMonthOfYear`, is populated with the names of all 12 months. As the `MonthOfYear` property has a range of 1 to 12, we need to subtract 1 from its value when displaying or add 1 to the selected list index when saving it, to allow for the `ListIndex` being zero-based. The next textbox, `txtYearlyDayOfMonth`, corresponds to the `DayOfMonth` property. We could also select the year interval for an appointment, but we're not going to.

The `CdoRecurTypeYearlyNth` type is similar to `CdoRecurTypeMonthlyNth` with an additional property, `MonthOfYear`. I will not explain it further, since that's the only difference. Just remember that you can also set a year interval for this type.

Let's finish off the `ShowRecurType` and `SaveRecurType` methods to handle the yearly recurrence types:

```
Private Sub ShowRecurType()
    With mobjPattern
        Select Case .RecurrenceType
...

        Case CdoRecurTypeMonthlyNth
            Call ShowRecurTypeFrame(rftMonthly)

            optMonthlyType(rtoMonthlyNth).Value = True
            cboMonthInstance.ListIndex = .Instance - 1
            cboMonthlyDayOfWeek.ListIndex = Log2(.DayOfWeekMask)
            txtMonthInterval(rtoMonthlyNth).Text = .Interval

        Case CdoRecurTypeYearly
            Call ShowRecurTypeFrame(rftYearly)

            optYearlyType(rtoYear).Value = True
            cboMonthOfYear(rtoYear).ListIndex = .MonthOfYear - 1
            txtYearlyDayOfMonth.Text = .DayOfMonth

        Case CdoRecurTypeYearlyNth
            Call ShowRecurTypeFrame(rftYearly)

            optYearlyType(rtoYearNth).Value = True
            cboYearInstance.ListIndex = .Instance - 1
            cboYearlyDayOfWeek.ListIndex = Log2(.DayOfWeekMask)
            cboMonthOfYear(rtoYearNth).ListIndex = .MonthOfYear - 1
        End Select
    End With
End Sub

Private Sub SaveRecurType()
    With mobjPattern
        Select Case True
...
        Else
            .RecurrenceType = CdoRecurTypeMonthlyNth
            .Instance = cboMonthInstance.ListIndex + 1
            .DayOfWeekMask = 2 ^ cboMonthlyDayOfWeek.ListIndex
            .Interval = CLng(txtMonthInterval(rtoMonthlyNth).Text)
        End If

        Case optPattern(rftYearly).Value
            If optYearlyType(rtoYear).Value = True Then
                .RecurrenceType = CdoRecurTypeYearly
                .DayOfMonth = CLng(txtYearlyDayOfMonth.Text)
```

```
                .MonthOfYear = cboMonthOfYear(rtoYear).ListIndex + 1
            Else
                .RecurrenceType = CdoRecurTypeYearlyNth
                .Instance = cboYearInstance.ListIndex + 1
                .DayOfWeekMask = 2 ^ cboYearlyDayOfWeek.ListIndex
                .MonthOfYear = cboMonthOfYear(rtoYearNth).ListIndex + 1
            End If
        End Select
    End With
End Sub
```

Now we have added code to handle difference recurrence types, but the Recurrence Pattern frame is way too big. This is convenient at design time but it does not look very good at run time. Since the ShowRecurTypeFrame method displays the sub-frames at the correct locations when the form loads, we can rearrange the sub-frames and resize the Recurrence Pattern frame to make it look better at run time:

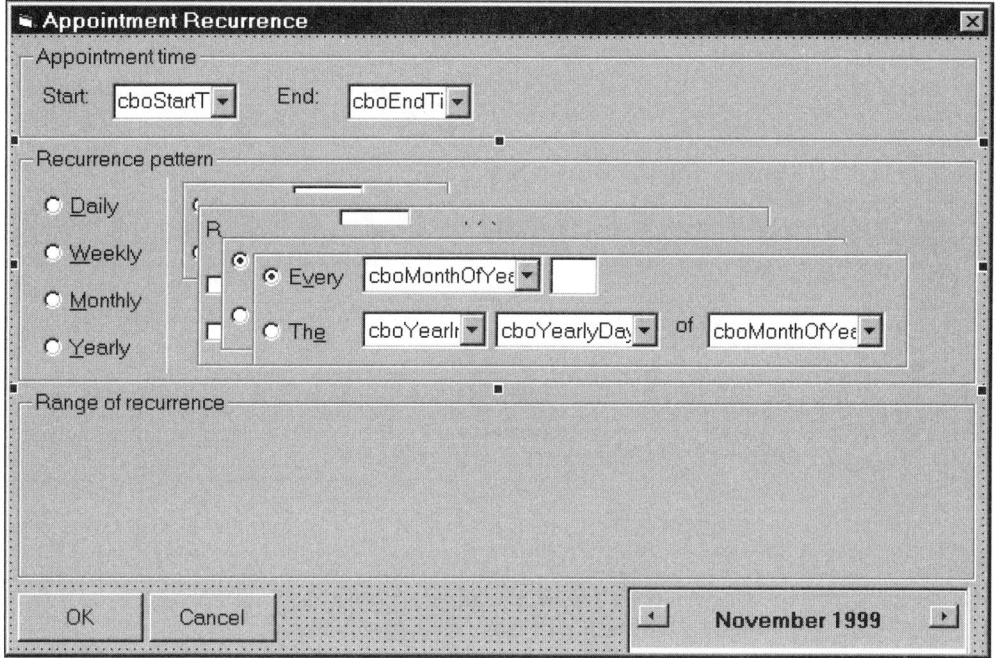

Ok, now we've got the most complex frame out of our way, let's move to the last frame, the recurrence range frame.

Working with the Range of Recurrence

A recurring appointment always starts from one day and can run infinitely into the future. Of course you can also set it to end at a particular day, or after a certain number of occurrences. The starting day of a recurring series is stored in the `PatternStartDate` property. If the appointment is to run infinitely, we set the `NoEndDate` property to `True`. By default, when you first call the `GetRecurrencePattern` method to create a `RecurrencePattern` object, CDO sets its `NoEndDate` property to `True`. To end the series on a specific date, set its `PatternEndDate` to the ending date. You can also set its `Occurrences` property to tell it to stop after a given number of occurrences. The `PatternEndDate` and `Occurrences` properties are dependent on each other. For instance, if you set a `PatternEndDate` after setting the `Occurrences` property, the latter will be recalculated. Setting the `Occurrences` property also causes the `PatternEndDate` to be recalculated. Setting either the `PatternEndDate` or the `Occurrences` property sets the `NoEndDate` flag to `False`. Add our last enumeration type to the General section of `FRecurrence`:

```
' Recurrence Range End Date Types
Private Enum EndDateTypeEnum
    edtNoEndDate = 0
    edtOccurrences = 1
    edtEndDate = 2
End Enum
```

The Range of recurrence frame contains controls that allow us to set those properties:

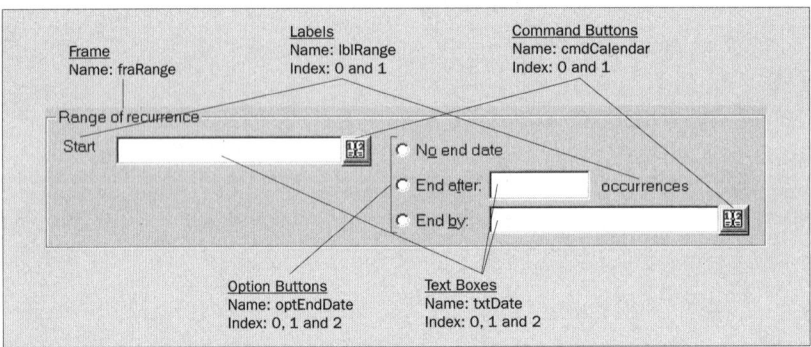

Note that the index of each option button corresponds to a constant in `EndDateTypeEnum`. Let's look at how we display the relevant properties to controls in this frame:

```
Private Sub ShowRange()
    With mobjPattern
        txtDate(dttStartDateTime).Text = Format(.PatternStartDate, gcstrDateFormat)
        If .NoEndDate Then
            optEndDate(edtNoEndDate).Value = True
        Else
            optEndDate(edtEndDate).Value = True
            txtOccurrence.Text = .Occurrences
            txtDate(dttEndDateTime).Text = Format(.PatternEndDate, gcstrDateFormat)
        End If
    End With
End Sub
```

It first displays the `PatternStartDate` in the date format specified in the string `gcstrDateFormat`. If the `NoEndDate` is `True`, it selects the corresponding option button. Otherwise, it displays both the `Occurrences` and `PatternEndDate` property values.

Like we did in the `FAppointment` form, we display the `MonthView` control when a user clicks one of the Calendar commands:

```
Private Sub cmdCalendar_Click(Index As Integer)
    With mvwDate
        .Move fraRange.Left + txtDate(Index).Left, _
            fraRange.Top + txtDate(Index).Top - .Height
        .Value = ToDate(txtDate(Index).Text)
        .Tag = Index
        .Visible = True
    End With
End Sub
```

Firstly, it moves the `mvwDate` control to just above the corresponding starting or ending date textbox and sets its value to the date string in the textbox. Next, it saves the `Index` of the clicked calendar command so that `mvwDate` knows where to output the selected date later on. Finally, it displays the control:

```
Private Sub mvwDate_DateClick(ByVal DateClicked As Date)
    Dim DateType As DateTimeTypeEnum
    DateType = CLng(mvwDate.Tag)

    With mobjPattern
        If DateType = dttStartDateTime Then
            .PatternStartDate = DateClicked
        Else
            .PatternEndDate = DateClicked
        End If
    End With

    mvwDate.Visible = False
    Call ShowRange
End Sub
```

When a user selects a date from the control, this event handler looks up the control's `Tag` property and displays the selected date to the corresponding date text box.

If a user changes the pattern ending criteria by clicking one of the three option buttons on the right, we update the pattern object accordingly using the following procedure:

```
Private Sub optEndDate_Click(Index As Integer)
    Select Case Index
        Case edtNoEndDate
            mobjPattern.NoEndDate = True

        Case edtOccurrences
            txtOccurrence.Text = mobjPattern.Occurrences
```

```
            Case edtEndDate
                txtDate(dttEndDateTime).Text = _
                    Format(mobjPattern.PatternEndDate, gcstrDateFormat)
        End Select
    End Sub
```

To save these settings, we simply update the appropriate properties:

```
    Private Sub SaveRange()
        With mobjPattern
            .PatternStartDate = ToDate(txtDate(dttStartDateTime).Text)
            Select Case True
                Case optEndDate(edtNoEndDate).Value
                    .NoEndDate = True

                Case optEndDate(edtOccurrences).Value
                    .Occurrences = CLng(txtOccurrence.Text)

                Case optEndDate(edtEndDate).Value
                    .PatternEndDate = ToDate(txtDate(dttEndDateTime).Text)
            End Select
        End With
    End Sub
```

Once a user has entered the relevant recurrence pattern settings, they can click the **OK** button to save them:

```
    Private Sub cmdOK_Click()
        Call SavePattern
        Unload Me
    End Sub

    Private Sub SavePattern()
        Call SaveTimes
        Call SaveRecurType
        Call SaveRange

        Call mobjAppItem.Update
    End Sub
```

The `SavePattern` method calls the originating appointment's `Update` method to commit the changes to the recurrence pattern. The form is then unloaded. The user may also click the **Cancel** button to discard the changes:

```
    Private Sub cmdCancel_Click()
        Unload Me
    End Sub
```

When the form unloads, it releases the references to the appointment and its recurrence pattern objects:

```
Private Sub Form_QueryUnload(Cancel As Integer, UnloadMode As Integer)
    On Error Resume Next
    Set mobjPattern = Nothing
    Set mobjAppItem = Nothing
End Sub
```

That is all for recurrence patterns. Now we just need to make this form accessible to the FAppointment form. Let's go back to its Toolbar_ButtonClick event handler and fix it up:

```
Private Sub Toolbar_ButtonClick(ByVal Button As MSComctlLib.Button)
    Select Case Button.Key
    Case mcstrButtonKeySave
        Call SaveAppointment
        Unload Me

    Case mcstrButtonKeySend
        Call SendMeeting
        Unload Me

    Case mcstrButtonKeyRecur
        Call ShowRecurrence

    Case mcstrButtonKeyCalendar
        Call ShowFreeBusy
    End Select
End Sub


Private Sub ShowRecurrence()
    Dim frmRecur As FRecurrence

    Call SaveAppointment

    Set frmRecur = New FRecurrence
    Call frmRecur.ShowForm(mobjAppItem)
    Set frmRecur = Nothing
End Sub
```

The ShowRecurrence method saves the current appointment and loads the FRecurrence form. From then on, it's up to the FRecurrence form to do the work to set up the associated recurrence pattern object.

After all that hard work, you can test drive the FRecurrence form and try to give it a thorough workout. There are still some rough edges to be ironed out, so feel free to polish it to make it more reliable. One obvious candidate is to add verification code to various textboxes so that they will not crash when given invalid entries. You know, CLng can be very unforgiving.

Next up, we look at how to respond to a meeting request.

Managing Meeting Requests and Responses

Let's start by adding a `FMeeting` form to the sample project.

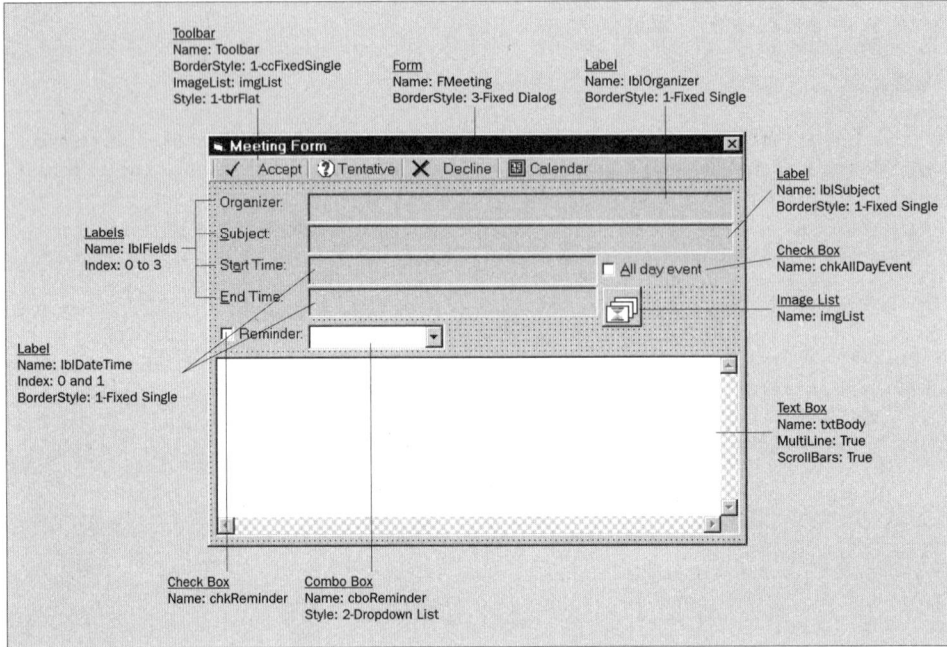

Here are the images for the image list. As usual, they're from the common graphics that come with Visual Studio:

Index	File Path	Key
1	Icons\Misc\Checkmrk.ico	`imgAccept`
2	Icons\Misc\Question.ico	`imgtent`
3	Icons\Misc\Misc19.ico	`imgDecline`
4	Bitmaps\Assorted\Calendar.bmp	`imgCalendar`

Now set up the toolbar buttons like this (the captions are as shown in the screenshot):

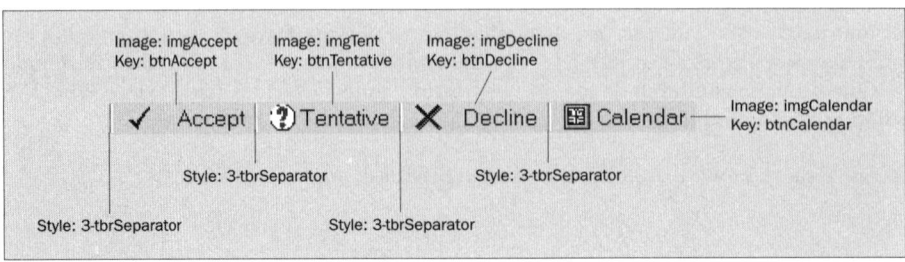

Most of the controls in this form correspond to the controls in the `FAppointment` form. Apart from the buttons on the toolbar, all other controls are for displaying the meeting properties. More precisely, they display the properties of the associated appointment item. CDO will save the associated appointment to the recipient's default Calendar folder when you accept or tentatively accept the request. So there is no need to save anything in our code.

Please note that you can modify some of the associated appointment's properties such as the starting and ending time. Since we have seen how we can handle this in the `FAppointment` form, I will not repeat it here. You will also need to remember that any changes made to that `AppointmentItem` object are local, CDO will not propagate the changes to the meeting organizer or other recipients.

The majority of code in this form should be very familiar to you by now:

```
Option Explicit

Private Const mcstrButtonKeyAccept As String = "btnAccept"
Private Const mcstrButtonKeyTentative As String = "btnTentative"
Private Const mcstrButtonKeyDecline As String = "btnDecline"
Private Const mcstrButtonKeyCalendar As String = "btnCalendar"

Private mobjMeeting As MAPI.MeetingItem

Private Sub Form_Load()
    Call PopulateReminderComboBox(cboReminder)
End Sub

Private Sub ProcReminder(ShouldSetReminder As Boolean)
    Dim objApp As MAPI.AppointmentItem
    Dim lngIndex As Long

    Set objApp = mobjMeeting.GetAssociatedAppointment
    If ShouldSetReminder Then
        chkReminder.Value = vbChecked

        With cboReminder
            .Visible = True
            For lngIndex = 1 To .ListCount
                If .ItemData(lngIndex) = objApp.ReminderMinutesBeforeStart Then
                    .ListIndex = lngIndex
                    Exit For
                End If
            Next

            If .ListIndex = -1 Then
                .Text = objApp.ReminderMinutesBeforeStart & " minutes"
            End If
        End With
    Else
        chkReminder.Value = vbUnchecked
        cboReminder.Visible = False
    End If
    Set objApp = Nothing
End Sub
```

The four constants specify the keys of the buttons on the toolbar. The module-level object, `mobjMeeting`, stores a reference to current meeting object. `ProcReminder` is almost identical to its counterpart in FAppointment form, except that it gets the `AppointmentItem` object using the `Meeting` object's `GetAssociatedAppointment` method. When the form loads, it populates the reminder combo box using the very same `PopulateReminderComboBox` method defined in MCommon.

The popular `ShowForm` method accepts a `MeetingItem` object:

```
Public Sub ShowForm(objMeeting As MAPI.MeetingItem)
    On Error GoTo ErrHandler

    Set mobjMeeting = objMeeting
    Call ShowMeeting
    Me.Show vbModal

ExitFunc:
    Exit Sub

ErrHandler:
    Call ReportError(Err)
    Resume ExitFunc
End Sub
```

Please note that meeting objects can only be created in one of two ways in CDO: when the meeting organizer sends a meeting request or cancellation, or when meeting participants send responses to meeting requests. Either way, CDO takes care of the creating of `MeetingItem` objects for us. We cannot create `MeetingItem` objects directly using CDO. Therefore the `ShowForm` method requires a `MeetingItem` object to be passed in. Otherwise, we will have nothing to work on. It then calls the `ShowMeeting` method to actually display the selected properties of the `MeetingItem` object:

```
Private Sub ShowMeeting()
    On Error Resume Next

    Const cstrAccepted As String = "IPM.Schedule.Meeting.Resp.Pos"
    Const cstrDeclined As String = "IPM.Schedule.Meeting.Resp.Neg"
    Const cstrTentAccepted As String = "IPM.Schedule.Meeting.Resp.Tent"

    Dim strMeetingType As String
    Dim objAssocAppItem As MAPI.AppointmentItem

    Select Case mobjMeeting.MeetingType
        Case CdoMeetingRequest
            strMeetingType = "has requested a meeting"

        Case CdoMeetingResponse
            Select Case mobjMeeting.Type
                Case cstrAccepted
                    strMeetingType = "has accepted this meeting"

                Case cstrTentAccepted
                    strMeetingType = "has tentatively accepted this meeting"
```

```
            Case cstrDeclined
                strMeetingType = "has declined this meeting"

            Case Else
                strMeetingType = mobjMeeting.Type
        End Select
    End Select

    Me.Caption = mobjMeeting.Sender.Name & " " & strMeetingType

    Set objAssocAppItem = mobjMeeting.GetAssociatedAppointment
    If Err.Number = 0 Then
        With objAssocAppItem
            lblOrganizer.Caption = .Organizer.Name
            lblSubject.Caption = .Subject
            txtBody.Text = .Text

            If .AllDayEvent Then
                lblDateTime(dttStartDateTime).Caption = _
                    Format(.StartTime, gcstrDateFormat)
                lblDateTime(dttEndDateTime).Caption = _
                    Format(.EndTime, gcstrDateFormat)
                chkAllDayEvent.Value = vbChecked
            Else
                lblDateTime(dttStartDateTime).Caption = _
                    Format(.StartTime, gcstrDateFormat & " " & gcstrTimeFormat)
                lblDateTime(dttEndDateTime).Caption = _
                    Format(.EndTime, gcstrDateFormat & " " & gcstrTimeFormat)
                chkAllDayEvent.Value = vbUnchecked
            End If
            Call ProcReminder(.ReminderSet)
        End With
    Else
        With mobjMeeting
            lblOrganizer.Caption = "The associated appointment is not accessible"
            lblSubject.Caption = .Subject
            txtBody.Text = .Text
        End With
    End If

    Set objAssocAppItem = Nothing
End Sub
```

If a MeetingItem object is a request for a meeting, it shows this fact on the form caption by saying that somebody has requested a meeting. If a MeetingItem object is a response to a meeting request, it checks to see what kind of response this is.

The type of response is stored in the Type property of the MeetingItem object. It has one of the three possible string values, IPM.Schedule.Meeting.Resp.Pos, IPM.Schedule.Meeting.Resp.Neg, and IPM.Schedule.Meeting.Resp.Tent. We define three constants in this method to store those values. Depending on the response type, the ShowMeeting method displays the appropriate information as the form caption. Note that the MeetingItem object's Sender is always the creator of the meeting.

Next, it displays some of the properties of the associated appointment object such as the name of the meeting organizer, the subject and body, the starting and ending time, and whether this is set as an all-day event. When you try this out, you will see that the ReminderSet and the ReminderMinutesBeforeStart properties are the same as those set by the meeting organizer. Normally everyone will have their own preference for reminders, so that doesn't make a lot of sense here. Nonetheless, such information is also passed along with the meeting request.

The main task of this form is to respond to a meeting request:

```
Private Sub Toolbar_ButtonClick(ByVal Button As MSComctlLib.Button)
    On Error GoTo ErrHandler

    Dim objResponse As MAPI.MeetingItem

    Select Case Button.Key
        Case mcstrButtonKeyAccept
            Set objResponse = mobjMeeting.Respond(CdoResponseAccepted)

        Case mcstrButtonKeyTentative
            Set objResponse = mobjMeeting.Respond(CdoResponseTentative)

        Case mcstrButtonKeyDecline
            Set objResponse = mobjMeeting.Respond(CdoResponseDeclined)

        Case mcstrButtonKeyCalendar
            Call ShowAvailability(gobjSession.CurrentUser, _
                    mobjMeeting.GetAssociatedAppointment.StartTime, _
                    mobjMeeting.GetAssociatedAppointment.EndTime)
    End Select

    If Not objResponse Is Nothing Then
        objResponse.Send
        mobjMeeting.Delete DeletedItems:=True
        Unload Me
    End If

ExitFunc:
    Set objResponse = Nothing
    Exit Sub

ErrHandler:
    Call ReportError(Err)
    Resume ExitFunc
End Sub
```

Responding to a meeting request is actually quite easy. You just call the MeetingItem object's Respond method and pass it a CDO constant representing one of the three standard responses: Accept, Tentatively Accept, or Decline. You then call its Send method to actually send it. As I mentioned before, CDO saves the associated appointment to the user's default Calendar folder when you accept or tentatively accept the request. If you decline a meeting, CDO will not save the AppointmentItem object. The MeetingItem object itself, however, remains in the user's Inbox. Depending on your application requirements, you might want to delete it as we do here.

If Outlook is running when a meeting request arrives, it will save the associated appointment to the Calendar folder. If you decline the request later, Outlook will remove the associated appointment from the Calendar folder. However, this is an Outlook feature that is separate from CDO.

As in the `FAppointment` form, a user can also click the Calendar button to check out his own availability for the scheduled meeting period.

Summary

In this chapter, we have examined the three remaining CDO objects. The `AppointmentItem`, `RecurrencePattern`, and `MeetingItem` objects provide rich support for team-based collaboration. CDO applications can use them to create appointments, request meetings, and respond to meeting requests.

We have also extended our sample application to utilize these objects. We spent quite a lot of time building a form that lets us edit recurrence patterns. I feel that the effort in building this form is well justified as it is fairly self-contained and can be easily reused in your own applications to provide the ability of manipulating recurrence patterns.

This concludes our sample CDO application. It demonstrates the capability and limitations of the CDO 1.21 library and each CDO object. I have put in error handling code for many of the commonly encountered error conditions and exceptions. However, it is still far from bulletproof. One of the notable shortcomings is input verification. Despite such shortcomings, it does achieve our goal of exploring the CDO library object model, which is what we wanted to do.

That's also the end of our tour of 'pure' CDO. By now, you should be reasonably familiar with the kinds of things you can do with CDO. From here we move off into a slightly different area: how to manage rules and folder permissions.

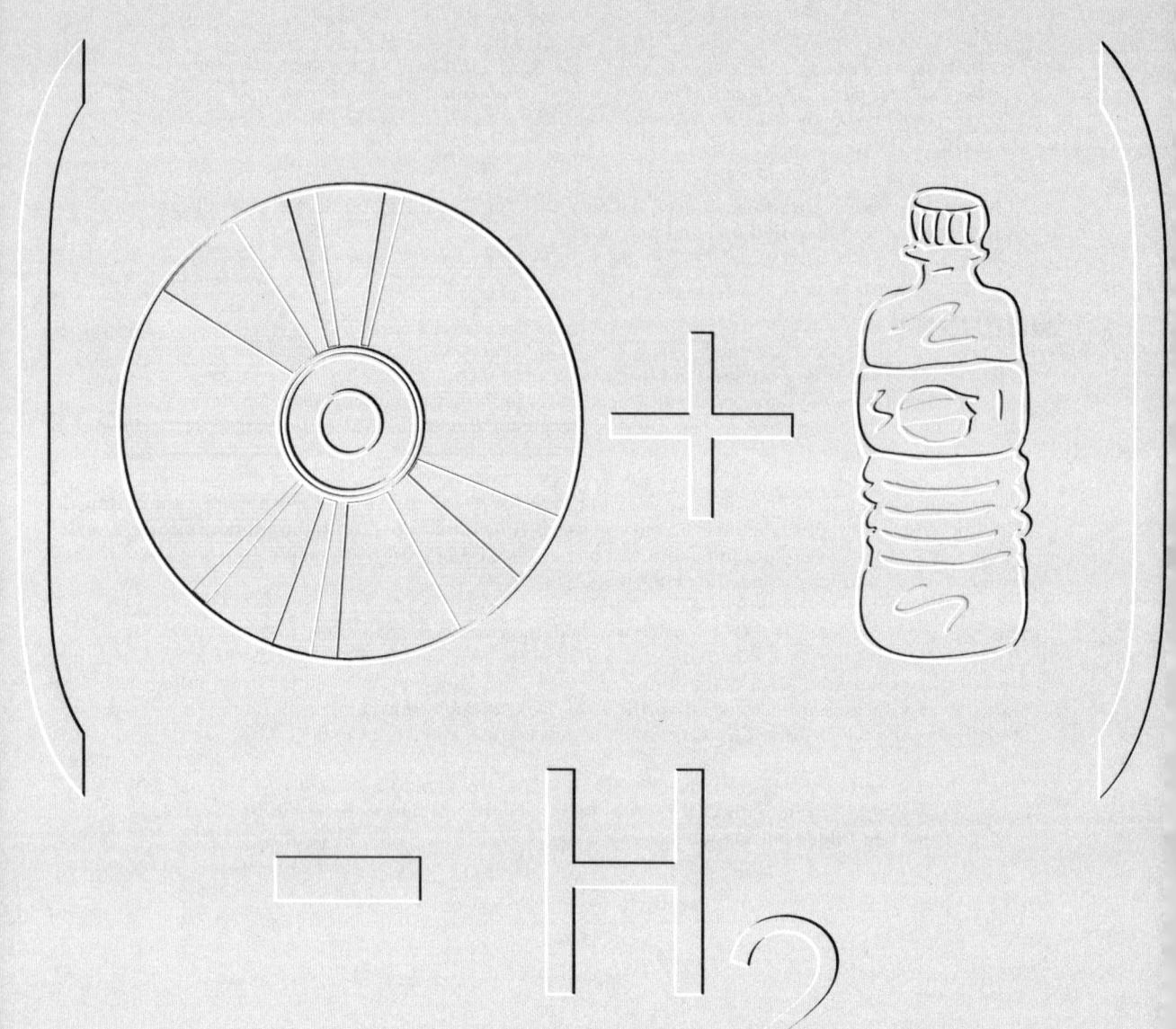

7

Managing Rules and Folder Permissions

Introduction

Microsoft Exchange Server provides powerful features to build collaborative solutions, including a public folder engine to store information in any format you choose. Another key feature is a server-based rules engine to run rules, created by a client application (usually Outlook), either on a mailbox or on a public folder. However, the CDO 1.21 for Exchange library object model exposes few features related to rules. You can access the Out of Office Assistant to enable or disable it, or change the Out of Office text. But Inbox Assistant, Outlook Rules Wizard and Public Folder Assistant rules cannot be created or manipulated with CDO itself.

For any folder, the folder owner (usually either the mailbox user or the creator of a public folder) can assign access permissions either to particular Exchange mailboxes or, for easier management, to distribution lists of mailboxes. Client applications can then depend on Exchange Server to show the content of the folder only to people that are allowed to read or modify its items. Although you can manage these permissions via the user interface of the Outlook or Exchange client, CDO provides no way to programmatically create or modify existing permissions of a folder.

With regard to these two areas absent from CDO – rules and access permissions – Microsoft has provided two additional COM components for use with Exchange Server 5.5. Both are included in the latest Microsoft Platform SDK, which can be downloaded from the Microsoft Web site.

> *Download the Microsoft Platform SDK from the Microsoft Web site at*
> `http://msdn.microsoft.com/developer/sdk/platform.htm`

Since they're COM components, you can use both in any development or scripting environment that supports the component object model standard. They are built with C/C++ and Extended MAPI 1.0 and, as you will see, require that you first obtain a `Folder` object with CDO. Therefore, as with other CDO applications, these components require a proper installed MAPI subsystem, as described in Chapter 1.

The ACL Component

First, we'll look at the ACL component (`Acl.dll`), a COM component that allows you to build applications to manage permissions on Exchange Server folders. You can use it to modify existing permissions and also to add or delete members from the particular folder permissions list.

> *ACL stands for Access Control List, and it's essentially a description of the permissions for a folder on either Exchange Server or Windows NT Server.*

After a brief discussion of the structure of Exchange folder permissions, we'll explore the ACL component's object model and build some code to manage folder access with it.

Folder Permission Architecture

Before we look at any code, you need to understand how Exchange Server manages permissions on a mailbox or public folder. Exchange Server actually uses two different types of permissions – one granting overall access to a mailbox or public folder using Windows NT accounts, the other granting more granular access to individual folders, based on Exchange mailboxes and distribution lists.

As far as client access goes, the broad, NT account type of security (normally set through the Microsoft Exchange Administrator program) is an all or nothing affair. It is not possible, for example, to grant read-only access at the mailbox level, only at the folder level. The ACL component manages those folder-level permissions by assigning client access rights to specific Exchange mailboxes and distribution lists.

Each mailbox or distribution list that has client access permissions for a folder is represented in the permissions architecture by an object called an **access control entry**, or **ACE**. A single folder can have multiple ACE objects. The different ACE objects can each have different permissions – one with full access perhaps, with others having read-only rights. In addition to ACE objects that represent mailboxes and distribution lists, folders also support permissions for Default and Anonymous users. You can set these with the ACL component, too.

These multiple ACE objects comprise a collection of access control entries, known as the ACEs collection. Each Exchange Server object to be given permissions to a particular folder is added to this ACEs list. But it's not enough just to add the object to the ACEs collection; you must still set the permissions for the single ACE. So, to recap:

> **An ACE, or access control entry, is an object that holds information about the permissions that a mailbox or distribution list has on an Exchange Server folder.**

If you have configured folder permissions using Outlook as the client, you have probably already seen that it is either possible to use a specific **Role** provided by Exchange Server, or configure specific rights to build more granular permissions.

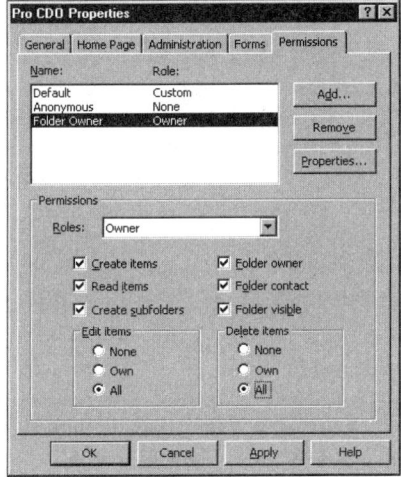

Installation and Registration

Before you can use the ACL component (either on your development system or on the customer's computer where your application will run), you must make sure that it is installed and registered properly. To provide proper access to the ACL.DLL file for your application you should copy it to the C:\Windows\System (on Windows NT C:\Winnt\System32) directory, assuming Windows is installed in the default location. To register the ACL component run regsvr32 from the Windows command prompt:

```
Regsvr32.exe acl.dll
```

To use the ACL component in a Visual Basic application, you need to set the reference in the current project references by selecting Project | References and selecting Microsoft Exchange 5.5 ACL Type Library 1.0. Once you add the ACL component to your project references, you can view its objects, properties and methods in the Object Browser by selecting the MSExchangeACLLib from the list of available libraries.

ACL Component Object Model

The ACL component exposes an object model that provides you with an easy-to-use interface to manipulate Exchange Server folder permissions.

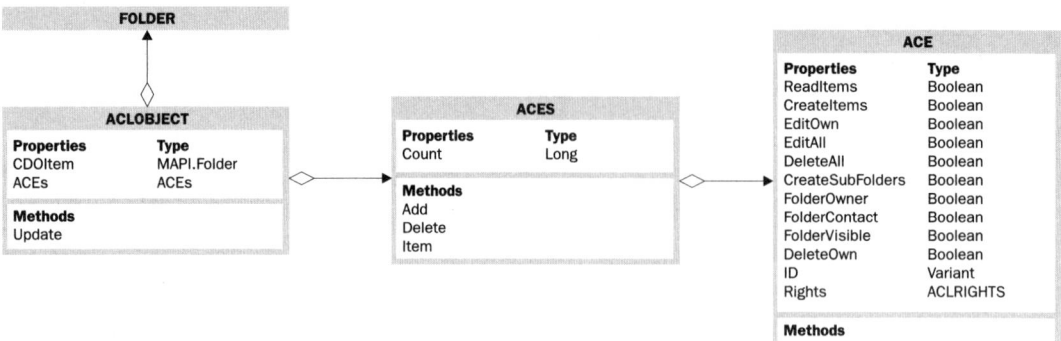

One important consideration is that the ACL component requires a valid CDO `Folder` object. The top-level `ACLObject` object exposes a property named `CDOItem` that must be set to a `Folder` object representing a particular Exchange Server folder. After this is done, the ACL component automatically creates the `ACEs` collection for the selected Exchange Server folder for your application to manipulate.

> *Note that in the object browser the ACEs collection is listed with the object class IACEs. We'll continue to call it ACEs, since that's the name of the property of the parent ACLObject.*

To add a new ACE, your program needs to add the `ACE` object to the `ACEs` collection, set its `ID` property to the ID of an Exchange Server `AddressEntry` object representing a mailbox or distribution list, and either assign a role or set the rights it should have. You can set rights by two different methods – either by setting individual named properties, such as `CreateItems` and `EditOwn`, to `True` or `False` or by using the `Rights` property, which is a 32-bit integer bit-mask. You'll see some examples of both methods in the upcoming code section.

Access Control Entry Rights

It is possible to set or read the specific rights of an ACE using the constants provided below. For some of the most commonly used rights, you also have a more convenient method – use the named properties that the ACE exposes. Both are listed in the table below, which shows all possible rights for an ACE, and you can choose which you prefer.

Constant	Value	Named Property	Right Description
RIGHTS_CREATE_ITEMS	&H2	CreateItems	Create Items
RIGHTS_READ_ITEMS	&H1	ReadItems	Read Items

Constant	Value	Named Property	Right Description
RIGHTS_ CREATE_SUBFOLDERS	&H80	CreateSubFolders	Create subfolders
RIGHTS_FOLDER_OWNER	&H100	FolderOwner	Folder owner
RIGHTS_FOLDER_CONTACT	&H200	FolderContact	Folder contact
RIGHTS_FOLDER_VISIBLE	&H400	FolderVisible	Folder visible
N/A	N/A	N/A	Edit None
RIGHTS_EDIT_OWN	&H8	EditOwn	Edit Own
RIGHTS_EDIT_ALL	&H20	EditAll	Edit All
N/A	N/A	N/A	Delete None
RIGHTS_DELETE_OWN	&H10	DeleteOwn	Delete Own
RIGHTS_DELETE_ALL	&H40	DeleteAll	Delete All
RIGHTS_NONE	&H0	N/A	No access to folder

It is possible to read and write each separate right using the values in the table above. We'll see this in action in a moment. However, working with individual rights can be troublesome. For example, to make a folder available to certain users to read (but not edit) the items, you could just set the ReadItems property to True. If you forget to also set the FolderVisible property to True, users will not be able to see the folder at all! To avoid that sort of problem, you may find it more convenient to use the roles discussed in the next section.

> *In the table above, a Folder Contact is a right that sets an administrative contact for a public folder. The contact's name is displayed to users of the folder.*

Also you may have recognized that there are two rights present in the user interface – Edit None and Delete None – that do not have counterparts among the named properties or constants. These rights are really just the absence of rights. To check or assign the Edit None right, your application would check the Edit Own and Edit All rights. If neither is set, then the particular ACE has what an Outlook user would see as the Edit None right. You'd use a similar procedure for the Delete None right.

Access Control Entry Roles

Instead of setting or reading individual rights, you can set or read a related group of rights called a role. The following table shows the constants representing the possible roles for an ACE. Assigning a role with the specific constant is a shortcut to assigning the individual rights listed in the Rights column:

Constant	Value	Role Description	Rights
ROLE_OWNER	&H7FB	Owner	Create Items Read Items Create Subfolders Folder Owner Folder Visible Edit All Delete All
ROLE_PUBLISH_EDITOR	&H4FB	Publishing Editor	Create Items Read Items Create Subfolders Folder Visible Edit All Delete All
ROLE_EDITOR	&H47B	Editor	Create Items Read Items Folder Visible Edit All Delete All
ROLE_PUBLISH_AUTHOR	&H49B	Publishing Author	Create Items Read Items Create Subfolders Folder Visible Edit Own Delete Own
ROLE_AUTHOR	&H41B	Author	Create Items Read Items Folder Visible Edit Own Delete Own
ROLE_NONEDITING_AUTHOR	&H413	Nonediting Author	Create Items Read Items Folder Visible Delete Own
ROLE_REVIEWER	&H401	Reviewer	Read Items Folder Visible
ROLE_CONTRIBUTOR	&H402	Contributor	Create Items Folder Visible
ROLE_NONE	&H400	No Rights	N/A

Predefined roles do not have named properties. Use the role constants when you want to set a group of rights for an ACE. However, when reading the permissions, you should use the built-in properties such as CreateItems or use the corresponding constants in conjunction with the Rights property.

Although predefined roles can ease the development of your application, they do not work quite right in all cases. Note in particular that, when you set the `Rights` property to the `ROLE_OWNER` constant, the Folder Contact right is not assigned, even though setting a folder owner through the Outlook user interface *does* add the Folder Contact right.

Now that we've reviewed the ACL component object model and the basics of rights and roles, let's move on to some code, to see how to connect to the Exchange Server and set or retrieve the permissions of a particular folder. Here, we'll review a little of the CDO we learned in the previous chapters.

Building ACL Applications

When working with the ACL component, there are a few common steps you'll need to follow:

1. Create a CDO `Session` object, and log on.

2. Obtain a CDO `Folder` object representing the folder whose permissions you want to change.

3. Create an `ACLObject` object, and set its `CDOItem` property to the folder obtained in Step 2.

After completing those three steps, your application will have an `ACEs` collection to work with. To read or modify existing permissions, your code obtains an individual `ACE` object, then reads or modifies either its built-in properties representing particular rights or evaluates the `Rights` property. The `Update` method on the `ACLObject` object commits the changes.

To add new permissions to the folder, you follow these steps:

1. Create an `ACE` object.

2. Set a role or individual rights using either the `Rights` property or the built-in properties representing specific rights.

3. Repeat steps 1 and 2 for each additional mailbox or distribution list for which you want to grant access to the folder.

4. Use the `Update` method on the top-level `ACLObject` object to commit the changes.

One important consideration is that you can only modify the permissions of a particular folder if you are already the owner of the folder. Otherwise, trying to update the permissions will fail.

Let's look at the details of using these techniques.

General Considerations

All code samples provided here are designed and tested only with Visual Basic 6.0 Service Pack 3. If you want to use the code within an Active Server Pages application there are some things that will need to be changed. For example, VBScript doesn't support early binding or variable type declarations.

So where in VB you can use the following code:

```
Dim objSession As MAPI.Session
Set objSession = New MAPI.Session
objSession.Logon "", "", True, True
```

With VBScript you must use the following syntax:

```
Dim objSession
Set objSession = CreateObject("MAPI.Session")
objSession.Logon "", "", True, True
```

Also to prevent major problems with your application you should always clean up the object variables after they are no longer required, to make sure that they don't stay in memory. Not doing that in either Visual Basic or VBScript can result in memory leaks and crashes of the computer running your application.

Be aware that you need to use different ProgIDs and type library names, depending on whether your application uses Visual Basic or VBScript. The following table shows the ProgIDs and the type library names for these two programming environments:

Class	Visual Basic	VBScript
ACLObject	MSExchangeACLLib.ACLObject	MSExchange.ACLObject
ACEs	MSExchangeACLLib.IACEs	N/A
ACE	MSExchangeACLLib.ACE	MSExchange.ACE

Creating a New CDO Session and Logon

Before we can access any Exchange Server folders, we need to create a valid CDO Session and perform a log-on. This is all stuff you've seen before. The following code creates a new CDO Session and displays a log-on dialog, to log the user on to the Exchange Server. Because a log-on dialog is displayed the user needs to choose an existing MAPI profile:

```
Dim objSession As MAPI.Session
Set objSession = New MAPI.Session
objSession.Logon NewSession:=True, ShowDialog:=True
```

If your application is an administrative tool, you might want to use a dynamic, profile-less logon to a user mailbox.

Once the application has successfully logged on to the Session, the next step is to gain access to the desired information store. As an example, we will access the public information store (in other words, the Public Folders hierarchy) so that we can later obtain a particular public folder whose permissions we want to modify.

Opening the Exchange Server Public Information Store

While it is possible to use the name of the public information store of the Exchange Server, which in the English international version is always "Public Folders", you should not rely on that name if you develop applications that are desired to run in a multilingual environment.

The following code retrieves the public information store without relying on the name. Instead, it uses an undocumented constant that always represents the ID property of the root of the public information store.

```
Const PR_IPM_PUBLIC_FOLDERS_ENTRYID = &H66310102

Dim objInfoStores As MAPI.InfoStores
Dim objInfoStore As MAPI.InfoStore
Dim strRootID As String
Dim objTopFolder As MAPI.Folder

Set objInfoStores = objSession.InfoStores
For Each objInfoStore In objInfoStores
    Err.Clear
    strRootID = objInfoStore.Fields(PR_IPM_PUBLIC_FOLDERS_ENTRYID).Value
    If Err.Number = 0 Then
        Set objTopFolder = objSession.GetFolder(strRootID, _
                            objInfoStore.ID)
        Exit For
    End If
Next
```

Finding the Desired Folder in the Information Store

After the information store is found, we still need a valid CDO `Folder` object as a reference to the desired folder in the hierarchy.

After adding the appropriate `Dim` statement to your application:

```
Dim objFolder As MAPI.Folder
```

...you can use code similar to this to gain access to your folder, as we've seen previously:

```
Set objFolder = objTopFolder.Folders("FirstFolder"). _
                Folders("SecondFolder").Folders("YourFolder")
```

If the operation completed successfully, we have a reference to the folder "YourFolder" in the public information store, whose full path is `\Public Folders\All Public Folders\FirstFolder\SecondFolder\YourFolder`. Now, we are going to create the `ACLObject` object and connect it to the `Folder` object.

Creating the ACL Object and Set the Folder Reference

The following code creates a new `ACLObject` object:

```
Dim objFolderACL As MSExchangeACLLib.ACLObject
Set objFolderACL = New MSExchangeACLLib.ACLObject
```

Now we set the `CDOItem` property of the `ACLObject` object and retrieve a reference to the access control entry collection:

```
Set objFolderACL.CDOItem = objFolder
Set objFolderACEs = objFolderACL.ACEs
```

After the `CDOItem` property of the `ACLObject` is set, it automatically populates the `ACEs` collection for you with the Exchange Server folder permissions. Now we can either create a new `ACE` or retrieve the rights of a particular existing `ACE`.

Reading the Permissions of an Access Control Entry

Before we can read the permissions, we need to retrieve a specific `ACE` from the `ACEs` collection. Then, we can use the named properties of the `ACE` to retrieve all rights held by the specific `ACE`.

The following code, using the `ACEs` collection and the CDO `Session` as arguments, loops through the access control entries collection and pulls out the rights of each access control entry:

```
Sub EnumRights(objFolderACEs As MSExchangeACLLib.IACEs, _
             objSession As MAPI.Session)
   Dim objFolderACE As MSExchangeACLLib.ACE
   Dim strID As String
   Dim strName As String
   Dim strRights As String
   Dim objAddrList As MAPI.AddressList

   Set objAddrList = objSession.AddressLists("Global Address List")
   For Each objFolderACE In objFolderACEs
      strID = objFolderACE.ID
      If strID = "ID_ACL_DEFAULT" Or strID = "ID_ACL_ANONYMOUS" Then
         strName = strID
      Else
         strName = objSession.GetAddressEntry(strID)
      End If
      strRights = "Create Items: " & CBool(objFolderACE.CreateItems) _
             & vbCrLf & "Read Items: " _
             & CBool(objFolderACE.ReadItems) & vbCrLf _
             & "Create Subfolders: " _
             & CBool(objFolderACE.CreateSubFolders) & vbCrLf _
             & "Folder Owner: " _
             & CBool(objFolderACE.FolderOwner) & vbCrLf _
             & "Folder Contact: " _
             & CBool(objFolderACE.FolderContact) & vbCrLf _
             & "Folder Visible: " _
             & CBool(objFolderACE.FolderVisible) & vbCrLf _
```

```
                      & "Edit Own: " & CBool(objFolderACE.EditOwn) & vbCrLf _
                      & "Edit All: " & CBool(objFolderACE.EditAll) & vbCrLf _
                      & "Delete Own: " & CBool(objFolderACE.DeleteOwn) & vbCrLf _
                      & "Delete All: " & CBool(objFolderACE.DeleteAll) & vbCrLf
            MsgBox strRights, , "Rights for " & strName
        Next
        Set objAddrList = Nothing
        Set objFolderACEs = Nothing
    End Sub
```

The ID property of the ACE object can have three possible values:

❑ "ID_ACL_DEFAULT" – corresponding to the Default access by users who are not represented by a specific ACE

❑ "ID_ACL_ANONYMOUS" – for public folders where anonymous access is permitted

❑ An ID corresponding to a recipient in the Global Address List. You use the CDO Session object's GetAddressEntry() method to return an AddressEntry object containing information about the recipient, including the Name property.

As you can see it is fairly easy to access the particular rights using the named properties. But how do you read the role that an ACE has?

Creating a New ACE and Set the Permissions

To add a new ACE to the ACEs collection, we first need to create a new access control entry object:

```
Dim objACE As MSExchangeACLLib.ACE
Set objACE = New MSExchangeACLLib.ACE
```

Next, we must supply a valid ID for an Exchange Server recipient, the "ID_ACL_DEFAULT" string for default access or the "ID_ACL_ANONYMOUS" string for anonymous public folder access. For an Exchange Server recipient, you obtain the ID from the recipient's AddressEntry object, as shown above. You can then set either a role or individual rights. Here we have already obtained an AddressEntry object, and we give the recipient it represents the Owner role:

```
objACE.ID = objAddressEntry.ID
objACE.Rights = ROLE_OWNER
```

Talking about the AddressEntry ID property, there's one thing we need to address (no pun intended...). In CDO and Extended MAPI 1.0, entry identifiers are used to find an object in the Exchange Server information store or the Exchange Server directory. Generally there are two different types of identifiers, **Long Term** and **Short Term**.

A Long Term Entry ID is associated permanently with a MAPI object and is unique in a global scope. It is stored with the object and in other appropriate places so that it can be used for multiple operations.

A Short Term Entry ID is considered to be of limited duration and scope. It is typically used only for a single operation and is not stored for later use. It can, however, be converted into a long-term entry identifier with Extended MAPI 1.0.

When you create a new ACE object, its ID property uses a short-term identifier. However, when you add it to the ACEs collection (see the next section), it is converted to a long-term identifier. Generally, this is not an issue in your code. One area where it can cause problems is when you create an ACE, add it to the ACEs collection, then want to retrieve information about that ACE later in your application. The ID that you gave to the ACE when you created it is not the same as the ID it is given once it's been stored in the ACEs collection.

Adding the ACE to the ACEs Collection

After the ACE is created and the permissions are set successfully, we now need to add it to the ACEs collection. It's very easy:

```
objFolderACEs.Add objACE
```

Note that this does not commit the changes to the access control entries collection. This must be done separately by calling the Update method as described later.

Modifying the Permissions of an Existing ACE

Modifying the rights of an existing ACE is also fairly easy. You just need to modify the named properties to fit your needs. The following code shows how to make an existing access control entry the owner of the folder, by setting all the rights a folder owner has:

```
objFolderACE.CreateItems = True
objFolderACE.ReadItems = True
objFolderACE.CreateSubFolders = True
objFolderACE.FolderOwner = True
objFolderACE.FolderContact = True
objFolderACE.FolderVisible = True
objFolderACE.EditAll = True
objFolderACE.DeleteAll = True
```

Finally, don't forget that only after the changes are committed with the Update method do all rights become effective on the desired Folder object. This provides a simple way to roll back if you want to decide not to change the rights of the desired access control entry.

Removing an ACE

To remove an ACE from the ACEs collection you only need a valid ACE object. Because each ACE has an entry ID it is fairly easy. You just need the person's AddressEntry object from the global address list. After you get this, you can use the AddressEntry object's ID to remove the ACE from the access control entries collection:

```
objFolderACEs.Delete objAddressEntry.ID
```

Committing Changes to the ACEs Collection

After all modifications on the `ACEs` collection are completed, we need to actually commit the changes to the Exchange Server.

The following code shows how to commit the changes using the `Update` method on the `ACLObject` object:

```
objFolderACL.Update
```

After the changes are committed with the `Update` method, all modifications are saved to the Exchange Server and the permissions should be in effect immediately.

Cleaning Up

At the end of all that, don't forget to log off from the CDO session and clean up all your objects, using code similar to this:

```
objSession.Logoff

Set objSession = Nothing
Set objInfoStores = Nothing
Set objInfoStore = Nothing
Set objTopFolder = Nothing
Set objFolder = Nothing

Set objFolderACL = Nothing
Set objFolderACE = Nothing
Set objACE = Nothing
```

Some developers still rely on Visual Basic's inherent behavior to do their garbage collection after an object gets out of scope. However, it is always a good idea to release all objects in your code yourself. Your customers will be happier if you do so because your application will run more stably.

That's all we're going to see about the ACL component. If you want to know more, check out the SDK documentation on the subject. We now move on to talk about managing rules in your CDO applications.

The Rule Component

There are a couple of parallels between the ACL component and the Rule component. Both add a programming interface to an important feature that was previously available only through the user interface of existing client programs. Both use CDO to bind to a `Folder` object. The Rule component is more complex, but after working with the ACL component, you should find its procedures logical.

Folder Rule Architecture

The Rule component is dedicated to provide read and write access to Exchange Server rules. Rules manipulate items arriving in a user's Inbox or in a particular public folder. Exchange Server has a built-in rules engine that is exposed to the client via the Inbox Assistant, Out-Of-Office Assistant, Folder Assistant and (in Outlook) the Rules Wizard.

The client applications create rules that are stored as hidden messages of the type `IPM.Rule.Message` in either the user's Inbox folder (in the case of mailbox rules), or a public folder (for Folder Assistant rules). The Outlook Rules Wizard is a little different, as it also stores a copy of the rules in a `.rwz` file. While you can use CDO to gain access to this hidden message itself, using the `HiddenMessages` collection of the `Folder` object, you can't manipulate it, because the rule data is stored in binary format inside the message.

With all the client tools (except the Folder Assistant), users create rules that can run unattended on the Exchange Server or that require the Exchange or Outlook client to be running in order to operate. Some rules contain elements of both – say, a rule to move an incoming item to a different folder (server-based rule) and notify the user by playing a sound (client-based rule). Actually, all rules are processed by the server. For those that require client-dependent actions, Exchange creates a "deferred action message," stored in the hidden Deferred Action folder in the user's mailbox. When the user starts the Exchange or Outlook client, the client processes these deferred action messages and takes appropriate action.

The Rule component is used mainly to create server-based rules. While it does allow applications to create a deferred action rule, there is virtually no documentation on the syntax for specific client-based actions, such as notification. Also, rules that you create with the Rules component are not visible to the client rule-creation tools. Therefore, you should exercise caution when using the Rules component to create rules on the Inbox folder of a mailbox; since the user cannot see your application's rules, they may create other rules that conflict with the ones your application creates.

Each rule consists of a condition that defines what types of items the rule will act upon and one or more actions that will be applied. If the condition is true, the actions are executed. The condition may be omitted if you want the rule to apply to all items. The Rule component also provides a special type of condition that you can use to join two or more conditions together.

Again, if some actions cannot be executed because they require the client application to be running, Exchange will create a deferred action message.

Rule Installation and Registration

Before you can use the Rule component, you must again make sure that it is installed and registered properly. Copy the `Rule.DLL` file to the `C:\Windows\System` (on Windows NT `C:\Winnt\System32`) directory, and register it as before with `regsvr32`.

To use the Rule component in your Visual Basic application you need to set a reference to it in the usual way. It should appear under the name Microsoft Exchange SDK 5.5 Rules 1.0. If it does not, you need to check if the `Rule.DLL` file is registered properly on your system.

Rule Component Object Model

The Rule component exposes its own object model to provide you with an interface to manipulate Exchange Server rules.

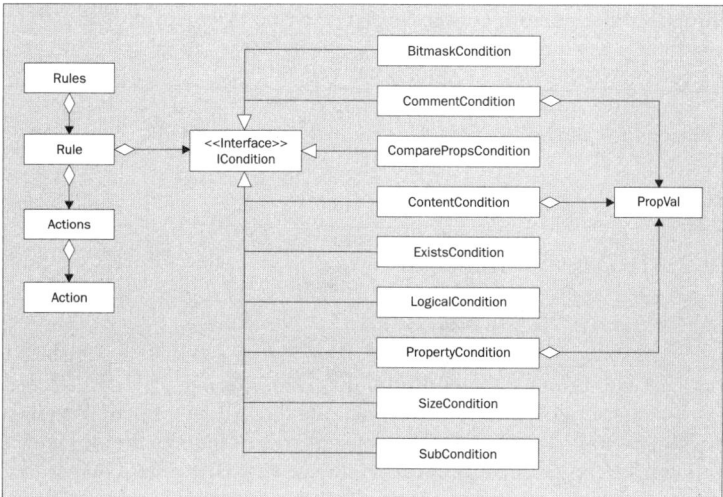

Let's look briefly at the `Rules` collection and `Rule` object before we go on to tackle the real meat of the topic: `Conditions` and `Actions`.

RULES	
Properties	**Type**
Count	Long
Folder	MAPI.Folder
Methods	
Add	
Clear	
Delete	
Item	
Update	
UpdateIndices	

As you can see, the `Rules` collection has the standard property and methods collections usually have. It also has a `Folder` property, which refers to the folder the rules in the collection will operate on. There's an `Update` method, which essentially saves any changes that have been made to rules in the collection. Finally, it has an `UpdateIndices` method, which allows you to commit changes to the ordering of individual rules.

RULE	
Properties	**Type**
Actions	Actions
Condition	ICondition
Index	Long
Level	Long
Name	String
NewIndex	Long
Provider	String
ReadOnly	Boolean
Sequence	Long
State	Long
Methods	

The `Rule` object exposes ten properties, the first of which are `Actions` and `Condition`. We'll get on to just how the objects they represent behave in a moment.

Next comes the `Index` property. This and the `Sequence` property are linked, detailing the order in which rules will be executed. You can alter the `Index` properties indirectly by setting the `NewIndex` property and calling the `Rules` collection's `UpdateIndices` method. The `Sequence` properties of consecutive `Rule` objects need not differ by 1 if you don't want them to – the `Index` properties will, though, just like any other collection of objects.

Now let's take a closer look at the `Condition` and `Actions` objects.

Rule Conditions

INTERFACE	
Properties	**Type**
ICondition	CONDITION_TYPES
Methods	

As you saw in the Rule component object model diagram, there are many different types of conditions. The Rule component enumerates constants that allow your application to determine the type of rule from the `Condition` object's `Type` property. In fact, as the object model shows, it isn't as simple as just having a `Condition` object. There are actually many classes of `Condition` object, all of which implement the `ICondition` interface.

Creating a rule condition is much more complicated than just setting its `Type`. In fact, the `Type` property is read-only. To set the `Condition` object property for a rule, you must create a condition of the class corresponding to the particular type, for example a `SizeCondition` condition if you want to check the size of an incoming item. Then, you set your `Condition` object to that newly created condition. Something like this:

```
Set objCondition = CreateObject("MSExchange.SizeCondition")
```

This updates the `Type` property automatically.

The following table shows all possible condition types for a rule, along with the associated condition classes:

Constant	Value	Class	Description
R_BITMASK	2	BitmaskCondition	Compare a property value against a bitmask
R_COMMENT	3	CommentCondition	Associate information with a condition
R_COMPAREPROPS	4	ComparePropsCondition	Compare two properties
R_CONTENT	5	CommentCondition	Test the contents of a property

Constant	Value	Class	Description
R_EXISTS	6	ExistsCondition	Test the existence of a property
R_LOGICAL	1	LogicalCondition	Combine conditions logically
R_PROPERTY	7	PropertyCondition	Test the value of a property
R_SIZE	8	SizeCondition	Test the size of a property
R_SUB	9	SubCondition	Specify an attachment or recipient condition

We will discuss the use of the condition classes later in this chapter.

Rule Actions

A rule must have at least one action. The rule action is used to fire an event specified in the rules Action object. The Rule object's Actions collection is a standard collection, with no extra methods or properties.

ACTION	
Properties	**Type**
ActionType	ACTION_TYPE
Arg	Variant
Methods	

To read and write actions the Rule component exposes a set of constant values for the appropriate ActionType property of the Action object. The following table shows all possible action values. Arg is the property representing the required arguments for the rule, such as the destination folder for an ACTION_MOVE action.

Constant	Value	Description
ACTION_MOVE	1	Move the message to folder specified in Arg
ACTION_COPY	2	Copy the message to folder specified in Arg
ACTION_DELETE	3	Delete the message
ACTION_REPLY	4	Respond to the message with the message specified in Arg
ACTION_OOFREPLY	5	Respond to the message with Out-Of-Office message specified in Arg

Table Continued on Following Page

Constant	Value	Description
`ACTION_FORWARD`	6	Forward the message to the recipient list specified in `Arg`
`ACTION_DELEGATE`	7	Delegate the message to the recipient list specified in `Arg`
`ACTION_BOUNCE`	8	Return the message back to the sender for the reason specified in `Arg`
`ACTION_TAG`	9	Tag the message to set the property specified in `Arg`
`ACTION_MARKREAD`	10	Mark as read
`ACTION_DEFER`	11	Defer action (create a client-based rule, e.g. an alert with popup window and display specific text)

> **You may see a discrepancy if you read a rule created with a client tool that deletes an incoming message from an Inbox folder. The Rule component will show it as an `ACTION_MOVE` rule, not an `ACTION_DELETE` rule. This is because the item is actually moved to the Deleted Items folder.**

Building Rule Component Applications

All applications built with the Rule component share several common steps (which are very similar to the initial steps involved in building an ACL component application; see the General Code Considerations section earlier in the chapter):

1. Create a CDO `Session` object, and log on.

2. Obtain a CDO `Folder` object representing the folder whose permissions you want to change.

3. Create a `Rules` object, and set its `Folder` property to the folder obtained in Step 2.

After completing those three steps, your application will have a `Rules` collection to work with. To read or modify existing rules, your code obtains an individual `Rule` object, then reads or modifies its properties.

To add a new rule to the folder, you follow these steps:

1. Create an optional `Condition` object using one of the condition classes in the table above, and set its properties (skip this step if you want the rule to apply to all items).

2. Create an `Action` object, and set its properties. Repeat if you plan to add multiple actions to the rule.

3. Create a `Rule` object.

4. Set the `Rule` object's `Condition` property to the condition object from Step 1 (skip this step if you want the rule to apply to all items).

5. Add each `Action` object to the `Rule` object's `Actions` collection.

6. Add the `Rule` to the `Rules` collection.

7. Repeat steps 1-6 for each additional rule you want to create.

8. Use the `Rules` collection's `Update` method to commit the changes.

You can also change the order in which rules are processed by changing the `NewIndex` property of the rules you want to reorder, then calling the `UpdateIndices` method on the `Rules` collection, followed by the `Update` method on the `Rules` collection.

You can only modify the rules for a particular folder if you are the owner of the folder.

Let's look at the details of creating conditions and actions, then using them to create rules.

Creating a Condition

Creating a condition is the hardest part of building a rule. The different types of conditions can be intimidating. How do you know what class to use to test for which sort of condition? Every condition is ultimately based on a CDO property tag. The table below summarizes some of the most frequently used conditions, the type of condition class to use, and the property tag to test.

Type of Condition	Condition Class	CDO Property Tag
From a particular sender	`PropertyCondition`	`CdoPR_SENDER_SEARCH_KEY`
To a particular recipient	`SubCondition`	`CdoPR_SEARCH_KEY`
Sent directly to me	`PropertyCondition`	`CdoPR_MESSAGE_TO_ME`
With text in Subject	`ContentCondition`	`CdoPR_SUBJECT`
With text in Message Body	`ContentCondition`	`CdoPR_BODY`
With a particular Importance	`PropertyCondition`	`CdoPR_IMPORTANCE`
With or without attachments	`BitmaskCondition`	`CdoPR_MESSAGE_FLAGS`
Of a particular size	`SizeCondition`	`CdoPR_MESSAGE_SIZE`
With a particular message class	`ContentCondition`	`Cdo_MESSAGE_CLASS`

As you can see, many of the most commonly used conditions are built with the `PropertyCondition` and `ContentCondition` classes. We'll look at those in more detail in the next sections. Other condition classes have particular uses:

- ❑ A `CommentCondition` is used to add useful information that is not used in evaluating the condition itself, such as the sender's name for a rule testing the `From` field.

- ❑ A `ComparePropsCondition` compares the value in one property to the value in a different property.

- ❑ The `ExistsCondition` class allows to you test whether a property has been set or not.

- ❑ The `LogicalCondition` class combines two conditions using logical `And`, `Or` and `Not` operators.

The SDK documentation contains more detailed information and examples of how to use each of the different condition classes.

Specifying the Property and the Value it should have

Before we can create the condition itself, we need to specify the CDO property and the value it should have to meet the condition. The following code does this:

```
Dim objPropVal As MSExchange.PropertyValue

Set objPropVal = New MSExchange.PropertyValue

objPropVal.Tag = CdoPR_BODY
objPropVal.Value = "To unsubscribe from this newsletter"
```

The code above will specify that the message body should contain the words "To unsubscribe from this newsletter" to meet the condition.

Setting the Condition Properties

CONTENTCONDITION	
Properties	**Type**
Operator	FUZZYLEVEL
PropertyType	Long
Value	Object
Methods	

After we have specified the CDO property and its value, we need to set the condition properties to meet the requirements of the particular condition class. Most condition classes expose an `Operator` property. This property can be used to specify how a string search is performed. For the `ContentCondition` class, the following table shows all possible values and their constants for the `Operator` property. Other classes have similar tables which can be found in the SDK documentation.

Constant	Value	Description
FULLSTRING	0	Match value to full string
SUBSTRING	1	Match value to a sub-string

Constant	Value	Description
PREFIX	2	Match value to the first part of the string
IGNORECASE	&H10000	Ignore case
IGNORENONSPACE	&H20000	Ignore non-spaces, such as accents, diacritics, and vowel marks
LOOSE	&H40000	Ignore high bits (maps Unicode to corresponding ANSI values)

Note that you can set the Operator property to only one of FULLSTRING, SUBSTRING, or PREFIX. You can combine any of those three with the any or all of the IGNORECASE, IGNORENONSPACE, and LOOSE.

For example, use FULLSTRING in your program to perform a full-string comparison that ignores case, IGNORENONSPACE to ignore non-space characters, and LOOSE to map Unicode characters when comparing text strings.

We can now use the following code to set the properties of a condition to test the body of a message for the presence of particular text, assuming we've already set objPropVal as above:

```
Dim objCondition As MSExchange.ContentCondition

Set objCondition = New MSExchange.ContentCondition

objCondition.PropertyType = CdoPR_BODY
objCondition.Operator = SUBSTRING + IGNORECASE + LOOSE
objCondition.Value = objPropVal
```

If we wanted to check for text in the subject, rather than the body of the message, we'd set the PropertyType property to CdoPR_SUBJECT.

Other Types of Rule Class

The PropertyCondition class uses a different set of constants for its Operator property, as shown in the table below.

PROPERTYCONDITION	
Properties	**Type**
Operator	RELOP_TYPES
PropertyTag	Long
Value	Object
Methods	

Constant	Value	Description
REL_EQ	7	Equal to
REL_GE	1	Greater than or equal to

Table Continued on Following Page

Constant	Value	Description
REL_GT	2	Greater than
REL_LE	3	Less than or equal to
REL_LT	4	Less than
REL_NE	5	Not equal to
REL_RE	6	Like

To create a condition that tests incoming items for `Importance` set to `High`, you would use this code to set the property values and create a `PropertyCondition` object. Instead of the `PropertyType` used in the `ContentCondition` class, you set the `PropertyTag` to the property being tested, then set the `Operator` appropriately:

```
Dim objPropVal As MSExchange.PropertyValue
Dim objCondition As MSExchange.PropertyCondition

Set objPropVal = New MSExchange.PropertyValue

objPropVal.Tag = CdoPR_IMPORTANCE
objPropVal.Value = CdoHigh

Set objCondition = New MSExchange.PropertyCondition

objCondition.PropertyTag = CdoPR_IMPORTANCE
objCondition.Operator = REL_EQ
objCondition.Value = objPropVal
```

Notice that the `Tag` property of the `PropVal` object matches the `PropertyTag` property of the `PropertyCondition` object.

By using different operators and combining different conditions with the `LogicalCondition` class, it is possible to create rules that are much more complex than those created with the Inbox Assistant or Rules Wizard.

Creating an Action

Compared with building a condition, creating the action is fairly easy. You just need to create a new `Action` object, specify the action that should take place using the `ActionType` property and supply any required arguments to the `Arg` property.

```
Dim objAction As MSExchange.Action

Set objAction = New MSExchange.Action
objAction.ActionType = ACTION_DELETE
```

Note that if you want to create an action that should (for example) forward a message, you must specify an additional property of the `Action` object which contains a list of the appropriate recipients like the following code shows:

```
Set objGAL = objSession.GetAddressList(CdoAddressListGAL)
Set objAddressEntries = objGAL.AddressEntries
For Each objAddressEntry In objAddressEntries
    If objAddressEntry.Name = "Postmaster" Then
        ActionList(0) = objAddressEntry.ID
        Exit For
    End If
Next

objAction.ActionType = ACTION_FORWARD
objAction.Arg = ActionList
```

The code above forwards the message to a recipient called "Postmaster". In this sample the `Arg` property is an array of strings. Each element in the array represents an address entry identifier. The SDK contains a list of the arguments for other actions.

Creating the New Rule

After the condition and actions are defined, we can now create the new rule:

```
Dim objRule As MSExchange.Rule

Set objRule = New MSExchange.Rule
objRule.Name = "New Rule"
objRule.Condition = objCondition
objRule.Actions.Add , objAction
```

If you have multiple actions, repeat the `objRule.Actions.Add` method for each action you need to add. The first parameter for the `Add` method that we're not supplying is the `Index` you want to insert the new rule at. Omitting the parameter like this places it at the end of the collection.

Note that the above code does not add the rule to the appropriate folder, nor does it add it to the folder's `Rules` collection. This must be done in a separate step.

Binding the Rule to the Folder

After we have created the rule, we need to create a `Rules` collection, associate it with the appropriate folder, then add the newly created rule:

```
Dim objRules As MSExchange.Rules

Set objRules = New MSExchange.Rules
objRules.Folder = objFolder
objRules.Add , objRule
```

This still doesn't activate the rule. You will need to commit the changes to the `Rules` collection with the `Update` method described below before the rule can become active.

Once you obtain the `Rules` collection for the folder, you can perform other operations with it, of course, enumerating existing rules by inspecting their properties, modifying existing rules, adding more rules, and deleting rules.

Deleting a Rule

To delete a rule from a particular folder, you need to obtain the `Rules` collection of the folder and find the rule you want to delete. You can only delete individual rules created with the `Rule` component. How do you know which ones you can delete? Check the `Provider` property for the rule. If the `Provider` is "`MSExchange.Rules`," then it is a Rules component rule and can be deleted individually.

The following code shows how to delete all Rules component rules associated with a folder:

```
For intCounter = objRules.Count to 1 Step -1
    If objRules.Item(intCounter).Provider = "MSExchange.Rules" Then
        objRules.Delete(intCounter)
    End If
Next
```

To remove all rules for all providers – including those created by users – you can use the `Clear` method on the `Rules` collection:

```
objRules.Clear
```

Updating the Rules Collection

After you have finished adding, modifying and deleting rules, you must update the `Rules` collection of the folder to commit the changes.

The following code shows how to commit the changes:

```
objRules.Update
```

After the changes are committed with the `Update` method, all modifications are saved to the Exchange Server, and the rules become active immediately.

Summary

The ACL and Rule components discussed in this chapter work with CDO to expand the amount of control you have over critical areas – folder permissions and automatic processing of new items. You will find sample applications that explore these components in greater depth at http://www.cdolive.com/code.htm. The ACL sample duplicates the look and feel of the Permissions dialog that you might see in Microsoft Outlook, while the Rules sample shows how to achieve the functionality of the client Inbox Assistant or Folder Assistant dialog.

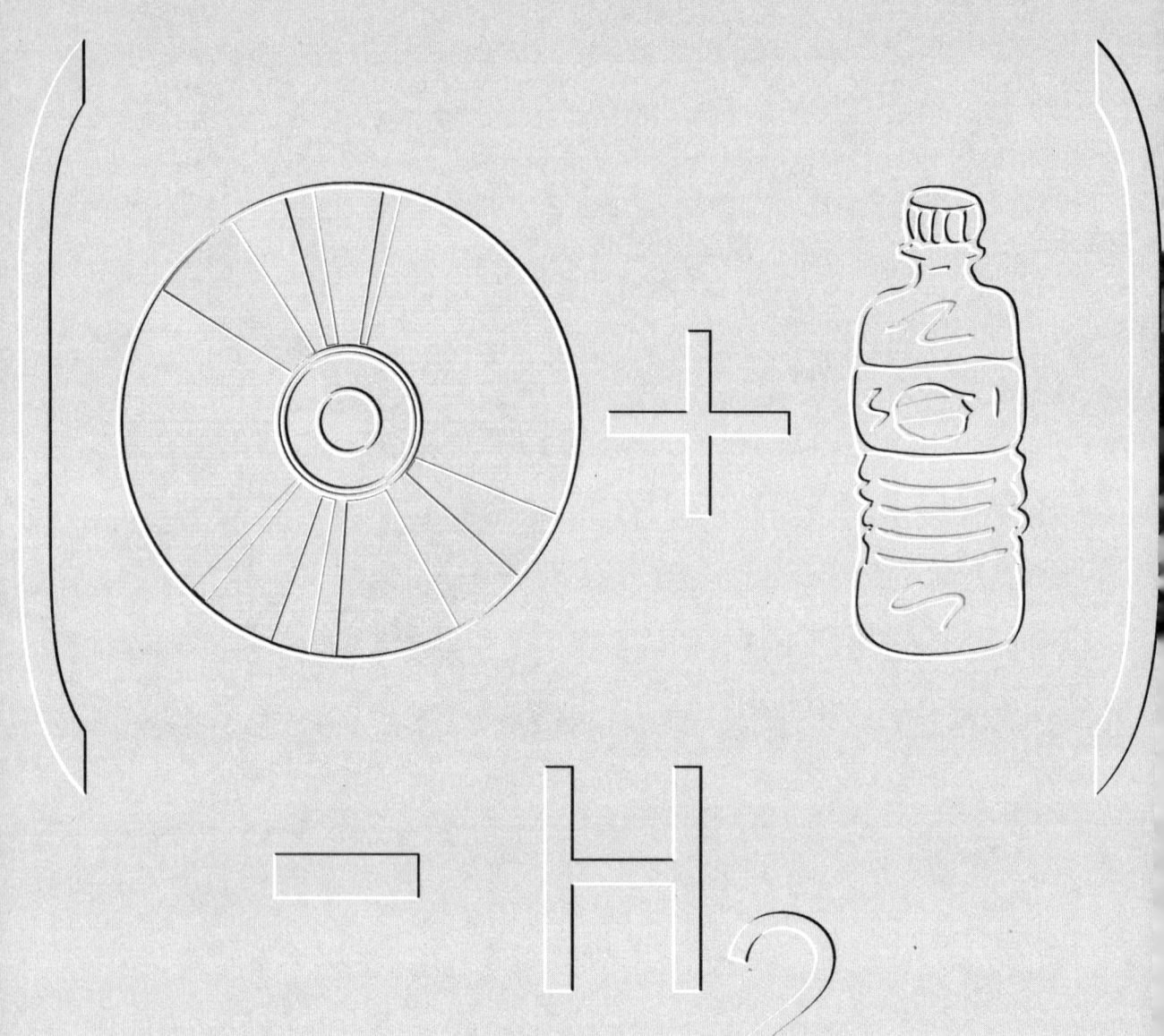

8

CDO For NT Server – CDONTS

Although the main focus of this book is on Collaboration Data Objects and programming using the CDO libraries, in this chapter we will be focusing on a functional *subset* of the Collaboration Data Objects library: the **Collaboration Data Objects for Windows NT Server (CDONTS) library.**

The first thing we will cover in this chapter is the differences between the CDO and CDONTS libraries, and also when it is preferable to use CDONTS instead of the full CDO library. We'll briefly consider how to set up the SMTP service before we cover the CDONTS object model. Whilst we do this, we will go through some sample applications written in both Visual Basic and in Active Server Pages VBScript code that demonstrate how to use CDONTS in our applications.

What is CDONTS?

> **CDONTS is a programming library intended to be used in conjunction with Microsoft Internet Information Server (IIS) and the SMTP (Simple Mail Transfer Protocol) service, though it is capable of executing in a Microsoft Exchange Server environment.**

As the rest of the book explains, the CDO library makes it easier for a developer to add support to their applications for messaging and some of the more advanced features, such as calendaring, provided by Microsoft Exchange Server. However, in some situations, you may not be interested in your application supporting these advanced features, and are only concerned with sending and receiving simple mail messages. That situation is the target for the CDONTS object library.

The first thing to know (or to ask) is: What is CDONTS? The short answer is that CDONTS is a simple object library for developers to create e-mail-capable applications. As an example of CDONTS' simplicity, this is all the code needed in order to send a mail message:

```
Dim objSendMail As CDONTS.NewMail
Set objSendMail = CreateObject("CDONTS.NewMail")

objSendMail.Send "Wesley@ThisPlace.com", "Jeanie@RightHere.com", _
                 "Greetings", "How have you been?"

Set objSendMail = Nothing
```

The longer answer is that CDONTS is an object library that provides developers with a functional subset of the CDO library's capabilities and is intended to provide reliable, fast, scalable messaging for server applications. What CDONTS doesn't provide is support for any of the more advanced features, like calendaring and workflow applications, that the combination of CDO and Exchange Server can provide.

Besides not supporting the advanced features of Exchange Server, there are a couple other important limitations to note:

❑   First, CDONTS is intended to *only* be executed on a Microsoft Windows NT Server.

❑   Second, CDONTS *only* supports communication using the SMTP protocol. However, this does not mean that a CDONTS application is unable to communicate with an Exchange Server.

❑   One other thing to note about CDONTS, is that it only communicates with the SMTP service of the machine on which it is running. It is *not possible* for CDONTS to connect to a *remote* SMTP server.

As the CDONTS library is intended to be used with the SMTP service of an Windows NT Server, when you install the SMTP service (either as a Windows 2000 Optional Component or from the Windows NT 4.0 Option Pack) you will also get the CDONTS library installed too. As mentioned above, this does not mean that a CDONTS application cannot communicate with an Exchange Server. But, there are a couple conditions that must be met in order for a CDONTS application to send and receive e-mail through an Exchange Server:

❑   First, and most importantly, the Internet Information Server service must be installed on the machine.

❑   Secondly, the administrator must use the **Exchange Internet Messaging Service (IMS) Wizard**. This wizard will add SMTP support to the Exchange Server, allowing Exchange to replace the SMTP service on the machine.

Doing this will allow the CDONTS objects to communicate with the Exchange Server instead of the Internet Information Server SMTP service.

CDONTS or CDO?

For the developer working on adding messaging support to their applications, there will be times when a decision must be made between using CDO and using CDONTS. If and when this decision must be made, there are two points to keep in mind:

- ❑ CDO excels at supporting and interacting with Exchange Server, and provides support for its more advanced features.

- ❑ CDONTS is best for creating fast, large-scale mail applications or adding mail and messaging support to existing applications.

If an application is required to support calendars, discussions, public folders, or workflow management, then CDO is the only choice. If, on the other hand, an application is just to send very simple mail messages, then CDONTS is the preferred library.

SMTP Service Configuration

In order to use CDONTS library and program utilizing a SMTP Server, it is necessary to setup the server machine and configure it correctly for CDONTS. Note that part of the name of CDONTS includes *Windows NT Server*. As such, it is necessary that you run on a machine with Microsoft Windows NT 4 Server. Once the SMTP Service has been installed on the machine, you then need to configure the service so that it can properly deliver e-mail.

For incoming mail, you may wonder how to setup a user's mailbox. For the SMTP service, this is not necessary. There is no such concept as individual user inboxes. All incoming e-mail is delivered to a central folder (the `MailRoot` folder you specified during installation), and each user's access to that folder is filtered so that they can only access the messages that are addressed to them. There may be five messages in the `MailRoot` folder, but only two addressed to a specific user. In that case, when the user logs in to their SMTP session, they will only see the two messages that are theirs. The SMTP service will not expose any messages to a user that are not addressed to that user.

For outbound messages, they can be sent in either of two ways: directly to a domain, or by using a **smarthost** mail server. If messages are delivered directly to a domain, then each message is sent only to the domain to which it was addressed. If messages are delivered through a smart host, then every message is sent to the smarthost machine. The smarthost will then determine and execute the correct routing for the message.

Setting Up Domains

In order to do domain routing, the SMTP Service needs to have routing information for each of the possible destination domains. To provide this routing information, each domain must be added to the SMTP Service and then its properties must be configured. This is done using the **Internet Service Manager**:

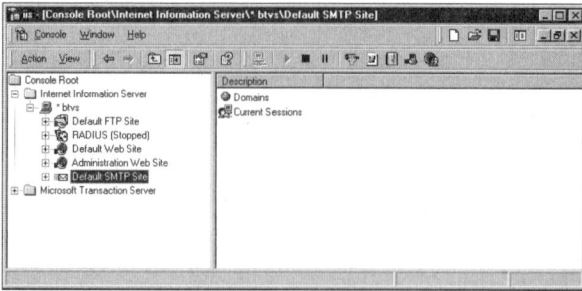

When the **Default SMTP Site** node is expanded, there is a **Domains** node shown. This is where you can see the list of domains, as well as where you add domains and specify their delivery settings. To add a new domain, right-click on the node, select **New**, and then select `Domain`. This will launch the **New Domain Wizard**, which will guide you through the addition of the domain. The first dialog asks whether the domain is **Local** or **Remote**:

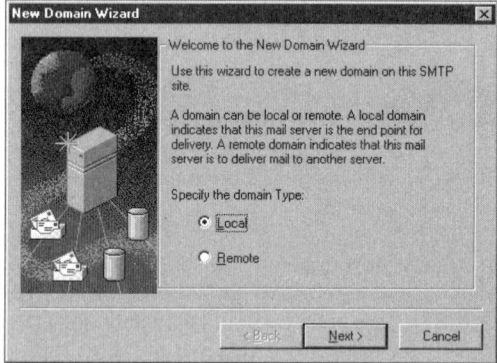

If this mail sent to the domain is to be kept on the local machine, then it is a local domain. If mail sent to the domain is to be forwarded on to another mail server, then it is a remote domain. In this case, we are going to setup a **Local** domain. The next dialog will ask for the name of the remote domain. In our case, we will be using **AnyWhere.com**:

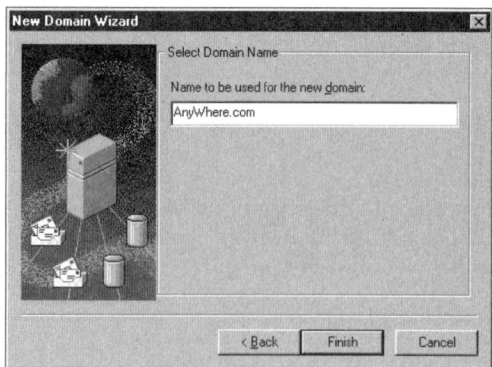

After the name is entered, and the Finish button is clicked, the new domain is created and shown in the list of domains:

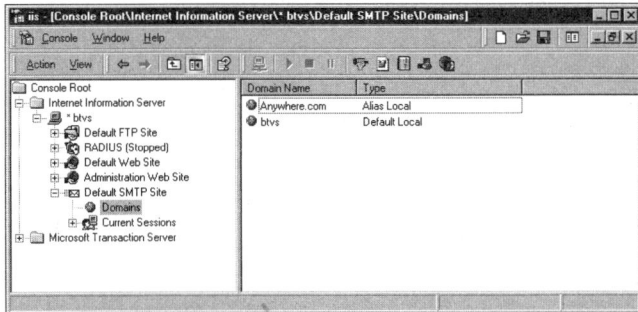

Alternatively, if you wanted to route the messages through a smarthost you would set up a Remote domain and then use the Domain Properties dialog to set up the routing information.

The CDONTS Object Library

Knowing the definition of an object library is useful, but to understand the object library it is important to investigate its object model. As this object model diagram shows, the CDONTS library is fairly straightforward and not very large:

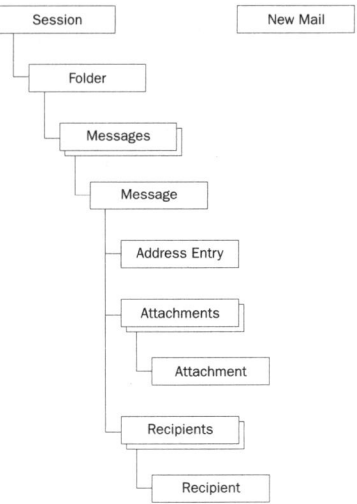

Looking at the diagram, there are two main top-level objects provided by the CDONTS library:

❑   **The** Session **object**

❑   **The NewMail object**

As the NewMail object is the simpler one, we will cover that first and then proceed to the Session object.

Referencing the CDONTS Library

As you program using the CDONTS library you will find it useful to be able to use constants (such as `CdoBodyFormatHTML`) instead of the value associated with them (0 for `CdoBodyFormatHTML`). In order to do this in either an ASP or a Visual Basic application you will need to reference the type library.

For an ASP Application, it is necessary to add a `META` tag to the `global.asa` of the project. If you are programming using Visual InterDev, this can be done through the **Project References** dialog. Otherwise, you can edit the `global.asa` yourself and add this tag:

```
<!--METADATA TYPE="TypeLib" NAME="Microsoft CDO for NTS 1.2 Library"
           UUID="{0E064ADD-9D99-11D0-ABE5-00AA0064D470}" VERSION="1.2"-->
```

To add the library reference to a Visual Basic project, you would use access the **References** dialog using the **Project | References** menu option. When the **References** dialog appears, scroll down to find **Microsoft CDO for NTS 1.2 Library**:

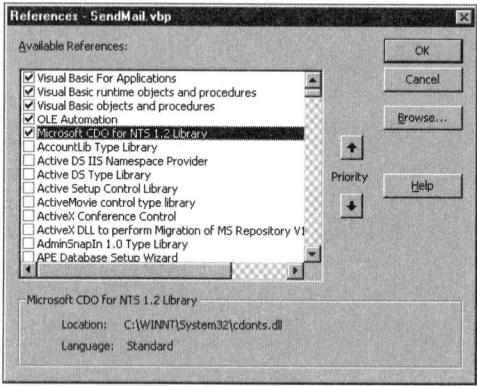

Now that we know how to reference the object library for use in our applications, we will take a look at what is included in the CDONTS library.

The NewMail Object

As the name implies, this object is provided so that a developer can easily, and quickly, add support for sending simple mail messages. Earlier we saw an example that used the `NewMail` object to send a mail message in only a couple of lines. Here again is that code:

```
Dim objSendMail As CDONTS.NewMail
Set objSendMail = CreateObject("CDONTS.NewMail")

objSendMail.Send "Wesley@ThisPlace.com", "Jeanie@RightHere.com", _
                 "Greetings", "How have you been?"

Set objSendMail = Nothing
```

When the code executes, a connection is made to the SMTP service and an SMTP message is sent to `"Jeanie@RightHere.com"`. When viewed by the recipient the message will have a subject line of `"Greetings"` and its body will be `"How have you been?"`. The message will also show that is was sent from `"Wesley@ThisPlace.com"`.

Now, we'll take a look at the code and see what is actually happening as it executes. In the first two lines, a new instance of the `NewMail` object is created. The third line of code is where all of the work for sending the message actually occurs. The `Send` method composes a message using the values passed in as parameters and then sends that message.

As an alternative to specifying all the message details in the parameters, it is possible to set values on the `NewMail` object and then execute the `Send` method. The following code would have the same results as the sample above:

```
Dim objSendMail As CDONTS.NewMail
Set objSendMail = CreateObject("CDONTS.NewMail")

With objSendMail
   .From = "Wesley@ThisPlace.com"
   .To = "Jeanie@WentWhere.com"
   .Subject = "Greetings"
   .Body = "How have you been?"
   .Send
End With

Set objSendMail = Nothing
```

These seven lines of code are functionally no different from the one line of code in the other example. The difference between the two is that the second code fragment is much more readable, and it is not necessary to know the syntax of the `Send` method in order to understand what the code is doing. Individually specifying each property is also helpful when there may be multiple values (such as multiple `To` recipients of a message) for a property, or the property value is large in size and/or length. In addition, for the rare time when there is a coding error, it is easier to debug when each property is individually set. However, specifying each property is not always the best method. If you want to send a simple message that will not be very complex, the parameterized `Send` method may be your best choice.

There is one thing that appears to be missing from these code snippets – logging in to a mailbox. With CDONTS and the `NewMail` object, this is not required to be able to send mails. While this makes it easier to send mails, it is a possible security issue.

> *Note that this security issue is not specific to CDONTS, but exists in SMTP. Since there is no logon required, it is possible to impersonate users and to send anonymous e-mails.*

Not setting the `From` property, or setting it to an empty string, would result in an e-mail in which the sender is not noted. It is up to the developer to decide on the appropriate security and whether to specify the sender of each message.

Having seen a quick glimpse of the `NewMail` object, we will now covers its properties and methods in more detail.

The From Property

As we noted above, it is possible to send an anonymous or impersonated message through CDONTS by setting (or not setting) the value of the From property. The value of the From property for a message is to be the SMTP address of the person sending the message. This value is set simply by using the following code:

```
objSendMail.From = "Wesley@ThisPlace.com"
```

For this example, when the message is viewed it will display as being sent from Wesley@ThisPlace.com. In addition to using the sender address for displaying the message, some mail clients use that address as the Reply To address. If you send a piece of mail with an invalid or incorrect SMTP address then replies to that mail will also be misdirected.

The To, Cc, and Bcc Properties

In the prior examples, you may have noticed that the recipient had to be fully qualified messaging addresses (Jeanie@RightHere.com).

> In the realm of CDONTS, there is no such thing as aliases or address books. Each of the recipients must be specified with the full SMTP address.

The NewMail object allows you to specify To, CC, and BCC recipients for the message. For example:

```
objSendMail.To = "Jeanie@RightHere.com"
objSendMail.Cc = "JeaniesBoss@RightHere.com"
objSendMail.Bcc = "Steve@RightHere.com"
```

Using these properties, the message would be sent to Jeanie@RightHere.com, JeaniesBoss@RightHere.com would get a copy of the message, and Steve@RightHere.com would get a blind copy of the message.

To send a message to multiple recipients, you simple separate the addresses with a semi-colon:

```
objSendMail.To = "John@Where.com; Jack@Where.com; Tina@Where.com"
```

You can specify multiple names/addresses for the To, Cc, and Bcc properties. A message can only have one sender though, so the From property should never be more than one e-mail address.

The Importance Property

Everyone familiar with e-mail knows that all messages can have an importance. Typically, these are Low, High, and Normal. When sending mail using the NewMail object, it is also possible to set the Importance property, which allows you to set the priority/importance for the mail message. Here are the possible values for a message's importance:

Importance	Value
High	2 (CdoHigh)
Normal	1 (CdoNormal)
Low	0 (CdoLow)

By default, each message is given an importance of Normal. For the developer to change the importance of a message, you simply set the value of the property, preferably using the constant to make it more readable:

```
objSendMail.Importance = CdoHigh
```

Earlier, we used the Send method to provide all the necessary information for sending a message. In that example, we did not specify a value for the Importance of the message. If we did want to specify the message importance in the Send method, the code would have looked like:

```
objSendMail.Send "Wesley@ThisPlace.com", "Jeanie@RightHere.com", _
                 "Greetings", "How have you been?", CdoHigh
```

The Body of the Mail Message

The primary purpose of e-mail is to send information, and the primary means of sending this information is to place it in the body of a message. On the NewMail object, the Body property allows you to specify the body contents of the message. This can be either plain text or HTML. For a simple, plain text body you would do the following:

```
objSendMail.Body = "How have you been?"
```

By default, all messages are plain text formatted. However, it is possible to send a message that has an HTML formatted body. In order to do this you need to change the BodyFormat property of the NewMail object to be CdoBodyFormatHTML (0). After that, you can set the Body property to an HTML formatted string:

```
Dim objSendMail As CDONTS.NewMail
Dim strHTML As String

strHTML = "<HTML>"
strHTML = strHTML & "<HEAD>"
strHTML = strHTML & "<TITLE>Greetings</TITLE>"
strHTML = strHTML & "</HEAD>"
strHTML = strHTML & "<BODY>"
strHTML = strHTML & "<P>What a <STRONG>Wonderful</STRONG> day!</P>"
strHTML = strHTML & "</BODY>"
strHTML = strHTML & "</HTML>"

Set objSendMail = CreateObject("CDONTS.NewMail")
```

```
With objSendMail
   .From = "Wesley@ThisPlace.com"
   .To = "Jeanie@RightHere.Com"
   .BodyFormat = CdoBodyFormatHTML
   .Body = strHTML
   .Send
End With

Set objSendMail = Nothing
```

If you send an HTML Formatted message to a client that is not HTML capable, then that client will display the message in plain text. This will cause the reader to see all the HTML tags and contents for the message. If you are not sure of the capabilities of the mail clients you will be sending to, it is best to use the Plain Text formatting.

Attachments

Sending files through e-mail is usually done by adding attachments to a message. For the `NewMail` object, the `AttachFile` method provides the means of including those file attachments in a message. The method has the following syntax:

```
objNewMail.AttachFile(Source [, FileName] [, EncodingMethod] )
```

Parameter	Description
Source	*Required.* This is the fully qualified path (either local or on a network share) to the file to include as an attachment.
FileName	*Optional.* This caption is displayed under the attachment when it is viewed in the mail client.
EncodingMethod	Optional. The method of encoding the attachment. The default method is UUENCODE. Possibly encoding methods are CdoEncodingUUencode (0) and CdoEncodingBase64 (1). (More details on this can be found in the upcoming Format Options section.)

As an example, to send a message with a excel file attachment, the code would look like:

```
Dim objSendMail As CDONTS.NewMail
Set objSendMail = CreateObject("CDONTS.NewMail")

With objSendMail
   .From = "Wesley@ThisPlace.com"
   .To = "Jeanie@RightHere.com"
   .Subject = "Inventory"
   .Body = "Here is the inventory report that you had requested."
   .AttachFile("C:\InventoryListing.xls", "Inventory Report")
   .Send
End with

Set objSendMail = Nothing
```

This `AttachFile` method would add the file `C:\InventoryListing.xls` as an attachment to the message. When the message is viewed, the caption for the attachment would be "`Inventory Report`".

The MailFormat Property

The `NewMail` object is capable of sending both plain text formatted messages and MIME formatted messages. By setting/changing the value of the `MailFormat` property the developer is able to change the format of the message. The default `MailFormat` is plain text. To change to use the MIME format we set the `MailFormat` property like this:

```
objSendMail.MailFormat = CdoMailFormatMIME
```

Any changes to the mail format will only apply to the current `NewMail` object. The changes will not affect the default mail format for the `NewMail` object. The default format will always be plain text for any `NewMail` objects instantiated in the future.

MailFormat vs. BodyFormat

Although they seem similar and it appears as though the value of one should affect the other, neither the `MailFormat` or `BodyFormat` property values affect the other. A message may be a MIME formatted message but still have a plain text body. By the same token, it is possible for a plain text formatted message to have HTML body text. This is because the `MailFormat` property affects how the entire message is formatted, while the `BodyFormat` property only describes whether the text of the message is plain text or HTML.

Format Options

Because there are a number of encoding and formatting possibilities, you may have to decide which one is best for your use. The answer is dependent on the purpose of the message being sent, as well as whom the intended recipients of the message are. Here are some guidelines to keep in mind when choosing the formatting:

❑ For using CDONTS to just send simple administrative or informative mails to a small group, or to yourself, you will be concerned with the content of the message and not the format. In this case, it would take a good bit of work to format the message to HTML and you would gain very little benefit from doing so. You could get the same information out of the message whether it was in HTML or plain text formatting, so you should probably just use the plain text format.

❑ If, on the other hand, you are using CDONTS to compose and send mails to a larger group such as a mailing list, or subscribers, then your presentation is more important. In this case, you would probably take the extra time to create some HTML that will show your best image. You could use Visual InterDev, FrontPage, or another HTML authoring tool to create the HTML and then use that HTML when setting the value of the `Body` property.

❑ Another consideration is the size of the message. If you want to keep the message small in size then you need to consider plain text formatting. When you use HTML formatting, you add a number of tags and other text to the message, possibly greatly increasing its size. Those bigger mails may take longer for the recipients to download. Although access speeds are always increasing, significantly large documents (with a number of pictures and/or attachments) may still take time and add costs in phone and ISP charges.

❑   The recipient's mail client should also not be left out of this decision. Although many mail clients today are capable of handling MIME and/or HTML messages, there are most likely a number of users out there whose mail client does not support MIME or HTML. If you are not sure of the capabilities of the recipients' mail clients, you may want to target the lowest common denominator format. For e-mail, that format would be plain text.

Modifying Message Headers

Although the intention of the `NewMail` object was to provide a quick and easy way of sending mail messages, it does have some more advanced capabilities. In our first example, we saw how you can send a message by writing four lines of code:

```
Dim objSendMail As CDONTS.NewMail
Set objSendMail = CreateObject("CDONTS.NewMail")

objSendMail.Send "Wesley@ThisPlace.com", "Jeanie@RigthHere.com", _
                 "Greetings", "How have you been?"

Set objSendMail = Nothing
```

Most mail clients allow you to view the full source of the message. In Outlook 2000, when the message is opened, you can click on View | Options and then see all the message headers in the Internet Headers text box. If we were to look at the headers for the message received after executing the previous code, it would look like this:

```
Received: from mail pickup service by MailSvr with Microsoft SMTPSVC;
          Sun, 22 Aug 1999 19:30:55 -0700
From: <Wesley@ThisPlace.com>
To: <Jeanie@Righthere.com>
Subject: Greetings
Date: Sun, 22 Aug 1999 19:30:55 -0700
X-Priority: 3
X-MSMail-Priority: Normal
Importance: Normal
X-MimeOLE: Produced By Microsoft MimeOLE V5.00.2314.1300
Message-ID: <003ab5530021789@MailSvr>

How have you been?
```

You will notice that there is much more included in the message than just the body of the message. There are a number of mail headers that are not displayed when the message is read in a mail client's message window. Most of the header information is generated based on the values set for the `NewMail` objects properties or as parameters on the `Send` method. The mail servers generate other information in the headers as they handle the message:

```
Received: from mail pickup service by MailSvr with Microsoft SMTPSVC;
          Sun, 22 Aug 1999 19:30:55 -0700
```

We can use the `NewMail` object's `Value` collection to set our own header values and to create our own headers for the messages we send. An example of when this would be useful would be in the case that all the recipients are known to have a mail client that is capable of reading and acting on a "Keywords" header in a mail message. In this case, we would want to add a `Keywords` header to the mail message.

To add a `Keywords` header we would add the following code:

```
Dim objSendMail As CDONTS.NewMail
Set objSendMail = CreateObject("CDONTS.NewMail")

objSendMail.Value("Keywords") = "Greetings"
objSendMail.Send "Wesley@ThisPlace.com", "Jeanie@Righthere.com", _
                 "Greetings", "How have you been?"

Set objSendMail = Nothing
```

When we again look at the source for that message you will note that there is now a `Keywords` header that has been added to the message:

```
Received: from mail pickup service by MailSvr with Microsoft SMTPSVC;
          Sun, 22 Aug 1999 19:30:55 -0700
From: <Wesley@ThisPlace.com>   ·
To: <Jeanie@Righthere.com>
Subject: Greetings
Date: Sun, 22 Aug 1999 19:30:55 -0700
Keywords: Greetings
X-Priority: 3
X-MSMail-Priority: Normal
Importance: Normal
X-MimeOLE: Produced By Microsoft MimeOLE V5.00.2314.1300
Message-ID: <003ab5530021789@MailSvr>

How have you been?
```

There is no limit to the number of items you can add to the `Value` collection. Each one you add will create another header for the message:

```
Dim objSendMail As CDONTS.NewMail
Set objSendMail = CreateObject("CDONTS.NewMail")

objSendMail.Value("Reply-To") = "Wesley@ThisPlace.com"
objSendMail.Value("Keywords") = "Greetings"
objSendMail.Send "Wesley@ThisPlace.com", "Jeanie@Righthere.com", _
                 "Greetings", "How have you been?"

Set objSendMail = Nothing
```

Since the `Value` property is the default property of the `NewMail` object, the previous code could also have been written like this:

```
objSendMail("Reply-To") = "Wesley@ThisPlace.com"
objSendMail("Keywords") = "Greetings"
```

Version Property

The NewMail object also exposes a Version property that returns the version of the CDONTS library that the code is executing within. To get a string containing the version information we would write this code:

```
strCurVersion = objNewMail.Version
```

Currently, the Version property will return the string "1.2".

The Send Method

Throughout this chapter, we have used the Send method of the NewMail object. Although using the Send method and listing the parameters may not be the easiest for readability and debugging, it is still useful in some applications and should not be overlooked completely. Here is a complete list of the parameters for the Send method:

```
objNewMail.Send( [From] [, To] [, Subject] [, Body] [, Importance] )
```

Parameter	Description
From	Optional. String value. Address of the sender of the message.
To	*Optional.* String value. Sets the list of To (primary) recipients of the message.
Subject	*Optional.* String value. Sets the Subject of the message.
Body	*Optional.* String value. Sets the Body of the message.
Importance	*Optional.* Long value. Sets the Importance for the message. Default is 1 (CdoNormal).

As you can see, each of the parameters is Optional. Leaving them blank will cause the NewMail object to just use its default values. All of the string parameters will default to an empty string, while the Importance value defaults to 1 (CdoNormal). Specifying the values as parameters is functionally no different from individually setting each property. If any there are any properties that are set individually on the NewMail object and then also specified in the parameters to the Send method, the values in the Send method will be used. One exception to that is if To recipients lists are specified in the Send method as well as in the To property on the NewMail object, the message will be sent to *all* recipients on *both* of the lists.

Summary of NewMail Object

Before moving on to the other objects provided by CDONTS, there are some important points to be made about the NewMail object.

- ❏ The CDONTS library supplies no user interface, and is not expected to interact with any human users. As such, none of the NewMail object's properties other than Version are intended to be read at runtime. All of the properties (again, other than Version) are write-only, and cannot be read. One implication of this is that once a header, or attachment is added to the message, it cannot be removed. In order to remove a single attachment from a message, the entire collection of attachments must be removed and only the desired attachments should be re-added.

- ❏ It is also important to know that the NewMail object is not re-usable. Once the Send method has been called on an instance, you cannot reuse that instance. If you do attempt to call the Send method without instantiating a new instance of the NewMail object, then you will get a runtime error in your code. Each additional message you send requires you to create a new instance of the NewMail object.

- ❏ Lastly, keep in mind that the NewMail object is separate from the other components provided by the CDONTS library. Most of the objects are in the hierarchy under the Session object. Those objects provide a much higher lever of functionality, and allow you to create more complex applications. When you may need to do something more than simply sending an e-mail, the other objects are better used for that task.

Before we move onto looking at the other object in the CDONTS object model, we will use our knowledge of the NewMail object to build a simple mail application in Visual Basic. This will only be capable of sending mails – we'll build a complementary inbox client after we have explored the other objects.

VB Send Mail Application

The first step in working with messaging applications is being able to send a message. To do this we will look at a simple application that was written in Visual Basic. Although CDONTS is intended to be used in a server environment, this client application will work as long as it is executing on the Windows NT Server that has IIS and the SMTP service installed.

For this application there is very little user interface necessary, CDONTS handles most of the work. We'll start by creating a new Standard EXE VB project called SendMail. Then we need to add a reference to the CDONTS library (as detailed in the earlier section on references). Next, we will create the user interface for the application. In this program, we only need to provide the user with one dialog that allows them to send a message. To do so, it is necessary to create a form in the VB Project that has the necessary fields. Here is what the dialog will look like:

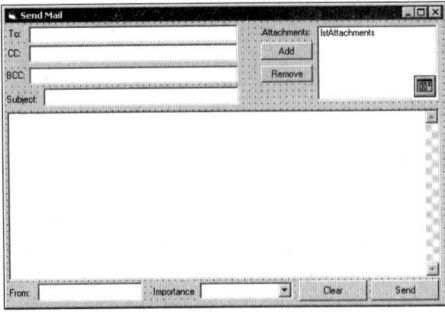

The form has the following controls on it:

Name	Type
cboImportance	Drop Down Combo Box
txtTo	Textbox
txtCC	Textbox
txtBCC	Textbox
txtSubject	Textbox
txtBody	Textbox – Multiline
txtFrom	Textbox
cmdSend	Command Button
cmdClear	Command Button
cmdAdd	Command Button
cmdRemove	Command Button
lstAttachments	List Box
dlgAttachments	Common Dialog Control

The purpose of this form is to provide the user with the graphical interface they need in order to send a simple mail message. The first thing to happen when the form loads is for the Importance combo box to be populated and the default importance of Normal is selected:

```
Private Sub Form_Load()

    cboImportance.AddItem "High"
    cboImportance.AddItem "Normal"
    cboImportance.AddItem "Low"
    cboImportance.ListIndex = 1

End Sub
```

The only other code that is needed is that to add and remove attachments. However, all that these two command buttons will do it control the attachments list box. We won't actually attach any file until the user presses the **Send** button:

```
Private Sub cmdAdd_Click()

   With dlgAttachments
     .ShowOpen
     lstAttachments.AddItem .FileName
   End With

End Sub

Private Sub cmdRemove_Click()

   lstAttachments.RemoveItem lstAttachments.ListIndex

End Sub
```

When the user does fill in the fields and clicks the **Send** button, the Click event handler will make a call to the SendMail function that we'll code shortly:

```
Private Sub cmdSend_Click()

   Dim strAttachments As String

   If lstAttachments.ListCount > 0 Then
     GetAttachments strAttachments
   End If

   If (modMail.SendMail(txtFrom, txtTo, txtCC, txtBCC, txtSubject, txtBody, _
                    GetImpValue(cboImportance.Text), strAttachments)) Then
      ClearFields

   Else
     MsgBox "There was an error sending the message, please check" & _
            " your values and try again.", vbCritical, "Error!"
   End If

End Sub
```

You'll notice that before we call the SendMail function we need to create a list of attachments. This is done by calling the GetAttachments method. All this method does is loop through the list box and creates a pipe-delimited string of attachments:

```
Private Sub GetAttachments(strAttachmentList As String)

   Dim intCounter As Integer

   For intCounter = 0 To lstAttachments.ListCount - 1
     strAttachmentList = strAttachmentList & _
```

```
                              lstAttachments.List(intCounter) & "|"
        Next

End Sub
```

Another thing to notice is that in the parameter list for `SendMail` is a call to the `GetImpValue` function. This function is in a separate BAS module that we'll look at shortly. The next thing you'll notice is that the return value from the `SendMail` function is checked. If an error occurred, and `SendMail` returned `False`, then the use will get a message box informing them of the error. If there was no error when attempting to send the message then a call is made to the `ClearFields` method of the form:

```
Private Sub ClearFields()

    txtBCC.Text = ""
    txtBody.Text = ""
    txtCC.Text = ""
    txtFrom.Text = ""
    txtTo = ""
    txtSubject = ""
    cboImportance.ListIndex = 1
    lstAttachments.Clear

End Sub
```

This method simply sets all the text box values to be an empty string, resets the importance combo box back to "Normal", and clears the attachments list box.

The last method on the form is the event handler for the **Clear Fields** button. All this handler does is call the `ClearFields` method to reset the dialog:

```
Private Sub cmdClear_Click()

    ClearFields

End Sub
```

In addition to the form, there is a standard module (`modMail`) where the real work of sending the message actually occurs. There are only two functions in the module, but they both perform important tasks. We'll start by looking at the `GetImpValue` function:

```
Function GetImpValue(strSelected As String) As Integer

  Select Case strSelected

    Case "Normal":
          GetImpValue = CdoNormal

    Case "High":
          GetImpValue = CdoHigh
```

```
          Case "Low"
              GetImpValue = CdoLow

      End Select

  End Function
```

This function is needed in order to get the correct value for the possible message importance choices. The function executes a `Select` statement and returns the correct value to use when setting the message's `Importance` property.

Lastly, we have the `SendMail` function:

```
Function SendMail(strFrom As String, strTo As String, strCC As String, _
                 strBCC As String, strSubject as String, strBody As String, _
                 intImportance As Integer, strAttachments As String) As Boolean

   On Error GoTo SendMail_Error

   Dim objNewMail As New CDONTS.NewMail

   With objNewMail
     .From = strFrom
     .To = strTo
     If strCC <> "" Then .Cc = strCC
     If strBCC <> "" Then .Bcc = strBCC
     .Body = strBody
     .Subject = strSubject
     .Importance = intImportance

     If strAttachments <> "" Then
       Dim varAttachments As Variant
       Dim intCount As Integer
       varAttachments = Split(strAttachments, "|")
       For intCount = 0 To UBound(varAttachments) - 1
         .AttachFile varAttachments(intCount)
       Next
     End If

     .Send
     SendMail = True
   End With

   Set objNewMail = Nothing

   Exit Function

SendMail_Error:

   SendMail = False

End Function
```

This function takes as parameters all of the information that is needed for creating a new mail message. If either the CC or BCC fields is left blank on the form then the method will not attempt to set those properties. Attempting to set the values to an empty string would result in an error, but it is acceptable to not assign any value.

If there are no errors when trying to send the message then the function's return value is set to `True` and the `objNewMail` object is set to `Nothing`, releasing the resources that it held. If there is an error then the function simply returns `False`. A good modification to this function could be the addition of better error handling and reporting.

Other CDONTS Objects

As we saw in the CDONTS object model diagram earlier in the chapter, there are two main objects provided by CDONTS. In this section, our focus will be on the `Session` object, and all of its child objects. Sending mail using the `NewMail` object was very simple. Is it possible for the `Session` object to make it easier to send mail? No, sending a message using the `Session` object is more code intensive than sending a message using the `NewMail` object. The payoff for the `Session` object is that a developer is given more control and capabilities when using the `Session` object than they would have with the `NewMail` object.

Common Properties

Before investigating the `Session` object and its child objects, we should note that similar to the CDO library, there are certain properties that every CDONTS object exposes. Since these are the same as those in CDO we will only mention them here and not go into any detail on the properties. The common properties are:

- ❑ Session
- ❑ Class
- ❑ Parent
- ❑ Application

The Session Object

> The `Session` object is used to store all of the information needed for accessing a user's default message information, Inbox/Outbox, and binding to a user's mailbox.

All of the user's session settings and options are stored in the `Session` object for each user's session. Any access to a user's messaging store is provided through the `Session` object. The `Session` object has four methods on it:

- ❑ LogonSMTP

❑ Logoff

❑ GetDefaultFolder

❑ SetLocaleIDs

The LogonSMTP Method

In the section on the NewMail object, we noted that there was no logging in required. When using the Session object it is necessary to login, and an error will occur if the object is used before successfully calling the LogonSMTP method. This is because before a Session object can be used, it must be instantiated, which is what the LogonSMTP method will handle. The LogonSMTP method initializes the Session object and then binds that Session object to the specified mailbox. The syntax of the LogonSMTP method is:

```
objSession.LogonSMTP(DisplayName, Address)
```

Parameter	Description
DisplayName	*Required.* This display name for the user logged on.
Address	*Required.* The complete e-mail address for the user logged on.

Before being able to access any messages, or any messaging stores, a new Session object must be created and the LogonSMTP command successfully executed. This can be done with the following code:

```
Dim objCurSession As CDONTS.Session
Set objCurSession = CreateObject("CDONTS.Session")

objCurSession.LogonSMTP("Jack Roberts", "JackR@AnyWhere.com")
```

First, the code will create a new Session object. In the last line, the session is initialized with the user's display name and messaging address settings. Additionally, the session is then bound to the specified SMTP mailbox (JackR@AnyWhere.com). Connecting to another mailbox would require either another Session object or calling the Logoff method and then calling the LogonSMTP method with the new settings.

> It is important to note that, although its name may imply otherwise, the LogonSMTP method does not perform any authentication. The method just sets properties for the Session object – they are not validated. It is possible to specify any display name and e-mail address in the call to LogonSMTP, and you will not get any errors returned. If an incorrect or invalid e-mail address is specified there is no error given, but messages may not be delivered correctly.

329

In SMTP there is no real physical mailbox. All of the messages for a server are stored in one folder (\Inetpub\MailRoot\Drop). When the Session object "binds" to a mailbox, all that is really happening is that it filters the messages in the store and only allows access to those addressed to the Address specified in the LogonSMTP method. If a user has a SMTP address of Wesley@ThisPlace.com but incorrectly calls LogonSMTP specifying Wexlex@ThisPlace.com then that Session object will only show the messages addressed to Wexlex@ThisPlace.com. Also, any messages that person sends will show an incorrect return address.

After the Session object has been instantiated and the LogonSMTP method has been called, you can then have access to the messaging store for that user. Since the LogonSMTP method does not perform validation, it will not return an error message. Instead, it will just initialize its values and attempt to bind to the specified mailbox.

The GetDefaultFolder Method

The GetDefaultFolder method returns the default Inbox or Outbox folder for a message store. The syntax of the method is:

```
Set objFolder = objSession.GetDefaultFolder(folderType)
```

There is only one parameter for the method – folderType. This can be one of two values:

Folder	FolderType Value
Inbox	CdoDefaultFolderInbox (1)
Outbox	CdoDefaultFolderOutbox (2)

Depending on the value specified for the folderType parameter, the method will return either the default Inbox or Outbox for the current messaging store.

Unlike Exchange Server, when using an SMTP server each user has only an Inbox and an Outbox.

The following code would create a new session and get the Inbox folder:

```
Dim objSession As CDONTS.Session
Dim objInbox As CDONTS.Folder

Set objSession = CreateObject("CDONTS.Session")
objCurSelection.LogonSMTP ("Jack Roberts", "JackR@AnyWhere.com")

Set objInbox = objSession.GetDefaultFolder(CdoDefaultFolderInbox)
```

The SetLocaleID Method

The SetLocaleID method allows the programmer to specify identifiers to define the session's locale. The locale is the features of the environment that are based on the language, culture, and/or conventions. This can include formatting of dates and times, displaying of currency, the sorting order, and the character set that is to be used. The syntax of the method is:

```
objSession.SetLocaleIDs(CodePageID)
```

The only parameter for the method is the `CodePageID` parameter. This is a Long value, and is a code page identifier.

More information and details on Code Pages can be found in the Windows NT documentation.

There are two key things to note about the `SetLocaleID` method. First, it must be called before the `LogonSMTP` method is executed. Secondly, the specified `CodePageID` is checked to validate that it is a valid value. If the value specified is incorrect, you will get an error of `CDOE_INVALID_PARAMETER` (&H80070057).

The LogOff Method

Once the session is finished with, we need to end the session and log off by calling the `LogOff` method and then releasing the `Session` object:

```
objCurSession.LogOff

Set objCurSession = Nothing
```

The `LogOff` method will end all activity on the `Session` object, terminate the binding to the SMTP message store and will clear the settings for the `Session` object. It is possible to reuse the `Session` object by calling the `LogonSMTP` method again.

The Session Object's Properties

The `Session` object also exposes some properties for the current session. In addition to the common properties for all CDONTS objects, it exposes some specific properties. Those properties and their return values are listed here:

Property	Description
Inbox	*Read-Only.* Folder object for the Inbox of the current session.
Outbox	*Read-Only.* Folder object for the Outbox of the current session.
MessageFormat	*Read/Write.* Returns or sets the formatting/encoding of messages. Can be either `CdoMime` (0, **MIME** Messages) or `CdoText` (1, **Plain Text** Messages).
Name	*Read-Only.* The display name for the current session.
Version	*Read-Only.* Version of the CDONTS Library.

The Folder Object

The `Folder` object represents a folder or a container for the message store of the current session.

A Folder object represents a folder in the users messaging store. Folders can contain messages, documents, and forms. For the SMTP service, the only folders are **Inbox** and **Outbox**:

❑ The Inbox is the delivery location for incoming mail. All mail addressed to the recipient will be delivered to the Inbox.

❑ The Outbox is the temporary location for outgoing mail. When a message is sent it is placed into the Outbox folder and sent when that folder is processed, which the server does automatically.

By using Folder objects, it is possible to programmatically access the contents of the folder. However, although it is possible to access the messages in a folder, the only changes that can be made to these messages are the deletion of entire messages. The CDONTS library does not allow: modifications to attachments (adding or deleting); modifications to any of the To, CC, or BCC recipient lists; modifications to any message properties. Even those properties that are writeable when a message is created cannot be modified on an existing message. In addition to the common properties, the Folder object also exposes the following properties:

Property	Description
Name	*Read-Only*. Display name for the folder.
Messages	*Read-Only*. Collection of messages in the folder.

The Messages Collection

For each Folder object there is a `Messages` property. This property will return a **Messages collection**, which is a collection of zero or more `Message` objects. Each folder's `Messages` property will return the collection of messages that exist in that folder, and only those that exist in the specified folder. A Messages collection has a number of properties to allow easier access to the messages, as well as methods to allow modifications to the collection of messages.

The Item Property

In the case where access to a single message is desired, there is the `Item` property. Using the `Item` property will return a single `Message` object from the Messages collection. The syntax of the property is:

```
colMessages.Item(index)
```

The value for the `index` parameter can be from 1 to the size of the collection. If we wanted to get the first message in the collection, we would use the following code:

```
Dim objMessage As CDONTS.Message
Set objMessage = colMessages.Item(1)
```

It may be useful to know that the default property for the Messages collection is the `Item` property, so this code would have the same effect:

```
Dim objMessage As CDONTS.Message
Set objMessage = colMessages(1)
```

The Add Method

A `Messages` collection also has an `Add` method, which is used for adding a `Message` object to the collection. When called, this method creates a new `Message` object, adds it to the collection, and then returns a reference to that object. In this way, a developer is able to add a new message to the collection and then immediately modify its properties without first having to find it within the collection. The syntax for `Add` is:

```
Set objMessage = colMessages.Add( [subject] [, text] [, importance] )
```

Parameter	Description
Subject	*Optional.* Subject line for the message.
Text	*Optional.* The body text for the message.
Importance	*Optional.* The importance setting for the message. Default is 1 (CdoNormal).

The following code would add a new message to the Outbox:

```
Set objOutbox = objSession.GetDefaultFolder(CdoDefaultFolderOutbox)
Set objNewMsg = objOutbox.Messages.Add

With objNewMsg
  .Text = "How are things going?"
  .Subject = "Status Needed"
  Set objRecip = .Recipients.Add(Name:="Jeanie", Type:=CdoTo, _
                             Address:="Jeanie@AnyWhere.com")

  .Send
End With
```

Right now, the lines relating to the `Recipients` collection may not be understandable. Don't concern yourself with that, as we will cover that later when we look at the `Message` object and its `Recipients` collection.

The Delete Method

If you can add a message to a collection, it is also useful to be able to delete a message from the collection. Your first inclination may be to call the `Delete` method on the `Messages` collection. If you did that, then you would delete all the messages in the collection and remove them from the message store. It is important to remember that the `Delete` method on the `Messages` collection immediately removes *all* of the messages from the collection.

> **The action cannot be undone, so use care when your code involves deleting messages.**

If you want to delete only a single message from a collection, you should call the `Delete` method on that `Message` object. On the other hand, if you wanted to delete all the messages in the Inbox, you would use this code:

```
Set objOutbox = objSession.GetDefaultFolder(CdoDefaultFolderInbox)
objOutbox.Messages.Delete
```

The GetFirst, GetNext, GetLast, GetPrevious Methods

The ability to add and delete messages in a collection is very useful, but it is also necessary to be able to navigate through the collection of messages. In order to allow navigation, there are four methods provided by the Messages collection:

- ❑ GetFirst
- ❑ GetNext
- ❑ GetLast
- ❑ GetPrevious

These methods return the first, next, last, or previous message (respectively) in the Messages collection. If there is a failure in getting the specified message, the methods will return `Nothing`. Keep in mind that the order of the messages within the collection is *unknown*, and the order that these methods return messages cannot be predicted. When navigating through a collection of messages using these methods it is best to treat the collection as unsorted and to not make any assumptions about the orders of the `Message` objects.

In order to iterate through the collection of messages in the Inbox, and list out the sender of each of the messages, we would use this code:

```
Set objInbox = objSession.GetDefaultFolder(CdoDefaultFolderInbox)
Set objMsg = objInbox.Messages.GetFirst

While Not objMsg Is Nothing
  Debug.Print "Sent By : " & objMsg.Sender
  Set objMsg = objInbox.Messages.GetNext
Wend
```

The Message Object

The most important part of any messaging application is the message itself. CDONTS provides a **Message object** that represents one message in the messaging store. This can be an e-mail message, a document, or a form in a folder. A `Message` object can be accessed through the Messages collection. Here is a listing of the properties of a `Message` object, also noting the name of the corresponding property from the `NewMail` object:

Property	NewMail Property	Description
Attachments	Attachments	`Attachment` object or collection of `Attachment` objects.
ContentBase	ContentBase	Content base header for a MIME message.
ContentID	ContentID	Content-ID header for a MIME message.
ContentLocation	ContentLocation	Content-Location header for a MIME message.
HTMLText	Body	HTML formatted message body.
Importance	Importance	The message's importance.
MessageFormat	BodyFormat	Encoding format for the message.
Recipients	To,CC,BCC	`Recipient` object or collection of `Recipient` objects.
Sender	From	An `AddressEntry` object for the user that sent the message.
Size	N/A	`Message` size, in bytes.
Subject	Subject	Subject of the message.
Text	Body	The plain test of the message body.
TimeReceived	N/A	Date/Time message was received.
TimeSent	N/A	Date/Time message was sent.

As all of these properties have been covered when we dealt with the `NewMail` object (or the new ones are self-explanatory), we will not go into further detail on them.

The Delete Method

Earlier it was mentioned that calling the `Delete` method on the `Messages` collection would delete all the messages in that collection. If you want to delete only one message in the collection, you need to use the `Delete` method on that `Message` object. To delete the first message in the inbox you would use the following code:

```
Set objInbox = objSession.GetDefaultFolder(CdoDefaultFolderInbox)
Set objMsg = objOutbox.Messages.GetFirst
objMsg.Delete
```

Just like the `Delete` method on the `Messages` collection, the deletion here happens immediately and *cannot be undone*.

The Send Method

Just as the `NewMail` object had a `Send` method, so does the `Message` object. The `Send` method on a `Message` object has the same effect – sending the message to its specified recipients. The same code we saw earlier for sending a message from the outbox provides an example of the `Send` method:

```
Set objOutbox = objSession.GetDefaultFolder(CdoDefaultFolderOutbox)
Set objNewMsg = objOutbox.Messages.Add

With objNewMsg
  .Text = "How are things going?"
  .Subject = "Status Needed"
  Set objRecip = .Recipients.Add(Name:="Jeanie", Type:=CdoTo, _
                                  Address:="Jeanie@AnyWhere.com")
  .Send
End With
```

The Attachments Collection

Each message exposed an `Attachments` property, which returns an **Attachments collection**.
This collection provides the developer with programmatic access to the attachments of a message.
Each `Attachments` collection that will contain zero or more attachments for that message. The
`Attachments` collection has only two unique properties: an `Item` property and a `Count` property.
An example of using the `Item` and `Count` properties to list all the attachments for a message would
look like this:

```
Set colAttachments = objMessage.Attachments

For intLoop = 1 To colAttachments.Count
    Debug.Print "Attachment: " & colAttachments.Item(intLoop).Name
Next
```

In addition to the properties provided by the collection, the collection also exposes `Add` and `Delete`
methods. For the `Delete` method, there are no parameters. Calling the `Delete` method will delete all
attachments from the collection and *cannot be undone*.

In order to add new attachments to a message, we would use the `Add` method. The syntax of the `Add`
method is:

```
Set objAttach = colAttachments.Add( [name] [, type] [, source] _
                                    [, ContentLocation] [, ContentBase] )
```

Parameter	Description
Name	*Optional.* Display name for the attachment.
Type	*Optional.* Attachment type. Either 1 (`CdoFileData`) or 4 (`CdoEmbeddedMessage`).
Source	*Optional.* Full path to the file to attach if type is `CdoFileData`, or a `Message` object if type is `CdoEmbeddedMessage`.
ContentLocation	*Optional.* MIME attachment content location header.
ContentBase	*Optional.* MIME attachment content base header.

If we wanted to add the file `C:\InventoryReport.xls` to the message, our code would look like:

```
Set colAttachments = objMessage.Attachments
colAttachments.Add ("Inventory Report", CdoFileData, "C:\InventoryReport.xls")
```

The Attachment Object

In order to access one of the Attachments for a message, we have the **Attachment object**. This object represents either a file or a message attached to the message. An Attachment object exposes these properties:

Property	Description
ContentBase	Content-Base header value for a MIME attachment.
ContentID	Content-ID header value for a MIME attachment.
ContentLocation	Content-Location header value for a MIME attachment.
Name	Display name for the attachment.
Source	Path or location for the attachment.
Type	Attachment type. Either CdoFileData (1) or CdoEmbeddedMessage (4).

There are three methods exposed on the Attachment object. The Delete method is used to delete an individual attachment from the Attachments collection for a message. This method will immediately remove the attachment from the collection and *cannot be undone*.

The Attachment object also has a method that allows the attachment source to be loaded from a file. That method is ReadFromFile and has this syntax:

```
objAttach.ReadFromFile(fileName)
```

The fileName parameter specifies the fully qualified path to the source file to load the attachment data from. This method allows the developer to load an attachment from a source location after the attachment object has already been created.

There is also a method that allows the developer to save the attachment data to a file. This method is the WriteToFile method and its syntax is:

```
objAttach.WriteToFile(fileName)
```

Where the fileName parameter is the fully qualified path for the destination file that the attachment data is to be saved to. This method is used when you want to save the attachment to a hard drive, or to a location other than the messaging store.

The Recipients Collection

Every message object has a collection of addresses for its recipients. These can be To, CC, or BCC recipients, but they are all contained within one **Recipients collection**. For a particular Message object, the Recipients collection will contain zero or more Recipient objects. Similar to the Attachments collection, it exposes a Count and Item property. There is also a Delete method on the collection. As with the other collection Delete methods for collections, this Delete method will remove all recipients from the collection.

Adding recipients for a message is done using the Add method on the Recipients collection. The Add method has the following syntax:

```
Set objRecip = collRecips.Add( [name] [, address] [, type])
```

Parameter	Description
Name	*Optional.* Recipient's display/friendly name.
Address	*Optional.* Recipient's e-mail address.
Type	*Optional.* Type of recipient. Can be one of three values: CdoTo (1), CdoCc (2), or CdoBcc (3)

The Name, Address, and Type parameters are the same as the Name, Address, and Type properties for the Recipient object (covered in the next section). If no parameters are specified, a Recipient object is still created but with empty values. This code example shows the adding of To, CC, and BCC recipients to a message:

```
objMsg.Recipients.Add ("Jeanie", CdoTo, "Jeanie@AnyWhere.com")
objMsg.Recipients.Add ("JeaniesBoss", CdoCc, "JeaniesBoss@AnyWhere.com")
objMsg.Recipients.Add ("Jack", CdoBcc, "Jack@AnyWhere.com")
```

Since CDONTS does not allow the modifying of messages in the inbox, attempting to call the Add method on a message in the Inbox will return an error of CdoE_No_Access. The only time that the Add method is useful is when you are creating a new Message object and not attempting to modify an existing message.

The Recipient Object

The **Recipient object** represents a single recipient of the message. The object exposes the following properties, which map exactly to the parameters for the Add method on the Recipients collection:

Property	Description
Name	Recipient's display/friendly name.
Address	Recipient's e-mail address.
Type	Type of recipient. Can be one of three values: CdoTo, CdoCc, or CdoBcc

The Recipient object also has a Delete method, which deletes only the current Recipient object from the Recipients Collection.

The AddressEntry Object

The Sender property on a Message object will return an **AddressEntry object**. This AddressEntry object contains all of the addressing information for the sender of the message. The object has the following properties:

Property	Description
Name	Sender's alias or friendly display name
Address	Senders's e-mail address.
Type	Type of address. For CDONTS, this is always "SMTP"

Other CDONTS Objects Summary

As you can see, the level of granularity and control provided by the Session object and its children is much greater than that of the NewMail object. This allows the creation of more powerful and capable applications, but does require some more work. There is a tradeoff of capabilities vs. ease of use. In this case, when you want to create that more complex application, you can still do so without a large amount of work. CDONTS does allow the developer to create both the simple and complex applications, and makes both of those easier to create.

The MailClient ASP Application

Earlier in the chapter we built a VB application that makes use of the CDONTS library and the NewMail object. Now we will look at an ASP application that uses the Session object. In this application we will look at the other side of messaging – the displaying of the received message. This application will have a user login and then present them with a listing of message in their Inbox. From the Inbox, the user will be able to click on a message and be taken to another page that will display the selected message.

As we noted earlier in the chapter, programming can be much easier when you can use constants instead of their literal values. For this application we have already added the required meta tag to the global.asa file, as we described earlier in this chapter, so that we can make use of those CDONTS constants.

Logging In

Unlike the NewMail object, when using the Session object it is necessary to login. This is done using the Login.asp page. On this page a user will enter their user name (display name) and the e-mail address of the account to which they wish to login. The source of the page is:

```
<%@ Language=VBScript %>
<HTML><HEAD>
<TITLE>Inbox login</TITLE>
</HEAD>
```

```
<BODY>
<STRONG><FONT SIZE=5>Please Login</FONT></STRONG>
<FORM ID = LoginFrm ACTION = "Inbox.asp" METHOD = "Get">

<TABLE WIDTH="300" BORDER = "0" CELLSPACING = "1" CELLPADDING = "1">
    <TR>
      <TD>User Name</TD>
          <TD><INPUT TYPE="Text" NAME=UserName></TD>
    </TR>
    <TR>
       <TD>E-mail Address</TD>
          <TD><INPUT TYPE="Text" NAME=UserE-mail></TD>
    </TR>
</TABLE>

<INPUT TYPE="Submit" VALUE="Login" ID=submit1>

</FORM>
</BODY>
</HTML>
```

When viewed in the browser, it appears like this:

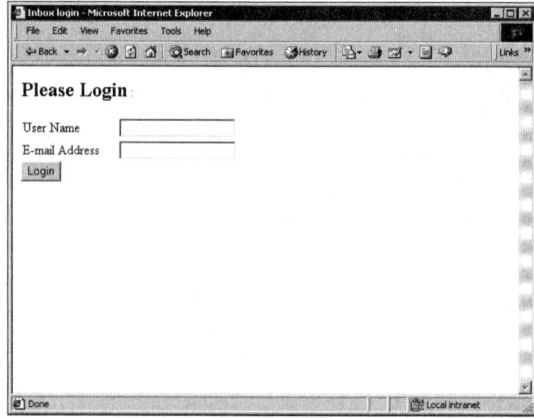

Atfirst you might wonder why there is no server to specify in the login page. This is because, as we noted earlier, the CDONTS objects are only able to communicated with the SMTP service of the machine on which the application is executing. All that is needed to access their messages is the user's display/user name and their e-mail address. These two pieces of information are passed on to the Inbox.asp page and used in the LogonSMTP call.

Listing Messages

Oncea user enters their login information, they are taken to their Inbox. The Inbox.asp page is the page that handles actually logging the user in and then listing the messages in their inbox. If there is an error during the login then there will not be any messages listed. The source of the page is:

```asp
<%@ Language=VBScript %>
<% Option Explicit %>
<HTML>
<HEAD>
<TITLE><% =Request.QueryString("UserName") %>'s Inbox</TITLE>
</HEAD>
<BODY>
<%
Dim objInbox
Dim colMsgs
Dim strUserName
Dim strUserE-mail
Dim objCurSession

' Assign the values from the query string into local variables
' since they will be needed more than once.
strUserName = Request.QueryString("UserName")
strUserE-mail = Request.QueryString("UserE-mail")

' Store the User Name and E-mail
' in ASP session variables for possible future use.
Session("UserName") = strUserName
Session("UserE-mail") = strUserE-mail

' Use the values passed in to create a new session and
' initialize its variables.
Set objCurSession = CreateObject("CDONTS.Session")
objCurSession.LogonSMTP strUserName, strUserE-mail

' Create an ASP session variable to store the current user's
' CDONTS Session instance
Set Session("curSession") = objCurSession

' Get the Inbox Folder object
Set objInbox = objCurSession.Inbox

' Using that object, get the collection of messages in the Inbox
Set colMsgs = objInbox.Messages

' Display a greeting to the user.
Response.Write "Welcome, " & Session("UserName") & ". You have " & _
            colMsgs.Count & " messages in your inbox. <BR><BR>"

' Then, display a listing of the messages in their inbox
' only if there are some messages to display

If (colMsgs.Count > 0) Then

%>

<TABLE BORDER=0 CELLPADDING=1 CELLSPACING=1 WIDTH=90% >

  <TR>
    <TD><STRONG>Importance</STRONG></TD>
```

```
      <TD><STRONG>From</STRONG></TD>
      <TD><STRONG>Subject</STRONG></TD>
      <TD><STRONG>Sent</STRONG></TD>
    </TR>

<%
Dim intLoop

For intLoop = 1 To colMsgs.Count
%>

  <TR>
    <TD ALIGN=Middle><% ShowImportanceIcon(colMsgs(intLoop).Importance) %>
    </TD>
    <TD><% =colMsgs(intLoop).Sender %></TD>
    <TD><A HREF="ViewMessage.asp?MsgID=<% =intLoop %>">
        <% =colMsgs(intLoop).Subject %></A></TD>
    <TD><% =colMsgs(intLoop).TimeSent %></TD>
  </TR>

<%
  Next
End If
%>
</TABLE>
</BODY>
</HTML>

<%
' Function to generate the correct IMG tag for the importance icon
Sub ShowImportanceIcon(intImpValue)

  Dim strIconFile

  Select Case intImpValue

    Case CdoNormal
        strIconFile = "Norm_Importance.gif"

    Case CdoHigh
        strIconFile = "High_Importance.gif"

    Case CdoLow
        strIconFile = "Low_Importance.gif"

  End Select

  Response.Write ("<IMG SRC=.\Images\" & strIconFile & ">")

End Sub
%>
```

And here is a sample of what the page would look like for a user:

Taking a look at the ASP code that is behind this page will give a much clearer view of using the `Session` object in an application.

After the declarations there are a couple of lines of code that stand out as not being directly related to the CDONTS `Session` object. Those lines take care of getting the logon information that the user entered on the logon page and then storing that in an ASP `Session` variable for future uses:

```
' Assign the values from the query string into local variables
' since they will be needed more than once.
strUserName = Request.QueryString("UserName")
strUserE-mail = Request.QueryString("UserE-mail")

' Store the Session Object, User Name and E-mail
' in ASP session variables for possible future use.
Session("UserName") = strUserName
Session("UserE-mail") = strUserE-mail
```

Once those ASP `Session` variables are created, the next step is to create the CDONTS `Session` object and then initialize it. By using the `UserName` and `E-mail` address values that were passed in, the instantiation of the object and the initialization of the `Session` values is done in these lines:

```
Set objCurSession = CreateObject("CDONTS.Session")
objCurSession.LogonSMTP strUserName, strUserE-mail
```

After the session is created and initialized, it is stored in an ASP `Session` variable:

```
Set Session("curSession") = objCurSession
```

This, like the `UserName` and `E-mail` name variables, allows the users CDONTS session to be more easily accessed from another page in the web application.

Once the session is created and the user is logged in, the `Session` object can be used to access the user's folders. In this case, the only folder that we are concerned with is the Inbox. Using the `Inbox` property of the `Session` object allows access to the `Messages` collection for the Inbox, as shown in this code:

```
' Get the Inbox Folder object
Set objInbox = objCurSession.Inbox

' Using that object, get the collection of messages in the Inbox
Set colMsgs = objInbox.Messages
```

Once we have access to the collection of messages in the Inbox, we can then access that collection and list the individual messages. This code handles generating the HTML code that lists the messages in the Inbox:

```
' Display a greeting to the user.
Response.Write "Welcome, " & Session("UserName") & ". You have " & _
               colMsgs.Count & " messages in your inbox. <BR><BR>"

' Then, display a listing of the messages in their inbox
' only if there are some messages to display
If (colMsgs.Count > 0) Then
```

By querying the value of the `Count` property on the messages collection it is possible to present the user with a message indicating the number of messages they have. This can be useful when the listing of messages would scroll off screen. The `Count` property is also used to determine whether there are any messages in the Inbox to list on the web page. If there are one or more messages in the collection then the code will iterate through the collection and display each message's importance, sender, subject, and when it was sent. There is one line of code in the loop that could use some more explaining. The line of code that generates the text for the subject display makes an anchor tag our of the text. The line looks like:

```
<TD><A HREF="ViewMessage.asp?MsgID=<% =intLoop %>">
    <% =colMsgs(intLoop).Subject %></A></TD>
```

An anchor tag is generated so that the user can click on a message and view the message. When the link is clicked, the index of the message within the messages collection is passed to the `ViewMessage` page. This allows the `ViewMessage` page to immediately access the desired message and then display its contents.

There is another function on the page for which its use may not be immediately apparent. The function, `ShowImportanceIcon`, will create the correct HTML `IMG` tag to display an each message's importance as an icon:

```
Sub ShowImportanceIcon(intImpValue)

  Dim strIconFile

  Select Case intImpValue

    Case cdoNormal
```

```
            strIconFile = "Norm_Importance.gif"

        Case cdoHigh
            strIconFile = "High_Importance.gif"

        Case cdoLow
            strIconFile = "Low_Importance.gif"

    End Select

    Response.Write ("<IMG SRC=.\Images\" & strIconFile & ">")

End Sub
```

Dependingon the value of the message's `Importance` property (which is passed into this sub as the `intImpValue` parameter), the sub will point to either the high, low, or normal importance image. The images used in this application were found at the Texas A&M University Computer Science Image Gallery (http://www.cs.tamu.edu/Images/small_buttons/), with some minor name changes done before use.

Displaying Messages

Oncea user has seen the listing of messages in their Inbox, they may want to view the contents of one or more of the message. In this application, a user can click on the subject of a message and be taken to a page that will show the message's contents. If the user had clicked on the message with the subject of **Game Friday Night** in the inbox, they would then see that message displayed like this:

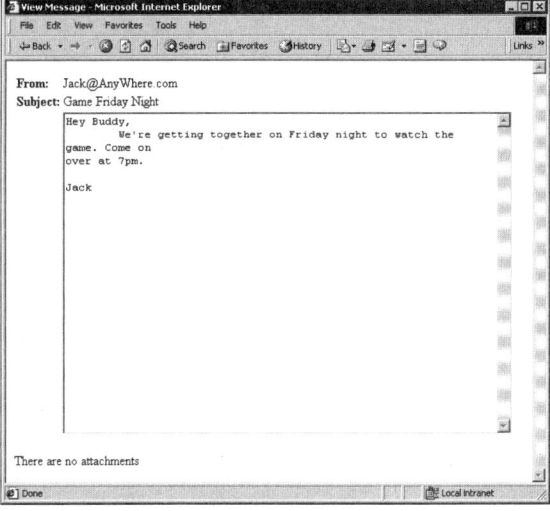

The source code for `ViewMessage.asp` is:

```asp
<%@ Language=VBScript %>
<% Option Explicit %>
<HTML>
<HEAD>
<TITLE>View Message</TITLE>
</HEAD>
<BODY>
<%
Dim colMsgs
Dim objCurMessage
Dim objSession
Dim intIndex

Set objSession = Session("curSession")
Set colMsgs = objSession.Inbox.Messages

intIndex = Request.QueryString("MsgID")
Set objCurMessage = colMsgs(intIndex)
%>

<TABLE BORDER = 0 CELLPADDING = 1 CELLSPACING = 1 WIDTH = "75%">

  <TR>
    <TD><STRONG>From:</STRONG></TD>
    <TD><LABEL><% = objCurMessage Sender %></LABEL></TD></TR>
  <TR>
    <TD><STRONG>Subject:</STRONG></TD>
    <TD><LABEL><% = objCurMessage Subject %></LABEL></TD></TR>
  <TR>
    <TD></TD>
    <TD><TEXTAREA ID=TEXTAREA1 NAME=TEXTAREA1 STYLE="HEIGHT: 390px;
               WIDTH: 547px"><% = objCurMessage Text %>
</TEXTAREA></TD></TR></TABLE></P>

<%
If objCurMessage.Attachments.Count = 0 Then
   Response.Write "There are no attachments"
Else
   Dim intCount
   Response.Write "<B>Attachments:</B> <BR>"
   For intCount = 1 To objCurMessage.Attachments.Count
       Response.Write objCurmessage.Attachments(intCount).Name & "<BR>"
   Next
End If
%>

</BODY>
</HTML>
```

At first glance, there does not appear to be a large amount of code necessary to display a message. That is because some of the more involved work has already been done by the `Login.asp` and `Inbox.asp` pages. The results of that work were maintained in ASP `Session` variables, which can be easily retrieved by other pages in the application. This saves the work of passing around the `UserName` and `UserE-mail` values as well as removes the need to keep creating new `Session` objects and calling `LogonSMTP` on them. All of that logon work is recalled with the following line:

```
Set objSession = Session("curSession")
```

This will assign to the local `objSession` object the CDONTS `Session` object that was created and initialized in code in the `Inbox.asp` page. After we have that `Session` object, we can use it to get back to the collection of messages in the Inbox. In this case, we are not concerned with the Inbox object, so we just get the collection of messages:

```
Set colMsgs = objSession.Inbox.Messages
```

Once we have that collection, we can then access the messages contained within it. In this case, we are only concerned with one of the messages in the collection, the one the user selected for display. To determine which one is to be displayed, we use the `MsgID` variable that was passed in the QueryString. Since we are dealing with the same collection as existed in the `Inbox.asp` page, we know the collection will be in the same order as it was there. Therefore, the index of the selected message will be the same. Since the `Message` object will be used multiple times in this page the value of `MsgID` is use to retrieve the message and store it in a local variable – `objCurMessage`. The code to query the properties of the selected message then uses the `objCurMessage` local variable:

```
    <TR>
      <TD><STRONG>From:</STRONG></TD>
      <TD><LABEL><% = objCurMessage.Sender %></LABEL></TD></TR>
    <TR>
      <TD><STRONG>Subject:</STRONG></TD>
      <TD><LABEL><% = objCurMessage.Subject %></LABEL></TD></TR>
    <TR>
      <TD></TD>
      <TD><TEXTAREA ID=TEXTAREA1 NAME=TEXTAREA1 STYLE="HEIGHT: 390px;
                    WIDTH: 547px"><% = objCurMessage.Text %>
</TEXTAREA></TD></TR></TABLE>

<%
If objCurMessage.Attachments.Count = 0 Then
    Response.Write "There are no attachments"
Else
    Dim intCount
    Response.Write "<B>Attachments:</B> <BR>"
    For intCount = 1 To objCurMessage.Attachments.Count
        Response.Write objCurmessage.Attachments(intCount).Name & "<BR>"
    Next
End If
%>
```

Summary

In this chapter, we have briefly looked at the CDONTS library, compared it to capabilities of CDO, and then seen sample applications both in Visual Basic and in a VBScript ASP Application. Although CDONTS is a capable object library, it still does not compare to CDO in terms of capabilities and flexibility. CDONTS is a limited library, and it is intended to be limited. What CDONTS does provide is a very useful and simple object library that allows developers to quickly add simple messaging capabilities to their applications. CDO and CDONTS each have their place in the messaging environment.

In the next chapter, we will once again look at CDO but this time a different subset, that of the CDO Rendering Library.

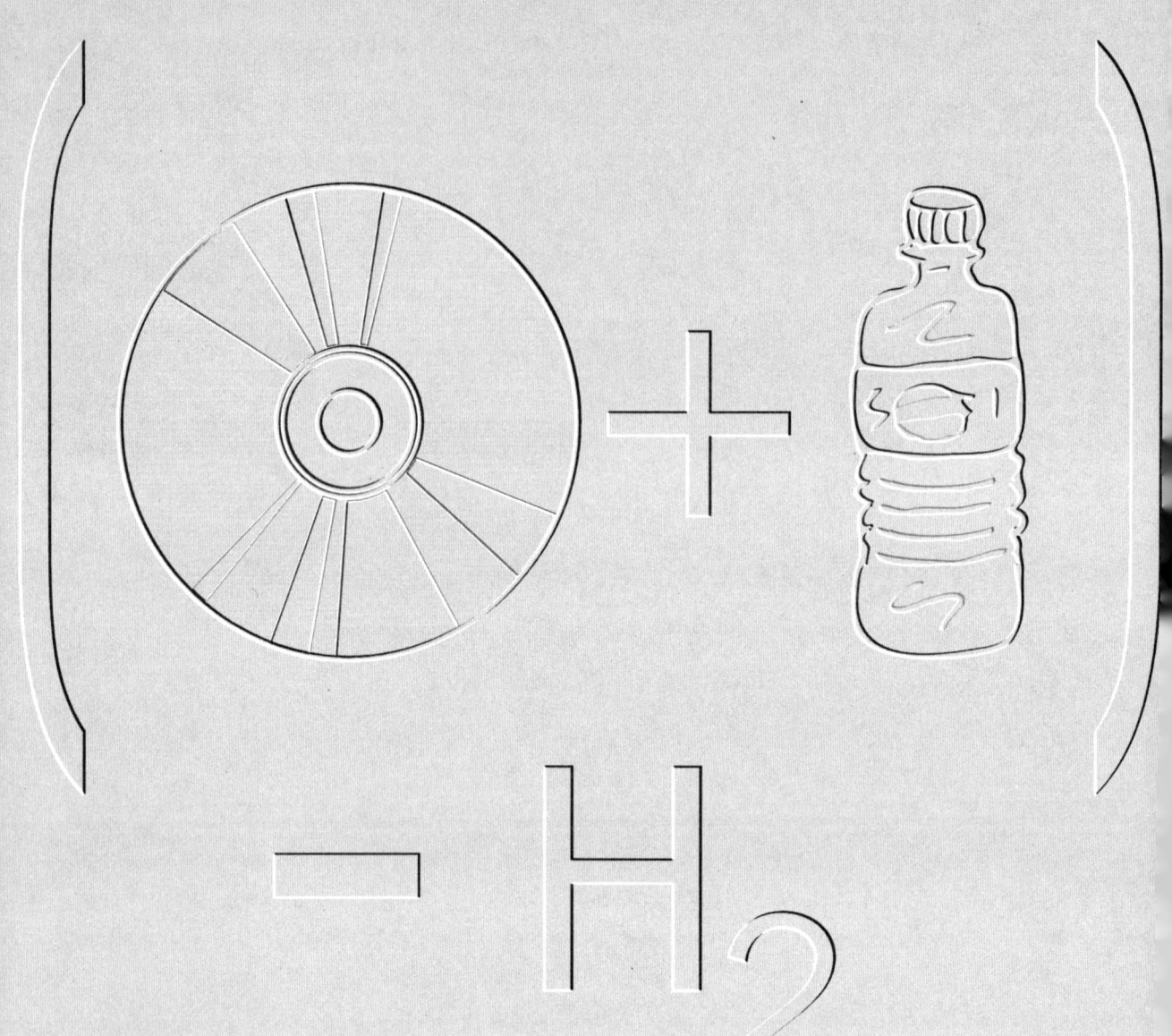

Working with the CDO Rendering Library

When Microsoft released Exchange Server 4.0 in early 1996, the Internet boom was well underway and yet the only Internet-related feature available to its users was the ability to send and receive SMTP-based e-mail messages.

With the boom continuing, the release of Exchange 5.0, and then 5.5 a couple of years later, saw the inclusion of some radical new features including the ability to access Exchange Server data via any simple Web browser that supported the downloading of Java controls and scripts.

To provide this functionality, Microsoft created the CDO Rendering library, a collection of objects for use in ASP pages designed specifically to convert Exchange data into HTML for display on the web or on an intranet.

In this chapter, then, we'll be looking at:

- ❑ How ASP and the CDO Rendering library interoperate.
- ❑ The CDO Rendering object model and its contents.
- ❑ The top-level objects in the model.
- ❑ Security and authentication concerns addressed by CDO Rendering.

With this done, Chapters 10 and 11 will look more closely at the other objects in the model and work with them in detail. Finally, in Chapter 12, we'll take a trip through Outlook Web Access, Microsoft's own CDO Rendering-based application and add some features to it, based on the knowledge we start learning here.

About CDO Rendering

Just like its bigger cousin, CDO 1.21, the CDO 1.2 Rendering Library is also a COM component written in C++ using Extended MAPI 1.0, this time specially designed for use in web pages. Being COM-based, it can be scripted with any ActiveScript-based language, such as VBScript, JScript, PerlScript, ECMAScript, and so on to the same effect – a page that dynamically generates views of mailboxes, personal details, contact lists and so on.

One slight restriction to its usefulness is that, also like CDO 1.21, CDO Rendering relies on a properly installed MAPI subsystem on the server to function properly. This limits you to installing at least one Extended MAPI 1.0 server to get this set up, which in turn narrows the field down to Exchange.

More specifically, it narrows you down to having to install Outlook Web Access (OWA), Microsoft's web interface for Exchange. It's only with this application that CDO Rendering is installed inside the file `cdohtml.dll`, which you'll find in your Windows system directory. If you want to use CDO Rendering functionality in your ASP application and you have not already installed OWA on your development server, then do so before you begin for three reasons:

❑ Installing OWA is the only way to properly install the library

❑ OWA is a very good example of using the technology and you can learn a lot from it

❑ Microsoft only supports CDO Rendering queries if OWA is installed

Do also remember to work on a development server before you deploy your new pages to a live server. Both OWA and any CDO\ASP pages you create require several small adjustments to get them working properly – read more on these and other OWA-related topics in Chapter 12. There's also a bug in the CDO Rendering library that causes a small memory leak each time the page is accessed, so be warned.

One point often raised is whether or not you can create custom ActiveX controls or custom COM components and use the CDO Rendering library functions inside them. There's no reason why you can't try, but Microsoft designed it only for use in an ASP environment, so such use could result in some undefined behavior. The reason seems to be that the CDO 1.2 Rendering library is optimized to interface only with Active Server Pages output provided by the `Response` object of ASP. This is a known and documented design limitation of the current version of the CDO 1.2 Rendering library and you can find the technical article Q188599 at the Microsoft Knowledge Base that talks about this issue. See Appendix G for the link.

As a result of this limitation it seems to be impossible to use CDO 1.2 Rendering library in development environments which support the COM standard (like Visual J++, Visual C++, Visual Basic, Visual Basic for Applications, Delphi) to build WebClasses, Java Applets or custom ActiveX controls even though the CDO 1.2 Rendering library is itself a COM component.

Past Generations of CDO Rendering

Just as with CDO 1.21, it's very important to make sure you have the most up to date version of the CDO Rendering library on your server. A lot of bugs have been fixed since Exchange 5.5 was initially released and those fixes, along with basic support for Contacts folders, can only be found in Exchange 5.5's service packs. The full history looks like this:

CDO Renderer Version	Where found
1.1	Exchange 5.0 Bug fixes in Service Packs 1 and 2
1.2	Exchange 5.5
1.21	Exchange 5.5 Service Pack 1
1.22	Exchange 5.5 Service Pack 2 Bug fixes in Service Pack 3

At time of going to press (December 1999), Microsoft had not made any announcements regarding the future of the CDO Rendering library in Exchange 2000, but it was believed to be the case that it would cease to be an entity on its own.

How ASP and CDO Fit Together

One of the things this book is not going to teach you is how to script ASP pages – we must assume you already know how to do that, but before we look at the object model itself, it would be a good idea to know how both CDO Rendering and CDO 1.21 fit into the grand ASP scheme of things.

> *If you do need to brush up on your ASP skills, try Professional Active Server Pages 2.0 by Homer et al. (ISBN 1-861001-26-6) if you've not upgraded to Windows 2000 yet, or Professional Active Server Pages 3.0 by Francis et al. (ISBN 1-861002-61-0) if you have.*

Since both libraries are COM components, they can be used within any ASP application using the scripting language interface of your choice on Internet Information Server. The following diagram, then, illustrates the ASP\CDO architecture:

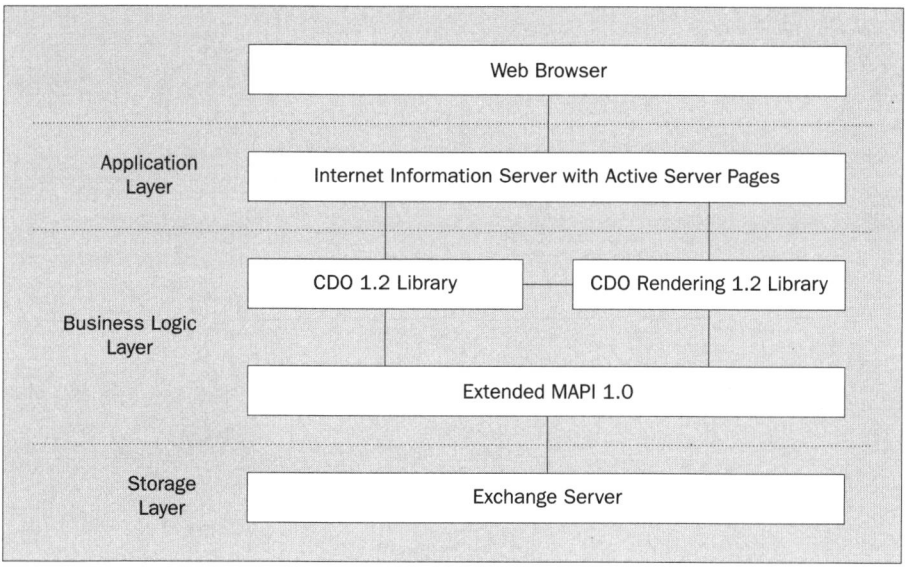

As you can see, the two form the interface between the underlying MAPI subsystem and our ASP application. They depend on each other very heavily in this set up – CDO Rendering needs the objects that CDO 1.21 exposes to function and CDO 1.21 needs CDO Rendering to display the information it generates on screen.

Note also that everything bar the browser is on the server-side. One advantage of the CDO Rendering library then is that you don't need any special client software to see what it generates – a simple browser or even a Windows CE device will do.

The CDO Rendering Object Model

With all the background and items to note taken care of, it's time to get down to business and look at the object model for the CDO Rendering library. Unlike the CDO 1.21 object model, this one is very easy to work with and understand. It too consists of a number of collections and objects as you can see:

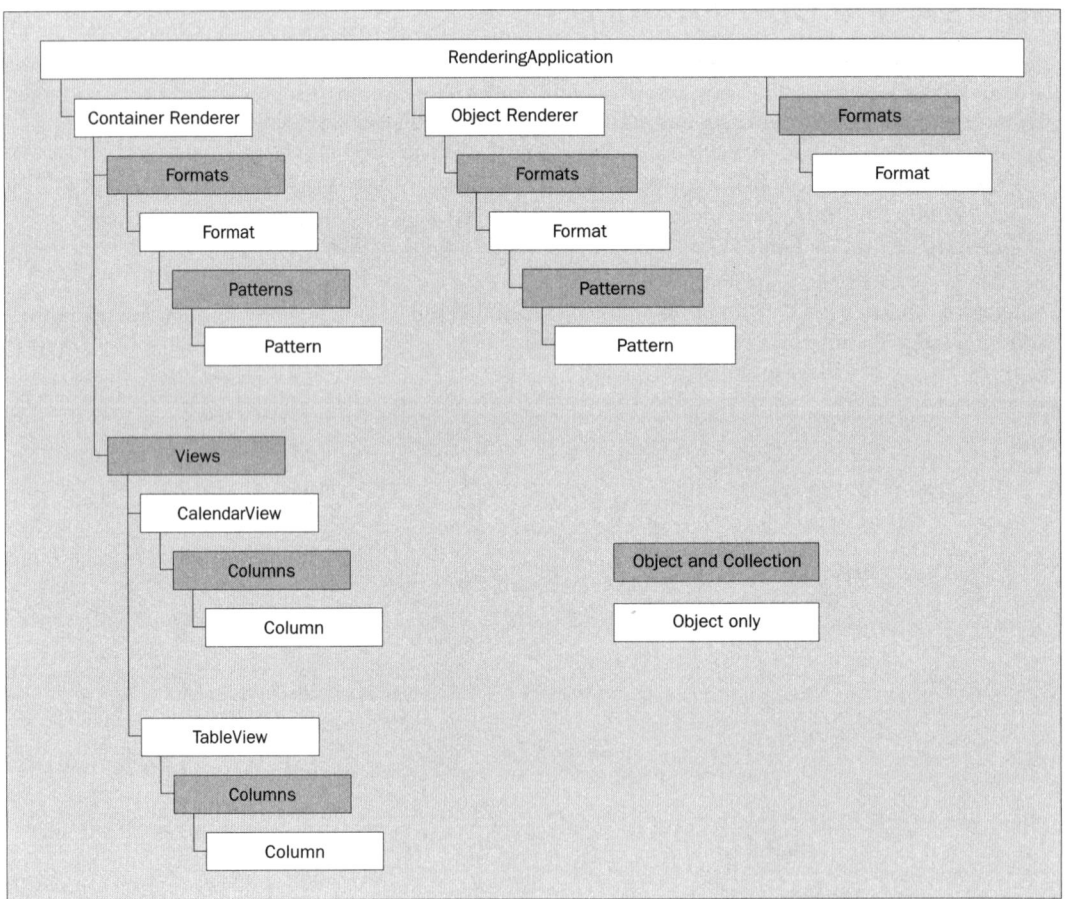

At the top of the hierarchy is the `RenderingApplication` object. It's with this object that your application can discover which Exchange server it needs to log onto and whom to log on as, define global styles for all the pages that it will create for the duration of the application.

You can also create the other two key objects – `ContainerRenderer` and `ObjectRenderer` – from the `RenderingApplication` object. As their names would suggest, each object has very specific roles. The `ContainerRenderer` object is created specifically to handle the rendering of any CDO collections into HTML. If, for example, you needed to display your mailbox (a collection of Messages) onscreen, you would create a `ContainerRenderer` object as the coverall in which to specify how you'd like it displayed. On the other hand, if you just want to read one of the messages in your inbox, this would count as a single CDO `Message` object that you would create an `ObjectRenderer` object to display onscreen.

We'll be looking at these three 'top-level' objects later on in this chapter.

Underneath both renderer objects, is a `Formats` collection and for each `Format` object within, a `Patterns` collection. If you remember back to the chapters on the CDO library, each object has a number of MAPI properties associated with it. For example, the `Message` object has associated with it `CdoPR_SUBJECT` and `CdoPR_DISPLAYTYPE` properties for the subject of the message and what kind of message (mail, meeting request, etc.) it is. By associating a `Format` for a property, you can then assign it a pattern (in the form of an HTML string) which will be incorporated into the page when it's all rendered. For example, `CdoPR_SUBJECT` might just be assigned a different to be displayed in. On the other hand, we might require a certain icon to be displayed for `CdoPR_DISPLAYTYPE` depending on its value. To do this, we would create a `Pattern` for each specific value of the property, place them inside a `Patterns` collection and assign that to the `Format` object for it.

You'll find all you need to know about Formats and Patterns in the next chapter.

Last but not least, you'll have noticed that the `ContainerRenderer` object also provides two view objects, easily distinguishable by their names alone. The `CalendarView` object provides a little bit of automatic processing for rendering calendaring information (imminent meetings, times when and when not out of the office etc) in an appropriate diary layout just as Outlook does. Appropriately, the `TableView` should be used to view Message folders and Address lists in a table and column format.

When it comes to defining views with the CDO Rendering library, you have two choices. You can either make use of the views that Exchange\Outlook has available by default or define your own. Defining your own gives you the greater flexibility than the built-in ones like 'Group By Conversation Topic' and 'Group by From'; you simply define a number of `Columns` in your view (for example, From, To, Subject and TimeSent for a message view) and, if required, specify by which column the items in your view should be sorted. You can find out exactly how to do this in Chapter 11.

The RenderingApplication Object

At the top of the hierarchy of the CDO 1.2 Rendering library is the `RenderingApplication` object, the recommended start point for all your ASP/CDO applications. It's from here that we can create a series of connected renderer objects, load the information we need about our Exchange server to be able to query it, and from here that we can set the user account we want to access our Exchange data with. Interestingly, it does not provide methods to log onto an Exchange server – this is left to the CDO 1.21 library.

To create a new `RenderingApplication` object with VBScript, we use the following code:

```
Set objRenderingApplication = Server.CreateObject("AMHTML.Application")
```

In a historical quirk of fate, this object retains its ProgID from its previous incarnation in the Active Messaging library – the previous name for CDO. Rather than being referred to as `CDOHTML.Application`, we must still instantiate it using the `AMHTML` prefix.

Once the object has been created, it gives us the following properties and methods to use:

RENDERINGAPPLICATION	
Properties	**Type**
Class	Long
CodePage	Long, Object or String
ConfigParameter	Variant
Formats	Formats
FormsRoot	String
ImpID	Long
LCID	Long
LoggingLevel	Long
Name	String
Parent	Object (Nothing)
Version	String
VirtualRoot	String
Methods	
CreateRenderer	
Impersonate	
ListComposerForms	
LoadConfiguration	

Two of the properties, `Class` and `Parent`, are **available to all the objects** in the CDO Rendering library. The `Class` property returns a long integer indicating what type of object it is. This integer corresponds to one of the `CdoObjectClasses` constants as detailed in Appendix D. The `Parent` property meanwhile returns the object that is the immediate parent of the object you're querying. In the case of the `RenderingApplication` object, however, this property returns `Nothing`.

There are also two CDO-like properties attached to this object, `Name` and `Version`, which return the strings 'Microsoft CDO Rendering 1.2.1 Library' and '1.1' respectively.

The two 'root' properties available here are also worth explaining. The `VirtualRoot` property contains the virtual path from the root of your web server to the base directory of your ASP/CDO application. By default, this is set to '\exchange', the location of Outlook Web Access. The `FormsRoot` meanwhile specifies the physical directory on your hard drive under which the server can find the forms and patterns that determine how different types of messages will be displayed.

Getting Configuration Information

These last two properties may allow you to configure your own forms and patterns, but that whole exercise is useless if your application doesn't know where to find your Exchange server.

Before you can create a CDO `Session` object and log onto your mailbox, public folders, etc., you first need some basic information to create a MAPI profile:

❑ The name of the Exchange server

❑ The organization and site your mailbox are located in

Fortunately, these three basic pieces of information are located in both the Windows registry and in Exchange's directory server and we can use the `RenderingApplication` object's `LoadConfiguration` method to obtain them from either source. The syntax for this is as follows:

```
objRenderApplication.LoadConfiguration
                    ConstSource, strSection, [objSession]
```

The first parameter, `ConstSource`, determines whether we retrieve our information from the registry or Exchange, according to which value we give it. There are two alternatives:

❑ `CdoConfigRegistry` (1) : Find the data in the Windows NT registry.

❑ `CdoConfigDS` (2) : Find the data in the Exchange directory server.

Next in the parameter list is `strSection`, which allows you to specify where in the registry the information you're looking for is specified. Unless you've deliberately altered something in Exchange, the registry key that holds this information is `HKEY_LOCAL_MACHINE\SYSTEM\CurrentControlSet\Services\MSExchangeWEB\Parameters`.

Last but not least, we can optionally pass `objSession` the CDO `Session` object we're currently using! This may come to you as a shock – surely we can't have created a `Session` object if we're still trying to find out where our mailbox is? Quite true. In actual fact, in most CDO/ASP applications, you'll call `LoadConfiguration` twice – once to get you to your Exchange server and once to get the HTTP protocol settings from Exchange.

The first call – to get our Exchange server organization, site and server – is aimed at the registry, with `constSource` set to `CdoConfigRegistry` as demonstrated below:

```
Dim objRendApp
Set objRendApp = Server.CreateObject("AMHTML.Application")

objRendApp.LoadConfiguration CdoConfigRegistry, _
"HKEY_LOCAL_MACHINE\System\CurrentControlSet\Services\MSExchangeWeb\Parameters"
```

Note that there's no point in specifying a value for `objSession` in this call – we haven't created a CDO `Session` object yet, so there isn't one to pass. Note also that it's not just the location of the server we pull from the registry, but more on that in a minute.

The second call – to get your Exchange server's HTTP protocol settings – can only happen once you've loaded the information from the registry with the above call since the Exchange organization, site, and server must be set in order to access the Exchange server directory. Here, we set `constSource` to `CdoConfigDS` and `strSection` to the empty string, as we do not need to specify a specific part of the Exchange directory server to query; it only has one configuration object:

```
objRendApp.LoadConfiguration CdoConfigDS, "", objSession
```

Now if the `constSource` parameter is set to `CdoConfigDS`, `LoadConfiguration` method will, by default, log on to the Exchange server anonymously to get the protocol settings we require. However, if you have already created a CDO `Session` object and logged on to the server, you can pass that object as the third parameter of `LoadConfiguration`, so the application need not log on again.

All being well, once the information has been acquired from the two sources, you can access the values of the various parameters with the following call to the `RenderingApplication`'s `ConfigParameter` property:

```
strConfParam = objRendApp.ConfigParameter("Parameter Name")
```

For example:

```
strEnterprise = objRendApp.ConfigParameter("Enterprise")
strSite = objRendApp.ConfigParameter("Site")
strServer = objRendApp.ConfigParameter("Server")

blnAnonAccess = objRendApp.ConfigParameter("Anonymous Access")
lngTimeout = objRendApp.ConfigParameter("AnonymousSessionTimeout")
lngHTTPEnabled = objRendApp.ConfigParameter("HTTP Enabled")
```

The table below gives a full list of parameter names, which source they come from and what they each govern. Note that you should include the spaces in the parameter names as set down here:

Configuration Parameter	Data Type	Source	Description
Admin Display Name	String	Exchange	Display name
Admin Note	String	Exchange	Administrative note
Anonymous Access	Boolean	Exchange	Can anonymous users access the public folders?
AnonymousSessionTimeout	Long	Registry	Session timeout for anonymous users (default 20 minutes)
AuthenticatedSessionTimeout	Long	Registry	Session timeout for authenticated users (default 60 minutes)
Debug	Long used as Boolean	Registry	Append more details to error messages sent to the browser if nonzero (defaults to 0)
Directory Name	String	Exchange	Directory name

Configuration Parameter	Data Type	Source	Description
Enterprise	String	Registry	Corresponds to the Exchange server's X.400 address "/o=" setting – its organization name
HTTP Enabled	Long used as Boolean	Exchange	Is the HTTP protocol service enabled?
Language Pack Directory	String	Registry	Physical path to the directory containing the language support DLLs
Publish GAL	Boolean	Exchange	Can anonymous users browse the global address list?
Publish GAL Limit	Long	Exchange	Number of entries from the global address list to be published per page
Published Public Folders	String array	Exchange	IDs of public folders which allow anonymous users to use them
RFC1867NoCleanupAtUnload	Long used as Boolean	Registry	Can the files in the temporary web server directory be deleted at shutdown? (defaults to 0)
RFC1867SaveDirectory	String	Registry	Physical path to the temporary web server directory for messages still being composed
RFC1867Trace	Long used as Boolean	Registry	Should all file uploads be logged to a TRCnnnnn.TMP file in the temporary web server directory? (defaults to 0)
Server	String	Registry	Corresponds to the Exchange server's X.400 address "/cn=" setting – its common name
Site	String	Registry	Corresponds to the Exchange server's X.400 address "/ou=" setting – its organizational unit.

Most of these configuration parameters may be new to you, but most of them can be explained away by the configuration section you'll find in Chapter 12 on Outlook Web Access. Using the syntax above, it's very easy to make a simple page listing all information you can retrieve using the `LoadConfiguration` method and `ConfigParameter` parameter. For example:

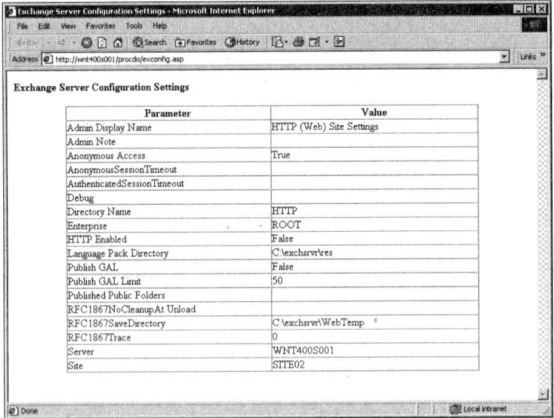

Security and Impersonation

Exchange Server is designed to maintain security so that Windows NT users cannot access Exchange Server mailboxes to which they do not have access rights. That means that each Exchange server mailbox usually has at least one Windows NT account – user or group – associated with it. This is what's known as its Primary Windows NT account. If you do specify more than one account to a mailbox, you can also create different access levels for each account, defined either by role-based access levels or single rights. Using single rights you can build your own custom role that holds the permissions of your choice.

At a higher level, an Exchange Server provides for two different types of access to the data that it stores:

❑ **Anonymous Access** means that a user need not be authenticated by Windows NT security to gain access to some of the data on the server.

❑ **Authenticated Access** requires a user to have logged on with a valid Windows NT account before access to the server was attempted.

As implied, those accessing the server anonymously cannot have access to everything contained therein. Indeed, user access is restricted as shown in the table below:

Access To	Required Authentication
Exchange Server Global Address List	Anonymous or authenticated access. The Exchange Server Administrator can decide if anonymous access is enabled or not.
Exchange Server Public Folder	Anonymous or authenticated access. The Exchange Server Administrator can decide if anonymous access is enabled globally and the owner of a folder can enable or disable anonymous access for the particular folder.
Exchange Server Mailbox	Authenticated access only. Each mailbox must have an associated Windows NT account that ***must*** be used to access the mailbox.

As you can see, it is only possible to send or receive e-mail with authenticated access to a particular Exchange server mailbox. Consider then that an application which sends feedback via e-mail cannot access Exchange anonymously – without proper Windows NT authentication, access to a mailbox will fail immediately, causing the ever present ASP 0115 error and stopping your application from continuing.

Problem enough except that with an Internet-based application, all users by default are given the security context of the anonymous user account `IUSR_MachineName`. This is fine for anyone who just wants anonymous access to Exchange, but not so good for those who want to access their mailbox. The solution however, is ready to hand in the form of the security level on the web server under which your ASP/CDO application runs.

Microsoft's web server, Internet Information Server (IIS) has three levels of security it can apply to a web-based application:

❑ **Allow Anonymous Access**. To provide access to a particular webpage without creating an Windows NT account for each user, IIS uses `IUSR_MachineName` as mentioned above. This Windows NT account is used each time a webpage is requested by a browser and no logon dialog is displayed. If it is not required to send e-mail via Exchange Server, or to open a particular mailbox, it is possible to use anonymous access to gain access to Exchange Server public folders and the Global Address List.

❑ **Basic Authentication**. IIS will challenge the client machine for a Windows NT account and password in the form `DOMAIN\UserID`. Usually, this means that a dialog will appear onscreen prompting the user for their account details. Note that although both are Base64-encoded, username and password are transmitted over the LAN or internet.

❑ **Windows NT Challenge/Response**. The most secure IIS authentication method, it challenges the client for a valid security token which must match that on the server. Should the client do this, he or she is authenticated as a valid user without having sent his or her password over the LAN or internet.

By making sure that our application's users authenticate their identity with Windows NT and thus with Exchange, they can be allowed to access their mailboxes even over the Internet. Because a lot of people don't know about these authentication requirements, their attempts to write a web-enabled application that leverages Exchange server data, be it public folder, mailbox or directory information, will fail.

To Authenticate a Windows User Account

If you've played with Outlook Web Access at all, you might have wondered why you can access your Exchange server mailbox without a separate authentication. The answer is in the Windows NT Challenge/Response authentication method we've just mentioned. This allows a user account to be verified without even prompting the user for their account information.

On the other hand, if you have had to log in twice to access your mailbox, you've probably come up against one of Challenge/Response's limitations:

❑ It is not possible to use Challenge/Response if Exchange and IIS are on different machines.

❑ Only Microsoft's own Internet Explorer web browser supports Challenge/Response.

❑ Challenge/Response also fails if a proxy server is installed between the browser and Exchange.

In these cases, your application must resort to using Basic Authentication as its user validation process.

Whichever method you employ to validate your users, once they have been validated you can always find out who they are and under which method they were accepted by querying the ASP Response object's ServerVariables collection. For example, we can run a little check that an anonymous user isn't viewing restricted content by including this code snippet at the top of the page:

```
If Request.ServerVariables("LOGON_USER") = "" Then
    Response.Buffer = True
    Response.Status = "401 Access Denied"
    Response.End
End If
```

The LOGON_USER property here contains the user's account name if he/she has been authenticated or nothing if he/she has not. This code simply refuses an anonymous user any information save an 'Access Denied' statement.

Other properties likewise contain some very useful information. In particular:

Property	Description
AUTH_PASSWORD	User's password, if the user has been authenticated with Basic Authentication.
AUTH_TYPE	The method of authentication. Set to Basic for Basic Authentication or NTLM for Challenge/Response
AUTH_USER	User's name, if user has been authenticated.

As an aside, the Response.ServerVariables collection contains a lot more useful information than just these four things. You can print the entire set out with the following code. If you'd like to know more, then pick up a copy of the ASP references mentioned earlier in this chapter:

```
<HTML>
<TABLE>
<TR>
    <TD><B>Server Variable</B></TD>
    <TD><B>Value</B></TD>
</TR>

<% For Each name In Request.ServerVariables %>
    <TR>
        <TD><%= Name %></TD>
        <TD><%= Request.ServerVariables(Name) %> </TD>
    </TR>

<% Next %>

</TABLE>
</HTML>
```

To Force a Logon Dialog

If you can't use NTLM authentication for any particular reason – we've mentioned three already – you'll need to switch to Basic Authentication and force the browser to display a logon dialog to the user. (Of course, this is only necessary if your ASP application needs the ability to send and receive e-mail using an Exchange Server mailbox.)

This can be done with the following code:

```
Const vbTextCompare = 1
blnAuthenticated = False
bstrAuthentication = Request.ServerVariables("AUTH_TYPE")
If InStr(1, "_BasicNTLM", bstrAuthentication, vbTextCompare) < 2 Then
  Response.Buffer = True
  Response.Status = ("401 Unauthorized")
  Response.AddHeader "WWW.Authenticate", "Basic"
  Response.End
Else
  blnAuthenticated = True
End If
```

The following code will retrieve the DOMAIN\UserID from the Internet Information Server variables and then manipulate the string to return just the UserID. This is especially useful if your Windows NT account is identical to the Exchange alias. Then you can pass the strUserID variable as a mailbox to the CDO Session Logon method:

```
If blnAuthenticated = True Then
    strNTAccount = Request.ServerVariables("LOGON_USER")
    strUserID = Right(strNTAccount, Len(strNTAccount) - InStr(strNTAccount, "\"))
End If
```

To Authenticate a Windows User Account in an Exchange Security Context

Whichever method we've used to authenticate the user, they now have 'a proper security context' to access their mailbox. However, because our CDO/ASP application is running in an IIS thread process, it is still running in IIS's security context as well and not that of the user. To get around this, the application must **impersonate** the user and then, finally, it will be allowed to access the user's mailbox.

In brief, to be granted authenticated access to the Exchange information store, a thread must be constantly associated with a set of valid security credentials. This is easily achieved by saving them, for example, into an ASP Session variable like so:

```
Session("hImp") = objRenderApplication.ImpID
```

The RenderingApplication's ImpID property holds a handle (or a pointer if you will) to the context we have just created by forcing the user to log on. This context might be lost just switching by pages or reloading a frame if we didn't store it somewhere safe and it avoids a great many ASP 0115 errors too. Once we have a handle to the context, whenever we load a new page in which we access Exchange, it a simple matter of adding the following two lines to the page to make sure we still have access to the mailbox we want to look at:

```
hImp = Session("hImp")
objRenderApplication.Impersonate(hImp)
```

Internationalization

One issue the whole web community is slowly coming around to is that not everybody out there speaks English. You've been able to specify which locale and character set you want to use on your page in both HTML and ASP for a while now and you can do just the same use the `RenderingApplication`'s `CodePage` property.

By setting this property like so, for example:

```
CodePage = objRendApp.CodePage "USA"
```

You can set the code page (character set) to be used by all rendering objects created with the `CreateRenderer` method, which we'll come to next. Note that setting this `CodePage` property does not affect the locale settings on a CDO `Session` object. Each session has it's own `SetLocaleIDs` method.

It does, however, affect further character selection and any dependent data considerations. The collating sequence, the sort order, and the formats for time, date, and currency representation are controlled by the `LCID` property, which is automatically set to correspond to the code page information whenever you set `CodePage`.

The `CodePage` property accepts a single parameter that can be in three different formats as set out in the following table:

Format	Description
Long Integer	Represents the code page used for character representation.
Object	Contains an `IDispatch` pointer to an `IRequest` object. The CDO Rendering Library obtains from this object an HTTP Accept-Language header and sets the ·code page to the value that most closely matches the header.
String	An International Standards Organization (ISO) language name. The code page is set from the Windows NT registry entry for that language.

There are a couple of things you have to take care of yourself. First, if you use a long integer value that is not a valid code page identifier, no changes take effect. Something similar happens if a string value is used which does not represent a valid language name. The code page will stick with the default value if this happens. Finally, if a code page is requested which is not installed on the Windows NT server you will get an error returned to the web browser and the execution of the ASP page will be terminated.

Having said that, you need to take care of those issues and double-check that your code does not run into some of these problems.

Creating The Other Renderer Objects

There's just one more method we need to look at that's a member of the `RenderingApplication` object – `CreateRenderer`. Simply put, it's this method that creates both `ContainerRenderer` and `ObjectRenderer` objects and it's these two that generate the HTML to display Exchange data onscreen.

The syntax for `CreateRenderer` is as follows:

```
Set objRenderer = objRendApp.CreateRenderer(Class)
```

To specify which kind of `Renderer` object we want to create, the `class` parameter takes one of two possible values:

Class	Value	Description
CdoClassContainerRenderer	3	Create a `ContainerRenderer` object to render CDO collections
CdoClassObjectRenderer	2	Create an `ObjectRenderer` object to render single CDO objects

The rendering object created by the `CreateRenderer` method inherits the code page and formats from this application, as well as logging capability.

You could also create the two renderer objects directly by calling `Server.CreateObject(ProgID)` if you wish them to work as standalone objects. In general, standalone renderer objects are best used for single operations, such as rendering certain properties of the current object. When you use standalone renderer objects, you generally do not intend to read more data from the object or access it in other ways.

The ContainerRenderer Object

The `ContainerRenderer` is the object we use to render CDO collections into HTML. It is a top-level object in the CDO Rendering library, meaning that, as we mentioned just above, it can either be created as a standalone object with the call:

```
Set objContRend = Server.CreateObject("AMHTML.ContainerRenderer")
```

Or it can be created by a call to a `RenderingApplication` object, inheriting the `codepage` and `Formats` from it, thus:

```
Set objContRend = objRenderingApplication.CreateRenderer(3)
```

Note that the same legacy glitch occurs with the `ContainerRenderer`'s `ProgID` that we saw earlier with the `RenderingApplication` object. It still has an `AMHTML` prefix rather than `CDOHTML` as you might have guessed.

No matter how you've instantiated the object, it still has the same properties and methods, some of which we've already seen and won't cover below.

CONTAINERRENDERER	
Properties	**Type**
BusinessDayEndTime	Variant (vbDate)
BusinessDays	Long
BusinessDayStartTime	Variant (vbDate)
CellPattern	String
Class	Long
CodePage	Long, Object or String
CurrentStore	InfoStore
CurrentView	TableView
DataSource	Collection Object
FirstDayOfWeek	Long
Formats	Format or Formats
HeadingCellPattern	String
HeadingRowPrefix	String
HeadingRowSuffix	String
Is24HourClock	Boolean
LCID	Long
LinkPattern	String
Parent	Object
PrivateStore	InfoStore
RowsPerPage	Integer
RowsPrefix	String
RowSuffix	String
TablePrefix	String
TableSuffix	String
TimeZone	Long
Views	CalendarView, TableView or Views
Methods	
Render	
RenderDate	
RenderHeading	
RenderProperty	
RenderTime	

Although the `ContainerRenderer` object provides a lot of features, there are still some major limitations in the current version of the CDO Rendering library. The most requested enhancements are to provide access to contacts, tasks and appointments.

While the first one, contacts, is implemented for the default contact folder of a mailbox, it is natively supported by neither the CDO 1.21 nor the CDO Rendering libraries. Microsoft has added a limited support for contacts to Outlook Web Access in the service packs for Exchange 5.5 but there are no officially announced plans to add support for tasks and journaling to it. With the imminent arrival of Exchange 2000, it doesn't look likely that there will ever be.

The same applies to appointment items stored in a calendar folder as it does to contacts in a mailbox. Appointments are natively supported in the default calendar folder of the mailbox, but there is no support for a calendar folder stored in any other place, even the Exchange server public folders.

What to Render?

So where do you start with this object? Well, we know that it looks after the rendering into HTML of the CDO collections so let's start there. Specifically, the CDO collections that you can render using a `ContainerRenderer` object are:

Collection	Description
Folders	A collection of folder objects
Messages	A collection of messages inside a folder
AddressEntries	A collection of address entries
Recipients	A collection of recipient objects of a message

Once you know which collection you want to render, you use the `DataSource` property to mark it out as the target for the renderer. For example, let's say you wanted to render the contents of your inbox. You'd use the following code to set this up:

```
Set objMessages = objSession.Inbox.Messages
objContainerRenderer.DataSource = objMessages
```

Alternatively, let's say you wanted to render the members of a distribution list:

```
Set objAddressEntries = objAddressList.AddressEntries
objContRend.DataSource = objAddressEntries
```

When you set the `DataSource` property, do make sure you set it to a valid collection object. There are quite a few similarly named objects in CDO and `objFolders` could easily get misplet (sic) as `objFolder`. If you do send a non-collection object to `DataSource`, an error will occur.

> Note that if you want to filter the CDO collection used as the `DataSource` you must set the filter on the CDO collection before it is passed to the `ContainerRenderer` object as `DataSource`, otherwise the filter does not take effect.

One point not made yet is that the `DataSource` property actually has two functions. The first we've already covered. Once we've assigned a collection to be rendered however, a new `Views` collection is created for the `ContainerRenderer`, This will contain any custom `View` objects already defined but not necessarily any views predefined by the CDO library (which equate those you see in Outlook).

If the `DataSource` property is set to a CDO `Messages` or CDO `Folders` collection, a default view is automatically assigned and can be found in the `CurrentView` property. However, if the `DataSource` is set to an `AddressEntries` or a `Recipients` collection, no default view is applied and we need to build our own view, as described in Chapter 11.

> Note also that you must set the `DataSource` property to `Nothing`, or set the `ContainerRenderer` object to `Nothing`, before you call the `Session` object's `Logoff` method. Failure to do so can result in unexpected behavior.

Specifying a Table Layout

One thing you'll quickly realize is that whatever view you define for your `DataSource`, your `ContainerRenderer` will generate an HTML table that displays it. The default table format it generates comes in three lovely shades of gray in the same style as Outlook Web Access, but there's no reason why you can't show your inbox in red, orange and yellow if you want – it's just a matter of setting the right properties.

When a collection is rendered, it's actually delivered as two tables, one for column headings and one for each item in the collection and in each table, you can determine the attribute values for both `TABLE` and `TR` tags as well as exactly what goes inside a table cell, delimited by `<TD>` and `</TD>`. It's perhaps easier if this is explained in a diagram:

Table Prefix	Heading RowPrefix	Heading CellPattern	...	Heading CellPattern	Heading RowSuffix	Table Suffix
Table Prefix						
	RowPrefix	CellPattern	...	CellPattern	RowSuffix	
	...	...		...	...	
	RowPrefix	CellPattern	...	CellPattern	RowSuffix	
						Table Suffix

Changing the Header Row

Both heading and content tables are initially defined by the `TablePrefix` property and closed with the `TableSuffix` property. For example:

```
objContRend.TablePrefix = "<TABLE BORDERCOLOR='orange' BGCOLOR='red'>"
objContRend.TableSuffix = "</TABLE>"
```

Similarly, you can change the format at a row and cell level as well, if you need to. Let's say we needed to alter the font, size and background color of the heading row:

```
objContRend.HeadingRowPrefix = "<TR VALIGN='top' BGCOLOR='orangered'>"
objContRend.HeadingRowSuffix = "</TR>"
objContRend.HeadingCellPattern = _
              "<FONT COLOR='yellow' SIZE='2'><B>%value%</B></FONT>"
```

Let's say for a minute, that we had previously defined a view for a `Messages` collection containing just Subject and Date Received columns. If we generated the table now, the HTML generated for the heading table would look like this:

```
<TABLE BORDERCOLOR='orange' BGCOLOR='red'>
<TR VALIGN='top' BGCOLOR='orangered'>
```

```
<TD><FONT COLOR='yellow' SIZE='2'><B>Subject</B></FONT></TD>
<TD><FONT COLOR='yellow' SIZE='2'><B>Date Received</B></FONT></TD>
</TR>
</TABLE>
```

You should be able to see the connection between the table generated and the properties we've given a value quite easily. One thing to note is the substitution of `%value%` in the `HeadingCellPattern` property to the name of the column. `%value%` is one of a number of substitution tokens that we'll use more frequently when working with `Pattern` objects. You can find out more about these tokens then in the next chapter.

It is also possible to hide the default heading table totally using the following code:

```
objContRend.HeadingRowPrefix = "<TR VALIGN='top'>"
objContRend.HeadingRowSuffix = "</TR>"
```

Actually you might be wondering about this because these are the default settings. However if you set the column headers in the view to empty strings, the heading row is totally removed and you can build some very smart looking HTML pages.

Changing the Content Rows

Just as we can redefine how the column headers look, so too can we format the actual contents of the table. As you might have guessed, `RowPrefix`, `CellPattern` and `RowSuffix` do jobs equivalent to `HeadingRowPrefix`, `HeadingCellPattern` and `HeadingRowSuffix` respectively. For example:

```
objContRend.CellPattern = _
    "<FONT FACE='Arial, sans-serif' SIZE='-1'>%value%</FONT>"
objContRend.RowPrefix = "<TR VALIGN='middle' BGCOLOR='#FFFFFF'>"
objContRend.RowSuffix = "</TR>"
```

You must bear in mind that these changes affect the whole HTML to be generated. However it does not affect the Exchange data itself, only its format, nor the number of rows the table could theoretically have – that is left to the actual number of items in the CDO collection and the `ContainerRenderer`'s `RowsPerPage` property. By default, the HTML output generated by the `ContainerRenderer` is limited to 25 rows per page, but to change that you just need to set the `RowsPerPage` property as the following code shows:

```
objContRend.RowsPerPage = 15
```

This is particular useful if you have a huge number of items, e.g. a Global Address List which holds more than 10,000 entries. Imagine how long it would take to build this table and send it to the Web browser as one huge HTML table. One quick point to be aware of though is that this property only changes how many rows a single `ContainerRenderer` HTML output contains. You still need to plug in the ability to move through the pages for your application to be of any use. Fortunately, we'll be doing exactly that a little later on.

Getting from Container to Object

Of course, there's one thing missing from our discussions so far – once we've rendered a collection on screen, how does a user select an item in the collection and view it? The easiest way by far is to add hyperlinks from each item in the collection to a new `ObjectRenderer` page that will then display their individual details to the user. To do this, we use the `LinkPattern` property. For example:

```
objContRend.LinkPattern = _
                    "<A HREF='read.asp?obj=%obj%'>" & "%value%" & "</a>"
```

Again we use substitution tokens to add us in generating the right HTML. We've already met `%value%` which is replaced by the current contents of the table cell. `%obj%` here is replaced by the unique identifier (note a GUID, please note) for the single object in question, giving the linked-to page a reference to the correct object to render.

Calendar Stuff

The astute amongst you might have noticed just a few properties we have left to cover and wonder what they're for. Essentially, they're there only to help render `CalendarViews` – collections of `AppointmentItems`. In alphabetical order, they are:

Property	Description
BusinessDayEndTime	The `BusinessDayEndTime` property returns or sets the time of day the business day is set to end.
BusinessDays	The `BusinessDays` property returns or sets a bitmask representing the days of the week that are to be considered business days.
BusinessDayStartTime	The `BusinessDayStartTime` property returns or sets the time of day the business day is set to start.
FirstDayOfWeek	The `FirstDayOfWeek` property returns or sets the day on which the week is set to start.
Is24HourClock	The `Is24HourClock` property indicates whether the calendar is to be rendered in 12-hour or 24-hour mode.
TimeZone	The `TimeZone` property returns or sets the time zone in which the calendar is to be rendered.

To reiterate, these properties are only available if the `ContainerRenderer`'s `DataSource` property is set to a valid calendar folder and, given the current limitations of the CDO libraries, this means they are only available if `DataSource` is set to the default calendar folder of a mailbox.

Pressing 'Go'

With all the setup done, the properties given a value and the collection chosen, all that remains in the `ContainerRenderer` object is the 'go switch' that gets it to generate the required HTML. This go switch then is the `Render` method and is invoked like so:

```
<HTML>
<HEAD>
    <TITLE>Your Application Title</TITLE>
</HEAD>

<BODY>
<%
    objContRend.Render intStyle, intCurrentPage, boolRaw, Response
%>
</BODY>
</HTML>
```

As you can see, Render takes four parameters. The first, intStyle, specifies exactly what will be elements of the collection chosen as DataSource will be rendered onscreen. There are two choices:

intStyle	Value	DataSource	What is Rendered
CdoFolderContents	1	AddressEntries, Messages, Recipients	Address entries, group headers and messages, or recipients, but not child folders
CdoFolderHierarchy	2	Folders, Messages	Child folders, but not address entries, group headers, messages, or recipients

As you can see, you have a choice between viewing the (singular) objects in a collection so that a user might view their details or the collections within this collection so a user can navigate to a collection lower down in the hierarchy.

The second parameter is directly related to the RowsPerPage property we mentioned earlier. By specifying this, we also know how many different HTML pages we need to create in order to completely list the contents of a collection. The second parameter then is the number of the page to be rendered. By default this is set to 1, the first page.

Of course the trick remains to navigate through these pages, but with a couple of buttons and JScript functions this is quite straightforward. So we don't go past the ends of the collection, we need first to discover the number of pages needed to render the entire collection:

```
intMaxPage = 1 + _
        ((objAddressEntries.Count - 1) \ objContRend.RowsPerPage)
intCurrentPage = 1
```

After we have determined the maximum page count we need to build two small functions used to step back and forward in the available pages. Actually, we use two little JScript helper functions in the HTML page to evaluate the current page against the last page and re-invoke the Render method with the appropriate intCurrentPage parameter like this:

```
<script language = "Javascript">
var CurrentPage = eval(<%= intCurrentPage %>);
var MaxPage = eval(<%= intMaxPage %>);
```

```
function PreviousPage()
{
   if (CurrentPage == 1)
   {
      alert('You are already at the beginning of the list');
   }
   else
   {
      CurrentPage = CurrentPage - 1;
      self.location = "browse.asp?page="+CurrentPage;
   }
}

function NextPage()
{
   if (CurrentPage >= MaxPage)
   {
      alert('You already at the end of the list');
   }
   else
   {
      CurrentPage = CurrentPage + 1;
      self.location = "browse.asp?page="+CurrentPage;
   }
}
```

All that remains then is to create two HTML buttons, label them Next and Previous and attach the relevant function to their OnClick event.

To finish up, Render's third property is reserved and should be left as 0, while the fourth parameter allows you to pass it a reference to an ASP Response object, which will store the HTML generated in a buffer to send to the browser for display. The alternative is leaving this parameter blank and having the HTML stored as a string in the variable you assign Render to. For example:

```
strHTML = objContRend.Render(1)
```

The Other Render Methods

Render is the main way to generate HTML for display, but it is not the only method. The ContainerRenderer object has four other Renderxxxx methods which translate slightly less into HTML:

- ❑ **RenderDate** (*Date/time, Format, Response*) : Renders the date segment of the *date/time* value in HTML in the given *format*.

- ❑ **RenderHeading** (*CellPattern, Response*) : Generates just a table of column headings for the current view. If need be, you can specify a pattern for the cell in the table overriding that one already specified in the CellPattern property.

- ❑ **RenderProperty** (*Property, boolRaw, Response*) : Renders the specified property of the immediate parent of the collection given by the DataSource property.

- ❑ **RenderTime** (*Date/time, Format, Response*) : Renders the time segment of the *date/time* value in HTML in the given *format*.

Both the *boolRaw* and *Response* parameters in these methods are exactly the same as those for the `Render` method.

And that's it for our whistle stop tour of the `ContainerRenderer` object. Finally in this chapter, we'll look at its smaller brother, the `ObjectRenderer` object.

ObjectRenderer

The `ObjectRenderer` is the object we use to render (singular) CDO objects into HTML. It is a top-level object in the CDO Rendering library, meaning that, as we mentioned just above, it can either be created as a standalone object with the call:

```
Set objObjRend = Server.CreateObject("AMHTML.ObjectRenderer")
```

Or it can be created by a call to a `RenderingApplication` object, inheriting the `codepage` and `Formats` from it, thus:

```
Set objObjRend = objRenderingApplication.CreateRenderer(2)
```

Having instantiated the object, it makes available the following properties and methods, most of which are exactly the same as those defined by the `ContainerRenderer` object that we've already seen:

OBJECTRENDERER	
Properties	**Type**
Class	Long
CodePage	Long, Object or String
DataSource	Collection Object
Formats	Format or Formats
LCID	Long
LinkPattern	String
Parent	RenderingApplication
Methods	
RenderDate	
RenderLink	
RenderProperty	
RenderTime	

Barring the obvious difference of purpose, there's a second fundamental difference in the way we work with the `ObjectRenderer` in comparison with the `ContainerRenderer`. Unlike the latter, there is no one 'go switch' which produces all the HTML you need, possibly because a table is not necessarily the best way to display the properties of an object. Instead, you need to write all the HTML for the page displaying the object and insert calls to the `ObjectRenderer`'s `RenderXxxx` methods as you go along.

> Note again that you must set the `ObjectRenderer` object to `Nothing`, or set its `DataSource` property to `Nothing`, before you call the `Session` object's `Logoff` method. Failure to do so can result in unexpected behavior.

What to Render?

So which CDO objects can we make use of with this object. We already know they can't be collection objects, and indeed the full list is:

Object	Description
AddressEntry	A single address entry
AppointmentItem	A single appointment item in a calendar
Attachment	A single attachment to a message
Folder	A single folder
MeetingItem	A single meeting item in a folder
Message	A single message

Again, once you know which object you want to render, you use the DataSource property to mark it out as the target for the renderer. For example, you could set it an AddressEntry object like so:

```
ObjObjectRenderer.DataSource = objAddressEntry
```

More common however is the scenario that the page containing this object has been called with the unique identifier of the object that needs to be rendered as part of the URL's querystring. To demonstrate, let's suppose the page being called prints a message onscreen and is called with the following URL:

```
http://server/exchange/read.asp?msgId=Full_Message_Id
```

The CDO Session object provides a number of GetXxxx methods that retrieve objects given their unique ID and we can make good use of them here:

```
strMessageID = Request.QueryString ("msgID")
Set objMsg = objSession.GetMessage(strMessageID)
ObjObjectRenderer.DataSource = objMsg
```

This method of retrieving specific objects for use as the DataSource of the ObjectRenderer applies to any of the above objects and once you've done this and set a LinkPattern, if needed, to the DataSource object, it's just a matter of constructing the HTML and calling the right methods.

How to Render

There are four RenderXxxx methods available from the ObjectRenderer. We've already seen RenderTime and RenderDate in the ContainerRenderer object above: their functionality and parameters are identical. RenderLink meanwhile is new but simply refers to the ObjectRenderer's LinkPattern method and renders a link to the object currently specified in the DataSource property.

The fourth and most important method is `RenderProperty` which renders not the value of the CDO object's properties, but the value of any associated MAPI property tags. For example:

```
<% objObjectRenderer.RenderProperty CdoPR_DEPARTMENT_NAME, 0, Response %>
```

As you can see, `RenderProperty` has three parameters. The second and third we've come across before, being the reserved parameter we saw in the `ContainerRenderer`'s `Render` method (which should only be set to 0) and a reference to an ASP `Response` object that we can pass the generated HTML to.

The first parameter meanwhile should contain the MAPI property you want to render. In the above example, we assumed that somehow we've access to type library constants and can therefore give the property its more straightforward name. You could always call the property by its code like so:

```
<% objObjectRenderer.RenderProperty &H3A18001F, 0, Response %>
```

But it's not that readable. The easiest thing to do is predefine the convenient names to their codes in an include file somewhere or just include the type library in each page. A full list of MAPI property tags can be found in Appendix B under the heading `CdoPropTags`.

Summary

Many people have never used the CDO Rendering library because they thought that the output would always look like Outlook Web Access. This is a major misunderstanding because if you do your homework and learn the methods and properties well you can actually build very high level solutions, starting with guest books, bulletin boards, discussion groups, customer feedback systems and many more that don't look in any way like the standard Outlook Web Access interface. You can also support online collaboration activities in several different languages thanks to its internationalization features.

In this chapter then, we saw:

❑ How the CDO Rendering library has evolved and how it fits in with CDO and ASP to produce online email and collaboration data access.

❑ That the `RenderingApplication` object provides us with several very key properties and methods that first gain us access to Exchange and second give us a limited kind of global control over everything else we do with our application.

❑ The two Renderer objects, `ContainerRenderer` and `ObjectRenderer`, what they each can do and how to personalise the output they produce by altering several of their properties.

In the next chapter, we turn to the subject of formats and patterns, which allow us to specify how properties are displayed onscreen, not just overall, but if need be on a value by value basis.

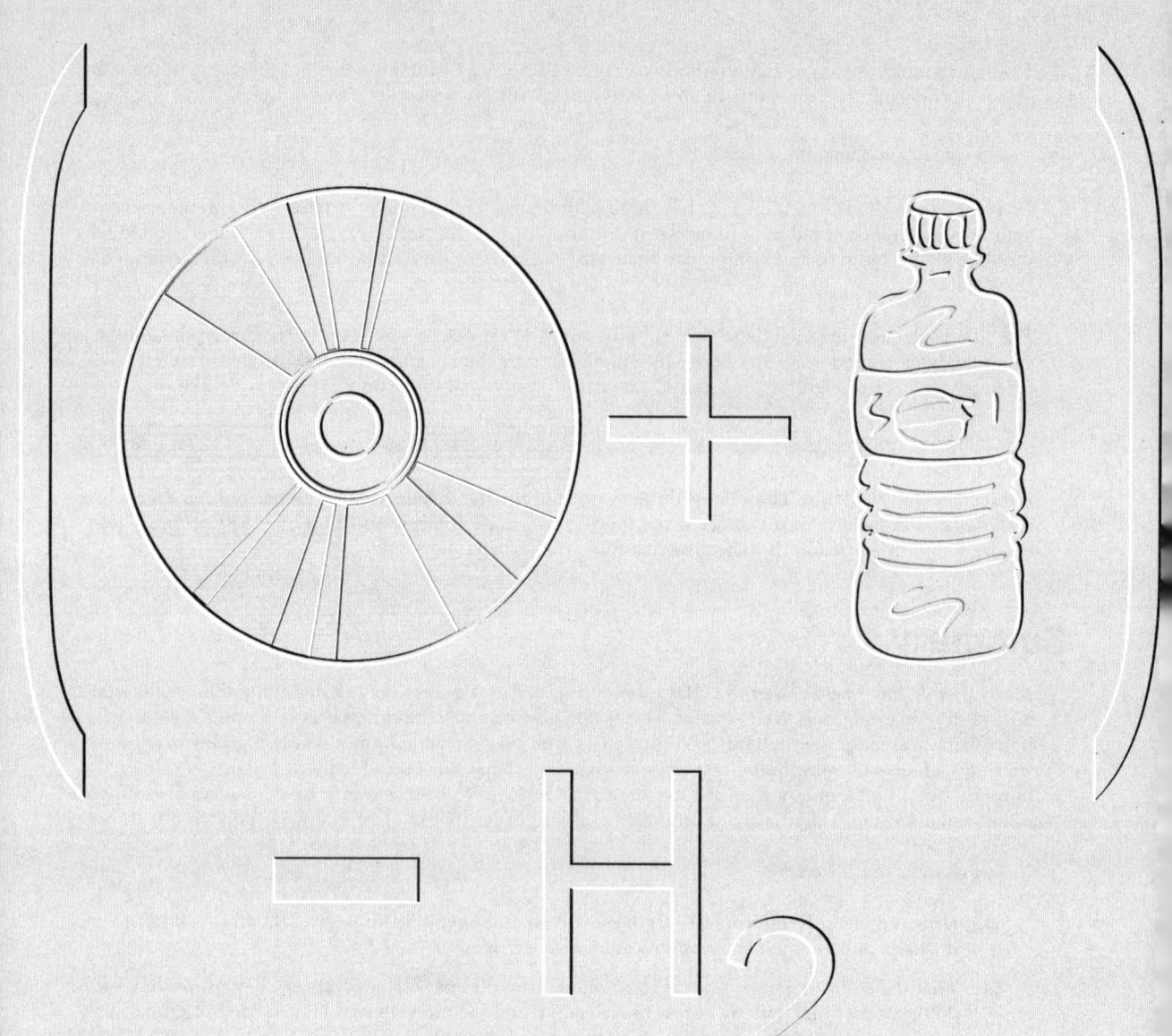

10

Formats and Patterns

Having talked about how to create a `ContainerRenderer` and `ObjectRenderer` object in the previous chapter, this chapter now provides an insight into using formats and patterns. But what are they?

Formats and patterns allow us to modify the HTML output that determines how each MAPI property is rendered. This is done through the use two relatively simple collections:

❑ The `Formats` collection and its child the `Format` object

❑ The `Patterns` collection and its child the `Pattern` object

Think of the formats and patterns as the templates that allow you to display Exchange data in HTML format.

Since formatting data is one of the most used parts in a `ContainerRenderer` object within a view, this chapter will give us a pretty good overview of how to handle formatting MAPI properties, so that we can go ahead and build our own views in the next chapter.

Therefore, in this chapter we will cover:

❑ Formats and why we use them with a container or object renderer

❑ How patterns are used in a container or object renderer and why we need them

How Formats and Patterns Fit into CDO

Before we go any further we need to be clear on how formats and patterns map onto what we know about the CDO library. Although the relationship can seem complex it is really quite simple once you've got it straight in your head. Basically there is a 1:1 mapping of elements of the CDO object library to formats and patterns. The diagram below demonstrates this:

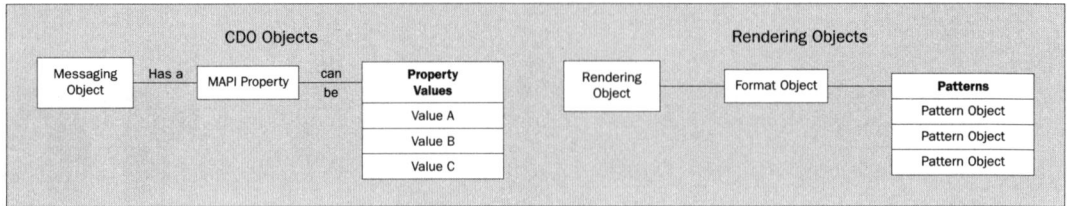

To make sure that's absolutely clear, the relationship can also be described thus:

❑ Each CDO Messaging object contains a set of MAPI properties. Each one of these MAPI properties can be represented in the Rendering library as a **Format object**.

❑ MAPI property values can also only be specific values defined in the Exchange Server. Each one of these property values maps to a **Pattern object**.

To provide a way to format a MAPI property and display its every possible value, the CDO 1.2 Rendering library provides the **Formats collection** with the ContainerRenderer, ObjectRenderer and RenderingApplication objects. This collection gives us the ability to use very simple code either in a HTML table view of a ContainerRenderer output, or a plain HTML page created with the ObjectRenderer, to display and format the information properly.

> *The* Formats *collection on the RenderingApplication object is used more to hold format information that is to apply throughout the entire applications (global values as it were) so that all object will use that formatting information.*

Each Format object in the Formats collection can only be assigned to one single MAPI property. Once we have assigned a Format object to a MAPI property we can then start to define the possible values for the property by adding Pattern objects to the **Patterns collection** of the Format object.

Formats and their Purpose

> Basically a format is used to define the style of a MAPI property, in other words it allows us to control how the property will actually be rendered in HTML.

That means we can define things like the font, the size, an image to be used, and so on for the MAPI property that we want to render as HTML output. So for example, by applying a format to the MAPI property `Importance` for a `Message` object, we can display a graphic indicating the message's importance rather than just getting a numeric value. This can be particularly useful, for example, if we want to build a highly sophisticated HTML table view with the `ContainerRenderer`.

*Don't be misled into thinking that you **have** to define formats to render properties. For example, if you use a ContainerRenderer object without adding any formatting information yourself, it would still render the MAPI properties but using default formatting values.*

The Formats Collection

The `Formats` collection is a fairly standard collection object:

FORMATS	
Properties	**Type**
Class	Long
Count	Long
Item	Format
Parent	ContainerRenderer or ObjectRenderer
Methods	
Add	

❑ The `Class` property will return a value of 5 or `CdoClassFormats`.

We will discuss how to use the `Add` method in the sections below on adding a format to the `ContainerRenderer` and `ObjectRenderer` objects.

The Format Object

The individual `Format` objects from the `Formats` collection is also quite straightforward:

FORMAT	
Properties	**Type**
Class	Long
Name	String
Parent	Formats
Patterns	Patterns
Property	Long or String
Methods	
Delete	

❑ The Class property returns a value of 4 or CdoClassFormat.

❑ The Delete method is used instead of having a Remove method on the Formats collection. Calling the Delete method means the object is no longer linked to the Formats collection but you can still hold a reference to the object. The object won't actually be destroyed until you release the object reference by setting it to Nothing. You can't add the object back into the Formats collection because the Add method always creates a new object.

Now that we have covered what formats are useful for, we will take a look at how we can use them in ContainerRenderer and ObjectRenderer objects.

Adding a Format to a ContainerRenderer Object

Let's take a look at the AddressEntry object's DisplayType property. This property is used to differentiate between the available object types the Exchange directory can contain.

Actually, the best way to gather information about this DisplayType property is to use the Outlook client, and look at the available address entries of the Global Address List:

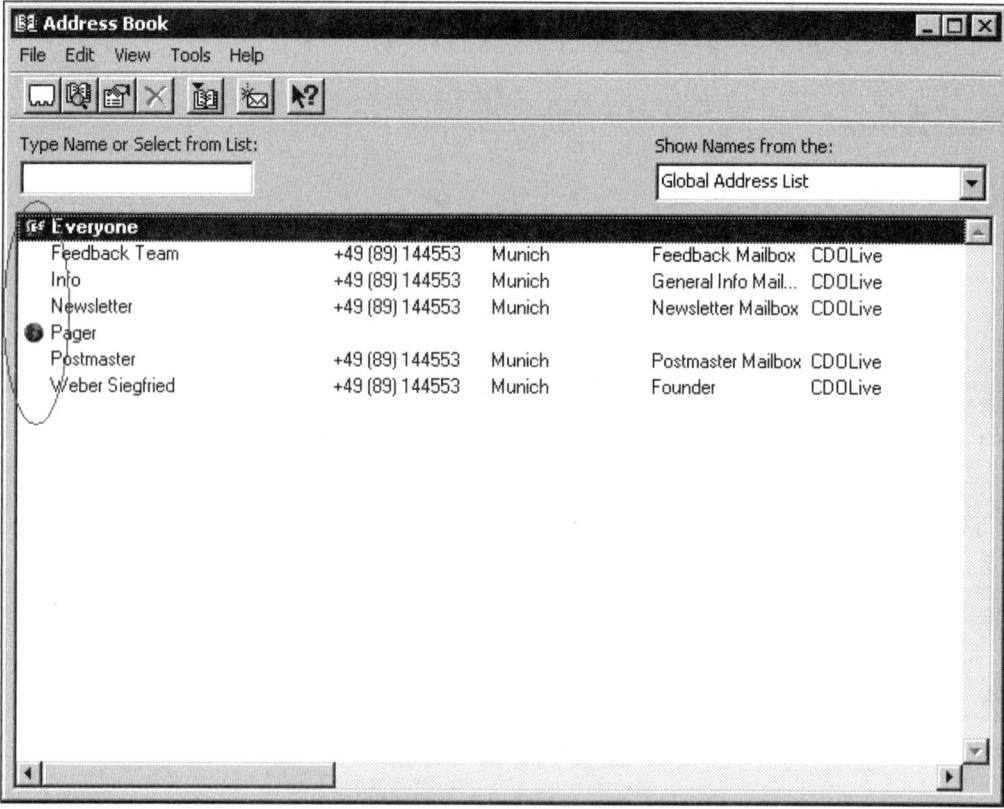

For example, in the screenshot above you can see that two different DisplayTypes are marked with icons.

The following table shows all the possible `DisplayType` values for an `AddressEntry` object:

DisplayType	Value	Description
CdoUser	0	An Exchange Server mailbox.
CdoDistList	1	An Exchange Server-side distribution list
CdoForum	2	An Exchange Public Folder
CdoAgent	3	An automated agent, such as Quote-of-the-Day
CdoOrganization	4	A special address entry defined for large groups, such as a helpdesk
CdoPrivateDistList	5	A private distribution list stored in your personal address book
CdoRemoteUser	6	An Exchange Server custom recipient

Outlook Web Access provides a list of MAPI properties in the `amprops.inc` file. This file holds many of the constants used in Outlook Web Access, including some undocumented ones, and also many of the possible values for MAPI properties.

The `amprops.inc` file is located in the `C:\exchsrvr\WEBDATA\USA\LIB` directory. Note that the USA directory in this case points to the US English version of Outlook Web Access. In German you should use GER, in French FRE etc.

Don't worry about the fact that the `amprops.inc` file of Outlook Web Access still uses the prefix `ActMsg` with all constants. This is only used for backwards compatibility.

So the MAPI property `DisplayType` will be mapped to a `Format` object and the above values can each be mapped to a `Pattern` object. So for the above screenshot, we would need the three `Pattern` objects (Mailbox, Dist List and Remote User) in the `Patterns` collection for the `DisplayType` `Format` object. Ideally, of course, you would have seven `Pattern` objects, covering each possible value.

To add a format for the `DisplayType` property of an `AddressEntry` object to the `ContainerRenderer` object we can use the following code:

```
Set objFormat = objContainerRenderer.Formats.Add(CdoPR_DISPLAY_TYPE, Null)
```

The first parameter of the `Add` method specifies the MAPI property tag or the name of a custom property and maps to the `Name` property on the created `Format` object. You can either use a constant, as in the sample code above, or use the decimal or hex value of the MAPI property.

I always recommend using constants declared in a separate file that is included in your ASP page. You can find a list of MAPI property tags in Appendix B.

The second parameter is used only for special-purpose formats that don't represent any one specific property. If you do use this parameter, the first parameter must be set to `Null`.

The code sample above will not add the possible pattern values; it just adds the `AddressEntry` object's `DisplayType` property to the `Formats` collection of the `ContainerRenderer` object. The next thing we should do is to add the appropriate patterns to the `Patterns` collection of the newly created `Format` object, and add all the possible values to them. We'll be doing this shortly.

Adding a Format to an ObjectRenderer Object

Adding a format to an `ObjectRenderer` object is similar to adding it to a `ContainerRenderer` object.

We will use the CDO `Message` object's `Importance` and `Sensitivity` properties. Let's look at the Outlook Options dialog of a new message to find out the possible values (patterns) for these properties (formats):

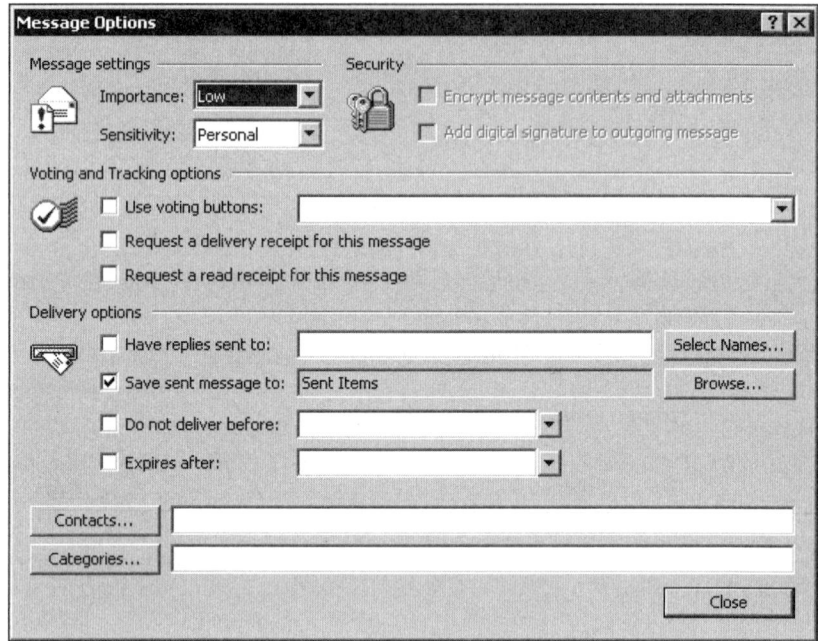

Note that a lot of the other message properties displayed on the Outlook Options dialog, such as the Voting boxes, are private to Outlook and are not exposed to CDO 1.2 for Exchange. The properties that are exposed to CDO are listed in Appendix B.

The `Importance` property has three possible values:

Constant	Value	Description
CdoLow	0	Low importance
CdoNormal	1	Normal importance (default)
CdoHigh	2	High importance

So to add a format for the `Importance` property we would use the following code:

```
Set objFormat = objObjectRenderer.Formats.Add(CdoPR_IMPORTANCE, Null)
```

The `Sensitivity` property has four possible values:

Constant	Value	Description
CdoNoSensitivity	0	No special sensitivity (default)
CdoPersonal	1	Personal
CdoPrivate	2	Private
CdoConfidential	3	Designated as company confidential

To add the `Sensitivity` format we would use this code:

```
Set objFormat = objObjectRenderer.Formats.Add(CdoPR_SENSITIVITY, Null)
```

Patterns and Why We Need Them

Now we have now learned how to use formats to prepare a single property that can contain multiple values, to be used in either a `ContainerRenderer` or `ObjectRenderer` object. We can now go ahead and take a look at how to define the HTML to be rendered.

Unfortunately we still don't have a fully-fledged example here because the final step would be to either create a new custom view or use an existing predefined view. Since this will be discussed in the next chapter, we'll look at code fragments that should prepare us for the next chapter, where we can put it all together.

Having said that, we can now start to take a look at the `Patterns` collection and its child `Pattern` object.

The Patterns Collection

The `Patterns` collection is actually nearly identical to the `Formats` collection:

PATTERNS	
Properties	**Type**
Class	Long
Count	Long
Item	Pattern
Parent	Format
Methods	
Add	

❑   The `Class` property will return a value of `6` or `CdoClassPatterns`.

We will describe how to use the `Add` method soon.

The Pattern Object

The `Pattern` object is also not very complex:

PATTERN	
Properties	**Type**
Class	Long
Parent	Patterns
RenderUsing	String
Value	Variant
Methods	
Delete	

❑   The `Class` property returns a value of `7` or `CdoClassPattern`.

❑   The `RenderUsing` property provides the mechanism to describe how the property, described in the parent `Format` object, is rendered in HTML. An example string for this property would be: `<FONT FACE='Arial, Helvetica, Sans-serif' SIZE='2'>%value%</FONT>`

❑   The `Value` property describes which values for the MAPI property being rendered will be rendered using the value of the `RenderUsing` property. An example for this property would be: `IPM*`

❑   The `Delete` method operates in a similar fashion to that of the `Format` object.

Before we can look at some code examples, we need to explore the `Value` and `RenderUsing` properties in a bit more detail.

Using Wildcards in a Pattern String

In the example value for the `Value` property you may have noticed that we have used a wildcard character. This is one of the important points with the `Pattern` object. It provides a convenient way to work with wildcards in properties that contain `String` values.

The method used to implement this is called **WILDMAT pattern matching**. So how does it work? First of all WILDMAT is a defined wildcard format, so this is not a Microsoft proprietary format. It defines exactly how wildcards are used to build string matches.

The following shows how WILDMAT pattern matching can be used:

❑ The wildcard * will return zero or more characters of any value. For example, `IPM.Note.*` will return all values that start with the characters `IPM.Note.` no matter what characters follow them. If you use this wildcard character on its own you will return *all* possible values.

❑ The wildcard ? will return exactly one character of any value to replace the wildcard. For example, `IPM.Note.S??ure` will return any value that starts with `IPM.Note.S`, followed by any two characters, and ends with `ure`, like `IPM.Note.Secure`.

❑ The wildcard [...] allows you to specify specific characters that can be returned. For example, `IPM.Note.[abcd]` will return only matches with a character or a, b, c, or d at that end position.

   You can also use this wildcard to search for a range of characters using the format **[x1-x2]**. For example, `IPM.Note.[a-f]` will return `IPM.Note.a` but not `IPM.Note.k`. If you specify a specific range then the matching is case-sensitive.

   In addition, you can use the caret character (^) to exclude specific characters from the range. For example, `IPM.Note.[^ab]` will return any character at that position except an a or b.

There are some cases in which the pattern matching works quite a bit differently. One case is if the MAPI property is of type `PT_BINARY`. In CDO 1.2 for Exchange and the CDO 1.2 Rendering libraries, binary MAPI properties are generally converted to a hexadecimal string value. Basically that means if the wildcard is a string of hexadecimal values it is automatically converted into a binary value and then the matching is performed.

If you want to search for the backslash character you must use a double backslash, as the backslash character contains a special meaning in pattern matching.

Now let's take a look at another important feature provided by the `Pattern` object, the ability to use tokens in the format string.

Using Substitution Tokens with a Pattern Object

In order to actually apply your formatting to a pattern you need a way to access specific values for the pattern's property. This is achieved through the use of **substitution tokens**. These tokens defined by enclosing percent signs, e.g. `%value%`, are replaced by the value the token represents in the Exchange Server when they are actually rendered.

For example, if the renderable property `value` contains the string "This is the subject of a message", then you can format this by using the following `RenderUsing` string:

```
objPattern.RenderUsing = "<B>%value%</B>"
```

This would actually be rendered as: **This is the subject of a message**

If you use an invalid or misspelled token:

```
objPattern.RenderUsing = "<B>%valu%</B>"
```

The token value would not be substituted, and would be rendered as: **valu**

Because of the many different types of information available, e.g. the size of a message in kilobytes, and the way Outlook Web Access is built to provide a convenient interface to the user, the CDO 1.2 Rendering library provides many substitution tokens:

Substitution Token	Description
%apptlength%	Replaced by the number of rows spanned by the appointment or free block, for an `AppointmentItem` object's MAPI property being viewed in `CdoModeCalendarDaily` mode.
%apptwidth%	Replaced by the number of columns spanned by the appointment or free block, for an `AppointmentItem` object's MAPI property being viewed in `CdoModeCalendarDaily` mode.
%classpath%	Replaced by the message class expressed as a lowercase string, such as `ipm.note`, for a `Message` object's MAPI property. For a report message class, only the first and last elements are retained, so that `REPORT.IPM.NOTE.NDR` is expressed as `report.ndr`.
%columns%	Replaced by the total number of columns in the view for an `AppointmentItem` object's MAPI property being viewed in `CdoModeCalendarDaily` mode.
%date%	Replaced by the day for which appointments are being rendered, expressed as a string, for an `AppointmentItem` object's MAPI property.
%kvalue%	Replaced by the value or a numeric property expressed in kilobytes, i.e. divided by 1024. Note that it is rendered without a "K" character.
%obj%	Replaced by the unique identifier of the object, expressed as a hexadecimal string, for any MAPI property.
%parentobj%	Replaced by the unique identifier of the parent folder of the message, expressed as a hexadecimal string, for any MAPI property.
%rowid%	Replaced by the position of the object in its containing table, for a MAPI property in a calendar view or a table view.
%tablewidth%	Replaced by the sum of the pixel widths of all the columns in the view, expressed in pixels, for a MAPI property in a calendar view.
%time%	Replaced by the time of the time slot currently being rendered, expressed as a string, for an `AppointmentItem` object's MAPI property being viewed in `CdoModeCalendarDaily` mode. If the slot begins on an hour boundary, the string contains the hour and either "AM" or "PM". Otherwise, the string contains the time separator character and the starting minute.
%value%	Replaced by the value of the property, rendered according to the property's data type, for any MAPI property.

The most widely used tokens are %obj% and %value%. The %value% token is the generic token used with most of the MAPI properties, while the %obj% token is used especially on a ContainerRenderer object to build the LinkPattern string, to open the selected object and display the properties.

Link Patterns

A **link pattern** is a pattern that when rendered displays a hyperlink. This allows you to create links between the hierarchy of objects which are being displayed. For example, if you were displaying a list of messages in a user's inbox, you could render a hyperlink on each message's subject, which would allow the user to read the message:

```
Set objFormat = objContainerRenderer.Formats.Add(CdoPR_SUBJECT, Null)
Set colPatterns = objFormat.Patterns

Set objPattern = colPatterns.Add "*", "<A HREF='ViewMessage.asp?" & _
                                      "obj=%obj%'>%value%</A>"
```

Note that there is nothing stopping you rendering more than two substitution strings.

Adding Patterns to a ContainerRenderer Object

The most important part of using Patterns with the ContainerRenderer is to know which possible values the designated MAPI property can hold. As mentioned before, one of the best places to gather this information is by using the Outlook client and finding the appropriate options which you then map to constants.

With the information we have gathered together it is now fairly easy to add a pattern to a ContainerRenderer Format object. For the example we saw earlier, we will use different images for each different DisplayType property of the AddressEntry object to distinguish between the different objects like mailboxes, custom recipients, and distribution lists that the Global Address List can hold. This provides a display that shows different images for each type of AddressEntry object.

The following code adds all possible patterns to the Format used in the DisplayType MAPI property:

```
Set objFormat = objContainerRenderer.Formats.Add(CdoPR_DISPLAY_TYPE, Null)
Set objPatterns = objFormat.Patterns

objPatterns.Add CdoUser, ""
objPatterns.Add CdoDistList, _
                "<IMG SRC='PubDL.gif' WIDTH='16' HEIGHT='16' BORDER='0'>"
objPatterns.Add CdoForum, _
                "<IMG SRC='PFolder.gif' WIDTH='16' HEIGHT='16' BORDER='0'>"
objPatterns.Add CdoAgent, _
                "<IMG SRC='Agent.gif' WIDTH='16' HEIGHT='16' BORDER='0'>"
objPatterns.Add CdoOrganization, _
                "<IMG SRC='HDesk.gif' WIDTH='16' HEIGHT='16' BORDER='0'>"
objPatterns.Add CdoPrivateDistList, _
                "<IMG SRC='PrivDL.gif' WIDTH='16' HEIGHT='16' BORDER='0'>"
objPatterns.Add CdoRemoteUser, _
                "<IMG SRC='Custom.gif' WIDTH='16' HEIGHT='16' BORDER='0'>"
```

There is no known limit for the count of Patterns you can add. However, practically you will use not more than maybe ten to fifteen patterns because there are not many MAPI properties used with CDO 1.2 for Exchange that hold more values.

The first parameter for the `Add` method contains the value of the designated MAPI property that is to rendered. The type of this parameter will depend on the type of MAPI property you want to work with. The sample above uses numeric values. For properties that contain `String` values you can use the wildcard pattern matching that we discussed earlier.

The following screenshot shows how the code we just saw would be rendered:

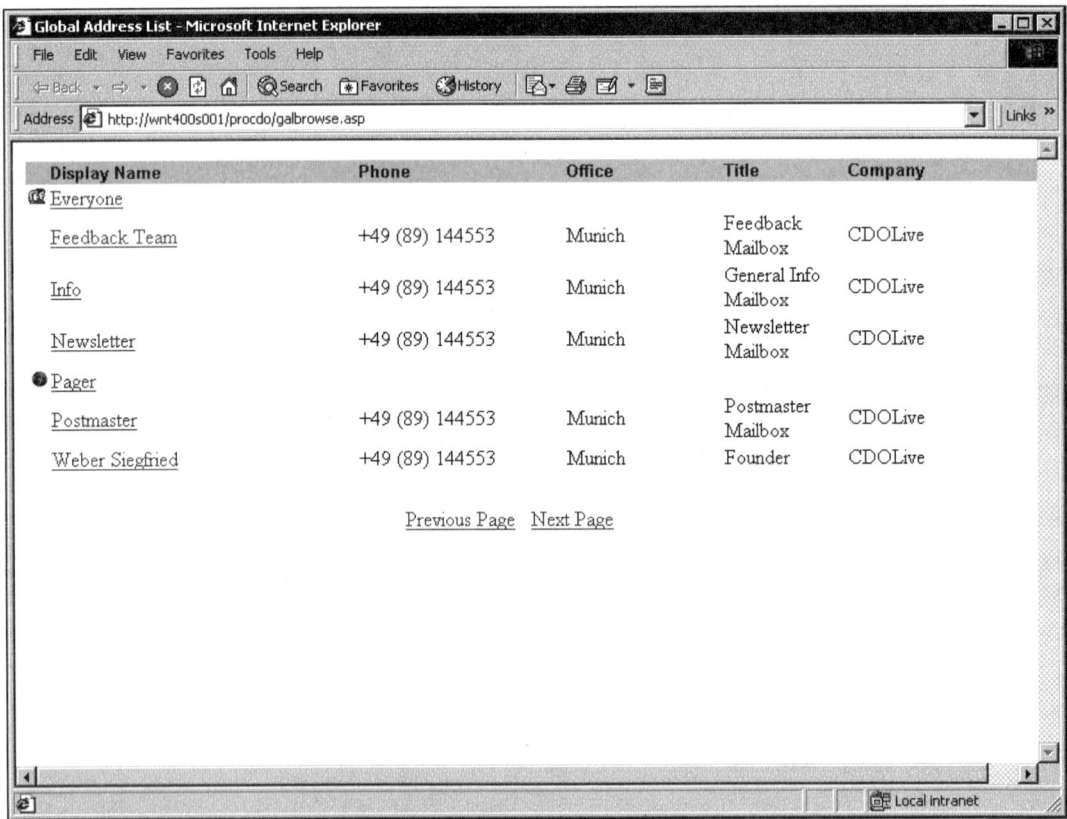

> We'll see the complete code that produced this screenshot when we cover views in the next chapter

Adding Patterns to an ObjectRenderer Object

Adding patterns to an `ObjectRenderer` object is very similar to adding patterns to the `ContainerRenderer` object. The only difference is that we will not use the pattern to generate output from a CDO collection into an HTML table view. Instead we will use the results in a single page grouped together with other MAPI properties of the designated object.

We'll be using the two MAPI properties we looked at earlier on the Outlook **Options** dialog. However, given that these two MAPI properties, the `Message Importance` and `Sensitivity` properties, are both available natively on the CDO `Message` object, you might ask yourself why we should even bother to use the Rendering library and not just use the CDO `Message` object's properties directly?

We could, for instance, use the following code:

```
If objMessage.Importance = CdoLow
    strImage = "<IMG SRC='Low.gif' WIDTH='13' HEIGHT='16' BORDER='0'>"
ElseIf objMessage.Importance = CdoHigh
    strImage = "<IMG SRC='High.gif' WIDTH='13' HEIGHT='16' BORDER='0'>"
End If

If objMessage.Sensitivity = CdoNoSensitivity
    strSensitivity = "Normal"
ElseIf objMessage.Sensitivity = CdoPersonal
    strSensitivity = "Personal"
ElseIf objMessage.Sensitivity = CdoPrivate
    strSensitivity = "Private"
ElseIf objMessage.Sensitivity = CdoConfidential
    strSensitivity = "Confidential"
End If
```

While it is not a big deal to code this without using the Rendering library, it runs slower because each time the page is requested all this code must be interpreted, because the code is running in a script language, and of course the message must be loaded into memory also.

This would probably create some overhead in your application because you have to check for all possible values in your code, and for properties with a large number of possible values this could slow down the overall performance a lot.

So what would it look like if we use the CDO 1.2 Rendering library and its `ObjectRenderer` object methods?

```
Set objFormat = objObjectRenderer.Formats.Add(CdoPR_IMPORTANCE, Null)
Set objPatterns = objFormat.Patterns

objPatterns.Add CdoLow, "<IMG SRC='Low.gif' WIDTH='13' HEIGHT='16' BORDER='0'>"
objPatterns.Add CdoNormal, ""
objPatterns.Add CdoHigh, "<IMG SRC='High.gif' WIDTH='13' HEIGHT='16' BORDER='0'>"
```

This code will add the relevant images to the `Patterns` collection of the `ObjectRenderer` object's `Format` property for the message's importance.

As mentioned earlier in this chapter we can either assign an HTML formatted image tag information to each specific value of the MAPI property, or use simple string values as used in the following code for the message's `Sensitivity` property:

```
Set objFormat = objObjectRenderer.Formats.Add(CdoPR_SENSITIVITY, Null)
Set objPatterns = objFormat.Patterns

objPatterns.Add CdoNoSensitivity, "Normal"
objPatterns.Add CdoPersonal, "Personal"
objPatterns.Add CdoPrivate, "Private"
objPatterns.Add CdoConfidential, "Confidential"
```

Summary

In this chapter we looked at the purpose of formats and patterns used with the rendering objects of the CDO 1.2 Rendering library. We now know that it is possible that a single MAPI property of a particular object can hold multiple values, and we can use the methods described in this chapter to easily build HTML output to display this information in our ASP applications.

To be honest I have cheated a bit in this chapter. The reason is that a `ContainerRenderer` that displays the Exchange server Global Address List in a HTML table view can't be built without creating a custom view. This is one of the limitations of the CDO 1.2 Rendering library `ContainerRenderer` object. Therefore, in the next chapter, we will now discuss in depth how custom views are built and how to customize existing predefined views. In the next chapter you will see a lot of the code in this chapter being put to use.

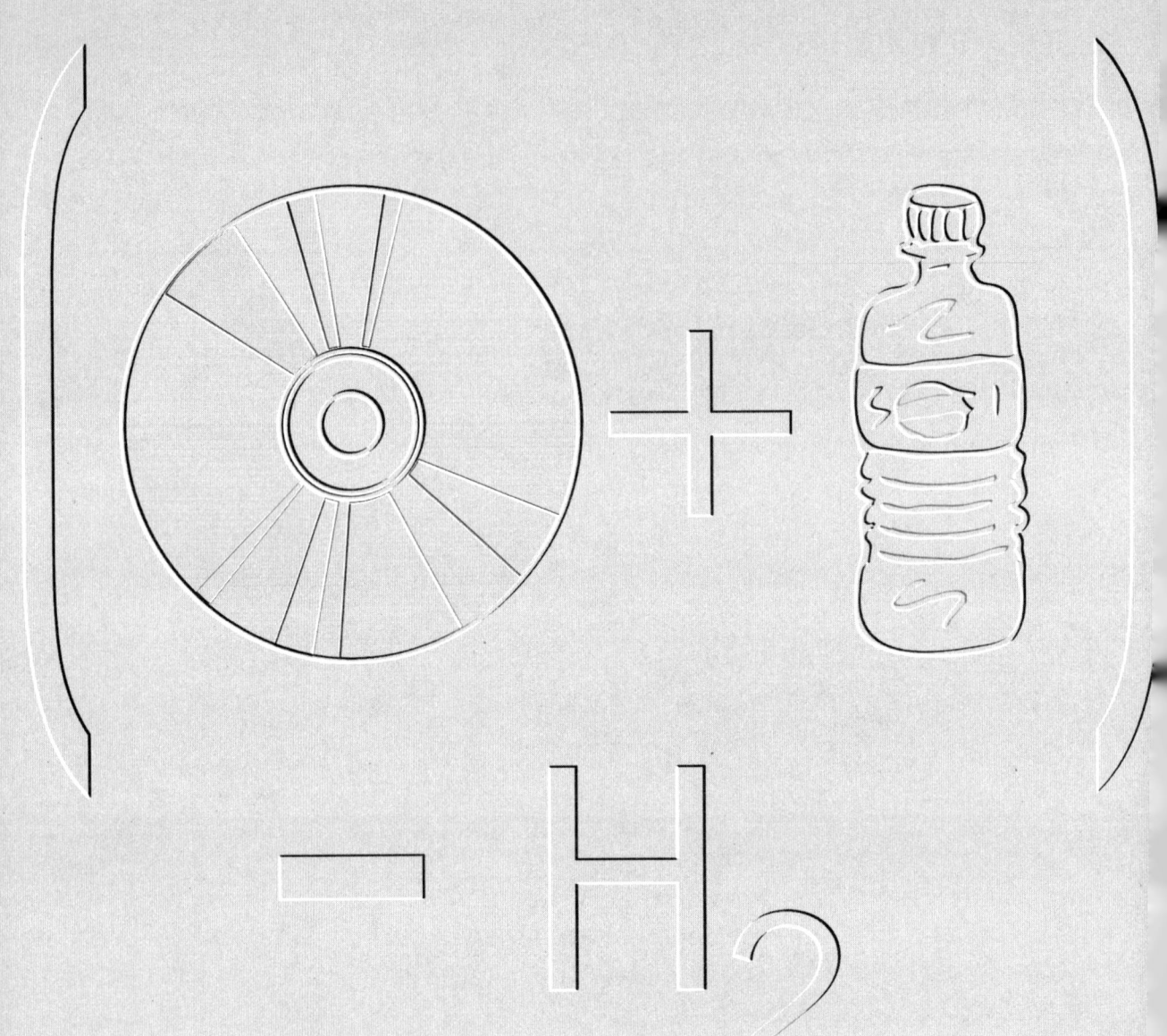

11

Views

Introduction

In the last three chapters we learned how to create a `RenderingApplication` and build a `ContainerRenderer`. The `ContainerRenderer` prepares a particular collection to be rendered into HTML later. It also provides methods and properties to apply either an existing view (defined with the Exchange client or Outlook), or a new dynamically created view.

> Note that views are only applicable to a `ContainerRenderer` and not to an `ObjectRenderer`.

In this chapter, we will discuss:

- ❏ Views and how to use them in a container renderer
- ❏ Accessing predefined views and modifying them
- ❏ Creating custom, non-persistent, views programmatically

Views and How to Use Them in a ContainerRenderer Object

The CDO Rendering library provides a neat feature that is available neither in the CDO 1.21 for Exchange library nor in the Outlook object model. It is the ability to either create new dynamic views, or to use the existing predefined views of a CDO collection. Views are basically used in a `ContainerRenderer` to provide a convenient view of the data stored in the particular CDO collection. Many people are not aware of the fact that each time we open a folder, for example, the content is presented with a particular view applied.

Views are an integral part of the Exchange client and Outlook to present data to the user. They are not a feature of the Exchange Server itself, though. If you are using Microsoft Outlook you can define custom persistent views on each folder. The type of view is tied to the type of folder. That means a view called "Day/Week/Month", which is a calendar view, can only be applied to calendar folders and not to mail folders.

As mentioned above, Exchange Server doesn't provide any built-in views. In fact, it doesn't know very much about the data at all – it's really only the storage for the underlying data.

Here's where the CDO Rendering library jumps in, because it can either be used to display a folder's built-in views, or custom views. Custom views will need a little bit more explanation. There are several ways to create custom views. Basically, persistent views can only be created with either Exchange Client or Outlook 9x/2000. Those persistent custom views can be stored in two different places. The first place is the user's mailbox. This is called a personal view and it can be used in any folder of the same type as the one it was defined in. The following picture shows a persistent custom view created in a mailbox. To open this dialog, start Microsoft Outlook and select View | Current View | Define Views:

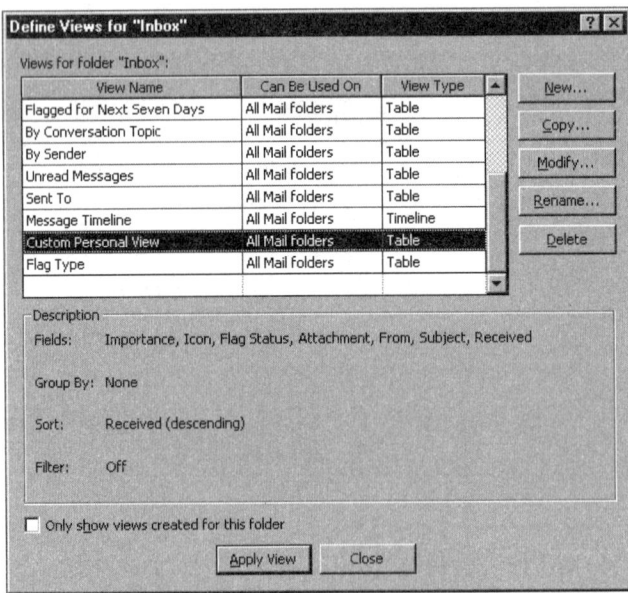

In the screenshot above, you'll see a lot of other views besides the custom view. While these views can be used with Outlook, they are unfortunately not available in the CDO Rendering library. The reason is that the CDO Rendering library can only access a folder's default view, and any views stored in the folder.

So what do we mean by 'a view stored in a folder'? This is the second type of view that can be created with the Exchange client and Outlook, the so-called **folder-associated** views. These views are stored in the folder where they have been defined and are only available in this folder. They're available to all users who have permissions to open the folder. The following picture shows a persistent custom view created in a folder:

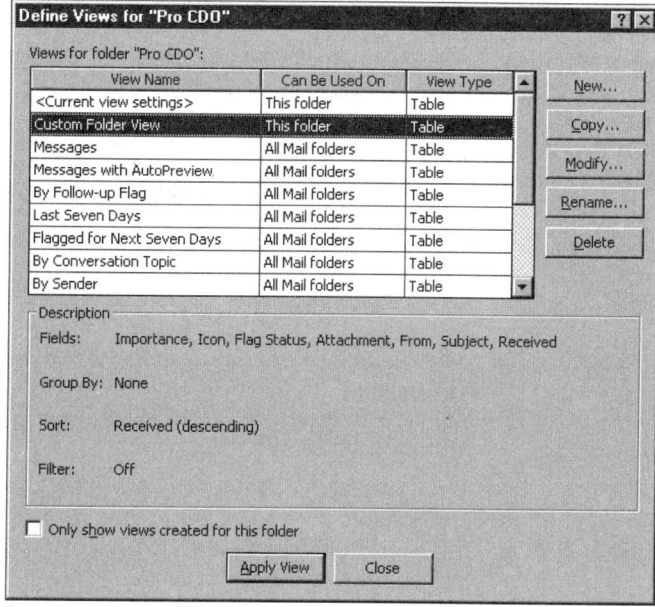

One important point to keep in mind is that we can have two different types of views. One for table-oriented views, the `TableView`, and the other one for displaying data of the default calendar folder, the `CalendarView`.

The timeline view is another Outlook view, so it's not available for the Renderer.

The following table shows which CDO collection can be rendered with which view:

View Type	Description
TableView	`AddressEntries`, `Folders`, `Messages`, or `Recipients`.
CalendarView	`Messages` collection containing `AppointmentItem` objects.

The same restriction as to the CDO 1.2 library applies here. An `AppointmentItem` object can only be retrieved from the default calendar folder.

We can now take a look at how the `ContainerRenderer` object works with views. The `ContainerRenderer` object exposes a property called `Views`. This property returns a CDO collection that holds all views available to the `ContainerRenderer`'s `DataSource`.

> **If the `DataSource` of the `ContainerRenderer` is set to a CDO `AddressList` object no default views are available and you have to build your own custom non-persistent view in code.**

Having said that it becomes pretty obvious that the primary purpose of the `Views` property on the `ContainerRenderer` object is to provide a way to access views of a CDO `Folder` object. Although this can be a folder holding mail items, appointments or anything else the CDO Rendering library does not distinguish between a folder containing tasks, contacts, journal entries or the little yellow sticky notes because they are not supported in the CDO Rendering library.

VIEWS	
Properties	**Type**
Class	Long
Count	Long
Item	TableView
Parent	ContainerRenderer
Methods	
Add	

By default a public folder accessed via anonymous access provides a set of predefined views. The following list shows the available views:

View Name	Description
Messages	All messages of a particular folder.
Unread Messages	Only unread messages of a particular folder.
By Sender	All messages grouped by sender.
By Subject	All messages grouped by subject.
By Conversation Topic	All messages grouped by conversation topic.
Unread by Conversation Topic	All unread messages grouped by conversation topic.

The views in the table above are available when accessing the Exchange Server in either authenticated or anonymous mode.

> **When connected to Exchange server in authenticated mode, one additional view "By Category", which is a grouped view, is available. It's not clear why you only get this view in authenticated mode, but that's the way it is.**

The following picture shows the existing views of a particular public folder in Outlook Web Access. As you can see we are in anonymous mode because there are only six predefined views available:

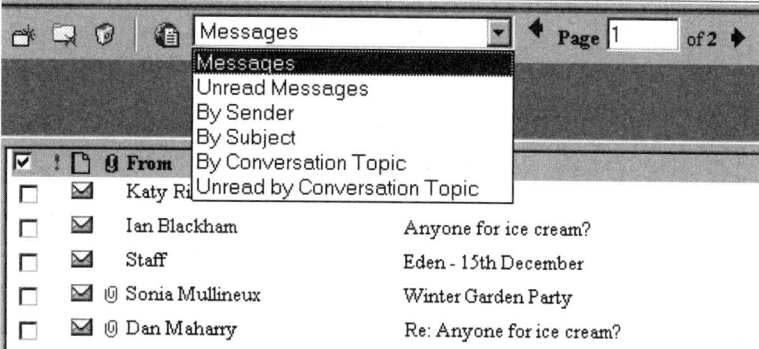

The following code shows how to loop through the `Views` collection of the inbox folder of a particular mailbox and display the name of each available view:

```
<%@LANGUAGE=VBSCRIPT CODEPAGE = 1252 %>
<%

blnAuthenticated = False
bstrAuthentication = Request.ServerVariables("AUTH_TYPE")
If InStr(1, "_BasicNTLM", bstrAuthentication, vbTextCompare) < 2 Then
    Response.Buffer = True
    Response.Status = ("401 Unauthorized")
    Response.AddHeader "WWW.Authenticate", "Basic"
    Response.End
Else
    blnAuthenticated = True
End If
%>
<html>
<head>
<title>Defined Views for Inbox Folder</title>
</head>
<body>
<%

Dim CdoDefaultFolderInbox
Dim intRenderingClass
Dim vbLF

Dim objRenderApplication
Dim objSession
Dim objFolder
Dim objContainerRenderer
Dim objViews
Dim strExchangeServer
Dim strMailbox
Dim objView
```

```
Set objRenderApplication = Nothing
Set objSession = Nothing
Set objFolder = Nothing
Set objContainerRenderer = Nothing
Set objViews = Nothing

CdoDefaultFolderInbox = 1
vbLF = Chr(10)
intRenderingClass = 3
strExchangeServer = "YourExchangeServer"
strMailbox = "YourMailbox"

Set objRenderApplication = Server.CreateObject("AMHTML.Application")

Set objSession = Server.CreateObject("MAPI.Session")
objSession.Logon "", "", False, True,, True, strExchangeServer & vbLF _
    & strMailbox
Set objFolder = objSession.GetDefaultFolder(CdoDefaultFolderInbox)

Set objContainerRenderer = _
    objRenderApplication.CreateRenderer(intRenderingClass)
objContainerRenderer.DataSource = objFolder.Messages

Set objViews = objContainerRenderer.Views

%>

<b> Defined Views for Inbox Folder</b>
<p>
<table border=1 width="80%">
<tr>
    <td><b>View Name</b></td>
</tr>
<% For Each objView In objViews %>
<tr>
    <td><%= objView.Name %> </td>
</tr>
<% Next %>
</table>

</center></div>
<%

Set objViews = Nothing
Set objFolder = Nothing
Set objContainerRenderer = Nothing
Set objRenderApplication = Nothing

objSession.Logoff
Set objSession = Nothing

%>
</body>
</html>
```

All these views are only applicable if the folder contains messages. The `ContainerRenderer` does not expose the same views if the folder contains appointment items. In fact, if a folder containing appointment items is used there are only two built-in views available – a daily and a weekly view. Unfortunately a monthly view is not available.

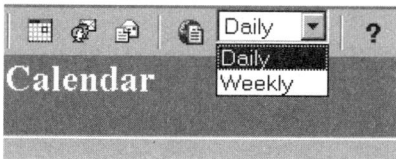

Whether you use a built-in or a custom view you need to specify it as the current view to apply it to the particular folder. This is accomplished by using the `CurrentView` property. This property needs to be set before the `ContainerRenderer` is invoked. This can be done by using either the numeric index of the view in the list, or using the name of the view.

The following code shows how to set the current view of a `ContainerRenderer` object using the name:

```
objContainerRenderer.CurrentView = "By Conversation Topic"
```

If you do not specify a view when creating the `ContainerRenderer` object, either by name or by index value, in the `CurrentView` property the CDO Rendering library uses the first view in the `Views` collection. Similarly, if you use an invalid name or index value to change the existing view, the current view will remain unchanged.

If you successfully change the `CurrentView` as discussed above, the `DataSource` collection is also repopulated. For example if you change the view from Messages to Unread Messages, the `DataSource` collection is altered to only contain messages which are unread and all other messages will be hidden. The count of messages in the collection also changes to show only the number of unread messages.

Columns and their Purpose

Each view, whether predefined or custom, includes a `Columns` collection. This `Columns` collection holds a single `Column` object for each column that is to be displayed when the `ContainerRenderer` is invoked.

COLUMNS	
Properties	**Type**
Class	Long
Count	Long
Item	Column
Parent	TableView
Methods	
Add	

Columns are the key to customizing a view because a `Column` object exposes a set of properties that need to be set to add a valid column to the `Columns` collection of the view in question.

To add a new column to a custom non-persistent view use the following code (remember, you can't add columns to persistent views). The third parameter in the `Add` method is the column width:

```
Set objCustomView = objContainerRenderer.Views.Add("CustomView")
Set objColumns = objCustomView.Columns
Set objColumn = objColumns.Add("Display Name", CdoPR_DISPLAY_NAME, 30, 0 , 2)
```

COLUMN

Properties	Type
Class	Long
Flags	Long
Index	Long
Name	String
Parent	Columns
Property	Variant
RenderingUsing	String
Width	Long

Methods

The Flags Property

The first important property is the `Flags` property. It is used to determine if the column should contain either a bitmap or a string value and also if the column can be used for sorting. The following table shows the possible values for the `Flags` property and their purpose:

Flag	Decimal Value	Description
CdoColumnBitmap	8	The property rendered in this column is displayed using a bitmap.
CdoColumnNotSortable	32	The display cannot be sorted on the property rendered in this column.

To set the `Flags` property use the following code:

```
objColumn.Flags = 32
```

Columns in predefined views have 12106 = &H2F4A in the `Flags` property. This default setting includes the `CdoColumnBitmap` flag together with several obsolete flags that are ignored by CDO.

Note that if you set the `Flags` property to indicate that the column should contain a bitmap instead of a string value the `Width` property is expressed in a pixel range and not in characters. If the column is in a `CalendarView` the value of the `Flags` property is ignored because the `CalendarView` object makes its own alignment calculations automatically.

The Name Property

The Name property is the next one necessary to define the column. The name holds a string value that will be displayed in the heading row of the ContainerRenderer when it is invoked.

To set the Name property use the following code:

```
objColumn.Name = "Display Name"
```

The RenderUsing Property

The RenderUsing property adds information used by the ContainerRenderer to determine how the column content should be rendered. It can include HTML formatting information if, for example, the column contains a character string to define the font style and size.

The following code sample shows how to set the RenderUsing property to display a character string:

```
objColumn.RenderUsing = _
    "<font face='Arial, Helvetica, sans-serif' size='-2'>%value%</font>"
```

As you can see in the code sample above, the RenderUsing property can contain substitution tokens like %value%. If such a token is present it will be replaced by the appropriate property value specified for this column. If you don't use a substitution token in the string the property value will be rendered without modifications as it is.

> If no information to render a particular column is defined, the ContainerRenderer searches for a Format object to be used for displaying the particular property. If no Format can be found, or if the format contains no Pattern object, the property is rendered with its default style according to the data type and value.

The Width Property

You need to use the Width property to define the horizontal space the column occupies when it is displayed in the HTML output.

The following code sample shows how to set the Width property:

```
objColumn.Width = "1"
```

> According to the documentation, for predefined views the column width is 'relative' and specified in characters.

Overall, the `ContainerRenderer`'s column widths are determined using the following rules:

❑ The `ContainerRenderer` determines the overall width of the `TableView` by adding the `Width` properties of every column.

❑ The `ContainerRenderer` computes the proportional width for each column by dividing its `Width` property by the overall table view width.

❑ The proportional width for each column is placed in the HTML output.

❑ The browser calculates each column's final display width from its proportional width and the available horizontal space in the browser window.

> **For custom views the column width is 'absolute' and specified in characters. If the column's Flags property is set to CdoColumnBitmap the column's width is expressed in pixels.**

Accessing and Modifying Predefined Views

As mentioned earlier the CDO Rendering library exposes six (or seven when running in authenticated mode – see above) predefined views in each folder that holds messages. These views are automatically added to the `Views` collection property of the `ContainerRenderer` object if the `DataSource` is set to a folder.

The trick here is to access the `Views` collection and loop through it to access the columns of each view. The following code hides particular columns on each of the available views in the `Views` collection by simply removing all formatting information:

```
<%@LANGUAGE=VBSCRIPT CODEPAGE = 1252 %>
<%
On Error Resume Next

blnAuthenticated = False
bstrAuthentication = Request.ServerVariables("AUTH_TYPE")
If InStr(1, "_BasicNTLM", bstrAuthentication, vbTextCompare) < 2 Then
    Response.Buffer = True
    Response.Status = ("401 Unauthorized")
    Response.AddHeader "WWW.Authenticate", "Basic"
    Response.End
Else
    blnAuthenticated = True
End If
%>

<html>
<head>
<title>Modified View for Inbox Folder</title>
</head>
```

```
<body>
<%

Const CdoPR_HASATTACH = &H0E1B000B
Const CdoPR_IMPORTANCE = &H00170003
Const CdoPR_SENT_REPRESENTING_NAME = &H0042001E
Const CdoPR_SUBJECT = &H0037001E
Const CdoPR_MESSAGE_DELIVERY_TIME = &H0E060040
Const CdoPR_MESSAGE_SIZE = &H0E080003
Const CdoPR_MESSAGE_CLASS = &H001A001E


Dim CdoDefaultFolderInbox
Dim intRenderingClass
Dim vbLF

Dim objRenderApplication
Dim objSession
Dim objFolder
Dim objContainerRenderer
Dim objViews
Dim objView
Dim objColumns
Dim objColumn
Dim strExchangeServer
Dim strMailbox

Set objRenderApplication = Nothing
Set objRenderApplication = Nothing
Set objSession = Nothing
Set objFolder = Nothing
Set objContainerRenderer = Nothing
Set objViews = Nothing
Set objView = Nothing
Set objColumns = Nothing
Set objColumn = Nothing

CdoDefaultFolderInbox = 1
vbLF = Chr(10)
intRenderingClass = 3
strExchangeServer = "YourExchangeServer"
strMailbox = "YourMailbox"

Set objRenderApplication = Server.CreateObject("AMHTML.Application")

Set objSession = Server.CreateObject("MAPI.Session")
objSession.Logon "", "", False, True,, True, strExchangeServer & vbLF _
   & strMailbox
Set objFolder = objSession.GetDefaultFolder(CdoDefaultFolderInbox)
'
Set objContainerRenderer = _
   objRenderApplication.CreateRenderer(intRenderingClass)
objContainerRenderer.DataSource = objFolder.Messages
```

403

```
Set objViews = objContainerRenderer.Views

For Each objView In objViews
   For Each objColumn In objView.Columns
      Select Case objColumn.Property
         Case CdoPR_HASATTACH
            objColumn.Name = ""
            objColumn.Width = 0
            objColumn.RenderUsing = ""

         Case CdoPR_IMPORTANCE
            objColumn.Name = ""
            objColumn.Width = 0
            objColumn.RenderUsing = ""

         Case CdoPR_SENT_REPRESENTING_NAME
            objColumn.Name = ""
            objColumn.Width = 20
            objColumn.RenderUsing = _
            "<font face='Arial, Helvetica, sans-serif' size='-2'>%value%</font>"
         Case CdoPR_SUBJECT
            objColumn.Name = ""
            objColumn.Width = 50
            objColumn.RenderUsing = _
            "<font face='Arial, Helvetica, sans-serif' size='-2'>%value%</font>"

         Case CdoPR_MESSAGE_DELIVERY_TIME
            objColumn.Name = ""
            objColumn.Width = 20
            objColumn.RenderUsing = _
            "<font face='Arial, Helvetica, sans-serif' size='-2'>%value%</font>"

         Case CdoPR_MESSAGE_SIZE
            objColumn.Name = ""
            objColumn.Width = 0
            objColumn.RenderUsing = ""

         Case CdoPR_MESSAGE_CLASS
            objColumn.Name = ""
            objColumn.Width= 5
            objColumn.RenderUsing = "<img src='note.gif'>"

      End Select
   Next'
Next

%>

<b> Modified View for Inbox Folder</b>
<p>
<table border=1 width="80%">

<% objContainerRenderer.Render 1, 0, 0, Response %>

</table>
```

```
</center></div>
<%

Set objRenderApplication = Nothing
Set objRenderApplication = Nothing
Set objFolder = Nothing
Set objContainerRenderer = Nothing
Set objViews = Nothing
Set objView = Nothing
Set objColumns = Nothing
Set objColumn = Nothing

objSession.Logoff
Set objSession = Nothing

%>
</body>
</html>
```

> Note that you can only modify *predefined* `TableViews`. This tweak won't work with `CalendarViews` because we don't get any predefined views in a calendar folder.

By formatting information, I mean the `Column` object's `Name`, `Width` and `RenderUsing` properties. If those properties are blanked out the column will simply vanish in that view. That means that we can use this to hide columns.

> Take care when you try to actually add or delete columns of the predefined views. This can result in undefined behavior because the `ContainerRenderer` seems not to recognize the changes properly. Hiding the column as described above is a more reliable alternative.

Creating Custom Non-Persistent Views Programmatically

Now that we've discussed how to modify predefined views, we will now move on to create our own custom views programmatically. One important thing you need to remember is that a custom view created with the CDO Rendering library can't be stored anywhere. That means it is only valid while your Active Server Pages application is running.

This might be an issue if your ASP is used in a heavy-load environment where a heavy load is expected because it can slow down the overall performance of your Internet Information Server. In this case a persistent view created with the Exchange client or Outlook and saved in the folder might be the better solution. Remember that you can still modify this kind of view as described earlier in this chapter.

While you can use existing grouped views, you can't create them programmatically. You need to use the Exchange client or Outlook to define such a view in the particular folder.

Creating a TableView

TABLEVIEW	
Properties	**Type**
Categories	Long
Class	Long
Columns	Columns
Index	Long
Name	String
Parent	Views
Source	Long
Methods	
IsSameAs	

So how do we create a custom table view? We just need to create a `ContainerRenderer` and set the `DataSource` like this:

```
Set objContainerRenderer = objRenderingApplication.CreateRenderer(3)
objContainerRenderer.DataSource = objFolder.Messages
```

After setting the `DataSource` to a valid `Folder` object we can access the `Views` collection and add a custom view using code like this:

```
CdoClassTableView = 9
Set objView = objContainerRenderer.Views.Add("Custom View", CdoClassTableView)
```

If you omit the optional second parameter, which specifies the view type, the `TableView`'s default settings will be used. The name supplied to the method is required, though. If you don't implement a view selection in your Active Server Pages application this name is only used to reference the view by name in the `Views` collection and later when the view is applied as the `CurrentView` on the `ContainerRenderer`.

> **Make sure the view name is unique in the `Views` collection and don't use names like "Messages" as your custom view name. While the CDO Rendering library does not require a unique view name, only the first one can be found by name if a duplicated view name exists.**

After we have created the view we can actually add the columns and apply the format we want. This is just done by using code like this:

```
<%@LANGUAGE=VBSCRIPT CODEPAGE = 1252 %>
<%
On Error Resume Next

blnAuthenticated = False
bstrAuthentication = Request.ServerVariables("AUTH_TYPE")
If InStr(1, "_BasicNTLM", bstrAuthentication, vbTextCompare) < 2 Then
    Response.Buffer = True
    Response.Status = ("401 Unauthorized")
```

```
      Response.AddHeader "WWW.Authenticate", "Basic"
      Response.End
Else
      blnAuthenticated = True
End If
%>

<html>
<head>
<title>Custom View for Inbox Folder</title>
</head>
<body>
<%

Const CdoPR_SUBJECT = &H0037001F
Const CdoPR_MESSAGE_DELIVERY_TIME = &H0E060040
Const CdoPR_MESSAGE_CLASS = &H001A001F


Dim CdoDefaultFolderInbox
Dim CdoClassTableView
Dim intRenderingClass
Dim vbLF

Dim objRenderApplication
Dim objSession
Dim objFolder
Dim objContainerRenderer
Dim objView
Dim objColumns
Dim objColumn
Dim objFormat
Dim objPatterns


Dim strExchangeServer
Dim strMailbox

Set objRenderApplication = Nothing
Set objRenderApplication = Nothing
Set objSession = Nothing
Set objFolder = Nothing
Set objContainerRenderer = Nothing
Set objView = Nothing
Set objColumns = Nothing
Set objColumn = Nothing
Set objFormat = Nothing
Set objPatterns = Nothing

CdoDefaultFolderInbox = 1
CdoClassTableView = 9
vbLF = Chr(10)
intRenderingClass = 3
strExchangeServer = "YourExchangeServer"
strMailbox = "YourMailbox"
```

```
Set objRenderApplication = Server.CreateObject("AMHTML.Application")

Set objSession = Server.CreateObject("MAPI.Session")
objSession.Logon "", "", False, True,, True, strExchangeServer & _
   vbLF & strMailbox
Set objFolder = objSession.GetDefaultFolder(CdoDefaultFolderInbox)

Set objContainerRenderer = _
   objRenderApplication.CreateRenderer(intRenderingClass)
objContainerRenderer.DataSource = objFolder.Messages

Set objFormat = objContainerRenderer.Formats.Add(CdoPR_MESSAGE_DELIVERY_TIME)
Set objPatterns = objFormat.Patterns.Add _
   ("*", "<font face='Arial, Helvetica, sans-serif' size='2'>%value%</font>")

Set objFormat = objContainerRenderer.Formats.Add(CdoPR_MESSAGE_CLASS)
Set objPatterns = objFormat.Patterns.Add("IPM*", "<img src=note.gif>")

Set objFormat = objContainerRenderer.Formats.Add(CdoPR_SUBJECT)
Set objPatterns = objFormat.Patterns.Add _
   ("*", "<font face='Arial, Helvetica, sans-serif' size='2'>%value%</font>")

Set objView = objContainerRenderer.Views.Add("Custom View", CdoClassTableView)
Set objColumns = objView.Columns

objColumns.Add " ", CdoPR_MESSAGE_CLASS, 1, 8, 1
objColumns.Add "Date", CdoPR_MESSAGE_DELIVERY_TIME, 18, 0, 2
objColumns.Add "Subject", CdoPR_SUBJECT, 50, 32, 3

objContainerRenderer.CurrentView = "Custom View"

objContainerRenderer.RowsPerPage = 50

objContainerRenderer.HeadingCellPattern = "<font face='Arial, Helvetica, sans-
serif' size='2'><b>%value%</b></font>"
objContainerRenderer.HeadingRowPrefix = "<tr valign='top' bgcolor='#C0C0C0'>"
objContainerRenderer.HeadingRowSuffix = "</tr>"

objContainerRenderer.CellPattern = "<font face='Arial, Helvetica, sans-serif'
size='-1'>%value%</font>"
objContainerRenderer.RowPrefix = "<tr valign='middle' bgcolor='#FFFFFF'>"
objContainerRenderer.RowSuffix = "</tr>"

%>

<b> Custom View for Inbox Folder</b>
<p>
<table border=1 width="80%">

<% objContainerRenderer.Render 1, 0, 0, Response %>

</table>
</center></div>
```

```
<%

Set objRenderApplication = Nothing
Set objRenderApplication = Nothing
Set objFolder = Nothing
Set objContainerRenderer = Nothing
Set objView = Nothing
Set objFormat = Nothing
Set objPatterns = Nothing

objSession.Logoff
Set objSession = Nothing

%>
</body>
</html>
```

The string properties above are in Unicode format. The standard property tag for PR_SUBJECT is &H0037001E, but we're using Unicode so it becomes &H0037001F. The same applies to other string properties – just change the E to an F or vice versa if you're having trouble.

Creating a CalendarView

CALENDARVIEW	
Properties	**Type**
BusyCell	String
BusyIndicator	String
Categories	Long
Class	Long
Columns	Columns
DailyEventCell	String
DailyTimeCell	String
FreeBusinessCell	String
FreeIndicator	String
FreeNonBusinessCell	String
Index	Long
Interval	Long
Mode	Long
Name	String
NumberOfUnits	Long
OOFIndicator	String
Parent	Views
Source	Long
TentativeIndicator	String
WeeklyAppointmentCell	String
WeeklyHeadingCell	String
Methods	
IsSameAs	
RenderAppointments	
RenderDateNavigator	
RenderEvents	

Creating a CalendarView is very similar to creating a TableView. One major difference is that we can only create it if we have a valid AppointmentItems collection of the default calendar folder of the mailbox.

CalendarView Properties

The `CalendarView` object has a lot of properties that relate to the display of appointments. It has two modes, the daily and the weekly views, as determined by the `Mode` property. By far the majority of its display properties apply to the daily mode, as you can see in this table:

Property	Daily	Weekly
BusyCell	✓	
BusyIndicator	✓	
DailyEventCell	✓	
DailyTimeCell	✓	
FreeBusinessCell	✓	
FreeIndicator	✓	
FreeNonBusinessCell	✓	✓
Interval	✓	
NumberOfUnits	✓	✓
OOFIndicator	✓	
TentativeIndicator	✓	
WeeklyAppointmentCell		✓
WeeklyHeadingCell		✓

The BusyCell Property

The `BusyCell` property is used to define a string that determines how appointments will be rendered. It applies only when the `Mode` property is set to `CdoModeCalendarDaily`. If your custom view is a weekly view you need to use the `WeeklyAppointmentCell` property.

To set the `BusyCell` property use the following code:

```
objView.BusyCell = <td rowspan=%apptlength% colspan=%apptwidth% bgcolor=#C0C0C0
valign=top align=left width=%percentwidth%>%value%</td>
```

There's a list of these tokens in chapter 11.

The BusyIndicator Property

The `BusyIndicator` property is used to define the style used to display the free/busy indicator bar between the time column and the appointment cells.

To set the `BusyIndicator` property use the following code:

```
objView.BusyIndicator = <td rowspan=%apptlength% colspan=1 bgcolor=0000ff
width=%percentwidth%> </td>
```

The DailyEventCell Property

To specify how individual events are rendered use the DailyEventCell property.

To set the DailyEventCell property use the following code:

```
objView.DailyEventCell = <td rowspan=%apptlength% colspan=%apptwidth%
bgcolor=c0c0c0 valign=top align=left width=%percentwidth%>%value%</td>
```

The DailyTimeCell Property

The DailyTimeCell property is used to define the style of the time slot cells in the column at the left of a daily view.

To set the DailyTimeCell property use the following code:

```
objView.DailyTimeCell = <td bgcolor=c0c0c0 valign=middle align=right
width=%percentwidth%><font size=-1><nobr>%time%</nobr></font></td>
```

The FreeBusinessCell Property

You can show business hours cells in a different style from cells outside business hours. The FreeBusinessCell property is used to define the style for displaying a free time slot during business hours.

To set the FreeBusinessCell property, use the following code:

```
objView.FreeBusinessCell =  <td rowspan=%apptlength% colspan=%apptwidth%
bgcolor=ffffff valign=top align=left width=%percentwidth%><br></td>
```

The FreeIndicator Property

Use the FreeIndicator property is to define the style for the free/busy indicator bar for a free time slot in a daily view.

To set the FreeIndicator property use the following code:

```
objView.FreeIndicator = <td rowspan=%apptlength% colspan=1 bgcolor=ffffff
width=%percentwidth%> </td>
```

The FreeNonBusinessCell Property

Use the FreeNonBusinessCell property to define the style for displaying a free cell outside of business hours.

To set the FreeNonBusinessCell property use the following code:

```
objView.FreeNonBusinessCell = <td rowspan=%apptlength% colspan=%apptwidth%
bgcolor=c0c0c0 valign=top align=left width=%percentwidth%><br></td>
```

The Mode Property

The Mode property of the CalendarView is necessary to distinguish between a daily or weekly view. The following table shows the two valid values:

Mode	Decimal Value	Description
CdoModeCalendarDaily	0	View is rendered in multiples of a day.
CdoModeCalendarWeekly	1	View is rendered in multiples of a week.

> Note that it is not possible to build a monthly view. This is a limitation of the CDO Rendering library.

Use the following code to set the Mode property:

```
CdoModeCalendarDaily = 0
objView.Mode = CdoModeCalendarDaily
```

> The default value for the Mode property is CdoModeCalendarDaily.

The Interval Property

The Interval property is used to define how big a time slot is in minutes.

Setting the Interval property is easy:

```
objView.Interval = 60
```

The default value of the Interval property is 30 minutes. If you change this, the CDO Rendering library may change the value such that it is between 5 and 60 and divides integrally into 60.

The NumberOfUnits Property

Use the NumberOfUnits property to define the number of time units (whether days or weeks) to be included in the CalendarView HTML output. Use it in conjunction with the Mode property to determine the overall time span of the CalendarView.

```
objView.NumberOfUnits = 5
```

> The default value for the NumberOfUnits property is 1.

The OOFIndicator Property

The `OOFIndicator` property is used to define the style for the indicator bar for an out-of-office time slot. The indicator bar is the thin vertical column between the time column and the appointments table.

To set the `OOFIndicator` property use the following code:

```
objView.OOFIndicator = <td rowspan=%apptlength% colspan=1 bgcolor=660066
width=%percentwidth%> </td>
```

> The `OOFIndicator` property only applies when the `Mode` property is set to `CdoModeCalendarDaily`.

The TentativeIndicator Property

The `TentativeIndicator` property holds a string for rendering the indicator bar for a tentatively busy time period.

The default value of the `TentativeIndicator` property is:

```
<td rowspan=%apptlength% colspan=1 bgcolor=99ccff width=%percentwidth%> </td>
```

Summary

In this chapter we have learned how we can access and modify predefined views, as well as how to create our own views. This is a very powerful feature of the CDO Rendering library because we can build HTML output that doesn't look just like a straight dump of the data stored in an Exchange Server public folder. This might be particularly useful if you already manage a lot of your information in Exchange Server and you want to be able to present it in a web site.

In the next chapter we will look at the Outlook Web Access interface that is built with CDO 1.21 and CDOR libraries. We'll also see how we can enhance it with some custom-built ASP.

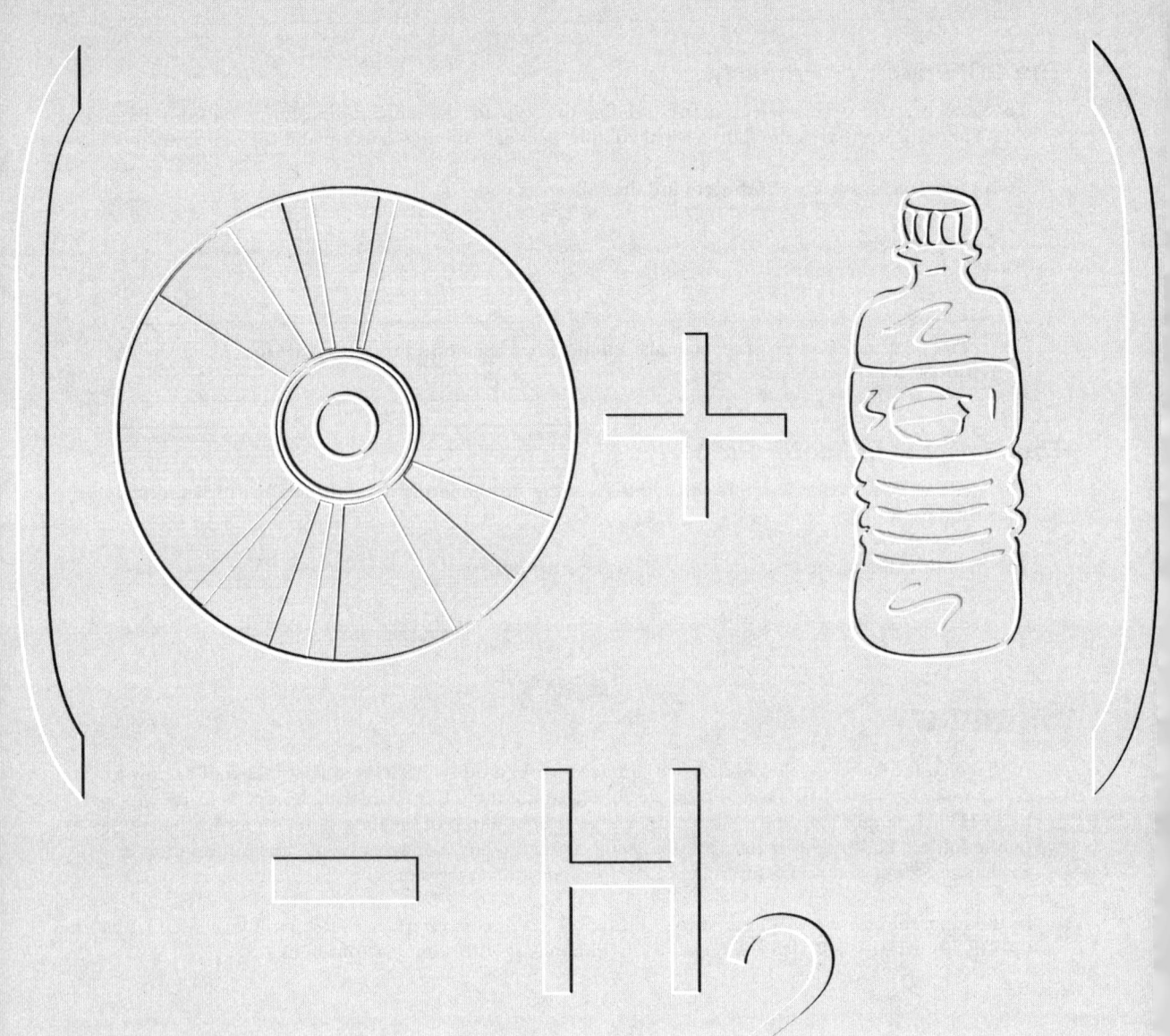

12

Outlook Web Access

Outlook Web Access (OWA) is Microsoft's web-based interface to your Exchange mailboxes and public folders. It was introduced with the release of Exchange Server 5.0 and has continued to grow in functionality with each new service pack and release of the software. It can be viewed in versions 3.0 and above of both Netscape Navigator and Microsoft Internet Explorer or indeed in any browser that supports HTML 3.2, JavaScript and frames.

From our perspective however, the best thing about OWA is that it is a fully functioning application that relies upon the CDO and CDO Rendering libraries to work. By delving into how it works, we can learn by example how to build up an ASP page that uses CDO Rendering to bring mailboxes and messages to the web.

In this chapter then, we'll

- ❑ Look at how to install and configure it.
- ❑ Examine its setup.
- ❑ Discover how to personalize the OWA logging in and out pages.
- ❑ Demonstrate CDO Rendering in ASP to build new functionality in OWA.
- ❑ Finally, look at how to mimic this functionality without writing a single line of code.

What OWA is and what it isn't

Stripped of its clothes, OWA is just an internet-enabled way to access Exchange data – that is, our mailboxes and public folders. Unfortunately, it suffers from the assumption that because it has the Outlook name, it has all the functionality of Outlook 9x/2000 too, which is not the case. Not only does it lack some of the usability features like drag and drop and context menus because of its web-based interface, OWA's messaging and collaboration features like support for calendar, contacts, tasks, journal and Outlook 9x/2000 forms are also quite limited. On the application-level too, apps built to work under Outlook are unlikely to work under OWA. The same applies to your custom Outlook forms.

Why? The simple reason is that instead of being natively built into Exchange à la Outlook 9x/2000, OWA uses ASP, CDO, CDO Rendering and IIS (Internet Information Server) to implement its functionality and not the Outlook object model or some other API. The figure below demonstrates how they fit in with each other.

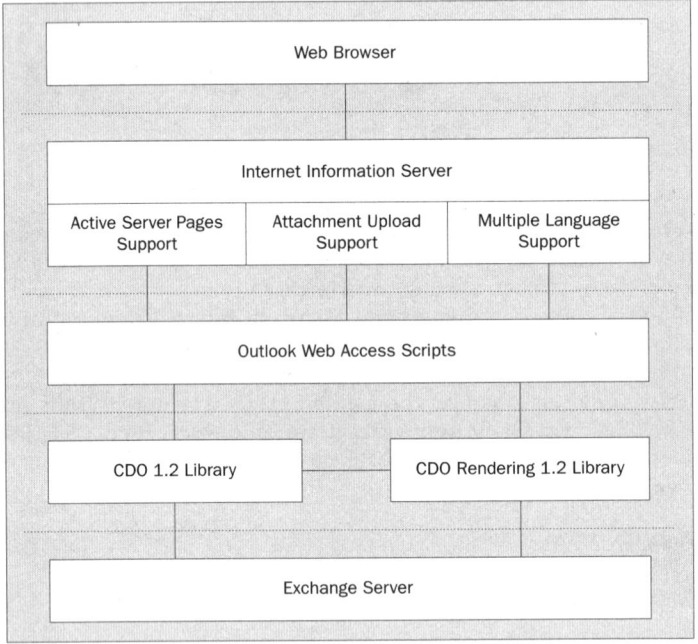

Having read the chapters on the CDO library so far you may have correctly assumed there are some fairly major limitations in the object models of both it and the CDO Rendering library and, as a result of those limitations, Outlook Web Access does have some major gotchas.

The most annoying problems come from the fact that there is no support for accessing calenders not stored in the primary mailbox and that there is only limited support for accessing any contacts folders at all so far. This limited support to access the main contact folder in your mailbox was added in service pack 1 for Exchange 5.5, but there is still no support for accessing contact folders and calendars in public folders as of service pack 3.

Also missing from the current version of OWA and indeed the CDO library is any support for tasks, journals and sticky notes that we have in Outlook 9x\2000. Unfortunately, it doesn't look likely that this will appear with the arrival of another service pack for Exchange 5.5. Microsoft is now focusing on the release of Exchange 2000, which is to appear in May/June 2000 at time of writing. This will deliver a lot of new features to CDO and an enhanced version of Outlook Web Access all of which we'll look at in the final chapter of this book.

It's not all doom and gloom though. One very neat feature of OWA is its ability to install multiple (20) language support for users in non-English speaking countries. This comes in the form of two language support packs which you can download from the Exchange website at http://www.microsoft.com/exchange/55/downloads/LangPacks.htm. Alternatively, they come included in service pack 3 for Exchange 5.5. Note though that to ensure the same functionality in OWA in different languages, one quick fix is to download service pack 3 in the appropriate language and copy the OWA files over the existing language version.

Getting It Up and Running

As nice as it would be to just be able to install OWA and go, there are some deployment considerations for you to be aware of.

First off is your server setup. Outlook Web Access requires Microsoft's IIS web server to run and access to an Exchange Server as well. The obvious solution then is to install all three on the same machine, but there's a large problem in the scalability of this option – 150 or so users using the same machine will slow it right down. Better then to consider a two-machine solution as follows.

Both machines need to be running Windows NT 4 with service pack 4 or higher and be members of the same domain. Neither application requires that their machine be a domain controller, but in the case of Exchange it's a recommended option. The figure below shows a typical setup with a list of software installed on each

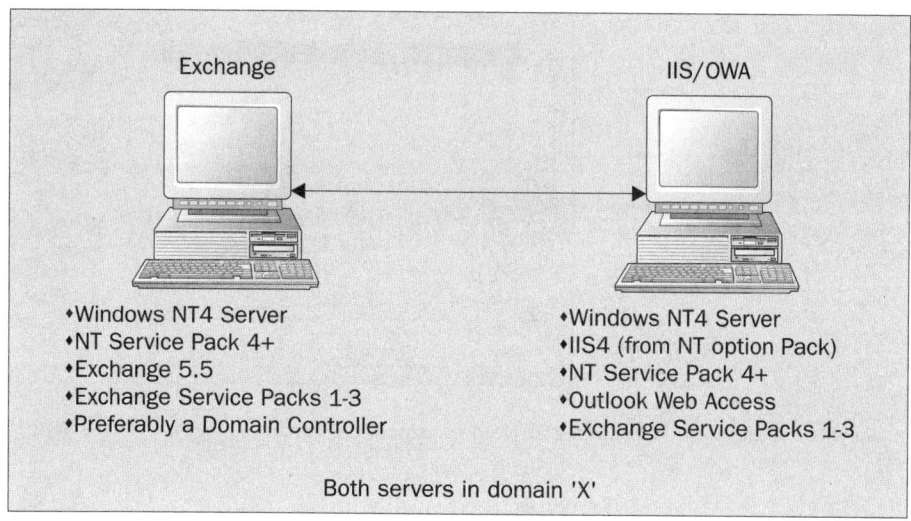

Exchange

IIS/OWA

•Windows NT4 Server
•NT Service Pack 4+
•Exchange 5.5
•Exchange Service Packs 1-3
•Preferably a Domain Controller

•Windows NT4 Server
•IIS4 (from NT option Pack)
•NT Service Pack 4+
•Outlook Web Access
•Exchange Service Packs 1-3

Both servers in domain 'X'

Installation of the Exchange machine should be fairly straightforward, but a word of caution is needed when installing IIS and NT Service Pack 4. To install version 4 of IIS, you'll need first to install service pack 3 for Windows NT, then IIS as part of the NT Option Pack (available for download from http://www.microsoft.com/ntserver/nts/downloads/ recommended/NT4OptPk/default.asp) and then service pack 4 for NT. This is annoying but SP4 contains a hotfix called **rollup** that *must* be installed or else the Outlook Web Access installation will be terminated with an error message.

It's also worth noting that it is perfectly valid to install OWA and any of the Exchange service packs for OWA updates on a machine that doesn't have Exchange installed on it. The installers will simply note its absence and install only the relevant files. Be aware however, that if you install a service pack on Exchange, you must apply it to Outlook Web Access too which means not forgetting to backup all your modified or additional files – the service pack will overwrite them all.

Installing Outlook Web Access

Assuming then that you have setup the Exchange server and both Windows NT and IIS on your web server box, you'll be able to get straight on with installing OWA, the option for which you'll find as part of the Exchange server setup program. Simply put your Exchange CD in the drive and wait for the install options to appear.

❑ When the autorun dialog appears, select Setup Server and Components and then Microsoft Exchange Server 5.5.

❑ Accept the license agreement to Exchange Server.

❑ Select a Complete/Custom installation. You'll see this dialog. Note that in Exchange 5.0, this looks a little different; in this case, OWA is referred to as Active Server Components.

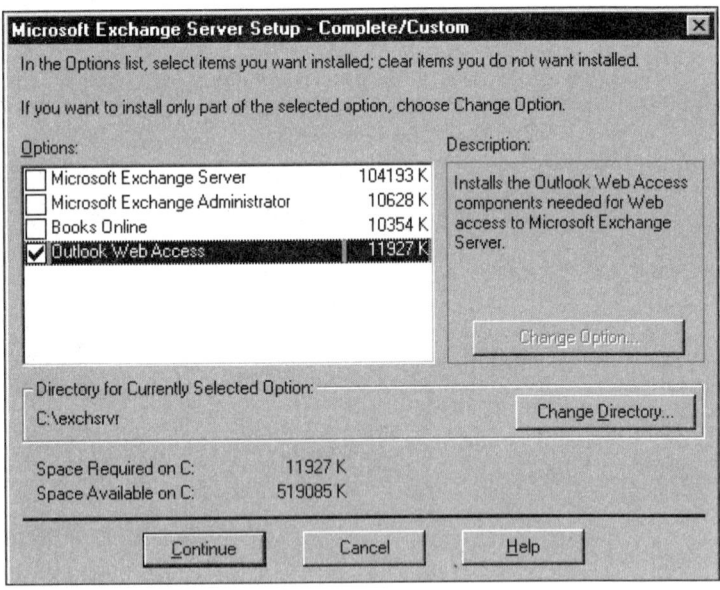

❑ To carry on the installation for your IIS box, deselect everything except Outlook Web Access and hit Continue.

❑ The installer will halt IIS and as your machine does not also have Exchange installed on it, query you for the name of your Exchange server.

❑ Type in the Exchange server name and hit **OK**. Installation will begin and after a short while, OWA will be ready for you to configure and use.

The Directory Structure

After you have installed OWA you will see a new virtual directory in the Internet Information Server management console, as the following picture shows:

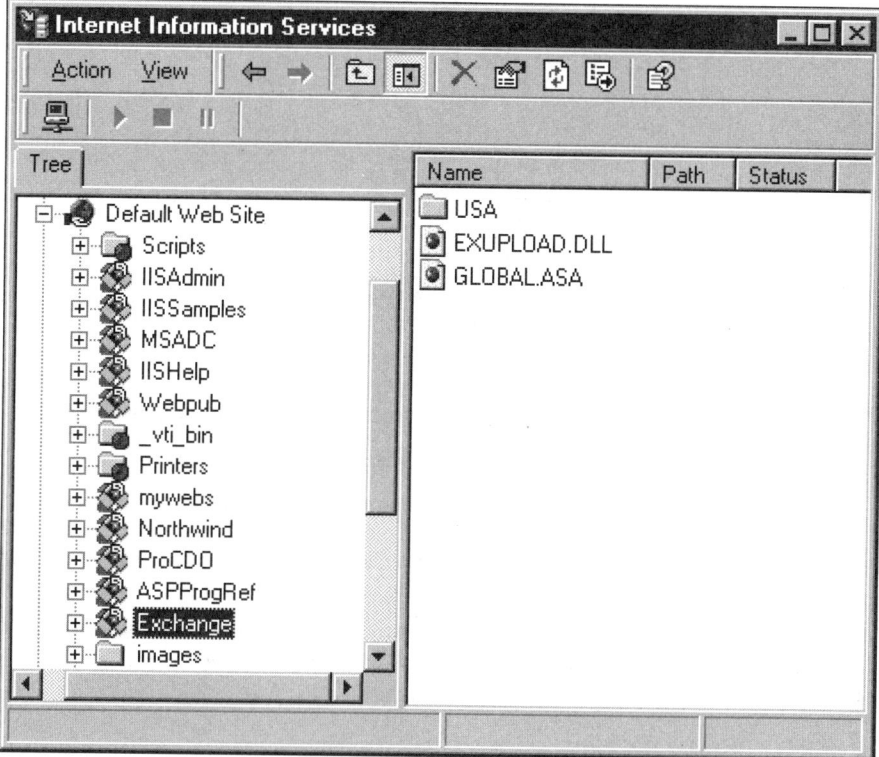

As you can see, the Exchange server setup creates a new virtual directory under the Default Web Site called Exchange. By default then, OWA can be accessed online at http://your_servers_name/exchange.

On the physical side of the installation meanwhile, OWA is installed in the WEBDATA directory directly underneath the base Exchange install directory. If you changed none of the defaults during installation then, you'll find it at C:\Exchsrvr\WEBDATA.

The following screenshot shows the directory structure of Outlook Web Access if installed in the English US language.

As you can see, the root directory of Outlook Web Access contains only three objects:

❑ Global.asa, which contains the initialization and shutdown information for OWA,

❑ Exupload.dll, which provides support for attachment uploads, and

❑ A subdirectory, which contains the files for the application in the default language. In the screenshot, the language is US English. Here, you'll find a set of files used to bring up the Outlook Web Access logon screen and provides the basic logon functions to authenticate a user either with anonymous or authenticated access. We'll come back to these files later.

Inside this support subdirectory are several other directories, each of which has a specific role. By having a quick look at these now, we can get some insight into how we can tweak them to enhance or modify the features already in OWA.

❑ ATTACH – Contains the files used when an attachment is opened in a message to send the attachment to the web browser client.

❑ CALENDAR – Contains files to create a ContainerRenderer to display the primary calendar folder of the mailbox.

❑ CONTACTS – Contains files to create a ContainerRenderer to display the primary contacts folder of the mailbox. N.B. CONTACTS is only created once the Exchange service packs have been installed.

❑ FINDUSER – Contains files to create a ContainerRenderer to display the search results of the Global Address List search dialog.

❑ FORMS – Contains the files used to create an ObjectRenderer to display messages. Each subdirectory holds the routines used to display a different type of message, e.g. delivery reports, non-delivery reports.

- ❑ HELP – Contains the online help files for Outlook Web Access.

- ❑ IMAGES – Contains several image files. They are used either in the `ContainerRenderer` to denote the different message types or in the OWA dialogs.

- ❑ INBOX – Contains several files used to display the contents of the inbox folder.

- ❑ LIB – Contains several include files holding the common functionality shared by all the modules of OWA.

- ❑ MOVCPY – Contains several files used when a message is moved or copied with OWA.

- ❑ NAVBAR – Contains several files used to display the left hand navigation bar.

- ❑ OPTIONS – Contains several files used to display the options dialog.

Configuring Outlook Web Access

One of the more confusing things about Outlook Web Access is that it has no dedicated configuration options within it. Instead, you'll find them divided between the registry on the OWA box and the Exchange Administrator program on the Exchange box.

In the Registry

You may recall that when setting up your OWA box, you were asked for the Exchange server's name. This is needed for OWA to connect to the correct Exchange box when a user logs on and is held along with some other important settings in the registry under the key HKEY_LOCAL_MACHINE\SYSTEM\CurrentControlSet\Services\MSExchangeWEB\ Parameters. They are:

Key	Description
Enterprise	The Exchange organization name.
HTMLQuoting	Reserved for internal use.
Language Pack Directory	Directory with dynamic link library resource files.
RFC1867NoCleanupAt Unload	Specifies if attachments are deleted after their upload. Reserved for internal use.
RFC1867SaveDirectory	The directory that holds all the attachments while the upload to Outlook Web Access is in progress. Reserved for internal use.
RFC1867Trace	Enables advanced logging for attachment upload feature. Reserved for internal use. Reserved for internal use.
Server	The Exchange server name.
Site	The Exchange site name.

Bear in mind that if you reinstall your Exchange server box under a different organization, site or server name than was specified in the Outlook Web Access setup, OWA will stop working and you need to change those settings manually with a registry editor tool such as `regedit`.

With Exchange Admin

It's on the Exchange server that you have the most options to choose from with respect to OWA. Unfortunately, none of them are particularly obvious so we'll work through them together.

Start off by firing up Exchange Admin on your server and expanding the left hand view until you can view the Protocols Configuration panel in the right-hand pane. It should look like this:

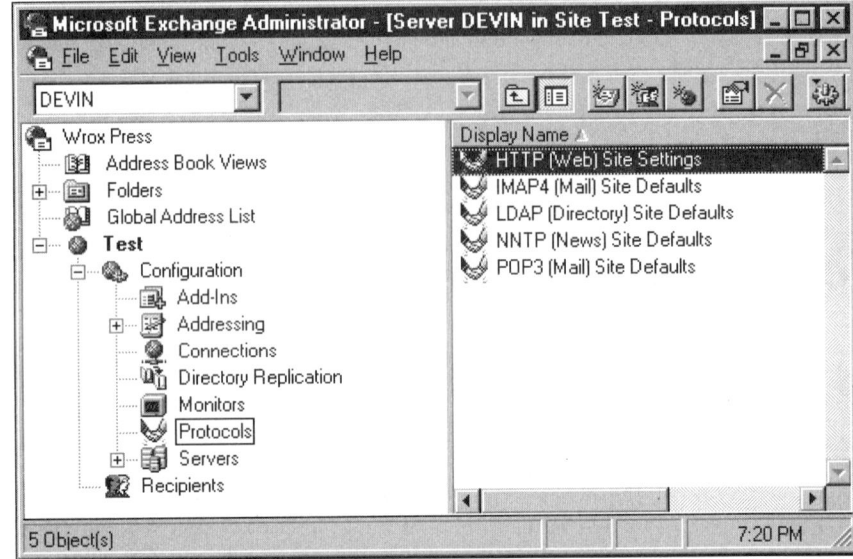

As you may have guessed, the options we're looking for are contained in the HTTP (Web) Site Settings which you can access by highlighting it and then choosing Properties from the File menu. Here you'll find a dialog with three tabs, General, Folder Shortcuts and Advanced.

The General tab contains three fundamental choices to OWA's operation.

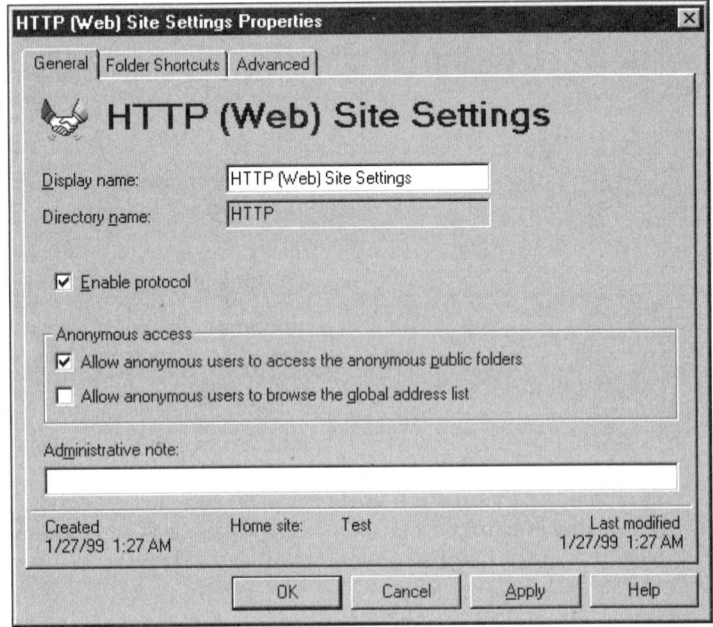

The most important of these is probably the Enable Protocol option. By unchecking this, you disable any and all HTTP access to Exchange, effectively shutting down Outlook Web Access completely. This doesn't shut down the web server though – just the gates to Exchange.

The other two options here concern what Exchange information OWA can disseminate for public access without users logging on, but we'll come back to that in a minute. There is a caveat here for administrators who need to allow users to log on to OWA and access their private mailboxes. In order for a user to do this, IIS needs to authenticate a NT user account on the machine it's running on. This can only happen if the administrator opens the NT User manager and gives the user account or user group containing the user, the right to Log on Locally as demonstrated below.

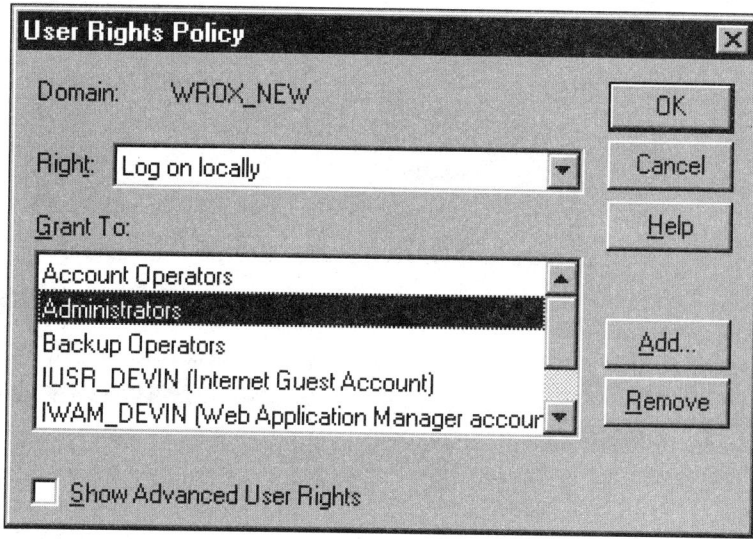

Back to the public access options: Exchange gives us the options to allow the public to view both our public folders and our global address list. Checking these requires to do a little more work in the other tabs of this Settings dialog.

Configuring Anonymous Public Folder Access

Once you've checked the Public Folder Access box, you'll also need to configure the permissions on the public folder itself to allow the anonymous access and create a shortcut to the public folder. Without the latter, Joe Public can't access a public folder through OWA even if you have enabled the HTTP access and set the permissions of the appropriate folder properly.

Let's take an example to demonstrate. Suppose I wanted to enable access to a public folder called Discussion Forum. In the Folder Shortcuts tab of our settings dialog, we hit New.. and navigate through the public folder hierarchy until we find our folder and hit OK. The settings dialog should look something like this.

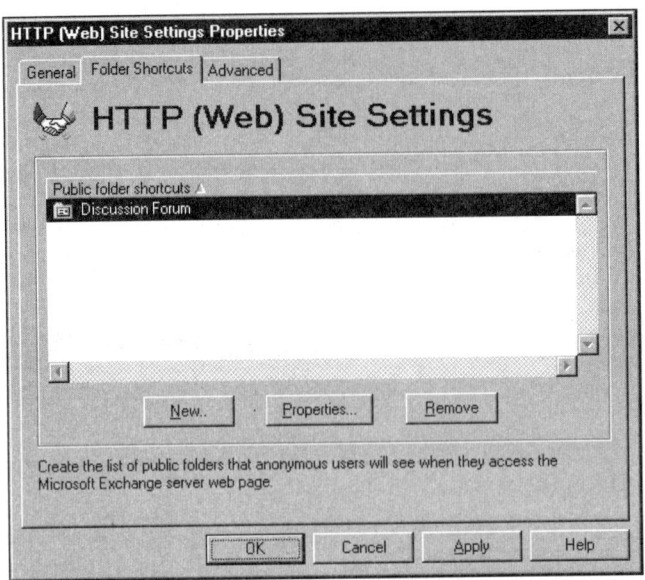

However, we're only half done. We need also to configure the folder permissions to allow anonymous access to its contents. Fortunately, this is a simple task. From the position above with the folder highlighted, we press the Properties button and then the Client Permissions... button in the resulting dialog to get here.

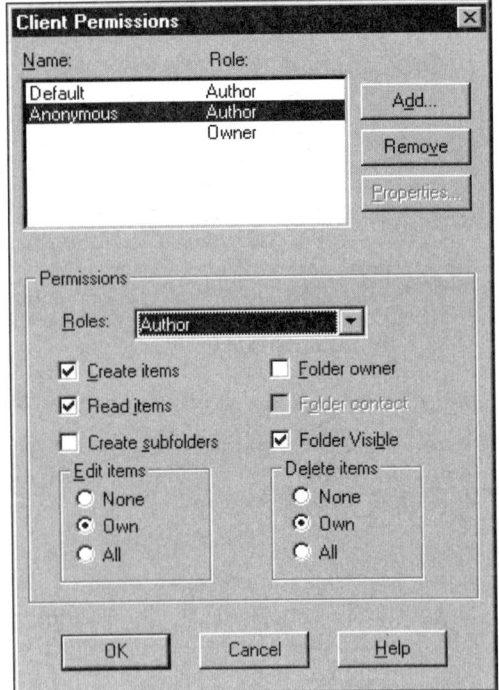

It's from here that we can set the permissions on the folder for our anonymous users. Initially, user Anonymous has no permissions at all, but that can be changed by selecting him and selecting a role from the drop-down box. In our example, we given him Author access meaning that he can read every message but only alter and delete his own.

With this done, public, anonymous access to our Discussion Forum folder is now granted be it either by using the standard Outlook Web Access interface or directly by opening a special URL that is described later in this chapter.

Configuring Anonymous Global Address List Access

The other option Exchange Admin gives OWA is to allow anonymous searches through the Global Address List (GAL). Simply check the box marked **Allow Anonymous Users To Browse The Global Address List**. For reasons unknown, it isn't actually possible to *browse* the GAL in OWA unless we write it in ourselves (see later). Instead, there's just the search facility and, with service pack 2 for Exchange 5.5, the ability to check names against the GAL when composing a new message.

The GAL search page in OWA is called **Find Names**. Unhappily, it does tend to slow down OWA if the GAL is large or the search is vague but it is possible to restrict the number of addresses returned by the search and speed it up. To do this, we turn to the **Advanced** tab of our **Site Settings** dialog. Here you'll find two radio buttons which either set no limit or allow you restrict the returned results back to a number. By default, it is set to return a maximum of fifty addresses.

Logging On

Users of course won't notice what you have and haven't allowed OWA to access. Instead, they'll simply want to know how to get it running and begin. As we saw before, OWA installs itself in a virtual directory called `Exchange`. From the internet then, users may get started by pointing their browsers to `http://yourserver.yourdomain.com/exchange` or, if they're accessing it internally across a LAN, from `http://OWA_Machine/exchange`.

Either way, they'll see the following screen to log on.

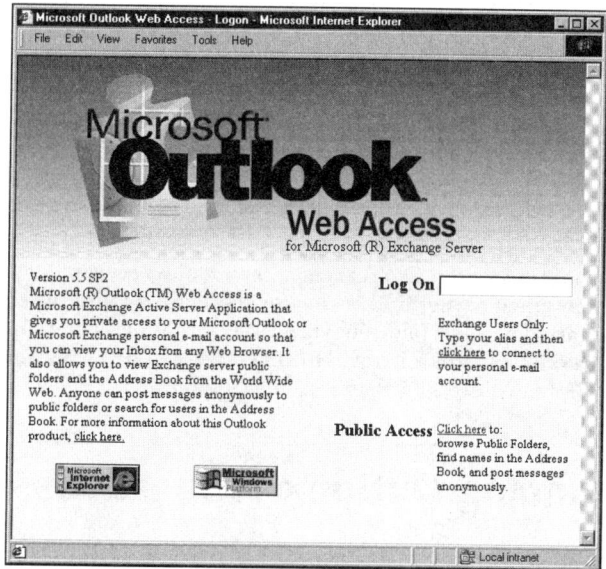

The default logon screen provides two methods to connect to Exchange server data. The lower one – Public Access – gives users anonymous access to Exchange. What exactly they see is dependant upon what you've set up following the config procedures we've outlined above.

The top one meanwhile – Log On – allows users to authenticate themselves and gain access to their personal mailbox. To do this they enter their mailbox alias in the text box and hit the Click here link. Depending on how IIS is set up to authenticate users, they will either be prompted with a windows NT logon dialog (if Basic Clear Text authentication is enabled) or will be passed straight along into the main Outlook Web Access screen.

> Note that if the logon dialog appears and the users' Windows NT accounts are in a different domain from the server running OWA, they'll need to enter their Windows NT account in the form **Domain\UserID**.

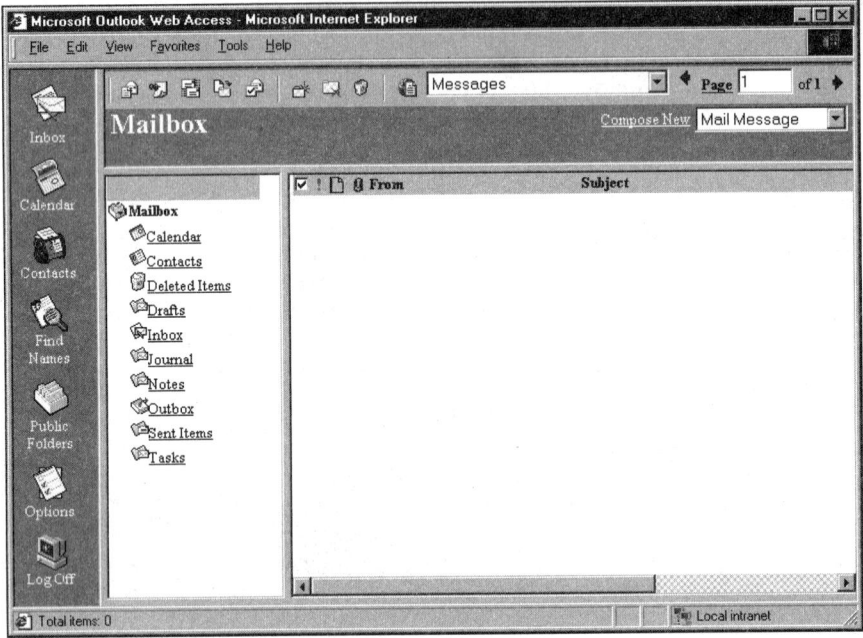

As you can see, the OWA main screen looks very similar to the Outlook 9x/2000 client interface but as mentioned earlier in this chapter there are a lot of differences. While an Outlook 9x/2000 like navigation bar and folder navigation is implemented an option to browse the Exchange server Global Address List is still missing. However, we will discuss a simple enhancement to enable us to browse the Global Address List later in this chapter.

Enhancing Outlook Web Access

Now we have a pretty good idea of Outlook Web Access' capabilities and limitations, we can take a look at how to modify and enhance some of its functionality without breaking it. Specifically, we'll be taking a look at how to:

❑ Personalize the OWA log on and log off screen.

❑ Browse the Global Address List and display the details of an entry when selected.

It doesn't sound much, but will demonstrate well each concept we've learnt in the previous chapters about using the CDO Rendering library.

Personalizing the Log On Screen

One of the most requested modifications to OWA is to change the log on and log off pages to include a company logo. Not that difficult, providing you know where to look. The files in question are called `logon.asp` and `logoff.asp`, which you'll find in `C:\Exchsrvr\WEBDATA\USA`. The code for displaying the OWA logo in both pages is the same and looks like this:

```
<BODY BACKGROUND="back.jpg" BGCOLOR="#ffff99"
    TEXT="#000000" LINK="#000000" VLINK="#000000">

<TABLE CELLSPACING="0" CELLPADDING="0" BORDER="0">
<TR>
    <TD VALIGN=TOP ROWSPAN="2">
        <A HREF="http://www.microsoft.com/outlook" ALT="Microsoft Outlook">
            <IMG SRC="part1.gif" ALIGN=LEFT HSPACE=0 VSPACE=0 BORDER=0
                WIDTH=273 HEIGHT=188 ALT="Microsoft Outlook"></A></TD>
    <TD VALIGN=TOP>
        <A HREF="http://www.microsoft.com/outlook" ALT="Microsoft Outlook">
            <IMG SRC="part2.gif" ALIGN=LEFT HSPACE=0 VSPACE=0 BORDER=0
                WIDTH=296 HEIGHT=169 ALT="Microsoft Outlook"></A></TD></TR>
<TR>
    <TD>for Microsoft (R) Exchange Server</TD></TR>
</TABLE>
```

The remainder of the page actually doesn't matter – we're more concerned with the two `<IMG>` tags at the top of the table that correspond to the OWA logos. If we changed the above code to read, say

```
<BODY TEXT="#000000" LINK="#000000" VLINK="#000000">
<P> </P>

<TABLE CELLSPACING="0" CELLPADDING="0" BORDER="0" WIDTH="100%">
<TR>
    <TD VALIGN=middle>
        <IMG BORDER="0" SRC="company.gif"></TD>
    <TD VALIGN=middle></TD></TR>
<TR>
    <TD VALIGN=middle></TD>
    <TD VALIGN=middle>
        <FONT FACE="Arial Black">
            The Premier Resource for Microsoft Collaboration Data Objects
        </FONT></TD></TR>
<TR>
    <TD VALIGN=middle ROWSPAN="2" COLSPAN="2">
        <P><FONT FACE="Arial Black" SIZE="7">
             E-Mail Web Access  - Logon Page
        </FONT></P></TD></TR>
</TABLE>
```

we would have a brand new logon screen with a different background color and new logos that looks like this.

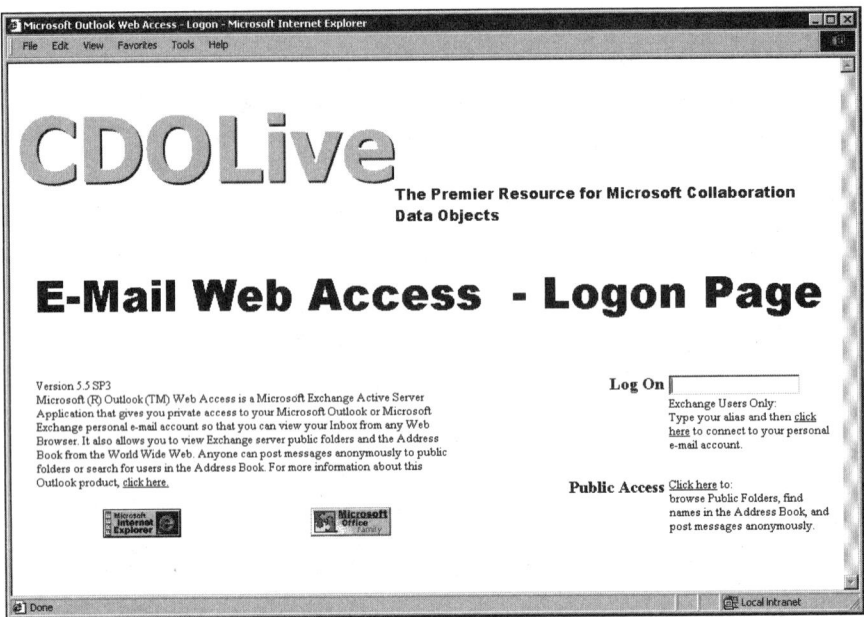

To complete the modifications, we could make the same changes to `logoff.asp` as we have in `logon.asp`, not forgetting of course to change the one line that says 'Logon Page' to 'Logoff Page'.

As you can see, it really is easy to modify the default logon/off screens. But, always keep in mind that Microsoft does not support this and that any service packs you install on top of this will erase all your changes.

Browsing the Global Address List

Our second modification to OWA takes into account the fact we noticed earlier that although we can run searches against the Global Address List, we cannot just browse it. To resolve this problem, we're going to make full use of our newfound CDO Renderer knowledge, modifying one page and creating two new ones from scratch and incorporating them into OWA as follows:

- ❑ First, add a button to the OWA navigation bar on the left that points to the browser.
- ❑ Second, create a `ContainerRenderer` page that displays the entries in the GAL.
- ❑ Third, create an `ObjectRenderer` page that displays an entry's details once we've selected it from our other page.

Bearing in mind that service packs will erase all our hard work, we'll create a new directory called `GALBROWSE` and store in it all the files needed to run the enhancement to display the Global Address List, including images etc. This will give us an easy way to back up those files before a new service pack is applied and we can restore this functionality later by just adding the appropriate change to the left hand navigation bar and copying the `GALBROWSE` folder back into the same place.

Modifying the OWA Navbar

Our first task then is to modify the left hand navigation bar to link to our GAL browser. The files that govern the navbar can be found in the `C:\Exchsrvr\Webdata\USA\Navbar` folder. In particular, it's `nbinbox.asp` that contains the navigation bar for authenticated access and `nbanon.asp` the navigation bar for anonymous access. The modification is the same for both files, so let's take `nbinbox.asp` and open it up in your preferred HTML/ASP editor.

You'll find that the navbar is a simple table with one row per button. All we need to do is add another row with the following code.

```
<!-- Browse GAL -->
<TR ALIGN=center>
   <TD NOWRAP>
   <A HREF="JavaScript:openNewWindow
        ('<%=bstrVirtRoot%>/galbrowse/root.asp', 'GALWindow',850,500)">
   <IMG SRC="../galbrowse/gal.gif" WIDTH=32 HEIGHT=32
        ALT="Browse GAL" BORDER=0><BR>
   <DIV ALIGN=center><FONT <%=bstrFace%> SIZE=2 COLOR=White>
        Browse<BR>Global<BR>Address<BR>List
   </FONT></DIV></A>
   </TD>
</TR>
```

In the example below, we inserted this code between the `<!-- Find Names -->` and the `<!-- Public Folders -->` sections of the code to produce the following results onscreen.

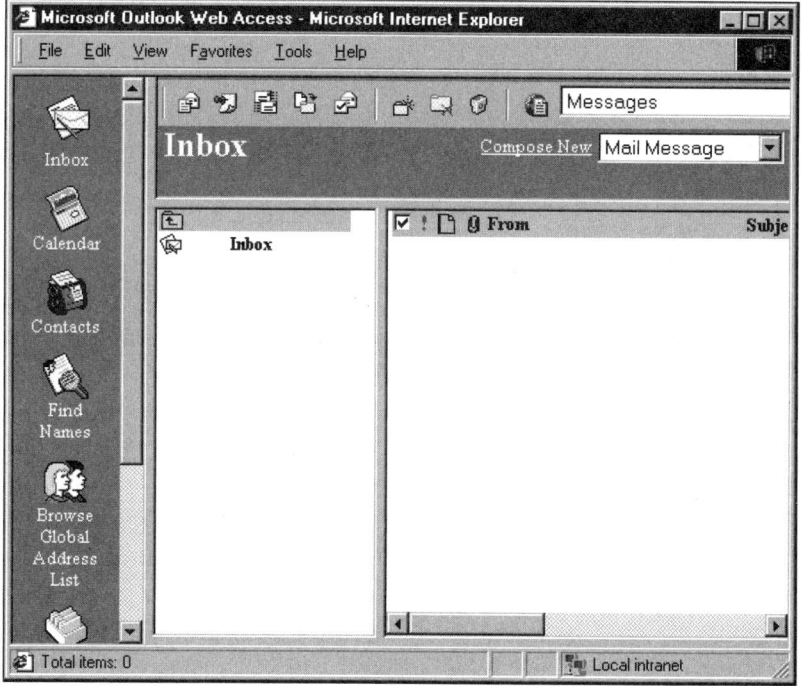

As you can see, we now have a handy icon and descriptive text in the navbar that link to our browser pages. All we need to do now is construct them.

Building The Address List Browser

The first page to tackle will be the one to render the Global Address List using a custom `ContainerRenderer` as described in Chapters 9 to 11, but modified slightly to work in OWA. The keen-eyed among you will have noted that our navbar addendum contains a link to a page called `root.asp` in the `GALBROWSE` folder and this is exactly what we're going to build now.

Note that all the code and graphics for this chapter and indeed for the book are available to download from the Wrox website at `http://www.wrox.com`.

So then, open a new file in your editor of choice and save it as `root.asp` in your `C:\exchsrvr\WEBDATA\USA\GALBROWSE` folder or equivalent. The code here is dependent on include files that have installed with OWA for authentication and a few other routines, so make sure to check the links where appropriate if you're saving this file elsewhere.

```
<% @ LANGUAGE=VBSCRIPT CODEPAGE = 1252 %>
<!--#include file="../constant.inc" -->
<!--#include file="../lib/session.inc" -->
<%
    On Error Resume Next
```

The constants below are the CDO and MAPI properties we'll need for our page. You can find a full list of CDO and MAPI properties in Appendix B under the heading **CdoPropTags**.

```
Const CdoAddressListGAL = 0
Const CdoPR_DISPLAY_NAME = &H3001001F
Const CdoPR_BUSINESS_TELEPHONE_NUMBER = &H3A08001F
Const CdoPR_OFFICE_LOCATION = &H3A19001F
Const CdoPR_TITLE = &H3A17001F
Const CdoPR_COMPANY_NAME = &H3A16001F
Const CdoPR_DISPLAY_TYPE = &H39000003
```

Next we declare and initialize the variables we'll need later on in our script. These are the same as those used in previous chapters to create a `ContainerRenderer` object and customize a view within it.

```
Dim objRenderApplication
Dim objAddressList
Dim objAddressEntries
Dim objCustomView
Dim objColumns
Dim objColumn
Dim objFormat
Dim objPatterns
Dim objPattern

Dim intRenderingClass
Dim intStyle
```

```
        Dim intCurrentPage
        Dim intMaxPage
        Dim intNewPage

        Set objRenderApplication = Nothing
        Set objOMSession = Nothing
        Set objAddressList = Nothing
        Set objAddressEntries = Nothing
        Set objCustomView = Nothing
        Set objColumns = Nothing
        Set objColumn = Nothing
        Set objFormat = Nothing
        Set objPatterns = Nothing
        Set objPattern = Nothing

        intRenderingClass = 3
        intStyle = 1
        intCurrentPage = 1
```

The next three variables are taken out of OWA and used to make sure our custom pages use the same color scheme.

```
        bcGrayM = "#c0c0c0"
        bcGray = "#909090"
        bcGrayD = "#707070"
```

Because OWA can either run with authenticated or anonymous access we need to use this OWA code to check the session state. Handily, OWA provides a function called CheckSession in session.inc that does just that.

```
        CheckSession
```

Our new file will be called with a parameter called page attached to the URL. For example, root.asp?page="2". This parameter includes the current page (set of address entries) that the ContainerRenderer object should display. If page is not set to anything in the URL, then we'll display page 1 of the GAL. If it is set, we'll return whatever page it specifies.

```
        intNewPage = Request.QueryString("page")
        If intNewPage <> "" Then
            intCurrentPage = intNewPage
        End If
```

Now we need to obtain the already existing instance of the RenderingApplication object. OWA stores this object in the ASP application variable bstrRenderApp:

```
        Set objRenderApplication = Application(bstrRenderApp)
```

The next lines are again taken out of OWA and are used to check if access to the Global Address List is enabled in the Exchange admin console as described earlier in this chapter. Otherwise the same error message used in the Find User option of OWA is displayed.

```
If objRenderApplication.ConfigParameter("Publish GAL") = False And _
    Session(bstrAuthenticated) = False Then
    ReportErrorClose L_errPageDisabled_ErrorMessage
End If
```

Note that the objOMSession variable used below is an object variable used by OWA and we don't need to explicitly dim it because it is dimmed already in the include file session.inc.

```
Set objAddressList = objOMSession.GetAddressList(CdoAddressListGAL)
Set objAddressEntries = objAddressList.AddressEntries
```

Following the formula for creating a custom view that we've seen in the last couple of chapters, we'll need to define a View ('CustomView') and then Patterns and Columns within it.

First then, we'll set up a ContainerRenderer, and define the Patterns for the Display Type property.

```
Set objAddressList = objOMSession.GetAddressList(CdoAddressListGAL)
Set objAddressEntries = objAddressList.AddressEntries

Set objContainerRenderer = _
                    objRenderApplication.CreateRenderer(intRenderingClass)
objContainerRenderer.DataSource = objAddressEntries

Set objCustomView = objContainerRenderer.Views.Add("CustomView")
Set objColumns = objCustomView.Columns

Set objFormat = objContainerRenderer.Formats.Add(CdoPR_DISPLAY_TYPE, Null)
Set objPatterns = objFormat.Patterns

Set objPattern = objPatterns.Add(0, "")
Set objPattern = objPatterns.Add(1, _
            "<img src='pubdl.gif' width='16' height='16' border='0'>")
Set objPattern = objPatterns.Add(2, _
            "<img src='pfolder.gif' width='16' height='16' border='0'>")
Set objPattern = objPatterns.Add(3, _
            "<img src='agent.gif' width='16' height='16' border='0'>")
Set objPattern = objPatterns.Add(4, _
            "<img src='hdesk.gif' width='16' height='16' border='0'>")
Set objPattern = objPatterns.Add(5, _
            "<img src='privdl.gif' width='16' height='16' border='0'>")
Set objPattern = objPatterns.Add(6, _
            "<img src='custom.gif' width='16' height='16' border='0'>")
```

With the patterns done, we'll go straight onto adding in the columns to be displayed in our view. For each entry in the GAL, we'll see the type of entry, its display name, phone number, office, title and company name.

```
Set objColumn = objColumns.Add(" ", CdoPR_DISPLAY_TYPE, 2, 8 , 1)
Set objColumn = objColumns.Add("Display Name", _
                               CdoPR_Display_NAME, 30, 0 , 2)
Set objColumn = objColumns.Add("Phone", _
                               CdoPR_BUSINESS_TELEPHONE_NUMBER, 20, 32 , 3)
Set objColumn = objColumns.Add("Office", CdoPR_OFFICE_LOCATION, 15, 32 , 4)
Set objColumn = objColumns.Add("Title", CdoPR_TITLE, 15, 32 , 5)
Set objColumn = objColumns.Add("Company", CdoPR_COMPANY_NAME, 20, 32 , 6)
```

To activate the view, we'll define it as the default view and set the `LinkPattern` property. This will provide us with the template HTML link for each address entry to our second custom page which will display the full details of the entry.

```
objContainerRenderer.CurrentView = objCustomView
objContainerRenderer.LinkPattern = _
    "<A HREF='JavaScript:parent.openNewWindow (""details.asp?obj=%obj%"", _
    ""%obj%"", 600, 400)'>%value%</A>"
```

Now we make sure that the table formation of the Global Address List looks similar to the OWA interface using the following code.

```
objContainerRenderer.HeadingCellPattern = _
    "<FONT FACE='Arial, Helvetica, sans-serif' SIZE='2'><B>%value%</B></FONT>"
objContainerRenderer.HeadingRowPrefix =
    "<TR VALIGN='top' BGCOLOR='#C0C0C0'>"
objContainerRenderer.HeadingRowSuffix = "</TR>"

objContainerRenderer.CellPattern = _
    "<FONT FACE='Arial, Helvetica, sans-serif' SIZE='-1'>%value%</FONT>"
objContainerRenderer.RowPrefix = "<TR VALIGN='middle' BGCOLOR='#FFFFFF'>"
objContainerRenderer.RowSuffix = "</TR>"
```

To reduce the amount of data received when the `ContainerRenderer` is invoked we'll limit it to 15 entries per page. At this point we'll also work out how many pages the `ContainerRenderer` object will use to render the entire GAL.

```
    objContainerRenderer.RowsPerPage = 15
    intMaxPage = 1 + _
            ((objAddressEntries.Count - 1) \ objContainerRenderer.RowsPerPage)
%>

<!DOCTYPE HTML PUBLIC "-//IETF//DTD HTML 3.2//EN">
<HTML>
<HEAD>
    <TITLE>Global Address List</TITLE>
```

Again, we're using an include file provided by OWA to provide some JavaScript utility functions for our HTML.

```
    <!--#include file="../lib/jsutil.inc" -->
</HEAD>
<BODY BGCOLOR="white">
<DIV ALIGN="center">
```

And now we invoke the `ContainerRenderer` to render (some of) the GAL in HTML.

```
<%
    objContainerRenderer.Render intStyle, intCurrentPage, 0, Response
%>
</DIV>
```

All that's left is to provide a way to walk forward and backward through the GAL. We'll do this with two JavaScript functions, `PreviousPage()` and `NextPage()`, which make use of the `page` parameter in the URL we saw earlier to change pages.

```
<SCRIPT language = "Javascript">
    var CurrentPage = eval(<%= intCurrentPage %>);
    var MaxPage = eval(<%= intMaxPage %>);

    function PreviousPage()
    {
       if (CurrentPage == 1)
       {
          alert('You are already at the beginning of the list');
       }
       else
       {
          CurrentPage = CurrentPage - 1;
          self.location = "root.asp?page="+CurrentPage;
       }
    }

    function NextPage()
    {
       if (CurrentPage >= MaxPage)
       {
          alert('You are already at the end of the list');
       }
       else
       {
          CurrentPage = CurrentPage + 1;
          self.location = "root.asp?page="+CurrentPage;
       }
    }
</SCRIPT>
```

```
<P>
<DIV ALIGN="center">
<CENTER>
    <TABLE BORDER="0" CELLPADDING="4" CELLSPACING="4" WIDTH="80%">
        <TD COLSPAN="4" ALIGN="middle">
            <INPUT TYPE="button" VALUE="Previous Page" onClick="PreviousPage()">
            <INPUT TYPE="button" VALUE="Close" onClick="parent.close()">
            <INPUT TYPE="button" VALUE="Next Page" onClick="NextPage()">
        </TD>
    </TABLE></CENTER>
</DIV>
</BODY>
</HTML>
```

And that's it. If you go ahead and save `root.asp`, when you next click on the Browse Global Address List option in the OWA navigation bar, you should see something like this.

Each of the display names is a hyperlink that follows the `linkpattern` property we set to a page showing all the details for the entry. It's this page that is our final task in this modification.

Displaying the Details of a Selected GAL Item

Because an `AddressEntry` item, which is effectively what we wish to render in this page is not a container object itself, this page will need to define a custom `ObjectRenderer` object. Again, we've already covered how to do this in previous chapters, so it should present no problems for you.

The file we're going to create is a slightly modified version of the built-in OWA file `details.asp` used by the Find Users option to display the details of a Global Address List address entry. You can find it in the `C:\Exchsrvr\Webdata\USA\Finduser` directory if you're curious. We can use it with a slight modification to remove the option to send a message to the selected address entry.

Create a new file in your editor and save the following code as `details.asp` in the GALBROWSE directory. You'll note once again that the code here is dependant on include files that have been installed with OWA, so make sure to alter the links where appropriate if you're saving this file elsewhere.

```
<% @ LANGUAGE=VBSCRIPT CODEPAGE = 1252 %>
<!--#include file="../constant.inc" -->
<!--#include file="../lib/session.inc" -->
<% SendHeader 1, 1 %>
<!--#include file="../lib/getrend.inc" -->
<%
    On Error Resume Next
```

Again, we'll use `CheckSession` to check if a valid CDO session, either authenticated or anonymous, exists. If one doesn't exist, it will be created automatically. We'll also retrieve the current `RenderingApplication` object that is being stored in an application variable by OWA.

```
    CheckSession

    bcGrayM = "#c0c0c0"
    bcGray = "#909090"
    bcGrayD = "#707070"

    set objRenderApp = Application( bstrRenderApp )
```

The next lines are also taken from OWA and are used to check if access to the Global Address List is enabled in the Exchange admin console as described earlier in this chapter. If not, the same error message used in the Find User option of OWA is displayed.

```
    If objRenderApp.ConfigParameter("Publish GAL") = False _
        And Session(bstrAuthenticated) = False Then
        ReportErrorClose L_errPageDisabled_ErrorMessage
    End If
```

Now we retrieve the `obj` variable that is passed by the `ContainerRenderer`'s `LinkPattern` property to determine which item is selected in the Global Address List and retrieve the selected address.

```
    strAddrEntryID = Request.QueryString("obj")
    Set objAddrEntry = objOMSession.GetAddressEntry(strAddrEntryID)
```

To make sure we have a valid item selected, we check that no error has been returned. If one has, we call a built-in error function and display a predefined (by OWA) error message to the user.

```
    If Err.Number <> 0 or objAddrEntry Is Nothing Then
        ReportErrorClose L_errOpeningAddressEntry_ErrorMessage
    End If
```

Finally we retrieve the `ObjectRenderer` and set the `DataSource` property to the selected address entry.

```
    Set objRender = GetObjectRenderer
    objRender.DataSource = objAddrEntry
%>


<!DOCTYPE HTML PUBLIC "-//IETF//DTD HTML 3.2//EN">
<HTML>
<HEAD>
    <TITLE>Detailed Information</TITLE>
```

Again, we are using an include file provided by OWA that provides some JavaScript utility functions.

```
    <!--#include file="../lib/jsutil.inc" -->
</HEAD>

<BODY BGCOLOR="white" TEXT="black" LINK="white" VLINK="white">
<FONT SIZE="3"><B>Details for:
<%
    objRender.RenderProperty ActMsgPR_DISPLAY_NAME, 0, Response
%>
</B></FONT>
```

The top bar creates the dark gray header that includes a link to close the details window.

```
<!-- Top Bar -->
<TABLE BORDER="0" CELLSPACING="0" CELLPADDING="0"
       WIDTH="100%" BGCOLOR="<%= bcGrayD %>">
<TR>
    <TD ALIGN="right" HEIGHT="20" VALIGN="center" COLSPAN="2" NOWRAP></TD>
    <TD ALIGN="right" HEIGHT="20" VALIGN="center" COLSPAN="1" NOWRAP>
        <A HREF="JavaScript:self.close()">
            <FONT FACE="<%=bstrFace%>" SIZE="2"><B>Close</B></FONT></A></TD>
</TR>
</TABLE>
```

With the preliminaries done, it's a matter now of creating rows in the table to display the various properties for the selected entry. In the first row, we'll display the addressee's name, a concatenation of First and Surname, where applicable.

```
<!-- First and Surname -->
<TABLE BORDER="0" CELLSPACING="0" CELLPADDING="6"
       WIDTH="100%" BGCOLOR="<%=bcGrayM%>">
<TR>
    <TD WIDTH="25%" VALIGN="baseline" ALIGN="right">
        <FONT SIZE="2"><B> Name: </B></FONT></TD>
    <TD WIDTH="25%" VALIGN="baseline" COLSPAN="3"><FONT SIZE="2">
    <%
        bstrFirstName = objAddrEntry.Fields.Item(ActMsgPR_GIVEN_NAME)
        bstrLastName = objAddrEntry.Fields.Item(ActMsgPR_SURNAME)
```

```
        If L_LastNameFirst_Number = 0 Then
            bstrName = bstrFirstName + " " + bstrLastName
        Else
            bstrName = bstrLastName + " " + bstrFirstName
        End If
        objRender.Write bstrName, Response
    %>
    </FONT></TD></TR>
```

Next up come the mailbox alias and the addressee's telephone number.

```
    <!-- Mailbox Alias and Telephone Number -->
    <TR>
        <TD WIDTH="25%" VALIGN="baseline" ALIGN="right" WIDTH="25%">
            <FONT SIZE="2"><B> Alias: </B></FONT></TD>
        <TD WIDTH="25%" VALIGN="baseline" COLSPAN="1"><FONT SIZE="2">
        <%
            objRender.RenderProperty ActMsgPR_ACCOUNT, 0, Response
        %>
        </FONT></TD>
        <TD WIDTH="25%" VALIGN="baseline" ALIGN="right">
            <FONT SIZE="2"><B> Phone: </B></FONT></TD>
        <TD WIDTH="25%" VALIGN="baseline" COLSPAN="1"><FONT SIZE="2">
        <%
            objRender.RenderProperty _
                                ActMsgPR_BUSINESS_TELEPHONE_NUMBER, 0, Response
        %>
        </FONT></TD></TR>
```

Now comes the account's display name.

```
    <!-- Account Display Name -->
    <TR>
        <TD WIDTH="25%" VALIGN="baseline" ALIGN="right">
            <FONT SIZE="2"><B> Display Name: </B></FONT></TD>
        <TD VALIGN="top" ALIGN="left" COLSPAN="3"><FONT SIZE="2">
        <%
            objRender.RenderProperty ActMsgPR_DISPLAY_NAME, 0, Response
        %>
        </FONT></TD></TR>
```

At this point, we have to deal with the issue of whether or not the selected entry was a distribution list.

```
    <%
        If objAddrEntry.DisplayType = 1 Then
    %>
    </TABLE>
```

If it is a distribution list, we'll need to check if the number of GAL entries we can display is restricted. We'll use the code from Find User's `details.asp` to deal with this situation in the same manner.

```
<%
        nPubLimit = objRenderApp.ConfigParameter("Publish GAL Limit")
        ' No limit enforced by DSA

        If CStr(nPubLimit) = "" Then
           nPubLimit = 9999
        End If
```

If we can't display the individual details for each member of the list then we'll put up a polite notice to that effect. If we can, then we do.

```
        If objAddrEntry.Members.Count > nPubLimit Then
%>
            <STRONG>This query would return too many addresses!</STRONG><BR>
<%
        Else
%>

<TABLE VALIGN="top" BORDER="0" CELLSPACING="0" CELLPADDING="0" WIDTH="100%">
<TR VALIGN="middle" BGCOLOR="330000">
    <TD ALIGN="left" VALIGN="middle" NOWRAP COLSPAN="5"></TD></TR>
<TR BGCOLOR="#c0c0c0">
    <TD WIDTH="40%"><B><FONT SIZE="2"> Name </FONT></B></TD>
    <TD WIDTH="14%"><B><FONT SIZE="2"> Alias </FONT><B></TD>
    <TD WIDTH="14%"><B><FONT SIZE="2"> Department </FONT></B></TD>
    <TD WIDTH="14%"><B><FONT SIZE="2"> Office </FONT></B></TD>
    <TD WIDTH="18%"><B><FONT SIZE="2"> Phone </FONT></B></TD></TR>
</TABLE>
<FONT SIZE="2">
<%
    objRender.RenderProperty ActMsgPR_CONTAINER_CONTENTS, False, Response
%>
</FONT>

<%
        End If
```

If the entry is not a distribution list, we'll continue building our table of entry details. First the job title and manager of the addressee.

```
    Else
%>

<!-- Job Title and Manager -->
<TR>
    <TD WIDTH="25%" ALIGN="right">
        <FONT SIZE="2"><B> Title: </B></FONT></TD>
    <TD WIDTH="25%" VALIGN="baseline" ALIGN="left" COLSPAN="1"><FONT SIZE="2">
    <%
```

```
        objRender.RenderProperty ActMsgPR_TITLE, 0, Response
    %>
    </FONT></TD>
    <TD WIDTH="25%" VALIGN="baseline" ALIGN="right">
        <FONT SIZE="2"><B> Manager: </B></FONT></TD>
    <TD WIDTH="25%" VALIGN="baseline" ALIGN="left" COLSPAN="1">
        <FONT COLOR="black" SIZE="2" FACE="<%=bstrFace%>">
        <%
            objRender.Write objAddrEntry.Manager.Name, Response
        %>
        </FONT></TD></TR>
```

Now their office and department.

```
<!-- Office and Department -->
<TR>
    <TD ALIGN="right"><FONT SIZE="2"><B> Office: </B></FONT></TD>
    <TD><FONT SIZE="2">
    <%
        objRender.RenderProperty ActMsgPR_OFFICE_LOCATION, 0, Response
    %>
    </FONT></TD>
    <TD ALIGN="right"><FONT SIZE="2"><B> Department: </B></FONT></TD>
    <TD><FONT SIZE="2">
    <%
        objRender.RenderProperty ActMsgPR_DEPARTMENT_NAME, 0, Response
    %>
    </FONT></TD></TR>
```

The company they work for and the city they're based in.

```
<!-- Company and City -->
<TR>
    <TD ALIGN="right"><FONT SIZE="2"><B> Company: </B></FONT></TD>
    <TD><FONT SIZE="2">
    <%
        objRender.RenderProperty ActMsgPR_COMPANY_NAME, 0, Response
    %>
    </FONT></TD>
    <TD ALIGN="right"><FONT SIZE="2"><B> City: </B></FONT></TD>
    <TD><FONT SIZE="2">
    <%
        objRender.RenderProperty ActMsgPR_BUSINESS_ADDRESS_CITY, 0, Response
    %>
    </FONT></TD></TR>
```

And finally, the state and country in which they're situated.

```
<!-- State and Country -->
<TR>
    <TD ALIGN="right"><FONT SIZE="2"><B> State: </B></FONT></TD>
    <TD><FONT SIZE="2">
    <%
        objRender.RenderProperty _
                    ActMsgPR_BUSINESS_ADDRESS_STATE_OR_PROVINCE, 0, Response
    %>
    </FONT></TD>
    <TD ALIGN="right"><FONT SIZE="2"><B> Country: </B></FONT></TD>
    <TD><FONT SIZE="2">
    <%
        objRender.RenderProperty ActMsgPR_BUSINESS_ADDRESS_COUNTRY, 0, Response
    %>
    </FONT></TD></TR>
</TABLE>
```

With the details over, all that remains is for us to list this entry's e-mail addresses and end the page.

```
<!-- Email addresses -->
<TABLE BGCOLOR="white" BORDER="0" CELLSPACING="1" CELLPADDING="2" WIDTH="100%">
<TR BGCOLOR=" <%=bcGray%> ">
    <TD WIDTH="100%">
        <FONT COLOR="white" SIZE="2"><B> Email Addresses<BR></B></FONT></TD></TR>
<%
        EmailAddresses = objAddrEntry.Fields.Item(ActMsgPR_EMS_AB_PROXY_ADDRESSES)
        Count = UBound(EmailAddresses)
        For i = LBound(EmailAddresses) To Count
%>
<TR>
    <TD>[ <% objRender.Write EmailAddresses(i), Response %>] </TD></TR>
<%
        Next
%>
</TABLE>
<%
    End If
%>

</BODY>
</HTML>
```

Once you've saved `details.asp`, if you now click on one of the display names a new window is opened and the details of the selected address entry are displayed. For example:

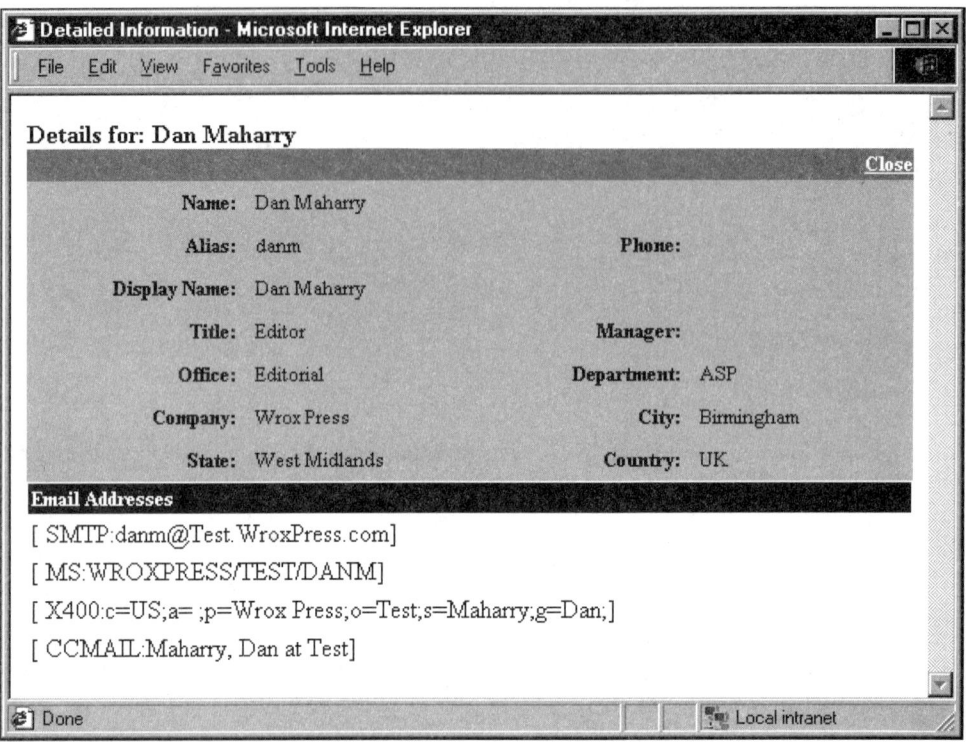

And that's it for this modification. We've one more to look at in this chapter and, handily, it involves us writing no code at all.

Accessing Public Folders Directly

One useful trick that OWA has up its sleeve but which not many know about is that you can access Exchange's public folders through a single URL without the need to go through a log on page first. This functionality is actually built into OWA's 'homepage', `root.asp`; the trick is simply to call it having attached five parameters to it in your HTML. These cover the logon method, the view used to display the folder content and a mode to determine if the standard OWA toolbar and folder picker are to be displayed.

The form the URL should take then is as follows:

```
http:\\OWA_Machine\exchange\root.asp?obj=...&store=...&view=...&acs=...&mode=...
```

where each parameter should take a value according to the following table. Note that all of these parameters must be passed to `root.asp`. None are optional.

Parameter	Description
Obj	The entry ID of the particular public folder. See below for how to obtain this.
Store	0 = Private Information Store 1 = Public Information Store
View	1 = Messages 2 = Unread Messages 3 = By Sender 4 = By Subject 5 = By Conversation Topic 6 = Unread by Conversation Topic
Acs	anon = Anonymous access auth = Authenticated access
Mode	0 = Message frame, folder picker and toolbar 1 = Message frame and folder picker 2 = Message frame 3 = Message frame and toolbar

The easiest way to obtain the public folder entry ID for the `obj` parameter is through OWA itself. Simply navigate to the public folder you want to link to and hit the "Update Page Address"

button – – in the Outlook Web Access toolbar. This will expose the public folder entry ID in

the URL of the browser's address bar and you can cut and paste it into your own HTML.

The entry ID is a very long hex string, so be careful to cut and paste it all, otherwise your link won't work. It might also be a good idea to hide the entire link to your public folder using another file like the one below. At the very least, it makes your own code easier to read. If you also force the address bar to disappear, you can prevent the entry ID from being seen by the client. Simply link to this file first and then it will redirect the browser to the public folder view.

```
<HTML>
<META HTTP-EQUIV="REFRESH" CONTENT="0;
URL=/exchange/root.asp?obj=000000001A447390AA6611CD9BC800AA002FC45A0300E4193D0DB73
FD31196D500001C0891E40000000098910000&store=1&view=5&acs=anon&mode=3">
</HTML>
```

Note that the entry ID above is only a sample to show you how to create the appropriate file. You'll still need to obtain your own folder's entry IDs using the method described above.

Summary

In this chapter we have seen how Outlook Web Access works and how we can customize and enhance it without being an advanced developer. Furthermore, we've seen how to put our knowledge of the CDO Rendering library to good use by making those enhancements.

Now that we've seen what we can do with both the CDO and CDO Rendering libraries using both Visual Basic and ASP scripts, the next chapter looks at a more advanced case study in ASP.

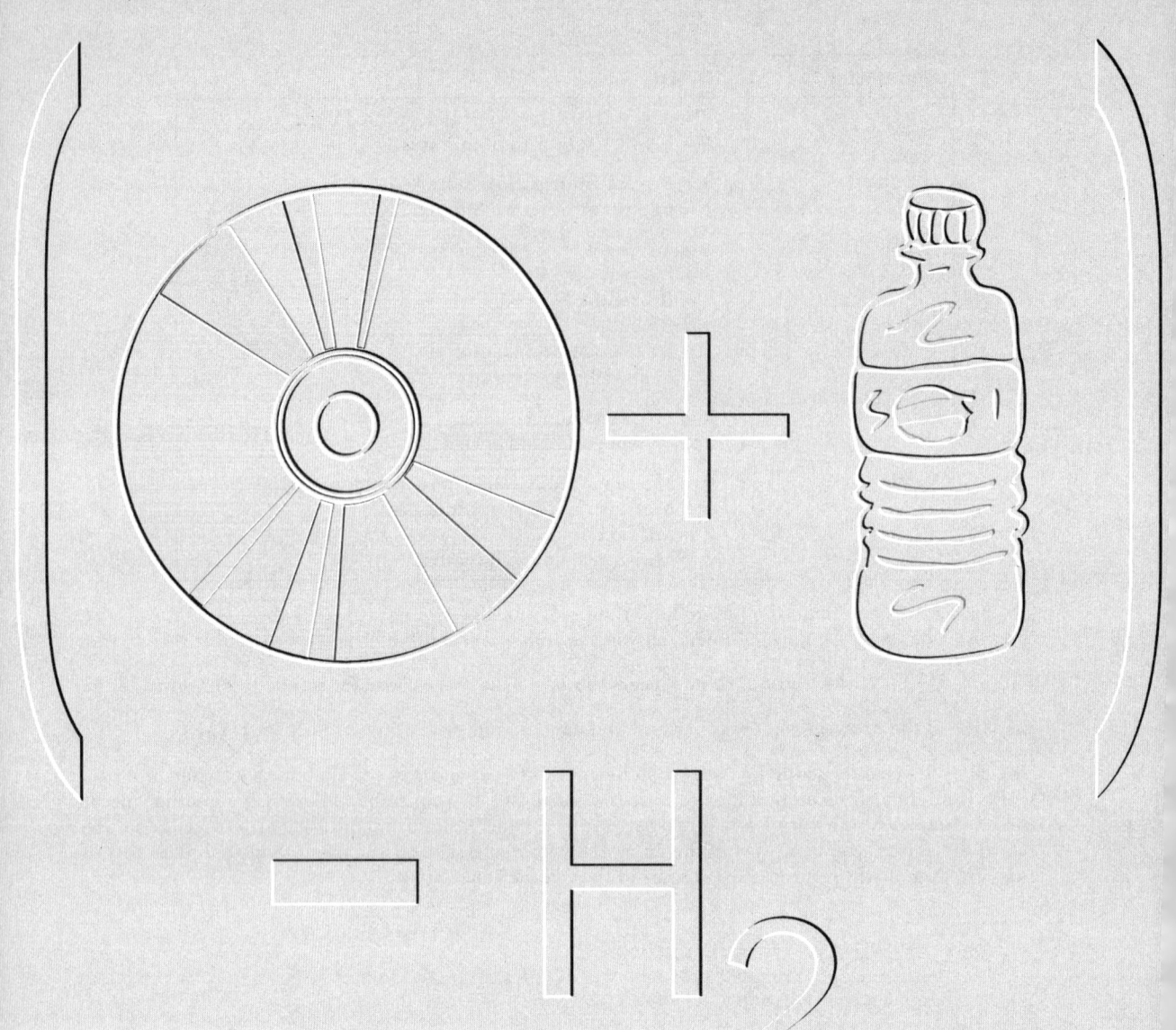

13

Case Study: People Finder

If you've got this far, then congratulations, you should now know the ins and outs of both the CDO and CDO Rendering object models. Time for another case study then. Taking on board the ideas introduced by the previous chapter's modifications to Outlook Web Access, in this case study we'll develop a standalone application that makes use of the CDO Rendering library.

At this early point in the chapter, it should be pointed out that the code contained herein is available as part of the download available at http://www.wrox.com *which accompanies the book.*

The Background

Invisible Inc. have a corporate intranet, but they are finding it difficult to keep up to date the contact details for their staff, because of the costs involved in maintaining the information when it is stored in so many different places. For example:

- ❏ **Human Resources** keep contact details in their records, which are updated only when they are notified of a change, and this usually occurs only when they instigate a change.

- ❏ **Reception** maintain a contact details list, which is again only updated when they are notified, this is usually when calls keep coming through to a person who is no longer at a location.

- ❏ **Various colleagues** keep scraps of contact information about each other in diaries, mobile phones, on personal digital assistants etc.

Invisible Inc. consequently decided to use one source for this information and just to keep that up to date, as the ultimate contact details information source. They decided to standardize the information they store in the Exchange mailboxes so that it becomes a single people contact point for e-mail, fax, and phone details.

They have a single intranet server, which hosts IIS, SQL Server, and Site Server. They also have an Exchange Server that they use just for e-mail. As the company grows, more people are starting to work remotely, so Invisible Inc decided to use Outlook Web Access. With IIS on the same machine as their Exchange Server, they have a number of options for making the information stored in Exchange available via a web interface, and more importantly via their intranet.

While in the office, there will be two options for accessing this information, via the Outlook client, or via the web interface of the corporate intranet. While out of the office, it will be possible to connect via the Outlook client providing there is a reasonable RAS connection, but it is anticipated that the most common method of accessing such data while off site is via the web interface.

This case study will take you through the process Invisible Inc. went through to get the information from Exchange on to the intranet to create the "People Finder" application.

The Structure

The code used in the case study is implemented as a small collection of ASP/VBScript files and some supporting include files. Much of the functionality would benefit from being component-based if the number of users becomes very large, and/or the application is expected to get a large number of hits.

As it stands, it would be very easy to put the code into a component-based solution, but for this case study the simplest way of demonstrating the concept, and the best way of exposing the concept to wider audience with as little "catch-up" as possible, is by writing the code in ASP.

> *This case study assumes you are familiar with VBScript, Active Server Pages, and Internet Information Server 4 or above.*

As mentioned in the introduction, the application will sit on the server running Exchange, and be linked to from the corporate intranet. In this way, the company has pushed one of its knowledge bases past the boundaries of its intranet server. As a consequence, this knowledge will remain available even if the application fails. It also has the attraction of being very easy to set up – it's Exchange-independent so 'installing' it is a case of copying the code to a directory on the server, making sure the directory is available through IIS and setting anonymous and basic authentication security on the folder only. On the software side, the application has the same dependencies as Outlook Web Access, i.e. Exchange Server 5.5 and upward, and Internet Information Server 4 and upward.

The structure of the application is quite simple. In the root are all the functional files, a few common include files, plus `global.asa`. If you are confident with CDO (which, given you're reading this book, you should be) and want to extend this application into an enterprise environment then the application should be placed in a virtual directory off the intranet server. A problem arises however when deciding what to do with the application's initialization routines in `global.asa`. One option is to copy its constants into the main `global.asa` at the root of the server. Unfortunately, this undermines the application somewhat, reducing its scalability and independence from the intranet server. This is where a more "component-based" solution may help.

Finding People...

As the application is about finding out about people, the first requirement is to have a facility for finding the people in the first place.

There are two ways we are going to make this possible:

❑ By browsing the Global Address List

❑ By searching the Global Address List

As you can see from the following screenshot, our application has two areas to do just that. The main table lists the entries in the GAL just as the extension to Outlook Web Access did in the previous chapter. Around two of its sides are the search functions. This is set up as a frameset that we define in our default page, `default.asp`.

At the top of the screen is a simple form that allows you to search against any of the attributes featured in the main table – Name, Department, Office, etc. – and a value for it. If any people are found in the GAL that match your criteria then they will be listed in the table below the form. You can find the code for it in `title.asp`.

In addition to the search form, on the right-hand side is a column of letters from the alphabet that is generated by `rolodex.asp`. By clicking on a letter, a list of people is returned with the first letter of their first name matching the letter you selected. Again, this list is presented in the main table area as drawn by `address.asp`.

You can get a more visual idea of the layout from the screenshot below.

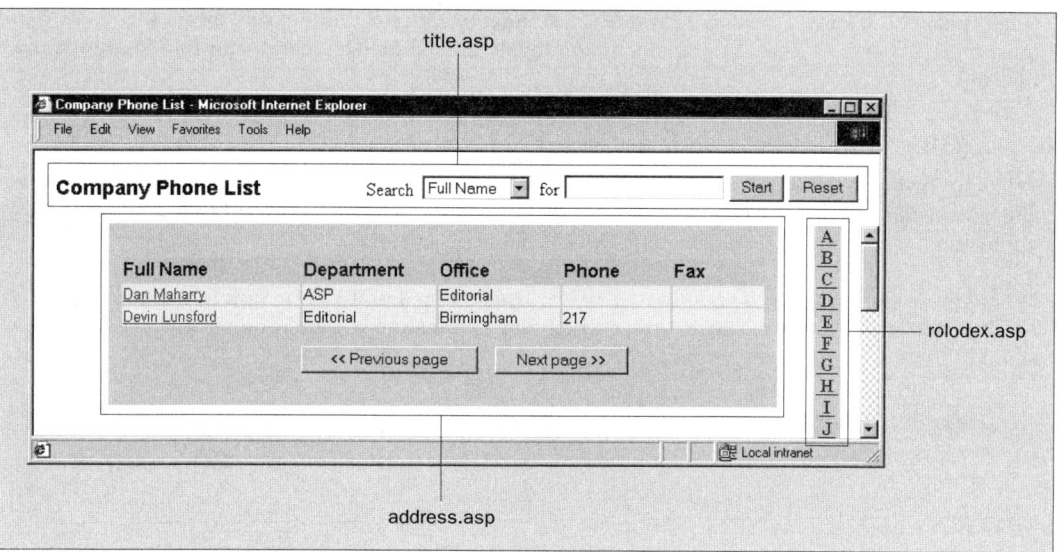

... And Viewing Their Details

Each address entry displayed in the main table contains a link. Following this link takes a user to the Personal Details page, `details.asp` that lists the information about that person. Like the page we created for Outlook Web Access in the previous chapter this contains many more personal details concerning the queried user. There's also a quick link to mail the person.

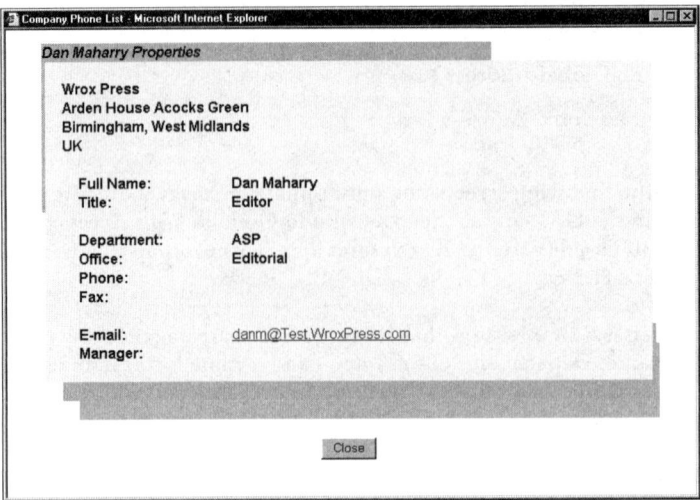

The Code

So then, to the code. Although most of the functionality is the same as the GALBROWSE extension to Outlook Web Access that we saw in the previous chapter, the work going on in the background is actually quite different. Consider that this is a standalone application not one inline with OWA and must create its own objects and impersonation levels. Also, both the search and rolodex functions are new too.

Global.asa

When an ASP application is first run under IIS, it goes to `global.asa` for its initialization routine. This file actually contains instructions for four key events – the beginning and termination of the application as a whole and the start and end of each user session.

When the application starts, `Application_OnStart` is called. Its basic task is to create the `RenderingApplication` object under which our application will be running and to exit gracefully should this go wrong.

```
<SCRIPT LANGUAGE=VBScript RUNAT=Server>
Sub Application_OnStart

    ' Create CDO HTML rendering application
    On Error Resume Next
    Set objRenderApp = Server.CreateObject("AMHTML.Application")

    ' Check for possible errors
    If Err.Number = 0 Then

        ' Create renderer application and CDO session object
        Set Application("RenderApplication") = objRenderApp
        Set Application("CDOAnonSession") = Nothing
    Else
```

```
        ' Display error description and number
        Application("startupFatal") = Err.Number
        Application("startupFatalDescription") = _
           "Failed to create application object<br>" & Err.Description
     End If

     ' Initialize application impersonation
     Application("hImp") = Empty
     Err.Clear
  End Sub
</SCRIPT>
```

When the application ends (which will occur if the web server is stopped for some reason), `Application_OnEnd` is called. Logically, this reverses what `Application_OnStart` set out to do, destroying the `RenderingApplication` object safely.

```
<SCRIPT LANGUAGE=VBScript RUNAT=Server>
Sub Application_OnEnd

   ' Set render application
   Set objRenderApp = Application("RenderApplication")
   fRevert = FALSE

   ' Get impersonation
   hImp = Application("hImp")

   ' Check if impersonation is not empty
   If Not IsEmpty(hImp) Then

      ' Save impersonation status
      fRevert = objRenderApp.Impersonate(hImp)
   End If

   ' Session is not impersonated
   If (fRevert) Then

      ' Retry impersonation
      objRenderApp.Impersonate(0)
   End if

   ' Destroy objects
   Set Application("CDOAnonSession") = Nothing
   Set Application("RenderApplication") = Nothing
End Sub
</SCRIPT>
```

As mentioned earlier, `global.asa` also holds functions which are set off each time a user begins to use our application ('starts a session') and each time one stops using it. As you may imagine then, the `Session_OnStart` routine sets aside some resources for what will eventually be the objects we should by now all recognize.

```
<SCRIPT LANGUAGE=VBScript RUNAT=Server>
Sub Session_OnStart

    ' Initialize variables
    Set Session("CDOAnonSession") = Nothing
    Set Session("objAddresslists") = Nothing
    Set Session("objAddresslist") = Nothing
    Set Session("objAddressEntries") = Nothing
    Set Session("objAddressEntry") = Nothing
    Set Session("objFilter") = Nothing
    Set Session("objFields") = Nothing
    Set Session("objField") = Nothing

    ' This is a handle to the security context. It will be set to the correct
    ' VALUE when a CDO session is created.
    On Error Resume Next
    Session("hImp") = Empty
    Session("WhoAmI")= "Default global.asa"
End Sub
</SCRIPT>
```

At the end of a session, the server's resources are freed, and if the CDO session is not logged off, then this is done here too:

```
<SCRIPT LANGUAGE=VBScript RUNAT=Server>
Sub Session_OnEnd

    ' Get rendering application
    On Error Resume Next
    Set objRenderApp = Application("RenderApplication")

    ' Get impersonation status
    fRevert = FALSE
    hImp = Session("hImp")

    ' Check if handle to impersonation is not empty
    If Not IsEmpty(hImp) Then

        ' Get impersonation status
        fRevert = objRenderApp.Impersonate(hImp)
    End If

    ' Get anonymous session
    On Error Resume Next
    Set objSession = Session("CDOAnonSession")

    ' Check if anonymous CDO session exists
    If Not objSession Is Nothing Then

        ' Logoff anonymous CDO session
        On Error Resume Next
        objSession.Logoff
        Set objSession = Nothing
```

```
      End If

      ' Do our cleanup set all CDO and CDOHTML objects
      ' inside the session to Nothing
      Set Session("CDOAnonSession") = Nothing
      Set Session("objAddresslists") = Nothing
      Set Session("objAddresslist") = Nothing
      Set Session("objAddressEntries") = Nothing
      Set Session("objAddressEntry") = Nothing
      Set Session("objFilter") = Nothing
      Set Session("objFields") = Nothing
      Set Session("objField") = Nothing

      ' Check handle to impersonation
      If (fRevert) Then

         ' Clear session object
         Session("hImp") = Empty

         ' Close impersonation status
         objRenderApp.CloseSysHandle(hImp)
         objRenderApp.Impersonate(0)
      End If
   End Sub
</SCRIPT>
```

As we've noted in a previous chapter there is a bug in CDO that causes a small memory leak to occur each time a user logs on. Administrators should be made aware of this so they can act accordingly if the application runs continuously over a long period of time.

The Include Files

Before we can move on to look through the main ASP pages in our application, it would be a good idea to look at the include files that they provide them with some common functionality and constants. The first two files, CDOProps.inc and lang.inc contain just a list of CDO constants and string variables respectively. The third file, global.inc, also contains constants, but these are specific to the application itself as follows.

```
<%
   Const APP_TITLE = "Company Phone List"

   ' Backround color of the main application window
   Const APP_BACKROUND_COLOR = "FFFF99"

   ' Frameborder color
   Const APP_FRAMEBORDER_COLOR = "99CCFF"

   ' Frameborder shadow color
   Const APP_FRAMEBORDER_SHADOW = "C0C0C0"

   ' Number of addresses to display per page
   Const APP_ITEM_COUNT = 25
%>
```

Logon.inc

Fourth of five is `logon.inc`, which contains a series of methods that our ASP pages can use to detect and logon to MAPI sessions. The first, `CheckCDOAnonSession`, checks that an anonymous MAPI session exists in the `Application` object, or creates it if necessary:

```
<%
Public Function CheckCDOAnonSession

    ' Declare variables
    Dim objSession

    ' Initialize variables
    CheckCDOAnonSession = False
    Set objSession = Nothing

    ' Set anonymous session
    On Error Resume Next
    Set objSession = Application("CDOAnonSession")

    ' Check if session is not set
    If objSession Is Nothing Then

        ' Try to logon again
        NoAnonSession

        ' Set session
        Set objSession = Application("CDOAnonSession")
    End If

    ' Check if session is set
    If Not objSession is Nothing Then

        ' Set return VALUE
        CheckCDOAnonSession = True
    End If
End Function
```

The next method, `NoAnonSession`, retrieves the configuration information, creates a dynamic profile for anonymous logon and then a CDO session. Again, this is nothing we've not seen already. First we declare and initialize our variables.

```
Sub NoAnonSession

    ' Declare variables
    Dim objRenderApp
    Dim objSession
    Dim objStores
    Dim bstrEnterprise
    Dim bstrSite
    Dim bstrServer
    Dim bstrProfileInfo
    Dim blnAddressList
```

```
        Dim intCounter
        Dim intTimeout

        ' Initialize variables
        Set objRenderApp = Nothing
        Set objSession = Nothing
        Set objStores = Nothing
        bstrEnterprise = ""
        bstrSite = ""
        bstrServer = ""
        bstrProfileInfo = ""
        blnAddressList = False
        intCounter = 1
        intTimeout = 0
```

With that done, we need to create a `RenderingApplication` object to set as the context for our anonymous session. In this instance, we're going to extract the exchange configuration from the registry and then dynamically create the anonymous profile.

```
        ' Set render application
        On Error Resume Next
        Set objRenderApp = Application("RenderApplication")

        ' Check if render application is set
        If Not objRenderApp Is Nothing Then

            ' Pull Exchange config out of the registry
            Err.Clear
            On Error Resume Next
            objRenderApp.LoadConfiguration 1, _
    "HKEY_LOCAL_MACHINE\System\CurrentControlSet\Services\MSExchangeWeb\Parameters"

            ' Check for possible errors
            If Err.Number = 0 Then
                bstrEnterprise = objRenderApp.ConfigParameter("Enterprise")
                bstrSite = objRenderApp.ConfigParameter("Site")
                bstrServer = objRenderApp.ConfigParameter("Server")

                ' Construct CDO profile
                bstrProfileInfo = "/o=" + bstrEnterprise + "/ou=" + bstrSite + _
                    "/cn=Configuration/cn=Servers/cn=" + bstrServer + vbLF + _
                    "anon" + vbLF + "anon"
            Else

                ' Display error message
                Call DebugAssert _
                    ("RenderingApplication.LoadConfiguration from registry", True)
            End If

            ' Check if CDO profile info is created
            If Not IsEmpty(bstrProfileInfo) Then
```

Provided all has gone well so far, we can go ahead with creating a session and logging onto the Exchange server with our anonymous profile.

```
' Create CDO session
Err.Clear
On Error Resume Next
Set objSession = Server.CreateObject("MAPI.Session")
If Not objSession Is Nothing Then

    ' Logon with anonymous CDO profile
    Err.Clear
    On Error Resume Next
    objSession.Logon "", "", False, True, 0, True, bstrProfileInfo

    ' Check for possible error
    If Err.Number = 0 Then

        ' Set application and impersonation
        Set Application("CDOAnonSession") = objSession
        Application("hImp") = objRenderApp.ImpID

        ' We need to force the store to open before
        ' anonymous access will work
        Set objStores = objSession.InfoStores
        For intCounter = 1 To objStores.Count
            Set objStore = objStores.Item(intCounter)
            lMask = objStore.Fields.Item(CdoPR_STORE_SUPPORT_MASK)
            If lMask And CdoPR_STORE_PUBLIC_FOLDERS Then
                Exit For
            End If
        Next
    Else
```

You may have noticed that at each stage of our building the session, we've used if statements in case the call failed. In this case, we call DebugAssert, which we'll come to in a minute, to display the error on screen.

```
        ' Error logon anonymously
        Call DebugAssert("Error logging on anonymously", True)
    End If

    ' Get anonymous session timeout VALUE
    intTimeout = objRenderApp.ConfigParameter("AnonymousSessionTimeout")

    ' Check if VALUE is set
    If intTimeout = 0 Then

        ' Set timeout of session to 10 minutes
        intTimeout = 10
    End If
    Session.Timeout = intTimeout
Else
```

```
                   ' Error creating CDO session
                   Call DebugAssert("Error creating CDO session", True)
              End If
         Else

                   ' Error creating CDO profile
                   Call DebugAssert("Error creating CDO profile", False)
              End If
         Else

              ' Error creating render application
              Call DebugAssert("Error creating RenderApp", False)
         End If

         ' Destroy objects
         Set objStore = Nothing
    End Sub
```

Finally, as mentioned above, `logon.inc` also contains the error notification method `DebugAssert`:

```
    Function DebugAssert(bstrContext, blnErrChkFlag)

         ' Check if error check flag is set
         If boolErrChkFlag = True Then

              ' Check if error found
              If Err.Number <> 0 Then

                   ' Pull out error details
                   Response.Write("Error: " & bstrContext & " : " & Err.Number & _
                                  ": " & Err.Description & "<br>")

                   ' Clear error object
                   Err.Clear
              End If
         Else

              ' Display error message
              Response.Write("Error: " & bstrContext & "<br>")
         End If
    End Function
%>
```

Address.inc

The final include file, `address.inc`, contains the code to instantiate and make use of the various renderer objects. The first function, `GetRenderer` sets up a `RenderingApplication` object, impersonation and either a `ContainerRenderer` or an `ObjectRenderer`, depending on the integer value passed to the function:

```
    <%

    Function GetRenderer(nType)
```

455

```
   ' Declare variables
   Dim objRenderApp
   Dim objRenderer

   ' Initialize variables
   Set objRenderApp = Nothing
   Set GetRenderer = Nothing

   ' Get render application object
   Set objRenderApp = Application("RenderApplication")

   ' Check if render application is not set
   If Not objRenderApp Is Nothing Then

      ' Create renderer
      Set objRenderer = objRenderApp.CreateRenderer(nType)
      If IsEmpty(Session("hImp")) Then
         Session("hImp") = objRenderApp.ImpID
      End If
   End If

   ' Set return VALUE
   Set GetRenderer = objRenderer
End Function
```

The second function, GetAddressRenderer, does the all the hard work for address.asp, setting up as it does the layout, columns, patterns and format for the main table of address entries in our application. As we'd expect, the first thing it does is initialise the variables we'll be needing and then create a ContainerRenderer for (a part of) the Global Address List.

```
Function GetAddressRenderer(objAddressEntries, intMaxCount)

   ' Declare variables
   Dim objRenderApp
   Dim objRenderer
   Dim objFormat
   Dim objPatterns
   Dim objView
   Dim objColumns
   Dim objColumn
   Dim objAddressEntry
   Dim intCounter

   ' Initialize variables
   Set GetAddressRenderer = Nothing
   Set objRenderApp = Nothing
   Set objRenderer = Nothing
   Set objFormat = Nothing
   Set objPatterns = Nothing
   Set objView = Nothing
   Set objColumns = Nothing
   Set objColumn = Nothing
   Set objAddressEntry = Nothing
```

```
        intCounter = 0

        ' Get render application object
        Set objRenderApp = Application("RenderApplication")

        ' Create container renderer and set datasource
        Set objRenderer = objRenderApp.CreateRenderer(3)
        objRenderer.DataSource = objAddressEntries
```

This is a simple table in comparison to that in OWA. The patterns we attach to our various CDO properties are just HTML font tags to display the properties' values in some sans-serif font.

```
        ' Create format and add patterns
        Set objFormat = objRenderer.Formats.Add(CdoPR_DISPLAY_NAME)
        Set objPatterns = objFormat.Patterns
        objPatterns.Add "*"," _
            <FONT FACE='Arial, Helvetica, sans-serif' SIZE='-1'>%VALUE%</FONT>"
        Set objFormat = objRenderer.Formats.Add(CdoPR_DEPARTMENT_NAME)
        Set objPatterns = objFormat.Patterns
        objPatterns.Add "*"," _
            <FONT FACE='Arial, Helvetica, sans-serif' SIZE='-1'>%VALUE%</FONT>"
        Set objFormat = objRenderer.Formats.Add(CdoPR_OFFICE_LOCATION)
        Set objPatterns = objFormat.Patterns
        objPatterns.Add "*"," _
            <FONT FACE='Arial, Helvetica, sans-serif' SIZE='-1'>%VALUE%</FONT>"
        Set objFormat = objRenderer.Formats.Add(CdoPR_BUSINESS_TELEPHONE_NUMBER)
        Set objPatterns = objFormat.Patterns
        objPatterns.Add "*"," _
            <FONT FACE='Arial, Helvetica, sans-serif' SIZE='-1'>%VALUE%</FONT>"
        Set objFormat = objRenderer.Formats.Add(CdoPR_PRIMARY_FAX_NUMBER)
        Set objPatterns = objFormat.Patterns
        objPatterns.Add "*"," _
            <FONT FACE='Arial, Helvetica, sans-serif' SIZE='-1'>%VALUE%</FONT>"
```

With the patterns set for each property, we need to add one column per property to a `View` object that we must also create.

```
        ' Create view and set columns
        Set objView = objRenderer.Views.Add("DefaultView")
        Set objColumns = objView.Columns

        ' Add columns to view
        ' Note: do not remove the first parameter otherwise the heading row
        ' will end up in an undefined state
        Set objColumn = objColumns.Add("Full Name", _
                                    CdoPR_DISPLAY_NAME, 40, 0, 0)
        Set objColumn = objColumns.Add("Department", _
                                    CdoPR_DEPARTMENT_NAME, 20, 32, 1)
        Set objColumn = objColumns.Add("Office", _
                                    CdoPR_OFFICE_LOCATION, 20, 32, 2)
        Set objColumn = objColumns.Add("Phone", _
```

```
                                          CdoPR_BUSINESS_TELEPHONE_NUMBER, 20, 32, 3)
        Set objColumn = objColumns.Add("Fax", _
                                       CdoPR_PRIMARY_FAX_NUMBER, 20, 32, 4)
        objRenderer.CurrentView = "DefaultView"
```

Finally, we have to set up the `LinkPattern` property that will eventually be used to link users' names to the personal information page and the miscellaneous headers and footers needed to render the table.

```
    ' Set url link
    objRenderer.LinkPattern = "<a href=" & Chr(34) & _
        "JavaScript:openNewWindow('details.asp?obj=%obj%', _
        'newAddressWindow', 770, 520)" & Chr(34) & _
        "onMouseOver='message(""Click to display details"");return true;'" & _
        ">" & "%VALUE%" & "</a>"

    ' Set maximum displayed rows
    objRenderer.RowsPerPage = intMaxCount

    ' Set heading row and cell rendering style
    ' Note: do not remove this lines otherwise the heading row
    ' will become visible with the default color
    objRenderer.HeadingCellPattern = _
        "<FONT FACE='Arial, Helvetica, sans-serif' SIZE='3' VALIGN='top' _
        ALIGN='left' NOWRAP><b>%VALUE%</b></FONT>"
    objRenderer.HeadingRowPrefix = "<TR VALIGN='top' bgcolor='#99CCFF'>"
    objRenderer.HeadingRowSuffix = "</TR>"

    ' Set row and cell rendering style
    ' Note: do not remove this lines otherwise each row
    ' will be displayed with the default backround color
    objRenderer.CellPattern = _
        "<FONT FACE='Arial, Helvetica, sans-serif' SIZE='1' VALIGN='top' _
        ALIGN='left' NOWRAP>%VALUE%</FONT>"
    objRenderer.RowPrefix = "<TR VALIGN='middle' bgcolor='#FFFF99'>"
    objRenderer.RowSuffix = "</TR>"

    ' Set table rendering style
    objRenderer.TablePrefix = "<TABLE BORDER=0>"
    objRenderer.TableSuffix = "</table>"

    ' Set return VALUE
    Set GetAddressRenderer = objRenderer
End Function
```

As we should already know, the personal details page renders a single `AddressEntry` object which must be rendered by an `ObjectRenderer` object. We use `GetObjectRenderer` to instantiate this and make it available throughout the session.

```
    Function GetObjectRenderer()

        ' Declare variables
```

```
    Dim objRenderer

    ' Initialize variables
    Set GetObjectRenderer = Nothing

    ' Get object renderer
    If IsEmpty(Session("ObjectRenderer")) Then

        ' Create object render
        Set objRenderer = GetRenderer(2)
        Set Session("ObjectRenderer") = objRenderer
    Else

        ' Set object renderer
        Set objRenderer = Session("ObjectRenderer")
    End If

    ' Set return VALUE
    Set GetObjectRenderer = objRenderer
End Function
```

Finally in `address.inc`, we have two utility functions for reporting errors. Note the `fClose` parameter in `DisplayError`. If this is set to `true`, the current window is closed otherwise the function will navigate to the previous location in the history list.

```
Public Function ReportError(bstrErr)
    DisplayError bstrErr, False
End Function

Public Function DisplayError(bstrErr, fClose)

    ' Declare variables
    Dim bstrMessage
    Dim objRenderer

    ' Initialize variables
    Set objRenderer = Nothing
    bstrMessage = bstrErr

    Set objRenderApp = Application("RenderApplication")
    If objRenderApp.ConfigParameter("Debug") = 1 Then
        If Err.Number <> 0 Then
            bstrMessage = bstrMessage & vbCRLF & hex(Err.Number) & _
                          ": " & Err.Description
            bstrMessage = bstrMessage & vbCRLF & _
                          Request.ServerVariables("SCRIPT_NAME")
        End If
    End If

    ' Display error message
    Response.Write( bstrMessage)
    Response.End
End Function
%>
```

The Frameset Page - Default.asp

The next key file in the application is `default.asp`; this is simply a frameset for the other pages. Before it does this though, it checks to make sure that the user can open an anonymous user session in CDO:

```
<!--#include file = "global.inc"-->
<!--#include file = "cdoprops.inc"-->
<!--#include file = "address.inc"-->
<!--#include file = "logon.inc"-->


<%
    ' Declare variables
    Dim objCDOAnonSession

    ' Initialize variables
    Set objCDOAnonSession = Nothing

    ' Check if anonymous CDO session exists
    On Error Resume Next
    If CheckCDOAnonSession Then

        ' Get anonymous CDO session object
        Set objCDOAnonSession = Application("CDOAnonSession")
    Else

        ' CDO session does not exist, display error message
        Response.Write("Default.asp: Can not logon to system." & "<br>")

        ' Exit application
        Response.End
    End If
%>
```

Once that is out of the way, the frameset can be built:

```
<HTML>
<HEAD>
    <TITLE><%= APP_TITLE %></TITLE>
</HEAD>

<FRAMESET FRAMESPACING="0" BORDER="True" ROWS="64,*" FRAMEBORDER="0">
    <FRAME NAME="Title_fr" SCROLLING="No"
            NORESIZE TARGET="Address_fr" SRC="Title.asp"
            MARGINHEIGHT=0 MARGINWIDTH=0 FRAMEBORDER=0>

    <FRAMESET COLS="*,75">
        <FRAME NAME="Address_fr" SRC="Address.asp" SCROLLING="Auto" MARGINHEIGHT=0
                MARGINWIDTH=0 FRAMEBORDER=0>
        <FRAME NAME="Rolodex_fr" TARGET="Main" SRC="Rolodex.asp" MARGINHEIGHT=0
                MARGINWIDTH=0 FRAMEBORDER=0>
    </FRAMESET>
```

```
<NOFRAMES>
  <BODY>
    <P>This page uses frames, but your browser doesn't support them.</P>
  </BODY>
</NOFRAMES>
</FRAMESET>
</HTML>
```

The Search Form - Title.asp

As you'll recall, `Title.asp` contains the search form where you can enter a value, select an attribute to search against, and submit the query. To remind you, it looks like this.

The first thing to do is set up the anonymous session with help from `logon.inc`.

```
<!--#include file = "global.inc"-->
<!--#include file = "cdoprops.inc"-->
<!--#include file = "address.inc"-->
<!--#include file = "logon.inc"-->

<%
  ' Declare variables
  Dim objCDOAnonSession

  ' Initialize variables
  Set objCDOAnonSession = Nothing

  ' Get field and search VALUE
  strField = Request.Form("SearchField")
  strVALUE = Request.Form("SearchString")

  ' Check if anonymous CDO session exists
  On Error Resume Next
  If CheckCDOAnonSession Then

    ' Get anonymous CDO session object
    Set objCDOAnonSession = Application("CDOAnonSession")
  Else

    ' MAPI session does not exist, display error message
    Response.Write("Default.asp: Can not logon to system." & "<br>")

    ' Exit application
    Response.End
  End If
%>
```

We use two helper functions in this page directly related to the search form. The first, `StartSearch`, pulls the values given in the form and constructs the correct query string to pass to address.asp which will create the filters and produce the results of the search.

```
<SCRIPT LANGUAGE="JavaScript">
function StartSearch()
{

   /* Get selected field and search VALUE */
   var strMaxEntries = <%= APP_ITEM_COUNT %>;
   var strSearchField = document.forms[0].elements[0].VALUE;
   var strSearchVALUE = document.forms[1].elements[0].VALUE;
   /* var strSearchField = document.forms[OptionForm].elements[0].VALUE; */
   /* var strSearchVALUE = document.forms[SearchForm].elements[0].VALUE; */

   /* Set search parameter */
   switch(strSearchField)
   {
      case "Full Name":
         strSearchField = "fname";
         break;
      case "Department":
         strSearchField = "dept";
         break;
      case "Office":
         strSearchField = "loc";
         break;
   }

   /* Build url with all search parameters and reload phone list frame */
   var strSearchURL = "address.asp?" + strSearchField + "=" +
                         strSearchVALUE + "&count=" + strMaxEntries;
   window.open(strSearchURL, 'address_fr');
}
```

The second function, ResetSearch, simply clears the values currently in the search form.

```
function ResetSearch()
{
   /* Reset the phone list frame to display all mailboxes without any filters */
   var strMaxEntries = <%= APP_ITEM_COUNT %>;
   var strSearchURL = "address.asp?type=mailbox&count=" + strMaxEntries;
   window.open(strSearchURL, 'address_fr');
}
</script>
```

The rest of this page is just the HTML to produce the form.

```
<!DOCTYPE HTML PUBLIC "-//IETF//DTD HTML 3.2//EN">
<HTML>
<HEAD>
   <TITLE><%= APP_TITLE %></TITLE>
</HEAD>
```

```
<BODY>
<DIV ALIGN="center">
<TABLE BORDER="0" CELLPADDING="0" CELLSPACNG="0" WIDTH="95%" ALIGN=middle>
   <TR>
      <TD WIDTH="100%" VALIGN="baseline" HEIGHT="5%">   </TD>
      <TD VALIGN="baseline" HEIGHT="5%" WIDTH="100%" NOWRAP></TD>
      <TD WIDTH="1%" VALIGN="baseline" HEIGHT="5%"></TD>
      <TD VALIGN="baseline" NOWRAP></TD>
      <TD WIDTH="64%" VALIGN="baseline" HEIGHT="5%"></TD>
      <TD WIDTH="64%" VALIGN="baseline" HEIGHT="5%"></TD>
   </TR>
   <TR>
      <TD WIDTH="100%" VALIGN="baseline" HEIGHT="5%">
         <FONT FACE="Arial" SIZE="4">
            <STRONG><%= APP_TITLE %></EM></STRONG></FONT></TD>
      <TD VALIGN="baseline" HEIGHT="5%" WIDTH="100%" NOWRAP>
            Search  </TD>
      <TD WIDTH="1%" VALIGN="baseline" HEIGHT="5%">

         <FORM NAME="OptionForm">
         <SELECT NAME="SelectField" SIZE="1">
            <OPTION
               <% If strField = "Full Name" then Response.Write("selected")%>
               VALUE="Full Name">Full Name</OPTION>
            <OPTION
               <% If strField = "Department" then Response.Write("selected")%>
               VALUE="Department">Department</OPTION>
            <OPTION
               <% If strField = "Office" then Response.Write("selected")%>
               VALUE="Office">Office</OPTION>
         </SELECT>
         </FORM></TD>
      <TD VALIGN="baseline" NOWRAP>
         <FORM NAME="SearchForm" METHOD="POST"
            ACTION="JavaScript:StartSearch()">
         <P> for 
         <INPUT TYPE="text" name="SearchField" SIZE="20"></P></FORM></TD>

      <TD VALIGN="baseline" WIDTH="64%" HEIGHT="5%">
         <FORM NAME"StartForm">
         <P> 
         <INPUT TYPE="submit" VALUE=" Start " onClick="StartSearch()">
         </P></FORM></TD>

      <TD WIDTH="64%" VALIGN="baseline" HEIGHT="5%">
         <FORM NAME"ResetForm">
         <P> 
         <INPUT TYPE="submit" VALUE="Reset" onClick="ResetSearch()">
         </P></FORM></TD>
   </TR>
</TABLE>
</DIV>
</BODY>
</HTML>
```

As a whole, the only part of this file worth mentioning here is that the attribute list must be changed here if it should be changed in the actual search code, for example if you add a new attribute to search against. Just as `Default.asp` does, it also contains code to ensure that the user can achieve an anonymous connection to the server.

A to Z - Rolodex.asp

Rolodex.asp has the least remarkable page of the solution. It simply produces the vertical list of letters as hyper links, which when clicked on constructs a similar query string to `Address.asp` to activate a search. The syntax is the same as that produced by `StartSearch` in `title.asp`. For example:

```
<TABLE BORDER="0" CELLPADDING="0" CELLSPACING="0"
       BGCOLOR="<%= APP_FRAMEBORDER_SHADOW %>">
<TR>
    <TD WIDTH="100%" VALIGN="Middle" ALIGN="Center">
    <STRONG>
        <A HREF="Address.asp?fname=a&Count=<%= APP_ITEM_COUNT %>"
           TARGET="Address_fr">  A  </A></STRONG></TD></TR>

<TR>
    <TD WIDTH="100%" VALIGN="Middle" ALIGN="Center">
    <STRONG>
        <A HREF="Address.asp?fname=a&Count=<%= APP_ITEM_COUNT %>"
           TARGET="Address_fr">  B  </A></STRONG></TD></TR>

<TR>
    <TD WIDTH="100%" VALIGN="Middle" ALIGN="Center">
    <STRONG>
        <A HREF="Address.asp?fname=a&Count=<%= APP_ITEM_COUNT %>"
           TARGET="Address_fr">  C  </A></STRONG></TD></TR>
```

And so on for each letter of the alphabet. You can find the full version of `rolodex.asp` in the code download along with the rest of this case study.

Address.asp

This is where most of the work is done, in displaying the main table and performing the searches passed to it from `rolodex.asp` and `title.asp` beforehand where necessary.

In the following diagram you can see a basic logic flow diagram describing what happens when `Address.asp` is executed. We will follow each part of the diagram with a description of what is happening at that point, then move on in to the code:

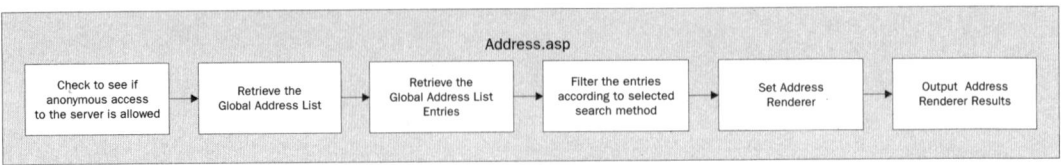

Having declared our variables, the first thing we need to do is parse the information that may be contained in the `QueryString` referring to the filter that needs to be applied to the search results. As you've already ascertained, there are only three filters we've set up in the previous pages – Full Name, Department, and Location. In addition we retrieve information for the number of rows per page, and an identifier to show what page the user is currently on if the search results have been paged. As usual though, the first thing to do is declare and initialize our variables.

```
<!--#include file = "global.inc"-->
<!--#include file = "cdoprops.inc"-->
<!--#include file = "address.inc"-->
<!--#include file = "logon.inc"-->

<%
  ' Declare variables
  Dim objCDOAnonSession   ' Anonymous CDO session
  Dim objAddressList      ' Global Address list
  Dim objAddressEntries   ' Address entries collection object
  Dim objAddressEntry     ' Address entry object
  Dim objFilter           ' Address entries filter
  Dim objRenderer         ' Renderer object
  Dim strFullName         ' Full name
  Dim strDepartment       ' Department
  Dim strLocation         ' Office location
  Dim intCounter          ' Counter
  Dim intRowsPerPage      ' Maximum count of GAL entries displayed on one page
  Dim intMaxCount         ' Maximum count of GAL entries displayed
  Dim intPageCount        ' Current displayed page

  ' Initialize variables
  Set objCDOAnonSession = Nothing
  Set objRenderApplication = Nothing
  Set objAddressList = Nothing
  Set objAddressEntries = Nothing
  Set objAddressEntry = Nothing
  Set objAEFilter = Nothing
  Set objFilter = Nothing
  Set objRenderer = Nothing
  strFullName = " "
  strDepartment = " "
  strLocation = " "
  intCounter = 0
  intRowsPerPage = 0
  intMaxCount = 0
  intPageCount = 0

  ' Get parameters
  strFullName = LCase(Request.QueryString("fname"))
  strDepartment = LCase(Request.QueryString("dept"))
  strLocation = LCase(Request.QueryString("loc"))
  intRowsPerPage = LCase(Request.QueryString("count"))
  intPageCount = LCase(Request.QueryString("page"))
```

Next up is to define what the maximum number of rows in the search results should be. This is identified by a constant titled APP_ITEM_COUNT, which we defined in `Global.inc`:

```
' Check if maximum count of GAL entries is empty
If Trim(intRowsPerPage) = "" Then

    ' Set maximum count to application default value
    intRowsPerPage = APP_ITEM_COUNT
End If
```

Here you can see that there is a check to make sure that if the results are not paged then the paging buttons are not displayed on the screen by designating the number of pages as one:

```
' Check if page count is empty
If Trim(intPageCount) = "" Then

    ' Set page count to application default value
    intPageCount = 1
End If
```

The next part is essential because it checks to make sure that the anonymous connection to CDO is valid. Obviously if you plan to use an authenticated session, you would adjust the code accordingly:

```
' Check if anonymous CDO session exists
On Error Resume Next
If CheckCDOAnonSession Then

    ' Get CDO session object
    Set objCDOAnonSession = Application("CDOAnonSession")
Else

    ' CDO session does not exist, display error message
    Response.Write("Address.asp: Cannot logon to system." & "<br>")

    ' Exit application
    Response.End
End If
```

Once you have established that the user session is valid, we can try to retrieve the global address list. We need this in order to retrieve the individual mailboxes/addresses from the server:

```
' Get global address list
Set objAddressList = objCDOAnonSession.GetAddressList(0)

' Check if global address list found
If objAddressList Is Nothing Then

    ' Display error message
    Response.Write("Address.asp: Cannot get global address list." & "<br>")

    ' Exit application
    Response.End
End If
```

Now we have successfully retrieved the global address list, we need to retrieve the address entries:

```
' Get address entries
On Error Resume Next
Set objAddressEntries = objAddressList.AddressEntries

' Check for possible errors
If Err.Number <> 0 then

    ' Try again to get address entries
    Set objAddressEntries = objAddressList.AddressEntries

    ' Again check for possible errors
    If Err.Number <> 0 Then

        ' Display error message
        Response.Write(objAddressList.Name & "<br>")
        Response.Write(Err.Number & ": " & Err.Description & "<br>")
        Response.Write _
                ("Address.asp: Cannot get requested address entry collection.")

        ' Exit application
        Response.End
    End If
End If
```

Upon successful retrieval of the address entries, it is time to apply the filter on the collection retrieved. It's important to make sure you set the filter to apply to mailboxes only, as it is only people that we are interested in retrieving information about.

Naturally if mailboxes have been for meeting rooms and office equipment etc, then they may also come up in the search. Another filter could be applied against such items that the code could take in to account of if you wanted to:

```
' Set filter to display only selected address entries
    Set objAddressEntries.Filter = Nothing
    Err.Clear
    Set objFilter = objAddressEntries.Filter

    ' Check for possible errors
    If Not objFilter Is Nothing Then

        ' Check if full name is found
        If Trim(strFullName) <> "" Then

            ' Set filter on display name
            objFilter.Fields.Add CdoPR_DISPLAY_NAME, strFullName
        End If

        ' Check if department is found
        If Trim(strDepartment) <> "" Then
```

```
            ' Set filter on department
            objFilter.Fields.Add CdoPR_DEPARTMENT_NAME, strDepartment
        End If

        ' Check if location is found
        If Trim(strLocation) <> "" Then

            ' Set filter on location
            objFilter.Fields.Add CdoPR_OFFICE_LOCATION, strLocation
        End If

        ' Set filter on display type to display only mailboxes
        objFilter.Fields.Add CdoPR_DISPLAY_TYPE, 0

        ' All filter restrictions are ANDed
        objFilter.Or = False
    Else

        ' Display error message
        ReportError("Address.asp: Could not set address entries filter." & "<br>")

        ' Exit application
        Response.End
    End If
```

Next up we need to loop through the filtered address entry collection. We need to do that to update the collection information otherwise the `ContainerRenderer` object does not recognize that a filter has been applied:

```
For Each objAddressEntry In objAddressEntries

    ' Increase counter
    intCounter = intCounter + 1
Next

' Check if maximum count of address entries is higher than the
' maximum rows per page count
If intCounter >= intRowsPerPage Then

    ' Calculate the maximum count
    intMaxCount = ((intCounter - 1) / intRowsPerPage) + 1
Else

    ' Set maximum count to the maximum GAL entry count
    intMaxCount = intRowsPerPage ' intCounter
End If

' Set container renderer
Set objRenderer = GetAddressRenderer(objAddressEntries, intRowsPerPage)

' Check if container renderer is not set
If objRenderer Is Nothing Then
```

```
        ' Display error message
        Response.Write("Address.asp: Cannot get address list information." & _
                    "<BR>")

        ' Exit application
        Response.End
    End If
%>
```

That completes all the pre page formatting functionality of Address.asp. Next we move onto some fairly simple client-side script that takes care of navigating through the results of our searches.

```
<SCRIPT LANGUAGE = "Javascript">

function PreviousPage()
{
    var intCurrentPage = eval(<%= intPageCount %>);
    var intMaxRows = eval(<%= intRowsPerPage %>);

    if (intCurrentPage == 1)
    {
        alert("You are already at the beginning of the list")
    }
    else
    {
        intCurrentPage = intCurrentPage - 1
        parent.address_fr.location = "address.asp?page=" + intCurrentPage +
                "&count=" + intMaxRows + "&fname=" + "<%= strFullName %>" +
                "&dept=" + "<%= strDepartment %>" + "&loc=" + "<%= strLocation %>"
    }
}
function NextPage()
{
    var intCurrentPage = eval(<%= intPageCount %>);
    var intMaxPage = eval(<%= intMaxCount %>);
    var intMaxEntries = eval(<%= intCounter %>);
    var intMaxRows = eval(<%= intRowsPerPage %>);

    intMaxPage = (intMaxEntries / intMaxRows);
    if (intCurrentPage >= intMaxPage)
    {
        alert("You are already at the end of the list")
    }
    else
    {
        intCurrentPage = intCurrentPage + 1
        parent.address_fr.location = "address.asp?page=" + intCurrentPage +
                "&count=" + intMaxRows + "&fname=" + "<%= strFullName %>" +
                "&dept=" + "<%= strDepartment %>" + "&loc=" + "<%= strLocation %>"
    }
}
```

We also define a function that will open a new window for us when we need to display a person's full details.

```
function openNewWindow(fileName,windowName,theWidth,theHeight)
{
   if (windowName == "newAddressWindow")
   {
      uniqueName = new Date();
      windowName = uniqueName.getTime();
   }
   window.open(fileName, windowName,"toolbar=0, location=0, directories=0,
             status=0, menubar=0, scrollbars=0, resizable=0,
             width="+theWidth+", height="+theHeight)
}
</SCRIPT>
```

Finally, we come to the HTML that defines the main table.

```
<!DOCTYPE HTML PUBLIC "-//IETF//DTD HTML 3.2//EN">
<HTML>
<HEAD>
   <TITLE><%= APP_TITLE %></TITLE>
</HEAD>

<BODY>
<%
   If intCounter = 0 Then
%>

   <SCRIPT language='JavaScript'>
      alert("No entries found for the selected search criteria");
      history.back();
   </SCRIPT>

<%
   Else
%>

   <DIV ALIGN="center">
   <TABLE BORDER="0" CELLPADDING="0" CELLSPACING="0" WIDTH="90%" ALIGN="right">
   <TR>
      <TD BGCOLOR="<%= APP_FRAMEBORDER_SHADOW %>"> 
         <DIV ALIGN="center">

         <TABLE BORDER="0" CELLSPACING="5" CELLPADDING="5" WIDTH="100%">
         <TR>
            <TD COLOR="<%= APP_BACKROUND_COLOR %>" VALIGN="top" COLSPAN="2">
               <% objRenderer.Render 1, intPageCount, 0, Response %>
               </TD></TR>
         <TR>
            <TD BGCOLOR="<%= APP_FRAMEBORDER_SHADOW %>" VALIGN="top">
               <FORM NAME="NextForm" METHOD="POST"
```

```
                    ACTION="JavaScript:self.PreviousPage()">
                <DIV ALIGN="right">
                <P>
                <INPUT TYPE="SUBMIT" VALUE="&lt;&lt; Previous page"></P></DIV>
            </FORM></TD>
        <TD BGCOLOR="<%= APP_FRAMEBORDER_SHADOW %>" VALIGN="top">
            <FORM NAME="PreviousForm" METHOD="POST"
                ACTION="JavaScript:self.NextPage()"> ,
                <DIV ALIGN="left">
                <P>
                <INPUT TYPE="SUBMIT" VALUE="Next page &gt;&gt;"></P></DIV>
            </FORM></TD></TR>
        </TABLE>
        </DIV></TD></TR>
    </TABLE>
    </DIV>

<%
    End If
%>

</BODY>
</HTML>
```

Most of note in the HTML is the line

```
<% objRenderer.Render 1, intPageCount, 0, Response %>
```

This line creates all the HTML for displaying the list of entries in the table. Running quickly through this call, Render takes four parameters:

- ❑ The rendering style – in this case CDOFolderContents
- ❑ The page number to start at
- ❑ VarBoolRaw – a reserved parameter, do not use
- ❑ A choice between assigning the output to the Response object otherwise it is written to a variable named strHTML

Details.asp

Our final page in this case study is Details.asp, the page that displays more information about the individual after you have clicked on a name from the results in address.asp.

It displays the following information:

- ❑ Full Company Name and Address
- ❑ Telephone Number
- ❑ Fax Number
- ❑ Managers Name
- ❑ Email Address (hyperlinked as a mailto)

We will now go through Details.asp to understand what is going on when the page is shown. In the following diagram, you can see a logical flow of what happens:

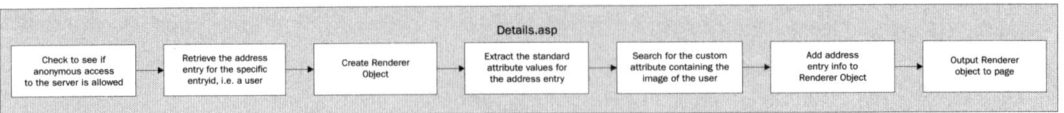

The first thing to do, having declared the necessary variables, is, as before to check to make sure the user has anonymous access to the server, and then to set the Rendering object for the page:

```
<!--#include file = "global.inc"-->
<!--#include file = "cdoprops.inc"-->
<!--#include file = "address.inc"-->
<!--#include file = "logon.inc"-->


<%
    On Error Resume Next

    ' Declare variables
    Dim objCDOAnonSession
    Dim objRenderApp
    Dim objRenderer
    Dim objAddressEntry
    Dim strAddressEntryID
    Dim strAddressCity
    Dim strPictureUrl
    Dim strEMailAddress
    Dim strManager
    Dim strManagerID
    Dim intCounter

    ' Initialize variables
    Set objCDOAnonSession = Nothing
    Set objRenderApp = Nothing
    Set objRenderer = Nothing
    Set objAddressEntry = Nothing
    intCounter = 1

    ' Check if anonymous CDO session exists
    If CheckCDOAnonSession Then

        ' Get anonymous CDO session object
        Set objCDOAnonSession = Application("CDOAnonSession")
    Else

        ' CDO session does not exist, display error message
        Response.Write("Details.asp: Can not logon to system." & "<br>")

        ' Exit application
        Response.End
    End If

    ' Create renderer object
    Set objRenderApp = Application("RenderApplication")
```

You then need to retrieve the address entry for the page, as we are only displaying information about a single user:

```
' Get address entry ID
strAddressEntryID = Request.QueryString("obj")

' Check for possible errors
If strAddressEntryID = "" then

    ' Address entry ID not found, display error message
    Response.Write("Details.asp: Can not get ID of address entry." & "<BR>")

    ' Exit application
    Response.End
End If

' Get address entry object
Err.Clear
Set objAddressEntry = objCDOAnonSession.GetAddressEntry(strAddressEntryID)

' Check for possible errors
If Err.Number <> 0 Or objAddressEntry Is Nothing Then

    ' Address entry object not found, display error message
    Response.Write("Details.asp: Can not get address entry object." & "<br>")

    ' Exit application
    Response.End
End If
```

You next have to set the ObjectRenderer object to prepare for it to output recipient details:

```
' Create renderer object for the recipient
Set objRenderer = objRenderApp.CreateRenderer(2)
```

With that done it's now a matter of extracting the details from the address entry in question and rendering them into a table. We've already seen how to do this in Chapter 13, so we'll refrain from repeating the technique here.

Possible Extensions

That completes the "People Finder" case study. Hopefully it demonstrates how easy it is to use Collaborative Data Objects to extend the use of your e-mail system – in this case Microsoft Exchange to be used in the broader environment of an intranet, or even potentially the Internet.

If you'd be interested in extending this case study, perhaps you'd like to consider implementing some or all of the following additions:

❑ **Viewing Peoples Diaries**
   You could extend the application where you could link from the personal details page to the user's calendar to check they're availability on certain dates.

❑ **Out of Office Assistant**
You could set up a flag to tell the person using the system if an individual has set their Out of Office Assistant on, notifying them that the person is unavailable. The Out of Office Text may also be displayed.

❑ **Quick Messaging**
When you go to the user details screen, you could incorporate into it the ability to send a quick message to the individual via e-mail. This may be useful if you are accessing the intranet from a machine that is not normally the one you would use e.g. in an Internet cafe or perhaps if you just have a couple of sentences to say which doesn't justify sending an e-mail through a web email client or a traditional email client.

❑ **User Grouping**
If you have an efficient strategy for grouping users, then you could allow an option to browse via groups, and even show information about users on a group wide basis. For example, say you wanted to speak to someone from accounts, but you weren't exactly sure who to speak to. You could just browse to the Accounts Group and see a screen detailing who is in the group.

The list goes on, the limit to being able to extend an application is only limited by the flexibility of your email architecture, the way you have designed your Exchange Server for accessing user information, and your ability to see an opportunity from your email system as a centralised data store.

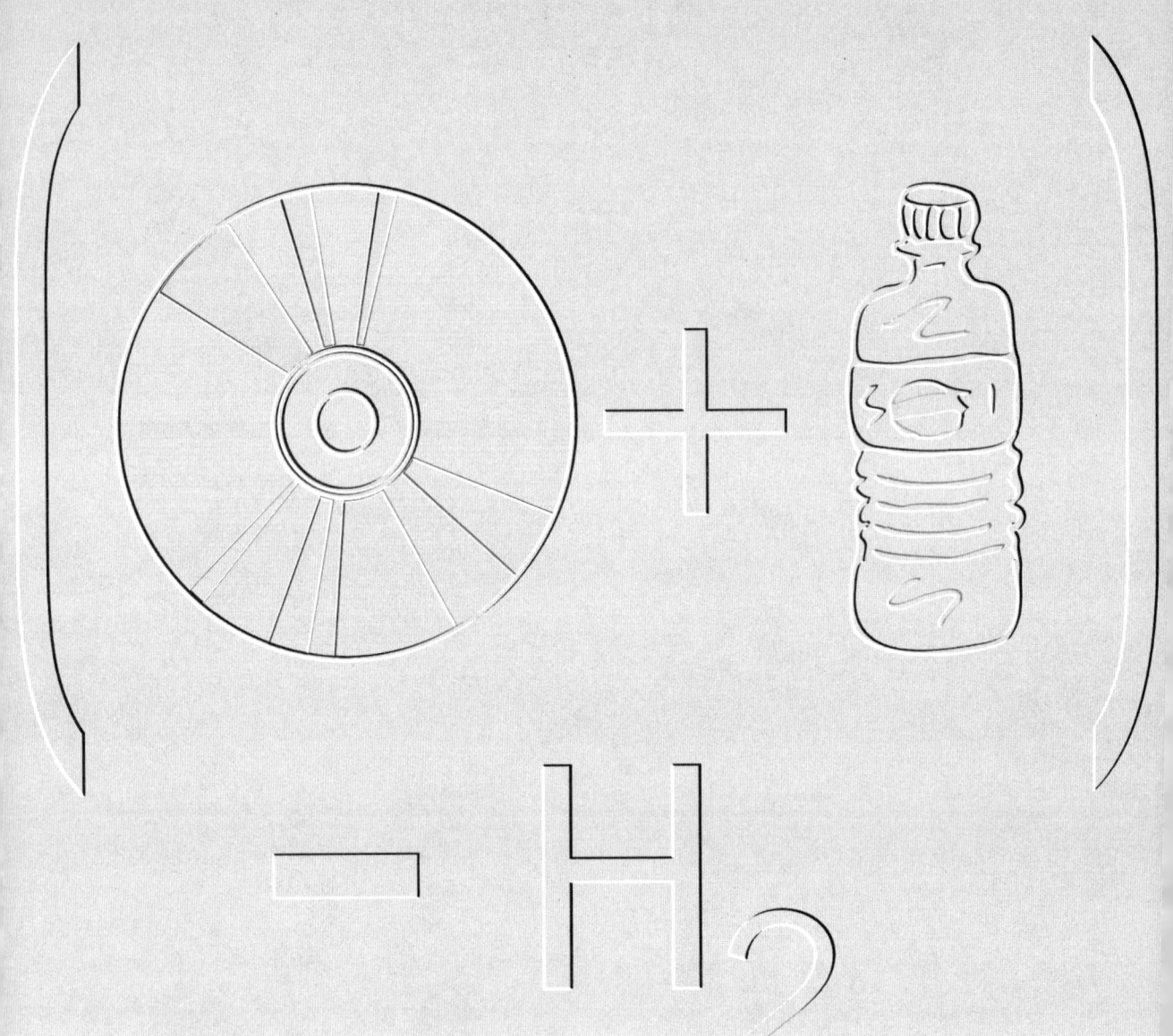

14

Using CDO from C++

Thus far, all the code we've looked at that uses CDO has been written in Visual Basic. If you want to use CDO from C++, it's not merely possible, it's actually relatively easy – but you'll need some knowledge of the fundamental technologies you'll be using to access the library if you want to have an easy time of it.

In this chapter, we'll write a simple C++ application to send mail using CDO, and look at the tricks you need to know to use CDO from C++ – once we've finished this application, you should know enough to be able to extend it to use any other features of CDO that you might want.

Then, we'll take a brief look at Extended MAPI, the low-level messaging system that underlies CDO, and show how we can take advantage of our ability to use that from C++ to do things we can't do in CDO – we'll write an application that sends mail with rich-text (RTF) bodies, and also write a small utility to edit the list of mail profiles on the system.

> There's a fair amount of code to follow in this chapter for you to type in. If you fancy giving your fingers a break, you can download the code for this chapter and for the rest of the book from the Wrox website at http://www.wrox.com.

Basic Assumptions

There are some things I'm going to assume you know about and not explain during this chapter – if you don't know about any of the following, you may still be able to follow what's going on, but things won't be as clear as they might be. In practice, you may very well be able to get away with simply copying the basic syntax we'll use, but your life will be much less confusing if you understand the following:

❑ **COM**. CDO is a library of COM components, so I'm going to assume you understand about reference counting issues, `QueryInterface`, CLSIDs, the `VARIANT` type and so forth.

❑ **Dispatch interfaces**. CDO is designed to be usable from Visual Basic, VBScript, ASP, and other scripting languages, so all the interfaces are pure Dispatch interfaces. They're not even dual interfaces so we have to use `IDispatch` to invoke their methods.

❑ **How to build MFC-based dialog applications**. We won't do anything too sophisticated here, but I'm assuming you know your way around the menus and dialogs of Visual Studio and don't need overly detailed instructions on how to do things.

❑ **CDO**. I'm assuming you've read the previous chapters covering the CDO object model and methods therein – there'll only be brief descriptions of what's going on when I use CDO in ways that have already been covered.

There are a profusion of good introductory books to all the above. You might like to try:

❑ *Beginning MFC COM Programming* by Julian Templeman (ISBN 1-874416-87-7).

❑ *Inside COM* by Dale Rogerson (ISBN 1-572313-49-8)

❑ *Essential COM* by Don Box (ISBN 0-201634-46-5)

❑ *Professional MFC with Visual C++ 6* by Mike Blaszczak (ISBN 1-861000-15-4)

As a final note, I should point out that it's possible to use CDO from C if you really insist, but it's infinitely more painful than using it from C++. But, if you're a stickler, even a dispatch interface is still a COM interface, and as you can talk to COM interfaces using C, you can talk to CDO using C. Note though that all the automatically generated code we'll be leveraging assumes C++, so you'll have an awful lot more effort in front of you.

A SendMail Application In C++

We'll start off by building a very basic send-mail application – all it will be able to do is send a simple plain text mail message to a single recipient. This may seem rudimentary when compared to the Visual Basic application we wrote earlier on, but in this chapter we're looking more at how CDO is used in C++ than the CDO object model itself – once you understand the principles of how to use CDO in C++, you can then apply your knowledge of CDO to extend this application or write entirely new ones.

Rather than introduce CDO from the very next paragraph, we'll start by assembling our dialog and code, and then look at CDO. We won't, then, be looking at CDO itself for a few pages more, but on the other hand, coverage won't be interspersed with instructions on which MFC dialog to build next.

Building The Main Dialog

Start up Visual Studio. Select File | New, and then Project | MFC AppWizard(exe). Select a directory for your new project. For this example, the project is called Book2 and is located in D:\Source\CDO\Book2 but where you put it and what you call it is of course up to you.

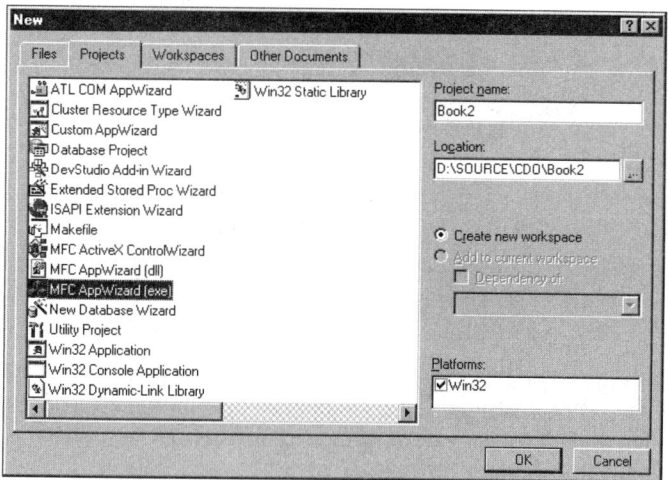

Hit OK, and select the Dialog Based application option from the next window. Those are all the non-default settings we need, so click Finish and let Visual C++ generate the application's boilerplate code.

You may be wondering why we aren't selecting the Automation option that appears in the next wizard page. This would allow us to turn our project into an ActiveX control, which isn't what we want in this situation. All we need to use CDO is access to COM, and we can do that easily enough ourselves.

Now select the main dialog of the project, resize it, move the OK and Cancel buttons to the bottom right corner, and add three static bits of text and three edit boxes to it, changing the properties from their defaults as illustrated:

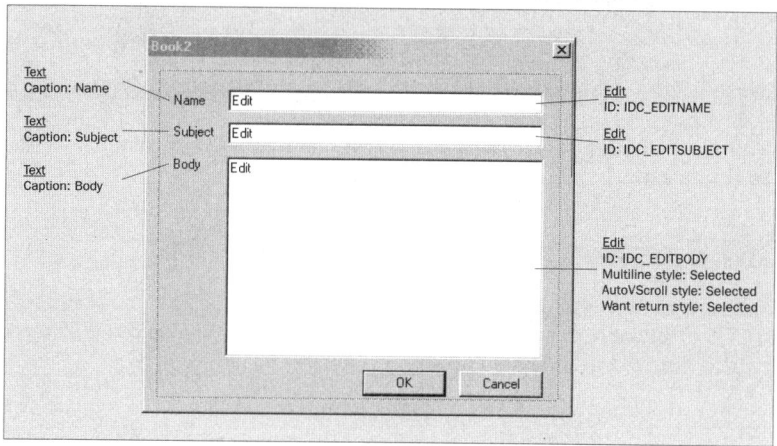

Finally, bring up the MFC ClassWizard (press Ctrl+W) and switch to the **Member Variables** tab. Now add m_csName, m_csSubject, and m_csBody as CString member variables for the Name, Subject and Body edit boxes, like so:

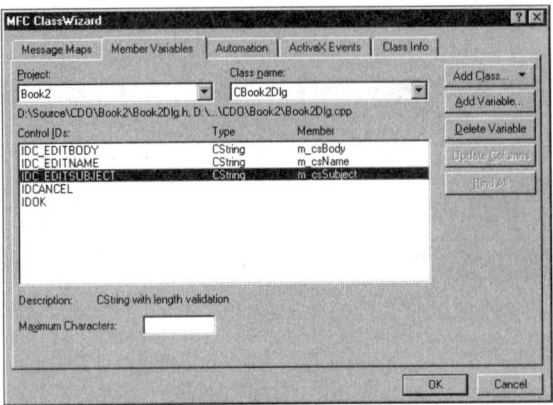

Still in ClassWizard but now on the **Message Maps** tab, we need to add a method for clicking the OK button on our form. Select object **IDOK** and then double click the **BN_CLICKED** message value. An **Add Member Function** dialog will appear for the function. We'll leave it with the name OnOK, so click OK. ClassWizard should now look like this:

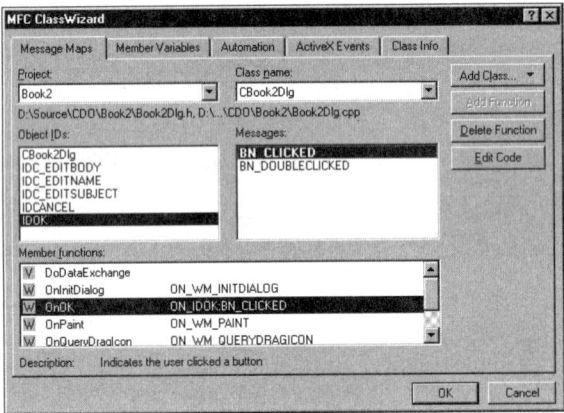

That should be all the explicitly MFC-based coding (or, rather, use of Visual Studio to do the coding for us) we'll need to do for now.

Adding COM Support

Adding COM support to our project is very simple – in order to use any COM interfaces, we first need to initialize the COM library with a call to CoInitialize(NULL). The obvious place to do this is in the InitInstance function of our main app.

So then, open up `book2.cpp` (or whatever the equivalent file is called in your project), and change `InitInstance` as follows:

```
/////////////////////////////////////////////////////////////////////////
// CBook2App initialization

BOOL CBook2App::InitInstance()
{
    HRESULT hr = CoInitialize(NULL);
    if (FAILED(hr))
    {
        CString csError;
        csError.Format("CoInitialize failed: HRESULT 0x%08x", hr);
        AfxMessageBox(csError, MB_OK | MB_ICONERROR);
        // FALSE -> exit application entirely, don't start the main
        // message pump.
        return FALSE;
    }

    AfxEnableControlContainer();

    // Standard initialization
```

This is the standard call to `CoInitialize` – we check to verify it's succeeded, and if not, warn the user and exit.

Introducing CDO To The Application

Now we've got the basic dialog framework in place, we need to look at how we can tell our program about the CDO object model.

One approach would be to use the ClassWizard again to add a reference to the library. This works, but has a major disadvantage: ClassWizard only generates code for the "*classes*" (strictly speaking, interfaces) that make up CDO. Thus, none of the large number of enumerations and other defines (CDO constants and the like) will get generated. We could get away without these – but it would be painful having to remember that `CdoDefaultFolderCalendar` is defined to be 0 every time we want to use it. The code that ClassWizard generates also doesn't contain the nice wrappers for properties that we'll find ourselves able to use; but I'm getting ahead of myself a bit here.

Instead of ClassWizard then, we're going to use the rather convenient compiler directive `#import`, which automatically generates wrapper code to let us use the interfaces defined in the type library we import – in this case, `cdo.dll`.

Open `book2dlg.cpp` and add the following to the start of the file:

```
// book2Dlg.cpp: implementation file
//

#include "stdafx.h"
#include "book2.h"
#include "book2Dlg.h"
```

```
#import <cdo.dll>
using namespace MAPI;

#ifdef _DEBUG
#define new DEBUG_NEW
#undef THIS_FILE
static char THIS_FILE[] = __FILE__;
#endif
```

Now Build the project (Press F7). I won't look at the code that `#import` generates in too much detail – for a great description of what's going on, see the first section of *Professional ATL COM Programming* by Richard Grimes (Wrox Press, ISBN 1-861001-40-1). However, I will mention some of the more problematic aspects of using `#import` that you may come across during development.

The File Locking Problem

When `#import` operates, it generates two files from the type library, putting these generated files in the output directory of your project (`book2\Debug`, for instance) – `cdo.tlh` and `cdo.tli`. The compiler then `#includes` those files into your main source file and compiles the contents.

One problem that can arise is where `#import` hasn't quite finished generating the files before the compiler starts to read them – you can tell this has happened, because you'll get an error like the following when you try to build your project:

> D:\source\cdo\book2\book2Dlg.cpp(8): fatal error C1083:
> Cannot open include file: 'd:\source\cdo\book2\debug\cdo.tlh': Permission denied

This just seems to be a glitch in the development environment – sometimes you won't see it at all, sometimes it'll pop up every time you try and build. If you never see this happen, you can just ignore the following section – if you do, though, here are some workarounds.

- ❑ Just re-compile. This isn't a great workaround, but if you try to build and hit this problem, you can usually make it go away by simply doing the build again. This is the simplest solution; however, I personally find it amazingly irritating to always have to build twice.

- ❑ Move the `#import` line into `stdafx.h`, which means that the file lock might only occur when you change the `stdafx.h` header file (and thus cause the header to be recompiled and the `#import` processing to happen again), and that is presumably something that you won't be doing very often. It is an easy fix, but it's a bit inelegant and has the side-effect that all your code now knows about CDO when chances are you're only going to refer to CDO from one object file. On the other hand, there might be many parts of your project that will need to know about CDO – in which case `stdafx.h` is the right place for it.

❏ Copy `cdo.tlh` from the output directory of your project into the main directory, rename it to `cdo.h`, and replace `#import <cdo.dll>` with `#include "cdo.h"`. This guarantees you'll only run `#import` once, because after that you just include the file as usual. (Of course, this assumes you've managed to successfully compile things at least once)

The gotcha with this method is that `#import` generates two files; `cdo.tlh`, the header file that declares the objects in the type library, and `cdo.tli` which contains the implementation of the `IDispatch` calls. `cdo.tlh` automatically includes `cdo.tli` when you `#include "cdo.tlh"` by some compiler directive magic – but it includes it from the directory it was originally generated in. This means that if you do your first build in Debug mode, move files as explained here, and then delete your Debug output tree and build again in Release mode, you'll hit problems because `cdo.tli` is no longer where `cdo.h` expects it to be. The solution is not difficult however – just edit `cdo.h` to point to the right place and move `cdo.tli` as before.

The other major nasty aspect of this way of doing things is that if you ever do upgrade your version of `cdo.dll`, you won't get any changes coming through to your code because you won't ever process the new version of CDO; if methods change between versions, all sorts of mismatch problems will appear.

The Generates-every-time Problem

More strange still is that `#import` shouldn't ever build the `.tlh` and `.tli` files more than once – according to the documentation, it should compare the timestamp of the generated files to the timestamp of the source DLL and only regenerate them if the DLL is newer than the output files. In practice, it doesn't seem to do this terribly well – this may not be the case on your particular system, but if this does happen, then the workarounds above will not only remove possible locking clash issues, they'll also speed up compilation time by not processing the `#import` every time.

The Mysterious Timestamp Edit Problem

The weirdest glitch I've come across with this (and this one, again, may not happen on your system if you're lucky) is that if you ever open either of the generated files in Visual Studio, for some reason Visual Studio seems to think that the files are constantly being updated. Even when nothing's happening, it will still pop up dialogs saying This file has been modified outside the editor – reload? for some strange reason best known to itself. This can be really annoying when you're trying to edit code, because they seem to pop up every 15 seconds once Visual Studio has decided to start popping them up. Closing the `.tlh` and/or `.tli` windows gets rid of this problem, and it only happens erratically – but it's another good reason for using the workarounds listed above.

A Brief Look at #import's Output

Assuming that you've managed to build the code one way or another, you'll now have the two files generated by `#import` in your debug directory. There aren't really any surprises here – we expect it to produce code that somehow wraps up the CDO library, and that's basically what it does. There are some need-to-be-aware-of aspects to the generated code that I'll point out, though:

Namespace Issues

Right at the top of `cdo.tlh`, after the boilerplate comments that `#import` generates, you'll see that everything is wrapped inside a namespace:

```
namespace MAPI {

// . . . rest of cdo.tlh . . .

}
```

which has its advantages and disadvantages. The obvious advantage is that we don't have to worry about name clashes between a CDO `Message` object and anything else called "Message" that we might have in our code already for whatever reason. The disadvantage is that we can't just say

```
MessagePtr ourMessage;
```

because the CDO `Message` object is in the `MAPI` namespace. Instead, we have two options for our code:

```
using namespace MAPI;
// . . .
MessagePtr ourMessage;
```

or

```
MAPI::MessagePtr ourMessage;
```

Of the two, the latter is safer – it reminds you which namespace you're in every time you declare an object. On the other hand, just putting `using namespace MAPI;` at the top of your source file allows you to avoid needing to do this – but you leave yourself more open to namespace clashes. I'm going to use the former method, just because in the source we'll look at here I know we won't have any possible clashes to worry about – you may want to be more careful, depending on which other objects you have defined. We'll look at why it's `MessagePtr` and not `Message` next.

Smart Pointers

If we go a bit further down through `cdo.tlh`, past the UUID declarations, we'll hit a section of smart pointer declarations looking very much like:

```
_COM_SMARTPTR_TYPEDEF(Message, __uuidof(IDispatch));
```

If we look at what `_COM_SMARTPTR_TYPEDEF` is actually defined as, we find (from `<comdef.h>`)

```
#define _COM_SMARTPTR           _com_ptr_t
#define _COM_SMARTPTR_LEVEL2 _com_IIID
```

```
#define _COM_SMARTPTR_TYPEDEF(Interface, IID) \
    typedef _COM_SMARTPTR<_COM_SMARTPTR_LEVEL2<Interface, &IID> > \
        Interface ## Ptr
```

Now _com_ptr_t is a built-in Visual C++ smart-pointer class – this basically wraps up the calls to AddRef and Delete for us, so we don't need to worry about them. The actual definition code here winds up defining MessagePtr to be a smart pointer wrapper for IDispatch.

Notice that the _COM_SMARTPTR_TYPEDEF line in cdo.tlh wraps IDispatch, not anything else; as mentioned before, all the CDO objects are only exposed through the IDispatch interface. This isn't a problem, because the #import-generated code does the right thing and we can just call methods on our generated classes, and they'll be the methods we expect to be present.

Extra Enums

Next we hit a large number of enum declarations; you'll notice that there are more of these than we've previously mentioned – for instance, we have the following three enumerations covering the type of recipient in a message:

```
enum mapiRecipientType
{
    mapiTo = 1,
    mapiCc = 2,
    mapiBcc = 3
};

// . . .

enum ActMsgRecipientType
{
    ActMsgTo = 1,
    ActMsgCc = 2,
    ActMsgBcc = 3
};

// . . .

enum CdoRecipientType
{
    CdoTo = 1,
    CdoCc = 2,
    CdoBcc = 3
};
```

Why do we have three definitions of the same thing? Easy – backwards compatibility. CDO was designed so that code written for the old OLE Messaging (v1.0) and Active Messaging (v1.1) versions of the library will still work. Thus it carries with it the names for the constants that these earlier technologies used as well as its own.

We don't see these in the Visual Basic object browser, because in the fundamental IDL file that defines the CDO type library (which we'll never see directly, because it presumably exists only on computers inside Microsoft), they all have attribute [hidden] assigned to them. This tells any user interface code browsing the type library not to display them; if you turn on **Show Hidden Items** in the Visual Basic object browser, all these will suddenly appear. This is a good thing when you're using Visual Basic, because you probably don't want to know about these redundant definitions; they're only there for backwards compatibility with old applications, and tend to clutter things up if you make them visible. When writing new code with CDO, you'd only be using the CdoRecipientType enums, so not seeing the old ones won't cause you any problems.

When #import generates code, however, it's not a user interface, it's an automatic code generator – people aren't expected to look at the code generated. Thus, it ignores this [hidden] attribute and just generates code for everything. This isn't a problem to us, because we can just ignore the old definitions with no harm done – I'm just mentioning this so that if you do browse through the cdo.tlh file you'll know what they're doing there.

Convenient member access functions

The final thing I'm going to mention is the convenient helpers that #import generates to let us get at the member properties of the CDO object model. If we take a look at, for instance, the Message object, we'll find:

```
struct __declspec(uuid("3fa7deaa-6438-101b-acc1-00aa00423326"))
Message: IDispatch
{
    //
    // Property data
    //

    // . . . snipped . . .
    __declspec(property(get=GetSubject,put=PutSubject))
    _variant_t Subject;
    // . . .
    _variant_t GetSubject ( );
    void PutSubject ( const _variant_t& _val );
```

What this is doing is declaring a Subject "member" of this class, which we can access as if it were a standard member variable in any class. While we can still read from the subject and write to it using GetSubject and PutSubject, we can also conveniently write code like:

```
pMessage->Subject = "This is the subject.";
```

and it'll be wrapped up into a call to PutSubject for us. This particular helpful aspect of the #import-generated code will make our lives enormously easier; as you'll see, even though all the methods we call and properties we write are still going through IDispatch::Invoke, we can still write code every bit as short as the Visual Basic equivalent.

cdo.tli

This is not terribly interesting to look at – it just contains an enormous number of object methods, all of which are wrappers to `IDispatch::Invoke` in one way or another. Here's an example (slightly reformatted):

```
#pragma implementation_key(165)
inline _variant_t MAPI::Message::Send (
        const _variant_t& SaveCopy, const _variant_t& ShowDialog,
        const _variant_t& ParentWindow )
{
    VARIANT _result;
    _com_dispatch_method(this, 0x83, DISPATCH_METHOD,
                         VT_VARIANT, (void*)&_result,
                         L"\x080c\x080c\x080c", &SaveCopy,
                         &ShowDialog, &ParentWindow);
    return _variant_t(_result, false);
}
```

There's nothing too special here – the thing that's worth noticing about this lot is just how painful it would be if we had to write all the calls to `IDispatch::Invoke` ourselves. You might have guessed already that `_com_dispatch_method` is just a wrapper for that function.

I won't go into any more detail about what's going on with COM and suchlike here. If you want to know more, you should consult the aforementioned books or the online documentation for more details.

Writing Code To Use CDO From C++

With all the preliminaries over and access granted to the CDO object model, let's write some code that actually uses it. We'll start off by just looking at the code we use to send mail; there's no error checking in this initial version, which makes it vulnerable to user abuse. We'll repair that omission later however.

Basic SendMail Code

Edit `CBook2Dlg::OnOk` to read as follows:

```
void CBook2Dlg::OnOK()
{
    UpdateData(TRUE);

    _SessionPtr pSession;
    HRESULT hr = pSession.CreateInstance("MAPI.Session");
    if (FAILED(hr))
    {
        CString cs;
        cs.Format("CreateInstance failed: 0x%08x", hr);
        AfxMessageBox(cs, MB_OK | MB_ICONEXCLAMATION);
        return;
    }
```

```
       pSession->Logon();

       FolderPtr pOutbox = pSession->Outbox;
       MessagesPtr pMessages = pOutbox->Messages;

       MessagePtr pMessage = pMessages->Add((const char *)m_csSubject);
       pMessage->Text = (const char *)m_csBody;

       RecipientsPtr pRecipients = pMessage->Recipients;
       RecipientPtr pRecipient = pRecipients->Add((const char *)m_csName);
       pRecipient->Type = (long)CdoTo;
       pRecipient->Resolve(true);

       pMessage->Send(false);
       pSession->Logoff();

       CDialog::OnOK();
   }
```

Let's take a look at that line-by-line:

```
       UpdateData(TRUE);
```

First, we read the contents of the dialog into our member variables m_csName et al.

```
       _SessionPtr pSession;
       HRESULT hr = pSession.CreateInstance("MAPI.Session");
       if (FAILED(hr))
       {
          CString cs;
          cs.Format("CreateInstance failed: 0x%08x", hr);
          AfxMessageBox(cs, MB_OK | MB_ICONEXCLAMATION);
          return;
       }
```

Now we create a session object. You'll note that this object is actually a pointer to _Session, not Session, as you might expect – the code that #import generates exposes the session object through _SessionPtr. The interface is in _Session, with a coclass of Session. We don't really need to worry about these details as long as we know they're there – this is just a consequence of the way the type library was originally written.

We actually create the session using _com_ptr_t::CreateInstance – it returns an HRESULT for success or failure which we check before proceeding.

The rest of this code is basically standard CDO, just with subtly different syntax.

```
       pSession->Logon();
```

Calling `Logon` is the same as it would be in Visual Basic. For now, we'll use the standard login dialog to choose a profile. One thing to notice, however, is that we can't directly pass named parameters to methods. If, for example, we wanted to use the `profileInfo` parameter of `Logon`, we have to pass in `vtMissing` for all the parameters we aren't specifying, as follows:

```
pSession->Logon(vtMissing, vtMissing, vtMissing,
                vtMissing, vtMissing, vtMissing,
                "server\ndanielm");
```

This isn't particularly difficult once you know to do this – the only trick is knowing that `vtMissing` is the thing to pass for "argument not present". Note that `vtMissing` is *not* the same as NULL – it's actually a variant of type `VT_ERROR` where the error is `0x80020004` – "Parameter not found". This seems reasonable enough and it allows us to distinguish between an argument which is empty (for instance, the string ""), a NULL pointer, and an argument that we're explicitly saying is missing.

```
FolderPtr pOutbox = pSession->Outbox;
MessagesPtr pMessages = pOutbox->Messages;
```

Notice that we can, as previously mentioned, just say `pSession->Outbox`, rather than `pSession->GetOutbox()` – this is the compiler helping us out with `__declspec(property)`. One thing that we do lose compared to Visual Basic, however, is the ability to have code like

```
Set msg = session.Outbox.Messages.Add
```

We can't do that because of return type issues – a `Session` object's `Outbox` property is of type `_variant_t`. This is fine if we then assign it directly to a `FolderPtr` object, because the constructor for `_com_ptr_t` (which, remember, is what `FolderPtr` boils down to) knows how deal with `_variant_t`.

The problem would arise if we tried to do `pSession->Outbox->Messages`, or even `pSession->GetOutbox()->GetMessages()` – those will fail, because the compiler doesn't know that there's a `GetMessages` method available on the `_variant_t` that `GetOutbox()` returns, even though we, as programmers, know that the returned object is actually an `IDispatch` interface implementing the `Folder` interface. We have to turn it into a `FolderPtr` object so we can use all the appropriate methods.

Again, this isn't difficult to deal with when you know it's there; you just have to make sure that every intermediate object is explicitly stored somewhere.

```
MessagePtr pMessage = pMessages->Add((const char*)m_csSubject);
pMessage->Text = (const char*)m_csBody;
```

Note that we have to explicitly cast our `CString`s for the subject and body text of the message to `const char*` – the `Add` method takes, as with every other method, `_variant_t` as arguments and there's no `CString` constructor for `_variant_t`. There is one for `const char*`, though, so we just cast our `CString` appropriately, and all is well.

```
RecipientsPtr pRecipients = pMessage->Recipients;
RecipientPtr pRecipient = pRecipients->Add((const char*)m_csName);
pRecipient->Type = (long)CdoTo;
```

Notice that we have to cast CdoTo to long here. CdoTo is defined as part of an enum, and there's no constructor for enum in _variant_t, so we cast it to a long and all is well.

> **In general, if we want to use any of the CDO constants, we'll have to cast them to long first.**

```
pRecipient->Resolve(true);

pMessage->Send(false);
pSession->Logoff();
```

Next, we call Resolve on the addresses in To field and tell it pop up a dialog if it can't resolve the name entered automatically. Assuming this resolution occurs happily, we call Send with the proviso not to include the message in our sent-messages folder. Finally, we log out of the session; this will happen automatically when the session object is released, but better safe than sorry.

Note that we're using true and false instead of TRUE and FALSE – our CDO methods are expecting Boolean arguments, and if we pass in TRUE, this will just expand to 1 (because TRUE is just a #define when it comes down to it), which is an integer, not a Boolean. So then, we need to use the C++ bool class when we want to use Boolean values.

Running the first version

If you build this version and run it, you should be able to send mail. However, as it stands, this is very vulnerable code; if you, for instance, just leave the edit fields blank and hit OK, you'll see something like the following:

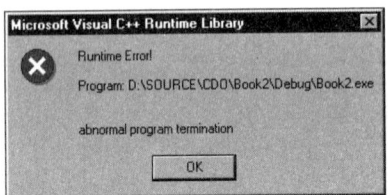

This is because when we try and call Resolve on a recipient with a blank name, CDO can't resolve it – even though we tell CDO to show a dialog to attempt to resolve things, CDO still doesn't have enough information to even do this – and throws an error. So let's look at error handling.

Error Handling

CDO does all its error reporting by throwing exceptions – so we need to catch those exceptions if we want to handle errors.

CDO throws exceptions when we use it through #import-generated code, because the smart pointer helper classes that #import generates throw exceptions to report errors. And, as #import is the only practical way to get at CDO, we'll only look at exceptions as a way of handling errors here).

Before we continue, please make sure that Exception Handling is turned on in your project. This is the default, but just in case, select Project | Settings and select the C/C++ tab in the dialog. By changing the Category list box to C++ Language, you should be able to check the Enable exception handling radio button if necessary.

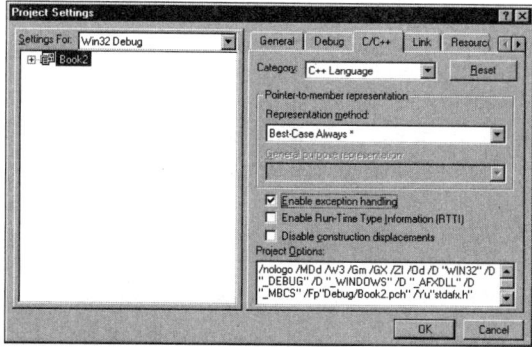

Basic Error Handling Techniques

We'll start off by wrapping all of our CDO code in a `try..catch` block; that way any exceptions thrown will be gracefully handled (or at least handled other than by Visual Studio), and after that we'll look at handling specific exceptions for error conditions we're expecting.

Change OnOk as follows:

```
void dump_com_error(_com_error& e);

void CBook2Dlg::OnOK()
{
    UpdateData(TRUE);

    _SessionPtr pSession;
    HRESULT hr = pSession.CreateInstance("MAPI.Session");
    if (FAILED(hr))
    {
        CString cs;
        cs.Format("CreateInstance failed: 0x%08x", hr);
        AfxMessageBox(cs, MB_OK | MB_ICONEXCLAMATION);
        return;
    }

    try
    {
        pSession->Logon();

        FolderPtr pOutbox = pSession->Outbox;
        MessagesPtr pMessages = pOutbox->Messages;

        MessagePtr pMessage = pMessages->Add((const char*)m_csSubject);
        pMessage->Text = (const char*)m_csBody;
```

```
        RecipientsPtr pRecipients = pMessage->Recipients;
        RecipientPtr pRecipient = pRecipients->Add((const char*)m_csName);
        pRecipient->Type = (long)CdoTo;
        pRecipient->Resolve(true);

        pMessage->Send(false);
        pSession->Logoff();
    }
    catch (_com_error e)
    {
        dump_com_error(e);
    }

    CDialog::OnOK();
}
```

We declare _dump_com_error, which we'll look at momentarily and then wrap all the code that uses the CDO objects in a try..catch block. Notice that the type of exception that CDO throws is _com_error – this is another Microsoft-specific COM helper class that comes with _com_ptr_t, _variant_t, and _bstr_t (which we haven't yet looked at).

```
void dump_com_error(_com_error& e)
{
    CString csError;
    _bstr_t bstrSource(e.Source());
    bstr_t bstrDescription(e.Description());
    _bstr_t bstrMessage(e.ErrorMessage());

    csError.Format("\
        Oops! Caught an exception.\n\
        Code = %08lx\n\
        WCode = %04x\n\
        HRESULT = %08x\n\
        Code meaning = %S\n\
        Source = %S\n\
        Description = %S",
            e.Error(), e.WCode(), e.WCodeToHRESULT(e.WCode()),
            (wchar_t*)bstrMessage, (wchar_t*)bstrSource,
            (wchar_t*)bstrDescription);

    AfxMessageBox(csError, MB_ICONERROR | MB_OK);
}
```

This is a convenient helper function for all sorts of COM debugging; it takes a _com_error exception and turns it into a useful diagnostic string containing the information about the error – in this case we display it in a message box, although you could also use TRACE to log it to the debugger, or some other logging mechanism, or whatever.

Most of this is pretty unremarkable, except for the fact that the strings in a _com_error are BSTRs so we use _bstr_t to wrap the extraction of these up and avoid memory leak problems (_bstr_t is a smart wrapper class for BSTR). We still have to convert these into standard characters to display, so we use the %S printf format specification to deal with this.

Now, if you build the project and try to send mail with no name, you'll see the following:

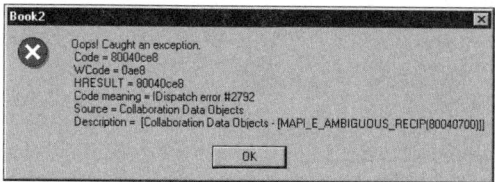

This contains a lot of numbers we don't have a particular use for at the moment, and some very helpful strings; firstly, we're told that the source of this exception is CDO – okay, we know this is the case here, but in more general debugging situations, we may not.

Another CDO Glitch

More interestingly, you'll note that while the error code is reported correctly in the `Description` field, as `0x80040700` (that's `MAPI_E_AMBIGUOUS_RECIP` if you look it up in `cdo.tlh`), the `HRESULT` that we extract from the `_com_error` reports as `0x80040ce8`. But why?

The reason for this particular mismatch is a bug in CDO – the errors that it throws, when caught by C++, contain invalid `HRESULT`s. If we read Microsoft Knowledge Base article Q235361 (see Appendix G), it tells us about this in somewhat more detail. In a nutshell,

> **We need to use a translation table to convert the WCode value in the `_com_error` to the correct HRESULT correctly.**

Hang on though. Why are we bothered about this at all? Because sometimes we do care which error was thrown – just catching all the errors the application generates and hoping that the user can interpret the resulting generic error dialog is not a good way of doing things. We have to do *something* to help CDO.

In the case of our current problem, for instance, we get the `MAPI_E_AMBIGUOUS_RECIP` error if CDO can't resolve the name from the information given. By entering nothing at all in the Name edit box, CDO doesn't even have enough name information to pop up the standard "Resolve Name" dialog. It would be good if we could display a dialog warning the user that they should be more specific with their name if this happened again. To do that, we need to be able to react to the specific error code when it's generated.

So, change `dump_com_error` as follows:

```
HRESULT GetHRESULTFromComError(_com_error& e);

void dump_com_error(_com_error& e)
{
    CString csError;
    _bstr_t bstrSource(e.Source());
    bstr_t bstrDescription(e.Description());
    _bstr_t bstrMessage(e.ErrorMessage());

    csError.Format("\
```

```
        Oops! Caught an exception.\n\
        Code = %081x\n\
        WCode = %04x\n\
        HRESULT = %08x\n\
        Real HRESULT = %08x\n\
        Code meaning = %S\n\
        Source = %S\n\
        Description = %S",
            e.Error(), e.WCode(), e.WCodeToHRESULT(e.WCode()),
            GetHRESULTFromComError(e),
            (wchar_t*)bstrMessage, (wchar_t*)bstrSource,
            (wchar_t*)bstrDescription);

    AfxMessageBox(csError, MB_ICONERROR | MB_OK);
}
```

Now add the following function at the end of `book2Dlg.cpp`. Remember, you can download the source code from `http://www.wrox.com`, if you don't feel up to typing all this in.

```
HRESULT GetHRESULTFromComError(_com_error& e)
{
    static HRESULT TranslationTable[][2] = {
        {1515,CdoW_NO_SERVICE},{1896,CdoW_ERRORS_RETURNED},
        {2153,CdoW_POSITION_CHANGED},{215,CdoW_APPROX_COUNT},
        {2408,CdoW_CANCEL_MESSAGE},{2664,CdoW_PARTIAL_COMPLETION},
        {17386,CdoE_INTERFACE_NOT_SUPPORTED},{17389,CdoE_CALL_FAILED},
        {1258,CdoE_NO_SUPPORT},{1259,CdoE_BAD_CHARWIDTH},
        {1261,CdoE_STRING_TOO_LONG},{1262,CdoE_UNKNOWN_FLAGS},
        {1263,CdoE_INVALID_ENTRYID},{1264,CdoE_INVALID_OBJECT},
        {1265,CdoE_OBJECT_CHANGED},{1266,CdoE_OBJECT_DELETED},
        {1267,CdoE_BUSY},{1269,CdoE_NOT_ENOUGH_DISK},
        {1270,CdoE_NOT_ENOUGH_RESOURCES},{1271,CdoE_NOT_FOUND},
        {1272,CdoE_VERSION},{1273,CdoE_LOGON_FAILED},
        {1274,CdoE_SESSION_LIMIT},{1275,CdoE_USER_CANCEL},
        {1276,CdoE_UNABLE_TO_ABORT},{1277,CdoE_NETWORK_ERROR},
        {1278,CdoE_DISK_ERROR},{1279,CdoE_TOO_COMPLEX},
        {1280,CdoE_BAD_COLUMN},{1281,CdoE_EXTENDED_ERROR},
        {1282,CdoE_COMPUTED},{1283,CdoE_CORRUPT_DATA},
        {1284,CdoE_UNCONFIGURED},{1285,CdoE_FAILONEPROVIDER},
        {1286,CdoE_UNKNOWN_CPID},{1287,CdoE_UNKNOWN_LCID},
        {1288,CdoE_PASSWORD_CHANGE_REQUIRED},{1289,CdoE_PASSWORD_EXPIRED},
        {1290,CdoE_INVALID_WORKSTATION_ACCOUNT},{1291,CdoE_INVALID_ACCESS_TIME},
        {1292,CdoE_ACCOUNT_DISABLED},{1512,CdoE_END_OF_SESSION},
        {1513,CdoE_UNKNOWN_ENTRYID},{1514,CdoE_BAD_VALUE},
        {1770,CdoE_INVALID_TYPE},{1771,CdoE_TYPE_NO_SUPPORT},
        {1772,CdoE_UNEXPECTED_TYPE},{1773,CdoE_TOO_BIG},
        {1774,CdoE_DECLINE_COPY},{1775,CdoE_UNEXPECTED_ID},
        {2024,CdoE_UNABLE_TO_COMPLETE},{2025,CdoE_TIMEOUT},
        {2026,CdoE_TABLE_EMPTY},{2027,CdoE_TABLE_TOO_BIG},
        {2029,CdoE_INVALID_BOOKMARK},{2280,CdoE_WAIT},
        {2281,CdoE_CANCEL},{2282,CdoE_NOT_ME},
        {2536,CdoE_CORRUPT_STORE},{2537,CdoE_NOT_IN_QUEUE},
        {2538,CdoE_NO_SUPPRESS},{2540,CdoE_COLLISION},
```

```
            {2541,CdoE_NOT_INITIALIZED},{2542,CdoE_NON_STANDARD},
            {2543,CdoE_NO_RECIPIENTS},{2544,CdoE_SUBMITTED},
            {2545,CdoE_HAS_FOLDERS},{2546,CdoE_HAS_MESSAGES},
            {2547,CdoE_FOLDER_CYCLE},{2792,CdoE_AMBIGUOUS_RECIP},
            {1005,CdoE_NO_ACCESS},{1014,CdoE_NOT_ENOUGH_MEMORY},
            {1087,CdoE_INVALID_PARAMETER}};

    HRESULT hrFake = e.WCode();
    hrFake = hrFake & 0xffff;

    for (int i=0; i < sizeof(TranslationTable) / sizeof(TranslationTable[0]); i++)
    {
        if (TranslationTable[i][0] == hrFake)
        {
            return TranslationTable[i][1];
        }
    }
    return E_UNEXPECTED;
}
```

This is just a big translation table from the WCode values we read from the exception into real HRESULT
values.

*Note that this bug is present as of writing this book – it may be fixed in future versions of CDO.
Checking the KnowledgeBase article above (235361) should allow you to find out if this has
happened or not, and if so, you can then remove this translation code.*

Watching For Individual Errors

Now let's add code to our project to check for the ambiguous recipient error and warn about it directly.
We'll insert the following piece of code into OnOK so that it reads:

```
    RecipientPtr pRecipient = pRecipients->Add((const char*)m_csName);
    pRecipient->Type = (long)CdoTo;

    try
    {
        pRecipient->Resolve(true);
        pMessage->Send(false);

    }
    catch (_com_error e)
    {
        if (GetHRESULTFromComError(e) == CdoE_AMBIGUOUS_RECIP)
        {
            CString cs;
            cs.Format("Couldn't resolve `%s' at all", m_csSubject);
            AfxMessageBox(cs, MB_ICONERROR | MB_OK);
        }
        else
        {
            throw(e);
```

```
            }
        }
    pSession->Logoff();
    }
    catch (_com_error e)
    {
        dump_com_error(e);
    }
    CDialog::OnOK();
}
```

We wrap the call to `Resolve` in an inner `try..catch` block, and if it fails with an error we know about, we pop up a more useful dialog box – if you now try sending mail with no recipient, you'll see a dialog like:

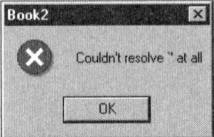

If the error isn't one we're looking for, we re-throw it so the outer `catch` block can deal with it – you can test this by typing in an ambiguous name that's not the empty string, hitting **OK**, and then hitting **Cancel** to the resolve dialog that pops up, you'll see:

As we'd expect, this new error tells us that the user cancelled an operation and appears in the generic error box because it was caught by the outer `catch` handler.

One final thing to note in this section on error handling is that there's a leak in the internal implementation of smart pointers. When an exception is thrown, three `BSTR`s and an `ICreateErrorInfo` interface are not released – see KnowledgeBase article 231872 for more on this.

There's not a great deal we can do about this problem, but, on the other hand, it only becomes apparent when an exception is raised. Consider this a note for future reference if you ever use BoundsChecker or do a lot of deliberate error catching.

Reading An Inbox

We've seen how to use CDO to send messages from C++. Let's move on now and add code to read the contents of the Inbox.

Code Reorganization

Now that we're going to be doing more than one thing before we exit, let's move the `Session` object we use into our dialog class to save logging in each time – open `Book2Dlg.h` and edit `CBook2Dlg` as follows, adding a member variable `m_pSession`:

```
#if _MSC_VER > 1000
#pragma once
#endif // _MSC_VER > 1000

#import <cdo.dll>
using namespace MAPI;

/////////////////////////////////////////////////////////////////////////
// CBook2Dlg dialog

class CBook2Dlg: public CDialog
{
// Construction
    //
    // . . . these lines not shown in this sample, but leave them in . . .
    //
// Implementation
protected:
    HICON m_hIcon;

    _SessionPtr m_pSession;

    // Generated message map functions
    //{{AFX_MSG(CBook2Dlg)
```

We can now remove the `#import <cdo.dll>` and `using namespace MAPI` lines from `Book2Dlg.cpp`, because they're now in the header file – so alter the top of `Book2Dlg.cpp` so that it begins:

```
#include "stdafx.h"
#include "book2.h"
#include "book2Dlg.h"

#ifdef _DEBUG
#define new DEBUG_NEW
#undef THIS_FILE
static char THIS_FILE[] = __FILE__;
#endif

void dump_com_error(_com_error& e);
HRESULT GetHRESULTFromComError(_com_error& e);
```

Note the lines mentioned have gone and we've moved the declarations of `dump_com_error` and `GetHRESULTFromComError` to the top of the file so that all our functions can use them. Accordingly, they should be removed from lower down in the file.

We're also going to make the log in occur as soon as the dialog initializes. This way we're already logged in by the time OnOK, or anything else we decide to add, gets to happen. So then, just edit CBook2Dlg::OnInitDialog as follows.

```
BOOL CBook2Dlg::OnInitDialog()
{
    // . . . leave all the original code here
    // Set the icon for this dialog. The framework does this automatically
    //  when the application's main window is not a dialog
    SetIcon(m_hIcon, TRUE);         // Set big icon
    SetIcon(m_hIcon, FALSE);        // Set small icon

    HRESULT hr = m_pSession.CreateInstance("MAPI.Session");
    if (FAILED(hr))
    {
        CString cs;
        cs.Format("CreateInstance failed: 0x%08x", hr);
        AfxMessageBox(cs, MB_OK | MB_ICONEXCLAMATION);
        return TRUE;
    }
    try {
        m_pSession->Logon();
    }
    catch (_com_error e)
    {
        dump_com_error(e);
    }

    return TRUE;  // return TRUE  unless you set the focus to a control
}
```

You'll also need to change OnOK() as follows, so that it uses our member session variable rather than the one generated. We'll also need to remove the calls to CreateInstance and Logon which are now in OnInitDialog():

```
void CBook2Dlg::OnOK()
{
    UpdateData(TRUE);

    try
    {

        FolderPtr pOutbox = m_pSession->Outbox;
        MessagesPtr pMessages = pOutbox->Messages;

        // . . . all as before . . .

        m_pSession->Logoff();
    }
    catch (_com_error e)
    {
        dump_com_error(e);
    }
    CDialog::OnOK();
}
```

Dialog Changes

Of course, we're also going to need some place to see the contents of our Inbox, so we'll need to change the layout of our main dialog. Add a listbox for the inbox contents to be displayed in and a button to update the listbox – you don't need to change their IDs.

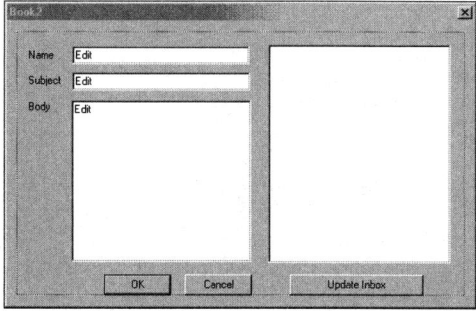

Open up ClassWizard and assign a member variable to the listbox control called m_ctlInbox of type CListBox and a method to the **Update Inbox** button called OnUpdateInbox() which you'll need to edit.

```
void CBook2Dlg::OnUpdateInbox()
{
    m_ctlInbox.ResetContent()
```

We start off by removing any old content from our listbox.

```
    try
    {
        FolderPtr pInbox = m_pSession->Inbox;
        MessagesPtr pMsgs = pInbox->Messages;
        MessagePtr pMsg;
```

All of this is wrapped, as usual, in a try..catch block. We get a pointer to the Messages collection of our Inbox, and prepare to start reading from it.

```
        try
        {
            pMsg = pMsgs->GetFirst();
        }
        catch(_com_error e)
        {
            // No messages at all!
            return;
        }
```

We wrap the call to GetFirst in an internal try..catch block. This may be being overly paranoid, but sometimes CDO will throw an exception if you try and read the first element of an empty collection and we don't want to show the generic error dialog just because someone has no messages in their Inbox, we just want to have an empty list.

499

```
        if (pMsg == NULL)
        {
            return;
        }
```

Alternatively, CDO may also just return an empty object if there are no messages in your Inbox – we need to deal with this situation as well.

```
        while(1)
        {
```

There are a number of ways of dealing with looping under CDO in C++ – we could, if we were feeling optimistic, try reading the number of messages from the Count property on our Messages object, and loop that many times. However, we know (see earlier chapters for more on this) that the Count property can return 0x7fffffff if CDO decides there are "too many" items in the collection we're looking at, so rather than add extra code to deal with that, we just start off assuming we'll have to loop until there are no more objects.

This is not perhaps the best way to do this in general – if the user's inbox has many thousands of messages, this loop will take a long time to operate. Adding a limit to the number of messages we'll process would be easy enough, but I'm not doing it here to keep the code as simple as possible.

> **Arrays we get from CDO are indexed starting from 1, not 0. This is because they may be generated by scripting languages, which index from 1.**

CDO thinks of the lists of objects that it returns as a collection, where the initial entry is the first – 1st – element 1. This is different to C++, where we're used to collections of things being arrays, where we index from 0 to reflect the layout of that array in memory. To reflect the distinction between arrays and lists then, the code for looping over items in a list should look like:

```
    for (int i=1; i <= nItems; i++) // start with 1, compare with <=
```

Fortunately, if you forget to do this it'll become obvious very rapidly, because CDO will throw an exception to tell you there's no item 0 in the list. Note that we won't actually need this particular type of loop in our code, but I've added this here as a potential trap for you to be aware of.

Given we're not looping over a known number of items, we use a while(1) loop – this is just personal style, some people prefer for(;;), or you could write while(pMsg != NULL) which would save a break further down.

```
        CString csSubject = (wchar_t*)(_bstr_t)pMsg->Subject;
        m_ctlInbox.AddString(csSubject);
```

Note that, again, we have to deal with BSTRs coming from the variants that CDO returns. In this case, the Subject that we read from our message returns a _variant_t. We extract the BSTR member of that into a _bstr_t, and then extract from that into a CString by casting the _bstr_t to (wchar_t*), so that the CString's constructor can deal with it – CString has a constructor for wchar_t* but not for _bstr_t. Once we've got the subject of this message in a useful format, we add it to our listbox.

```
try
{
    pMsg = pMsgs->GetNext();
}
catch (_com_error e)
{
    // No more messages.
    break;
}
if (pMsg == NULL)
{
    break;
}
```

Once again, we need to trap both the case where we come to the end of the messages collection and the case where we've been given a NULL object. Note that because we're in a while(1) loop here, we have to use break to exit the loop. If we'd made the loop condition while(pMsg != NULL), we wouldn't need to do a break here if pMsg actually did become NULL, but I've used while(1) to keep the checks for loop termination consistent with those that we did for no objects at all when we called GetFirst.

```
        }
    }
    catch (_com_error e)
    {
        dump_com_error(e);
    }
}
```

And we end with the usual top-level catch block.

If you now try this and click on the **Update Inbox** button, you should wind up with a dialog looking something like:

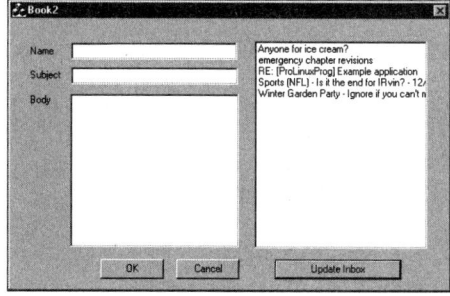

Note that if you hit OK you'll still get the Couldn't resolve " at all dialog, because OK still tries to send mail. This probably needs changing if you want to take this application as a starting point for further development.

At this point, we've covered the essential points you need to know to use CDO from C++. From here on, you should be able to extend this application to add new features, or write entirely new ones from scratch, as you wish. There's only so much you need to know to use CDO in C++, and we've covered it here. For further information on CDO, see the other chapters on the object model and how to use it.

Summary So Far

In this first half of the chapter then, we've covered the key aspects of writing C++\CDO applications. In particular:

- ❑ The use of `#import`, and some tricks you may need to employ if `#import` misbehaves.
- ❑ The files that `#import` generates and the helpful methods and wrappers for object properties within.
- ❑ How to send mail using CDO in C++.
- ❑ Adding simple error handling to deal with the fact that in C++, CDO throws exceptions to notify us of error conditions.
- ❑ Enhancing the error handling to account for the badly formed information in those exceptions and to deal with specific errors we know how to handle.
- ❑ Finally, we looked at reading information from the system using CDO – we reorganized our code for a more general way of doing mail in applications, and we dealt with the issues that arise from the variant types that CDO uses to return information.

In the second half, we'll go under the covers of CDO to reveal Extended MAPI calls and the things you can't do with CDO.

Using Extended MAPI with CDO

Extended MAPI (from now on referred to as just MAPI) is the COM-based messaging system API that CDO uses to talk to Exchange. While we implement our code in CDO, it turns out that CDO is just a set of wrappers to make MAPI more accessible and easier to use.

For this chapter, we'll assume that we're trying to talk to Exchange, but note that there are MAPI implementations to allow you to talk to, for instance, Lotus Notes. However, bear in mind that every implementation of MAPI has restrictions of some sort or another, usually undocumented. In general, you're probably best advised to use the API most directly designed to be used with your messaging server; Lotus Notes, for instance, has Notes-specific C and C++ APIs you can use to talk to it, and using these should be much less risky than relying on their implementation of MAPI.

> If you want to use Simple or Extended MAPI (or, for that matter, CDO) to talk to any sort of mail system other than Microsoft Exchange, be very careful to make sure that your code is working as you expect, and beware of undocumented bugs sneaking in.

CDO, which lives on top of Extended MAPI, will thus suffer from the same problems as writing direct MAPI code – you may well be able to get away with writing CDO code to talk to a non-Exchange server, but relying on it in production code would best be described as courageous...

Why use MAPI?

Why would we want to use MAPI at all? CDO provides a lot of messaging/collaboration functionality, certainly, but there are still some things you can't do with CDO – for instance, if you want to write a message with RTF in the body, there's no way to do this directly with CDO. (KnowledgeBase article 172038 has details on a workaround using an external DLL, however). Similarly, if you want to manage the list of profiles on your machine, you need to use MAPI or if you just want to guarantee yourself absolute fine-grained control over what's going on, you should use MAPI.

Advantages

MAPI has its pros and cons like everything else. The fundamental advantage is that, because it's the lowest level at which you can talk to Exchange Server (without opening a socket and reverse-engineering the wire protocol that MAPI uses, at least), you have the greatest possible level of control over what happens. You *can* access all the features that are available to you, whereas CDO only makes available a (large, but) limited subset of this functionality.

One other advantage of using this low-level an interface to the mail system is that you always know what's happening – CDO can occasionally behave in mysterious ways and, because CDO is wrapping up underlying functionality, it can be difficult to tell exactly what's going on and why you're seeing particular types of behavior. With MAPI, while it may take more effort to do things, when you *do* have your code written you can be that much more sure of what's going on and confident that the system isn't hiding things from you.

This is, to be honest, the only real advantage – wherever and whenever you can use MAPI, you can use CDO, and CDO is so much easier to use I can't see any reason you would want to use MAPI if you don't have to. Saying that though, when you have to use MAPI, you tend to *really* have to use MAPI.

Disadvantages

There is more than one reason for not using MAPI of course. In the end, it's a case of trading off your needs against what MAPI can offer that CDO can't.

Language Dependence

The most important disadvantage of MAPI, from one point of view, is that you can only use it from a language that speaks raw COM. In a Microsoft world, this means C++ and nothing else – Visual Basic, VBScript, Java, JScript, etc are all incapable of using MAPI directly. You *can* use MAPI from Delphi with some extra header files to define the interfaces, or C if you jump through the requisite hoops to use COM from C, but we won't go into either here.

If you need to use Visual Basic (or VBScript, etc), then you can't use MAPI directly – but you can still get at it indirectly, with some extra effort. If you write a DLL in C++ that contains your MAPI code, you can then call that DLL from your VB code – this is how the RTF-writing code in the KnowledgeBase article mentioned above works. Of course, you still need to be able to develop in C++, but it's possible to minimize the amount of C++ coding you need to do.

Complexity

The other obvious disadvantage of using MAPI is that it's much more complex to use. For one thing, all the interfaces you get don't come conveniently wrapped up in smart pointers; there's nothing to stop you using _com_ptr_t yourself, of course, but you have to remember to do this.

Memory allocation for MAPI is also *much* more complex than in CDO. Essentially, there aren't any memory allocation issues in CDO – you just pass strings in/out of it, and everything automatically does the right thing. MAPI, on the other hand, has much more arcane requirements. You need to explicitly allocate memory for everything you pass into the system, and free up the memory that the system allocates for the buffers it returns to you. What's more, the structures you need to use to talk to MAPI are, well, a pain. They're documented, but the learning curve you need to climb to get things working is a nasty steep one.

Calendaring

One other disadvantage of MAPI is another aspect of not having nice wrapper classes – you don't have any of the calendaring features of CDO. Now, at one level, all the objects that CDO uses are fundamentally messages with different lists of properties (or Field objects, in CDO terminology) so you can, in theory, do all the things that CDO does yourself using MAPI. It's just that you may not know *how* to do them – CDO wraps up the undocumented calendar properties stored in messages and turns them into useful things using Microsoft's internal knowledge of how this all works.

To take a concrete example, we'll look at the RecurrencePattern object that CDO gives us for appointments and meetings. In CDO, it's a nice tidy object that we can read all sorts of useful information from – how often does this appointment recur, which days of the week does it occur on, etc. In MAPI, however, there's no such thing as a RecurrencePattern object. What we have instead is a list of anonymous properties on the message, one of which we have to assume must contain recurrence information because it must be there somewhere. It is, in fact, possible to work out which property the recurrence information is stored in by changing the recurrence on a meeting and watching the low-level meeting to see which properties change.

Once we start doing this, we hit all sorts of excitement. First, we find that the recurrence information is stored in a named property – that's not fatal, but it means that we have to jump through the hoops that MAPI imposes on us to deal with named properties. If we do this, we discover that the names for properties are remarkably uninformative, and, instead of being RECURRENCE_PROP, the property is actually called 0x8216. Yes, the name *is* a six-character-long string looking like a hexadecimal number.

Secondly, we find that the recurrence information is stored in a large chunk of binary data.

At this point, one might want to give up and use CDO. However, with sufficient persistence, it is actually possible to reverse-engineer the undocumented set of bytes that makes up the recurrence information and thus decode a recurrence in code. This sort of thing leads to madness – one of the *less* cryptic aspects of this data that I found when doing this is that (for instance) the month, on which monthly recurrences occur, is stored not as a number from 1 to 12, but *as the number of minutes from the start of the year to the first day of that month.* Or, at least, that was the best guess I could make as to what that code did – there's no documentation, so everything needs to be reverse-engineered. It was, I can assure you, an enormous relief to be able to discard that code and use CDO.

Another exciting aspect of recurring meetings are that if you have, say, a meeting every Tuesday, but one instance of that meeting is moved to Wednesday, the moved instance is actually stored as an attachment on the "base" meeting, rather than as an entry in the calendar; CDO wraps up the extraction of this sort of thing for us, as well as generally expanding recurrences when we search for meetings over a given range of dates.

If you want to do calendaring, you *really* should use CDO rather than MAPI.

Documentation

One other problem with using MAPI is that the best reference book on MAPI, "Inside MAPI" (Irving de la Cruz and Les Thaler, Microsoft Press) is out of print. It's still by far the best reference; none of the information in there is out-of-date, and it contains the only really good explanations of how to use some of he more high-powered aspects of MAPI coding (which I won't go into here) – but Microsoft have let it go out of print for some reason. You may be able to find a copy of this in a bookstore, but count yourself very lucky if you do. The online documentation is adequate for most of the basic MAPI tasks you may need to perform (actually, it's surprisingly good, all things considered), but it suffers from the same problem as a lot of online documentation, namely that it's much more of a reference source than a way to learn what's actually going on.

One very, *very* useful source of information is the Microsoft sample projects you can download from `ftp://ftp.microsoft.com/developr/MAPI/Samples/MFCAPPS/` `MFCAPPS.ZIP`. Most of note in this zip file is the source to `MDBView`, an application to view the contents of your message store at a very low level. This utility in itself will prove incredibly useful if you start doing low-level things to talk to the messaging system, be it in CDO or MAPI, just because it's always helpful to see exactly what's going on – but the source code is also an amazing source of examples on how to do things.

There is also a `common` directory contains source code for a lot of utility functions that you'll find essential when you start developing – things to turn MAPI error codes into strings, MAPI property IDs into strings, dump MAPI properties to a file, etc. I really can't recommend strongly enough that you download, build, and look at these samples – if you ever do any MAPI development, you will *not* be sorry.

There are also samples in the Platform SDK, which are in general smaller and more focussed; however, I haven't found those anything like as helpful as the `MFCAPPS` sample code.

Sample Projects Using MAPI

Let's look at some sample code that uses MAPI and CDO at the same time, so you can see the added functionality to be gained.

Sending RTF mail

We'll start with the first thing we mentioned, sending mail with RTF (Rich Text Format) text in the body. If you understand what we're doing here, you might like to try extending this app to send HTML mail too – see KnowledgeBase article 216344 for more details.

At this point, we could theoretically take our previous send-mail application and upgrade it to send RTF; however, the number of changes we'd need to make would end up just confusing things, so let's start from scratch.

On The Basics Of RTF Editing

First, we'll quickly look at how to generate RTF text in the first place, before we worry about sending it as mail.

Main Dialog Layout

Start a new project, choose the MFC AppWizard (exe), make it dialog-based, and hit Finish.
Edit the main dialog to look like this, but do be careful, some things aren't what they appear to be.
Please read the notes in the diagram before you start on this.

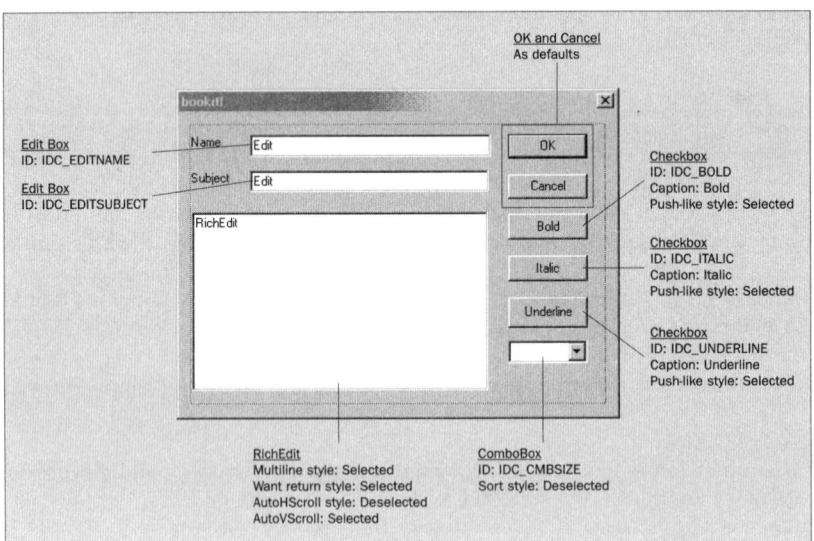

Now, use the ClassWizard, and add member variables as follows:

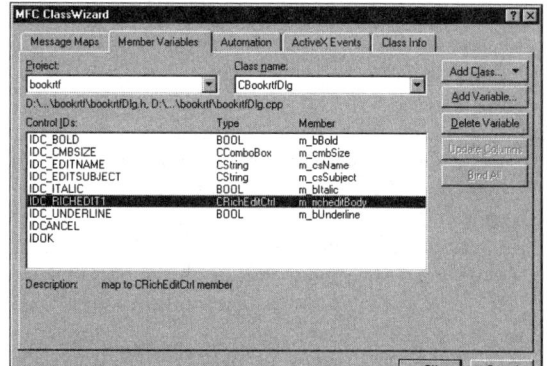

Finally, add methods in the **Message Maps** tab as follows:

❑   For BN_CLICKED on the buttons, add OnBold(), OnItalic(), and OnUnderline(). We'll
    leave OnOK() alone for now.

❑   For CBN_SELCHANGE on the combo box, add OnSelchangeCmbsize().

Using the CRichEditCtrl Control

Let's implement the rich-text edit part of this project first and then go onto the MAPI and CDO section.
Open bookrtf.cpp, and add the following line – we need to do this to be able to use the rich text edit
control.

```
BOOL CBookrtfApp::InitInstance()
{
    AfxEnableControlContainer();

    AfxInitRichEdit();

    // Standard initialization
```

Now open bookrtfDlg.cpp, and edit OnBold as follows:

```
void CBookrtfDlg::OnBold()
{
    // Read the state of our checkbox.
    UpdateData(TRUE);
    CHARFORMAT cfm;
    cfm.cbSize = sizeof(cfm);
    cfm.dwMask = CFM_BOLD;
    cfm.dwEffects = m_bBold ? CFE_BOLD: 0;

    // Next one doesn't change the default, it changes everything.
    // Docs lie!
    // m_richeditBody.SetDefaultCharFormat(cfm);
```

```
    // Have to do this instead.
    m_richeditBody.SendMessage(EM_SETCHARFORMAT, SCF_SELECTION, (long)&cfm);

    m_richeditBody.SetFocus();
}
```

Here, we're telling the rich-text edit control to change the default format for text to be bold; details of the CHARFORMAT structure are in the documentation, but, basically, the dwMask field is used to describe which of the other elements of CHARFORMAT are valid.

You might think from the documentation that we could use SetDefaultCharFormat to tell the edit box to start adding characters in bold – however, that method actually turns the entire contents of the edit box bold. We have to use SendMessage to get the required level of control.

Finally, we set focus to the edit box – this is because you'll usually be typing, hit the Bold button to start typing in bold, and want to just keep typing without having to re-click on the edit box to move focus there.

```
void CBookrtfDlg::OnItalic()
{
    UpdateData(TRUE);
    CHARFORMAT cfm;
    cfm.cbSize = sizeof(cfm);
    cfm.dwMask = CFM_ITALIC;
    cfm.dwEffects = m_bItalic ? CFE_ITALIC: 0;
    m_richeditBody.SendMessage(EM_SETCHARFORMAT, SCF_SELECTION, (long)&cfm);
    m_richeditBody.SetFocus();
}

void CBookrtfDlg::OnUnderline()
{
    UpdateData(TRUE);
    CHARFORMAT cfm;
    cfm.cbSize = sizeof(cfm);
    cfm.dwMask = CFM_UNDERLINE;
    cfm.dwEffects = m_bUnderline ? CFE_UNDERLINE: 0;
    m_richeditBody.SendMessage(EM_SETCHARFORMAT, SCF_SELECTION, (long)&cfm);
    m_richeditBody.SetFocus();
}
```

These two methods do the same thing as OnBold but for italics and underlining.

Before we implement the size combo, let's check that this works. Build the project and run it – you should be able to toggle the bold/italic/underlined state of your typing with the buttons, like so:

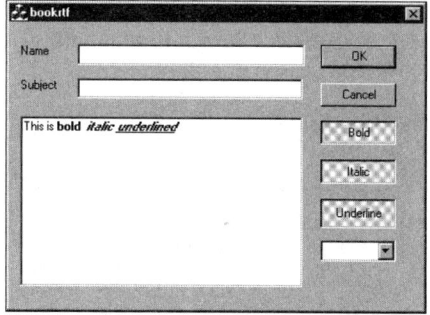

Changing font size

Changing the size of the characters in your message is also nice and easy – add the following to `OnInitDialog`:

```
BOOL CBookrtfDlg::OnInitDialog()
{
    // . . . rest of function in here stays untouched . . .

    // TODO: Add extra initialization here

    for (int i=6; i < 36; i+= 2)
    {
        CString cs;
        cs.Format("%d", i);
        m_cmbSize.AddString(cs);
        m_cmbSize.SetItemData(m_cmbSize.GetCount()-1, i);
    }
    m_cmbSize.SetCurSel(1); // default is 8 point

    return TRUE;  // return TRUE  unless you set the focus to a control
}
```

We add a list of strings containing the point sizes we want to use for text to the combo box, and use the associated item data to store the appropriate size for each entry (remember, we turned sorting off on the combo box, so we don't have to worry about mysterious reordering getting in the way here).

Now edit the `OnSelchangeCmbsize()` method as follows:

```
void CBookrtfDlg::OnSelchangeCmbsize()
{
    CHARFORMAT cfm;
    cfm.cbSize = sizeof(cfm);
    cfm.dwMask = CFM_SIZE;
    // next one measures in twips = 20ths of a point.
    cfm.yHeight = m_cmbSize.GetItemData(m_cmbSize.GetCurSel()) * 20;
    m_richeditBody.SendMessage(EM_SETCHARFORMAT, SCF_SELECTION, (long)&cfm);
    m_richeditBody.SetFocus();
}
```

This is pretty much the same as the code to set things for bold et al, but we use the `yHeight` member of the `CHARFORMAT` structure. Note that the size in that structure is measured in twips, which are 1/20th of a point – we have to scale up from the value we read from our combo box.

Again, let's quickly build this and test it before we get to the mail. You should now be able to change the font size as well as the font style:

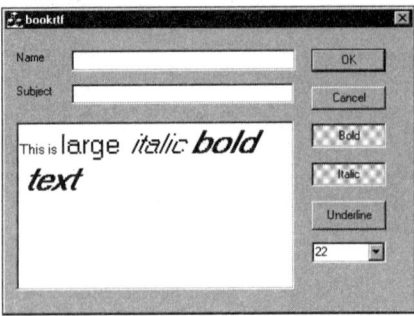

We could now continue and add color/font selection boxes to our project, but for now we'll leave it as it stands – we have enough options to allow us a lot of formatting possibilities, and we want to get onto the mail stuff before the rich-text aspect of things gets out of hand. See the WordPad MSDN sample if you want much, much more code covering rich text support.

Adding Mail Functionality

Let's get down to our basic functionality for this control. If you remember from our first example, we need to `#import` the contents of `cdo.dll` to make CDO available. Of our three strategies for this, we'll put the `#import` line in `stdafx.h`, because we'll have more than one file that uses it, and need to make sure we don't do any more `#import` processing than we need to, to speed builds. Thus, edit `stdafx.h` as follows:

```
#include <afxcmn.h>          // MFC support for Windows Common Controls
#endif // _AFX_NO_AFXCMN_SUPPORT

#import <cdo.dll>
using namespace MAPI;

//{{AFX_INSERT_LOCATION}}
```

At this stage, we'll also set up our error handling routines, but in code-conscious, easy-to-reuse mode, we'll add them in their own files. Add a new header file and source file to the project and name them `dump_com_error.h` and `dump_com_error.cpp`. If you haven't guessed already, we're going to reuse the `dump_com_error` and `GetHRESULTFromComError` functions from our previous application.

`dump_com_error.h` should contain:

```
#pragma once

HRESULT GetHRESULTFromComError(_com_error& e);
void dump_com_error(_com_error& e);
```

dump_com_error.cpp meanwhile should contain the following lines at the top of the file

```
#include "stdafx.h"
#include "dump_com_error.h"
```

followed by a copy of dump_com_error and GetHRESULTFromComError from Book2dlg.cpp in our previous application.

Including MAPI

Next, we need to add the MAPI include files to our main project. Add the following to the start of bookrtfDlg.cpp: (check_hresult.h is not yet in the project – we'll cover that after the main body of code).

```
#ifdef _DEBUG
#define new DEBUG_NEW
#undef THIS_FILE
static char THIS_FILE[] = __FILE__;
#endif

#include <mapix.h>
#include <mapiutil.h>

#include "check_hresult.h"
#include "dump_com_error.h"

/////////////////////////////////////////////////////////////////////////////
// CAboutDlg dialog used for App About
```

We're including mapix.h, the main MAPI header file, and mapiutil.h, which contains a lot of useful helper functions we'll be using later on.

Priming the OK Button

Add an OnOK method (for the BN_CLICKED method of the OK button, as you'd expect). Now before we add any code to the actual function we need to declare the smart pointer types for the MAPI interfaces we'll be using further down, using _COM_SMARTPTR_TYPEDEF as before. We'll also declare a helper function, RichTextCallback, that we'll need to extract text from the rich text edit control.

```
_COM_SMARTPTR_TY*PEDEF(IMAPISession, IID_IMAPISession);
_COM_SMARTPTR_TYPEDEF(IMessage, IID_IMessage);
DWORD CALLBACK RichTextCallback(DWORD dwCookie, \
                LPBYTE pbBuff, LONG cb, LONG *pcb);

void CBookrtfDlg::OnOK()
{
    UpdateData(TRUE);
```

We start OnOK() itself by reading the contents of the Name and Subject edit boxes into our member variables so we know who to send the message to, and what to title it.

```
    CoInitialize(NULL);
```

We'll just do `CoInitialize` here, rather than in `InitInstance` – we won't need to use COM before this function, so there's no real need to do this earlier, and it keeps the number of functions we change to a minimum.

```
try {
```

As usual, we'll wrap all this stuff in a `try..catch` block.

Logging into the default profile

While we're doing MAPI things, let's also demonstrate another very useful trick – logging into the default profile without knowing its name. We already know that the default profile name is stored in the `DefaultProfile` value in the following keys:

Win9x	`HKEY_CURRENT_USER\Software\Microsoft\` `Windows Messaging Subsystem\Profiles`
WinNT	`HKEY_CURRENT_USER\Software\Microsoft\Windows NT` `\CurrentVersion\ Windows Messaging Subsystem\Profiles`

but let's save ourselves having to use the registry and log into the default profile directly.

```
IMAPISessionPtr pMAPISession;
```

To do this, we have to log into a MAPI `IMAPISession` and then convert that session into a CDO `_SessionPtr`.

```
HRESULT hr;
hr = MAPIInitialize(NULL);
```

Before we can use any MAPI methods, we have to call `MAPIInitialize`. We don't pass in any extra parameters here – we could use these to tell the MAPI system that we're running as an NT service, but that's a whole other chapter.

```
if (!CHECK_HRESULT1(hr, "MAPIInitialize"))
{
    return;
}
```

The `CHECK_HRESULT` (and `CHECK_HRESULT1`) methods are helper functions I've used to decode MAPI errors into strings – we'll cover these after the main body of the `OnOK` function. For now, you can safely assume that they have the same effect as the `SUCCEEDED` macro, i.e. they return `FALSE` if the `HRESULT` passed in indicates failure.

```
FLAGS flags;
flags = MAPI_EXTENDED    // use extended MAPI, not simple MAPI
    | MAPI_NEW_SESSION   // don't connect to any current session
    | MAPI_NO_MAIL       // don't tell the MAPI spooler about this session
    | MAPI_USE_DEFAULT;  // use default username and password
```

We need to tell MAPI how we want to log in – the comments cover this in as much depth as we'll go into here – for more, see the online MAPI documentation.

```
hr = MAPILogonEx(
    0,          // no parent window
    NULL,       // don't supply profile name
    NULL,       // don't supply password
    flags,
    &pMAPISession);
```

Now we actually log in. We aren't giving MAPI a profile name to log in with because we're telling it to log into the default profile for the system. If MAPILogonEx succeeds, it returns a pointer to the logged-in session in the pMAPISession argument we're passing in.

```
if (!CHECK_HRESULT1(hr, "MAPILogonEx"))
{
    return;
}
```

We need to make sure that the logon succeeded – there may not even be a default profile to log into, or we might not have the appropriate permissions, etc.

```
_SessionPtr pSession;
hr = pSession.CreateInstance("MAPI.Session");

if (FAILED(hr))
{
    AfxMessageBox("CreateInstance for the session failed",
    MB_ICONERROR | MB_OK);
    return;
}

pSession->MAPIOBJECT = (LPUNKNOWN)pMAPISession;
```

Now we build ourselves a CDO session as usual. Then comes the clever bit – we can turn the logged-in MAPI session into a CDO session by assigning to the MAPIOBJECT property of our CDO session. At this point, we could safely Release the MAPI session because the CDO session will keep things alive, but we're using a smart pointer for our MAPI session so there's no real need to do that explicitly. Instead, we can just wait for the smart pointer to go out of scope and do this for us.

```
FolderPtr pOutbox = pSession->Outbox;
MessagesPtr pMessages = pOutbox->Messages;
MessagePtr pMessage = pMessages->Add((const char*)m_csSubject);

RecipientsPtr pRecipients = pMessage->Recipients;
RecipientPtr pRecipient = pRecipients->Add((const char *)m_csName);
pRecipient->Resolve(true);
```

This is very similar to the code we used before to create a message, except that we're passing arguments to the Add methods rather than creating the object and then assigning to the subject/name. I'm not wrapping the call to Resolve in an inner try..catch block to keep things as concise as possible here – the main try..catch block will still do the right thing but the error message won't be as pretty as it might be.

Getting RTF from the rich-edit control

```
CString csRTF;
EDITSTREAM es;
es.dwCookie = (DWORD)&csRTF;
es.pfnCallback = RichTextCallback;
m_richeditBody.StreamOut(SF_RTF, es);
```

One disadvantage of the `CRichEditCtrl` control is that there's no convenient way to get its contents in RTF format. We have to tell it to stream its contents to us via a callback function which we'll look at the end of `OnOK`, but briefly, we fill out the `EDITSTREAM` structure with a "cookie" that our callback function can use to track where the contents are going, and a pointer to the callback function to use.

Writing RTF to the message

```
IMessagePtr lpmpNew = pMessage->MAPIOBJECT;
```

As with the session logging in, we need to take advantage of the fact that many of the CDO objects provide a `MAPIOBJECT` property to allow us to get at the underlying MAPI object that the CDO object wraps up. In this case, we're reading from the `pMessage` object to get the `IMessage` pointer from it.

```
ULONG lMsgStoreFlags = 0;
```

Now we hit an unfortunate side effect of using RTF – some message stores can't store RTF in compressed form, so we need to read flags from the message store to check this ability. In practice, we're almost certainly going to be talking to a Microsoft Exchange Server, and we could just hardcode the flags we expect from it but let's do things properly.

Hang on though, why compress RTF in the first place? Well, RTF can take up a large amount of space compared to plain text, especially when there are graphical elements to the RTF, so compression is a good idea. Furthermore, it compresses very nicely, so message stores can take advantage of this to reduce the amount of space used.

```
LPSPropValue lpspvStoreFlags;
HrGetOneProp(lpmpNew, PR_STORE_SUPPORT_MASK, &lpspvStoreFlags);
CHECK_HRESULT(hr, "Reading store support mask", lpmpNew);
```

`HrGetOneProp` is a MAPI helper function that reads a single property from a MAPI object – in CDO terms, think of a MAPI property as a `Field`. We store this property as a `SPropValue`, which is a very similar structure to a `VARIANT`, in that it contains a large union which can store many different types of data. In contrast however, a `SPropValue` also contains information on the property ID that is stored therein. (See "Inside MAPI" or the online documentation for a much more in-depth explanation of this).

We actually pass a pointer to a pointer to a `SPropValue` to `HrGetOneProp`, and it allocates memory for the property it returns and puts the address of that property in our pointer.

```
lMsgStoreFlags = lpspvStoreFlags->Value.l;
MAPIFreeBuffer(lpspvStoreFlags);
```

We read the value of the store flags from the appropriate element of the union in the property value we got back, and free up the buffer. Note that we have to use MAPIFreeBuffer to free it – HrGetOneProp and the MAPI system in general use MAPIAllocate to allocate memory. We should also use MAPIAllocate if we need to pass things to MAPI.

```
IStreamPtr strRTFCompressed;

hr = lpmpNew->OpenProperty(
    PR_RTF_COMPRESSED,              // open the compressed rtf property
    &IID_IStream,                   // we want a stream back
    0,                              // data for IID_IStream. Hopefully nothing..
    MAPI_MODIFY                     // we're going to want to write to it,
    | MAPI_CREATE,                  // and create this property if there isn't
                                    // one there yet
    (LPUNKNOWN *)&strRTFCompressed);

if (!CHECK_HRESULT(hr, "OpenProperty on compressed RTF stream", lpmpNew))
{
    return;
}
```

Now we have to open the RTF body of our new message (actually, the compressed version of the RTF body; more in just a second). We can't just write a string to this however. Instead, we have to open it as an object supporting the IStream interface, and use IStream methods to write to it. Conveniently, comdef.h contains the _COM_SMARTPTR_TYPEDEF smart pointer wrapper for IStream already, so we don't have to do that ourselves. You'll notice also that CHECK_HRESULT takes a pointer to an object – again, we'll cover this later.

```
IStreamPtr strRTFUncompressed = NULL;

hr = WrapCompressedRTFStream(
    strRTFCompressed,       // stream we've got on the RTF body
    MAPI_MODIFY             // because we want to write to it
    | (lMsgStoreFlags & STORE_UNCOMPRESSED_RTF),
                            // we have to check the store's capabilities
    &strRTFUncompressed);   // puts the stream we have to write to in this.

if (!CHECK_HRESULT1(hr, "WrapCompressedRTFStream"))
{
    return;
}
```

As I mentioned above, we actually open up the compressed version of the RTF body of the message. This is just the way we have to do things, peculiar though it may seem. Because we don't want to deal with the particular method of compression used by the message store, we then convert the compressed RTF stream into an uncompressed RTF stream using the WrapCompressedRTFStream method. In return, we get back a stream which we can write to, and, by some internal MAPI magic, appropriately compressed RTF will be written to the base property on the message. This is where we have to use the store properties; we need to pass the STORE_UNCOMPRESSED_RTF bit from the store flags to this function in order to handle the various types of store properly.

```
        ULONG cBytesWritten;

    hr = strRTFUncompressed->Write(
        csRTF,                // where's the data
        csRTF.GetLength(),    // how much of it?
        &cBytesWritten);      // how many bytes did we write?

    if (!CHECK_HRESULT(hr, "Write to uncompressed RTF stream",
                       strRTFUncompressed))

    {
        return;
    }
```

Now we actually write to the stream and, via the series of wrappers, to the compressed body property in the main message. This is just a standard `IStream::Write` call; we've read the RTF from our rich text edit control into `csRTF`, so this is nice and easy.

```
    hr = strRTFUncompressed->Commit(STGC_OVERWRITE);

    if (!CHECK_HRESULT(hr, "Commit-and-overwrite RTF", strRTFUncompressed))
    {
        return;
    }
```

Now we call `Commit` on the stream to ensure that everything's flushed through and there's nothing sitting in buffers.

```
    // Do we have to sync up the RTF and plaintext parts of the message?

    if (!(lMsgStoreFlags & STORE_RTF_OK))
    {
        BOOL bMessageUpdated;

        hr = RTFSync(
            lpmpNew,
            RTF_SYNC_RTF_CHANGED,
            &bMessageUpdated);

        if (!CHECK_HRESULT1(hr, "final RTFSync"))
        {
            return;
        }
    }
```

The last RTF thing we have to do is another message store thing – we may need to call `RTFSync` to get the plain text body and RTF body of the messages synchronized if the store doesn't do this automatically. This is needed because if we're sending this message to someone who can't receive RTF messages, we'll want to send them a plain text version of the message containing our best approximation to the RTF contents.

```
        pMessage->Send(false, false);
    }
    catch (_com_error e)
    {
        dump_com_error(e);
    }

    CoUninitialize();

    CDialog::OnOK();
}
```

Finally, we're done. We send the message, with no saving of copy to our sent-mail folder and no dialog shown, we hit the `catch` end of the `try..catch` block this is all wrapped in, and finally call `CoUninitialize` to shut COM down now that we're finished with it.

Rich-text callback function

Dazed and confused, you may vaguely recall the callback helper function used midway through `OnOK()`. Here is its code to add at the end of `bookrtfDlg.cpp`:

```
DWORD CALLBACK RichTextCallback(DWORD dwCookie, LPBYTE pbBuff,
                                LONG cb, LONG *pcb)
{
    CString* pcsOutput = (CString *) dwCookie;
    CString csTemp = pbBuff;
    *pcsOutput += csTemp;
    *pcb = cb;
    return 0;
}
```

This just takes the chunk of data that the rich text edit control streams to us and appends it to the `CString` that we're using to hold the contents. This is where we use the "cookie" value to keep track of where our data is going.

That's the end of our additions to `bookrtfDlg.cpp` but not to the project. We still have a couple of loose ends to tie up.

CHECK_HRESULT

As previously mentioned, I use a pair of helper functions `CHECK_HRESULT` and `CHECK_HRESULT1` to translate MAPI errors into text strings. We can use the `GetLastError()` method which the main MAPI objects provide to get error text describing whatever it was that went wrong when they returned an error code to print out more helpful error dialogs.

Once again, for neatness, we'll incorporate these into our application by adding two new files, `check_hresult.h` and `check_hresult.cpp`, to our project. The header file, `check_hresult.h` should contain:

```
#pragma once

BOOL CHECK_HRESULT(HRESULT hr, CString csDoing, IUnknown * pObject);
BOOL CHECK_HRESULT1(HRESULT hr, CString csDoing);
```

and the source file, `check_hresult.cpp` should contain:

```
#include "stdafx.h"
#include <mapix.h>
#include <mapispi.h>  // for IMAPISupport
#include <mapiform.h> // for IPersistMessage
#include <mapi.h>     // for simple MAPI error codes.
```

We need to include a fair number of header files here – even though we won't use a lot of them, I'm going to cover all the MAPI objects that support `GetLastError`. This should give you a good foundation for any future MAPI development you do. You can just use these files verbatim and not have to worry about adding new object types.

```
struct errdesc
{
    HRESULT lErrCode;
    LPCSTR lpszValue;
};
```

Initially, we just have a large table translating HRESULTs to a corresponding string. Again, the code for this is downloadable from the Wrox web site (`http://www.wrox.com`) if you don't feel up to typing this all in.

```
static errdesc errors[98] =
{
    {SUCCESS_SUCCESS, "SUCCESS_SUCCESS"},
    {MAPI_E_CALL_FAILED, "MAPI_E_CALL_FAILED"},
    {MAPI_E_NOT_ENOUGH_MEMORY, "MAPI_E_NOT_ENOUGH_MEMORY"},
    {MAPI_E_INVALID_PARAMETER, "MAPI_E_INVALID_PARAMETER"},
    {MAPI_E_INTERFACE_NOT_SUPPORTED, "MAPI_E_INTERFACE_NOT_SUPPORTED"},
    {MAPI_E_NO_ACCESS, "MAPI_E_NO_ACCESS"},
    {MAPI_E_NO_SUPPORT, "MAPI_E_NO_SUPPORT"},
    {MAPI_E_BAD_CHARWIDTH, "MAPI_E_BAD_CHARWIDTH"},
    {MAPI_E_STRING_TOO_LONG, "MAPI_E_STRING_TOO_LONG"},
    {MAPI_E_UNKNOWN_FLAGS, "MAPI_E_UNKNOWN_FLAGS"},
    {MAPI_E_INVALID_ENTRYID, "MAPI_E_INVALID_ENTRYID"},
    {MAPI_E_INVALID_OBJECT, "MAPI_E_INVALID_OBJECT"},
    {MAPI_E_OBJECT_CHANGED, "MAPI_E_OBJECT_CHANGED"},
    {MAPI_E_OBJECT_DELETED, "MAPI_E_OBJECT_DELETED"},
    {MAPI_E_BUSY, "MAPI_E_BUSY"},
    {MAPI_E_NOT_ENOUGH_DISK, "MAPI_E_NOT_ENOUGH_DISK"},
    {MAPI_E_NOT_ENOUGH_RESOURCES, "MAPI_E_NOT_ENOUGH_RESOURCES"},
    {MAPI_E_NOT_FOUND, "MAPI_E_NOT_FOUND"},
    {MAPI_E_VERSION, "MAPI_E_VERSION"},
    {MAPI_E_LOGON_FAILED, "MAPI_E_LOGON_FAILED"},
    {MAPI_E_SESSION_LIMIT, "MAPI_E_SESSION_LIMIT"},
    {MAPI_E_USER_CANCEL, "MAPI_E_USER_CANCEL"},
    {MAPI_E_UNABLE_TO_ABORT, "MAPI_E_UNABLE_TO_ABORT"},
    {MAPI_E_NETWORK_ERROR, "MAPI_E_NETWORK_ERROR"},
    {MAPI_E_DISK_ERROR, "MAPI_E_DISK_ERROR"},
    {MAPI_E_TOO_COMPLEX, "MAPI_E_TOO_COMPLEX"},
    {MAPI_E_BAD_COLUMN, "MAPI_E_BAD_COLUMN"},
```

```
{MAPI_E_EXTENDED_ERROR, "MAPI_E_EXTENDED_ERROR"},
{MAPI_E_COMPUTED, "MAPI_E_COMPUTED"},
{MAPI_E_END_OF_SESSION, "MAPI_E_END_OF_SESSION"},
{MAPI_E_UNKNOWN_ENTRYID, "MAPI_E_UNKNOWN_ENTRYID"},
{MAPI_E_MISSING_REQUIRED_COLUMN, "MAPI_E_MISSING_REQUIRED_COLUMN"},
{MAPI_W_NO_SERVICE, "MAPI_W_NO_SERVICE"},
{MAPI_E_BAD_VALUE, "MAPI_E_BAD_VALUE"},
{MAPI_E_INVALID_TYPE, "MAPI_E_INVALID_TYPE"},
{MAPI_E_TYPE_NO_SUPPORT, "MAPI_E_TYPE_NO_SUPPORT"},
{MAPI_E_UNEXPECTED_TYPE, "MAPI_E_UNEXPECTED_TYPE"},
{MAPI_E_TOO_BIG, "MAPI_E_TOO_BIG"},
{MAPI_W_ERRORS_RETURNED, "MAPI_W_ERRORS_RETURNED"},
{MAPI_E_UNABLE_TO_COMPLETE, "MAPI_E_UNABLE_TO_COMPLETE"},
{MAPI_E_TABLE_EMPTY, "MAPI_E_TABLE_EMPTY"},
{MAPI_E_TABLE_TOO_BIG, "MAPI_E_TABLE_TOO_BIG"},
{MAPI_E_INVALID_BOOKMARK, "MAPI_E_INVALID_BOOKMARK"},
{MAPI_W_POSITION_CHANGED, "MAPI_W_POSITION_CHANGED"},
{MAPI_W_APPROX_COUNT, "MAPI_W_APPROX_COUNT"},
{MAPI_E_WAIT, "MAPI_E_WAIT"},
{MAPI_E_CANCEL, "MAPI_E_CANCEL"},
{MAPI_E_NOT_ME, "MAPI_E_NOT_ME"},
{MAPI_W_CANCEL_MESSAGE, "MAPI_W_CANCEL_MESSAGE"},
{MAPI_E_CORRUPT_STORE, "MAPI_E_CORRUPT_STORE"},
{MAPI_E_NOT_IN_QUEUE, "MAPI_E_NOT_IN_QUEUE"},
{MAPI_E_NO_SUPPRESS, "MAPI_E_NO_SUPPRESS"},
{MAPI_E_COLLISION, "MAPI_E_COLLISION"},
{MAPI_E_NOT_INITIALIZED, "MAPI_E_NOT_INITIALIZED"},
{MAPI_E_NON_STANDARD, "MAPI_E_NON_STANDARD"},
{MAPI_E_NO_RECIPIENTS, "MAPI_E_NO_RECIPIENTS"},
{MAPI_E_SUBMITTED, "MAPI_E_SUBMITTED"},
{MAPI_E_HAS_FOLDERS, "MAPI_E_HAS_FOLDERS"},
{MAPI_E_HAS_MESSAGES, "MAPI_E_HAS_MESSAGES"},
{MAPI_E_FOLDER_CYCLE, "MAPI_E_FOLDER_CYCLE"},
{MAPI_W_PARTIAL_COMPLETION, "MAPI_W_PARTIAL_COMPLETION"},
{MAPI_E_AMBIGUOUS_RECIP, "MAPI_E_AMBIGUOUS_RECIP"},
{MAPI_USER_ABORT, "MAPI_USER_ABORT"},
{MAPI_E_USER_ABORT, "MAPI_E_USER_ABORT"},
{MAPI_E_FAILURE, "MAPI_E_FAILURE"},
{MAPI_E_LOGON_FAILURE, "MAPI_E_LOGON_FAILURE"},
{MAPI_E_LOGIN_FAILURE, "MAPI_E_LOGIN_FAILURE"},
{MAPI_E_DISK_FULL, "MAPI_E_DISK_FULL"},
{MAPI_E_INSUFFICIENT_MEMORY, "MAPI_E_INSUFFICIENT_MEMORY"},
{MAPI_E_ACCESS_DENIED, "MAPI_E_ACCESS_DENIED"},
{MAPI_E_TOO_MANY_SESSIONS, "MAPI_E_TOO_MANY_SESSIONS"},
{MAPI_E_TOO_MANY_FILES, "MAPI_E_TOO_MANY_FILES"},
{MAPI_E_TOO_MANY_RECIPIENTS, "MAPI_E_TOO_MANY_RECIPIENTS"},
{MAPI_E_ATTACHMENT_NOT_FOUND, "MAPI_E_ATTACHMENT_NOT_FOUND"},
{MAPI_E_ATTACHMENT_OPEN_FAILURE, "MAPI_E_ATTACHMENT_OPEN_FAILURE"},
{MAPI_E_ATTACHMENT_WRITE_FAILURE, "MAPI_E_ATTACHMENT_WRITE_FAILURE"},
{MAPI_E_UNKNOWN_RECIPIENT, "MAPI_E_UNKNOWN_RECIPIENT"},
{MAPI_E_BAD_RECIPTYPE, "MAPI_E_BAD_RECIPTYPE"},
{MAPI_E_NO_MESSAGES, "MAPI_E_NO_MESSAGES"},
{MAPI_E_INVALID_MESSAGE, "MAPI_E_INVALID_MESSAGE"},
{MAPI_E_TEXT_TOO_LARGE, "MAPI_E_TEXT_TOO_LARGE"},
```

```
        {MAPI_E_INVALID_SESSION, "MAPI_E_INVALID_SESSION"},
        {MAPI_E_TYPE_NOT_SUPPORTED, "MAPI_E_TYPE_NOT_SUPPORTED"},
        {MAPI_E_AMBIGUOUS_RECIPIENT, "MAPI_E_AMBIGUOUS_RECIPIENT"},
        {MAPI_E_AMBIG_RECIP, "MAPI_E_AMBIG_RECIP"},
        {MAPI_E_MESSAGE_IN_USE, "MAPI_E_MESSAGE_IN_USE"},
        {MAPI_E_NETWORK_FAILURE, "MAPI_E_NETWORK_FAILURE"},
        {MAPI_E_INVALID_EDITFIELDS, "MAPI_E_INVALID_EDITFIELDS"},
        {MAPI_E_INVALID_RECIPS, "MAPI_E_INVALID_RECIPS"},
        {MAPI_E_NOT_SUPPORTED, "MAPI_E_NOT_SUPPORTED"},
        {E_NOTIMPL, "E_NOTIMPL"}, {E_UNEXPECTED, "E_UNEXPECTED"},
        {E_OUTOFMEMORY, "E_OUTOFMEMORY"}, {E_INVALIDARG, "E_INVALIDARG"},
        {E_NOINTERFACE, "E_NOINTERFACE"}, {E_POINTER, "E_POINTER"},
        {E_HANDLE, "E_HANDLE"}, {E_ABORT, "E_ABORT"}
};

LPCSTR szUnknown = "Unknown error code";

LPCSTR GetMAPIError(HRESULT hr)
{
    for (int i=0; i < sizeof(errors)/sizeof(errors[0]); i++)
    {
        if (errors[i].lErrCode == hr)
        {
            return errors[i].lpszValue;
        }
    }
    return szUnknown;
}
```

The `GetMAPIError` function just translates from an `HRESULT` to the appropriate string, or returns an unknown code if the error code isn't a recognized MAPI error. MAPI errors don't necessarily tag in with some standard Windows error codes, but we're not going to cover translating those in text here anyway. If you do want to do this, you should use the `FormatMessage` function, a demonstration of which can be handily found in the online documentation for `FormatMessage` itself. Alternatively, you could just add more `HRESULT`s to the list above. Note though that this is a messier option – we can't know that we've added every `HRESULT` that we'll ever encounter.

```
BOOL CHECK_HRESULT1(HRESULT hr, CString csDoing)
{
    CString s;
    if (hr != S_OK)
    {
        s.Format("Error: %s failed (internal: 0x%08x %s).\n", csDoing, hr,
            GetMAPIError(hr));
        AfxMessageBox(s, MB_ICONERROR | MB_OK);
        return FALSE;
    }
    return TRUE;
}
```

The simpler of the two functions here is CHECK_HRESULT1, which just takes the HRESULT passed in, turns it into a string if possible, and uses AfxMessageBox to tell the user about it. You may want to change AfxMessageBox to some other error logging method in your own code – for now, it does the job well enough. CHECK_HRESULT1 returns TRUE or FALSE so it's a viable alternative to using SUCCEEDED with the added bonus of an error message neatly tacked into your code.

```
BOOL CHECK_HRESULT(HRESULT hr, CString csDoing, IUnknown * pObject)
{
    CString s;
    if (hr != S_OK)
    {
        s.Format("Error: %s failed (internal: 0x%08x %s). ", csDoing, hr,
            GetMAPIError(hr));
```

CHECK_HRESULT is the main error checking function, and it calls GetLastError on the MAPI object passed in.

```
    if (pObject != NULL)
    {
        LPMAPIERROR pErr = NULL;
        HRESULT hr2 = 0;


#define QI_AND_GET_ERROR(IID, Interface) \
        do { \
            HRESULT hr1; \
            Interface* pInterface;\
            hr1 = pObject->QueryInterface(IID, (void **)&pInterface);\
            if (hr1 == S_OK) \
            {\
                hr2 = pInterface->GetLastError(hr, 0, &pErr); \
                pInterface->Release(); \
            }\
        } while(0)
```

Here is where we hit a really painful aspect of getting error information from MAPI. There's no convenient interface we can look for to use GetLastError. Ideally, we could just QueryInterface on our object for some ideal ISupportsMAPIGetLastError interface, and then use that interface to read the error information. Sadly, there is no such interface – the only common interface that these objects all support is IUnknown, and there's no GetLastError method on IUnknown.

To avoid writing the same code over and over again, I've used a small preprocessor macro to reduce the amount of repeated text. There are a couple of tricks here to note, although I'll grant you that these are just personal style and not necessarily the best way to do things. [Editor's Note – Make sure there are no blank lines in this #define clause or extra spaces after the \ at the end of the lines. VC++ will throw up several errors if there are.]

❏ I've wrapped the definition up in a `do{...}while(0)` loop. This guarantees that the code will only be called once and enables us to call `QI_AND_GET_ERROR();` That is, we can put a semicolon on the end of the call without compiler warnings about empty statements. This is important if you use smart indenting in your editor.

❏ Use of types as macro arguments. Perhaps a template function would be nicer here, but this does the job when written as a `#define`, and it's the way I am personally used to doing things.

Anyway, preprocessor abuse aside, this macro simply checks to see if we can get the desired interface on our object, and if so, it calls `GetLastError` on that interface to populate the `pErr` error object with the details of our error.

```
        QI_AND_GET_ERROR(IID_IABLogon, IABLogon);
        QI_AND_GET_ERROR(IID_IMAPIControl, IMAPIControl);
        QI_AND_GET_ERROR(IID_IMAPIProp, IMAPIProp);
        QI_AND_GET_ERROR(IID_IMAPISession, IMAPISession);
        QI_AND_GET_ERROR(IID_IMAPISup, IMAPISupport);
        QI_AND_GET_ERROR(IID_IMAPITable, IMAPITable);
        QI_AND_GET_ERROR(IID_IMsgServiceAdmin, IMsgServiceAdmin);
        QI_AND_GET_ERROR(IID_IMSLogon, IMSLogon);
        QI_AND_GET_ERROR(IID_IPersistMessage, IPersistMessage);
        QI_AND_GET_ERROR(IID_IProfAdmin, IProfAdmin);
        QI_AND_GET_ERROR(IID_IProviderAdmin, IProviderAdmin);

#undef QI_AND_GET_ERROR
```

We now use the macro appropriately for the various interfaces that support `GetLastError`. Unfortunately, we can't just pass in `IABLogon` and use the preprocessor's `##` token-pasting operator to automatically convert `IABLogon` into `IID_IABLogon` because `IMAPISupport` has associated IID `IID_IMAPISup`, not `IID_IMAPISupport`. We can't use `__uuidof()` either because there are no IIDs associated that way in the MAPI header files, annoyingly.

```
    if (pErr != NULL && hr2 == S_OK)
    {
        CString s1;
        s1.Format("Internal error: '%s' in '%s'.", pErr->lpszError,
                    pErr->lpszComponent);
        s += s1;
        MAPIFreeBuffer(pErr);
    }
  }
  AfxMessageBox(s, MB_ICONERROR | MB_OK);
  return FALSE;
}
  return TRUE;
}
```

Now we check to see if we succeeded in getting an error from the object passed in, and if so, we adjust our error string appropriately and display that. Note that we have to free up the error info if we did get any.

Are We Done Yet?

At this point, we might feel as if we should, by rights, be able to compile. Sadly, that's not quite the case. The first, easiest, thing we need to do is add `mapi32.lib` to the list of libraries that need to link into the project. Open the Project Settings dialog (Alt+F7) and switch to the Link tab. Make the changes as shown below.

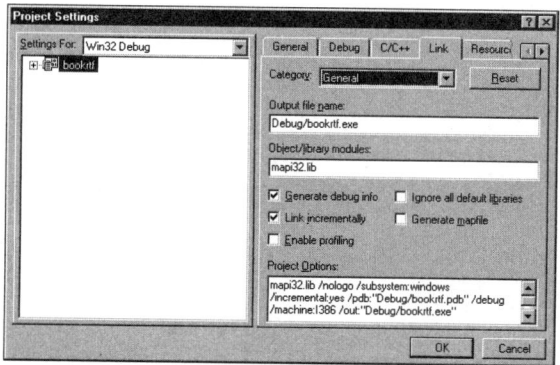

Final problem: no IIDs!

We should, arguably, be done now – but if we try and build our project, we'll get the following error(s):

```
bookrtfDlg.obj: error LNK2001: unresolved external symbol _IID_IMessage
check_hresult.obj: error LNK2001: unresolved external symbol _IID_IMAPISession
check_hresult.obj: error LNK2001: unresolved external symbol _IID_IMAPITable
check_hresult.obj: error LNK2001: unresolved external symbol _IID_IMAPIControl
check_hresult.obj: error LNK2001: unresolved external symbol _IID_IProfAdmin
check_hresult.obj: error LNK2001: unresolved external symbol _IID_IMsgServiceAdmin
check_hresult.obj: error LNK2001: unresolved external symbol _IID_IProviderAdmin
check_hresult.obj: error LNK2001: unresolved external symbol _IID_IMAPIProp
check_hresult.obj: error LNK2001: unresolved external symbol _IID_IMAPISup
check_hresult.obj: error LNK2001: unresolved external symbol _IID_IMSLogon
check_hresult.obj: error LNK2001: unresolved external symbol _IID_IABLogon
check_hresult.obj: error LNK2001: unresolved external symbol _IID_IPersistMessage
Debug/bookrtf.exe: fatal error LNK1120: 12 unresolved externals
Error executing link.exe.

bookrtf.exe - 13 error(s), 0 warning(s)
```

What is this telling us? It's telling us that, though all the IIDs that we're referring to are declared, none of them are actually defined anywhere.

This is one of the nastier gotchas of MAPI development – unless you actually explicitly tell the system to link in the IIDs, they won't be in there. Fortunately, we can get all of the IIDs linked in at once fairly easily; add a file `mapiguid.cpp` to the project, containing:

```
#include "stdafx.h"

#define USES_IID_IUnknown
```

```
#define USES_IID_IMAPISession
#define USES_IID_IMAPITable
#define USES_IID_IMAPIAdviseSink
#define USES_IID_IMAPIControl
#define USES_IID_IProfAdmin
#define USES_IID_IMsgServiceAdmin
#define USES_IID_IMAPIProgress
#define USES_IID_IMAPIProp
#define USES_IID_IProfSect
#define USES_IID_IMAPIStatus
#define USES_IID_IMsgStore
#define USES_IID_IMessage
#define USES_IID_IAttachment
#define USES_IID_IAddrBook
#define USES_IID_IMailUser
#define USES_IID_IMAPIContainer
#define USES_IID_IMAPIFolder
#define USES_IID_IABContainer
#define USES_IID_IDistList
#define USES_IID_IMAPISup
#define USES_IID_IMSProvider
#define USES_IID_IABProvider
#define USES_IID_IXPProvider
#define USES_IID_IMSLogon
#define USES_IID_IABLogon
#define USES_IID_IXPLogon
#define USES_IID_IMAPITableData
#define USES_IID_IMAPISpoolerInit
#define USES_IID_IMAPISpoolerSession
#define USES_IID_ITNEF
#define USES_IID_IMAPIPropData
#define USES_IID_IMAPISpoolerService
#define USES_PS_MAPI
#define USES_PS_PUBLIC_STRINGS
#define USES_IID_IPersistMessage
#define USES_IID_IMAPIViewAdviseSink
#define USES_IID_IStreamDocfile
#define USES_IID_IMAPIFormProp
#define USES_IID_IMAPIFormContainer
#define USES_IID_IMAPIFormAdviseSink
#define USES_IID_IStreamTnef
#define USES_IID_IMAPIMessageSite
#define USES_IID_IProviderAdmin
#define USES_IID_ISpoolerHook
#define USES_IID_IMAPIViewContext
#define USES_IID_IMAPIFormMgr
#define USES_IID_IMAPIForm
#define USES_IID_IMAPIFormRegistry

#include <initguid.h>
#include <mapiguid.h>
```

The way we get at the IIDs is by defining, for instance, `USES_IID_IMAPIMessage`, and then `#include`-ing `initguid.h` and `mapiguid.h` which are already part of the system. Quite why these aren't defined in the library is a mystery; however, as with a lot of mysterious aspects of MAPI and CDO development, once you know about it you can just add `mapiguid.cpp` to any project you develop, and forget about this problem thereafter.

This does the trick nicely, and we should now be able to build and send messages – testing should give you something like:

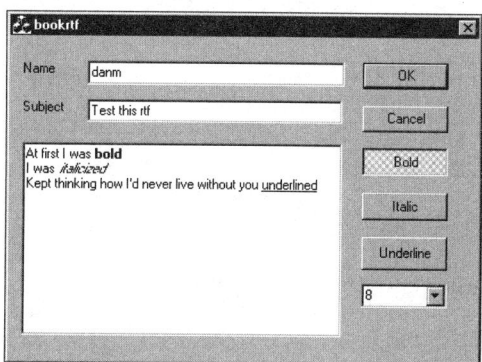

which will arrive as:

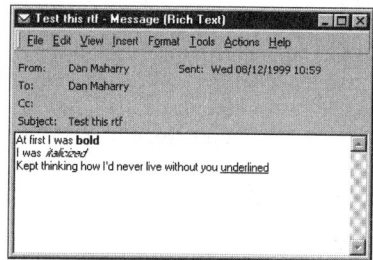

which is just what we'd hope to see.

Testing `CHECK_HRESULT` is actually relatively tricky – as it stands, none of the MAPI code herein should fail without particularly abnormal circumstances coming to play. We would be surprised if any of the `HRESULT`s were actually failure codes because our code is very unlikely to hit error conditions without the server doing strange things. However, by deliberately breaking the code, we can get failures – just change (**and remember to change this back once we're done**) the call to `OpenProperty` as follows:

```
hr = lpmpNew->OpenProperty(
        PR_RTF_COMPRESSED,        // open the compressed rtf property
        &IID_IMAPIProp,           // WRONG IID!
        0,                        // data for IID_IStream. Hopefully nothing..
        MAPI_MODIFY               // we're going to want to write to it,
        | MAPI_CREATE,            // and create this property if there
                                  // isn't one there yet
        (LPUNKNOWN *)&strRTFCompressed);
```

If you now build and run our project, enter a valid name (or we'll hit a CDO exception when trying to resolve the name before we ever try any RTF-related things) and hit "OK", you should see the following dialog:

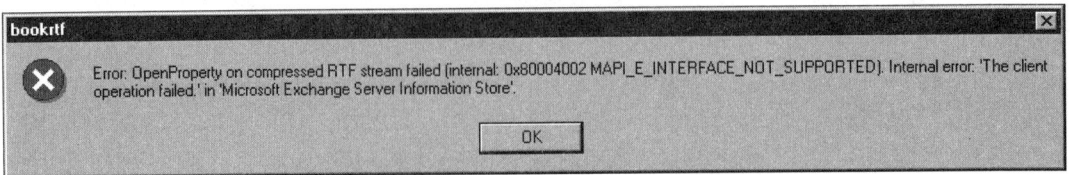

This is telling us exactly what we'd expect to see – the particular failed HRESULT that we were returned is MAPI_E_INTERFACE_NOT_SUPPORTED – this makes sense, because we probably can't get an IMAPIProp interface on an IStream. The internal error text in this case is not the most helpful message you may have seen, but it does at least tell us which part of the system failed; the information store. This makes sense, because it was an operation on a message (i.e. something stored in an information store) that failed.

Don't forget to change the code back to remove the deliberate "bug"!

Summary Number Two

So far in our coverage of MAPI, we've looked at why you would want to incorporate it into your code and the pros and cons of doing so. We've also looked at a hybrid CDO/MAPI application that sends RTF mail. In doing so, we saw briefly how to use CRichEditCtrl and change the format of text in that control.

We looked at how we can leverage MAPI's ability to log into the default profile without knowing its name to easily log our CDO session into the default profile, and then looked at how we go about setting a message to have RTF in the body rather than just plain text. We covered some ways to get more useful error information when error conditions occur, and we finally looked at the need to manually tell the compiler to link in the IIDs for all our objects.

It's really convenient that we can write hybrid code like this – this is, in general, the easiest way to do things. You should use CDO whenever possible because it's easier to code with and then drop down to raw Extended MAPI when you need that level of fine-grained control. Essentially, this offers you the best of both worlds. Once past the initial learning curve, development can be astonishingly easy and you can just copy the common files for error handling et al into any new project and start writing "real" code almost immediately. The hoops you have to jump through will still be there, but it's possible to get all that jumping done very quickly once you know about it.

Managing Mail Profiles

As a second example of the things that you can do with MAPI, let's look at something that CDO very definitely doesn't cover – managing profiles. To be fair, CDO sort of does this as it generates dynamic profiles but that's not the same thing as managing the list of profiles that Outlook uses. There's no way to do this with CDO, because the object model just doesn't cover this aspect of mail. We have to use MAPI if we want to edit the system's profiles – so let's do that.

The Main Dialog

Again, we'll start by building the main dialog first, but leaving the majority of the buttons unhooked. Start a new **MFC AppWizard (EXE)** project in Visual C++, dialog based and call it `bookprofile`.

Edit the main dialog to look like this with the control properties set as indicated where they're not the default:

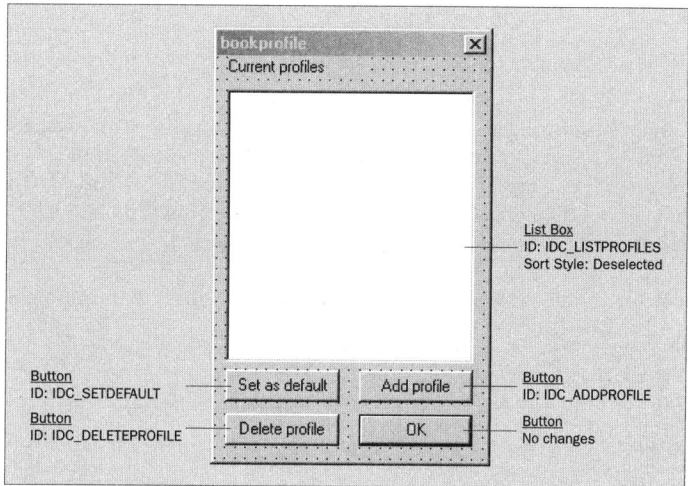

Open the **ClassWizard** and add `BN_CLICKED` methods for all of the buttons except the `OK` button. Leave the methods with their default names of `OnAddprofile`, `OnDeleteprofile` and `OnSetdefault`. Still in **ClassWizard**, you should also add a member variable for the ListBox control of type CListBox called `m_listProfiles`.

Adding Code

We'll use the same `CHECK_HRESULT` functions as before, so copy `check_hresult.cpp` and `check_hresult.h` from the previous project's directory to this one, and add them to the project. Also, we'll need the MAPI IIDs, so copy and add `mapiguid.cpp` as well.

In the previous example, we did all our MAPI work in a short burst in the `OnOK` method. Here, however, we're may want to do many things before exiting. As such, we want to keep the objects that we'll be using all the time in our main dialog class.

Listing Profiles

Edit `bookprofileDlg.h` as follows:

```
#if _MSC_VER > 1000
#pragma once
#endif // _MSC_VER > 1000

#include <comdef.h>
#include <mapix.h>
```

```
_COM_SMARTPTR_TYPEDEF(IProfAdmin, IID_IProfAdmin);

/////////////////////////////////////////////////////////////////////
// CBookprofileDlg dialog

{
    // Construction
public:
    CBookprofileDlg(CWnd* pParent = NULL);    // standard constructor
    virtual ~CBookprofileDlg();
// . . . and then continues untouched for a while
```

We'll be using an object supporting the `IProfAdmin` interface as the main way to access the profiles on this system, so we declare a smart pointer type using `_COM_SMARTPTR_TYPEDEF` to allow us to do this. Note also that we've included `<comdef.h>` and `<mapix.h>` for COM and MAPI functionality respectively, but that there's no sign of `<cdo.dll>`. We're not going to use CDO at all here so there's no point in including it.

We also add a destructor to our dialog class so that we can do some cleanup on shutdown – we'll look at that shortly.

```
// Implementation
protected:
    HICON m_hIcon;

    void StartMAPI();
    void StopMAPI();
    void UpdateProfileList();

    IProfAdminPtr m_pProfileAdmin;

    // Generated message map functions
    //{{AFX_MSG(CBookprofileDlg)
```

We add three methods to our dialog class; two to start and stop the MAPI system that we're using at startup/shutdown (this is only our instance of the MAPI system; these methods won't, for instance, kill a running instance of Outlook), and one to update the list of profiles when we make changes to it. We also add a smart pointer to the `IProfAdmin` interface that we'll be using.

Now, open `bookprofileDlg.cpp` and edit the start as follows:

```
#include "stdafx.h"
#include "bookprofile.h"
#include "bookprofileDlg.h"

#include <mapiutil.h>
#include "check_hresult.h"

#include <edkmdb.h> // for PR_PROFILE_UNRESOLVED_NAME

_COM_SMARTPTR_TYPEDEF(IMAPITable, IID_IMAPITable);
_COM_SMARTPTR_TYPEDEF(IMsgServiceAdmin, IID_IMsgServiceAdmin);
```

```
#ifdef _DEBUG
#define new DEBUG_NEW
#undef THIS_FILE
static char THIS_FILE[] = __FILE__;
#endif
```

We're including `<mapiutil.h>` because we'll use some of the helper functions from in there, `check_hresult.h` because we want to trap errors, and `edkmdb.h` because, though we don't use it immediately, we'll need it when we come to adding new profiles. We also declare two more smart pointer types for `IMAPITable` and `IMsgServiceAdmin`, the interfaces we'll be using.

Next, edit `OnInitDialog` as follows:

```
BOOL CBookprofileDlg::OnInitDialog()
{
    // . . . unchanged until . . .
    // Set the icon for this dialog. The framework does this automatically
    //  when the application's main window is not a dialog
    SetIcon(m_hIcon, TRUE);    // Set big icon
    SetIcon(m_hIcon, FALSE);   // Set small icon

    // TODO: Add extra initialization here

    StartMAPI();
    UpdateProfileList();

    return TRUE;  // return TRUE  unless you set the focus to a control
}
```

Now to add the destructor we mentioned earlier for our class to shut MAPI down. Strictly speaking, we don't need to do this, but it's good practice to always clean up after ourselves. It doesn't actually matter where in the file you add this, but after the constructor is probably a sensible spot to find it again.

```
CBookprofileDlg::~CBookprofileDlg()
{
    StopMAPI();
}
```

Now we'll add the methods that actually do the work:

```
void CBookprofileDlg::StartMAPI()
{
    HRESULT hr = MAPIInitialize(NULL);
    CHECK_HRESULT1(hr, "MAPIInitialize");

    m_pProfileAdmin = NULL;
    hr = MAPIAdminProfiles(0, &m_pProfileAdmin);
    CHECK_HRESULT1(hr, "MAPIAdminProfiles");
}
```

`StartMAPI` calls `MAPIInitialize`, which in turn calls `CoInitialize`. We aren't using any CDO objects anywhere, so we know this is safe – we won't be doing any COM things until after we've started MAPI up.

Once we've checked `MAPIInitialize`'s return value for an error, we call `MAPIAdminProfiles` – this is a global-level function that returns an `IProfAdmin` pointer we can use to access the profile information.

Note that in the interest of clarity, we aren't actually doing anything with the values returned from `CHECK_HRESULT1`. In a real world solution, we should really be trapping possible `FALSE` returns from `CHECK_HRESULT1` and aborting or handling them in some way.

```
void CBookprofileDlg::StopMAPI()
{
    m_pProfileAdmin = NULL;
    MAPIUninitialize();
}
```

`StopMAPI` just clears out our smart pointer, thus releasing our `IProfAdmin` interface. Then we close down the MAPI system because we're finished with it.

Reading The List Of Profiles

There's one other function we've defined to run at startup. `UpdateProfileList` will populate the list box in our dialog with the profiles currently available to us. Subsequently it will get used again when we add to or delete profiles with our program.

```
void CBookprofileDlg::UpdateProfileList()
{
    m_listProfiles.ResetContent();
```

We start off by removing any strings that might be in the list box.

```
    IMAPITablePtr lpProfileTable;

    HRESULT hr = m_pProfileAdmin->GetProfileTable(0, &lpProfileTable);
    CHECK_HRESULT(hr, "GetProfileTable", m_pProfileAdmin);
```

Now we get the table of profiles from our profile administration object as an `IMAPITable`. This structure is basically a two-dimensional array of rows and columns that we can query for information – let's look at how we do that.

```
    // How many profiles do we have?
    ULONG iCount;
    lpProfileTable->GetRowCount(0, &iCount);
    CHECK_HRESULT(hr, "GetRowCount on lpProfileTable", lpProfileTable);
```

We start by getting the number of rows in the table. This is, strictly speaking, a bit iffy – we should be prepared to handle the case where we can't find the number of rows because it's either too large to count (compare with the CDO collections' `count` property), or because MAPI just doesn't want to tell us about it.

Should this happen, we would loop reading rows a few (or perhaps just one) at a time until the table tells us there are no more rows. To keep things simple however, we'll assume that we always have a profile table small enough that we're given an accurate count.

```
for (unsigned int i=0; i < iCount; i++)
{
    LPSRowSet lpRow;
    hr = lpProfileTable->QueryRows(1, 0, &lpRow);
    CHECK_HRESULT(hr, "QueryRows on lpProfileTable", lpProfileTable);
```

To read rows from an IMAPITable interface, we use the QueryRows method. The first argument here is the number of rows we want to read, the second is optional flags, and the third is where we want to have the rows returned put. As before, when we were reading properties from objects, we pass in the address of a pointer that the system will point at allocated memory for the objects it returns, and we'll have to free that memory up.

```
// Two columns in the profile table: name, and "is-this-the-default".
//
// Note we query for one row at a time, but we get an array of rows
// back - this is why we do aRow[0].

CString csName;
csName = lpRow->aRow[0].lpProps[0].Value.lpszA;
```

In the profile table there are only ever two columns; the first one is the name of the profile, and the second one is a flag which is TRUE if that row contains the default profile (note that here we're using the integer versions of TRUE and FALSE rather than the C++ bool type). It won't be that often your tables will have so few columns but here we have a thankfully simple set of information to deal with.

The last line above reads the name of this profile out and stores it. It's also a typical example of lines common in MAPI coding that involve reading multiply-nested elements. To clarify at least this one, let's have a closer look at what's going on.

csName =	The CString that we put the name into.
lpRow	Starting from the pointer to an SRowSet that we returned,
->aRow[0]	we read from the first row (we only asked for one row, so this is a safe assumption to make),
.lpProps[0]	the first property from the list of properties in that row (i.e., the first column of that row), and take
.Value	the value of that property (as opposed to it's property ID),
.lpszA;	and, because we know the type of this property, we can safely read from the string element of the union storing the value

```
// we have a default.
if (lpRow->aRow[0].lpProps[1].Value.b != 0)
{
    csName = "* " + csName;
}
```

Now we check the second column, and if this is the default profile, we add "* " to the name of the profile to show that this is the default.

```
        m_listProfiles.AddString(csName);
```

We add this string to our listbox,

```
        FreeProws(lpRow);
    }
}
```

and we finally free the rows that `QueryRows` returned to us and loop. We have to use `FreeProws` to release a `SRowSet` that has been allocated. MAPI provides us with many, similarly useful functions to free up this sort of multi-level memory structure, which is a very good thing because they can get extremely nested if we're not careful.

Now, add `mapi32.lib` to the list of libraries linked into this project, and let's do a quick test of this. You should see something roughly resembling:

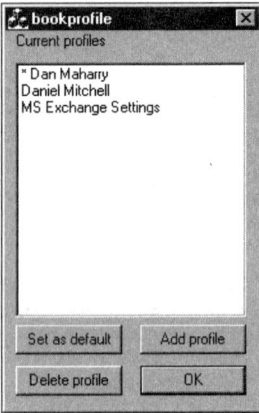

Your list of profiles will undoubtedly vary from mine. All we can do at the moment is view the profiles and then press OK to terminate the program. That said, let's add the rest of the functionality to our program.

Setting the Default Profile

First, we'll add code to set the default profile. Edit `OnSetdefault` as follows:

```
void CBookprofileDlg::OnSetdefault()
{
    int iIndex = m_listProfiles.GetCurSel();
    if (iIndex == -1)
    {
        AfxMessageBox("You must select a profile to set as the default", \
            MB_OK | MB_ICONEXCLAMATION);
        return;
    }
```

We start by making sure the user has actually selected a profile to set as the default, and warn them if not – we rely on them to have selected an entry from the list, or we can't proceed any further.

```
HRESULT hr;
// Remove the current default profile.
hr = m_pProfileAdmin->SetDefaultProfile(NULL, 0);
CHECK_HRESULT(hr, "Remove default profile", m_pProfileAdmin);
```

Next, we remove the current default profile. If we call `IProfAdmin::SetDefaultProfile (NULL, 0)`, this has the effect of setting the default profile to be "null", i.e. there is no default profile. The second argument here is a flag we could use if we were using Unicode – we're not, so we can leave that as 0.

Note that this call doesn't depend on the existence of a current default profile. We're just setting the new default to be "null" and any old default settings are automatically removed by the system if there were any to begin with. If not, the call will just do nothing.

```
CString csProfileName;
m_listProfiles.GetText(iIndex, csProfileName);

if (csProfileName.Left(2) == "* ")
{
    csProfileName = csProfileName.Mid(2);
}
```

Next, we read the name of the profile to become the default, and remove the "* " from the start should there be one there already, as the case would be if a user is reselcting the current default profile. Note that the string in the listbox for the current default profile isn't the actual name of the profile – we've added things to it to show it as the default.

```
char* szProfileName = (char*)(const char*)csProfileName;
```

For some reason, the `SetDefaultProfile` call takes a simple `char*` (LPTSTR) as it's first argument so we have to do nasty casting things to get the contents of our `CString` as one of these.

```
hr = m_pProfileAdmin->SetDefaultProfile(szProfileName, 0);
CHECK_HRESULT(hr, "SetDefaultProfile", m_pProfileAdmin);
```

Now we call `SetDefaultProfile` again to set the default profile to our new value.

```
// Need to flush things through by logging out and in, or we never see
// updates.
StopMAPI();
StartMAPI();

UpdateProfileList();
}
```

Finally, we have to exit the MAPI system and restart it. If we don't do this, we never see any updates to the list of profiles – the profile admin object seems to only read the list when it's first instantiated. We don't actually need to call `MAPIUninitialise` but it's one line shorter to call `StopMAPI` and then `StartMAPI` than it is to clear out m_pProfileAdmin and then call `MAPIAdminProfiles` and check the return value again, so we do things this way instead.

> *If you needed to keep the MAPI system running while you did things, you could change this code to just clear out and reinitialize the* m_pProfileAdmin *object instead; this would also save a tiny amount of time because we wouldn't be calling* `MAPIInitialize` *and* `MAPIUninitialize` *each time.*

At this point, we could build our project and entertain ourselves by bouncing the default profile around among the list of profiles, but let's press on and implement the remaining functionality.

Deleting Profiles

Edit `OnDeleteprofile` as follows:

```
void CBookprofileDlg::OnDeleteprofile()
{
    int iIndex = m_listProfiles.GetCurSel();
    if (iIndex == -1)
    {
        AfxMessageBox("You must select a profile to set as the default", \
            MB_OK | MB_ICONEXCLAMATION);
        return;
    }
```

As before, we check they've selected a profile in the list box before continuing.

```
    CString csProfileName;
    m_listProfiles.GetText(iIndex, csProfileName);

    if (csProfileName.Left(2) == "* ")
    {
        csProfileName = csProfileName.Mid(2);
    }
```

We read the name of the selected profile and trim it appropriately.

```
    CString csWarning = "Are you sure you want to delete the " + \
        csProfileName + " profile?";
    if (AfxMessageBox(csWarning, MB_ICONWARNING | MB_YESNO) == IDNO)
    {
        return;
    }
```

A quick warning dialog to make sure they really want to delete this profile before continuing.

```
char* szProfileName = (char*)(const char*)csProfileName;

HRESULT hr = m_pProfileAdmin->DeleteProfile(szProfileName, 0);
CHECK_HRESULT(hr, "DeleteProfile", m_pProfileAdmin);
```

And now we call `DeleteProfile` to delete the profile. Again, the second argument is an optional Unicode flag.

```
// Need to flush things through by logging out and in,
// or we never see updates.
StopMAPI();
StartMAPI();

UpdateProfileList();
}
```

As before, we need to make sure we've flushed out any possible caches before updating the list of profiles.

Be careful when testing this; if you delete all your profiles, you won't be able to start up Outlook and suchlike without first building new ones. When testing this code, I'd advise you to create some dummy profiles using either the Add-Profile code we provide here or the Mail and Fax control panel, so that you can safely delete these profiles and not affect your normal mail-reading activities.

Adding New Profiles

The basic steps taken to build a new profile are as follows:

❑ Build a new empty profile object.

❑ Add a message service to the profile. (For instance, "Microsoft Exchange Server", or "Personal Folders")

❑ Set the details for the message service by using the appropriate dialog as provided by the message service DLL.

❑ Repeat steps 2 and 3 as appropriate.

This is fine for things such as the Mail and Fax control panel, where we have a user to fill out the appropriate dialogs for us. On the other hand, we may want to add profiles automatically without any user intervention at all. This is possible, but we need to know how the particular message service in question needs to be configured.

We'll just look at configuring the Microsoft Exchange Server message service here – it's relatively simple to configure, and it should give you enough basic code to expand this for other message services if you need to do that later.

We know that we'll need two bits of information – the name of the Exchange Server to connect to, and the name of the mailbox on that server to use. Let's add a dialog to our project to enter that data:

Add a new dialog, give it dialog ID `IDD_PROFILEDETAILSDIALOG`, and set it up as shown:

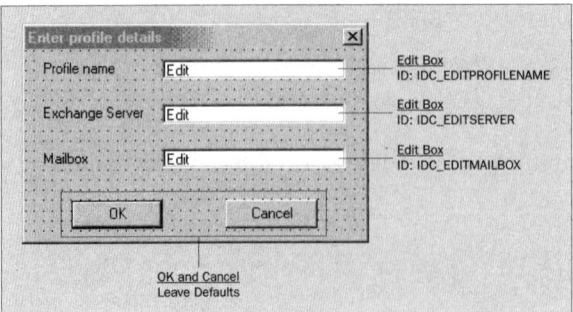

Open the ClassWizard and add member variables to your edit boxes. Call them `m_csProfileName`, `m_csServer` and `m_csMailbox` respectively. Use the class name `CProfileDetailsDlg` when you're asked for a name for your new dialog class.

Back to `bookprofileDlg.cpp`, and include the header file for this new class:

```
#include "stdafx.h"
#include "bookprofile.h"
#include "bookprofileDlg.h"

#include "profiledetailsdlg.h"

#include <mapiutil.h>
#include "check_hresult.h"
```

Now, let's look at the code that actually does the adding of this new profile. Add to `OnAddprofile` as follows:

```
void CBookprofileDlg::OnAddprofile()
{
    CProfileDetailsDlg dlg;

    if (dlg.DoModal() == IDCANCEL)
    {
        return;
    }

    CString csProfileName = dlg.m_csProfileName;
    CString csServer = dlg.m_csServer;
    CString csMailbox = dlg.m_csMailbox;
```

We start by using the dialog we've just built to get the information about the new profile from the user – now, while this may seem strange after I just explained how we don't need any UI, the point here is that this is *our own* UI, rather than that supplied by the system. We could just as well have read this information from a file on disk, or the command line given to our program, or something else that didn't require UI.

```
        char* lpszProfile = (char*)(const char*)csProfileName;

        HRESULT hr;

        // Create a new profile.
        // If the attempt to create the profile fails, remove the profile

        hr = m_pProfileAdmin->CreateProfile(lpszProfile, // name
            "", // password
            0,  // UI handle
            0); // flags
```

We call `CreateProfile` to build ourselves a new, empty, profile. We don't need a profile password here – this whole password thing is a hangover from the olden days of Microsoft Mail that still taints the interfaces of MAPI and CDO to this day.

```
        if (!CHECK_HRESULT(hr, "Creating new profile", m_pProfileAdmin))
        {
            // make sure it's gone.
            hr = m_pProfileAdmin->DeleteProfile(lpszProfile, 0);
            return;
        }
```

In this code, unlike the other stuff, we'll actually use CHECK_HRESULT because there's definite cleanup to do if we hit a failure condition. We don't want to leave half-formed profiles sitting around, so if any of the steps on the way to creating it fail, we delete the profile to tidy up after ourselves. We've already covered how `DeleteProfile` works, so I won't go into it again here.

```
        IMsgServiceAdminPtr pSvcAdmin;

        // Open the admin object on our new service.

        hr = m_pProfileAdmin->AdminServices (lpszProfile,  // name
            NULL,      // password
            0,         // UI handle
            0,         // flags
            &pSvcAdmin); // result

        if (!CHECK_HRESULT(hr, "AdminServices to open new profile", m_pProfileAdmin))
        {
            hr = m_pProfileAdmin->DeleteProfile(lpszProfile, 0);
            return;
        }
```

Now we've got our profile built, we need an `IMsgServiceAdmin` interface to edit the services on this profile. This is basically a wrapper for the list of message services stored in the profile – we need to use this to build ourselves a new message service for Exchange Server.

```
        // Add a message service to the newly created profile
        hr = pSvcAdmin->CreateMsgService("MSEMS", // service
            "Microsoft Exchange", // display name
```

```
        NULL,                  // UI handle
        0);                    // flags

    if (!CHECK_HRESULT(hr, \
        "Creating Microsoft Exchange service in new profile", pSvcAdmin))
    {
        hr = m_pProfileAdmin->DeleteProfile(lpszProfile, 0);
        return;
    }
```

Finally, we can start to use our knowledge of how the Exchange Server message service works to our advantage. The name of the service must come from the list of possible services stored in the `mapisvc.inf` file (which will be in your `Windows\System32` directory).

In this case, we're using `MSEMS`, which corresponds to "Microsoft Exchange Server" in `mapisvc.inf` – the second "M" in the abbreviation doesn't seem to have an obvious purpose. The display name is just that, the name used to display this service in lists of services. This field may be ignored if it's overridden in the `mapisvc.inf` file, but it won't hurt to pass it in. As ever, we specify no flags and no UI.

```
    // Get the message service table for our new profile so we can fill
    // out the details for Exchange.

    IMAPITablePtr pMsgSvcTable;
    hr = pSvcAdmin->GetMsgServiceTable(0, &pMsgSvcTable);

    if (!CHECK_HRESULT(hr, \
        "Opening message service table for new profile", pSvcAdmin))
    {
        hr = m_pProfileAdmin->DeleteProfile(lpszProfile, 0);
        return;
    }
```

Before we can actually do anything to this new message service we've added, we have to open the service up. Unfortunately, it's not quite as simple as you'd imagine – we have to pass the UID for this service to the service admin object and to get the UID, we have to search through the table of services that the service admin object gives us. As such, we start by getting the message service table. This is another `IMAPITable`.

```
    // Get the row from the message service table which represents the
    // Microsoft Exchange Server service provider

    // Build a restriction to search with.
```

For variety's sake, we'll search this table by building a MAPI restriction and searching with that. In practice, we know there's only one row in this table because we've just created this profile and we know there's only one service there. However, this basic technique will prove very useful in the future if you ever want to search tables for a particular row. We could also do the search manually by repeatedly doing `QueryRows` and checking a row at a time although that's probably the slowest possible way to do things. If we use restrictions, the search is done on the server, so the amount of data transferred is minimized.

```
      SRestriction sres;
      SPropValue pSvcProps;

      sres.rt = RES_CONTENT;
      sres.res.resContent.ulFuzzyLevel = FL_FULLSTRING;
      sres.res.resContent.ulPropTag = PR_SERVICE_NAME;
      sres.res.resContent.lpProp = &pSvcProps;
```

The structure we use for searches in MAPI is called `SRestriction` – it contains two members: the type of search we want to do, and the appropriate extra data for that search.

In this case, we're searching based on the content of the properties we're looking at. Alternative types of search include AND/OR/NOT searches, where the extra information would be pointers to the other restrictions combined to make up the overall restriction, or a search for the existence of the property at all. We won't look at that level of detail here, because that starts to get *really* complex. For more on how to do this, see the `mfcapps.zip` sample mentioned earlier on, and/or MSDN under "Building a Restriction" and "Sample Restriction Code".

Because we're doing a `RES_CONTENT` restriction here, we fill out the `resContent` entry of the `SRestriction` structure. We're doing a full-text search, on the name of the service, and we point the restriction at the `SPropValue` structure we're just about to build:

```
      pSvcProps.ulPropTag = PR_SERVICE_NAME;
      pSvcProps.Value.lpszA = "MSEMS";
```

This is the property we want to search for in the table. Notice that we have `PR_SERVICE_NAME` twice, once here and once in the `SRestriction` structure. This is required, because a `SPropValue` has to have the property tag defined, as does the restriction. If we don't fill one of these out, MAPI, sadly, won't read the relevant information from the other one.

```
      SizedSPropTagArray (2, sptCols) = {2, PR_SERVICE_NAME, PR_SERVICE_UID};
```

The next thing we need to do is tell the table which columns we're interested in retrieving. Whereas previously the table of all profiles only ever had two columns, the table of services within a profile can have many columns. Once again though we only care about two, the service name (which we need so we can search based on that), and the UID of the service that we'll use later to open the service.

`SizedSPropTagArray` is a helper macro used to build ourselves a `SPropTagArray` – this is another of the nested MAPI structures that you become accustomed to when doing MAPI development, which contains an array of `SPropTags` and the count of the number of `SPropTags` in that array – `SizedSPropTagArray` builds this for us. We have to cast to `LPSPropTagArray` when we use the resulting structure, but the convenience of not having to manually allocate or free memory for this structure is well worth it.

```
      LPSRowSet pRows = NULL;

      hr = HrQueryAllRows(pMsgSvcTable, // table
         (LPSPropTagArray)&sptCols,    // columns we want
         &sres,                        // restriction
         NULL,                         // sort order
```

```
                0,                              // max. rows to return
                &pRows);                        // results

        if (!CHECK_HRESULT(hr, \
             "Searching for Microsoft Exchange row in service table", pMsgSvcTable))
        {
             hr = m_pProfileAdmin->DeleteProfile(lpszProfile, 0);
             return;
        }
```

Now we call `HrQueryAllRows` – this is a helper function that makes searching tables easier (despite appearances, this is genuinely easier than the alternative). The comments pretty much describe what's going on here; we don't want any particular sort order on the rows that are returned, and we don't want to limit the number of rows returned.

The aforementioned alternative, without helper functions, would require us to manually set the restriction on the table, set the columns, and do a `QueryRows` call as before, with possible looping. `HrQueryAllRows` does all these things at once, and saves us needing to do multiple `QueryRows` calls to cover all the results. This is convenient here where we know the size of the results is limited but we run the risk of having all our memory taken up by enormous search results if we're not careful with what we search, and the resulting hard drive thrashing problems that you'd see with any application that's using up more than its fair share of memory.

```
        SPropValue rgval[2];

        for (int i=0; i<2; i++)
        {
             ZeroMemory(&rgval[i], sizeof(SPropValue));
        }
```

Now we build an array of properties that we're going to use to configure the newly built message service. We start by clearing out the memory to make sure there's nothing there other than what we want.

```
        // Set the values for PR_PROFILE_UNRESOLVED_NAME and
        // PR_PROFILE_UNRESOLVED_SERVER

        rgval[0].ulPropTag = PR_PROFILE_UNRESOLVED_NAME;
        rgval[0].Value.lpszA = (char *)(const char *)csMailbox;

        rgval[1].ulPropTag = PR_PROFILE_UNRESOLVED_SERVER;
        rgval[1].Value.lpszA = (char *)(const char *)csServer;
```

The properties we write to the new service are the name of the mailbox and the name of the server; they are both "unresolved", i.e. they are just strings at this time, not yet turned into references to the specific objects in question.

```
        hr = pSvcAdmin->ConfigureMsgService(
             (LPMAPIUID)pRows->aRow->lpProps[1].Value.bin.lpb, // uid of service
             0, // UI handle
```

```
      0, // flags
      2, // number of properties
      rgval); // pointer to props
```

Now we call `ConfigureMsgService`. The first argument is the UID of the service we want to configure. We've already got this from the message service table from searching under MSEMS. Again, notice the nesting required to go from the rows that were returned from `HrQueryAllRows` to the actual data stored therein. We read from `lpProps[1]` because the UID is in the second column here; the first column is the name, remember.

```
      FreeProws(pRows);

      if (!CHECK_HRESULT(hr, "Configuring message service", pSvcAdmin))
      {
         hr = m_pProfileAdmin->DeleteProfile(lpszProfile, 0);
         return;
      }
```

We free the row we got from `HrQueryAllRows`, and then check to see if the call to `ConfigureMsgService` succeeded; we're done with the memory for this row either way, so we may as well free it up before the check.

```
      // Get rid of the service admin object now so it doesn't get destroyed
      // after the profile object it lives in.
      pSvcAdmin = NULL;
```

Now we hit a nasty smart pointer trick – we're about to call `StopMAPI` to shut the MAPI system down so that we can update the list of profiles. However, our `pSvcAdmin` object is still alive at this point – at the end of this function, it'll be destroyed. If this happens *after* we've called `StopMAPI`, bad things start to creep up on us. To be precise, when we exit the dialog, we get a crash on the final `Release` of our `m_pProfileAdmin` object. Exactly why this happens isn't clear – but if we don't get rid of our service admin object before we call `StopMAPI`, we're in trouble. So at this point, we set our `pSvcAdmin` pointer to be `NULL` – the smart pointer will then release this object, and we can then safely call `StopMAPI`.

Beware of smart pointers; they are a very good thing most of the time, but sometimes you need to make sure you release objects at the right time, and because smart pointers remove the need to call `Release` at all, you can get caught out in nasty ways.

```
      // Need to flush things through by logging out and in, or we never see
      // updates. Caching, I guess.

      StopMAPI();
      StartMAPI();

      UpdateProfileList();
   }
```

Finally, we flush things out and update our list of profiles again.

You should now be able to build and test this project – and you can now build yourself new profiles with which to hook up to Exchange Server.

Testing

Testing the creation of profiles is relatively easy; just build a valid profile – one that points at a real Exchange Server and mailbox – and try to log into it with Outlook. All should be well.

We can also check the error handling more easily, because we have more opportunities to deliberately enter invalid data; try building a profile with a server name pointing at a nonexistent machine, and you'll see:

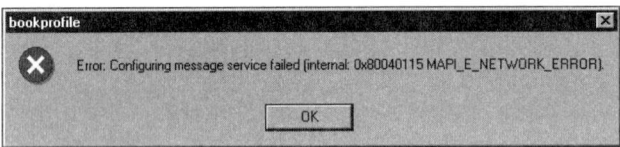

This seems like a reasonable error to get if we're trying to connect to a nonexistent machine, so all would appear to be well.

Extensions To This Project

Note that these profiles only contain the Exchange Server service. They don't contain the Personal Address Book service, for instance, but you should be able to extend this project to set that up if you need. Looking in `mapisvc.inf`, you'll find that the name of the message service for a PAB is "MSPST AB", and that the code for this lives in `mspst.dll`. If we then open `mspst.h`, we'll see a description of the properties we need to set to create a PAB entry in our profile. I won't go into any more detail here, because there's a lot of description in that file. Just change the code above to add another message service with name "MSPST AB" and change the properties you set on that new service appropriately.

Summary Of This Section

In the final part of this chapter, we wrote a MAPI-only application which edits the table of profiles. We looked at how you would access that table from the MAPI system, and how you can set the default profile. We then added code to delete profiles, and finally to create new profiles that connect to Microsoft Exchange Server. We also covered some more ways to get information from MAPI – building restrictions to search tables and using the `HrQueryAllRows` helper function to make querying tables easier.

With all the basics of CDO\C++ programming in your head along with a good knowledge of working with MAPI, in the next chapter, we're going to look at CDO in a different scenario – incorporated into an NT service.

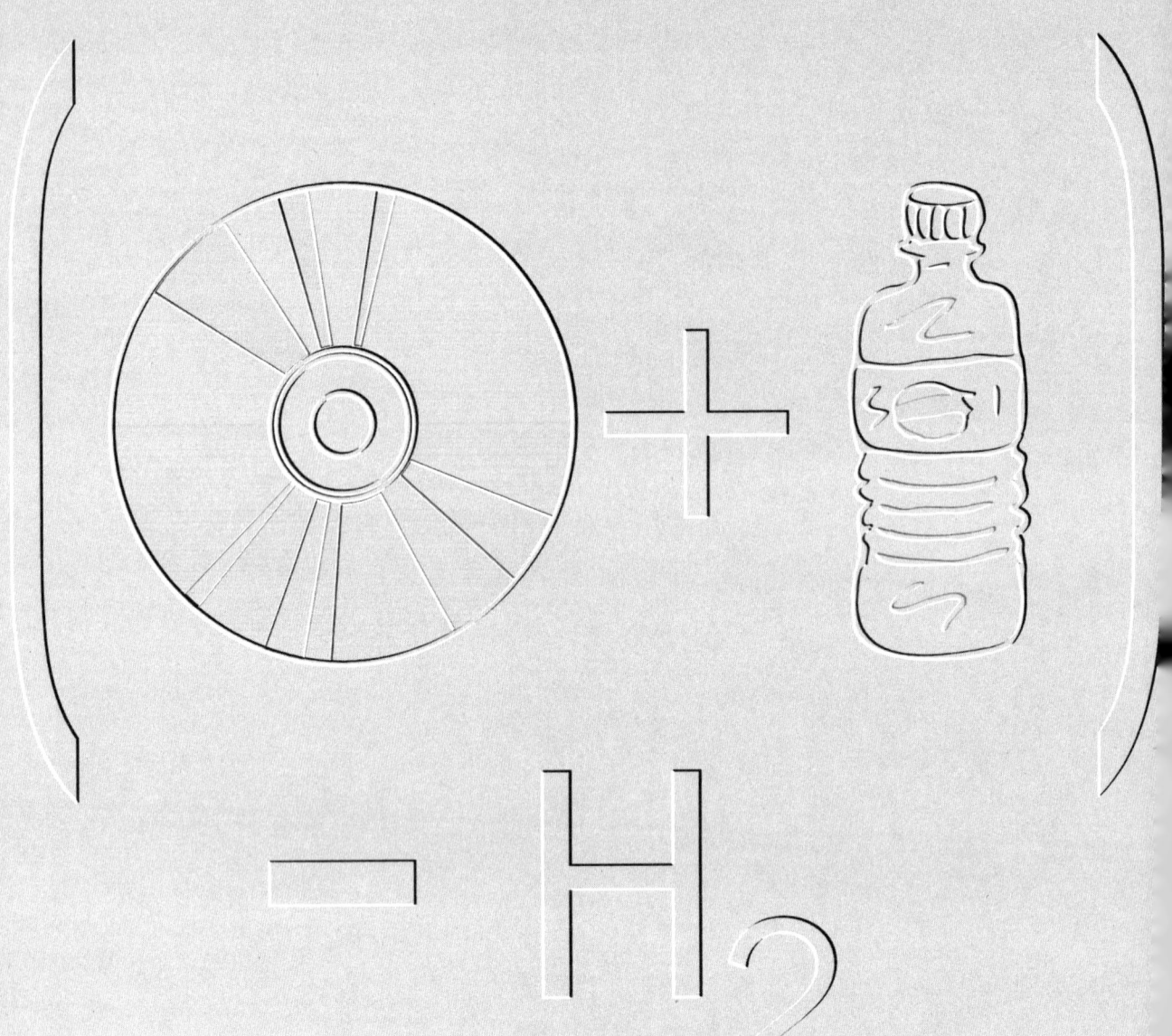

15

Case Study: Using CDO in NT Services

There are times when you may want to have an unattended automatic process running on your system to perform tasks without human interaction. On an NT system, the method provided for doing this (other than simply running an executable and leaving it alone) is to write an **NT service**.

> This chapter assumes you are running Windows NT 4.0. Windows 9x does not have the concept of a 'service', and the operating system doesn't provide any support for the automatic startup of programs. You can use scheduled execution utilities and the **Startup** group in the **Start** menu to launch things at a given time/reboot, but this is much less sophisticated than the facilities that NT provides.

The major advantage of an NT service over a normal application is that NT services run without needing a user to be logged in. This makes them ideally suited to automated server tasks where you don't want to have to worry about logging into the machine in question at startup each time or not being able to log out; you just want a program to run in the background doing whatever it is it does. NT services provide just this ability.

There are many possible things you might want to do in this sort of situation; user-independent tasks like performing backups, monitoring the system, or providing services to other computers (for example, Microsoft Internet Information Server, the Microsoft web server, runs as an NT service).

In this chapter, we'll be covering the following:

- ❏ Why you might want to send mail from a service

- ❏ The problems we'll encounter with sending mail from services

- ❏ A basic introduction to writing NT services – we start by looking at how to debug a process that runs unattended in the background

- ❏ Registering and unregistering our service with the system

- ❏ What our code has to do to act as a service

- ❏ How we go about adding mail functionality to our service

- ❏ Finally, we end up with a working service that sends mail warning of low disk space

Why Do We Want to Send Mail From a Service?

The advantage of an NT service is also simultaneously a disadvantage – they run in the background without user intervention, so you don't need to be logged in – but this means that it can be difficult for the service to tell you about error conditions. The NT event logs exist for this sort of thing, and it's a good fallback method – but this still needs someone to log into the system every so often and view the log to check for errors. You can interact with the desktop from an NT service, but this isn't quite as useful as it might seem; more on this later.

A more immediate way of warning people about this sort of thing is to send them e-mail; this means that information about the error can get off the machine the service is running on and into the inbox of an administrator in question; the administrator can then deal with the problem as they deem fit. In this situation, you want your service to be able to send mail. One other reason we might send mail is to track changes to the system event log and mail any errors logged there to the system administrator – that way they'll be notified immediately without needing to check the system logs manually.

Other Examples of Mail-Enabled Services

Of course, you don't have to use mail purely as a way of reporting errors – this is adding mail capability to an already-existing service. There are also services you might want to perform on the mail system itself – for instance, something that regularly measures the size of users' mailboxes and logs this to a file for the administrator to review. (This is the opposite of the previous example, in that it takes information from the mail system to a local file, rather than reporting a local error condition to the mail system.)

You could also write a service to perform data mining operations on your mailbox; write a service that processes your inbox at regular intervals and (for instance) prints out any new messages that have arrived there. (This somewhat defeats the point of e-mail, I admit, but it's a surprisingly common thing for people to want.)

One thing to beware of with this type of code is that it has the possibility of missing some messages – because your code only runs, say, once a minute, if the user deletes a message quickly enough after receiving it, your code will never see that message.

A solution to this is to use the Microsoft Exchange Server Scripting Agent (introduced with Exchange Server 5.5), which runs on the server and thus can operate on messages immediately after they arrive – for more information on this topic, see the file AGENTS.HLP *on the Exchange Server CDROM, and also* http://www.cdolive.com/agent.htm.

Before We Begin

Make Sure You're an Administrator

One thing to do before trying any of the things in this chapter is to make sure you're logged into the system as a local administrator. If you try and change the settings of the system's services while not logged in as an administrator, you'll just hit an awful lot of errors all over the place, which will not make developing any easier.

Outlook 97 + New Versions of CDO + NT Service Doesn't Mix

A second problem you may find is that if your server has Outlook 97 installed on it and cdo.dll installed manually later, the chances are fairly good that none of this will work either. Microsoft changed the way that CDO initializes MAPI with Exchange 5.5 SP2, and they changed it in such a way that it's no longer compatible with the version of MAPI that ships with Outlook 97 in one important way – you can no longer run CDO in services.

The recommended fix for this is to install Outlook 98/2000 on your server, thus upgrading the MAPI subsystem – this seems to be the only thing that's mentioned anywhere as changing with the MAPI versions, interestingly enough. Another possibility is to try and locate an older version of cdo.dll – the one that ships initially with Outlook 98 is older than the Exchange 5.5 SP2 version, and so doesn't have this "upgrade". Of course, installing CDO from Outlook 98 on top of an Outlook 97 install is a bit pointless when you could just install Outlook 98, but if you, for some reason, find yourself needing to do this, it will probably work. I don't recommend this unless there's no other way around it, though.

See KnowledgeBase article 239785 for more on this topic.

The Trouble with Services

The problem with NT services and mail is that the service runs as a particular user. This user is normally the "system" user – this is an NT-specific user that represents the operating system (to simplify things somewhat). Let's take a quick look at how you find which user a service is running as:

Firstly, from your NT system, open the Control Panel, and from there, the **Services** dialog (note that this and the other dialogs may look different under Windows 2000 – the screenshots here are from NT 4):

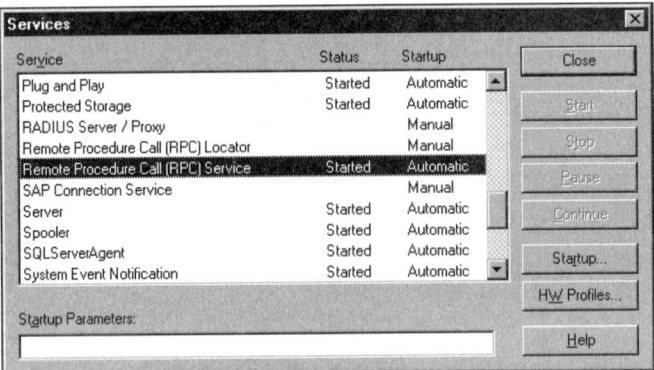

We'll open up the RPC service as an example here – double-click on the service you want to look at the properties of, and you'll see:

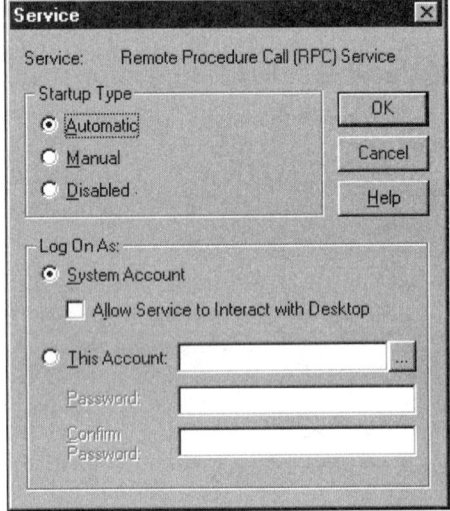

You'll notice the **Log On As** section of this dialog is, in this case, set to log on as the **System Account**.

The problem that this poses when sending mail is that the system account is local to the machine in question – in particular, it doesn't have network access privileges. This means that if you try and send mail from this account, you won't have the required access to the mail system and will get "access denied" type errors.

The second problem is the **Allow Service to Interact with Desktop** issue. This lets your service pop-up dialogs to the person currently logged in – but you can only set this if the service is set to run as the System Account. This would provide a way of telling the current user of the system that an error condition has occurred – but this is only useful if people actually use the server machine in question. If, as is commonly the case for servers, the machine is locked away somewhere out of harm's reach, then nobody will be logged in to see the errors.

Note that, strictly speaking, it is possible for non-interactive services to open dialogs on the main desktop by jumping through some hoops; this is more complicated than we want to go into here, though; see the MSDN entry "Interactive Services" for more detail on this.

So, assuming we're doing things by sending mail, we have to have the service running as a "real" user – but that means that we can't set "interact with desktop" to be true. This means we need to be very careful with our sending mail calls – there is no desktop for our application, so any operation that tries to pop-up a dialog will lock the service waiting for a click that will never come. (For instance, resolving a name to send mail to can optionally pop up the "resolve name" dialog if the automatic resolve fails – this is fine in a program used by real people, because the user can then do the right thing. If this is running as an NT service, there is nobody there to help the program out.).

This implies two things about your code – firstly, that it should always make sure that no methods called can ever create a dialog. In the case of CDO, this means passing `False` as the `ShowDialog` argument to any functions where this applies – in general, you need to make sure that any functions you call can't pop-up an unexpected dialog as a side-effect. Obviously, you can't call any dialog functions yourself.

Secondly, you should be even more paranoid than usual about trapping errors – if you try to send mail to a user that's not in the Global Address List, you need to make sure you trap the failed call to `Resolve` and do something appropriate with your code, because the system can't call on users to help out.

The Other Trouble with Services

Now, at this point, you might think, "okay, no problem; I just set my service to run as myself, and all will be well". Unfortunately, that's not true.

The first problem is a fairly obvious one; just because you have a mail profile set up on your main PC, you may well not have one set up on the PC that the service is running on – especially if this is a box locked away in a back room somewhere. Secondly, even if you were to set the profile up for yourself on the server PC, things still wouldn't work.

The problem is that just because your service is running with your identity, that doesn't mean it's logged in to the system in the same way as you are when you log in from the desktop. This is a subtlety in the way NT manages processes – the service has the same security settings and access as you would when you're logged in, but it doesn't see the registry the same way as you would. In particular, this means that it won't find the list of profiles that you would have when you're logged in.

This is a big pain. You can't simply have code like:

```
Dim objSession As MAPI.Session
Set objSession = New MAPI.Session
objSession.Logon "Default Profile"
```

Because `Default Profile` doesn't exist from the service's point of view.

If you were to write code that built a mail profile, and make your service run that code, then you would have a profile set up correctly that your service could use – however, building profiles from code requires MAPI rather than CDO, and is far from trivial even using MAPI.

If you want to use Extended MAPI from a service, you'll hit all sorts of other problems beyond the lack of profiles – see KnowledgeBase article 198720 for more details on this.

So What Do We Do?

Fortunately, we can create profiles from a service; we just have to create dynamic profiles, not permanent ones. This is fine, as it turns out – we don't really care that the profile will vanish when our service logs out, because the profile was only accessible by our service anyway. It's marginally less convenient than using standard profiles because we need to know the name of the mail server and mailbox we want to log into, rather than just reading the default profile from the registry and logging in or popping up a dialog (remember, we can't pop up dialogs because there may not be anyone there to deal with it).

The default profile can be found in the registry by reading the `DefaultProfile` *value from:*

Win9x: `HKEY_CURRENT_USER\Software\Microsoft\Windows Messaging Subsystem\Profiles`

For WinNT: `HKEY_CURRENT_USER\Software\Microsoft\Windows NT\CurrentVersion\ Windows Messaging Subsystem\Profiles.`

See KnowledgeBase article 171422 for a code sample to read this.

However, it works, and that's very very important at this point. Remember, to log in with a dynamic profile, you do:

```
Dim objSession As MAPI.Session
Set objSession = New MAPI.Session
objSession.Logon ProfileInfo := "Server" & vbLF & "Mailbox"
```

Where the combination of `Server` and `Mailbox` maps to a valid mailbox, and, remember, `Mailbox` is the alias of the mailbox that we find from the addressbook in Outlook rather than the display name of the user that owns that mailbox.

Small Gotcha

One slight trick you should be aware of is that a given NT account needs to have the Log on as a service account right granted to it before it can log on. It's possible to do this from code, but the code to do that is long and painful; if you want to write it, the particular function call you need is `LsaAddAccountRights` – but there's a fair amount of setup needed to be able to call that. A much easier way of doing this is to simply set a particular service to log on as a user using the Service Manager control panel– the system notices this happening, and automatically grants that user the Log on as a service right.

To save ourselves forgetting to do this later on, I'd advise you to do that now; pick any of the services from the Services control panel, double-click on it, set it to run as the user you're going to want to use, and then reset it to the account it was running as originally. When you set the service to run as a user, the system will notify you that it has added the Log on as a service right to that user – if you don't get this notification, it's because that user already had that right. Something like the Computer Browser service is a good one to pick here, because it runs as the system account under normal circumstances and it's easy to reset things to run to that. Ideally, you should choose a service that's not currently running, to avoid confusing matters any more than is necessary.

Another way to do this is from the User Rights section of the User Manager application – note that Log on as a service is an advanced right, so you'll have to enable those rights:

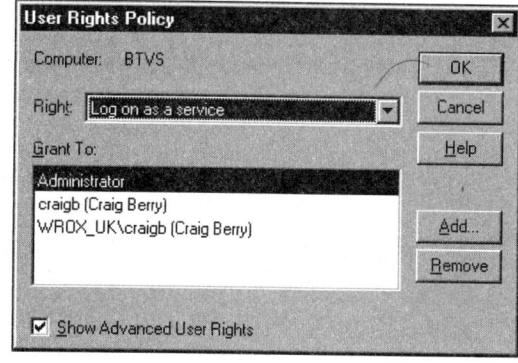

Creating an NT Service

We'll do this in C++ to start with, because the way you build a service relies on a lot of Win32 API calls and those are easier to do in C++ than Visual Basic. We'll cover the Visual Basic issues in more detail later in this chapter when we cover writing services in Visual Basic.

So, let's start off with a simple Win32 Console Application; start it as an empty project and call it something appropriate like CDOTestService. Then add a single .cpp source file, called main.cpp.

Put the following code into main.cpp as a nice standard starting point:

```
#include <windows.h>
#include <stdio.h>

int main(int argc, char* argv[])
{
    return 0;
}
```

Debugging Services

Now, the next thing we'll do is to digress slightly – before we start writing any real code, it's always good to know that the code we're writing is working. In standard DOS/console applications like the ones we used before with CDO in C++, we had access to the stdout stream to print messages; as a service, however, we don't have an output console. If we were writing Win32 applications, we could use a MessageBox to show progress (this is a pretty ugly way of doing things, I admit) – but we can't pop up windows from a service, for the reasons mentioned previously (i.e. that there's no user there to see and dismiss them).

One possibility would be to install and set up the Windows system debugger (remember, this is a service, so doesn't run in the same way as normal programs); this is possible, but pretty painful. What's more, it's a much lower-level debugger than the one that comes with Visual Studio, and messing with system-level debugging is never fun (unless you like that sort of thing, I suppose).

Alternatively, you could install Visual Studio on the server machine and use the Debug I Attach To Process feature to hook up to your service when it's running – however, you may wish to avoid installing an entire development environment on a server. This also only allows you to debug your service while you are actually sitting there at the machine; services are designed to run unattended, so in the long run we'll need a way to debug that doesn't require manual intervention.

I'm going to take a more classical approach to debugging; log progress to a file. This is messy compared to "real" debugging, but it'll do the job for now; and it doesn't require installing any extra software on the server machine our stuff runs on, which is always a bonus. Now, we could write ourselves a little `CLogFile` class that would dump messages to a log file `c:\ourlog.txt` or somesuch – but that seems a bit obtuse, as after all, NT provides the event logs for this sort of thing. The other advantage of the event logs are that they provide built-in size limits and a basic sort of data compression, which we'll cover when we look at writing to the logs; just dumping messages to a text file can run the risk of filling up your server's hard drive.

Using the Event Logs

There are actually three types of event log file; the main System log, the Security log, and the Application log. We'll do our logging to the application log, because we're an application. The System log is meant for the Windows NT system itself to log events to, so we'll steer clear of that.

At this stage, you might hope that there'd be some sort of convenient Win32 API call along the lines of:

```
WriteToSystemLog(LOG_APPLICATION, "Sending mail to %s", lpszName);
```

Sadly, that isn't the way. The actual call you have to use to log system messages is:

```
BOOL ReportEvent(
    HANDLE    hEventLog,      // handle to event log
    WORD      wType,          // event type
    WORD      wCategory,      // event category
    DWORD     dwEventID,      // event identifier
    PSID      lpUserSid,      // user security identifier
    WORD      wNumStrings,    // number of strings to merge
    DWORD     dwDataSize,     // size of binary data
    LPCSTR    *lpStrings,     // array of strings to merge
    LPVOID    lpRawData       // binary data buffer
);
```

We get a handle to an event log using `RegisterEventSource`, which we'll come to later. The event type `wType` can have the following values (from `<winnt.h>`):

EVENTLOG_SUCCESS	0x0000
EVENTLOG_ERROR_TYPE	0x0001
EVENTLOG_WARNING_TYPE	0x0002
EVENTLOG_INFORMATION_TYPE	0x0004
EVENTLOG_AUDIT_SUCCESS	0x0008
EVENTLOG_AUDIT_FAILURE	0x0010

And it's fairly clear which of these are which. The audit events only apply when auditing is turned on on the system, and we can ignore those; we'll use the EVENTLOG_INFORMATION_TYPE for our debugging information.

The event category wCategory is specific to the source and can have any value, so we can ignore it for now.

The problem comes when we look at the event identifier dwEventID. You can't just pass a string to ReportEvent and tell it to log that to the system – you have to pass an identifier for a string in a message table that you build separately. This has two advantages – firstly, it makes internationalization easier in the same way as string tables in general Win32 programming does; because all your strings are kept in one place, translating them is easier. Secondly, the system doesn't actually log the text of these messages, it just stores a reference to the message ID and executable containing that ID; this allows the log files to avoid storing redundant data and thus fill up more slowly. It makes our life more painful in the short term because we have to go through the effort of generating a string table and performing the particular magic required to let our program access it – but it's the right way to do things, so the effort is worthwhile.

The user's SID lpUserSID allows us to pass a SID (Security Identifier) to log with this event if we want to track which user is associated with it; we can alternatively just pass NULL for no identity, which we'll do for now.

At this point you may be asking yourself how you can write things to the log file that aren't in the message table – this is where the wNumStrings and lpStrings parameters enter the picture. In a similar (but not identical) way to printf, you can have % entries in your string, and those entries will be populated with the relevant entries from the table of strings passed in.

One interesting twist on this is that the event log file on disk only contains the index of the message within your executable code's message list, and the body of any insertions; this saves space if you have messages that appear multiple times.

The dwDataSize and lpRawData allow you to log raw binary data to the logs; we won't want to do that ourselves, because we only need to log text messages. If your application were processing images, say, then you might want to dump the contents of your image file to the event log.

Building a Message File

A message file is a plain text file in a very specific format – here's a very basic one to start with:

```
MessageId=0x1000
SymbolicName=EVENTLOG_DEBUG
Language=English
Debug: %1
.
```

The format should be relatively clear – notice that we only have to define one MessageId, the first one; the message compiler will fill in the rest of them for us. We then have the symbolic name of this – this is what we'll use in our code to refer to this message, the language for this particular bit of text, the text, and a line containing just a full stop to tell the system that this is the end of this message. Make sure that there's a new line after the last full stop.

Add the code above to your project as a new text file; call this file `servicemsgs.mc`, and save it.

The next thing we need to do is process this file so that we can use it in our code. In this case, we could do it by hand because we know this particular file isn't going to change. However, let's do things properly; right-click on the file in the Workspace view, and select Settings. You'll see a dialog like the following:

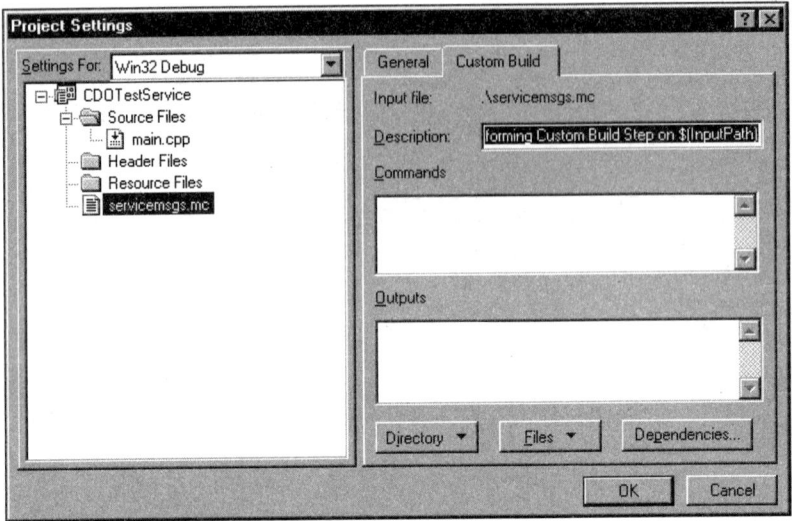

Change the Commands section to read `mc $(InputPath)`, and the Outputs section to contain `servicemsgs.h`, `servicemsgs.rc`, and `msg00001.bin`.

What's going on here? The utility we're using is `mc.exe`, the message compiler; it turns our message file into a header file we use in our code to refer to the messages; a `.rc` file we include as a resource file, and a `.bin` file that the resource file refers to. Build the project, and it should say:

```
——————————Configuration: bookntservice - Win32 Debug——————————
Performing Custom Build Step on .\servicemsgs.mc
MC: Compiling .\servicemsgs.mc
```

...in the Output window.

Now add `servicemsgs.h` and `servicemsgs.rc` to the project in the Header and Resource sections respectively; the Project window should now look like this:

The reason we're adding the message file and these files to the workspace is that if we do ever want to change the contents of the message file, Visual Studio will detect that the file's changed, compare its date to the date of the files that depend on it, and rebuild the right things automatically. This is a big improvement over having to remember to open up a DOS window and run `mc.exe` manually each time. We have to tell Visual Studio what the output files it should check against are, however, which is why we put those in the list of outputs in the Settings window.

If we take a look at the files generated by `mc.exe` here, we'll find that `servicemsgs.h` contains (after a lot of boilerplate header):

```
// MessageId: EVENTLOG_DEBUG
//
// MessageText:
//
//  Debug: %1
//
#define EVENTLOG_DEBUG                  0x00001000L
```

Which isn't terribly surprising; `servicemsgs.rc` contains (you'll need to open it with a non-Visual Studio editor to see this, or Visual Studio will go to its resource view):

```
LANGUAGE 0x9,0x1
1 11 MSG00001.bin
```

Which is not all that illuminating, but at least shows that it refers to the `.bin` file generated, so there is a reason for that being there.

Let's test this stuff before we go any further. Change `main.cpp` to read as follows:

```cpp
#include <windows.h>
#include <stdio.h>

#include "servicemsgs.h"

int main(int argc, char* argv[])
{
    HANDLE hEventLog = RegisterEventSource(NULL, "Testing");

    const char* msgs[1] = {"This is a test message"};

    BOOL bRetval = ReportEvent(hEventLog,
        EVENTLOG_INFORMATION_TYPE,
        0,
        EVENTLOG_DEBUG,
        NULL,
        1,
        0,
        msgs,
        NULL);

    DeregisterEventSource(hEventLog);

    return 0;
}
```

This basically just does what we've talked about so far – registers with the system so we can log messages, calls `ReportEvent`, and unregisters so we clean up after ourselves.

`RegisterEventSource` takes two arguments; the first one is the name of the machine to perform the event on (in this case, the local machine, where we can pass in NULL), and the second is the name of the source referenced by the handle we get back. There's a slight twist where that second value needs to have an associated registry entry created before we can log events with it properly, but we'll get back to that.

Notice that when you built this project, Visual Studio didn't rebuild the messages file, because we've told it what the dependencies are correctly. If you try running the resulting executable, and open up the Event Viewer, you should see that the Application Log now contains a record of our message:

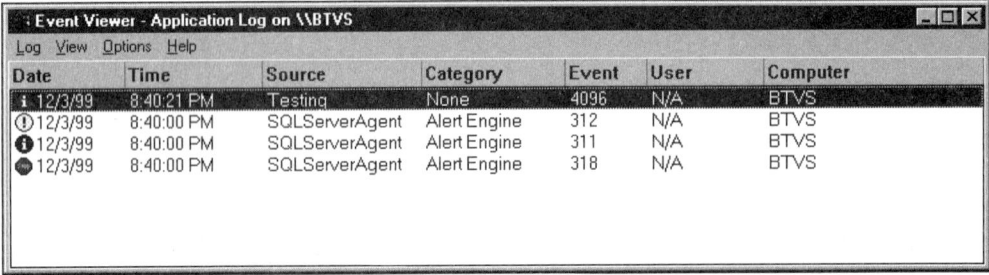

There's no category, because we didn't give one; the event has ID 4096 which is fine because we defined it to have ID `0x1000` which is 4096 in decimal; there's no user, because we didn't specify one. Things aren't quite all hunky-dory – when we double-click on the message to read it, we find:

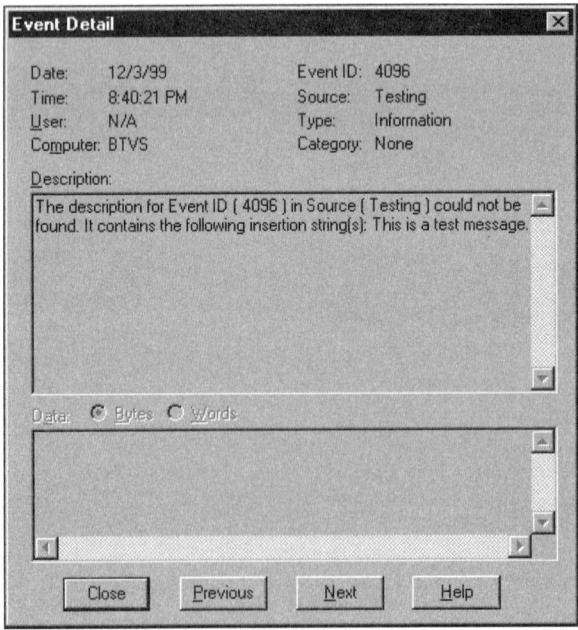

This is reasonable; it's complaining that it couldn't find the source message with code 4096 to insert our message in. As mentioned earlier, the logging subsystem only stores the index of the message and the executable code in which it can find that message. In our case, we haven't registered with the system properly yet, so it can't find the message to insert our text in.

Fortunately, this isn't too critical for now; all we're missing is the prefix Debug: on the front of our message, and we still have a way of logging messages before we've got our service properly installed, which will be useful when we're debugging the installation code. If worst came to worst, we could live with this – we'd have to have a manual copy of the table of message IDs to strings on paper or something to translate with, but that's not fatal. However, we want to do things properly.

So now we're ready to "debug" things, let's get back to actually building a service.

Writing an NT Service

I'm going to skim very lightly over the surface of this, because there's an awful lot of ground to cover. If you have access to MSDN (find it on the web at http://msdn.microsoft.com/library/) then you'll find an enormous amount more detail on this in the Platform SDK section, under Base Services : DLLs, Processes and Threads : Services, and in the Wrox book *Professional NT Services*, by Kevin Miller.

> *As a side note, you can also create a service using the Visual Studio ATL COM AppWizard – this will build the shell of a service for you, and if you simply don't add any COM interfaces, you can then use this code as an equivalent to some of the code we'll explain below. You'll need to alter the boilerplate code supplied to set the service to run as a particular user, and deal with the fact that the main loop of execution expects Windows messages. This is not necessarily the easiest way to do things, despite the fact that it builds code for you, but you may find it interesting to compare the code that Visual Studio builds for a basic service with the code we'll build below.*

An NT service, then, needs to supply three functions to the system; a main function where the overall execution starts, a ServiceMain function which is called to start the service running, and a Handler function which is where the actual code that does this stuff lives.

Now, we could write our service exactly like this; we only need three functions, and the minimal amount of code needed to be a service is pretty tiny. However, let's spend a little more time on this and write code that we can extend at a later date – the extra effort is tiny compared to the details of making things into a service at all, and it gives us a much better foundation.

The obvious way to go, then, is to have an object that represents our service. To be precise, we'll have an object of type CNTService (this is just the name we'll use, not a system-specific keyword) which we'll instantiate from main – that object will then provide a ServiceMain and Handler function to the system.

The first problem we'll come across when trying to do this is that the Win32 API calls we're going to use to register our service and its functions with the system take pointers to functions – but we can't just pass a pointer to a member function because C++ doesn't let us do that without a lot of awkwardness; there may well not be an object for that function to operate on.

We could solve this by having static member functions in our class; we are allowed to pass the address of those around, and we could then have a static member in our class which points to an instance of the class. That would work, but is pretty messy.

What we'll do instead is rely on the fact that we know we're going to instantiate one of our `CNTService` objects before we do any of the calls that need it; we have a global pointer to the object, and we have two non-member `ServiceMain` and `Handler` functions which simply pass their arguments on to that object. This is still messy, but keeps our object a bit cleaner at the expense of the code that calls it. Either way, things are pretty grotty, it has to be said – but for the sake of brevity we'll go this way for now. The only real restriction this imposes (other than the moral ugliness of this sort of thing) is that we can only have one service object at a time, because the global variable can only point at one object at once; that's a restriction we can, in the case of most services, live with. (If you want to have multiple objects in a service, the easiest way to do it is to write a COM server and that's a whole other kettle of fish.)

The Service Control Manager

We could at this point write ourselves a service – but we still aren't ready to do that. The problem we have is that if we wrote a bare-bones service in this way, it wouldn't appear in the Services Control Panel – and we need it to appear there so we can set it to run as a particular user (because, some long time ago, we wanted to send mail, remember). The bit of the Windows NT system that handles this is called the **Service Control Manager (SCM)**, and there's yet another lot of API calls that deal with it.

Before we write any code to actually run a service, then, let's get ourselves registered with the SCM. One side benefit of this is that while we're registering ourselves as a service, we can also do the required things to make logging work correctly.

The DebugLog Function

The first thing we'll do is add a helper function to let us log messages. These will still be broken "no-such-message-ID" messages, but they'll turn out to be very helpful when debugging. In practice, we could actually still get away with using `printf`, because at this point in development we run the install and uninstall from a DOS window and so have a console to print messages to. That particular ability won't be there forever, so let's do things properly.

Add a source file `debuglog.cpp` and corresponding header file `debuglog.h` to the project. `debuglog.h` should contain:

```
void DebugLog(const char* message, ...);
```

And `debuglog.cpp` should contain:

```
#include <windows.h>
#include <stdio.h>
#include <stdarg.h>

#include "debuglog.h"
#include "servicemsgs.h"

HANDLE hEventLog_G;
```

```
class EventSourceRegisterer
{
public:
    EventSourceRegisterer()
    {
        hEventLog_G = RegisterEventSource(NULL, "Debugging");
    }
    ~EventSourceRegisterer()
    {
        DeregisterEventSource(hEventLog_G);
    }
};
EventSourceRegisterer esr;

void DebugLog(const char* message, ...)
{
    char tb[10000];
    va_list arglist;
    va_start(arglist, message);
    _vsnprintf(tb, 9999, message, arglist);
    va_end(arglist);

    const char* msgs[1];
    msgs[0] = tb;

    BOOL bRetval = ReportEvent(hEventLog_G,
        EVENTLOG_INFORMATION_TYPE, 0, EVENTLOG_DEBUG, NULL,
        1, 0, msgs, NULL);
}
```

There's nothing terribly sophisticated going on here; we use `<stdarg.h>` to let us make `DebugLog` take print-style format specifications, because that's very useful indeed. We use `_vsnprintf` to do the printing; this is like `vsprintf`, in that it operates on variable-argument lists, but it will output at most a given number of characters – this means we can't overflow our buffer.

We then build a one-element array of strings, and call `ReportEvent` to log that. We use a static object to handle registering/unregistering the event source – the class `EventSourceRegisterer` registers an event source when it's constructed, and unregisters it when it's destroyed. We have one of those object declared in this file; so we know that the event source is registered at static constructor time (i.e. before any of our code gets to run) and unregistered automatically when our object is destroyed at the end of execution.

To test this, change `main.cpp` to read:

```
#include "debuglog.h"

int main(int argc, char* argv[])
{
    DebugLog("Testing logging: string `%s' number %d", "blah", 123);
    return 0;
}
```

And rebuild. You can leave `main.cpp` containing this; we'll edit it appropriately when we next need to, and we'll look at other files in the meantime. When you run this, you should see an event log message reading something like:

The description for Event ID (4096) in Source (Debugging) could not be found. It contains the following insertion string(s): Testing logging: string 'blah' number 123.

Which is what we'd expect.

Now we've got ourselves a convenient logging function, let's start writing code.

Installing and Uninstalling the Service

Add another source and header file to the project, called `ntservice.h` and `ntservice.cpp`. `ntservice.h` should contain:

```
#include <windows.h>

class CNTService
{
public:
    CNTService();
    virtual ~CNTService();

    BOOL AreWeInstalled();
    BOOL Install(LPCSTR szUserName, LPCSTR szPassword);
    BOOL Uninstall();

protected:
    LPCSTR m_szServiceName;
    HANDLE m_hEventLog;

    void LogMessage(WORD wType, DWORD dwMessageID, LPCSTR szInsertion);
};
```

We'll explain what all these functions do in a second; worth noting is the `LogMessage` function; this is what the service uses to log messages. It's more basic than `DebugLog` in that it doesn't take `printf`-style format specification, but it has the advantage that it'll use the messages we're about to define in the message file.

The Basic Structure of CNTService

`ntservice.cpp` should contain:

```
#include "ntservice.h"
#include "debuglog.h"
#include "servicemsgs.h"

CNTService::CNTService()
{
    m_szServiceName = "CDO Test service";
```

```
        m_hEventLog = RegisterEventSource(NULL, m_szServiceName);
}

CNTService::~CNTService()
{
    DeregisterEventSource(m_hEventLog);
}
```

Nothing too clever so far, as with our `DebugLog` helper object, we register an event source at constructor time and deregister at destructor time so we don't have to worry about remembering to do this. We store the name of our service in a member variable – this could just as well go in a `#define` at the top of `ntservice.cpp` after the `#include` lines, but this is perhaps more extensible.

CNTService::LogMessage

```
    void CNTService::LogMessage(WORD wType, DWORD dwMessageID, LPCSTR szInsertion)
    {
        const char* msgs[1];
        msgs[0] = szInsertion;

        BOOL bRetval = ReportEvent(m_hEventLog, wType,   0, dwMessageID,
                                   NULL, 1, 0, msgs, NULL);
    }
```

This is our logging function – it only supports messages from the message file with a single string inserted, though we could adapt it if we needed to. Otherwise, it's just a call to `ReportEvent` which we've already discussed.

CNTService::AreWeInstalled

Next we have a helper function that lets us tell if we're already installed – if you try and install a service that's already installed, the service manager gives errors, so we want to avoid that if possible:

```
    BOOL CNTService::AreWeInstalled()
    {
        // Open the service control manager.

        SC_HANDLE hSCM = OpenSCManager(
            NULL, // on the local machine
            NULL, // default services database
            GENERIC_READ); // want read access
```

First we open the Service Control Manager. We want to open it on the local machine; the second argument tells it which services database to open – as it turns out, this should always be set to `SERVICES_ACTIVE_DATABASE`, but `NULL` selects this, the default option, and is shorter. We only need read access because all we want to do is get information from this:

```
        if (hSCM == NULL)
        {
            // Couldn't get at the service control manager. Oops.
            //
            // Have to use generic log because we don't know the
            // registry's set up yet.
```

```
        DebugLog("Couldn't open SCM to check installation : 0x%08x",
                GetLastError());
        return FALSE;
    }
```

If `OpenScManager` fails, Thisit returns NULL – in this case, we want to log this failure to a file. The error code is reported by `GetLastError`, and, foresightedly, we can just print that error out using `DebugLog`:

```
    // Now try and open our entry in the SCM.

    SC_HANDLE hService = OpenService(
        hSCM,              // open on the manager object we just got.
        m_szServiceName,   // name of the service
        SERVICE_QUERY_STATUS); // want to ask about its status

    if (hService == NULL)
    {
        // Couldn't find the entry in the SCM.
        // This is fine, it tells us that we're not installed
        // yet.
        CloseServiceHandle(hSCM);
        return FALSE;
    }
```

This is the same sort of thing as before – we ask the Service Manager for a handle to our service. We open services by name, notice. At this point, if we get a "failure", i.e. returned value of Null, that's fine – that just tells us that our service isn't installed, so we close our service control manager handle, return `FALSE`, and we're done.

```
    // We successfully opened it; close the handles and return TRUE.

    CloseServiceHandle(hService);
    CloseServiceHandle(hSCM);

    return TRUE;
}
```

If we didn't get NULL as a service handle, we know the service is there. This is all we needed to know for now, so we'll just close the handles and return `TRUE`.

Installing the Service

Now we'll cover the code used to actually do the installing and uninstalling of the service.

CNTService::Install

```
BOOL CNTService::Install(LPCSTR szUserName, LPCSTR szPassword)
{
```

This is the function used to install the service. You'll notice that we pass in a username and password – one convenient aspect of the way we do things is that we can set the user to run this service as during the install – this means that when the time comes to start doing mail operations, we'll already be set up as a user with the required mailbox permissions:

```
if (AreWeInstalled())
{
    // Uninstall, then reinstall; this way they can
    // change password in one step.
    Uninstall();
}
```

As mentioned before, we have to make sure we don't try and install if we're already installed. However, if we just want to change our identity (i.e. name and password) then we let users do this in one step, and automatically uninstall ourselves (we cover the Uninstall function next) before reinstalling with possibly new identity information:

```
SC_HANDLE hSCM = OpenSCManager(
    NULL, // on the local machine
    NULL, // default services database
    SC_MANAGER_ALL_ACCESS); // want full access

if (hSCM == NULL)
{
    // Couldn't get at the service control manager. Oops.
    //
    // Again, have to use the generic logging features.
    DebugLog("Couldn't open SCM to install: 0x%08x",
            GetLastError());
    return FALSE;
}
```

As before, open the Service Manager, and log errors if they occur. This time around, though, we need to open it with full access because we're going to install a service:

```
// Get the path to our executable.
char szExecPath[_MAX_PATH];
GetModuleFileName(NULL, szExecPath, _MAX_PATH);
```

We need the path of the executable our service lives in; GetModuleFileName does this for us.

Calling CreateService

```
// Tell the SCM to create an entry for us.
SC_HANDLE hService = CreateService(
    hSCM,               // use our manager object
    m_szServiceName, // name of the service
    m_szServiceName, // display name
    SERVICE_ALL_ACCESS, // want full access to it.
    SERVICE_WIN32_OWN_PROCESS, // runs in its own process
                        // (ie normal)
    SERVICE_DEMAND_START,    // start on demand (ie not
                        // automatically)
```

```
        SERVICE_ERROR_NORMAL,         // pop up dialog (because we're
                                      // starting  manually, this is
                                      // okay for now)
        szExecPath,        // path to the executable
        NULL,              // load ordering group (ignore)
        NULL,              // tag within load group (ignore)
        NULL,              // services we depend on
        szUserName,        // name to start this service with
        szPassword);       // password for this service
```

There's plenty of arguments to `CreateService` – most of them are pretty obvious, so I won't go into too much detail. Things to note, though:

❑ The name of the service is not necessarily the same as the "display name" of the service; the name is the string used by the service control manager that is the one we'll use to query for installed-ness and suchlike. The display name is the string that appears in the "services" control panel.

❑ The flags basically tell the system that we're a simple single-process self-contained service; that we want to start on demand (i.e. from the Services control panel, rather than at system boot time), and that if errors happen when starting up it's okay to pop up a dialog to tell us about it. This may seem to fly in the face of everything I've been saying about the evils of dialogs, but for the moment we know we'll only be starting the service manually – and this only refers to startup errors, so we know that there'll always be someone at the computer starting the service, so that person can dismiss dialogs. If we want our service to start up at system boot time, we'd have to select other values. (See the documentation for more details, omitted here for brevity.)

❑ The "load ordering group" we could use to specify the order in which the system would load services; we don't care about that for now. Our service doesn't depend on any other services being loaded, so we can skip that argument as well.

❑ Finally, we pass in the name and password we want to use to authenticate this service's identity. These are the things you would type in the "Log on as this account" dialog accessed by double-clicking on the service in the services control panel – because it's a big pain having to do this every time we reinstall our service because we've changed it while developing, we set these at startup time.

```
    if (hService == NULL)
    {
        // Didn't register for some reason.
        DebugLog("Couldn't register service: 0x%08x", GetLastError());
        CloseServiceHandle(hSCM);
        return FALSE;
    }
```

There's error checking as usual.

Setting Up the Registry for Log Messages

```
// Now we're registered, set up the registry to let ourselves log
// messages properly.
//
// Want to put an entry in the registry under
// HKLM\CurrentControlSet\Services\EventLog\Application

char szKeyToBuild[256];
wsprintf(szKeyToBuild,
        "SYSTEM\\CurrentControlSet\\Services\\EventLog\\Application\\%s",
        m_szServiceName);
```

If we want to log messages to the application log properly, in other words using our message file, we have to build a couple of registry values in a key HKEY_LOCAL_MACHINE\
CurrentControlSet\Services\EventLog\servicename. First, then, we have to create that key:

```
HKEY hKey = NULL;

LONG lRetVal = RegCreateKey(HKEY_LOCAL_MACHINE, // local machine
    szKeyToBuild,    // key name
    &hKey);          // return into this

if (lRetVal != ERROR_SUCCESS)
{
    DebugLog(
 "Couldn't create registry key for log messages: 0x%08x",
 lRetVal);
    CloseServiceHandle(hService);
    CloseServiceHandle(hSCM);
    return FALSE;
}
```

Try and create it, if we can't, log this and clean-up:

```
// Now we have to create a value "EventMessageFile" in that key.

long lExecPathLen = strlen(szExecPath);
lExecPathLen++; // need null terminator

lRetVal = RegSetValueEx(hKey,   // create in this key
    "EventMessageFile",         // needs this name
    0,                          // reserved, must be 0
    REG_EXPAND_SZ,              // type of value -
                                // string with %PATH%-type expansion
    (const BYTE*)szExecPath,    // data to write
    lExecPathLen);              // size of data

if (lRetVal != ERROR_SUCCESS)
{
    RegCloseKey(hKey);
```

```
            DebugLog("Couldn't create EventMessageFile subkey: 0x%08x", lRetVal);
            CloseServiceHandle(hService);
            CloseServiceHandle(hSCM);
            return FALSE;
    }
```

We now create a value `EventMessageFile` in this key, containing the path to our executable. (This is so the event log can locate our executable to read the message table from it, reasonably enough.) Nothing too clever here: pass the pointer to and length of our data to `RegSetValueEx` and check it succeeded; if not, log the error and cleanup as usual:

```
    // Set the types of event we're going to want to log.

    DWORD dwFlagTypes =
        EVENTLOG_ERROR_TYPE |
        EVENTLOG_WARNING_TYPE |
        EVENTLOG_INFORMATION_TYPE;

    const BYTE* pData = (const BYTE*)&dwFlagTypes;

    lRetVal = RegSetValueEx(hKey,       // create in this key
        "TypesSupported",               // name we want
        0,                              // reserved
        REG_DWORD,                      // type
        pData,                          // data to write
        sizeof(DWORD));                 // size of data

    RegCloseKey(hKey);

    if (lRetVal != ERROR_SUCCESS)
    {
        DebugLog("Couldn't create TypesSupported subkey: %d", lRetVal);
        CloseServiceHandle(hService);
        CloseServiceHandle(hSCM);
        return FALSE;
    }
```

Same thing as before, but this time we need a DWORD key containing the types of event we're going to log; in our case, errors, warnings, and information. (We may not necessarily do all those, but it can't hurt to be aware we might need to at some point.) Note that we close the registry key as soon as we've finished with it, because, errors or not, we don't have any further use for it and it saves us having to have more calls to `RegCloseKey` than we need:

```
    CloseServiceHandle(hService);
    CloseServiceHandle(hSCM);

    // Log the fact we're successfully installed. Use proper logging now
    // that we're set up to do so.
    LogMessage(EVENTLOG_INFORMATION_TYPE, EVENTLOG_INSTALLED,
            m_szServiceName);

    return TRUE;
}
```

Now we've finished installing, close up all the things we opened, and log the fact that we installed ourselves successfully. Note that now we're installed, we can use `LogMessage` to log messages with our message table! The message table needs to be updated to contain a message `EVENTLOG_INSTALLED` but we'll get to that.

Uninstalling the Service

```
BOOL CNTService::Uninstall()
{
    if (!AreWeInstalled())
    {
        DebugLog("Tried to uninstall service that wasn't installed!");
        return FALSE;
    }
```

We can't uninstall a service if it's not been installed; trap this before we start hitting errors, and log it so we know someone tried to do this:

```
SC_HANDLE hSCM = OpenSCManager(
    NULL, // on the local machine
    NULL, // default services database
    SC_MANAGER_ALL_ACCESS); // want full access

if (hSCM == NULL)
{
    // Couldn't get at the service control manager. Oops.
    DebugLog("Couldn't open SCM to uninstall: 0x%08x", GetLastError());
    return FALSE;
}
```

This is the same as in the previous function – we need to open the Service Control Manager with full access so we can delete things; check to see this succeeded:

```
SC_HANDLE hService = OpenService(
    hSCM,             // open on the manager object we just got.
    m_szServiceName,  // name of the service
    DELETE);          // access levelwant to delete it

if (hService == NULL)
{
    DebugLog("Couldn't open service: 0x%08x", GetLastError());
    CloseServiceHandle(hSCM);
    return FALSE;
}
```

Now we open the service from the Service Control Manager, but this time we need `DELETE` access; this is not the same as full access, it turns out.

Calling DeleteService

```
BOOL bRetVal = DeleteService(hService);
```

Try and delete the service. Interestingly, this service management function doesn't take a handle to the Service Control Manager, whereas `CreateService` did. This may well just be an API peculiarity, but it's still strange to note these sort of differences.

After the complexity of calling `CreateService`, it's noticeable how much easier it is to delete a service once we have the appropriate access and service handle:

```
if (bRetVal == FALSE)
{
    // Okay, we know we're installed, so we can use proper logging.
    DebugLog("Couldn't uninstall: 0x%08x", GetLastError());
    LogMessage(EVENTLOG_INFORMATION_TYPE, EVENTLOG_UNINSTALLFAILED,
               m_szServiceName);
}
```

If the uninstall failed for some reason, we want to log this. We do this twice; once with `DebugLog` so we can log the error message, and once with `LogMessage` so it'll appear marked for our service. At this point we might want to upgrade `LogMessage` to take `varargs` parameters, but we'll live with the slight awkwardness for the time being:

```
    else
    {
        DebugLog("Successfully uninstalled");
        // This is still okay; the service doesn't vanish completely
        // until we release the last handle to it - so we can
        // still do logging.
        LogMessage(EVENTLOG_INFORMATION_TYPE, EVENTLOG_UNINSTALLED,
                   m_szServiceName);
    }
```

If we uninstalled successfully, we can still log messages tagged to our service. This is because the service doesn't actually go out of memory and the registry and suchlike until the last handle on the service is released – and we still have a handle open, so we can log messages appropriately.

Actually, the registry entries we created manually to enable the logging aren't deleted – arguably, we should tidy up after ourselves a bit further and remove that key, but I'm not going to do that here for brevity's sake. The main body of registry entries created by the system are removed, and those are the important ones.

```
    CloseServiceHandle(hService);
    CloseServiceHandle(hSCM);
    return (bRetVal != 0);
}
```

Finally, we close the handles, and return TRUE or FALSE as appropriate.

That's not quite all the changes we need to make to our project; we still have to update the message file to contain the messages. Alter servicemsgs.mc to contain:

```
MessageId=0x1000
SymbolicName=EVENTLOG_DEBUG
Language=English
Debug: %1
.
MessageId=
SymbolicName=EVENTLOG_INSTALLED
Language=English
Installed service %1
.
MessageId=
SymbolicName=EVENTLOG_UNINSTALLED
Language=English
Uninstalled service %1
.
MessageId=
SymbolicName=EVENTLOG_UNINSTALLFAILED
Language=English
Failed to uninstall service %1
.
```

Which adds the install/uninstall/fail-to-uninstall messages to the message table.

Finally, change main.cpp to read (this is the entire file; replace the previous contents with this):

```
#include "ntservice.h"

CNTService ntService_G;

int main(int argc, char* argv[])
{
    if (argc > 1 && stricmp(argv[1], "/install") == 0)
    {
        ntService_G.Install(argv[2], argv[3]);
    }
    else if (argc > 1 && stricmp(argv[1], "/uninstall") == 0)
    {
        ntService_G.Uninstall();
    }

    return 0;
}
```

You'll notice that we're doing things with a global variable – we don't need to quite yet, but it doesn't hurt (other than the existential pain of using global variables, at least). The command-line parser is very, very basic indeed; it doesn't do any validity checks or suchlike to keep things as short as possible. There are two possible things we can tell our program to do at this point – we can install it, in which case the second and third command-line arguments should be the username and password to run the service as; and we can uninstall it, in which case we don't need any extra arguments.

Build the project, and let's test it.

Testing Installing

First of all, let's try installing it with an invalid username, just to check that the error trapping does the right thing; run it with (literally this text this time around):

```
CDOTestService /install nosuchdomain\nosuchuser nosuchpassword
```

Where `CDOTestService` is the name of the executable built by the project.

Nothing should happen; if you open the Service Control Manager, you'll see that, unsurprisingly, there's no new services in there. What's more, if you look at the application log, you'll find an error saying:

The description for Event ID (4096) in Source (Debugging) could not be found. It contains the following insertion string(s): Couldn't register service: 0x00000421.

If we use the Error Lookup tool (in the **Tools** menu of Visual C++) to see what error $0x421$ means, we find that it's "The account name does not exist or is invalid". That's just what we'd expect – which is a good sign, because it means that our error trapping is actually telling us useful things.

Now let's try registering it properly – run it with:

```
CDOTestService /install realdomain\realuser realpassword
```

Where `realdomain\realuser` is a valid existing user and domain, and `realpassword` is that user's password. One slight ugliness now rears its head – we wind up typing a password in plaintext visible to all to this program; this is somewhat less secure than we might want. We could fix this easily (read a string with echo turned off, for instance; or more sophisticated still, build a dialog box to read name, domain, and password, and set the password entry field to produce "x" for each character – remember, we can safely use dialog boxes here because we're just installing the service, which we do by hand. When the service is running, we can't have dialogs) but for the time being we'll leave it as it is and assume nobody's looking over your shoulder when you're doing these tests.

One small flaw in the error reporting system is that if we type in an invalid password, we can't detect it at this stage. Windows only tries to log the user in when we start the service, and we can't start the service at this point of development. When we do try and start the service, we'll get errors, but it would be nice to have them trapped earlier on – that's not the way it goes, sadly.

Be careful – if you have a local account on the machine you're testing on, make sure you register the service to run with your network account name. A common setup is to have a local account on an NT machine with the same name and password as your network account – this will mean that both the following will work, but the second one will hit problems when we start to use mail:

```
CDOTestService /install networkdomain\username password

CDOTestService /install username password
```

We'll talk about this again when we look at the mail code.

Anyway, assuming you did have a valid username and password, if you open the Application log again (or hit *F5* to refresh, you'll see an entry saying:

Installed service CDO Test service

Which is exactly what we're looking for. Not only has it successfully installed (well, it's logged itself as having done so, but we can check that by external means in a second), it's also logging messages correctly and using the message table as we'd hoped.

If you're running Windows 2000, you may not see this. You may, instead, see a message saying Couldn't uninstall: 0x430 or Couldn't register: 0x430 or some other warning with error code 0x430. If we look up what this error code means, it's the code for "The specified service has been marked for deletion". This basically tells us that the Service Manager isn't letting us access this service because it's going to vanish any time soon now, but it hasn't quite got around to actually removing it yet. This causes problems when we're installing; because we uninstall the service prior to reinstalling it, if the service manager hasn't yet cleared out the old service, we hit problems reinstalling it because it finds the service that's marked for deletion and not yet gone, and gives us an error.

The easiest way to fix this is simply to try installing again; the second time around, our service won't be installed at the start so it won't get uninstalled – and so when we try and install, we won't hit a marked-for-deletion service. Another fix would be to put in a delay between uninstalling and installing; however, it's not clear how long this delay should be because it depends on how long the service manager takes to actually delete things; we could also check explicitly for this error and only if we hit it, wait, and then retry. I haven't implemented any of these in the code above to keep things simple – but if you do get this sort of problem, these are ways around it.

One problem with the event log viewer is that it locks the executable file containing the messages in memory – when developing, you may want to copy a new version of the executable over the old one (or build a new version, or whatever). If you try and do this, you'll get the following error from Windows:

The requested operation cannot be performed on a file with a user mapped section open.
    0 file(s) copied.

This basically tells us that somewhere on the system a process has mapped a section of our file into memory – in this case, it's the event log viewer mapping the message table into memory. This means we can't overwrite the file; to solve this, just close the event log viewer and all will be well. This is a bit awkward, because we have to keep opening and closing the event log viewer – but that's what desktop shortcuts are for...

Anyway, now we want to check that the service is actually installed – open up the Services control panel, and you'll see something like:

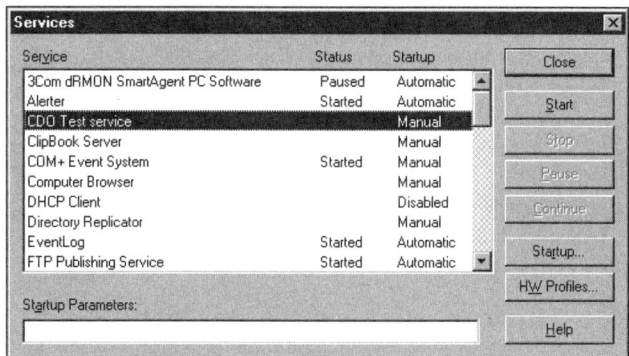

Where we can see that **CDO Test service** has made its way into the list of services. If you double-click on this, you'll see something like the following:

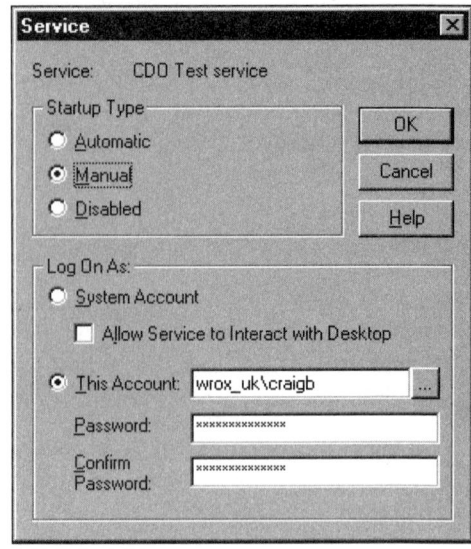

Where you should see your name and domain in place of wrox_uk\craigb. The number of "x"s in the password is, in this case, completely unrelated to the length of password used – they are just there to remind you that you've typed a password in at all, rather than to give you a hint that you've typed in one with the wrong length, and the number of "x"s is always the same.

If you try and start the service, nothing will happen for a long time, and then you'll get an error from the service manager saying that it couldn't start the service; to save you waiting the minute and a bit, here's the resulting dialog:

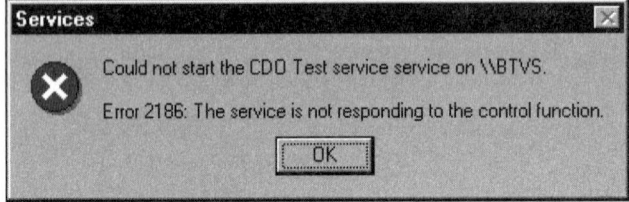

Which basically tells us that when the Service Manager tried to call `ServiceMain` to start our service, it didn't get any response. This is reasonable, because we don't even have a `ServiceMain` function yet – the system times out trying to get a valid response from our service.

If you want to test uninstalling the service, you can type:

```
CDOTestService /uninstall
```

And you'll find that the appropriate message appears in the application log, and the service vanishes from the list of services in the Service control panel, as we'd expect.

Functioning as a Service

Now we can install and uninstall our service, let's make it actually do what services do. Note that if you are developing on the same machine you're using for testing, you should uninstall the service and close the Event log before trying to compile your service, or you will hit the file locking issues mentioned before.

Global Functions

We'll start off by adding a new source and header file to the system to contain the global functions we're going to pass to the system for service management: add `globalfuncs.h` which contains:

```
#include <windows.h>

void WINAPI ServiceMain_G(DWORD dwArgc, LPTSTR* lpszArgv);
void WINAPI Handler_G(DWORD dwOpcode);
```

Note that the second argument to `ServiceMain_G` is of type `LPTSTR*` – this means that it'll compile as wide-characters if we're in a Unicode environment. If this does happen, the rest of our code won't be expecting wide characters, and bad things will happen. However, adding Unicode/MBCS functionality to the rest of our code would add complexity we don't need at the moment – we could safely change this to be `LPCSTR*` here, but I'm leaving it as it is because that's the "official" definition of `ServiceMain` from the documentation.

Add `globalfuncs.cpp` which contains:

```
#include "ntservice.h"

extern CNTService ntService_G;

void WINAPI ServiceMain_G(DWORD dwArgc, LPTSTR* lpszArgv)
{
    ntService_G.ServiceMain(dwArgc, lpszArgv);
}

void WINAPI Handler_G(DWORD dwOpcode)
{
    ntService_G.Handler(dwOpcode);
}
```

These are, as mentioned a while ago, just stub functions that pass their arguments onto the global `CNTService` object that does the real work.

Changes to main.cpp

Change `main.cpp`, by adding:

```
int main(int argc, char* argv[])
{
    if (argc > 1 && stricmp(argv[1], "/install") == 0)
    {
        ntService_G.Install(argv[2], argv[3]);
```

```
    }
    else if (argc > 1 && stricmp(argv[1], "/uninstall") == 0)
    {
        ntService_G.Uninstall();
    }
    else
    {
        ntService_G.DoStartup();
        return ntService_G.m_stStatus.dwWin32ExitCode;
    }

    return 0;
}
```

So that it now will call the DoStartup function on our service if it's not installing or uninstalling it. When the system control manager launches our service, it will run the executable, we won't have /install or /uninstall as command-line arguments, so we'll drop through and start the service going. When the DoStartup function returns, we read the exit code from our service (more on this shortly) and return it to the system.

Additions to the Class Definition

Next, change ntservice.h as follows:

```
#include <windows.h>

class CNTService
{
public:
    CNTService(LPCSTR szName);
    virtual ~CNTService();

    BOOL AreWeInstalled();
    BOOL Install(LPCSTR szUserName, LPCSTR szPassword);
    BOOL Uninstall();

    BOOL DoStartup();

    void WINAPI ServiceMain(DWORD dwArgc, LPTSTR* lpszArgv);
    void WINAPI Handler(DWORD dwOpcode);

protected:

    void SetStatus(DWORD dwNewStatus);

    virtual BOOL InitializeInServiceMain();

    virtual void HandleStop();
    virtual void HandleInterrogate();
    virtual void HandlePause();
    virtual void HandleContinue();
    virtual void HandleShutdown();
```

```
        virtual BOOL HandleUserOpcode(DWORD dwOpcode);
        virtual void Run();

    public:

        // public so the caller can get at our return code.

        SERVICE_STATUS m_stStatus;
        SERVICE_STATUS_HANDLE m_hStatus;

    protected:
        LPCSTR m_szServiceName;
        HANDLE m_hEventLog;
        BOOL m_bRunning;
        BOOL m_bPaused;
        int m_iNumber;

        void LogMessage(WORD wType, DWORD dwMessageID, LPCSTR szInsertion);
    };
```

We modify the constructor to take the name of the service as an argument – this will make it easier to change when we start deriving classes from CNTService later on.

Here, we're adding a set of functions to handle the assorted events that may happen to a service – starting up, being told to pause/continue/shutdown, and the main function that operates while the service is running – a quick summary:

- ❏ DoStartup – called by main to start the service.
- ❏ ServiceMain, Handler – our classes versions of the main service function.
- ❏ SetStatus – used to tell the system the current status of our service.
- ❏ InitializeInServiceMain – internal function we can override in derived classes to do setup.
- ❏ HandleStop, HandleInterrogate, HandlePause, HandleContinue, HandleShutdown, HandleUserOpcode – handlers for particular operations the system may ask us to perform. Note that these should perhaps return booleans, so our code can tell the system if it is unable to (for instance) pause at this point. We won't do that at the moment to keep things simple.
- ❏ Run – the main loop of execution for our service when it is running.

You'll notice that a number of the new functions are virtual – this is to allow us to simply derive a new class from this one and override those functions as necessary. This means that when we add in code to send mail, we won't have to worry about breaking the basic service functionality because we're in a new, derived, object. We only let the user override the functions that they can safely override – ServiceMain has certain essential functionality which never changes, so they can't do anything to that.

We add a SERVICE_STATUS member which is where the current status of the service is stored; this is needed for the system to track what our service is doing during startup and the like; more details on this later. We also add a member variable m_bRunning and m_bPaused that our service uses to track its state.

We also add a member variable `m_iNumber` that we'll use for debugging purposes only.

Alterations to the Main Object's Code

CNTService::CNTService()

Alter the constructor for `CNTService` as follows (and add a `#include` for `"globalfuncs.h"`):

```
#include "globalfuncs.h"

CNTService::CNTService(LPCSTR szName)
{
    m_szServiceName = szName;
    m_hEventLog = RegisterEventSource(NULL, m_szServiceName);
    m_bRunning = FALSE;
    m_bPaused = FALSE;

    m_hStatus = NULL;
    m_stStatus.dwServiceType = SERVICE_WIN32_OWN_PROCESS;
    m_stStatus.dwCurrentState = SERVICE_STOPPED;
    m_stStatus.dwControlsAccepted =
        SERVICE_ACCEPT_STOP | SERVICE_ACCEPT_PAUSE_CONTINUE |
        SERVICE_ACCEPT_SHUTDOWN;
    m_stStatus.dwWin32ExitCode = 0;
    m_stStatus.dwServiceSpecificExitCode = 0;
    m_stStatus.dwCheckPoint = 0;
    m_stStatus.dwWaitHint = 0;
}
```

We register as an event source as before; and we set our `m_bRunning` and `m_bPaused` flags to `FALSE` because we aren't yet running, and nobody's asked us to pause.

When we register ourselves with the Service Control Manager, we need to keep track of the handle it returns so we can unregister ourselves; thus `m_hStatus` which starts at `NULL`.

The details of the `m_stStatus` structure are fairly simple; the service type we've already covered. The initial state of the service is `SERVICE_STOPPED`, which is sensible because we've not started anything yet. We accept stop, pause, and continue events, and we want to be notified when the whole system is about to shut down.

We set our Win32 exit code to be 0 – this is what our main executable returns to the system when it exits – because the `main()` function needs to read this, our `m_stStatus` variable has to be public. We could alternatively add a `GetExitCode()` method to our class which just passes the `dwWin32ExitCode` member back out, but we might eventually want to read other elements of the status structure, so we'll leave it all accessible to the caller just in case.

The service-specific exit code only applies if we set the Win32 exit code to `ERROR_SERVICE_SPECIFIC_ERROR` – we don't do that in our service at the moment, so we can ignore that.

The last two variables are used to allow us to tell the service control manager about our progress at startup time – when you start a service, you see a little clock ticking up, like so:

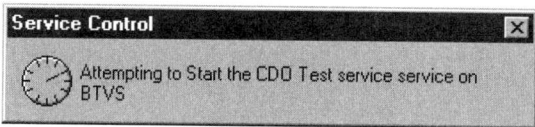

We can use the `dwCheckPoint` variable to tell the service control how far we have got through the progress of our startup – and the `dwWaitHint` variable can be used to tell the system how long it should expect to wait before the `dwCheckPoint` variable's next increment (or a status change); if we take longer than our hint time, the system should assume our startup has failed and deal with things appropriately. We'll leave these at zero for now; if we set them both to zero, the system ignores them, though we can still fail if our service doesn't respond before an overall timeout of about a minute and a half, as we found earlier on when we didn't have a `ServiceMain` function.

CNTService::DoStartup

Now add the following functions to the `ntservice.cpp`:

```
BOOL CNTService::DoStartup()
{
    DebugLog("In DoStartup");

    SERVICE_TABLE_ENTRY servicetable[2] =
    {
        {(char*)m_szServiceName,  // name of service
         ServiceMain_G},    // pointer to ServiceMain function

        {NULL, NULL} // "null terminator"
    };

    BOOL bRetVal;
    bRetVal = StartServiceCtrlDispatcher(servicetable);
    // doesn't return until our service's thread returns.
```

This is the function that `main` calls to start the service running. We have to build a table of services that are contained in this executable and pass them to the Service Control Dispatcher. This table is simply an array of pairs of service name and pointers to a `ServiceMain` function, terminated by a `NULL,NULL` pairing. In our case, the service name is, as usual, stored in our member variable (we have to cast to `char*` because that's what a `SERVICE_TABLE_ENTRY` contains), and the `ServiceMain` function pointer is the global `ServiceMain_G` function we're using. It's worth noting that the service name is only relevant when we have multiple services in the same executable – this doesn't apply to us, because we're using `SERVICE_WIN32_OWN_PROCESS` as our type. It's still tidier to set this up correctly.

When we call `StartServiceCtrlDispatcher`, the system connects our main thread to the service control manager, and sets our thread to be the control dispatcher for our process. We should call this as soon as possible after startup of our main executable, because it's not until this point that the system can start doing proper service monitoring stuff.

At this point, when the system calls `ServiceMain` to start up a new service, it spawns a thread for this service to run in; this isn't obviously important at the moment, but it will become more relevant when we start doing COM things.

The `StartServiceCtrlDispatcher` function doesn't return until all the services it starts up have finished running; so it's okay to call this and return immediately after it's finished – we won't exit back to `main` before we should:

```
    if (bRetVal == FALSE)
    {
        DebugLog("StartServiceCtrlDispatcher failed: 0x%08x", GetLastError());
    }
    return bRetVal;
}
```

We can get errors from `StartServiceCtrlDispatcher` – mainly these will happen if we pass in an invalid table of services, but if the registry isn't set up correctly those can fail as well; we trap such errors and log them.

CNTService::SetStatus

```
    void CNTService::SetStatus(DWORD dwState)
    {
        DebugLog("Service %s setting status to %d", m_szServiceName, dwState);
        m_stStatus.dwCurrentState = dwState;
        SetServiceStatus(m_hStatus, &m_stStatus);
    }
```

This is a little helper function we use to set our state and tell the system about it; we log these state changes with `DebugLog`, just in case we need to track things.

CNTService::ServiceMain

```
    void WINAPI CNTService::ServiceMain(DWORD dwArgc, LPTSTR* lpszArgv)
    {
        DebugLog("in CNTService::servicemain");

        m_stStatus.dwCurrentState = SERVICE_START_PENDING;
```

Now we get to `ServiceMain` – this will be called "at one remove", because the system will actually call `ServiceMain_G`, the function we passed to the dispatcher. However, from the point of view of our service, we can just assume that the system called this directly. We log the fact we've got this far, and set our state to `SERVICE_START_PENDING`, because we're not started yet, but we expect to be started in the immediate future. This allows the system to keep track of our progress through the stages of startup – in this code, we'll just start immediately, but if there are time-consuming operations that we perform during startup, we want to let the system know that we're awake and expect to start up soon, but haven't actually done so yet:

```
    m_hStatus = RegisterServiceCtrlHandler(m_szServiceName, Handler_G);

    DebugLog("tried to register control handler");

    if (m_hStatus == NULL)
    {
        DebugLog("RegisterServiceCtrlHandler failed: 0x%08x",
                GetLastError());
        LogMessage(EVENTLOG_ERROR_TYPE,
                EVENTLOG_CONTROLHANDLERINSTALLFAILED, m_szServiceName);
    }
```

Now we register our `Handler` function with the system. In our case, again, we're using a global function to get around the pointer-to-member-function problem. This is where we pass the name of the service to the system, in case you were wondering how it gets in, given that the entry in the service table earlier is ignored.

We store the handle to the service control handler in a member variable, because we need this to update our status:

```
    BOOL bRetVal = InitializeInServiceMain();
```

Next we call the virtual function `InitializeInServiceMain` – this is what we'll use in classes inheriting from this one to do any extra initialization we might need:

```
    DebugLog("done our init");

    if (bRetVal == FALSE)
    {
        // Our own initialize failed. Set things up so we can handle
        // this and mark ourselves as stopped.

        m_stStatus.dwWin32ExitCode = GetLastError();
        LogMessage(EVENTLOG_ERROR_TYPE,
                EVENTLOG_OURINITIALIZEFAILED, m_szServiceName);
        SetStatus(SERVICE_STOPPED);
        return;
    }
```

We should be aware that our own initialization may fail for some reason – if this happens, we don't want to continue when we know things aren't as they should be – so we mark ourselves as stopped using the `SetStatus` function, log this, and exit this function:

```
    LogMessage(EVENTLOG_INFORMATION_TYPE, EVENTLOG_SERVICESTARTED,
            m_szServiceName);
    SetStatus(SERVICE_RUNNING);
```

Assuming our internal initialization code succeeded, we want to log that, set our status to SERVICE_RUNNING, and continue by calling our Run function:

```
m_stStatus.dwWin32ExitCode = 0; // exiting happily for now.

m_bRunning = TRUE;

// When the Run function returns, we've stopped.

Run();
```

We now continue until the Run function exits – it's the responsibility of that function to keep track of our status and exit when appropriate. We don't actually need to have a separate Run function; we could just embed that code in here. However, that would stop us inheriting objects from this one, which is a bad thing:

```
    // Log the fact that we're done.
LogMessage(EVENTLOG_INFORMATION_TYPE, EVENTLOG_SERVICESTOPPED,
           m_szServiceName);

    // And tell the system about this
    SetStatus(SERVICE_STOPPED);
}
```

We need to be careful when exiting our service; as soon as we set our state to SERVICE_STOPPED, the call to StartServiceCtrlDispatcher can exit. As such, we have to make sure that our main code is finished before we set this state (this is why we have the m_bRunning flag) and that we've done any logging we wanted to do before we set this state. Once we've done this, the call to StartServiceCtrlDispatcher will exit, which will let our DoStartup function exit; it'll return to main, and execution will terminate.

CNTService::Handler

```
void WINAPI CNTService::Handler(DWORD dwOpcode)
{
    DebugLog("Service %s handling event %d", m_szServiceName, dwOpcode);
```

This is the other function that's called at one remove; it is, fundamentally, what the system calls to tell us to do things. Services are controlled by the system in a similar sort of way to Windows applications – we are sent messages, and we act on those messages. Unlike Windows, these messages only have an index, they don't have any extra parameters – this is because the things that the system can tell us to do are fairly basic. The dwOpcode argument describes the type of event we're meant to handle (roughly equivalent to the Windows message identifier):

```
    switch (dwOpcode) {

    case SERVICE_CONTROL_STOP:
        DebugLog("Event was SERVICE_CONTROL_STOP");
        SetStatus(SERVICE_STOP_PENDING);
        m_bRunning = FALSE;
        HandleStop();
//      SetStatus(SERVICE_STOPPED);
        break;
```

If the system tells us to stop, we start by logging the fact we've recognized this message. We then set our state to SERVICE_STOP_PENDING, so the system knows we're about to stop. At this stage, we should, again, be using the dwCheckPoint and dwWaitHint members of our SERVICE_STATUS variable to tell the system about our progress towards a real stopped state. In this case, though, we just stop immediately so we wouldn't gain much by doing that.

Once we've set our state to SERVICE_STOP_PENDING, we set our state to need-to-stop so that our main loop knows about this, and call our overrideable HandleStop function to let any derived classes do what they think appropriate. We set our internal state flag as well, so that our main service code in Run knows we should stop – the main flow of execution in ServiceMain won't start up until Run has finished, and until that happens we won't set our state to SERVICE_STOPPED.

At this point you may be wondering how this code can ever get called – didn't our code go into a loop in the Run function a while ago? Yes, that's true – but as long as our Run function isn't eating up 100% of the CPU time (not that this should ever be able to happen under Win32, though it's possible to slow a system down an awful lot with badly-behaved code), the system can call other functions in our object code – and Handler is one of those functions:

```
case SERVICE_CONTROL_PAUSE:
    DebugLog("Event was SERVICE_CONTROL_PAUSE");
    SetStatus(SERVICE_PAUSE_PENDING);
    m_bPaused = TRUE;
    HandlePause();
    SetStatus(SERVICE_PAUSED);
    break;

case SERVICE_CONTROL_CONTINUE:
    DebugLog("Event was SERVICE_CONTROL_CONTINUE");
    SetStatus(SERVICE_CONTINUE_PENDING);
    m_bPaused = FALSE;
    HandleContinue();
    SetStatus(SERVICE_RUNNING);
    break;
```

These are basically the same as the code for SERVICE_CONTROL_STOP; the system can put us into a paused state if we want to stop execution temporarily without stopping the whole service and requiring a restart of the service. We also set the internal flag to tell our main code in RUN that we're paused:

```
case SERVICE_CONTROL_INTERROGATE:
    DebugLog("Event was SERVICE_CONTROL_INTERROGATE");
    HandleInterrogate();
    break;
```

This just tells us to immediately update our status (i.e. our m_stStatus variable) and tell the system about it. We do that at the end of the switch statement we're in, so there's no need to do it here:

```
case SERVICE_CONTROL_SHUTDOWN:
    DebugLog("Event was SERVICE_CONTROL_SHUTDOWN");
    HandleShutdown();
    break;
```

This lets us handle system shutdown events should they occur. As usual, we have a virtual function that classes inheriting from us can use to deal with this in their own way:

```
default:
    if (dwOpcode < 128) // 128-255 = user messages
    {
        // Don't recognise this one at all, and it's not
        // in user-specific range.
        DebugLog("Service %s got invalid opcode %d", m_szServiceName,
                 dwOpcode);
        LogMessage(EVENTLOG_ERROR_TYPE, EVENTLOG_BADOPCODE, m_szServiceName);
    }
```

If the opcode passed into `Handler` is not one of the standard ones, it may still be an opcode specific to this particular service – opcodes in the range 128 to 255 are reserved for this sort of service-specific use. If it's not in that range and we didn't already handle it, though, we know it's a bad opcode; so we log this to the system. (this is one case where it would be nice if `LogMessage` was a bit more versatile):

```
    else
    {
        // Pass it on to our own handler.
        if (!HandleUserOpcode(dwOpcode))
        {
            // Oops, couldn't handle it.
            LogMessage(EVENTLOG_ERROR_TYPE, EVENTLOG_BADOPCODE,
                       m_szServiceName);
        }
    }
    break;
}
```

If it's a user opcode, then deal with it appropriately. Again, this is something that inheriting objects should do, because the base `CNTService` class is meant to do the minimum possible:

```
    SetServiceStatus(m_hStatus, &m_stStatus);
}
```

We always set our status at the end of handling an opcode – this may be redundant in many cases, but it's better to be safe than sorry, and the extra overhead is minimal.

CNTService::InitializeInServiceMain

```
BOOL CNTService::InitializeInServiceMain()
{
    m_iNumber = 0;
    return TRUE;
}
```

As a basic example service, the functionality we provide is going to consist of logging a message every 10 seconds containing an incrementing counter. Thus, reset our `m_iNumber` value to 0, and return `TRUE` to tell the calling `ServiceMain` function that we initialized ourselves successfully.

CNTService::HandleStop et al.

```
void CNTService::HandleStop()
{
}
void CNTService::HandleInterrogate()
{
}
void CNTService::HandlePause()
{
}
void CNTService::HandleContinue()
{
}
void CNTService::HandleShutdown()
{
}
BOOL CNTService::HandleUserOpcode(DWORD dwOpcode)
{
    // We don't expect any other opcodes, so bail.
    return FALSE;
}
```

These are all blank – a safe default behavior is to do nothing here. The base `CNTService` class will do the right thing with status, so we don't need to do anything else extra when pausing, continuing, and suchlike. We know we aren't expecting any user opcodes, so we return `FALSE` to tell the `Handler` function that we didn't recognize any that we might get.

CNTService::Run

```
void CNTService::Run()
{
    while (m_bRunning)
    {
```

This is the function where all the work really takes place. We loop for as long as our `m_bRunning` flag is true – when it becomes false, it's because we've handled a stop request, so we should exit this loop:

```
if (!m_bPaused)
{
    DebugLog("Service %s running: number is %d", m_szServiceName,
            m_iNumber);
    m_iNumber++;
}
```

We need to be slightly careful here – if we're paused, we don't want to keep logging messages; that's what pausing a service is meant to do, after all – we don't want to exit and reset our counter, but we also don't want to increment it either – so we check our state to make sure we're not paused, and only then do we do things.

It might seem tempting to put these checks for service status being stopped/running/paused in the base class to force any inheriting classes to only do things when in running state – but we don't know that people won't want to have some code running even when paused; it's just a request from the system, not a demand in the way that a Stop request is:

```
        Sleep(10*1000);
    }
}
```

The functionality of our Run function, other than keeping track of the service status, basically boils down to incrementing a counter and logging its value every ten seconds. We call Sleep to tell the system that we're not going to be doing anything for the next 10 seconds; this way we don't use up CPU cycles while waiting for time to pass.

One small problem with this is that it means our service can take up to 10 seconds to stop – it won't stop properly until the Run function has exited, so even if the Handler function sets m_bRunning to FALSE, we may still have 10 seconds of Sleep time to wait before Run will notice this. You should be wary of this when writing your own services; if you only want to do something once a minute, it's better to loop sleeping for 10 seconds and only do something every 6th time around the loop.

Note that in derived classes, as soon as we override Run, we'll lose this functionality. That probably isn't a great loss – this is mainly for testing purposes. You should be careful of trying to keep the base functionality in there by calling CNTService::Run from your derived class – that will just go into the base class's loop and stay there until our service is told to stop – at which point it'll drop out into your derived class and, almost certainly, not do what you expect.

Changes to main.cpp

Now our service class takes its name as a constructor argument, you'll need to change main.cpp to read:

```
#include "ntservice.h"

CNTService ntService_G("CDO Test service");

int main(int argc, char* argv[])
```

Message File Changes

The final thing to do is add all the new messages to the servicemsgs.mc file – append the following to that file:

```
MessageId=
SymbolicName=EVENTLOG_CONTROLHANDLERINSTALLFAILED
Language=English
Failed to install control handler for service %1
.

MessageId=
SymbolicName=EVENTLOG_OURINITIALIZEFAILED
Language=English
Failed in internal initialize for service %1
```

```
MessageId=
SymbolicName=EVENTLOG_SERVICESTARTED
Language=English
Service %1 started successfully
.

MessageId=
SymbolicName=EVENTLOG_SERVICESTOPPED
Language=English
Service %1 stopped
.

MessageId=
SymbolicName=EVENTLOG_BADOPCODE
Language=English
Service %1 received bad opcode.
.
```

Testing our Basic Service

You should now be able to build this service correctly; install it, launch the Services control panel, and tell our service to run.

> *Don't forget that if you have Event Viewer open, you'll have problems overwriting the executable when you build and/or copy the executable onto your server machine.*

You'll see the aforementioned "starting service" clock pop up, tick around for a bit, and then vanish; and because we're telling the system about our status, the Service control panel should now look something like:

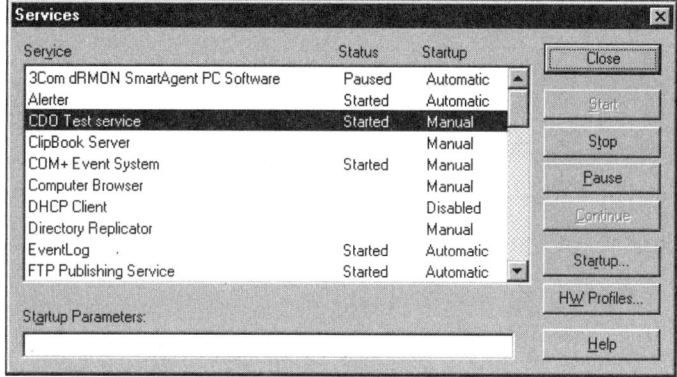

Notice that the status of the CDO Test service is now Started. This is a good sign. You'll also notice that the Pause button is now enabled – we told the system that we can be paused, so that's also pleasing to see.

If you open Event Viewer again and check the logs, you should see a series of events occurring; firstly, the service starts up, changes state to 4 (which is SERVICE_RUNNING), and logs a counter. If you wait 10 seconds (and tell Event Viewer to refresh it's view) then another counter message should appear; wait another 10 seconds, and you get another message, and so on.

One thing to watch for is that the Application log messages have a finite size. On the PC here, it filled up after 2,625 messages (file size allowed was 512 kilobytes); this is plenty of messages for most practical uses, but if we're logging something every 10 seconds that's only 7 ½ hours before the log is full. In the real world, of course, you probably wouldn't want to log something every time around your Run function's loop – but be aware that this sort of thing can happen. To work around the limitation on log size, you can do this from the Log | Log Settings menu in Event Viewer; you can change the maximum size of a log, or tell the system to overwrite old messages as new ones come in. See the Event Viewer help for more details on this.

The next thing to try is pausing the service; hit the Pause button, say OK when it asks you if you're sure, and watch the status change to Paused:

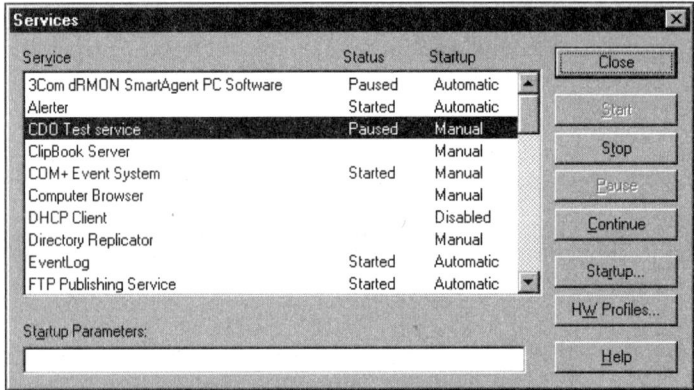

Notice that the status is now Paused, and that the Pause button has been disabled and the Continue button enabled. If you look at the logs, you'll be able to track the opcode coming into the Handler function, notice that SERVICE_CONTROL_PAUSE has a value of 2, see the state change to 6 (SERVICE_PAUSE_PENDING) and then 7 (SERVICE_PAUSED).

If you wait for 10 seconds or so, you'll see (or, rather, won't see) that no more messages appear in the log. This is what we would expect; our Run function is still going, because we're not stopped – but we're not running, either, so it won't log any messages.

You can then tell the service to continue – the state will shuffle through SERVICE_CONTINUE_PENDING to SERVICE_RUNNING, the counter will start incrementing again, and it'll keep filling the log up.

The final thing to test is stopping the service – this will do pretty much what you'd expect. One final thing to try while we're testing things is to pop up the Task Manager and watch how your executable is only running while the service is running – when it's stopped, because our code returns from main and exits, the executable will vanish.

Using CDO From A Service, Again

Finally, now that we know how to write services, we can get back to using CDO from a service. This is relatively simple – because we've designed our service to be easily overrideable, we can just derive a new class CCDOService from CNTService, and go from there. We'll make our service monitor the amount of free hard drive space and send warning mails to an administrator if free space starts to run low; this is a reasonably useful thing to do that doesn't require a lot of coding.

The very first thing we want to do is let our code get at the CDO library. As before, we'll use #import to generate the files, and you can then optionally rename them and shuffle them around as before if you have permissions problems.

The CCDOService Class

Add a header file cdoservice.h to the project; it should contain:

```
#include "ntservice.h"

#import <cdo.dll>
using namespace MAPI;

class CCDOService : public CNTService
{
public:
    CCDOService(LPCSTR szName);

protected:
    BOOL InitializeInServiceMain();
    void Run();
    _SessionPtr m_pSession;
};
```

> *You may need to enter the full path to the* cdo.dll *on your machine. On mine it was at*
> C:\Program Files\Common Files\System\Mapi\1033\NT\

This simply overrides the InitialiseInServiceMain and Run functions from CNTService, and keeps a member pointer to a CDO Session object.

CCDOService Functions

Add a source file cdoservice.cpp to the project; this should contain:

```
#include "cdoservice.h"
#include <comdef.h>
#include "debuglog.h"

using namespace MAPI;

HRESULT GetHRESULTFromComError(_com_error& e)
{
    static HRESULT TranslationTable[][2] = {
        {1515,CdoW_NO_SERVICE},{1896,CdoW_ERRORS_RETURNED},
```

```
            {2153,CdoW_POSITION_CHANGED},{215,CdoW_APPROX_COUNT},
            {2408,CdoW_CANCEL_MESSAGE},{2664,CdoW_PARTIAL_COMPLETION},
            {17386,CdoE_INTERFACE_NOT_SUPPORTED},{17389,CdoE_CALL_FAILED},
            {1258,CdoE_NO_SUPPORT},{1259,CdoE_BAD_CHARWIDTH},
            {1261,CdoE_STRING_TOO_LONG},{1262,CdoE_UNKNOWN_FLAGS},
            {1263,CdoE_INVALID_ENTRYID},{1264,CdoE_INVALID_OBJECT},
            {1265,CdoE_OBJECT_CHANGED},{1266,CdoE_OBJECT_DELETED},
            {1267,CdoE_BUSY},{1269,CdoE_NOT_ENOUGH_DISK},
            {1270,CdoE_NOT_ENOUGH_RESOURCES},{1271,CdoE_NOT_FOUND},
            {1272,CdoE_VERSION},{1273,CdoE_LOGON_FAILED},
            {1274,CdoE_SESSION_LIMIT},{1275,CdoE_USER_CANCEL},
            {1276,CdoE_UNABLE_TO_ABORT},{1277,CdoE_NETWORK_ERROR},
            {1278,CdoE_DISK_ERROR},{1279,CdoE_TOO_COMPLEX},
            {1280,CdoE_BAD_COLUMN},{1281,CdoE_EXTENDED_ERROR},
            {1282,CdoE_COMPUTED},{1283,CdoE_CORRUPT_DATA},
            {1284,CdoE_UNCONFIGURED},{1285,CdoE_FAILONEPROVIDER},
            {1286,CdoE_UNKNOWN_CPID},{1287,CdoE_UNKNOWN_LCID},
            {1288,CdoE_PASSWORD_CHANGE_REQUIRED},
            {1289,CdoE_PASSWORD_EXPIRED},
            {1290,CdoE_INVALID_WORKSTATION_ACCOUNT},
            {1291,CdoE_INVALID_ACCESS_TIME},
            {1292,CdoE_ACCOUNT_DISABLED},{1512,CdoE_END_OF_SESSION},
            {1513,CdoE_UNKNOWN_ENTRYID},{1514,CdoE_BAD_VALUE},
            {1770,CdoE_INVALID_TYPE},{1771,CdoE_TYPE_NO_SUPPORT},
            {1772,CdoE_UNEXPECTED_TYPE},{1773,CdoE_TOO_BIG},
            {1774,CdoE_DECLINE_COPY},{1775,CdoE_UNEXPECTED_ID},
            {2024,CdoE_UNABLE_TO_COMPLETE},{2025,CdoE_TIMEOUT},
            {2026,CdoE_TABLE_EMPTY},{2027,CdoE_TABLE_TOO_BIG},
            {2029,CdoE_INVALID_BOOKMARK},{2280,CdoE_WAIT},
            {2281,CdoE_CANCEL},{2282,CdoE_NOT_ME},
            {2536,CdoE_CORRUPT_STORE},{2537,CdoE_NOT_IN_QUEUE},
            {2538,CdoE_NO_SUPPRESS},{2540,CdoE_COLLISION},
            {2541,CdoE_NOT_INITIALIZED},{2542,CdoE_NON_STANDARD},
            {2543,CdoE_NO_RECIPIENTS},{2544,CdoE_SUBMITTED},
            {2545,CdoE_HAS_FOLDERS},{2546,CdoE_HAS_MESSAGES},
            {2547,CdoE_FOLDER_CYCLE},{2792,CdoE_AMBIGUOUS_RECIP},
            {1005,CdoE_NO_ACCESS},{1014,CdoE_NOT_ENOUGH_MEMORY},
            {1087,CdoE_INVALID_PARAMETER}};

    HRESULT hrFake = e.WCode();
    hrFake = hrFake & 0xffff;

    for (int i=0; i < sizeof(TranslationTable) / sizeof(TranslationTable[0]); i++)
    {
        if (TranslationTable[i][0] == hrFake)
        {
            return TranslationTable[i][1];
        }
    }
    return E_UNEXPECTED;
}
```

```
void dump_com_error(_com_error& e)
{
   DebugLog("Oops - hit an error!");
   DebugLog("Code = %08lx"), e.Error();
   DebugLog("WCode = %04x"), e.WCode();
   DebugLog("Real HRESULT = %08x", GetHRESULTFromComError(e));
   _bstr_t bstrSource(e.Source());
   _bstr_t bstrDescription(e.Description());
   _bstr_t bstrMessage(e.ErrorMessage());
   DebugLog("Code meaning = %S", (wchar_t*)bstrMessage);
   DebugLog("Source = %S", (wchar_t*)bstrSource);
   DebugLog("Description = %S", (wchar_t*)bstrDescription);
}
```

This is the boilerplate stuff we use to make debugging CDO applications easy – we've changed `dump_com_error` to call `DebugLog` instead of `printf` or `AfxMessageBox`, but otherwise it's pretty much the same as before – I've just inserted these files into our source code here rather than adding them as separate files as we did in the previous chapter.

CCDOService::CCDOService

```
CCDOService::CCDOService(LPCSTR szName)
: CNTService(szName)
{
}
```

The constructor does nothing but pass the name on to the base class:

```
CCDOService::InitializeInServiceMain()
{
   CoInitialize(NULL);
```

We have to call `CoInitialize(NULL)` before we can do any COM things such as creating `Session` objects – but we also have to make sure we call this in the correct thread. If we were to put this in `main`, for instance, that would only apply to the thread that `main` runs in, not the thread our service runs in. By putting this call in `InitializeInServiceMain`, we know we're in the service's thread and all is well:

```
   try {
      m_pSession.CreateInstance(__uuidof(Session));

      m_pSession->Logon(vtMissing, vtMissing, false, true,
         vtMissing, false, "server\nmailbox");
   }
   catch (_com_error e)
   {
      dump_com_error(e);
      return FALSE;
   }
   return TRUE;
}
```

Notice that, as explained, we log in using dynamic profiles. You'll have to change server\nmailbox to be a real server and mailbox name separated by \n (remember, this is the alias for your mailbox as found in the "Alias" field of the addressbook view of a person, not the display name of that user) for your system or things won't log in correctly. If you try running the service without changing this as necessary, then you'll get an error when you try and start the service, and looking in the log file will contain an error as we'd expect.

> *Reminder: don't forget to make sure you install the service to run as your network account, not any local identities you may have. If you have a local account with the same name and password as your main network account, the install will succeed, but when the service tries to log into CDO it will fail with error MAPI_E_LOGON_FAILED – this is because the local account won't have the same access to the network as your real network account, and so the local account can't open your mailbox. (You may have things set up so that even machine-local accounts can read your mailbox, in which case this will work; however, the most common setup is to only allow network accounts access.)*

The other parameters to Logon tell it to start a new session, not show dialog boxes, etc; there's nothing particularly out-of-the-ordinary going on there.

We return FALSE if we get an error trying to log in; we use try..catch as usual to detect errors, and dump_com_error as normal. Next we'll look at the main Run() function:

```
void CCDOService::Run()
{
    BOOL bWarned = FALSE;
```

We keep track of if we've already warned the admin about the current low space – we do a test every 10 seconds, but we don't want to send mail every 10 seconds once we run out of space, just the first time that we go below that amount of space:

```
    while (m_bRunning)
    {
        if (!m_bPaused)
        {
```

We'll do things in the normal way, i.e. running until we're told to stop and pausing when appropriate:

```
            // Read the amount of hard drive space left on C:
            ULARGE_INTEGER liFreeUs;
            ULARGE_INTEGER liTotal;
            ULARGE_INTEGER liTotalFree;

            GetDiskFreeSpaceEx("C:\\", &liFreeUs, &liTotal, &liTotalFree);
```

The API call to get the amount of disk space free is GetDiskFreeSpaceEx – it returns the amount of hard drive space free that is available to our process, the total amount of space on the drive, and the total amount of space free to all processes. Because hard drives can be very large, it uses the ULARGE_INTEGER structure to store the result; ULARGE_INTEGER contains two 32-bit words, one for the high 32 bits and one for the low 32 bits of the 64-bit result:

```
        // Is there less than 10% space free?

        __int64 iTotal = liTotal.QuadPart;
        __int64 iFree = liTotalFree.QuadPart;
        if (iFree < iTotal / 10)
        {
            if (!bWarned)
            {
                bWarned = TRUE;
```

Conveniently, Visual C++ comes with a built-in 64-bit integer type we can use for arithmetic on 64-bit quantities (this is a Microsoft language extension, so may not be in other C++ compilers); so we can check if we're below 10% free space with very little effort. We check to see if we've already warned the admin about this before sending mail off – if we've done so once for this particular drop below our threshold, we don't do it again:

```
            try {
                FolderPtr pOutbox = m_pSession->Outbox;
                MessagesPtr pMsgs = pOutbox->Messages;
                MessagePtr pMsg = pMsgs->Add
                    ("Low disk space warning");
                RecipientsPtr pRecips = pMsg->Recipients;
                RecipientPtr pRecip = pRecips->Add
                    ("Daniel J. Mitchell");
                pRecip->Resolve(false);
                pMsg->Send(false, false);
            }
            catch (_com_error e)
            {
                dump_com_error(e);
            }
        }
    }
```

This should by now be reasonably familiar code; we build a message in the outbox of our session, we add the sysadmin as a recipient (again, you'll have to change this to a real value for your system), we resolve the name, and we send the mail off.

Notice that the call to Resolve and Send both explicitly pass false to the CDO system to tell it not to pop-up dialogs (the second false argument in the call to Send tells it to not save a copy in the sent-mail folder):

```
        else
        {
            bWarned = FALSE;
        }
```

If we get above 10% free disk space, we reset our counter so we'll warn the admin again the next time we drop below that amount of space:

```
        }
        Sleep(10*1000);
    }
    try {
        m_pSession->Logoff();
        m_pSession = NULL;
    }
    catch (_com_error e)
    {
        dump_com_error(e);
    }

    CoUninitialize();
}
```

We pause for 10 seconds, and keep looping.

Note that we tell our session to log out here, at the end of Run – you may wonder why we aren't using, say, HandleStop for this – it's exactly the sort of thing that those functions are meant for, after all. The reason for this is that all the functions called by Handler are called from a different thread – now, we've built our session in InitializeInServiceMain which is in the same thread as Run, so we can safely log out from there. If we try and log out from a handler function, however, the Session object dies mysteriously because of thread clash problems. To add to the excitement, this only happens if the session's actually been used to send any mail; the initialization of the Session object that causes it to die only happens when we open the Outbox folder prior to sending mail from that folder. We also clear out our Session object before calling CoUninitialize – we don't want to risk our session trying to do COM things when it's destroyed with our main service object, because that'll happen after the call to CoUninitialize.

This sort of thing can be a real pain – beware of these problems if you write services yourself, because they can bite you in very unexpected ways.

Before we can build this, we need to tell the rest of our code that we're now using an object of type CCDOService rather than CNTService; change main.cpp as follows:

```
#include "cdoservice.h"

CCDOService ntService_G("CDO Test service");

int main(int argc, char* argv[])
{
    // . . . and then it continues as before . . .
```

And change `globalfuncs.cpp` to read:

```
#include "cdoservice.h"

extern CCDOService ntService_G;

void WINAPI ServiceMain_G(DWORD dwArgc, LPTSTR* lpszArgv)

// . . . and then it continues as before . . .
```

You should now be able to build this project; if you copy it onto your server machine (or not, if you're developing on that server), install it, and try making copies of files until you get below 10% disk space free, you should find that it sends mail to the system admin. It should only send one bit of mail while you remain below 10% free space; if you then clear up some space, wait 10 seconds (because that's the smallest amount of time we can wait to be sure our code has noticed we've got enough space free), and copy files so you're below 10% free again, it should send another message.

Further Directions

This should be enough to get you started with mail-enabling services, or writing services to send mail. Some obvious improvements to the current disk-space checker would include sending a more detailed message about how much disk space is free, rather than one with simply the title set. It would also be good to check more than just one hard drive.

Getting into more advanced situations, you could change it to monitor people's disk space usage against quotas and send mail to individual users when they run out of space; this would require checking for disk space usage in a more sophisticated way and probably having some sort of mapping from directory to username.

Writing Services in Visual Basic

At this point, you may be wondering how to create a service in Visual Basic. In theory, it should be possible to simply use the same Win32 API functions as we use in C++ to make a service in Visual Basic, with a lot of `Declare Function` stuff to let us use the relevant functions. We would also need to jump through some hoops to pass function pointers as required by the `StartServiceTableDispatcher` calls, and set things up to allow the system to call back into our code while our code is executing elsewhere. In general, it's pretty awkward, and covering this in full is beyond the scope of this book. If you want more information, the Microsoft KnowledgeBase has some sample code in article Q175948. There's also a Microsoft plugin control that basically wraps up the functionality of the C++ code we wrote which in theory you can use to turn your program into a service; that can also be found in the KnowledgeBase article above.

A Simpler Solution

Rather than cover the previous ground again in Visual Basic, we'll look at a couple of much simpler ways of creating a service in Visual Basic. To summarize the basic important points of running any code as a service from the first section of this chapter, there are four things we need to ensure we do to be able to successfully send mail from a service:

❑ We need to ensure we never rely on the user clicking on a dialog box – there will be no user present to do this, so we must make sure we always pass `ShowDialog:=False` to any methods that might pop up dialogs, and make sure no dialogs can appear as unexpected side effects. Actually, we don't want any sort of UI at all – no main form, nothing.

❑ We need to use the `ProfileInfo` parameter to the `Logon` call to create a dynamic profile, because of registry issues; see the start of this chapter for an explanation of this.

❑ We need some way to have our program start up without a user there to manually launch it.

❑ We need to ensure the program is running as a user with appropriate mailbox access.

Problems 1 and 2 have to be dealt with in our code; let's write a tiny sample program to obey those constraints, and then we'll get onto problems 3 and 4 once we have a program to run.

Creating the Main Application

We're going to duplicate the project we wrote in the C++ section of this chapter, namely a small application that monitors hard drive usage and sends mail to an administrator when free space gets below a certain threshold.

Start Visual Basic, and start a new **Standard EXE** project and call is something appropriate like `VBCDOService`. Add the CDO library to the list of project references, as usual. We now want to turn off all UI elements of this project – let's start by removing the main form from the project.

Writing an Application with No Main Form

We now have no form – so where will our code live? Add a new module to the project and call it `modService`.

We now need to tell Visual Basic how to start our project; because there's no main form, we have to add a `Sub Main` and launch that instead. To do this, open the Project Properties dialog, and check Unattended Execution:

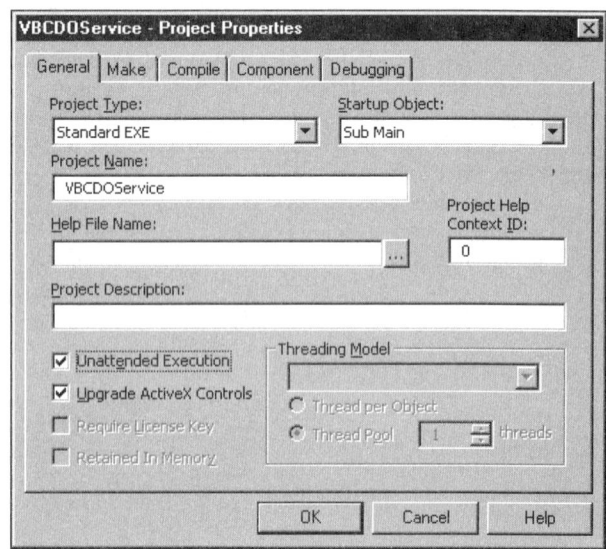

You'll notice that the Startup Object has automatically changed to Sub Main – so let's write one. We'll provide the same functionality as in the C++ service; warn when disk space gets below a certain threshold by mailing someone, and a bit of extra logic to ensure we don't send too many or too few messages for when we dip below the threshold.

Main Application Code

Add the following to the module:

```
Option Explicit
```

```
Private Declare Sub Sleep Lib "kernel32" (ByVal dwMilliseconds As Long)
Private Declare Function GetDiskFreeSpaceEx Lib "kernel32" _
      Alias "GetDiskFreeSpaceExA" _
      (ByVal lpRootPathName As String, _
      lpFreeBytesAvailableToCaller As Currency, _
      lpTotalNumberOfBytes As Currency, _
      lpTotalNumberOfFreeBytes As Currency) As Long
```

Here we declare the Win32 functions we're going to need; we want our program to loop checking every five seconds so as to not consume all the CPU time – to do this, we have to use `Sleep`. We don't have a form, remember, so we can't use the standard Visual Basic timer object.

We also declare `GetDiskFreeSpaceEx` because that's the function that tells us if we're running out of room. Note that it returns `Currency` – this is the Visual Basic 8-byte type. There are scaling issues with `Currency` that we'll ignore, because we only care about the proportion of space free at the moment.

> Note that `GetDiskFreeSpaceEx` is not declared in `win32api.txt` – it's a standard Win32 API function, nonetheless.

Sub Main()

```
Sub Main()

  Dim bWarned As Boolean
  bWarned = False

  Dim lFreeForUs As Currency
  Dim lTotalSpace As Currency
  Dim lFreeSpace As Currency
```

Here we simply declare variables to keep track of if we've warned for this instance of dropping below the relevant threshold, and to return the disk information into. Note that, as explained, the variables we use for amounts of disk space are of type `Currency`:

```
  Dim objSession As MAPI.Session
  Set objSession = New MAPI.Session
  objSession.Logon ShowDialog:=False, NewSession:=True, _
                   ProfileInfo:="Server" & vbLf & "Mailbox"
```

Log in, as usual – notice we explicitly tell it to not show a dialog.

> **Note that as usual you'll have to change `Server` and `Mailbox` as appropriate for your environment.**

```
MsgBox "Logged in"
```

What is this, you may ask? Didn't we just say that we can't ever show message boxes? Well, that's true, but there's a very convenient bit of code in Visual Basic that logs all message box text to the system's application log – this means we don't have to jump through the hoops that the C++ code did to do debugging, we can just use `MsgBox` to do this. (For more on the Application log, see the first section of this chapter.)

This doesn't mean we can get away with ignoring the lack of message boxes – we still have to explicitly tell the system not to show any dialogs. Message boxes are one thing, and the system can just press OK on them for us – a dialog is another thing entirely.

Note that this particular message isn't terribly helpful in terms of actually assisting debugging – I'm just doing this to prove that it works, and so that you'll know about this when you start writing your own code:

```
While True
```

Loop forever:

```
GetDiskFreeSpaceEx "c:", lFreeForUs, lTotalSpace, lFreeSpace
```

We'll check the disk space on the C drive:

```
If (lFreeSpace < (lTotalSpace / 10)) Then
    If Not bWarned Then
```

As in the previous sample, we check for being under 10% free space, and if we've not already warned for low space by sending out a warning mail, we send out a warning:

```
Dim objMessage As MAPI.Message
Set objMessage = objSession.Outbox.Messages.Add("Warning: " & _
                                        "low disk space")
Dim objRecip As MAPI.Recipient
Set objRecip = objMessage.Recipients.Add("Daniel J. Mitchell")
```

Change this to the appropriate administrator for your environment:

```
objRecip.Resolve False
```

Pass `False` to the `Resolve` call to tell it to not pop up a dialog. At this point, we should really do error checking, but for brevity I'm omitting that – we should be checking to see that the `Resolve` call succeeded and logging a warning if we couldn't resolve the user we're trying to send to:

```
objMessage.Text = "Only " & _
                  (100 * lFreeSpace / lTotalSpace) _
                  & " percent space left"
objMessage.Send SaveCopy:=False, ShowDialog:=False
```

Two `False` arguments here; first one tells it not to save a copy of this mail in the Sent Mail folder, and the second one tells it to not pop up a dialog. Again, error handling would be nice here, but we'll omit it for brevity's sake – handling CDO errors has already been covered in the rest of the book, so I'll avoid duplicating the explanation here:

```
    End If
        bWarned = True
    Else
        bWarned = False
    End If

    DoEvents
    Sleep 5000
Wend
```

Wait five seconds before checking again, and loop. Note that we call `DoEvents` before the call to `Sleep` to allow the system to process messages – this means that if we're debugging in Visual Basic, we can still stop our process from running (rather than having to kill the entire Visual Basic environment, as would otherwise be the case):

```
    objSession.Logoff
    Set objSession = Nothing
    Set objRecip = Nothing
    Set objMessage = Nothing

End Sub
```

Usual cleanup at the end. Build this as an executable, and test it. You should find that you'll get sent mail appropriately; that no dialogs pop up (if you run this under Windows 95, you probably will get a dialog; however, I'm assuming that you're doing this under Windows NT); and that the text "Logged in" appears in the system Application log.

Adding "Service" Functionality

So we now have a suitable program to run as a service – it never shows dialogs, it logs in correctly. Now we have problems 3 and 4 to solve:

- ❑ No dialogs – done.
- ❑ Use `ProfileInfo` – done.
- ❑ We need some way to have our program start up without a user there to manually launch it, and
- ❑ We need to ensure we are running as a user with appropriate mailbox access.

NT Scheduler?

One way to solve problem 3 is to use the NT Scheduler service – that's already running on most systems (and is installed by default), and can be used to automatically launch programs at a given time by using the `AT` command-line interface. This works, but is messy for two reasons – firstly, because it only tells our program to launch at a scheduled time – if we want something to run every five minutes, we have to schedule a lot of executions over the day, and that's not nice (especially because of the login/out memory leak problem). Alternatively, we could tell it to only launch once a day and stay logged in; but that will still wind up with multiple processes running after the first day, and has the problem that it won't start up for up to 24 hours after the server is turned on depending on when it's scheduled to start.

The second problem with the NT scheduler is problem 4 – now, we could set the scheduler service itself to run as the required user – but that means that *every* scheduled program now runs as that user, which may well not be plausible. Alternatively, we could set it to run a batch file which uses the `SU` utility to change it's identity – but then we have the problem of getting the user's password through to `SU` – we have to store the password in a file somehow to do this, and that's really not a good idea.

We'll ignore this solution for now – I'm just mentioning it for completeness' sake. If you read the Microsoft Knowledge Base article Q177851, you'll find more details on using `AT` to run CDO applications at a particular time.

Using SRVANY

The solution we'll use is a utility from the NT Resource Kit called `srvany.exe`. This basically allows you to run any executable as an NT service. The NT Resource Kit can be purchased from your local Microsoft vendor, and most bookstores should have it; it's a set of books and CDs. Alternatively, as we only need two files from this (`instsrv.exe` and `srvany.exe`), you can just download from Microsoft.

Once you have them on your computer open up a command prompt window, and type:

```
instsrv SrvAny c:\ntreskit\srvany.exe
```

Where `c:\ntreskit` is the directory you installed the resource kit to – this may vary depending on how you installed things. This installs the `SrvAny` service.

> *Note:* `instsrv` *may look as if it's something that'll do the general task of installing executables as a service, but it's not that simple, sadly. While it may put the executable in the Service Manager's list of services, unless our executable knows how to behave as a service, we still haven't gained anything.* `SrvAny` *knows how to behave as a service, which is why we'll use it here.*

Now, if you pop up the NT Service manager (again, see the first part of this chapter for screenshots and suchlike) you'll notice a new service `SrvAny` in the list of services. Double-click on `SrvAny`, and set it to run as the user we want to use. Note that this way we save typing the password into anywhere permanent – the service manager doesn't store the password, it just stores the fact that you logged in successfully when typing it in.

Now we need to set some registry keys to tell `SrvAny` which executable it's going to run: launch `regedit`.

Note that, as with any registry editing, you do this at your own risk. The chances of you bringing your system down just by adding keys here are, admittedly, fairly small, but you should always be very careful when editing the registry just in case.

Open up the key:

HKEY_LOCAL_MACHINE\System\CurrentControlSet\Services\SrvAny

And add a subkey called `Parameters` to that key. In the `Parameters` key, add a string value with name `Application` and value `c:\temp\project1.exe` where this would actually be where you've put the executable for your service. After this, `regedit` should look like this:

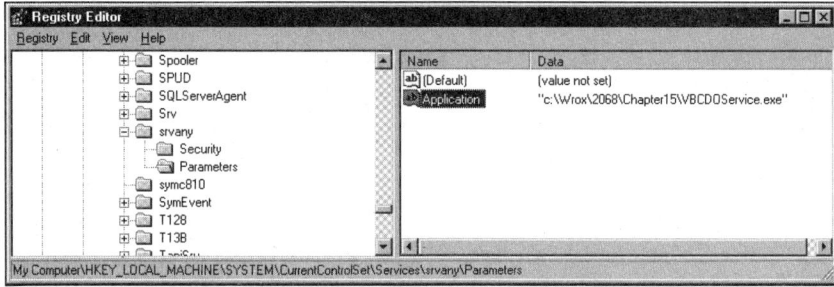

You should now be able to start the `SrvAny` service – it'll then start our VB service executable, and all should basically run as you'd expect.

Again, this is only a basic sample application; it has useful functionality, but there is obvious room for expansion; see the end of the previous section for further directions in which you might want to take this sample.

Summary

In this chapter, we looked at how adding send-mail functionality allows an unattended NT service to notify the outside world of events by leveraging the mail setup already in place.

We covered the requirements of identity and access that adding mail functionality to a service brings up; we looked in some detail at how you go about writing a service in C++, and implemented a basic disk space monitor in C++. We then wrote a Visual Basic application to perform the same task, though we used some workarounds to avoid the restrictions Visual Basic imposes on service writers.

This was a fairly basic service that we wrote which merely added mail functionality to an existing system. You can write services whose purpose is to perform unattended operations on the mail system.

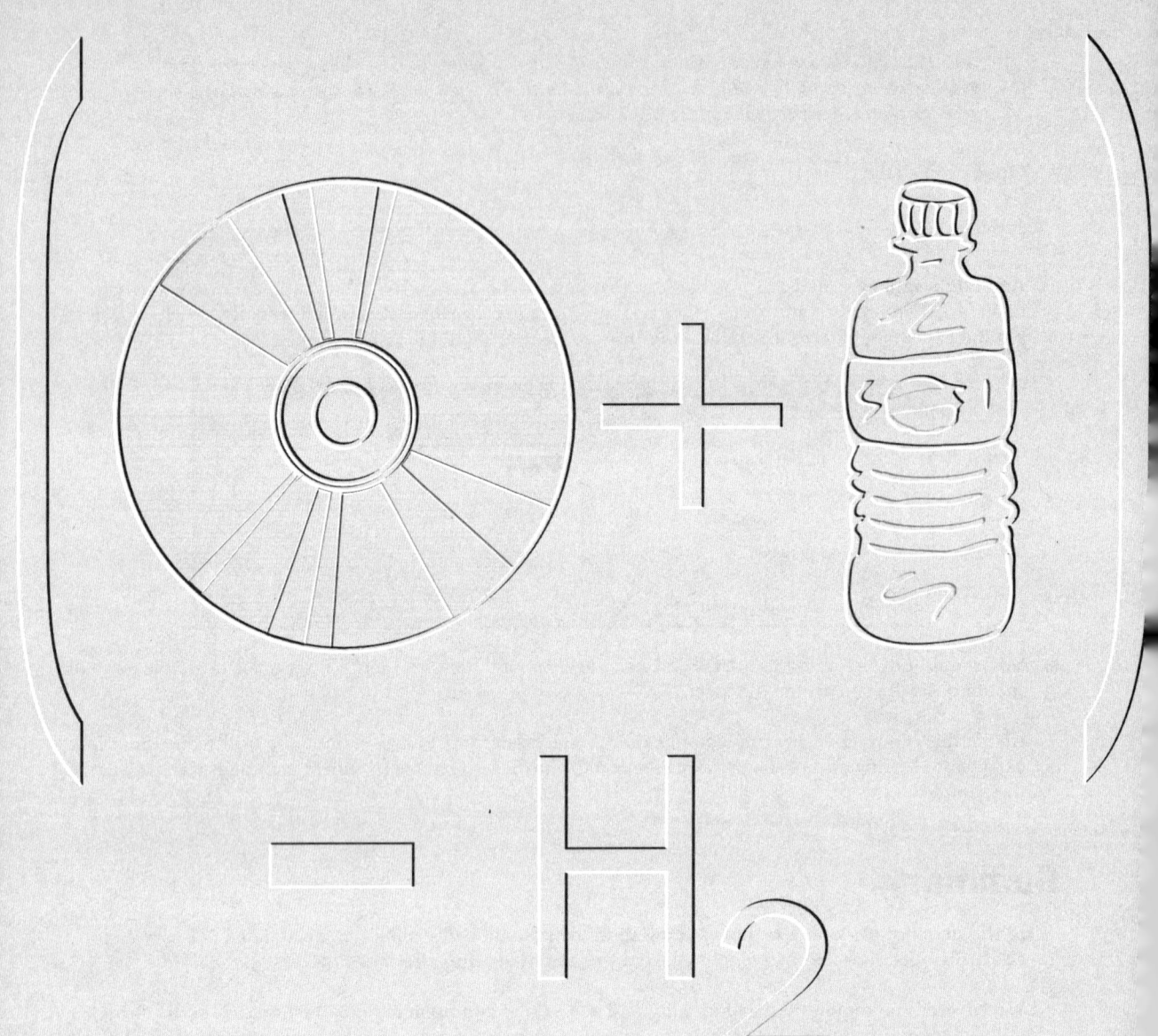

16

The Future of CDO

Having covered all of the different versions and flavors of CDO we are now going to take a look at the future direction that this technology may/will take. With the dawn of a new millennium, the latest releases from Microsoft of its operating system and premier messaging and collaboration system will bring a lot of new features and changes.

In this chapter we will take a look what messaging abilities Windows 2000 and Exchange 2000 will give us and what influences they might have to the development of our collaborative applications.

This chapter provides an overview of:

❑   The future of CDO in the Windows operating system environment

❑   The future of CDO in the Exchange messaging and collaboration platform

> Note that at the time this book went to press neither Windows 2000 nor Exchange 2000 are released products. So all information provided about CDO for Windows 2000 and CDO for Exchange 2000 are subject to change by Microsoft without any notice.

What Happens in the Future?

The next versions of Microsoft Windows and Exchange Server will add new features to help developers build sophisticated solutions that will work even better with Internet standards. For Windows 2000, some of the relevant new features include:

❑   The **Active Directory**, which combines information previous held separately in Windows NT and Exchange Server directories.

❑   **Enhanced security**, including support for the Kerberos authentication protocol.

❑   The new **CDO for Windows 2000 library**, adding support for MIME message body parts and adding NNTP protocol features for posting in Internet newsgroups.

> *MIME (Multipurpose Internet Mail Extensions) is an encoding method, supported by an Internet RFC (Request for Comments document) that makes it possible to send more than just plain text in Internet messages.*

Another sign of major change is that the Windows 2000 operating system does *not* ship with the MAPI-based Windows Messaging component. This option was available in Windows 9x and Windows NT 4.x to provide a minimal MAPI client for systems that do not have Microsoft Outlook installed. That means that if you develop an application that needs MAPI support, e.g. a Visual Basic application that leverages CDO 1.21 for Exchange, you will need to have either Microsoft Outlook or Exchange Server installed on the same Windows 2000 system as your application.

> *If Outlook 2000 is your preferred client, don't forget to ensure that the CDO component is included, since it is not part of the default setup.*

Exchange 2000 can only run on Windows 2000 servers, because of its integration with the Active Directory. It too, adds many new features:

❑   A **web store** merging the standard Exchange Server private and public information stores with a streaming database, storing MIME data types, such as Office documents and multimedia files, without conversion.

❑   **Full-text indexing**, including both message attachments and documents stored in Exchange folders.

❑   Access to any Exchange folder or item as a **URL**, or via **ActiveX Data Objects (ADO) 2.5**, with properties exposed as an ADO `Fields` collection.

❑   An enhanced version of **Outlook Web Acces**s – built into Exchange rather than implemented via thousands of lines of ASP code.

❑   The ability to host **more than one** private and public information store on a single Exchange Server.

Perhaps more importantly, will your current CDO applications continue to run with Windows 2000 and Exchange 2000? Yes, because Windows 2000 installs the CDONTS library, and Exchange 2000 installs the CDO 1.21 library for backward compatibility.

> *OLE DB 2.5 and ADO 2.5 are the strategic interfaces developed by Microsoft to provide universal data access to many types of data. You can find more information about both at the Microsoft Universal Data Access Website at http://www.microsoft.com/data.*

The Future of CDO in Windows 2000

CDO for Windows 2000 (previously known as CDO 2.0) ships as a COM component (`cdosys.dll`) that can be used in applications written in all programming languages that support the component object model, e.g. Visual Basic, Visual C++, Visual J++, Delphi, and scripting languages like VBScript, JavaScript, etc.

For example a web-based newsreader can be written using Active Server Pages on Internet Information Server (also included with Windows 2000) and the new CDO for Windows 2000 library without purchasing additional third-party components. While you can use ADO 2.5 for raw data access to the Exchange stores, CDO provides a higher-level language with many capabilities that help keep coding to a minimum.

The machine where your application is running must have access to either local or network SMTP and NNTP services. If you want to build applications that depend on SMTP or NNTP transport events, the SMTP or NNTP service *must* be running on the *same* machine as your application. In addition, the CDO for Windows 2000 object model includes a **Configuration object,** consisting of a `Fields` collection, whose settings control the way your application will work with the SMTP and NNTP services. For each service, you have these options:

❑ Send via a drop directory that a local SMTP or NNTP service uses to pick up waiting messages

❑ Send over the network using the SMTP or NNTP protocol

❑ Send through an Exchange Server

The following diagram depicts the basic architecture of the CDO for Windows 2000 library:

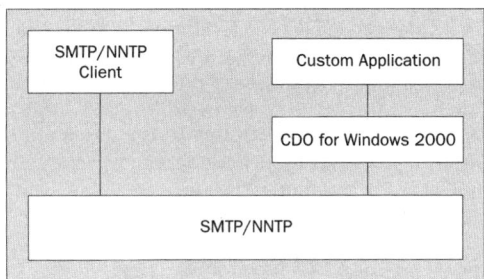

As you can see in the picture above, the CDO for Windows 2000 library is just a single layer between the supported protocols and your custom application. *There is no MAPI or any other API involved.*

You can use CDO for Windows 2000 either in a client or server-side application, e.g. to create and send MIME-formatted messages or newsgroup client applications. However, since most companies probably will not roll out Windows 2000 to the desktop quickly, server-based applications will be far more common than client programs. Where client interaction is required, such server-based applications can use a web interface.

While they share the Message object, the CDO for Windows 2000 object model is otherwise quite different from the CDONTS model. The `NewMail` and `Session` objects are eliminated and a key new object, the **BodyParts object**, makes it possible to build complex messages combining document attachments, embedded style sheets, images and other components of HTML-formatted messages. With CDO for Windows 2000, it becomes possible to send an entire web page – including its style sheet and any images – with a single line of code using the `Message` object's `CreateMHTMLBody` method.

The new features discussed so far focus on enhancements to sending messages – vastly improved support for HTML-formatted messages and support for posting to NNTP newsgroups. However, an additional new area for developers to explore is the new support for **transport event sinks.** Both the SMTP and NNTP services support events that will allow you, for example, to build applications that add a company disclaimer to each message transferred via SMTP, filter messages based on words in the subject posted to newsgroups via the NNTP protocol or perform other actions on messages as they are passing through the SMTP and NNTP services.

To be fluent in CDO for Windows 2000, you will not only want to familiarize yourself with the new object model, but also make sure you know how to access data with ADO 2.5.

> The `Fields` collections of the Message and BodyParts objects are implemented as ADO `Fields` collections stored as name-value pairs.

The Future of CDO in Exchange 2000

The **CDO for Exchange 2000 library** (previously known as CDO 3.0) also ships as COM components that can be used in applications written in all programming languages that support COM. An example might be a web-based customer registration application using an Exchange 2000 public contacts folder, written using Active Server Pages and the new CDO for Exchange 2000 library.

A key difference between CDO 1.21 and CDO for Exchange 2000 is that the latter is a *server-only* component. You cannot create client applications with it (except those using a web interface), even if you are running the workstation version of Windows 2000.

The following diagram shows the different ways applications can access Exchange 2000 – through CDO, directly through ADO 2.5 or via MAPI. Notice, however, that client applications operating with Outlook are not supported by CDO for Exchange 2000:

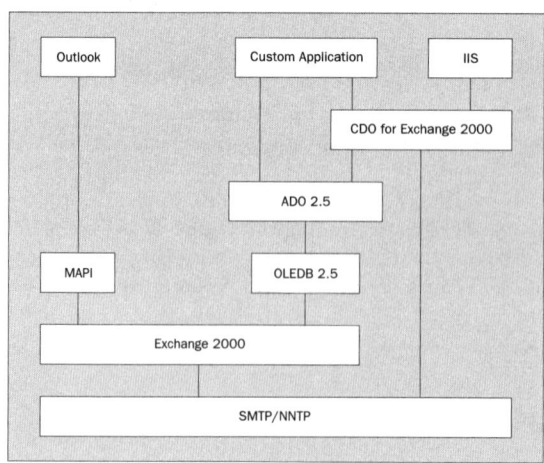

How does CDO for Exchange 2000 compare with CDO for Windows 2000? After all, both use the name CDO for their type libraries. The Exchange 2000 library is a **superset** of the Windows 2000 library. In fact, when Exchange 2000 is installed, the CDO for Windows 2000 component is automatically deregistered. In other words, on a machine with Exchange 2000, you simply use the single CDO for Exchange 2000 library to obtain all the functionality found in the CDO for Windows 2000 library, plus the whole range of messaging and collaboration enhancements provided by Exchange 2000.

Exchange 2000 actually includes three separate COM components, as shown in the following table:

Component	Description
CDO for Microsoft Exchange (cdoex.dll)	CDO component to create collaborative applications based upon the Windows 2000 and Exchange 2000.
CDO Workflow Objects for Microsoft Exchange (cdowf.dll)	CDOWF component to build workflow functionality on top of Exchange 2000.
CDO for Exchange Management (emo.dll)	CDOEXM component to manage an Exchange server. Can be used to create, move and delete mailboxes or manage users, contacts, and groups etc.

In addition to these new components, Exchange 2000 also installs the cdo.dll and cdohtml.dll to provide backward compatibility for your CDO 1.21 and HTML Rendering Library 1.21 applications.

CDO for Microsoft Exchange

CDO for Microsoft Exchange is the successor of CDO 1.2 for Exchange 5.x, implemented as a COM component for creating collaborative applications on top of Exchange 2000. Among its major enhancements is full support for calendaring and contact management in either Exchange mailboxes or Public Folders.

The bad news is that it does not support tasks and journal entries as separate objects, only as Message objects.

As with CDO for Windows 2000, the CDO for Microsoft Exchange library fully supports MIME and MHTML messages to build HMTL formatted e-mail messages.

ADO skills are essential. Applications typically use ADO to manipulate folders as rowsets and use structured query language (SQL) queries to retrieve particular items.

Because CDO in Exchange 2000 is tightly coupled with ADO 2.5 it is required to include the ActiveX Data Objects 2.5 Library (ADODB) library in all applications. ADO 2.5 ships with Windows 2000.

CDO Workflow Objects for Microsoft Exchange

The **CDO Workflow Objects for Microsoft Exchange** component is the successor to the Exchange Routing Objects introduced in Exchange Server 5.5 Service Pack 1 as a feature running on top of the Exchange Server Event Service.

Workflow objects can be used in two different kinds of applications that deal with item routing and decision-making:

❑ Applications connecting directly to the Exchange 2000 data store use what is called **database-style workflow**. In this case, a connection to the Exchange 2000 data store is required for the whole time while the workflow process is running, e.g. a document is edited.

❑ Offline users interact with a workflow application by sending messages to a workflow-enabled folder on the Exchange 2000 Server. For such messaging-style workflows, CDO Workflow Objects provide mechanisms for identifying a message as part of an ongoing workflow process instance, initiating a new process instance based on an incoming message, and ensuring that the sender of the message has the proper authority to participate in the workflow:

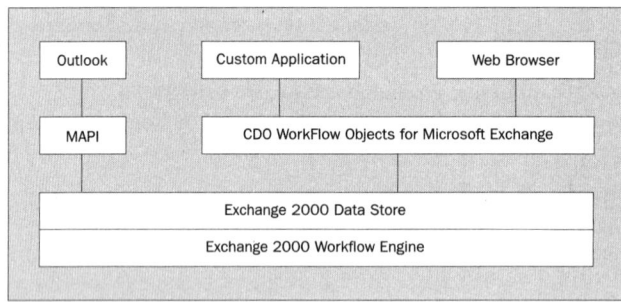

CDO for Exchange Management

The **CDO for Exchange Management** component provides another set of new features to support applications that manage mailboxes, e.g. create, move, or delete mailboxes and manage users, external recipients and groups. While those features are also available via OLE DB 2.5 and ADSI, CDO for Exchange Management provides a high-level method to perform those tasks without going into raw OLE DB 2.5 and Active Directory management.

Outlook Web Access in Exchange 2000

Exchange 2000 does not provide an updated version of the `cdohtml.dll` rendering library. You no longer need to build ASP pages in order to display messages, appointments, or contacts in web pages in Exchange 2000. Instead, the rendering is handled natively by the new version of Outlook Web Access (OWA) in Exchange 2000. Items can be opened simply by specifying a URL, which includes the folder path and the name of the item.

Other new features in OWA include:

- ❑ Rendering via either DHTML for more recent browsers or HTML 3.2 for earlier browsers
- ❑ Default web forms for public folders
- ❑ A web store forms registry
- ❑ Support for cascading style sheets to define the formatting of folder views

Exchange Server Events in Exchange 2000

Server-based events in Exchange 2000 expand vastly from those available in Exchange Server 5.5. In addition, you can use Visual Basic to create event agents, not just VBScript or languages like C++. Events fire upon changes to not just individual items, but folders as well.

If you've ever been frustrated by the lack of a true `Delete` event in Exchange 5.5, you will want to examine the new `OnSyncDelete` event. Both it and the new `OnSyncSave` event are synchronous events: They give your program exclusive control over an item *before* it is saved or deleted and are cancellable events. These and other events are listed in the following table:

Event	Description
OnDelete	Fires when a folder or item is deleted. Replaces the `OnMessageDeleted` event in Exchange Server 5.5. (*Asynchronous*)
OnMDBShutdown	Fires when the Exchange store stops. (*New*)
OnMDBStartUp	Fires when the Exchange store starts. (*New*)
OnSave	Fires when a folder or item is saved. Replaces the `OnMessageCreated` and `OnChange` events in Exchange Server 5.5. (*Asynchronous*)
OnSyncDelete	Fires when a folder or item is deleted. (*New, synchronous*)
OnSyncSave	Fires when a folder or item is saved. (*New, synchronous*)
OnTimer	Fires at an interval defined when the event-based application is installed.

Exchange Server 5.5 supported only asynchronous item events so there was no guarantee that when the event fired, the item would still be available. With the introduction of synchronous events in Exchange 2000, you get greater control over what happens when items or folders are created, modified, or removed

Don't forget that, because CDO for Exchange 2000 replaces CDO for Windows 2000, you also have access to the SMTP and NNTP protocol events discussed earlier.

Summary

In this chapter, we took a brief look at the directions Microsoft is taking with its Windows 2000 operating system and the Exchange 2000 messaging and collaboration platform. We looked at how the new object libraries that will ship with these products will shape and change the possible development directions that our collaborative applications may take.

As these products are likely to play a formidable role in the IT market, it might be a good idea to get your hands on these technologies as soon as possible to starting learning how to enhance the applications you designed with earlier versions of CDO.

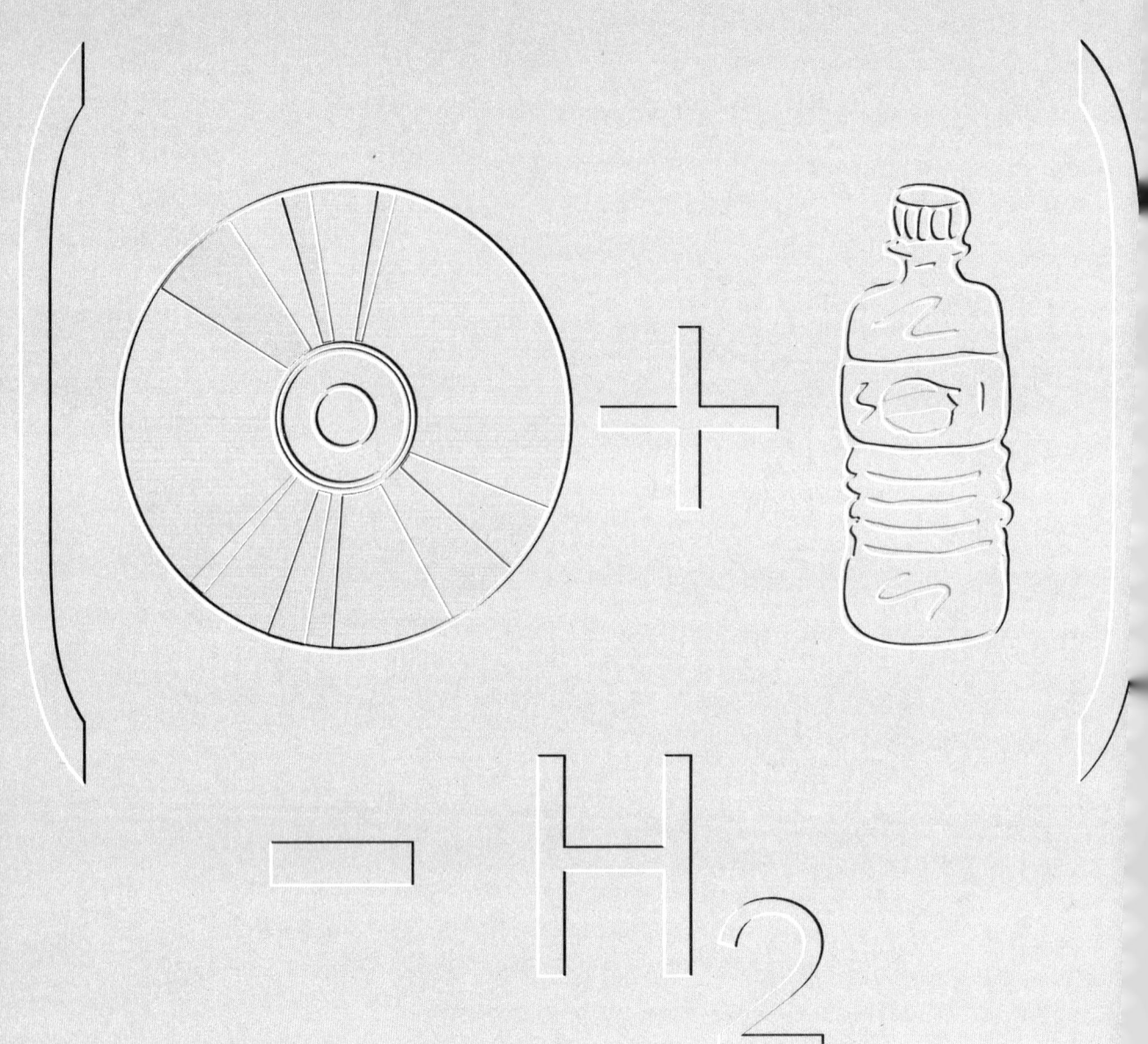

CDO 1.21 Object Model Reference

In this Appendix, you'll find a complete list of the objects, methods and properties in the CDO 1.21 object model. Note that any parameters in square brackets are optional arguments to a method.

Objects

Object	Description
AddressEntries	Collection containing a number of AddressEntry objects.
AddressEntry	Defines addressing information valid for a given messaging system. An address usually represents a person or process to which the messaging system can deliver messages.
AddressEntryFilter	The AddressEntryFilter object specifies criteria for a search on an AddressEntries collection.
AddressList	The AddressList object supplies a (distribution) list of address entries to which a messaging system can deliver messages.
AddressLists	Collection containing a number of AddressList objects.
AppointmentItem	The AppointmentItem object represents an appointment in a calendar folder.
Attachment	The Attachment object represents a document that is an attachment of a message.

Object	Description
Attachments	Collection containing a number of `Attachment` objects.
Field	A `Field` object represents a MAPI property on a CDO Library object.
Fields	Collection containing a number of `Field` objects.
Folder	The `Folder` object represents a folder or container within the MAPI system. A folder can contain subfolders and messages.
Folders	Collection containing a number of `Folder` objects.
GroupHeader	The `GroupHeader` object represents the header for a grouping of messages within a table view.
InfoStore	The `InfoStore` object provides access to the folder hierarchy of a message store.
InfoStores	Collection containing a number of `InfoStore` objects.
MeetingItem	The `MeetingItem` object represents a meeting in a folder.
Message	The `Message` object represents a single message, item, document, or form in a folder.
MessageFilter	The `MessageFilter` object specifies criteria for restricting a search on a `Messages` collection.
Messages	Collection containing a number of `AppointmentItem`, `GroupHeader`, `MeetingItem` and `Message` objects.
Recipient	The `Recipient` object represents a recipient of a message.
Recipients	Collection containing a number of `Recipient` objects.
RecurrencePattern	The `RecurrencePattern` object describes the recurrence pattern for an `AppointmentItem` object.
Session	The `Session` object contains session-wide settings and options. It also contains properties that return top-level objects, such as `CurrentUser`.

AddressEntries Collection

This object represents a **large** collection of `AddressEntry` objects.

Methods

Name	Returns	Description
Add (*addresstype* [, *name*] [, *address*])	AddressEntry	The `Add` method creates and returns a new `AddressEntry` object in the `AddressEntries` collection containing the *addresstype* (CdoPR_ADDRTYPE) and optionally the display *name* and *address* for the entry.
Delete()	None	The `Delete` method deletes all the address entries in the `AddressEntries` collection.
GetFirst()	AddressEntry	The `GetFirst` method returns the first `AddressEntry` object in the `AddressEntries` collection. It returns `Nothing` if there is no address entry in the collection.
GetLast()	AddressEntry	The `GetLast` method returns the last `AddressEntry` object in the `AddressEntries` collection. It returns `Nothing` if there is no address entry in the collection.
GetNext()	AddressEntry	The `GetNext` method returns the next `AddressEntry` object in the `AddressEntries` collection. It returns `Nothing` if no next object exists, for example if already positioned at the end of the collection.
GetPrevious()	AddressEntry	The `GetPrevious` method returns the previous `AddressEntry` object in the `AddressEntries` collection. It returns `Nothing` if no previous object exists, for example if already positioned at the beginning of the collection.
Sort ([*SortOrder*] [, *PropTag*]) Sort ([*SortOrder*] [, *name*])	None	The `Sort` method sorts the address entries in the collection on the specified property – either a named *CdoPropTag* constant or a tag *name* – according to the specified *sort order* (a constant of type CdoSortOrder). The default order is ascending if none is given. If no proptag or name is specified, a repeat is made of the last sort performed.

Properties

Name	Returns	Description
Application	String	The string 'Collaboration Data Objects'.
Class	CdoObjectClass	The class of the CDO object. In this case, CdoAddressEntries (21)
Count	Long	The number of AddressEntry objects in the collection or if this is not possible, returns &H7FFFFFFF.
Filter	AddressEntryFilter	The AddressEntryFilter object for the AddressEntries collection.
Item(*index*) Item(*search*)	AddressEntry	Returns a single AddressEntry object from the collection identified by either its *index* in the collection or some *search* criteria.
Parent	AddressList	The parent AddressList object.
RawTable	IUnknown	An IUnknown pointer to the MAPI table that underlies the AddressEntries collection.
Session	Session	The current CDO Session object.

AddressEntry Object

Represents the address of a user or distribution list. Also contains information related to address owner's availability.

Methods

Name	Returns	Description
Delete()	None	Deletes the AddressEntry object.
Details ([*parentWindow*])	None	Displays a dialog containing detailed (at least the display name and address) information about an AddressEntry object. Optionally, the method can take a long integer reference to the *parent window* where the call originated.
GetFreeBusy (*StartTime*, *EndTime*, *Interval*)	String	Returns a string indicating the free/busy status of the user for each time interval specified in minutes between the start and end times given. The string contains one character (0, 1, 2 or 3) per interval corresponding to the CdoBusyStatus constants.

Name	Returns	Description
IsSameAs (*AEObject2*)	Boolean	True if the AddressEntry object is the same as *AEObject2*.
Update ([*makePermanent*] [, *refreshObject*])	None	Saves any changes made to the AddressEntry object. Update takes two boolean parameters. *makePermanent* commits all changes to the object and *refreshObject* loses all changes not yet made permanent. The default call is Update(*True, False*).

Properties

Name	Returns	Description
Address	String	Specifies the messaging address of an address entry or message recipient. (e.g. an email address)
Application	String	The string 'Collaboration Data Objects'.
Class	CdoObjectClass	The class of the CDO object. In this case, CdoAddressEntry (8)
DisplayType	CdoDisplayType	A CdoDisplayType constant representing the display type of the address entry (User, Distribution List, Forum, etc)
Fields Fields (*index*) Fields (*proptag*) Fields (*name*)	Object (Field or Fields)	Returns the specified field attached to the AddressEntry object based on either *index* value (integer), *cdoPropTag* (long) or *name*. Returns Fields collection if no parameter is specified.
ID	String	The unique identifier of the AddressEntry object.
Manager	AddressEntry	The AddressEntry object corresponding to the manager of the user whose AddressEntry object this is.
MAPIOBJECT	IUnknown	An IUnknown pointer to this object.
Members	AddressEntries	Returns an AddressEntries collection containing the AddressEntry objects for those users in this distribution list.
Name	String	The display name or alias for the object.
Parent	AddressEntries, Recipient	The parent AddressEntries collection or Recipient object.

Name	Returns	Description
Session	Session	The current CDO Session object.
Type	String	The Type property specifies the address type, such as SMTP, fax, or X.400.

AddressEntryFilter Object

The AddressEntryFilter object specifies the criteria for a search on an AddressEntries collection.

Methods

Name	Returns	Description
IsSameAs (*AEFObject2*)	Boolean	True if the AddressEntryFilter object is the same as *AEFObject2*.

Properties

Name	Returns	Description
Address	String	The *full* address for the AddressEntry object being filtered.
Application	String	The string 'Collaboration Data Objects'.
Class	CdoObjectClass	The class of the CDO object. In this case, CdoAddressEntryFilter (9)
Fields Fields (*index*) Fields (*proptag*) Fields (*name*)	Object (Field or Fields)	Returns the specified field attached to the AddressEntryFilter object based on either *index* value (integer), *cdoPropTag* (long) or *name*. Returns Fields collection if no parameter is specified.
Name	String	Specifies a value for the default filter property. This value will be used in an ambiguous name resolution search. e.g 'tom' would find 'Tom', 'Tomas', 'Tomkinson' etc.
Not	Boolean	True if values should be negated before being ANDed or ORed to the filter.
Or	Boolean	True if the values in the filter should be ORed together rather than ANDed, which is the default.
Parent	AddressEntries	The parent AddressEntries collection.
Session	Session	The current CDO Session object.

AddressList Object

Methods

Name	Returns	Description
IsSameAs (*ALObject2*)	Boolean	True if the AddressList object is the same as *ALObject2*.

Properties

Name	Returns	Description
AddressEntries AddressEntries (*index*)	AddressEntry, AddressEntries	Returns either the collection of AddressEntry objects in the AddressList, or AddressEntry number *index*. Note that using *index* is only safe if the collection's count property returns a value other than &H7FFFFFFF.
Application	String	The string 'Collaboration Data Objects'.
Class	CdoObjectClass	The class of the CDO object. In this case, CdoAddressList (7)
Fields Fields (*index*) Fields (*proptag*) Fields (*name*)	Field, Fields	Returns the specified field attached to the AddressList object based on either *index* value (integer), *cdoPropTag* (long) or *name*. Returns Fields collection if no parameter is specified.
ID	String	The unique identifier of the AddressList object.
Index	Long	The index value of this AddressList object within its parent AddressLists collection.
IsReadOnly	Boolean	True if the current AddressList is read-only. Note this does not apply to the AddressEntry objects in the list.
Name	String	The name of the AddressList as a string.
Parent	AddressLists	The parent AddressLists collection.
Session	Session	The current CDO Session object.

AddressLists Collection

A collection of one or more `AddressList` objects. Note that `AddressLists` is regarded as a small collection for which the `Count` property is reliable. This object has no methods.

Properties

Name	Returns	Description
Application	String	The string 'Collaboration Data Objects'.
Class	CdoObjectClass	The class of the CDO Object. In this case, `CdoAddressLists` (20).
Count	Long	The exact number of `AddressList` objects in the collection.
Item(*index*) Item(*name*)	AddressList	Returns a single `AddressList` object from the collection identified by either its *index* in the collection or by being the first object in the collection whose name property matches *name*.
Parent	Session	The current CDO `Session` object.
Session	Session	The current CDO `Session` object.

AppointmentItem Object

The `AppointmentItem` object represents an appointment in a calendar folder. Only the properties and methods unique to the `AppointmentItem` object are listed here. It also inherits all the properties and some of the methods (`CopyTo`, `Delete`, `IsSameAs`, `MoveTo`, `Options`, `Send` and `Update`) defined in the `Message` object.

Methods

Name	Returns	Description
ClearRecurrence Pattern()	None	Removes any recurrence settings from this appointment.
GetRecurrence Pattern()	RecurrencePattern	Returns a `RecurrencePattern` object defining the recurrence settings for this appointment.
Respond (*RespondType*)	MeetingItem	Returns a `MeetingItem` object for responding to a meeting request for an appointment.

Properties

Name	Returns	Description
AllDayEvent	Boolean	Indicates whether this appointment is an all-day event.
BusyStatus	CdoBusyStatus	The busy flag for this user with respect to this appointment.
Class	CdoObjectClass	The class of the CDO Object. In this case, CdoAppointment (26).
Duration	Long	The duration of this appointment.
EndTime	Variant (vbDate)	The end date/time of this appointment.
IsRecurring	Boolean	True if this appointment is recurring.
Location	String	Returns or sets the location of this appointment.
MeetingResponse Status	CdoResponseStatus	The user's response status (Accepted, Declined, etc) to this AppointmentItem.
MeetingStatus	CdoMeetingStatusType	The current meeting status for this AppointmentItem.
Organizer	AddressEntry	The user who called the meeting.
ReminderMinutes BeforeStart	Long	How many minutes before the start of this appointment a reminder should be issued.
ReminderSet	Boolean	True if the user will be reminded of this appointment.
ReplyTime	Variant (vbDate)	The date/time a recipient replied to the meeting request for this appointment.
ResponseRequested	Boolean	True if a response is required to the meeting request for this appointment.
StartTime	Variant (vbDate)	The start date/time of this appointment.

Attachment Object

The Attachment object represents a document that is an attachment of a message.

Methods

Name	Returns	Description
Delete	None	Deletes the Attachment object.
IsSameAs (*AttObject2*)	Boolean	True if the Attachment object is the same as *AttObject2*.
ReadFromFile (*FileName*)	None	Loads the contents of an attachment from a file or OLE docfile source.
WriteToFile (*FileName*)	None	Saves the attachment to a file or OLE docfile in the file system. Note this overwrites any previous contents of the file without warning.

Properties

Name	Returns	Description
Application	String	The string 'Collaboration Data Objects'.
Class	CdoObjectClass	The class of the CDO Object. In this case, CdoAttachment(5)
Fields Fields (*index*) Fields (*proptag*) Fields (*name*)	Object (Field or Fields)	Returns the specified field attached to the AddressList object based on either *index* value (integer), *cdoPropTag* (long) or *name*. Returns Fields collection if no parameter is specified.
Index	Long	The index number for the Attachment object within its parent Attachments collection.
MAPIOBJECT	IUnknown	An IUnknown pointer to the Attachment object.
Name	String	The display name of the Attachment object
Parent	Attachments	The parent Attachments collection.
Position	Long	The position of the attachment within the text of the message.
Session	Session	The current CDO Session object.

Name	Returns	Description
Source	Variant (String or Message object)	The full path and file name, OLE class name, or unique message identifier for the attachment.
Type	CdoAttachmentType	The attachment type with one of the CdoAttachmentType constant values.

Attachments Collection

The Attachments collection object contains zero or more Attachment objects. Note that Attachments is regarded as a small collection for which the Count property is reliable.

Methods

Name	Returns	Description
Add ([*Name*] [, *Position*] [, *Type*] [, *Source*])	Attachment	Creates and returns a new Attachment object in the Attachments collection. Allows you to specify a display *name*, *position* in message, *type* and *source* for the attachment.
Delete()	None	Deletes all the attachments in the Attachments collection.

Properties

Name	Returns	Description
Application	String	The string 'Collaboration Data Objects'.
Class	CdoObjectClass	The class of the CDO Object. In this case, CdoAttachments(18)
Count	Long	The exact number of Attachment objects in the collection.
Item (*index*) Item (*recordKey*)	Attachment	Returns either Attachment number *index* from the collection or the first Attachment whose MAPI *recordKey* matches the one given as a parameter.
Parent	Message	The parent Message object.
Session	Session	The current CDO Session object.

Field Object

A `Field` object represents a MAPI property that is defined on a CDO object. A full list of MAPI properties can be found in Appendix B under the heading `CdoPropTags`.

Methods

Name	Returns	Description
Delete()	None	Deletes the user-defined or optional `Field` object from the `Fields` collection.
ReadFromFile (*FileName*)	None	Loads the value of a string or binary field from a file.
WriteToFile (*FileName*)	None	Saves the field value to a file in the file system.

Properties

Name	Returns	Description
Application	String	The string 'Collaboration Data Objects'.
Class	CdoObjectClass	The class of the CDO Object. In this case, `CdoField(6)`
ID	Long	The long integer value corresponding to the MAPI property value. See the `CdoPropTag` section of Appendix B for a complete list.
Index	Long	The index of the current `Field` object in the `Fields` collection.
Name Name (*PropsetID*)	String	The name of the current `Field` object.
Parent	Fields	The parent `Fields` collection.
Session	Session	The current CDO `Session`.
Type	Integer	The type of the value stored in the current `Field` object. (`vbArray`, `vbBoolean`, `vbLong`. etc)
Value	Variant	The value of the `Field` object.

Fields Collection

The Fields collection object contains zero or more Field objects. Note that Fields is regarded as a small collection for which the Count property is reliable.

Methods

Name	Returns	Description
Add (*Name*, *Type* [, *Value*] [, *PropsetID*]) Add (*PropTag*, *value*)	Field	Creates and returns a new Field object in the Fields collection. For a custom field, you must specify its *name* and the *type* of value it holds. Optionally, you can also give it a *value* and specify the *property set* it belongs to. For predefined MAPI properties, you must specify the *property tag* and its new *value*.
Delete ()	None	Deletes all user-defined and optional fields in the Fields collection object.
SetNamespace (*PropsetID*)	None	Selects the property set that is to be used for accessing named properties in the Fields collection.

Properties

Name	Returns	Description
Application	String	The string 'Collaboration Data Objects'.
Class	CdoObjectClass	The class of the CDO Object. In this case, CdoFields(19)
Count	Long	The exact number of Field objects in the collection.
Item (*index*) Item (*Proptag*) Item (*name* [, *PropsetID*])	Field	Returns a single Field from the collection based on its *index* number, the MAPI *property tag* it has a value for, or its custom *name* and *property set* if necessary.
Parent	Object	This collection's immediate parent.
Session	Session	The current CDO Session object.

Folder Object

The Folder object represents a folder or container within the MAPI system. As in client programs, a Folder object can contain other folders and messages.

Methods

Name	Returns	Description
CopyTo (*folderID* [, *storeID*] [, *name*] [, *copySubfolders*])	Folder	Makes and returns a copy of the Folder object at another folder hierarchy location (and InfoStore if need be). You can also specify a new name for the copy of the folder and whether or not to copy its subfolders.
Delete()	None	Deletes the Folder object from its parent Folders collection or InfoStore object.
IsSameAs (*FolObject2*)	Boolean	True if the Attachment object is the same as *FolObject2*.
MoveTo (*folderID* [, *storied*])	Folder	Relocates the Folder object to another folder hierarchy location.
Update([*makePermanent*] [, *refreshObject*])	None	The Update method saves changes to the Folder object. Update takes two boolean parameters. *makePermanent* commits all changes to the object and *refreshObject* loses all changes not yet made permanent. The default call is Update(*True*, *False*)

Properties

Name	Returns	Description
Application	String	The string 'Collaboration Data Objects'.
Class	CdoObjectClass	The class of the CDO Object. In this case, CdoFolder(2)
FolderID	String	The unique ID of this object's parent folder.
Folders	Folders	The Folders collection of subfolders in the current folder.
HiddenMessages	Messages	A collection of hidden messages in the current folder.
ID	String	The unique identifier of the current folder.
MAPIOBJECT	IUnknown	An IUnknown pointer to the current folder.
Messages	Messages	A collection of messages in the current folder.

Name	Returns	Description
Name	String	The name of the current folder.
Parent	Folders	The parent `Folders` collection.
Session	Session	The current CDO `Session` object.
StoreID	String	The ID of the parent information store.

Folders Collection

This object represents a **large** collection of `Folder` objects.

Methods

Name	Returns	Description
Add (*Name*)	Folder	Creates and returns a new `Folder` object in the Folders collection.
Delete()	None	Deletes all the folders in the `Folders` collection.
GetFirst()	Folder	Returns the first `Folder` object in this `Folders` collection or Nothing if there is no folder in the collection.
GetLast()	Folder	Returns the last `Folder` object in the `Folders` collection or `Nothing` if there is no folder in the collection.
GetNext()	Folder	Returns the next `Folder` object in the `Folders` collection or `Nothing` if no next object exists, for example if already positioned at the end of the collection.
GetPrevious()	Folder	Returns the previous `Folder` object in the `Folders` collection or `Nothing` if no previous object exists, for example if already positioned at the beginning of the collection.
Sort ([*SortOrder*] [, *PropTag*]) Sort ([*SortOrder*] [, *name*])	None	The `Sort` method sorts the address entries in the collection on the specified property – either a named *CdoPropTag* constant or a tag *name* – according to the specified *sort order* (a constant of type `CdoSortOrder`). The default order is ascending if none is given. If no proptag or name is specified, a repeat is made of the last sort performed.

Properties

Name	Returns	Description
Application	String	The string 'Collaboration Data Objects'.
Class	CdoObjectClass	The class of the CDO Object. In this case, CdoFolders(15)
Count	Long	The number of Folder objects in this collection or if this is not possible, returns &H7FFFFFFF.
Parent	Folder	The parent Folder object.
RAWTABLE	IUnknown	An IUnknown pointer to current folder table.
Session	Session	The current CDO Session object.

GroupHeader Object

The GroupHeader object represents the header for a group of messages within a table view. This group has been brought into existence by defining which categories messages should be grouped by.

Properties

Name	Returns	Description
Application	String	The string 'Collaboration Data Objects'.
Class	CdoObjectClass	The class of the CDO Object. In this case, CdoGroupHeader(25)
Count	Long	The number of messages in the group or if this is not possible, returns &H7FFFFFFF.
Level	Long	The indentation level of the group header within the table view. Takes a value between 1 and 4.
Name	String	The display name for the grouping of message objects. Generally describes the category.
Unread	Long	The number of unread messages in the group or if this is not possible, returns &H7FFFFFFF.
Parent	Messages	The parent Messages collection.
Session	Session	The current CDO Session object.

InfoStore Object

The InfoStore object provides access to the folder hierarchy of a message store.

Methods

Name	Returns	Description
IsSameAs (*ISObject2*)	Boolean	True if the InfoStore object is the same as *ISObject2*.

Properties

Name	Returns	Description
Application	String	The string 'Collaboration Data Objects'.
Class	CdoObjectClass	The class of the CDO Object. In this case, CdoInfoStore(1)
Fields Fields (*index*) Fields (*proptag*) Fields (*name*)	Object (Field or Fields)	Returns the specified field attached to the InfoStore object based on either *index* value (integer), *cdoPropTag* (long) or *name*. Returns the Fields collection if no parameter is specified.
ID	String	The unique identifier of the current store.
MAPIOBJECT	IUnknown	An IUnknown pointer to the current store.
Name	String	The display name of the current store.
ProviderName	String	The name of the InfoStore's message store provider.
RootFolder	Folder	The root of the IPM subtree for the InfoStore object.
Parent	InfoStores	The parent InfoStores collection.
Session	Session	The current CDO Session object.

InfoStores Collection

The Infostores collection object contains zero or more Infostore objects. Note that Infostores is regarded as a small collection for which the Count property is reliable. This object has no methods.

Properties

Name	Returns	Description
Application	String	The string 'Collaboration Data Objects'.
Class	CdoObjectClass	The class of the CDO Object. In this case, CdoInfoStores(14)

Table Continued on Following Page

Name	Returns	Description
Count	Long	Returns the exact number of `InfoStore` objects in the collection.
Item(*Index*) Item(*StoreName*)	InfoStore	Returns an InfoStore object from the collection specified either by *index* or by its *name*.
Parent	Session	The current CDO `Session` object.
Session	Session	The current CDO `Session` object.

MeetingItem Object

The `MeetingItem` object represents a meeting in a folder. It has all properties and most methods defined in the `Messages` object. Only the properties and methods unique to the `MeetingItem` object are listed here. It also inherits all the properties and some of the methods (`CopyTo`, `Delete`, `Forward`, `IsSameAs`, `MoveTo`, `Options`, `Reply`, `ReplyAll`, `Send` and `Update`) defined in the `Message` object.

Methods

Name	Returns	Description
GetAssociated Appointment()	AppointmentItem	Returns the `AppointmentItem` object associated with this meeting.
Respond(*RespType*)	MeetingItem	Returns a `MeetingItem` object for responding to this meeting request.

Properties

Name	Returns	Description
Class	CdoObjectClass	The class of the CDO Object. In this case, `CdoMeetingItem(27)`
MeetingType	String	The type of this meeting item with one of the `CdoMeetingType` constant values.

Message Object

The `Message` object represents a single message, item, document, or form in a folder.

Methods

Name	Returns	Description
CopyTo (*folderID* [, *storeID*])	Message	Makes and returns a copy of the `Message` object in another folder, located in a different `InfoStore` if needed.

Name	Returns	Description
Delete (*DeletedItems*)	None	Deletes the Message object. Boolean parameter determines whether object is moved to the Deleted Items folder or deleted permanently.
Forward()	Message	Returns a new Message object with which to forward the current Message object.
IsSameAs (*MsgObject2*)	Boolean	True if the Attachment object is the same as *MsgObject2*.
MoveTo (*folderID* [, *storeID*])	Message	Moves the Message object to another folder (in a different InfoStore if necessary).
Options ([*parentWindow*])	None	Displays a modal dialog box where the user can change the submission options for a message.
Reply()	Message	Returns a new Message object that can be used to reply to the sender of the current message.
ReplyAll()	Message	Returns a new Message object that that can be used to reply to the sender and all recipients of the current message.
Send ([*saveCopy*] [, *showDialog*] [, *parentWindow*])	None	Sends the message to the recipients through the messaging system.
Update ([*makePermanent*] [, *refreshObject*])	None	Saves the message in the messaging system.

Properties

Name	Returns	Description
Application	String	The string 'Collaboration Data Objects'.
Attachments Attachments (*index*)	Object (Attachments or Attachment)	Either Attachment object number *index* or the entire Attachments collection for the message if *index* is not specified.
Categories	String Array	An array of the categories (up to 4) assigned to the message.
Conversation	Do not use	**The Conversation property is obsolete.** Use the ConversationIndex and ConversationTopic properties instead.

Table Continued on Following Page

Name	Returns	Description
ConversationIndex	String	Specifies the message's index number in the conversation thread.
ConversationTopic	String	Specifies the subject of the conversation thread of the message.
Class	CdoObjectClass	The class of the CDO Object. In this case, CdoMsg(3)
DeliveryReceipt	Boolean	True if a user requires an acknowledgement of the message being delivered.
Encrypted	Boolean	True if a message has been encrypted or encryption has been requested for this message.
Fields Fields(*index*) Fields(*proptag*) Fields(*name*)	Object (Field or Fields)	Returns the specified field attached to the Message object based on either *index* value (integer), *cdoPropTag* (long) or *name*. Returns all fields if no parameter is specified.
FolderID	String	The unique identifier of the Folder containing the message.
ID	String	The unique identifier of the current message.
Importance	CdoImportance	The importance of the message as CdoNormal (the default), CdoLow, or CdoHigh.
MAPIOBJECT	IUnknown	An IUnknown pointer to the current message.
Parent	Messages	The Messages collection containing this Message.
ReadReceipt	Boolean	True if a user requires an acknowledgement of the message being read.
Recipients Recipients(*index*)	Recipients	Returns one or all of the recipients to receive this Message object.
Sender	AddressEntry	Returns the sender of a message as an AddressEntry.
Sensitivity	CdoSensitivity	The sensitivity of the message. Takes one of the CdoSensitivity constants.
Sent	Boolean	True if the message has been sent through the messaging system.

Name	Returns	Description
Session	Session	The current CDO Session.
Signed	Boolean	True if the message has been tagged with a digital signature.
Size	Long	The approximate size in bytes of the message.
StoreID	String	The ID for the InfoStore holding the Message object.
Subject	String	The subject of the message.
Submitted	Boolean	True when the message has been submitted.
Text	String	The text of the message.
TimeCreated	Variant (vbDate)	The date/time the message was first saved.
TimeExpired	Variant (vbDate)	The date/time the message will expire.
TimeCreated	Variant (vbDate)	The date/time the message was first saved.
TimeLastModified	Variant (vbDate)	The date/time the message was most recently saved.
TimeReceived	Variant (vbDate)	The date/time the message was received.
TimeSent	Variant (vbDate)	The date/time the message was sent.
Type	String	The message class for the message.
Unread	Boolean	True if the message has not been read by the current user.

MessageFilter Object

Represents the criteria used to search for specific Message objects in a Messages collection.

Methods

Name	Returns	Description
IsSameAs (*MsgFObject2*)	Boolean	True if the MessageFilter object is the same as *MsgFObject2*.

Properties

Name	Returns	Description
Application	String	The string 'Collaboration Data Objects'.
Class	CdoObjectClass	The class of the CDO Object. In this case, CdoMessageFilter(10)

Name	Returns	Description
Conversation	String	Sets a filter to match only messages with the conversation topic given.
Fields Fields (*index*) Fields (*proptag*) Fields (*name*)	Object (Field or Fields)	Returns the specified field attached to the Message object based on either *index* value (integer), *cdoPropTag* (long) or *name*. Returns all fields if no parameter is specified.
Importance	CdoImportance	Sets a filter to match only messages with the same importance value.
Not	Boolean	True if all search criteria are to be negated before being ANDed or ORed to the filter.
Or	Boolean	True if the restriction values are to be ORed instead of ANDed to search criteria.
Parent	Messages	The Messages collection holding this MessageFilter.
Recipients	Recipients	Sets a filter to match only messages with a specific Recipient object. Note this matches the *name* of the Recipient, not the address.
Sender	String	Sets a filter to match only messages with a specific sender. Note this matches the *name* of the sender, not the address.
Sent	Boolean	Sets a filter to match only messages that have been sent through the messaging system.
Session	Session	The current CDO Session object.
Size	Long	Sets a filter to match only messages that have a *greater* total size than the value given
Subject	String	Sets a filter to match only messages whose subject contains this value as a substring.
Text	String	Sets a filter to match only messages whose main text contains this value as a substring.
TimeFirst	Variant (vbDate)	Sets a filter to match only messages received at or after the specified time/date.
TimeLast	Variant(vbDate)	Sets a filter to match only messages received at or before the specified time/date.
Type	String	Sets a filter to match only messages with the same MAPI message class.
Unread	Boolean	Sets a filter to match only messages that haven't been read.

Messages Collection

This object represents a **large** collection of one or more `AppointmentItem`, `GroupHeader`, `MeetingItem`, and `Message` objects.

Methods

Name	Returns	Description
Add([*subject*] [, *text*] [, *type*] [, *importance*])	Object (AppointmentItem or Message)	Creates and returns a new `Message` or `AppointmentItem` object in the `Messages` collection. Optionally, you can specify the *subject*, body *text*, *type* and *importance* level of the message.
Delete()	None	Deletes all the objects in the `Messages` collection.
GetFirst ([*type*])	Nothing or Object (AppointmentItem, GroupHeader, MeetingItem or Message)	Returns the first object in the `Messages` collection or first object with specific *type* property (`IPM.Note`, etc) if specified. It returns `Nothing` if there is no messages in the collection.
GetLast ([*type*])	Nothing or Object (AppointmentItem, GroupHeader, MeetingItem or Message)	Returns the last object in the `Messages` collection or last object with specific *type* property (`IPM.Note`, etc) if specified. It returns `Nothing` if there is no messages in the collection.
GetNext()	Nothing or Object (AppointmentItem, GroupHeader, MeetingItem or Message)	Returns the next object in the `Messages` collection. It returns `Nothing` if no next object exists, for example if already positioned at the end of the collection.
GetPrevious()	Nothing or Object (AppointmentItem, GroupHeader, MeetingItem or Message)	Returns the previous object in the `Messages` collection. It returns `Nothing` if no previous object exists, for example if already positioned at the beginning of the collection.
Sort([*SortOrder*] [, *PropTag*]) Sort([*SortOrder*] [, *name*])	None	The `Sort` method sorts the address entries in the collection on the specified property – either a named *CdoPropTag* constant or a tag *name* – according to the specified *sort order* (a constant of type `CdoSortOrder`). The default order is ascending if none is given. If no proptag or name is specified, a repeat is made of the last sort performed.

Properties

Name	Returns	Description
Application	String	The string 'Collaboration Data Objects'.
Class	CdoObjectClass	The class of the CDO Object. In this case, CdoMessages (16)
Count	Long	The number of AppointmentItem, MeetingItem, or GroupHeader and Message objects in the collection, or if this is not possible, &H7FFFFFFF.
Filter	MessageFilter	The MessageFilter object for the Messages collection.
Item (*index*) Item (*search*)	Object (AppointmentItem, GroupHeader, MeetingItem or Message)	Returns a single object from the Messages collection identified by either its *index* in the collection or some *search* criteria.
Parent	Folder	The Folder object containing this collection.
RAWTABLE	IUnknown	An IUnknown pointer to current message table.
Session	Session	The current CDO Session object.

Recipient Object

The Recipient object represents a recipient of a message.

Methods

Name	Returns	Description
Delete ()	None	Deletes the Recipient object from its parent Recipients collection.
GetFreeBusy (*StartTime*, *EndTime*, *Interval*)	String	A string indicating the free/busy status of the user for each *Interval* (in minutes) between *StartTime* and *EndTime*.
IsSameAs (*RecObject2*)	Boolean	True if the Recipient object is the same as *RecObject2*.
Resolve ([*ShowDialog*])	None	Assembles the recipient's address entry information into a full messaging address. Optionally, if ambiguities occur, *ShowDialog* can be set to true to prompt the user for clarification.

Properties

Name	Returns	Description
Address	String	The full address for the recipient.
AddressEntry	AddressEntry	The AddressEntry object representing the recipient.
AmbiguousNames	AddressEntries	The AddressEntries collection of suggestions that might resolve the ambiguity in an AddressEntry object.
Application	String	The string 'Collaboration Data Objects'.
Class	CdoObjectClass	The class of the CDO Object. In this case, CdoRecipient(4)
DisplayType	CdoDisplayType	The display type of the recipient (User, Distribution List, etc)
ID	String	The unique identifier of the current Recipient object.
Index	Long	The index number of the Recipient object within the Recipients collection.
MeetingResponse Status	CdoResponseStatus	The status of this recipient's response to a meeting request.
Name	String	The name of the Recipient object.
Parent	Recipients	The Recipients collection containing this object.
Session	Session	The current CDO Session object.
Type	CdoRecipientType	The type of the Recipient object, either To, Cc, or Bcc.

Recipients Collection

The Recipients collection object contains zero or more Recipient objects. Note that Recipients is regarded as a small collection for which the count property is reliable.

Methods

Name	Returns	Description
Add([*name*] [, *address*] [, *type*] [, *entryID*])	Recipient	Adds and returns a new Recipient object to the Recipients collection. Optionally you can specify the recipient's display name, full address, recipient type and unique ID for the corresponding AddressEntry object if appropriate.

Table Continued on Following Page

Name	Returns	Description
AddMultiple (*names* [, *type*])	None	Adds zero or more new Recipient objects in the Recipients collection as specified by a list of display *names* or addresses. You can also specify what *type* of recipient they are.
Delete()	None	Deletes all the recipients in the Recipients collection.
GetFirstUnresolved ()	Recipient	Returns the first unresolved Recipient in the collection or Nothing if there aren't any.
GetFreeBusy (*StartTime*, *EndTime*, *Interval*)	String	Returns a string indicating the combined free/busy status of all the recipients for each *Interval* (in minutes) between *StartTime* and *EndTime*.
GetNextUnresolved ()	Recipient	Returns the next unresolved Recipient in the collection or Nothing if there aren't any.
Resolve ([*ShowDialog*])	None	Assembles in turn each of the recipients' address entry information into a full messaging address. Optionally, if ambiguities occur, *ShowDialog* can be set to true to prompt the user for clarification.

Properties

Name	Returns	Description
Application	String	The string 'Collaboration Data Objects'.
Class	CdoObjectClass	The class of the CDO Object. In this case, CdoRecipients(17)
Count	Long	The exact number of Recipient objects in the collection.
Item(*Index*)	Recipient	Returns Recipient object number *index* from the collection.
RAWTABLE	IUnknown	An IUnknown pointer to the current Recipient table.
Parent	Message	The Message collection holding this collection.

Name	Returns	Description
Resolved	Boolean	True if all of the recipients in the collection have had their address information resolved.
Session	Session	The current CDO Session object.

RecurrencePattern Object

The RecurrencePattern object describes the recurrence pattern for an AppointmentItem object. This object has no methods.

Properties

Name	Returns	Description
Application	String	The string 'Collaboration Data Objects'.
Class	CdoObjectClass	The class of the CDO Object. In this case, CdoRecurrencePattern(28)
DayOfMonth	Long	The day of the month on which the appointment recurs.
DayOfWeekMask	Long	The mask for the days of the week on which the appointment recurs.
Duration	Long	The duration of the recurring appointment in minutes.
EndTime	Variant (vbDate)	The finish time for each recurrence of the appointment.
Instance	Long	The specific day of the month on which an appointment occurs when described as 'First Wednesday of the month'.
Interval	Long	The number of recurrence units between each appointment. See RecurrenceType property.
MonthOfYear	Long	The month of the year in which the appointment recurs.
NoEndDate	Boolean	True if the recurrence pattern has no end date.
Occurrences	Long	The number of times the appointment reoccurs.
Parent	AppointmentItem	The parent AppointmentItem object.

Name	Returns	Description
PatternEndDate	Variant (vbDate)	The last possible date for the last appointment to occur.
PatternStartDate	Variant (vbDate)	The first possible date that the appointment may reoccur.
RecurrenceType	CdoRecurTypes	The recurrence unit and the frequency with which the appointment recurs. (Daily, Weekly, etc).
Session	Session	The current CDO Session object.
StartTime	Variant (vbDate)	The starting time for each recurrence of the appointment.

Session Object

The Session object is CDO's topmost object, offering access to a CDO application's mail and collaboration objects.

Methods

Name	Returns	Description
AddressBook ([recipients] [, caption] [, oneAddress] [, forceResolution] [, recipLists] [, toLabel] [, ccLabel] [, bccLabel] [, parentWindow])	Recipients	Displays the users address book in a dialog box. Addresses then selected are returned in a Recipients collection. Optionally, you can specify the recipients collection to add addresses to, a caption for the book, whether users must select one address at a time, whether the addresses selected must be resolved, which of the To, Cc and Bcc list boxes to display, their display labels, and finally a handle to the parentWindow.
CompareIDs (ID1, ID2)	Boolean	Returns True if ID1 and ID2 represent the same CDO object, or False if not.
CreateConversation Index ([ParentIndex])	String	Creates or updates a new conversation index or a child conversation index based on a parent conversation index.
DeliverNow()	None	Requests the immediate delivery of all undelivered messages submitted in the current session.
GetAddressEntry (ID)	AddressEntry	Returns the AddressEntry object with the ID specified.

Name	Returns	Description
GetAddressList (*ALType*)	AddressList	Returns either the default global or personal address list as specified by *ALType*.
GetArticle (*ArticleID*, *FolderID* [, *StoreID*])	Message	Returns a `Message` object with ID *ArticleID* from the folder (and infostore) as specified.
GetDefaultFolder (*Type* [, *mailbox*])	Folder	Returns the default folder of the specified *type* (from the specified *mailbox* if needed).
GetFolder (*folderID* [, *storeID*])	Folder	Returns a `Folder` object with ID *folderID* (from a certain message store if needed).
GetInfoStore (*storeID*)	InfoStore	Returns an `InfoStore` object with the given ID.
GetMessage (*messageID* [, *storeID*])	Object	Returns a `Message` object with ID *messageID* (from a certain message store if needed).
GetOption (*OptType*)	Variant	Returns the user preference for displaying the calendar.
Logoff()	None	Logs off and ends the session.
Logon ([*profileName*] [, *profilePassword*] [, *showDialog*] [, *newSession*] [, *parentWindow*] [, *NoMail*] [, *ProfileInfo*])	None	Logs on to the messaging system, optionally supplying the *profile name* and *password* to use, whether to display the **Show Profile** dialog box, if the application should start a new CDO session, the handle to the *parentWindow*, if mail should be disabled and the info needed to create a new profile for the session.
SetLocaleIDs (*LocaleID*, *CodePageID*)	None	Sets the *Locale* and *Codepage IDs* for the current session.
SetOption (*OptType*, *OptValue*)	None	Sets the user preference for displaying the calendar either by *name* or by *value*.

Properties

Name	Returns	Description
AddressLists AddressLists (*index*) AddressLists (*name*)	Object (AddressLists or AddressList)	Returns an AddressList as specified by its *index* in the AddressLists collection or its *name*. If neither is specified, returns the entire AddressLists collection.
Application	String	The string 'Collaboration Data Objects'.
Class	CdoObjectClass	The class of the CDO Object. In this case, CdoSession(0)
CurrentUser	AddressEntry	The AddressEntry object for the user currently using the application.
Inbox	Folder	The current user's Inbox folder.
InfoStores InfoStores (*index*) InfoStores (*name*)	InfoStores	Returns an InfoStores as specified by its *index* in the InfoStores collection or its *name*. If neither is specified, returns the entire InfoStores collection.
MAPIOBJECT	IUnknown	An IUnknown pointer to the session object.
Name	String	The display name of the profile logged on to this session.
OperatingSystem	String	The Name and version number of the current operating system.
Outbox	Folder	The current user's Outbox folder
OutOfOffice	Boolean	True if the user is currently considered out of the office.
OutOfOfficeText	String	The text of the message others receive if they send mail to this user while the user is out of the office.
Parent	Nothing	Nothing.
Session	Session	The current CDO Session object.
Version	String	The version number of CDO as a string, for example "1.2.1".

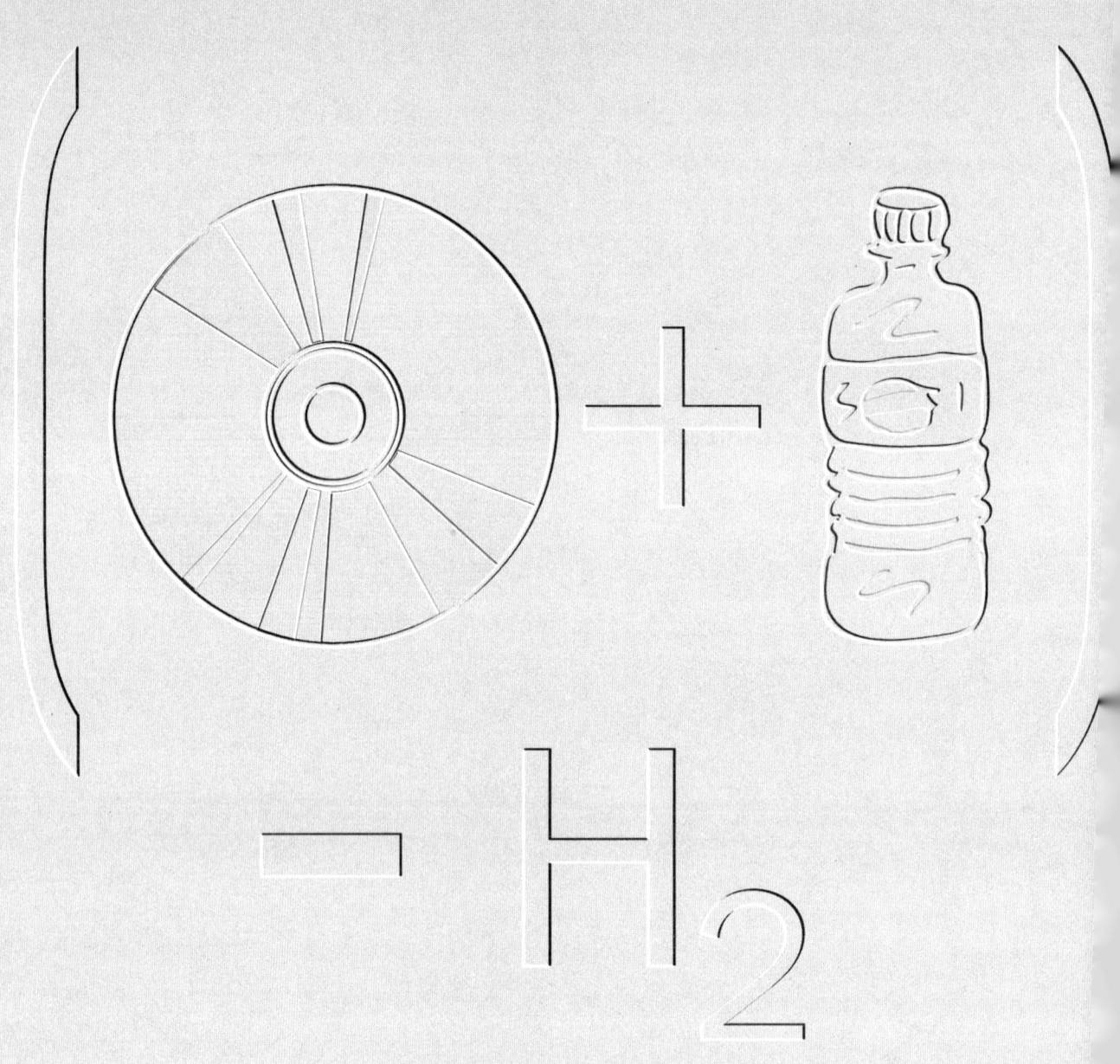

B

CDO 1.21 Constants

The following constants are predefined in CDO 1.21. To include them in ASP code, set a reference to the type library with a METADATA tag:

```
<!-- METADATA TYPE="typelib" uuid="{3FA7DEA7-6438-101B-ACC1-00AA00423326}" -->
```

You can include this METADATA tag in individual pages or in the global.asa page. For Visual Basic these constants are included automatically when you reference the CDO library.

Note that the cdo.dll file also holds a number of constants with the prefixes ActMsg and mapi that are not detailed here. This is because both groups of constants are redefined in CDO with the following constants.

CdoAddressListTypes

Used in conjunction with the Session object's GetAddressList method. Corresponds to the type of AddressList the user is trying to access.

Name	Value	Description
CdoAddressListGAL	0	Global address list
CdoAddressListPAB	1	Personal address book

CdoAttachmentType

Defines the type of attachment fixed to this message. Also implies how to stream the attachment to the message, as follows.

Name	Value	Description
CdoEmbeddedMessage	4	Message attachment. Use ID property of Message object to be attached
CdoFileData	1	File attachment. Use Attachment object's ReadFromFile method.
CdoFileLink	2	File link attachment. Use Attachment object's Source method.
CdoOle	3	OLE docfile attachment. Use Attachment object's ReadFromFile method.

CdoBusyStatus

Specifies a user's busy status for the duration of an appointment.

Name	Value	Description
CdoBusy	2	This messaging user already has at least one meeting he has agreed to at this time.
CdoFree	0	This messaging user has no other meeting invites so far at this time.
CdoOutOfOffice	3	This messaging user has marked some or all of this time as being out of the office.
CdoTentative	1	This messaging user has at least one

CdoDaysOfWeek

Used with the RecurrencePattern object to define on what day(s) an appointment occurs.

Name	Value	Description
CdoSunday	1	The AppointmentItem recurs on Sundays
CdoMonday	2	The AppointmentItem recurs on Mondays
CdoTuesday	4	The AppointmentItem recurs on Tuesdays
CdoWednesday	8	The AppointmentItem recurs on Wednesdays
CdoThursday	16	The AppointmentItem recurs on Thursdays
CdoFriday	32	The AppointmentItem recurs on Fridays
CdoSaturday	64	The AppointmentItem recurs on Saturdays

CdoDefaultFolderTypes

Used primarily with the `Session.GetDefaultFolder` method to specify which default folder is to be retrieved.

Name	Value	Description
CdoDefaultFolderCalendar	0	Calendar
CdoDefaultFolderContacts	5	Contacts
CdoDefaultFolderDeletedItems	4	Deleted Items
CdoDefaultFolderInbox	1	Inbox
CdoDefaultFolderJournal	6	Journal
CdoDefaultFolderNotes	7	Notes
CdoDefaultFolderOutbox	2	Outbox
CdoDefaultFolderSentItems	3	SentItems
CdoDefaultFolderTasks	8	Tasks

CdoDisplayType

Determines the type of address entry that has been added to an `AddressEntries` collection. Enables ability to create patterns for addressee types based on this property.

Name	Value	Description
CdoAgent	3	An automated mail agent
CdoDistList	1	A public distribution list
CdoForum	2	A public folder
CdoOrganization	4	An organization
CdoPrivateDistList	5	A private distribution list
CdoRemoteUser	6	A remote user
CdoUser	0	A local user

CdoErrorType

When a method is called, if the return value is 0, the method has worked and no ill effects have occurred. If the return value is non-zero, it will correspond to one of the following values that specify the various CDO errors.

Name	Value
CdoE_ACCOUNT_DISABLED	&H80040124
CdoE_AMBIGUOUS_RECIP	&H80040700
CdoE_BAD_CHARWIDTH	&H80040103
CdoE_BAD_COLUMN	&H80040118
CdoE_BAD_VALUE	&H80040301
CdoE_BUSY	&H8004010B
CdoE_CALL_FAILED	&H80004005
CdoE_CANCEL	&H80040501
CdoE_COLLISION	&H80040604
CdoE_COMPUTED	&H8004011A
CdoE_CORRUPT_DATA	&H8004011B
CdoE_CORRUPT_STORE	&H80040600
CdoE_DECLINE_COPY	&H80040306
CdoE_DISK_ERROR	&H80040116
CdoE_END_OF_SESSION	&H80040200
CdoE_EXTENDED_ERROR	&H80040119
CdoE_FAILONEPROVIDER	&H8004011D
CdoE_FOLDER_CYCLE	&H8004060B
CdoE_HAS_FOLDERS	&H80040609
CdoE_HAS_MESSAGES	&H8004060A
CdoE_INTERFACE_NOT_SUPPORTED	&H80004002
CdoE_INVALID_ACCESS_TIME	&H80040123
CdoE_INVALID_BOOKMARK	&H80040405
CdoE_INVALID_ENTRYID	&H80040107
CdoE_INVALID_OBJECT	&H80040108
CdoE_INVALID_PARAMETER	&H80070057

Name	Value
CdoE_INVALID_TYPE	&H80040302
CdoE_INVALID_WORKSTATION_ACCOUNT	&H80040122
CdoE_LOGON_FAILED	&H80040111
CdoE_MISSING_REQUIRED_COLUMN	&H80040202
CdoE_NETWORK_ERROR	&H80040115
CdoE_NO_ACCESS	&H80070005
CdoE_NO_RECIPIENTS	&H80040607
CdoE_NO_SUPPORT	&H80040102
CdoE_NO_SUPPRESS	&H80040602
CdoE_NON_STANDARD	&H80040606
CdoE_NOT_ENOUGH_DISK	&H8004010D
CdoE_NOT_ENOUGH_MEMORY	&H8007000E
CdoE_NOT_ENOUGH_RESOURCES	&H8004010E
CdoE_NOT_FOUND	&H8004010F
CdoE_NOT_IN_QUEUE	&H80040601
CdoE_NOT_INITIALIZED	&H80040605
CdoE_NOT_ME	&H80040502
CdoE_OBJECT_CHANGED	&H80040109
CdoE_OBJECT_DELETED	&H8004010A
CdoE_PASSWORD_CHANGE_REQUIRED	&H80040120
CdoE_PASSWORD_EXPIRED	&H80040121
CdoE_SESSION_LIMIT	&H80040112
CdoE_STRING_TOO_LONG	&H80040105
CdoE_SUBMITTED	&H80040608
CdoE_TABLE_EMPTY	&H80040402
CdoE_TABLE_TOO_BIG	&H80040403
CdoE_TIMEOUT	&H80040401
CdoE_TOO_BIG	&H80040305
CdoE_TOO_COMPLEX	&H80040117
CdoE_TYPE_NO_SUPPORT	&H80040303

Name	Value
CdoE_UNABLE_TO_ABORT	&H80040114
CdoE_UNABLE_TO_COMPLETE	&H80040400
CdoE_UNCONFIGURED	&H8004011C
CdoE_UNEXPECTED_ID	&H80040307
CdoE_UNEXPECTED_TYPE	&H80040304
CdoE_UNKNOWN_CPID	&H8004011E
CdoE_UNKNOWN_ENTRYID	&H80040201
CdoE_UNKNOWN_FLAGS	&H80040106
CdoE_UNKNOWN_LCID	&H8004011F
CdoE_USER_CANCEL	&H80040113
CdoE_VERSION	&H80040110
CdoE_WAIT	&H80040500
CdoW_APPROX_COUNT	&H00040482
CdoW_CANCEL_MESSAGE	&H00040580
CdoW_ERRORS_RETURNED	&H00040380
CdoW_NO_SERVICE	&H00040203
CdoW_PARTIAL_COMPLETION	&H00040680
CdoW_POSITION_CHANGED	&H00040481

CdoFieldType

Defines constants representing the basic types for Visual Basic.

Name	Value	Description
CdoArray	8192	Multiple values
CdoBlob	65	Binary block
CdoBoolean	11	Boolean
CdoCurrency	6	Currency
CdoDataObject	13	Embedded OLE
CdoDate	7	Date and time
CdoDouble	5	Long floating point
CdoEmpty	0	Empty field

Name	Value	Description
CdoInteger	2	Short integer
CdoLong	3	Long integer
CdoNull	1	No value
CdoSingle	4	Floating point
CdoString	8	String

CdoImportance

Defines the three levels of importance a message can have.

Name	Value	Description
CdoHigh	2	High importance
CdoLow	0	Low importance
CdoNormal	1	Normal importance

CdoLimits

Name	Value	Description
CdoMaxCount	&H7FFFFFFF	Indicating that the count of a large collection is not accurate.

CdoMeetingStatusTypes

Used with the `AppointmentItem`'s `MeetingStatus` property to define the status of the meeting.

Name	Value	Description
CdoMeeting	1	The `AppointmentItem` has been or is to be made into a meeting
CdoMeetingCanceled	5	The meeting has been canceled
CdoMeetingReceived	3	The requests for the meeting have been received by the intended attendees
CdoNonMeeting	0	The `AppointmentItem` has been scheduled by this messaging user alone and does not represent a meeting

CdoMeetingType

Used with the `MeetingItem` object's `MeetingType` property to define the type of this meeting item.

Name	Value	Description
CdoMeetingRequest	1	This meeting item is a meeting request
CdoMeetingResponse	2	This meeting item is a response to a meeting request

CdoObjectClass

A read-only value contained in every CDO object that identifies the class of the object. Read with the object's class property.

Name	Value	Description
CdoAddressEntries	21	`AddressEntries` collection
CdoAddressEntry	8	`AddressEntry`
CdoAddressFilter	9	`AddressFilter`
CdoAddressList	7	`AddressList`
CdoAddressLists	20	`AddressLists` collection
CdoAppointment	26	`AppointmentItem`
CdoAttachment	5	`Attachment`
CdoAttachments	18	`Attachments` collection
CdoException	30	`Exception`
CdoExceptions	29	`Exceptions` collection
CdoField	6	`Field`
CdoFields	19	`Fields` collection
CdoFolder	2	`Folder`
CdoFolders	15	`Folders` collection
CdoGroupHeader	25	Group Header
CdoHiddenMessages	32	`HiddenMessages` collection
CdoInfoStore	1	`InfoStore`
CdoInfoStores	14	`InfoStores` collection
CdoMeetingItem	27	`MeetingItem`
CdoMeetingPlanner	31	`MeetingPlanner`

Name	Value	Description
CdoMessageFilter	10	MessageFilter
CdoMessages	16	Messages collection
CdoMsg	3	Message
CdoRecipient	4	Recipient
CdoRecipients	17	Recipients collection
CdoRecurrencePattern	28	RecurrencePattern
CdoSession	0	Session
CdoUnknown	-1	Undefined

CdoPropTags

Name	Value
CdoPR_7BIT_DISPLAY_NAME	&H39FF001E
CdoPR_AB_DEFAULT_DIR	&H3D060102
CdoPR_AB_DEFAULT_PAB	&H3D070102
CdoPR_AB_PROVIDER_ID	&H36150102
CdoPR_AB_PROVIDERS	&H3D010102
CdoPR_AB_SEARCH_PATH	&H3D051102
CdoPR_AB_SEARCH_PATH_UPDATE	&H3D110102
CdoPR_ACCESS	&H0FF40003
CdoPR_ACCESS_LEVEL	&H0FF70003
CdoPR_ACCOUNT	&H3A00001E
CdoPR_ACKNOWLEDGEMENT_MODE	&H00010003
CdoPR_ADDRTYPE	&H3002001E
CdoPR_ALTERNATE_RECIPIENT	&H3A010102
CdoPR_ALTERNATE_RECIPIENT_ALLOWED	&H0002000B
CdoPR_ANR	&H360C001E
CdoPR_ASSISTANT	&H3A30001E
CdoPR_ASSISTANT_TELEPHONE_NUMBER	&H3A2E001E
CdoPR_ASSOC_CONTENT_COUNT	&H36170003
CdoPR_ATTACH_ADDITIONAL_INFO	&H370F0102

Name	Value
CdoPR_ATTACH_DATA_BIN	&H37010102
CdoPR_ATTACH_DATA_OBJ	&H3701000D
CdoPR_ATTACH_ENCODING	&H37020102
CdoPR_ATTACH_EXTENSION	&H3703001E
CdoPR_ATTACH_FILENAME	&H3704001E
CdoPR_ATTACH_LONG_FILENAME	&H3707001E
CdoPR_ATTACH_LONG_PATHNAME	&H370D001E
CdoPR_ATTACH_METHOD	&H37050003
CdoPR_ATTACH_MIME_TAG	&H370E001E
CdoPR_ATTACH_NUM	&H0E210003
CdoPR_ATTACH_PATHNAME	&H3708001E
CdoPR_ATTACH_RENDERING	&H37090102
CdoPR_ATTACH_SIZE	&H0E200003
CdoPR_ATTACH_TAG	&H370A0102
CdoPR_ATTACH_TRANSPORT_NAME	&H370C001E
CdoPR_ATTACHMENT_X400_PARAMETERS	&H37000102
CdoPR_AUTHORIZING_USERS	&H00030102
CdoPR_AUTO_FORWARD_COMMENT	&H0004001E
CdoPR_AUTO_FORWARDED	&H0005000B
CdoPR_BEEPER_TELEPHONE_NUMBER	&H3A21001E
CdoPR_BIRTHDAY	&H3A420040
CdoPR_BODY	&H1000001E
CdoPR_BODY_CRC	&H0E1C0003
CdoPR_BUSINESS_ADDRESS_CITY	&H3A27001E
CdoPR_BUSINESS_ADDRESS_COUNTRY	&H3A26001E
CdoPR_BUSINESS_ADDRESS_POST_OFFICE_BOX	&H3A2B001E
CdoPR_BUSINESS_ADDRESS_POSTAL_CODE	&H3A2A001E
CdoPR_BUSINESS_ADDRESS_STATE_OR_PROVINCE	&H3A28001E
CdoPR_BUSINESS_ADDRESS_STREET	&H3A29001E
CdoPR_BUSINESS_FAX_NUMBER	&H3A24001E

Name	Value
CdoPR_BUSINESS_HOME_PAGE	&H3A51001E
CdoPR_BUSINESS_TELEPHONE_NUMBER	&H3A08001E
CdoPR_BUSINESS2_TELEPHONE_NUMBER	&H3A1B001E
CdoPR_CALLBACK_TELEPHONE_NUMBER	&H3A02001E
CdoPR_CAR_TELEPHONE_NUMBER	&H3A1E001E
CdoPR_CELLULAR_TELEPHONE_NUMBER	&H3A1C001E
CdoPR_CHILDRENS_NAMES	&H3A58101E
CdoPR_CLIENT_SUBMIT_TIME	&H00390040
CdoPR_COMMENT	&H3004001E
CdoPR_COMMON_VIEWS_ENTRYID	&H35E60102
CdoPR_COMPANY_MAIN_PHONE_NUMBER	&H3A57001E
CdoPR_COMPANY_NAME	&H3A16001E
CdoPR_COMPUTER_NETWORK_NAME	&H3A49001E
CdoPR_CONTACT_ADDRTYPES	&H3A54101E
CdoPR_CONTACT_DEFAULT_ADDRESS_INDEX	&H3A550003
CdoPR_CONTACT_EMAIL_ADDRESSES	&H3A56101E
CdoPR_CONTACT_ENTRYIDS	&H3A531102
CdoPR_CONTACT_VERSION	&H3A520048
CdoPR_CONTAINER_CLASS	&H3613001E
CdoPR_CONTAINER_CONTENTS	&H360F000D
CdoPR_CONTAINER_FLAGS	&H36000003
CdoPR_CONTAINER_HIERARCHY	&H360E000D
CdoPR_CONTAINER_MODIFY_VERSION	&H36140014
CdoPR_CONTENT_CONFIDENTIALITY_ALGORITHM_ID	&H00060102
CdoPR_CONTENT_CORRELATOR	&H00070102
CdoPR_CONTENT_COUNT	&H36020003
CdoPR_CONTENT_IDENTIFIER	&H0008001E
CdoPR_CONTENT_INTEGRITY_CHECK	&H0C000102
CdoPR_CONTENT_LENGTH	&H00090003
CdoPR_CONTENT_RETURN_REQUESTED	&H000A000B

Name	Value
CdoPR_CONTENT_UNREAD	&H36030003
CdoPR_CONTENTS_SORT_ORDER	&H360D1003
CdoPR_CONTROL_FLAGS	&H3F000003
CdoPR_CONTROL_ID	&H3F070102
CdoPR_CONTROL_STRUCTURE	&H3F010102
CdoPR_CONTROL_TYPE	&H3F020003
CdoPR_CONVERSATION_INDEX	&H00710102
CdoPR_CONVERSATION_KEY	&H000B0102
CdoPR_CONVERSATION_TOPIC	&H0070001E
CdoPR_CONVERSION_EITS	&H000C0102
CdoPR_CONVERSION_PROHIBITED	&H3A03000B
CdoPR_CONVERSION_WITH_LOSS_PROHIBITED	&H000D000B
CdoPR_CONVERTED_EITS	&H000E0102
CdoPR_CORRELATE	&H0E0C000B
CdoPR_CORRELATE_MTSID	&H0E0D0102
CdoPR_COUNTRY	&H3A26001E
CdoPR_CREATE_TEMPLATES	&H3604000D
CdoPR_CREATION_TIME	&H30070040
CdoPR_CREATION_VERSION	&H0E190014
CdoPR_CURRENT_VERSION	&H0E000014
CdoPR_CUSTOMER_ID	&H3A4A001E
CdoPR_DEF_CREATE_DL	&H36110102
CdoPR_DEF_CREATE_MAILUSER	&H36120102
CdoPR_DEFAULT_PROFILE	&H3D04000B
CdoPR_DEFAULT_STORE	&H3400000B
CdoPR_DEFAULT_VIEW_ENTRYID	&H36160102
CdoPR_DEFERRED_DELIVERY_TIME	&H000F0040
CdoPR_DELEGATION	&H007E0102
CdoPR_DELETE_AFTER_SUBMIT	&H0E01000B
CdoPR_DELIVER_TIME	&H00100040

Name	Value
CdoPR_DELIVERY_POINT	&H0C070003
CdoPR_DELTAX	&H3F030003
CdoPR_DELTAY	&H3F040003
CdoPR_DEPARTMENT_NAME	&H3A18001E
CdoPR_DEPTH	&H30050003
CdoPR_DETAILS_TABLE	&H3605000D
CdoPR_DISC_VAL	&H004A000B
CdoPR_DISCARD_REASON	&H00110003
CdoPR_DISCLOSE_RECIPIENTS	&H3A04000B
CdoPR_DISCLOSURE_OF_RECIPIENTS	&H0012000B
CdoPR_DISCRETE_VALUES	&H0E0E000B
CdoPR_DISPLAY_BCC	&H0E02001E
CdoPR_DISPLAY_CC	&H0E03001E
CdoPR_DISPLAY_NAME	&H3001001E
CdoPR_DISPLAY_NAME_PREFIX	&H3A45001E
CdoPR_DISPLAY_TO	&H0E04001E
CdoPR_DISPLAY_TYPE	&H39000003
CdoPR_DL_EXPANSION_HISTORY	&H00130102
CdoPR_DL_EXPANSION_PROHIBITED	&H0014000B
CdoPR_EMAIL_ADDRESS	&H3003001E
CdoPR_END_DATE	&H00610040
CdoPR_ENTRYID	&H0FFF0102
CdoPR_EXPIRY_TIME	&H00150040
CdoPR_EXPLICIT_CONVERSION	&H0C010003
CdoPR_FILTERING_HOOKS	&H3D080102
CdoPR_FINDER_ENTRYID	&H35E70102
CdoPR_FOLDER_ASSOCIATED_CONTENTS	&H3610000D
CdoPR_FOLDER_TYPE	&H36010003
CdoPR_FORM_CATEGORY	&H3304001E
CdoPR_FORM_CATEGORY_SUB	&H3305001E

Name	Value
CdoPR_FORM_CLSID	&H33020048
CdoPR_FORM_CONTACT_NAME	&H3303001E
CdoPR_FORM_DESIGNER_GUID	&H33090048
CdoPR_FORM_DESIGNER_NAME	&H3308001E
CdoPR_FORM_HIDDEN	&H3307000B
CdoPR_FORM_HOST_MAP	&H33061003
CdoPR_FORM_MESSAGE_BEHAVIOR	&H330A0003
CdoPR_FORM_VERSION	&H3301001E
CdoPR_FTP_SITE	&H3A4C001E
CdoPR_GENDER	&H3A4D0002
CdoPR_GENERATION	&H3A05001E
CdoPR_GIVEN_NAME	&H3A06001E
CdoPR_GOVERNMENT_ID_NUMBER	&H3A07001E
CdoPR_HASATTACH	&H0E1B000B
CdoPR_HEADER_FOLDER_ENTRYID	&H3E0A0102
CdoPR_HOBBIES	&H3A43001E
CdoPR_HOME_ADDRESS_CITY	&H3A59001E
CdoPR_HOME_ADDRESS_COUNTRY	&H3A5A001E
CdoPR_HOME_ADDRESS_POST_OFFICE_BOX	&H3A5E001E
CdoPR_HOME_ADDRESS_POSTAL_CODE	&H3A5B001E
CdoPR_HOME_ADDRESS_STATE_OR_PROVINCE	&H3A5C001E
CdoPR_HOME_ADDRESS_STREET	&H3A5D001E
CdoPR_HOME_FAX_NUMBER	&H3A25001E
CdoPR_HOME_TELEPHONE_NUMBER	&H3A09001E
CdoPR_HOME2_TELEPHONE_NUMBER	&H3A2F001E
CdoPR_ICON	&H0FFD0102
CdoPR_IDENTITY_DISPLAY	&H3E00001E
CdoPR_IDENTITY_ENTRYID	&H3E010102
CdoPR_IDENTITY_SEARCH_KEY	&H3E050102
CdoPR_IMPLICIT_CONVERSION_PROHIBITED	&H0016000B

Name	Value
CdoPR_IMPORTANCE	&H00170003
CdoPR_INCOMPLETE_COPY	&H0035000B
CdoPR_INITIAL_DETAILS_PANE	&H3F080003
CdoPR_INITIALS	&H3A0A001E
CdoPR_INSTANCE_KEY	&H0FF60102
CdoPR_INTERNET_APPROVED	&H1030001E
CdoPR_INTERNET_ARTICLE_NUMBER	&H0E230003
CdoPR_INTERNET_CONTROL	&H1031001E
CdoPR_INTERNET_DISTRIBUTION	&H1032001E
CdoPR_INTERNET_FOLLOWUP_TO	&H1033001E
CdoPR_INTERNET_LINES	&H10340003
CdoPR_INTERNET_MESSAGE_ID	&H1035001E
CdoPR_INTERNET_NEWSGROUPS	&H1036001E
CdoPR_INTERNET_NNTP_PATH	&H1038001E
CdoPR_INTERNET_ORGANIZATION	&H1037001E
CdoPR_INTERNET_PRECEDENCE	&H1041001E
CdoPR_INTERNET_REFERENCES	&H1039001E
CdoPR_IPM_ID	&H00180102
CdoPR_IPM_OUTBOX_ENTRYID	&H35E20102
CdoPR_IPM_OUTBOX_SEARCH_KEY	&H34110102
CdoPR_IPM_RETURN_REQUESTED	&H0C02000B
CdoPR_IPM_SENTMAIL_ENTRYID	&H35E40102
CdoPR_IPM_SENTMAIL_SEARCH_KEY	&H34130102
CdoPR_IPM_SUBTREE_ENTRYID	&H35E00102
CdoPR_IPM_SUBTREE_SEARCH_KEY	&H34100102
CdoPR_IPM_WASTEBASKET_ENTRYID	&H35E30102
CdoPR_IPM_WASTEBASKET_SEARCH_KEY	&H34120102
CdoPR_ISDN_NUMBER	&H3A2D001E
CdoPR_KEYWORD	&H3A0B001E
CdoPR_LANGUAGE	&H3A0C001E

Name	Value
CdoPR_LANGUAGES	&H002F001E
CdoPR_LAST_MODIFICATION_TIME	&H30080040
CdoPR_LATEST_DELIVERY_TIME	&H00190040
CdoPR_LOCALITY	&H3A27001E
CdoPR_LOCATION	&H3A0D001E
CdoPR_MAIL_PERMISSION	&H3A0E000B
CdoPR_MANAGER_NAME	&H3A4E001E
CdoPR_MAPPING_SIGNATURE	&H0FF80102
CdoPR_MDB_PROVIDER	&H34140102
CdoPR_MESSAGE_ATTACHMENTS	&H0E13000D
CdoPR_MESSAGE_CC_ME	&H0058000B
CdoPR_MESSAGE_CLASS	&H001A001E
CdoPR_MESSAGE_DELIVERY_ID	&H001B0102
CdoPR_MESSAGE_DELIVERY_TIME	&H0E060040
CdoPR_MESSAGE_DOWNLOAD_TIME	&H0E180003
CdoPR_MESSAGE_FLAGS	&H0E070003
CdoPR_MESSAGE_RECIP_ME	&H0059000B
CdoPR_MESSAGE_RECIPIENTS	&H0E12000D
CdoPR_MESSAGE_SECURITY_LABEL	&H001E0102
CdoPR_MESSAGE_SIZE	&H0E080003
CdoPR_MESSAGE_SUBMISSION_ID	&H00470102
CdoPR_MESSAGE_TO_ME	&H0057000B
CdoPR_MESSAGE_TOKEN	&H0C030102
CdoPR_MHS_COMMON_NAME	&H3A0F001E
CdoPR_MIDDLE_NAME	&H3A44001E
CdoPR_MINI_ICON	&H0FFC0102
CdoPR_MOBILE_TELEPHONE_NUMBER	&H3A1C001E
CdoPR_MODIFY_VERSION	&H0E1A0014
CdoPR_MSG_STATUS	&H0E170003
CdoPR_NDR_DIAG_CODE	&H0C050003

Name	Value
CdoPR_NDR_REASON_CODE	&H0C040003
CdoPR_NEWSGROUP_NAME	&H0E24001E
CdoPR_NICKNAME	&H3A4F001E
CdoPR_NNTP_XREF	&H1040001E
CdoPR_NON_RECEIPT_NOTIFICATION_REQUESTED	&H0C06000B
CdoPR_NON_RECEIPT_REASON	&H003E0003
CdoPR_NORMALIZED_SUBJECT	&H0E1D001E
CdoPR_OBJECT_TYPE	&H0FFE0003
CdoPR_OBSOLETED_IPMS	&H001F0102
CdoPR_OFFICE_LOCATION	&H3A19001E
CdoPR_OFFICE_TELEPHONE_NUMBER	&H3A08001E
CdoPR_OFFICE2_TELEPHONE_NUMBER	&H3A1B001E
CdoPR_ORGANIZATIONAL_ID_NUMBER	&H3A10001E
CdoPR_ORIG_MESSAGE_CLASS	&H004B001E
CdoPR_ORIGIN_CHECK	&H00270102
CdoPR_ORIGINAL_AUTHOR_ADDRTYPE	&H0079001E
CdoPR_ORIGINAL_AUTHOR_EMAIL_ADDRESS	&H007A001E
CdoPR_ORIGINAL_AUTHOR_ENTRYID	&H004C0102
CdoPR_ORIGINAL_AUTHOR_NAME	&H004D001E
CdoPR_ORIGINAL_AUTHOR_SEARCH_KEY	&H00560102
CdoPR_ORIGINAL_DELIVERY_TIME	&H00550040
CdoPR_ORIGINAL_DISPLAY_BCC	&H0072001E
CdoPR_ORIGINAL_DISPLAY_CC	&H0073001E
CdoPR_ORIGINAL_DISPLAY_NAME	&H3A13001E
CdoPR_ORIGINAL_DISPLAY_TO	&H0074001E
CdoPR_ORIGINAL_EITS	&H00210102
CdoPR_ORIGINAL_ENTRYID	&H3A120102
CdoPR_ORIGINAL_SEARCH_KEY	&H3A140102
CdoPR_ORIGINAL_SENDER_ADDRTYPE	&H0066001E
CdoPR_ORIGINAL_SENDER_EMAIL_ADDRESS	&H0067001E

Name	Value
CdoPR_ORIGINAL_SENDER_ENTRYID	&H005B0102
CdoPR_ORIGINAL_SENDER_NAME	&H005A001E
CdoPR_ORIGINAL_SENDER_SEARCH_KEY	&H005C0102
CdoPR_ORIGINAL_SENSITIVITY	&H002E0003
CdoPR_ORIGINAL_SENT_REPRESENTING_ADDRTYPE	&H0068001E
CdoPR_ORIGINAL_SENT_REPRESENTING_EMAIL_ADDRESS	&H0069001E
CdoPR_ORIGINAL_SENT_REPRESENTING_ENTRYID	&H005E0102
CdoPR_ORIGINAL_SENT_REPRESENTING_NAME	&H005D001E
CdoPR_ORIGINAL_SENT_REPRESENTING_SEARCH_KEY	&H005F0102
CdoPR_ORIGINAL_SUBJECT	&H0049001E
CdoPR_ORIGINAL_SUBMIT_TIME	&H004E0040
CdoPR_ORIGINALLY_INTENDED_RECIP_ADDRTYPE	&H007B001E
CdoPR_ORIGINALLY_INTENDED_RECIP_EMAIL_ADDRESS	&H007C001E
CdoPR_ORIGINALLY_INTENDED_RECIP_ENTRYID	&H10120102
CdoPR_ORIGINALLY_INTENDED_RECIPIENT_NAME	&H00200102
CdoPR_ORIGINATING_MTA_CERTIFICATE	&H0E250102
CdoPR_ORIGINATOR_AND_DL_EXPANSION_HISTORY	&H10020102
CdoPR_ORIGINATOR_CERTIFICATE	&H00220102
CdoPR_ORIGINATOR_DELIVERY_REPORT_REQUESTED	&H0023000B
CdoPR_ORIGINATOR_NON_DELIVERY_REPORT_REQUESTED	&H0C08000B
CdoPR_ORIGINATOR_REQUESTED_ALTERNATE_RECIPIENT	&H0C090102
CdoPR_ORIGINATOR_RETURN_ADDRESS	&H00240102
CdoPR_OTHER_ADDRESS_CITY	&H3A5F001E
CdoPR_OTHER_ADDRESS_COUNTRY	&H3A60001E
CdoPR_OTHER_ADDRESS_POST_OFFICE_BOX	&H3A64001E
CdoPR_OTHER_ADDRESS_POSTAL_CODE	&H3A61001E
CdoPR_OTHER_ADDRESS_STATE_OR_PROVINCE	&H3A62001E
CdoPR_OTHER_ADDRESS_STREET	&H3A63001E

Name	Value
CdoPR_OTHER_TELEPHONE_NUMBER	&H3A1F001E
CdoPR_OWN_STORE_ENTRYID	&H3E060102
CdoPR_OWNER_APPT_ID	&H00620003
CdoPR_PAGER_TELEPHONE_NUMBER	&H3A21001E
CdoPR_PARENT_DISPLAY	&H0E05001E
CdoPR_PARENT_ENTRYID	&H0E090102
CdoPR_PARENT_KEY	&H00250102
CdoPR_PERSONAL_HOME_PAGE	&H3A50001E
CdoPR_PHYSICAL_DELIVERY_BUREAU_FAX_DELIVERY	&H0C0A000B
CdoPR_PHYSICAL_DELIVERY_MODE	&H0C0B0003
CdoPR_PHYSICAL_DELIVERY_REPORT_REQUEST	&H0C0C0003
CdoPR_PHYSICAL_FORWARDING_ADDRESS	&H0C0D0102
CdoPR_PHYSICAL_FORWARDING_ADDRESS_REQUESTED	&H0C0E000B
CdoPR_PHYSICAL_FORWARDING_PROHIBITED	&H0C0F000B
CdoPR_PHYSICAL_RENDITION_ATTRIBUTES	&H0C100102
CdoPR_POST_FOLDER_ENTRIES	&H103B0102
CdoPR_POST_FOLDER_NAMES	&H103C001E
CdoPR_POST_OFFICE_BOX	&H3A2B001E
CdoPR_POST_REPLY_DENIED	&H103F0102
CdoPR_POST_REPLY_FOLDER_ENTRIES	&H103D0102
CdoPR_POST_REPLY_FOLDER_NAMES	&H103E001E
CdoPR_POSTAL_ADDRESS	&H3A15001E
CdoPR_POSTAL_CODE	&H3A2A001E
CdoPR_PREFERRED_BY_NAME	&H3A47001E
CdoPR_PREPROCESS	&H0E22000B
CdoPR_PRIMARY_CAPABILITY	&H39040102
CdoPR_PRIMARY_FAX_NUMBER	&H3A23001E
CdoPR_PRIMARY_TELEPHONE_NUMBER	&H3A1A001E
CdoPR_PRIORITY	&H00260003
CdoPR_PROFESSION	&H3A46001E

Name	Value
CdoPR_PROFILE_NAME	&H3D12001E
CdoPR_PROOF_OF_DELIVERY	&H0C110102
CdoPR_PROOF_OF_DELIVERY_REQUESTED	&H0C12000B
CdoPR_PROOF_OF_SUBMISSION	&H0E260102
CdoPR_PROOF_OF_SUBMISSION_REQUESTED	&H0028000B
CdoPR_PROVIDER_DISPLAY	&H3006001E
CdoPR_PROVIDER_DLL_NAME	&H300A001E
CdoPR_PROVIDER_ORDINAL	&H300D0003
CdoPR_PROVIDER_SUBMIT_TIME	&H00480040
CdoPR_PROVIDER_UID	&H300C0102
CdoPR_RADIO_TELEPHONE_NUMBER	&H3A1D001E
CdoPR_RCVD_REPRESENTING_ADDRTYPE	&H0077001E
CdoPR_RCVD_REPRESENTING_EMAIL_ADDRESS	&H0078001E
CdoPR_RCVD_REPRESENTING_ENTRYID	&H00430102
CdoPR_RCVD_REPRESENTING_NAME	&H0044001E
CdoPR_RCVD_REPRESENTING_SEARCH_KEY	&H00520102
CdoPR_READ_RECEIPT_ENTRYID	&H00460102
CdoPR_READ_RECEIPT_REQUESTED	&H0029000B
CdoPR_READ_RECEIPT_SEARCH_KEY	&H00530102
CdoPR_RECEIPT_TIME	&H002A0040
CdoPR_RECEIVE_FOLDER_SETTINGS	&H3415000D
CdoPR_RECEIVED_BY_ADDRTYPE	&H0075001E
CdoPR_RECEIVED_BY_EMAIL_ADDRESS	&H0076001E
CdoPR_RECEIVED_BY_ENTRYID	&H003F0102
CdoPR_RECEIVED_BY_NAME	&H0040001E
CdoPR_RECEIVED_BY_SEARCH_KEY	&H00510102
CdoPR_RECIPIENT_CERTIFICATE	&H0C130102
CdoPR_RECIPIENT_NUMBER_FOR_ADVICE	&H0C14001E
CdoPR_RECIPIENT_REASSIGNMENT_PROHIBITED	&H002B000B
CdoPR_RECIPIENT_STATUS	&H0E150003

Name	Value
CdoPR_RECIPIENT_TYPE	&H0C150003
CdoPR_RECORD_KEY	&H0FF90102
CdoPR_REDIRECTION_HISTORY	&H002C0102
CdoPR_REFERRED_BY_NAME	&H3A47001E
CdoPR_REGISTERED_MAIL_TYPE	&H0C160003
CdoPR_RELATED_IPMS	&H002D0102
CdoPR_REMOTE_PROGRESS	&H3E0B0003
CdoPR_REMOTE_PROGRESS_TEXT	&H3E0C001E
CdoPR_REMOTE_VALIDATE_OK	&H3E0D000B
CdoPR_RENDERING_POSITION	&H370B0003
CdoPR_REPLY_RECIPIENT_ENTRIES	&H004F0102
CdoPR_REPLY_RECIPIENT_NAMES	&H0050001E
CdoPR_REPLY_REQUESTED	&H0C17000B
CdoPR_REPLY_TIME	&H00300040
CdoPR_REPORT_ENTRYID	&H00450102
CdoPR_REPORT_NAME	&H003A001E
CdoPR_REPORT_SEARCH_KEY	&H00540102
CdoPR_REPORT_TAG	&H00310102
CdoPR_REPORT_TEXT	&H1001001E
CdoPR_REPORT_TIME	&H00320040
CdoPR_REPORTING_DL_NAME	&H10030102
CdoPR_REPORTING_MTA_CERTIFICATE	&H10040102
CdoPR_REQUESTED_DELIVERY_METHOD	&H0C180003
CdoPR_RESOURCE_FLAGS	&H30090003
CdoPR_RESOURCE_METHODS	&H3E020003
CdoPR_RESOURCE_PATH	&H3E07001E
CdoPR_RESOURCE_TYPE	&H3E030003
CdoPR_RESPONSE_REQUESTED	&H0063000B
CdoPR_RESPONSIBILITY	&H0E0F000B
CdoPR_RETURNED_IPM	&H0033000B

Name	Value
CdoPR_ROW_TYPE	&H0FF50003
CdoPR_ROWID	&H30000003
CdoPR_RTF_COMPRESSED	&H10090102
CdoPR_RTF_IN_SYNC	&H0E1F000B
CdoPR_RTF_SYNC_BODY_COUNT	&H10070003
CdoPR_RTF_SYNC_BODY_CRC	&H10060003
CdoPR_RTF_SYNC_BODY_TAG	&H1008001E
CdoPR_RTF_SYNC_PREFIX_COUNT	&H10100003
CdoPR_RTF_SYNC_TRAILING_COUNT	&H10110003
CdoPR_SEARCH	&H3607000D
CdoPR_SEARCH_KEY	&H300B0102
CdoPR_SECURITY	&H00340003
CdoPR_SELECTABLE	&H3609000B
CdoPR_SEND_INTERNET_ENCODING	&H3A710003
CdoPR_SEND_RICH_INFO	&H3A40000B
CdoPR_SENDER_ADDRTYPE	&H0C1E001E
CdoPR_SENDER_EMAIL_ADDRESS	&H0C1F001E
CdoPR_SENDER_ENTRYID	&H0C190102
CdoPR_SENDER_NAME	&H0C1A001E
CdoPR_SENDER_SEARCH_KEY	&H0C1D0102
CdoPR_SENSITIVITY	&H00360003
CdoPR_SENT_REPRESENTING_ADDRTYPE	&H0064001E
CdoPR_SENT_REPRESENTING_EMAIL_ADDRESS	&H0065001E
CdoPR_SENT_REPRESENTING_ENTRYID	&H00410102
CdoPR_SENT_REPRESENTING_NAME	&H0042001E
CdoPR_SENT_REPRESENTING_SEARCH_KEY	&H003B0102
CdoPR_SENTMAIL_ENTRYID	&H0E0A0102
CdoPR_SERVICE_DELETE_FILES	&H3D10101E
CdoPR_SERVICE_DLL_NAME	&H3D0A001E
CdoPR_SERVICE_ENTRY_NAME	&H3D0B001E

Name	Value
CdoPR_SERVICE_EXTRA_UIDS	&H3D0D0102
CdoPR_SERVICE_NAME	&H3D09001E
CdoPR_SERVICE_SUPPORT_FILES	&H3D0F101E
CdoPR_SERVICE_UID	&H3D0C0102
CdoPR_SERVICES	&H3D0E0102
CdoPR_SPOOLER_STATUS	&H0E100003
CdoPR_SPOUSE_NAME	&H3A48001E
CdoPR_START_DATE	&H00600040
CdoPR_STATE_OR_PROVINCE	&H3A28001E
CdoPR_STATUS	&H360B0003
CdoPR_STATUS_CODE	&H3E040003
CdoPR_STATUS_STRING	&H3E08001E
CdoPR_STORE_ENTRYID	&H0FFB0102
CdoPR_STORE_PROVIDERS	&H3D000102
CdoPR_STORE_RECORD_KEY	&H0FFA0102
CdoPR_STORE_STATE	&H340E0003
CdoPR_STORE_SUPPORT_MASK	&H340D0003
CdoPR_STREET_ADDRESS	&H3A29001E
CdoPR_SUBFOLDERS	&H360A000B
CdoPR_SUBJECT	&H0037001E
CdoPR_SUBJECT_IPM	&H00380102
CdoPR_SUBJECT_PREFIX	&H003D001E
CdoPR_SUBMIT_FLAGS	&H0E140003
CdoPR_SUPERSEDES	&H103A001E
CdoPR_SUPPLEMENTARY_INFO	&H0C1B001E
CdoPR_SURNAME	&H3A11001E
CdoPR_TELEX_NUMBER	&H3A2C001E
CdoPR_TEMPLATEID	&H39020102
CdoPR_TITLE	&H3A17001E
CdoPR_TNEF_CORRELATION_KEY	&H007F0102

Name	Value
CdoPR_TRANSMITABLE_DISPLAY_NAME	&H3A20001E
CdoPR_TRANSPORT_KEY	&H0E160003
CdoPR_TRANSPORT_MESSAGE_HEADERS	&H007D001E
CdoPR_TRANSPORT_PROVIDERS	&H3D020102
CdoPR_TRANSPORT_STATUS	&H0E110003
CdoPR_TTYTDD_PHONE_NUMBER	&H3A4B001E
CdoPR_TYPE_OF_MTS_USER	&H0C1C0003
CdoPR_USER_CERTIFICATE	&H3A220102
CdoPR_USER_X509_CERTIFICATE	&H3A701102
CdoPR_VALID_FOLDER_MASK	&H35DF0003
CdoPR_VIEWS_ENTRYID	&H35E50102
CdoPR_WEDDING_ANNIVERSARY	&H3A410040
CdoPR_X400_CONTENT_TYPE	&H003C0102
CdoPR_X400_DEFERRED_DELIVERY_CANCEL	&H3E09000B
CdoPR_XPOS	&H3F050003
CdoPR_YPOS	&H3F060003

CdoRecipientType

Used when adding recipients to a message to define how the message is sent to them

Name	Value	Description
CdoBcc	3	BCC to recipient
CdoCc	2	CC to recipient
CdoTo	1	Primary recipient

CdoRecurTypes

Used with the RecurrenceType property of the RecurrencePattern object to define how often a appointment recurs.

Name	Value	Description
CdoRecurTypeDaily	0	The AppointmentItem recurs daily
CdoRecurTypeMonthly	2	The AppointmentItem recurs monthly

Name	Value	Description
CdoRecurTypeMonthlyNth	3	The AppointmentItem recurs monthly for a specific pattern
CdoRecurTypeWeekly	1	The AppointmentItem recurs weekly
CdoRecurTypeYearly	5	The AppointmentItem recurs yearly
CdoRecurTypeYearlyNth	6	The AppointmentItem recurs yearly for a specific pattern

CdoResponseStatus

Defines a user's status with respect to a meeting.

Name	Value	Description
CdoResponseAccepted	3	This messaging user has responded to the meeting request with a firm acceptance
CdoResponseDeclined	4	This messaging user has responded to the meeting request by declining.
CdoResponseNone	0	This messaging user has not responded to the meeting request
CdoResponseNotResponded	5	This messaging user has not responded to the meeting request
CdoResponseOrganized	1	This messaging user initiated the meeting request
CdoResponseTentative	2	This messaging user has responded to the meeting request with a tentative acceptance

CdoSensitivity

Defines the possible values for the Message.Sensitivity property.

Name	Value	Description
CdoConfidential	3	Confidential sensitivity
CdoNoSensitivity	0	Normal sensitivity
CdoPersonal	1	Personal sensitivity
CdoPrivate	2	Private sensitivity

CdoSortOrder

Defines the possible sort orders for use with the various `Sort` methods in CDO.

Name	Value	Description
CdoAscending	1	Ascending sort
CdoDescending	2	Descending sort
CdoNone	0	Unsorted

CdoTimeZones

Defines the possible values for the `ContainerRenderer.Timezone` property that specifies the timezone in which the calendar should be set.

Name	Value	Difference from GMT
CdoTmzAbuDhabi	24	+4:00
CdoTmzAdelaide	19	+9:30
CdoTmzAlaska	14	-9:00
CdoTmzAlmaty	46	+6:00
CdoTmzArizona	38	-7:00
CdoTmzAthens	7	+2:00
CdoTmzAtlanticCanada	9	-4:00
CdoTmzAzores	29	-1:00
CdoTmzBaghdad	26	+3:00
CdoTmzBangkok	22	+7:00
CdoTmzBeijing	45	+8:00
CdoTmzBerlin	4	+1:00
CdoTmzBogota	35	-5:00
CdoTmzBombay	23	+5:30
CdoTmzBrisbane	18	+10:00
CdoTmzBuenosAires	32	-3:00
CdoTmzCairo	49	+2:00
CdoTmzCaracas	33	-4:00
CdoTmzCentral	11	-6:00

Name	Value	Difference from GMT
CdoTmzDarwin	44	+9:30
CdoTmzEastern	10	-5:00
CdoTmzEasternEurope	5	+2:00
CdoTmzEnewetak	39	-12:00
CdoTmzFiji	40	+12:00
CdoTmzGMT	1	+0
CdoTmzGuam	43	+10:00
CdoTmzHarare	50	+2:00
CdoTmzHawaii	15	-10:00
CdoTmzHobart	42	+10:00
CdoTmzHongKong	21	+8:00
CdoTmzIndiana	34	-5:00
CdoTmzIslamabad	47	+5:00
CdoTmzIsrael	27	+2:00
CdoTmzKabul	48	+4:30
CdoTmzLisbon	2	+0
CdoTmzMagadan	41	+11:00
CdoTmzMax	52	Not a time zone. Counts as first unused time zone value
CdoTmzMexicoCity	37	-6:00
CdoTmzMidAtlantic	30	-2:00
CdoTmzMidwayIsland	16	-11:00
CdoTmzMonrovia	31	+0
CdoTmzMoscow	51	+3:00
CdoTmzMountain	12	-7:00
CdoTmzNewfoundlad	28	-3:30

Name	Value	Difference from GMT
CdoTmzNoDST	&H400 0	Specifies no change in time zone for summertime.
CdoTmzOrigin	0	+12:00
CdoTmzPacific	13	-8:00
CdoTmzParis	3	+1:00
CdoTmzPrague	6	+1:00
CdoTmzRiodeJaneiro	8	-3:00
CdoTmzSaskatchewan	36	-6:00
CdoTmzTehran	25	+3:30
CdoTmzTokyo	20	+9:00
CdoTmzUTC	16385	+0
CdoTmzWellington	17	+12:00

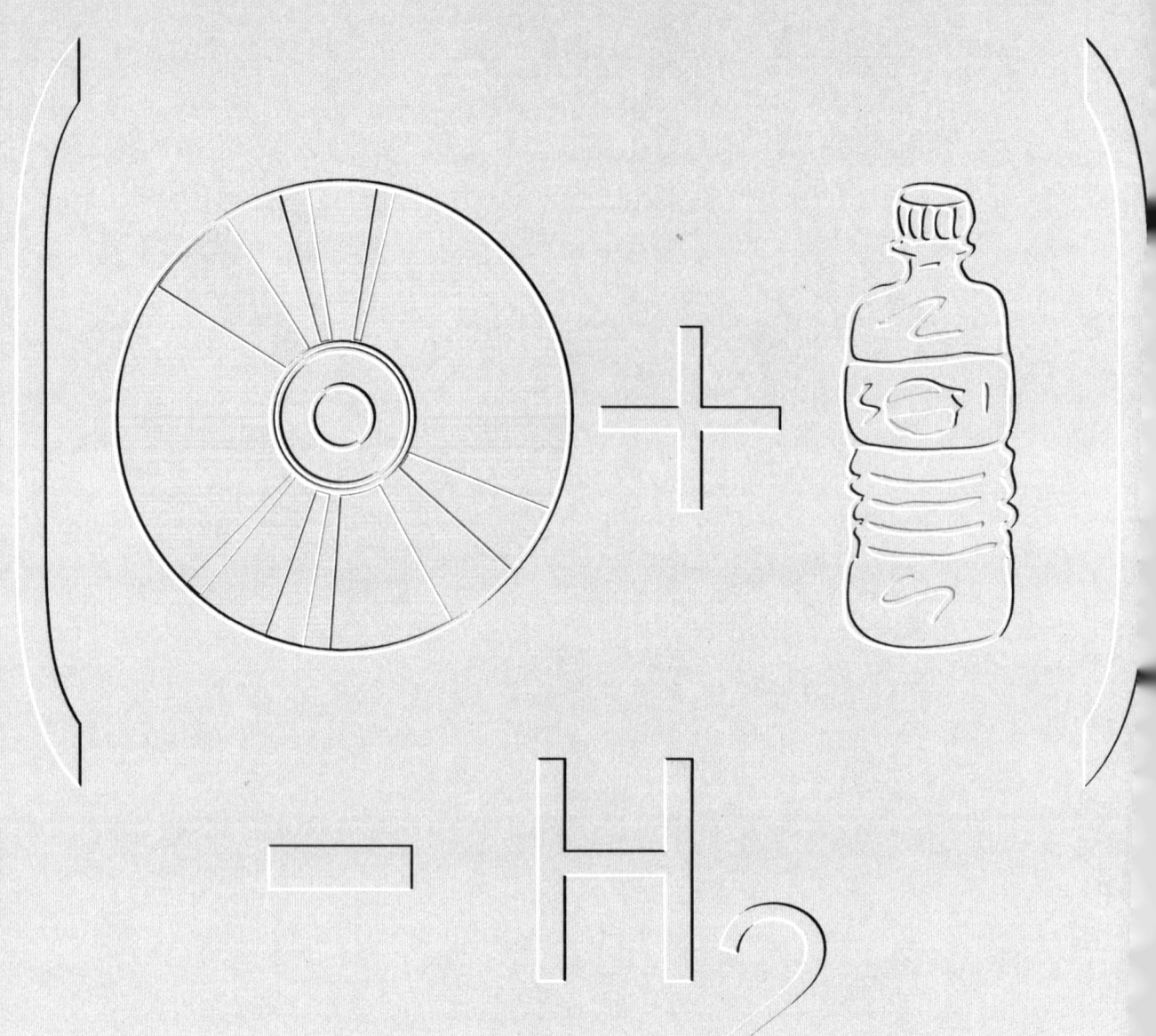

CDO Renderer Object Model Reference

In this Appendix, you'll find a complete list of the objects, methods and properties in the CDO Renderer object model. Note that any parameters in square brackets are optional arguments to a method.

Object	Description
CalendarView	The CalendarView object represents a view of a schedule calendar.
Column	The Column object represents a column within a view.
Columns	The Columns collection object contains zero or more columns in a view.
ContainerRenderer	The ContainerRenderer object renders the rows of a container object as an HTML table.
Format	The Format object contains information that controls how a particular property is to be rendered.
Formats	The Formats collection object contains zero or more formats for a rendering.
ObjectRenderer	The ObjectRenderer object renders selected properties of a specified CDO object.

Object	Description
Pattern	The Pattern object represents a rendering pattern within a format.
Patterns	The Patterns collection object contains zero or more patterns in a format.
RenderingApplication	The RenderingApplication object provides a framework and support for specific rendering objects.
TableView	The TableView object represents a tabular view of an address book container or a folder.
Views	The Views collection object contains one or more views for a container object.

CalendarView Object

Methods

Name	Returns	Description
IsSameAs (*CVObject*)	Boolean	Returns True if the AddressEntry object is the same as the one specified by the parameter.
RenderAppointments ([*StartDate*] [, *RespObject*])	String	Render a day's appointments. Specify the day with *StartDate* parameter (default is today). Returns HTML as string unless you specify an ASP response object to pass the HTML to.
RenderDateNavigator ([*StartDate*] [, *Months*] [, *RespObject*])	String	Render a date navigator. Specify the start date with *StartDate* parameter (default is today) and the number of *months* to render (default is 2). Returns HTML as string unless you specify an ASP response object to pass the HTML to.
RenderEvents ([*StartDate*] [, *RespObject*])	String	Render a day's events. Specify the day with *StartDate* parameter (default is today). Returns HTML as string unless you specify an ASP Response object to pass the HTML to.

Properties

Name	Returns	Description
BusyCell	String	Pattern used to format cells with appointments.
BusyIndicator	String	Pattern used to format indicator bar for a busy time.
Categories	Long	Number of categories in the view.
Class	CdoObjectClasses	The object's type as a value. In this case, CdoClass_CalendarView (12).
Columns Columns (*index*)	Columns	Returns specific column number *index* attached to the view or entire Columns collection if not specified.
DailyEventCell	String	Pattern used to format daily event cell.
DailyTimeCell	String	Pattern used to format daily time cell.
FreeBusinessCell	String	Pattern used to format free cells during business hours.
FreeIndicator	String	Pattern used to format indicator bar for free time.
FreeNonBusinessCell	String	Pattern used to format free cells outside business hours.
Index	Long	The index of this view in the Views collection.
Interval	Long	Length of time slot displayed in daily view. Default is 30 minutes.
Mode	CdoCalendarMode	Sets Calendar mode as day view or week view. Uses CdoCalendarMode constants detailed in Appendix D.
Name	String	The display name of this view.
NumberOfUnits	Long	Number of days or weeks to display. Determined by Mode property.
OOFIndicator	String	Pattern used to format indicator bar for out of office time.
Parent	Views	The parent Views collection.

Name	Returns	Description
Source	CdoViewSource	The source of this view (Common, Personal, Custom, or Folder).
TentativeIndicator	String	Pattern used to format indicator bar for tentatively busy time.
WeeklyAppointmentCell	String	Pattern used to format weekly appointment cell.
WeeklyHeadingCell	String	Pattern used to format weekly heading cell.

Column Object

The Column object has no methods attached to it.

Properties

Name	Returns	Description
Class	CdoObjectClasses	The object's type as a value. In this case, CdoClass_Column (11).
Flags	Long	The flags set on this column denoting that this column uses bitmaps (8) and/or that this column cannot be used as the basis for a sort (32).
Index	Long	The index of this column in the Columns collection.
Name	String	The display name of this column.
Parent	Columns	The parent Columns collection.
Property	Variant (Long or String)	The name or tag of the property rendered in this column.
RenderUsing	Variant (String)	Render the property values of this column using this string.
Width	Long	The width of this column (in pixels or characters based on Flags property).

Columns Collection

Methods

Name	Returns	Description
Add (*Name,* *Property,* *Width,* *Flags,* *InsertAfter* [, *Type*])	Column	Adds a new column to the collection of columns, specifying its display *name*, the *property* it holds, its *width*, any *flags* set on it, which column to insert it after and, optionally, if this is a custom property column.

Properties

Name	Returns	Description
Class	CdoObjectClasses	The object's type as a value. In this case, CdoClass_Columns (10).
Count	Long	Number of Column objects in this collection.
Item(*index*) Item(*proptag*)	Column	Returns Column object from collection matching the index or property tag specified.
Parent	TableView	The parent TableView object.

ContainerRenderer Object

Methods

Name	Returns	Description
Render (*Style* [, *PageNum*] [, *Raw*] [, *RespObject*])	String	Render the contents of this container as specified by the *style* parameter – either Folder Contents (1) or the Folder Hierarchy (2). Can also specify which *page number* to begin with and an ASP *Response object* to send the HTML to. N.B. The *Raw* parameter is reserved for future use and should not be used.
RenderDate (*Date,* *Format* [, *RespObject*])	String	Render the specified *date* using the specified *format* string and sends HTML to *Response Object* if given.

Name	Returns	Description
RenderHeading ([*CellPatt*] [, *RespObject*])	String	Renders a table containing the column headers specified for the current view so far. You can give a specific *pattern* for the cell header and a target *Response object* if needed.
RenderProperty (*Property* [, *Raw*] [, *RespObject*])	String	Renders the *Property* named of the current containers parent object. The *Raw* parameter is reserved and should not be used. You can send the method results to a *Response Object* if needed.
RenderTime (*Date*, *Format* [, *RespObject*])	String	Render the specified time (contained in *Date* object) using the specified *format* string. You can send the method results to a *Response Object* if needed.

Properties

Name	Returns	Description
BusinessDayEndTime	Variant (Date)	Time the business day ends.
BusinessDays	Long	Mask defining the business days of the week with the CdoDaysOfWeek constants.
BusinessDayStartTime	Variant (Date)	Time the business day starts.
CellPattern	String	Pattern used to format each content cell.
Class	CdoObjectClasses	The object's type as a value. In this case, CdoClass_ContainerRenderer (3).
CodePage	Variant (Long, Object or String)	This object's code page setting.
CurrentStore	InfoStore	The message store containing the data source.
CurrentView	TableView	The currently applied view.
DataSource	Object (AddressEntries, Folders, Messages, Recipients)	The object from which we will pull our data to be rendered.

Name	Returns	Description
FirstDayOfWeek	Long	The first day of the week. Note this long value is not taken from the CdoDaysOfWeek constants.
Formats Formats (*index*) Formats (*name*)	Object (Format or Formats)	Returns specific format number *index* or with certain *name* attached to the ContainerRenderer or entire Formats collection if not specified.
HeadingCellPattern	String	Pattern used to format each column heading.
HeadingRowPrefix	String	Pattern inserted at beginning of the header row in a view.
HeadingRowSuffix	String	Pattern inserted at end of each header row in view.
Is24HourClock	Boolean	Specifies if container should be rendered in 24-hour time format or not.
LCID	Long	This object's locale setting.
LinkPattern	String	Pattern used to format a link to another object.
Parent	Rendering Application or Nothing	The parent of this instance.
PrivateStore	InfoStore	Private message store (of container object).
RowsPerPage	Long	Sets the number of rows to be rendered for each page.
RowPrefix	String	Pattern inserted at the beginning of a table contents row in a view.
RowSuffix	String	Pattern inserted at the end of a table contents row in a view.
TablePrefix	String	Pattern inserted at beginning of each rendered container table.

Name	Returns	Description
TableSuffix	String	Pattern inserted at end of each rendered container table.
TimeZone	Long	Timezone used for rendering calendar information. Takes one of the CdoTimeZone constants.
Views Views (*index*)	Object (Views, TableView or CalendarView)	Returns specific view number *index* in Views collection or entire collection if not specified.

Format Object

Methods

Name	Returns	Description
Delete()	None	Delete this format from the collection.

Properties

Name	Returns	Description
Class	CdoObjectClasses	The object's type as a value. In this case, CdoClass_Format(4).
Name	String	A name to refer to this format.
Parent	Formats	The Formats collection holding this Format object.
Patterns Patterns (*index*)	Object (Pattern or Patterns)	Returns specific pattern number *index* in Patterns collection or entire collection if not specified.
Property	Variant (Long or String)	The property formatted by this collection of patterns.

Formats Collection

Methods

Name	Returns	Description
Add (*Property* [, *Name*])	Format	Adds a new Format for the specified *property* to the Formats collection. If it is a non-MAPI property, use *Name* property to let you reference it.

Properties

Name	Returns	Description
Class	CdoObjectClasses	The object's type as a value. In this case, CdoClass_Formats(5).
Count	Long	Number of Format objects in this collection.
Item(*index*) Item(*name*) Item(*propTag*)	Format	Returns Format object number *index* from the Formats collection. Alternatively, you can use either the *property tag* or its custom *name* to retrieve the Format.
Parent	Object (ContainerRenderer, ObjectRenderer, or RenderingApplication)	The immediate parent of this Formats collection.

ObjectRenderer Object

Methods

Name	Returns	Description
RenderDate (*Date*, *Format* [, *RespObject*])	String	Render the specified *date* using the specified *format* string and sends HTML to *Response Object* if given.
RenderLink [, *RespObject*])	String	Renders an HTML link to an object specified in the DataSource property. You can send the method results to a *Response Object* if needed.
RenderProperty (*Property* [, *Raw*] [, *RespObject*])	String	Renders the *Property* named of the current containers parent object. The *Raw* parameter is reserved and should not be used. You can send the method results to a *Response Object* if needed.
RenderTime (*Date*, *Format* [, *RespObject*])	String	Render the specified time (contained in *Date* object) using the specified *format* string. You can send the method results to a *Response Object* if needed.

Properties

Name	Returns	Description
Class	CdoObjectClasses	The object's type as a value. In this case, CdoClass_ObjectRenderer(2).
CodePage	Variant (Long, Object or String)	This object's code page setting.
DataSource	Object (AddressEntry, AppointmentItem, Attachment, Folder, MeetingItem, or Message)	The object from which we will pull our renderable data.
Formats Formats (*index*) Formats (*name*)	Object (Format or Formats)	Returns specific Format number *index* or with certain *name* attached to the ObjectRenderer or entire Formats collection if not specified.
LCID	Long	This object's locale setting.
LinkPattern	String	Pattern used to format a link to another object.
Parent	RenderingApplication or Nothing	The immediate parent of this instance. Either the RenderingApplication or Nothing.

Pattern Object

Methods

Name	Returns	Description
Delete	None	Delete this pattern from the Patterns collection.

Properties

Name	Returns	Description
Class	CdoObjectClasses	The object's type as a value. In this case, CdoClass_Pattern(7).
Parent	Patterns	The Patterns collection containing this object.

Name	Returns	Description
RenderUsing	Variant (String)	Render the property value using this string.
Value	Variant	When the property matches this value, the rendering string is used.

Patterns Collection

Methods

Name	Returns	Description
Add (*Value, RenderUsing*)	Pattern	Adds a new Pattern object to this collection. Specifies which property *value*s are to be rendered and *using* which html.

Properties

Name	Returns	Description
Class	CdoObjectClasses	The object's type as a value. In this case, CdoClass_Patterns(6).
Count	Long	Number of Pattern objects in this collection.
Item(*Index*)	Pattern	Returns Pattern object number *index* from the collection.
Parent	Format	Returns the parent Format object for this collection.

RenderingApplication Object

Methods

Name	Returns	Description
CreateRenderer (*class*)	Object (ContainerRenderer or ObjectRenderer)	Create either an ObjectRenderer or ContainerRenderer attached to this Application by specifying the class parameter with either 2 or 3 respectively.
Impersonate (*ImpID*)	Long	Use a saved security context handle with ID *ImpID* to impersonate an authenticated messaging user.

Name	Returns	Description
ListComposeForms (*LinkPatt* [, *LangDir*])	String Array	Creates HTML to link to custom forms with according to the *Link Pattern* given.
LoadConfiguration (*eSource*, *Section* [, *Session*])	None	Loads configuration data from the specified *source* (The Registry (1) or Exchange's Directory server (2)) or just a specific *section* of data as required. If using source 2, you can also specify the *session* object the user is logged onto.

Properties

Name	Returns	Description
Class	CdoObjectClasses	The object's type as a value. In this case, CdoClass_Application (1).
CodePage	Variant (Long, Object or String)	This object's code page setting.
ConfigParameter (*parameter*)	String	Returns the requested configuration *parameter*.
Formats Formats (*index*) Formats (*name*)	Object (Format or Formats)	Returns specific global Format object number *index* or with certain *name* attached to the RenderingApplication or entire global Formats collection if not specified.
FormsRoot	String	The physical directory containing ASP files to generate custom "classpath" formats.
ImpID	Long	The security context handle for the current user.
LCID	Long	This object's locale setting.
LoggingLevel	Long	Set the information level for a given logging category.
Name	String	The display name for this rendering application.
Parent	Nothing	The parent of this instance. In this case, Nothing.

Name	Returns	Description
Version	String	Returns the version number of CDOHTML.DLL.
VirtualRoot	String	Sets the virtual root of the application. Defaults to /exchange.

TableView Object

Methods

Name	Returns	Description
IsSameAs (*TVObject*)	Boolean	Returns True if the TableView object is the same as the one specified by the parameter.

Properties

Name	Returns	Description
Categories	Long	Returns the number of categories that objects in this table view are grouped by.
Class	CdoObjectClasses	The object's type as a value. In this case, CdoClass_TableView(9).
Columns Columns (*index*)	Columns	Returns specific column number *index* attached to the view or entire Columns collection if not specified.
Index	Long	The index of this view in the Views collection.
Name	String	The display name for this table view.
Parent	Views	The Views collection that contains this TableView object.
Source	CdoViewSource	The source of this view (Common, Personal, Custom, or Folder).

Views Collection

Methods

Name	Returns	Description
Add (*Name* [, *Class*] [, *sortBy*] [, *SortOrder*])	Object (TableView or CalendarView)	Add a new View to the Views collection with the specified display *name*, the *class* of view to be created, the property to sort the view by, and the order in which to display the sort.

Properties

Name	Returns	Description
Class	CdoObjectClasses	The object's type as a value. In this case, CdoClass_Views(8).
Count	Long	Number of View objects in this collection.
Item(*index*) Item(*name*)	View	Returns View object number *index* from the collection or the View with the specific *name*.
Parent	ContainerRenderer	The ContainerRenderer object holding this Views collection.

CDO Renderer Constants

The following constants are predefined in CDO Rendering Library 1.21. To include them in ASP code, set a reference to the type library with a METADATA tag:

```
<!-- METADATA TYPE="typelib" FILE="C:\ExchSrvr\bin\cdohtml.dll" -->
```

You can include this METADATA tag in individual pages or in the global.asa page.

Alternatively, you can download an include file – cdoprops.inc – declaring these constants from http://www.cdolive.com/sample16.htm.

Note that cdohtml.dll includes two sets of constants; those listed here with the prefix Cdo and those with the prefix AMHTML which are included only for backwards compatibility and should no longer be used.

CdoCalendarMode

Used in conjunction with the CalendarView object's Mode property to set what time range a calendar view should span.

Name	Value	Description
CdoMode_Calendar_Daily	0	This calendar view is rendered in multiples of a day.
CdoMode_Calendar_Weekly	1	This calendar view is rendered in multiples of a week.

CdoColumnSettings

Used in defining views and patterns for single columns in conjunction with the `Column` object's `Flags` property.

Name	Value	Description
CdoColumn_Bitmap	8	A bitmap will be used to render the property in this column
CdoColumn_NotSortable	32	Entries in a view may not be sorted with respect to this column.

CdoConfigSources

Used in conjunction with the `RenderingApplication` object's `LoadConfiguration` method to determine where to load the application's configuration information from.

Name	Value	Description
CdoConfig_DS	2	Load from the Windows Registry.
CdoConfig_Registry	1	Load from the Exchange directory server.

CdoObjectClasses

Specifies the type of CDO Rendering object.

Name	Value	Description
CdoClass_Application	1	`RenderingApplication` object
CdoClass_CalendarView	12	`CalendarView` object
CdoClass_Column	11	`Column` object
CdoClass_Columns	10	`Columns` collection object
CdoClass_ContainerRenderer	3	`ContainerRenderer` object
CdoClass_Format	4	`Format` object
CdoClass_Formats	5	`Formats` collection object
CdoClass_ObjectRenderer	2	`ObjectRenderer` object
CdoClass_Pattern	7	`Pattern` object
CdoClass_Patterns	6	`Patterns` collection object
CdoClass_TableView	9	`TableView` object
CdoClass_Views	8	`Views` collection object

CdoViewSource

Predetermines how a view is characterized with respect to the container currently being rendered. Note that the common and custom constants apply to both table and calendar views, but the folder and personal constants refer only to table views.

Name	Value	Description
CdoView_Common	0	This view is predefined globally for all folders and all messaging users.
CdoView_Custom	2	This view has been defined in the context of the current setting of the DataSource property of the ContainerRenderer object. However, it is still available when the DataSource property is changed.
CdoView_Folder	3	This table view is predefined for the particular folder currently being rendered. It is no longer available when the DataSource property is changed.
CdoView_Personal	1	This table view is predefined for the messaging user associated with the current session represented by the Session object.

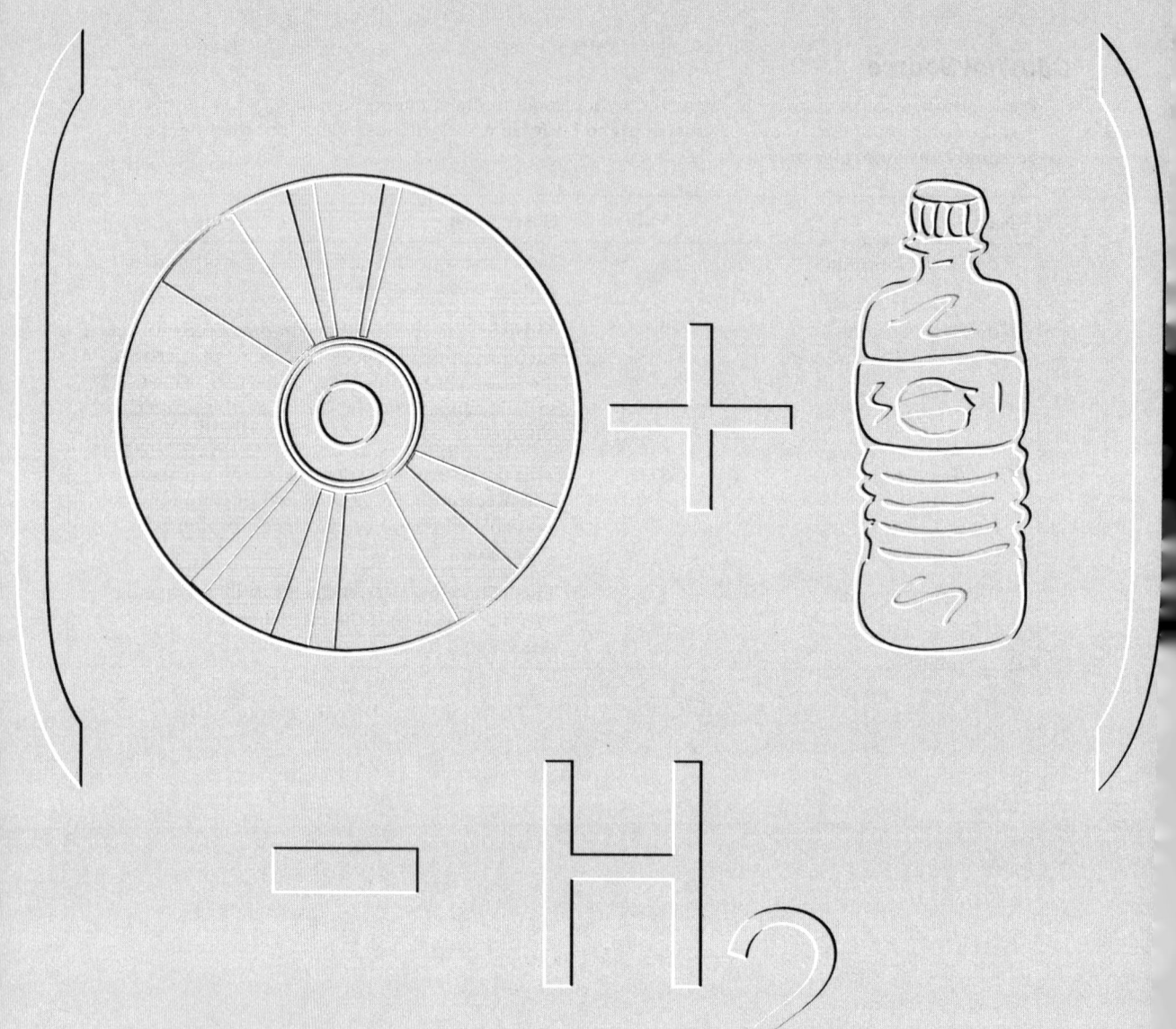

CDO for NTS 1.2 Object Model Reference

In this Appendix, you'll find a complete list of the objects, methods and properties in the CDONTS object model. Note that any parameters in square brackets are optional arguments to a method.

Objects

Object	Description
AddressEntry	Holds addressing information for an individual.
Attachment	Allows the manipulation of attachments.
Attachments	Collection of Attachment objects. Allows access to all attachments on a message, and lets you create new attachments.
Folder	Allows you to open the default Inbox or Outbox folder in a message store.
Message	Allows you to work with e-mail messages.
Messages	Collection of Message objects. Enables the access of all messages in a folder, and the ability to create new messages.
NewMail	Lets you send a message without having to log on to a session.
Recipient	Holds information for the recipient of a message.
Recipients	A collection of Recipient objects. Allows access to all recipients of a message, and the creation of new recipients.
Session	Establishes a connection between an application and the messaging system.

AddressEntry Object

The `AddressEntry` object has no methods.

Properties

Name	Returns	Description
Address	String	Specifies the messaging address of an address entry or message recipient.
Application	Variant	Returns the name of the active application, namely the Collaboration Data Objects for NTS Library.
Class	Long	Returns a numeric constant that identifies the class of the object.
Name	String	Returns or sets the display name or alias of the `AddressEntry` object as a string.
Parent	Variant	Returns the `AddressEntry` object's parent object, usually a Message object.
Session	Variant	Returns the top-level `Session` object associated with the specified `AddressEntry`.
Type	String	Specifies the address type, such as SMTP, fax, or X.400.

Attachment Object

Methods

Name	Description
Delete()	Deletes the `Attachment` object.
ReadFromFile (*filename*)	Loads the contents of an attachment from a file. Depends on the `Type` property of the `Attachment` – this method isn't supported for a `Type` of `CdoEmbeddedMessage`.
WriteToFile (*filename*)	Saves the attachment to a file in the file system. Depends on the `Type` property of the `Attachment` – this method isn't supported for a `Type` of `CdoEmbeddedMessage`.

Properties

Name	Returns	Description
Application	Variant	Returns the name of the active application, namely the Collaboration Data Objects for NTS Library.
Class	Long	Returns a numeric constant that identifies the class of the object.
ContentBase	Variant	Indicates a base URL to use if the ContentLocation is a relative URL.
ContentID	Variant	The universally unique ID for this attachment.
ContentLocation	Variant	Indicates a URL as the location of the attachment.
Name	String	Returns or sets the display name of the Attachment object as a string.
Parent	Variant	Returns the parent of the object, usually an Attachments collection.
Session	Variant	Returns the top-level Session object associated with the specified Attachment object.
Source	Variant	Returns or sets the full path and file name, OLE class name, or unique message identifier for the attachment.
Type	Long	Describes the attachment type.

Attachments Collection

Methods

Name	Returns	Description
Add ([*name*] [, *type*] [, *source*] [, *ContentLocation*] [, *ContentBase*])	Variant	Creates and returns a new Attachment object in the Attachments collection.
Delete()		Deletes all the attachments in the Attachments collection.

Properties

Name	Returns	Description
Application	Variant	Returns the name of the active application, namely the Collaboration Data Objects for NTS Library.
Class	Long	Returns a numeric constant that identifies the class of the object.
Count	Long	Returns the number of Attachment objects in the collection.
Item	Variant	Returns a single Attachment object from the Attachments collection, according to its index.
Parent	Variant	Returns the parent object of the Attachments collection, usually a Message object.
Session	Variant	Returns the top-level Session object associated with the specified Attachments collection.

Folder Object

The Folder object has no methods.

Properties

Name	Returns	Description
Application	Variant	Returns the name of the active application, namely the Collaboration Data Objects for NTS Library.
Class	Long	Returns a numeric constant that identifies the class of the object.
Messages	Variant	Returns a Messages collection object within the folder.
Name	String	Returns or sets the name of the Folder object as a string.
Parent	Variant	Returns the parent of the object, which will be a Session object.
Session	Variant	Returns the top-level Session object associated with the specified Folder object.

Message Object

Methods

Name	Description
Delete()	Deletes the Message object.
Send()	Sends the message to the recipients through the messaging system.

Properties

Name	Returns	Description
Application	Variant	Returns the name of the active application, namely the Collaboration Data Objects for NTS Library
Attachments	Variant	Returns a single Attachment object or an Attachments collection.
Class	Long	Returns a numeric constant that identifies the object.
ContentBase	Variant	Indicates a base URL to use if the ContentLocation is a relative URL.
ContentID	Variant	The universally unique ID for this message body.
ContentLocation	Variant	Indicates a URL as the location of the message body.
HTMLText	Variant	Returns or sets the HTML formatted text of the message.
Importance	Long	Returns or sets the importance of the message as CdoNormal (the default), CdoLow, or CdoHigh.
MessageFormat	Long	Determines how the message text will be encoded.
Parent	Variant	Returns the parent of the object, a Messages collection.
Recipients	Variant	Returns a single Recipient object or a Recipients collection.
Sender	Variant	Returns or sets the sender of a message as an AddressEntry object.
Session	Variant	The Session property returns the top-level Session object associated with the Message object.
Size	Long	Returns the approximate size in bytes of the message.
Subject	String	Returns or sets the subject of the message as a string.

Name	Returns	Description
Text	Variant	Returns or sets the text of the message as a variant data type.
TimeReceived	Variant	Sets or returns the date and time the message was received.
TimeSent	Variant	Sets or returns the date and time the message was sent as a vbDate variant data type.

Messages Collection

Methods

Name	Returns	Description
Add ([*subject*] [, *text*] [, *importance*])	Variant	Creates and returns a new Message object in the Messages collection.
Delete()		Deletes all the messages in the Messages collection.
GetFirst()	Variant	Returns the first Message object in the Messages collection. It returns Nothing if no first object exists.
GetLast()	Variant	Returns the last Message object in the Messages collection. It returns Nothing if no last object exists.
GetNext()	Variant	Returns the next Message object in the Messages collection. It returns Nothing if no next object exists, for example if already positioned at the end of the collection.
GetPrevious()	Variant	Returns the previous Message object in the Messages collection. It returns Nothing if no previous object exists, for example if already positioned at the beginning of the collection.

Properties

Name	Returns	Description
Application	Variant	Returns the name of the active application, namely the Collaboration Data Objects for NTS Library.

Name	Returns	Description
Class	Long	Returns a numeric constant that identifies the class of the object.
Count	Long	Returns the number of Message objects in the collection, or a very large number if the exact count is not available.
Item	Variant	Returns a single Message object from the Messages collection.
Parent	Variant	Returns the parent of the object, as a Folder object.
Session	Variant	Returns the top-level Session object associated with the specified object.

NewMail Object

Methods

Name	Description
AttachFile (*Source* [, *FileName*] [, *EncodingMethod*])	Attaches a file to the mail.
AttachURL (*Source,* *ContentLocation* [, *ContentBase*] [, *EncodingMethod*])	Attaches a file or data as a URL.
Send ([*From*] [, *To*] [, *Subject*] [, *Body*] [, *Importance*])	Sends the mail.
SetLocaleIDs (*codepageID*	Sets the Codepage ID for the new message.

Properties

Name	Returns	Description
Bcc	String	Adds to the list of Bcc recipients.
Body	Variant	Sets the body text of the object.
BodyFormat	Long	Sets the text format.
Cc	String	Adds to the list of Cc recipients.
ContentBase	String	Sets a base for all URLs relating to the NewMail object's message body.
ContentLocation	String	Sets an absolute or relative path for all URLs relating to the NewMail object's message body.
From	String	Sets the full address for the sender of the mail.
Importance	Long	Sets the mail's importance: low, normal or high.
MailFormat	Long	Sets the format for the encoding of the mail – MIME or plain text (the default).
Subject	String	Sets the subject text for the mail.
To	String	Adds to the list of To recipients.
Value	String	Allows you to specify custom headers alongside To, Subject, and so on.
Version	String	Returns the version number of the Collaboration Data Objects Library.

Recipient Object

Methods

Name	Description
Delete()	Deletes the Recipient object.

Properties

Name	Returns	Description
Address	String	Specifies the full address for the recipient.
Application	Variant	Returns the name of the active application, namely the Collaboration Data Objects for NTS Library.

Name	Returns	Description
Class	Long	Returns a numeric constant that identifies the class of the object.
Name	String	Returns or sets the name of the Recipient object as a string.
Parent	Variant	Returns the parent of the object, which will be a Recipients collection.
Session	Variant	Returns the top-level Session object associated with the specified Recipient object.
Type	Long	Specifies the type of the Recipient object, either To, Cc, or Bcc.

Recipients Collection

Methods

Name	Returns	Description
Add ([*name*] [, *address*] [, *type*])	Variant	Creates and returns a new Recipient object in the Recipients collection.
Delete()		Deletes all the recipients in the Recipients collection.

Properties

Name	Returns	Description
Application	Variant	Returns the name of the active application, namely the Collaboration Data Objects for NTS Library.
Class	Long	Returns a numeric constant that identifies the class of the object.
Count	Long	Returns the number of Recipient objects in the collection.
Item	Variant	Returns a single Recipient object from the Recipients collection.
Parent	Variant	Returns the parent of the object, which will be a Message object.
Session	Variant	Returns the top-level Session object associated with the specified Recipients collection.

Session Object

Methods

Name	Returns	Description
GetDefaultFolder (*folderType*)	Variant	Returns the requested folder object.
Logoff()		Logs off from the messaging system.
LogonSMTP (*displayname,* *address*)		Logs on to the messaging system.
SetLocaleIDs (*codepageID*)		Sets the Codepage ID for the current session.

Properties

Name	Returns	Description
Application	Variant	Returns the name of the active application, namely the Collaboration Data Objects for NTS Library.
Class	Long	Returns a numeric constant that identifies the class of the object.
Inbox	Variant	Returns a Folder object representing the current messaging user's Inbox folder.
MessageFormat	Long	Determines how messages will be encoded by default.
Name	String	Returns the display name of the profile logged on to this session.
Outbox	Variant	Returns a Folder object representing the current messaging user's Outbox folder.
Parent	Variant	The Parent property returns the Session object itself, since it has no logical parent.
Session	Variant	The Session property returns the Session object itself.
Version	String	Returns the version number of the CDO Library.

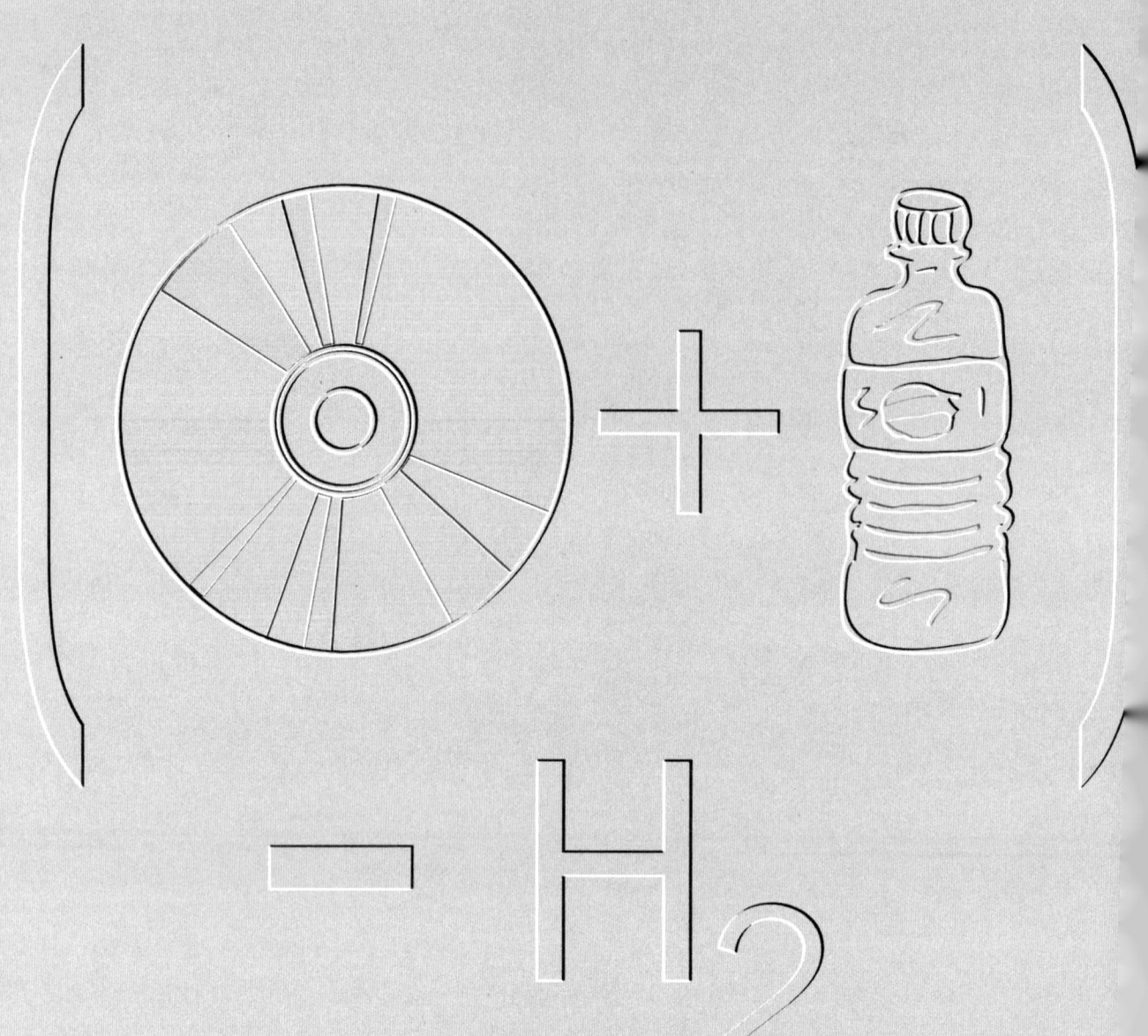

CDO for NTS Constants

The following constants are predefined in CDO 1.21. To include them in ASP code, set a reference to the type library with a METADATA tag:

```
<!-- METADATA TYPE="typelib" uuid="{0E064ADD-9D99-11D0-ABE5-00AA0064D470}" -->
```

You can include this METADATA tag in individual pages or in the global.asa page. For Visual Basic these constants are included automatically when you reference the CDONTS library.

CdoAttachmentTypes

Specifies the type of an attachment.

Name	Value	Description
CdoEmbeddedMessage	4	Message contains an embedded message
CdoFileData	1	Message has embedded file

CdoBodyFormats

Shows how the body of the text is formatted.

Name	Value	Description
CdoBodyFormatHTML	0	Specifies body is HTML formatted
CdoBodyFormatText	1	Specifies body is Text formatted

CdoEncodingMethod

Specifies the encoding type of a message.

Name	Value	Description
CdoEncodingBase64	1	File is Base64 encoded
CdoEncodingUUencode	0	File is UUencoded

CdoFolderTypes

Constants for accessing the Inbox and Outbox folders.

Name	Value	Description
CdoDefaultFolderInbox	1	Inbox folder
CdoDefaultFolderOutbox	2	Outbox folder

CdoImportance

Specifies the importance of a message: low, medium, or high.

Name	Value	Description
CdoHigh	2	High importance
CdoLow	0	Low importance
CdoNormal	1	Normal importance

CdoMailFormats

Specifies the encoding format for the current mail.

Name	Value	Description
CdoMailFormatMime	0	Format with MIME
CdoMailFormatText	1	Format with RFC 822 and UUEncode

CdoMessageFormats

Specifies the encoding format for mails in the current session.

Name	Value	Description
CdoMime	0	Format with MIME
CdoText	1	Format with RFC 822 and UUEncode

CdoRecipientTypes

Specifies the type of recipient: To, CC, or BCC.

Name	Value	Description
CdoBcc	3	BCC to recipient
CdoCc	2	CC to recipient
CdoTo	1	Primary recipient

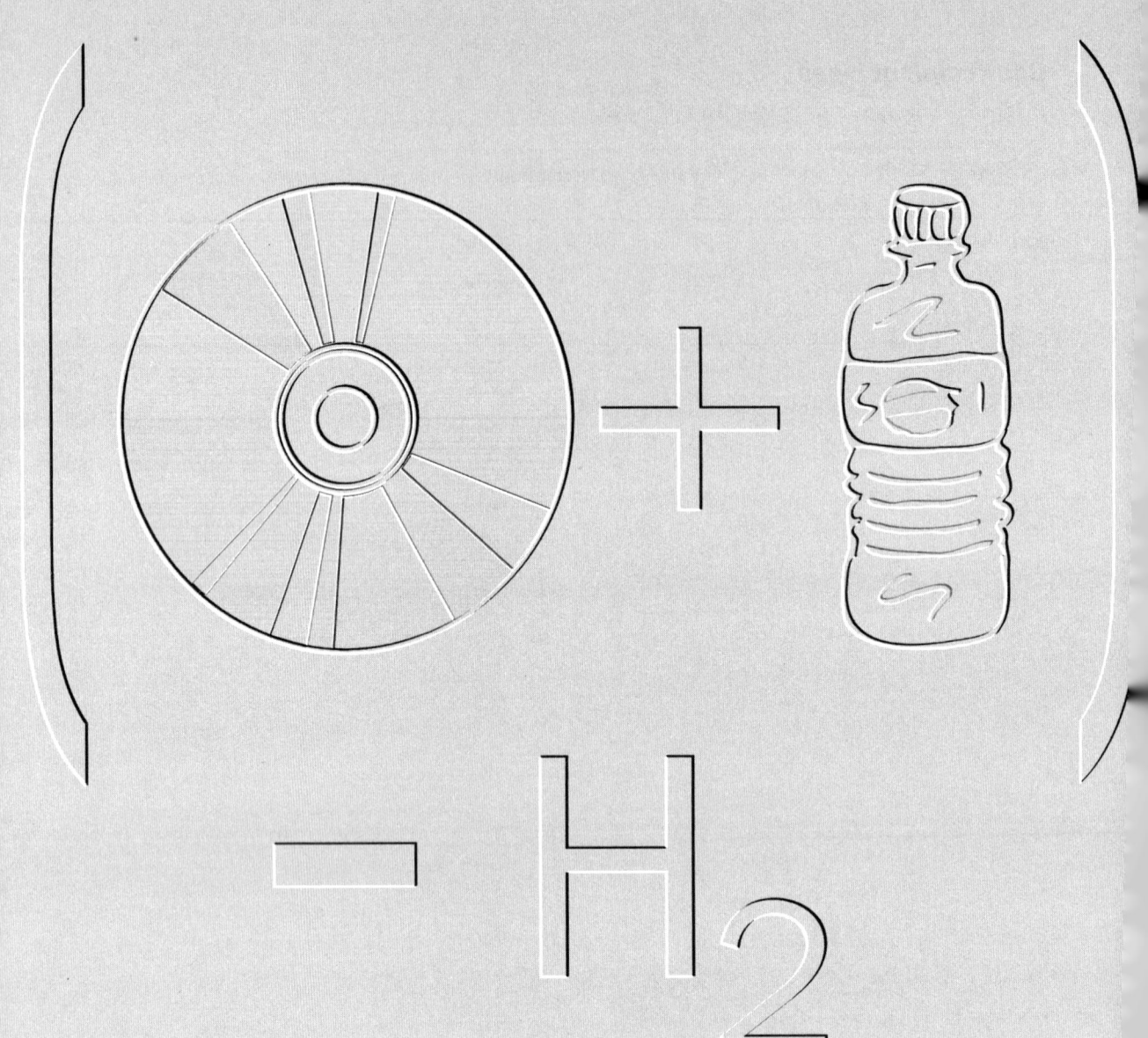

KnowledgeBase Articles

The following appendix consists of a complete list (to December 1999) of articles available on Microsoft's Knowledge Base website that concern CDO. Each article title is accompanied by a six digit number, xxxxxx. In order to access the correct web page, simply plug this number into the following template:

```
http://support.microsoft.com/support/kb/articles/qxxx/x/xx.asp
```

For example,

```
http://support.microsoft.com/support/kb/articles/q194/8/70.asp
```

The example here points to the first article in the first table: Accessing SMTP Headers of a Message Using CDO. Just change the numbers to get the article you want.

To discover any other post-Dec '99 articles relating to CDO, you could visit either of the following pages:

- ❑ `http://www.cdolive.com/kb.htm` is the page this appendix was adapted from and is maintained by one of the authors of this book, Siegfried Weber. It is an up-to-date list of the Exchange, Outlook and CDO related articles on the Knowledge Base.

- ❑ `http://support.microsoft.com/support/MessagingSDK/CDOArticles.asp` is the start page in the Knowledge Base itself for CDO related articles.

On The CDO Library

HOWTO

HOWTO articles give help and examples on performing certain tasks.

Article	Title
161833	Send Mail from Visual Basic Using OLE Messaging
169031	Embedding a Document in a Message using Active Messaging
172038	DLL to Read and Write RTF with Active Messaging
176914	Send Mail to Remote Exchange Server in ASP with VB DLL
177851	Build a VB/Messaging Application to Run from a Service
178508	Write a VB MessageFilter for Your Appointment Collection
178787	Work with Distribution Lists Using CDO from VB
178789	Forwarding Messages Using CDO Version 1.2 (VB Sample)
179083	Read Address Book Properties in Visual Basic
181035	Determine If a CDO Session Is Online or Offline from VB
181408	Use CDO to Set Up Reply to Alternate Recipient
183917	Find a User's Home Exchange Server from a MAPI Session
186753	Check Someone Else's Schedule for Free/Busy Information
191365	Retrieve Original Message from Non-Delivery Receipt
194070	Use CDO to Programmatically Resolve Ambiguous Recipients
194623	Determine if a Message is Signed and/or Encrypted
194870	Accessing SMTP Headers of a Message Using CDO
195381	Use CDO to Set the Message Delivery Options
195545	Use CDO/VC++ to Get Properties on Received Messages
195569	Finding a Sent Message using Collaboration Data Objects
195662	Log On to Exchange with the ProfileInfo Parameter
195681	Configure an Exchange Mailbox for Anonymous Access

Article	Title
195842	Set the Default Reply-Recipient with CDO Using C++
196507	Remove Published Forms from a Folder Using CDO
196507	Retrieve Alternate E-mail Addresses Using CDO
198752	Get Message Store Information on Mailboxes Programmatically
200150	Call a Visual Basic ActiveX DLL to Send Mail
200180	Remove a Published Form from a Folder Using Visual C++
231958	Programmatically Copy a Message Type Attachment to a Folder
240911	Use ACL Object To List All Permissions For a MAPI Folder
243900	Correlate Delivery and Read Receipt to the Original Message

PRB

PRB articles deal with common problems encountered in CDO and other programming.

Article	Title
171671	Changing Properties of AddressEntry object of a Recipient
178554	DateValue Does Not Return Time Information
179233	GetDefaultFolder Method of CDO Session Fails with VARIANT
179638	Folders.Item('tag_name') Returns Wrong Folder Item
179639	Error MAPI_E_NOT_FOUND (8004010F) Using CDO
183069	GetFirst/GetLast methods of CDO Cannot Filter Appointments
183094	MAPI_E_NOT_FOUND Err Setting Value of Property with CDO
183095	E_INVALIDARG Error Returned From CDO Reply Method
183250	CDO Error: Run-time error "-2147221233" with GetFreeBusy
190548	CDO: Session.Logon Fails with E_AccessDenied (0x80070005)
191816	Run-Time Error -2147467259 with MoveTo Method
192083	Setting PR_SENTMAIL_ENTRYID in CDO is Not Retained

Article	Title
192119	MAPI/CDO Applications Fail After Outlook Express Install
192404	CDO Filter on AppoinmentItems has Unexpected Behavior
194069	MAPI_E_NO_SUPPORT Calling Session.Logon on Windows 95/98
194077	Problems with CDO after Upgrading to Outlook 98
194806	Message.Class Incorrect After Calling GetMessage()
195380	CDO Cannot See New Incoming Messages in Personal Folders
195586	Problems Using CDO Against an Exchange 4.x Server
196080	ReadFromFile() Fails for Attachment of Type CdoOle
196258	GetMessage Returns Message Object Instead of MeetingItem
196508	Cannot Retrieve AppointmentItem from Other Folders
196509	Accepting Meeting Request Loses Categories Information
197145	E_FAIL on SaveChanges() with Too Many Properties
223446	CurrentUser of CDO Session Object Returns Wrong User Name
228890	MAPI_E_TOO_COMPLEX when Sorting the Messages by Subject
232626	CDO: MAPI_E_NO_SUPPORT When Using ClearRecurrencePattern
234213	ACL/Rules Samples and Some CDO Apps May Fail Installing Exch Server 5.5 SP2
235514	Cannot Set TimeSent and TimeReceived Properties Manually
237602	ACL: New ACE ID Not the Same As Original AddressEntry ID
237924	ACL: Outlook 2000 Doesn't Properly Read ACL Settings
239785	CDO Will Not Run in an NT Service with Outlook 97 Installed

BUG

BUG articles detail known bugs as well as possible workarounds.

Article	Title
174394	IAdrBook::OpenEntry() Fails on Outlook Contacts
177630	Anonymous Logon Causes Spooler to Hang During Logoff

Article	Title
183095	E_INVALIDARG Error Returned From CDO Reply Method
183248	CDO in C/C++ RawTable->Release() Hangs at Logoff
192910	CDO Message.Text Property May Return Truncated
195656	Accessing Custom Properties using CDO
195928	Type Mismatch Error Using CDO in MS Transaction Server
215463	MAPILogonEx Memory Leak
219691	CDO copies unnecessary MAPI properties to new messages in Forwarding and Replying
235361	CDO With #import Causes Incorrect HRESULT Error Code Values

On The CDO Rendering Library

INFO

INFO articles detail some background knowledge around the subject.

Article	Title
158229	Security Ramifications for IIS Applications
172024	Server Side Include Directives Not Processed by ASP
172925	Security Issues with Objects in ASP and ISAPI Extensions
173317	ASP's Request.Form and Request.QueryString Return Objects
185874	How to Troubleshoot Permissions in IIS 4.0
186137	IIS Security Settings for CDO Web-Based Messaging
196074	How to Store the Authenticated User Name in a Session Variable

HOWTO

Article	Title
176914	Send Mail to Remote Exchange Server in ASP with VB DLL
178509	Write a VBScript MessageFilter in an ASP Page

Article	Title
178552	View Public Folder Contents from an ASP Page
179082	Read Address Book Properties from ASP Page with VBScript
181483	Render Calendar To an ASP Page with CDO
192435	Render a Folder to an ASP Page with CDO
192436	Render the Global Address List with CDO
195591	Display Free/Busy Information from an ASP Page

PRB

Article	Title
173852	Load Library Failed Error Registering Active Messaging
179639	Error MAPI_E_NOT_FOUND (8004010F) Using CDO
181739	IIS 4.0 Automatic Password Synchronization and CDO
183094	MAPI_E_NOT_FOUND Err Setting Value of Property with CDO
188599	CDO Rendering Library Not Available Outside of ASP
189533	MAPI_E_FAILONEPROVIDER Accessing Public Folder Through ASP
192119	MAPI/CDO Applications Fail After Outlook Express Install
193451	"Error 8002009 - MAPI_E_NOT_INITIALIZED 80040605" w/ CDO
194190	ASP 0115 a Trappable Error Has Occurred
195379	CDO Application in an ASP Page Causes ASP 0115 Error
195849	Error: MAPI_E_FAILONEPROVIDER (8004011D) Using CDO

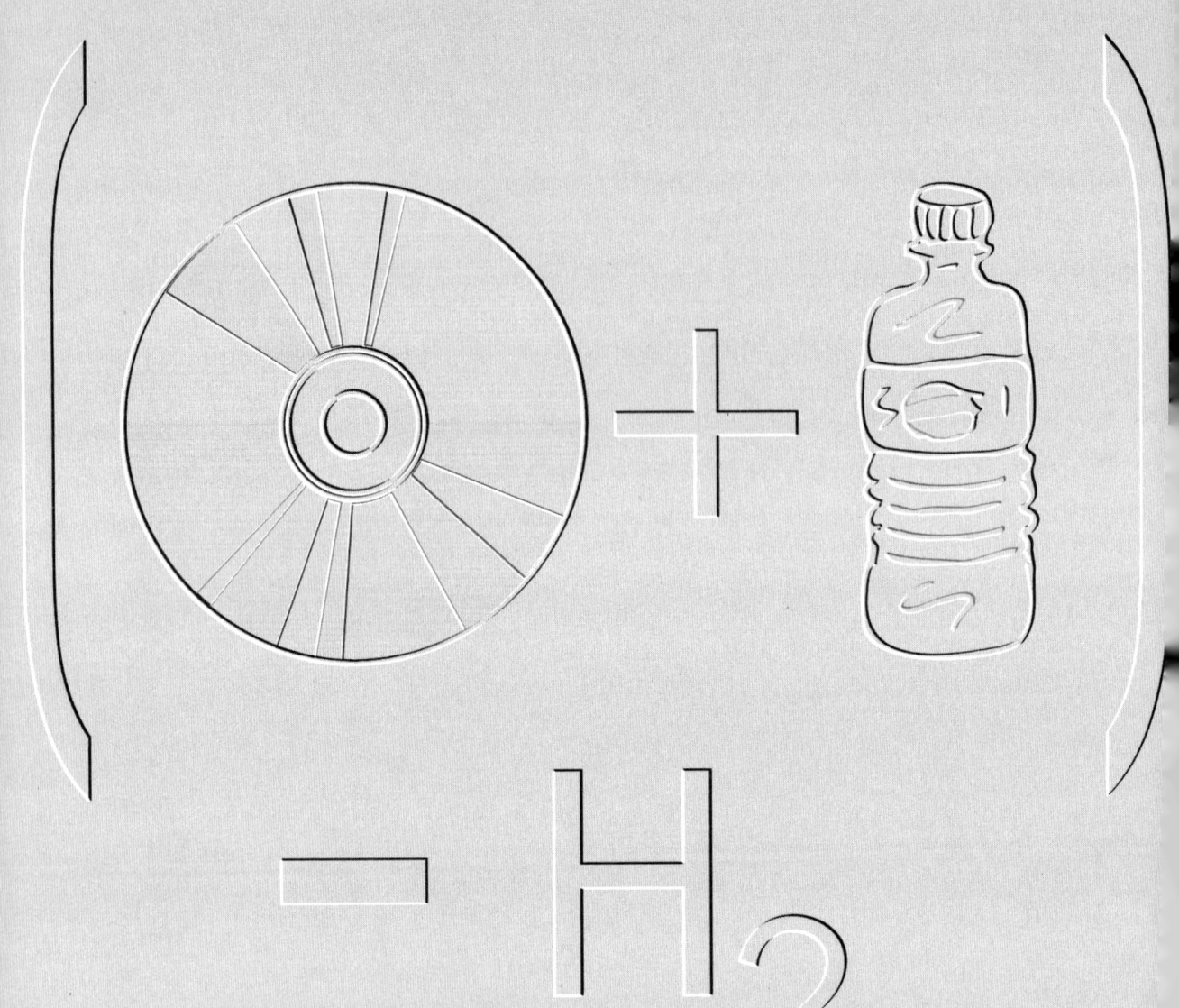

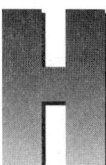

Support and Errata

One of the most irritating things about any programming book is when you find that bit of code you've just spent an hour typing simply doesn't work. You check it a hundred times to see if you've set it up correctly and then you notice the spelling mistake in the variable name on the book page. Of course, you can blame the authors for not taking enough care and testing the code, the editors for not doing their job properly, or the proofreaders for not being eagle-eyed enough, but this doesn't get around the fact that mistakes do happen.

We try hard to ensure no mistakes sneak out into the real world, but we can't promise that this book is 100% error free. What we can do is offer the next best thing by providing you with immediate support and feedback from experts who have worked on the book and try to ensure that future editions eliminate these gremlins. The following section will take you step by step through the process of posting errata to our web site to get that help. The sections that follow, therefore, are:

❑   Wrox Developers Membership

❑   Finding a list of existing errata on the web site

❑   Adding your own errata to the existing list

❑   What happens to your errata once you've posted it (why doesn't it appear immediately)?

There is also a section covering how to e-mail a question for technical support. This comprises:

❑   What your e-mail should include

❑   What happens to your e-mail once it has been received by us

So that you only need view information relevant to yourself, we ask that you register as a Wrox Developer Member. This is a quick and easy process, that will save you time in the long-run. If you are already a member, just update membership to include this book.

Wrox Developer's Membership

To get your FREE Wrox Developer's Membership click on Membership in the top navigation bar of our home site – http://www.wrox.com. This is shown in the following screenshot:

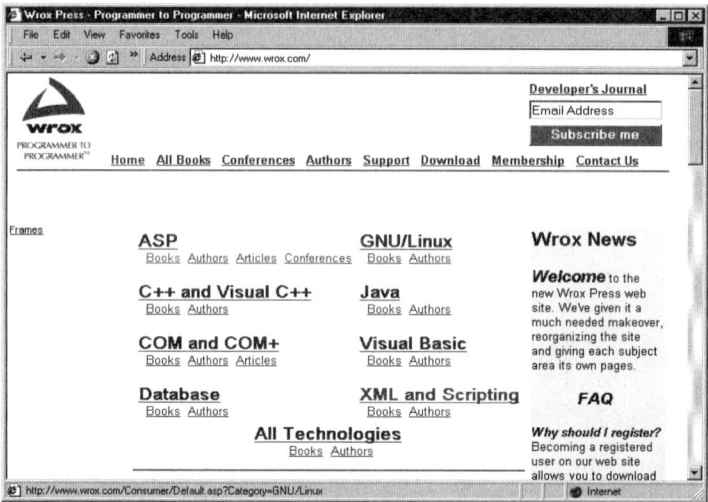

Then, on the next screen (not shown), click on New User. This will display a form. Fill in the details on the form and submit the details using the Register button at the bottom. Before you can say 'The best read books come in Wrox Red' you will get the following screen:

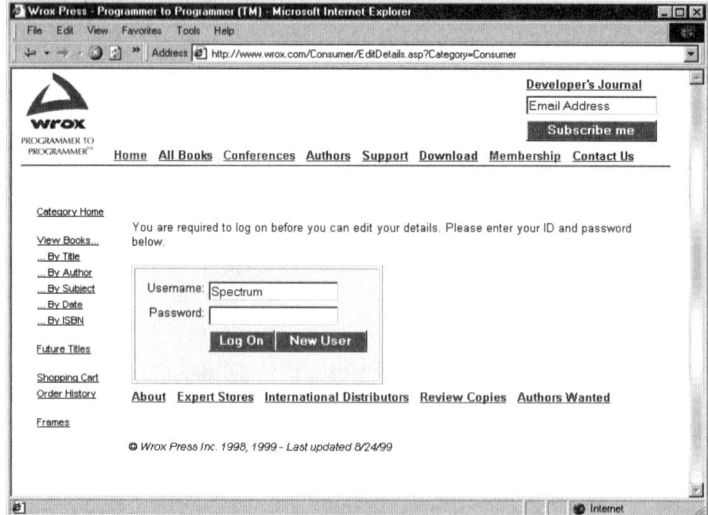

Type in your password once again and click Log On. The following page allows you to change your details if you need to, but now you're logged on, you have access to all the source code downloads and errata for the entire Wrox range of books.

Finding an Errata on the Web Site

Before you send in a query, you might be able to save time by finding the answer to your problem on our web site – `http:\\www.wrox.com`.

Each book we publish has its own page and its own errata sheet. You can get to any book's page by clicking on Support from the top navigation bar.

Halfway down the main support page is a drop down box called Title Support. Simply scroll down the list until you see Professional CDO Programming. Select it and then hit Errata.

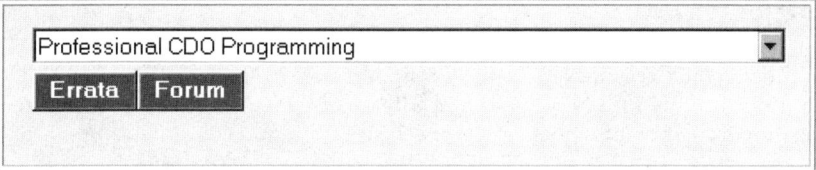

This will take you to the errata page for the book. Select the criteria by which you want to view the errata, and click the Apply criteria button. This will provide you with links to specific errata. For an initial search, you are advised to view the errata by page numbers. If you have looked for an error previously, then you may wish to limit your search using dates. We update these pages daily to ensure that you have the latest information on bugs and errors.

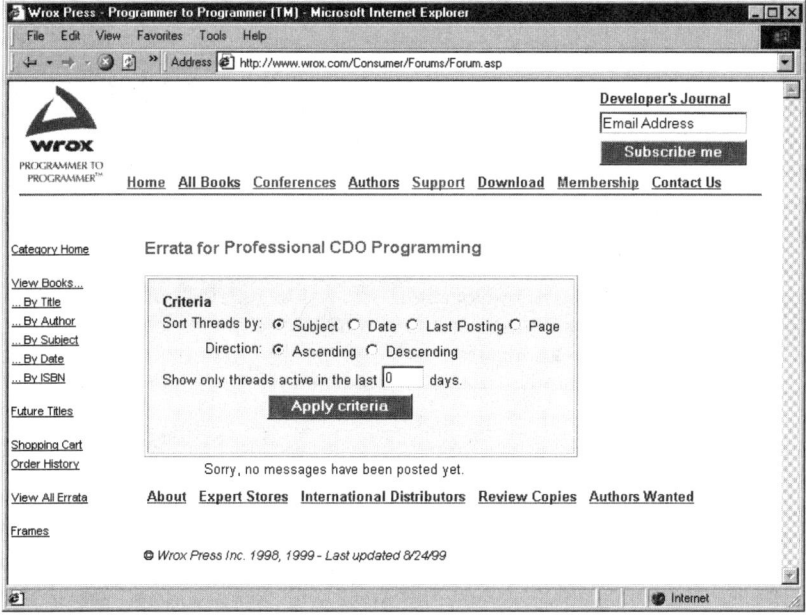

Add an Errata : E-mail Support

If you wish to point out an errata to put up on the website or directly query a problem in the book page with an expert who knows the book in detail then e-mail `support@wrox.com`, with the title of the book and the last four numbers of the ISBN in the subject field of the e-mail. A typical email should include the following things:

- ❑   The **name**, **last four digits of the ISBN** and **page number** of the problem in the Subject field.
- ❑   Your **name**, **contact info** and the **problem** in the body of the message.

We won't send you junk mail. We need the details to save your time and ours. If we need to replace a disk or CD we'll be able to get it to you straight away. When you send an e-mail it will go through the following chain of support:

Customer Support

Your message is delivered to one of our customer support staff who are the first people to read it. They have files on most frequently asked questions and will answer anything general immediately. They answer general questions about the book and the web site.

Editorial

Deeper queries are forwarded to the technical editor responsible for that book. They have experience with the programming language or particular product and are able to answer detailed technical questions on the subject. Once an issue has been resolved, the editor can post the errata to the web site.

The Authors

Finally, in the unlikely event that the editor can't answer your problem, s/he will forward the request to the author. We try to protect the author from any distractions from writing. However, we are quite happy to forward specific requests to them. All Wrox authors help with the support on their books. They'll mail the customer and the editor with their response, and again all readers should benefit.

What We Can't Answer

Obviously with an ever-growing range of books and an ever-changing technology base, there is an increasing volume of data requiring support. While we endeavor to answer all questions about the book, we can't answer bugs in your own programs that you've adapted from our code. But do tell us if you're especially pleased with the routine you developed with our help.

How to Tell Us Exactly What You Think

We understand that errors can destroy the enjoyment of a book and can cause many wasted and frustrated hours, so we seek to minimize the distress that they can cause.

You might just wish to tell us how much you liked or loathed the book in question. Or you might have ideas about how this whole process could be improved. In which case you should e-mail `feedback@wrox.com`. You'll always find a sympathetic ear, no matter what the problem is. Above all you should remember that we do care about what you have to say and we will do our utmost to act upon it.

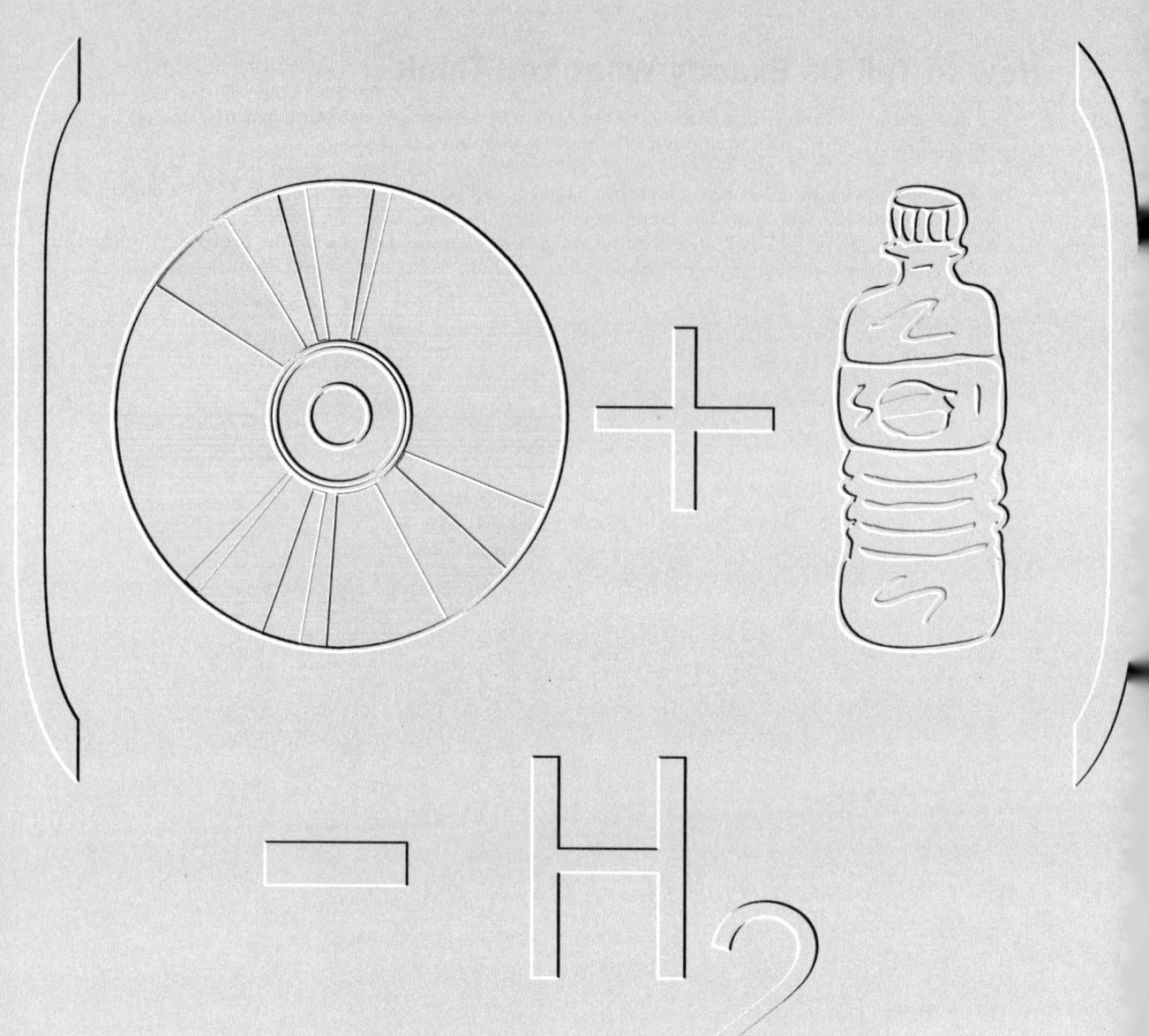

Index

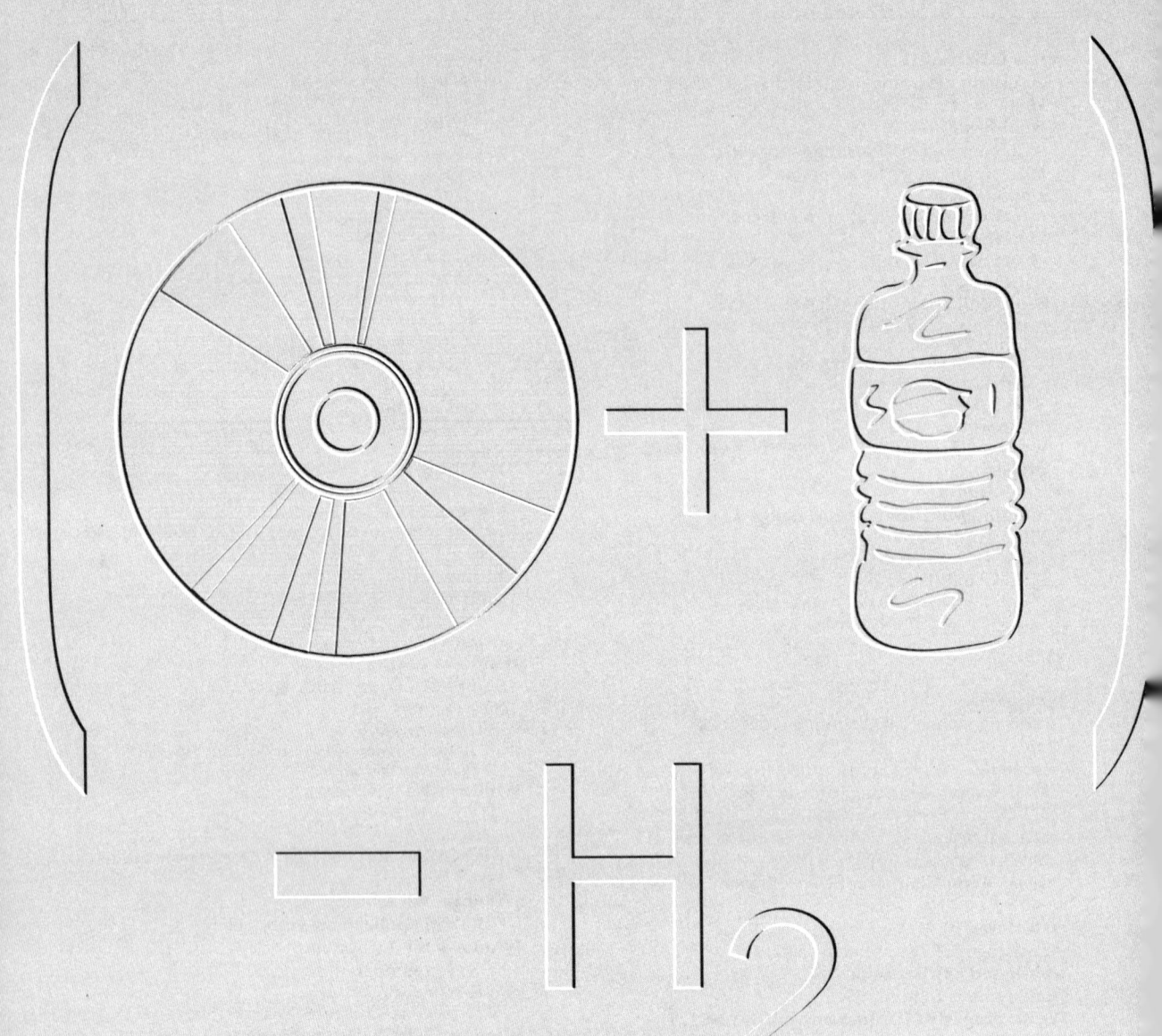

wrox
PROGRAMMER TO PROGRAMMER™

Wrox writes books for you. Any suggestions, or ideas about how you want
information given in your ideal book will be studied by our team.
Your comments are always valued at Wrox.

Free phone in USA 800-USE-WROX
Fax (312) 893 8001

UK Tel. (0121) 687 4100   Fax (0121) 687 4101

Professsional CDO - Registration Card

Name _____

Address _____

_____

_____

City_____ State/Region _____

Country_____ Postcode/Zip _____

E-mail _____

Occupation _____

How did you hear about this book? _____

☐ Book review (name) _____

☐ Advertisement (name) _____

☐ Recommendation _____

☐ Catalog _____

☐ Other _____

Where did you buy this book? _____

☐ Bookstore (name)_____ City _____

☐ Computer Store (name)_____

☐ Mail Order _____

☐ Other _____

What influenced you in the
purchase of this book?

☐ Cover Design

☐ Contents

☐ Other (please specify) _____

How did you rate the overall
contents of this book?

☐ Excellent   ☐ Good

☐ Average   ☐ Poor

What did you find most useful about this book? _____

What did you find least useful about this book? _____

Please add any additional comments. _____

What other subjects will you buy a computer
book on soon? _____

What is the best computer book you have used this year?

_____

*Note: This information will only be used to keep you updated
about new Wrox Press titles and will not be used for any other
purpose or passed to any other third party.*

wrox
PROGRAMMER TO PROGRAMMER™

NB. If you post the bounce back card below in the UK, please send it to:

Wrox Press Ltd., Arden House, 1102 Warwick Road,
Acocks Green, Birmingham B27 6BH. UK.

Computer Book Publishers